PEARSON — ALWAYS LEARNING

Exploring the Hospitality Industry

John R. Walker
McKibbon Professor of Hotel and Restaurant Management
University of South Florida, Sarasota – Manatee

Josielyn T. Walker

with additional information on the Past, Present, and
Future of Hospitality and Tourism

HFT 1000: Introduction to the Hospitality and Tourism Industry

Second Custom Edition for
Rosen College of Hospitality Management
University of Central Florida

Taken from:
Exploring the Hospitality Industry, Second Edition
by John R. and Josielyn T. Walker

Cover Art: Courtesy of PhotoDisc/Getty Images.

Taken from:

Exploring the Hospitality Industry, Second Edition
by John R. and Josielyn T. Walker
Copyright © 2008 by Pearson Education, Inc.
Published by Prentice Hall
Upper Saddle River, New Jersey 07458

Copyright © 2013, 2008, 2007 by Pearson Learning Solutions
All rights reserved.

Permission in writing must be obtained from the publisher before any part of this work may be reproduced or transmitted in any form or by any means, electronic or mechanical, including photocopying and recording, or by any information storage or retrieval system.

All trademarks, service marks, registered trademarks, and registered service marks are the property of their respective owners and are used herein for identification purposes only.

Pearson Learning Solutions, 501 Boylston Street, Suite 900, Boston, MA 02116
A Pearson Education Company
www.pearsoned.com

Printed in the United States of America

1 2 3 4 5 6 7 8 9 10 V0ZN 17 16 15 14 13 12

0002000102716739 53

JL

ISBN 10: 1-256-85857-9
ISBN 13: 978-1-256-85857-7

On behalf of the University of Central Florida's Rosen College of Hospitality Management, and the Central Florida community, it is my sincere pleasure to extend a warm welcome to our Introduction to Hospitality students.

The Central Florida area is surrounded with tourism and hospitality industry leaders. Here at the Rosen College, we are fortunate to have some of the best industry leaders sharing knowledge with our students in the classroom. Students in our programs are actively involved in learning the fundamentals of event preparation and design concepts. They also develop the skills necessary to provide world class service to visitors and guests.

We offer students the opportunity to take part in a variety of professional events and activities. Students are excited to combine what they are learning in the classroom with what they can grasp within the industry by working in the field and during their internships.

As the hospitality industry continues to grow and expand, we value each guest that visits the Central Florida area whether it is for business or pleasure. We look forward to sharing more about the hospitality industry with you as you proceed through this course.

We sincerely hope that you consider the Rosen College of Hospitality Management as part of your college experience as we offer a truly remarkable hands on curriculum. You are the future of the hospitality industry!

Best Wishes,

Dean Abraham Pizam

Rosen College History

In 1983, the hospitality management program was established as a department within the College of Business Administration at the University of Central Florida. In 2000, the program was elevated to the status of autonomous school and renamed the Rosen School of Hospitality Management following an $18.2 million donation by hotelier Harris Rosen. In January 2004, the school officially became the Rosen College of Hospitality Management and moved to a new campus custom-built to its specific needs. The campus is situated on approximately 20 acres of land that includes classroom facilities and apartment style living for students.

The Rosen College is the largest free standing learning laboratory in the world for hospitality management with its location right in Orlando, a city that boasts over 120,000 hotel rooms in 400 hotels, over 5,000 restaurants and four of the largest theme parks in the world, and the second largest convention center in the United States.

The Rosen College offers students hands on training facilities to properly learn aspects of the hospitality industry. Students are actively involved in learning the fundamentals of hospitality management as well as developing the managerial skills necessary to provide world class service to visitors and guests.

The college's facilities include:

- The Walt Disney World teaching dining room seats 150 and gives students the opportunities to serve guests and host events.
- Two training kitchens totaling 4,000 square feet of learning space.
- The Anheuser-Busch wine and beer lab that has the capability to store 1600 bottles of wine in a climate controlled area and where student's have the ability to microbrew there own beer and participate in tasting wines from around the world.
- The Darden Auditorium that seats 400 guests and allows guest speakers to discuss the hospitality industry with large groups of students all in one location.
- Three instructional computer labs
- The Universal Orlando Foundation Library which has been designated a UNWTO depository library that contains over 6,000 volumes and 130 subscriptions to hospitality & tourism periodicals

The College's 43 full-time faculty members and 20+ adjuncts represent 20 different nationalities and each one brings unique experiences to students at the Rosen College. In addition, students are able to participate in exchange programs taking place throughout the world.

Currently, the Rosen College offers three Bachelor degree programs; Hospitality Management, Event Management and Restaurant Management. Within the Hospitality Management degree, students can follow one of six tracks in the following areas: General, Tourism, Theme Parks and Attractions Management, Golf Management, Vacation Ownership, Lodging and Hospitality and Financial Management and Technology. All three degree programs require students to take three semesters of internship, allowing students to gain valuable industry experience in the hospitality capital of the world.

The Rosen College is based on the core values of professionalism, leadership and service. Each of these components contributes to the overall successes of the Rosen College and the way in which we conduct hospitality business.

Past, Present, and Future of Hospitality and Tourism

by Mary Jo Ross, Ph.D.
Michael Terry, Ph.D.

Introduction

Hospitality and tourism is the largest and fastest growing industry in the world. The World Travel and Tourism Council (WTTC) estimates that consumer-driven travel and tourism as a global economy are directly and indirectly responsible for 10 percent of gross domestic product, 200 million jobs, 7.5 percent of total employment and 5.0 million new jobs per year until 2010. The sheer size, however, does not do justice to the comprehensive nature of the interrelated components of products and services.

Whether for business or travel, luxury or economy, people have traveled since the beginning of time. As a result, tourism entrepreneurs have seized this opportunity to provide accommodating products and services throughout the world. From the Biblical story of the Inn in Bethlehem to the European Medieval Castle feasts to the Orient Express to the Titanic Maiden voyage to the transatlantic Supersonic Concorde to the Las Vegas' 5500 suite MGM Grand Resort, hospitality is arguably the most fascinating field on the planet. The diversity of the Industry includes stadium hot dog stands, underwater hotels, trips to the Grand Canyon and Victoria Falls, Africa, gambling junket cruises to nowhere, military facilities, resorts in Bora Bora, Tahiti, college campuses across the globe, health care facilities and business/industrial facilities in Russia.

In order to truly gain an appreciation for the industry, it is important to understand the historical roots of hospitality and tourism. The great sages agree that there is little way of projecting the future without understanding the past.

Tim Garvey says it another way: "Knowledge is telling the *past*. Wisdom is predicting the *future*." In keeping with this philosophy, we now explore the past, the present, and the future of this incredible field called hospitality and tourism.

Scope

In order to gain an understanding of the evolution of hospitality and tourism, we need to apply an organized perspective that defines the various segments of the industry. Therefore, the historical scope will reflect the following four major subdivisions:

LODGING: Inns, Motels, Hotels and Time Shares
FOOD/ BEVERAGE: Taverns, Restaurants, Bars, Catering and Vending
TRAVEL: Railroads. Automobiles, Cruise Ships, and Airlines
RECREATION: Festivals, Parks, Gaming, and Attractions

Eras of Hospitality Tourism

Volumes of pertinent history can be (and have been) written about the literally millions of lodging, food/beverage, travel and recreational aspects and facilities surrounding the business. This diary of events is but a thumbnail sketch of the highlights. It is meant to educate the reader from a "big picture" point of view, and will not, by definition, cover every moment of the world's illustrious hospitality history. In order to create the best "world video," this section divides The Past into eight convenient segments. These periods are outlined by significant travel or tourism milestones and outstanding industry "players" that defined their eras.

The second section, The Present, focuses on the existing products, services, and philosophical viewpoints at the turn of the twenty-first century. This section takes a particularly close look at the industry icons, which are now shaping the evolutionary process. The final segment, The Future, is a look into the possible horizons (social, technical, economical, environmental, political) of tomorrow for hospitality and tourism: types of travel, labor concepts, threats and opportunities regarding employees and guests et al. Enjoy this accelerated stroll down hospitality memory lane.........

The Past: Hospitality and Tourism "Yesterday"

Prior to 1700

As early as 300 B.C. Egyptians sailed up and down the Nile River, carrying huge rocks with which to build pyramids as tombs for their leaders. The Phoenicians were among the first real travelers, and both the Mediterranean and the Orient travelers were motivated by trade, commerce and food supplies. The Roman Empire provided safe passage for travelers via a vast road system that stretched from Egypt to Britain. The wealthy Romans traveled to Egypt and Greece to experience the Pyramids, the Sphinx, baths, shrines, and seaside resorts. The excavated ruins of the Roman town Pompeii, which was buried by an eruption of Mt. Vesuvius, yielded several restaurants, taverns and inns that tourists visit even today. The ancient Egyptians and Babylonians recorded the fermentation process, and the very first records about winemaking date back about 7,000 years. The Greeks received the vine from the Egyptians and later the Romans contributed to the popularization of wine in Europe by planting vines in the territories they conquered.

As far back as the year 1000, the Roman soldiers tasted PICEA and thought it lacked FOCUS (the Latin word for hearth). On a hearth, along with oil, herbs and cheese… pizza was born. The modern precursor to what we call pizza occurred in pre-Renaissance Naples. Poor housewives had only flour, olive oil, lard, cheese and herbs with which to feed their families, so combing them in a tasty and delicious manner became a goal. All of Italy proclaimed the Neapolitan pies to be the best.

Medieval travel was mostly confined to religious travel, such as the Crusades (1095–1300). Later, aristocrats undertook Grand Tours of Europe, stopping at major cities for weeks or months at a time. It was considered a necessary part of "rounding out" a young lady's or gentleman's education. During the seventeenth century, Pineapples were brought back to Europe from the West Indies by early European explorers. It became the favored fruit to serve the royalty and the elite, and was later introduced into the North American hospitality culture. The pineapple is now recognized as the international symbol of hospitality: friendliness, warmth, cheer, graciousness, and conviviality.

1637   The first European coffeehouse opened in England; within thirty years, coffee houses had replaced taverns as the inland's social, commercial, and political melting pots.

1665   The first racetrack in North America was built on Long Island in 1665.

1700s

The word "hotel" was first used in England in about 1760 by the Fifth Duke of Devonshire to name a lodging establishment in London, whereas similar establishments in North America began as inns or taverns, and later became known as hotels.

1770s   Taverns sprang up in the colonies and became a focal point of the community. These eating and drinking establishments in Boston were called "the candles of liberty" by Patrick Henry.
A half-dozen lotteries sponsored by prominent individuals such as Ben Franklin, John Hancock and George Washington operated in each of the 13 colonies to raise funds for building projects.

1794   The first hotel opened in the United States at Broadway in New York City. This was a 70-room hotel called City Hotel.

1800s

Tourism first appeared in the English language in the early nineteenth century. At the time, tour was associated with the idea of a voyage or theatrical tour. Today, the WTTC's definition is "comprising the activities of persons traveling to and staying in places outside of their usual environment for not more than one consecutive year for leisure, business and other purposes."

Inns were well established in England and elsewhere on the Continent in the Middle Ages. Most of them were privately run by couples and these Inns came to be known as "Pop and Mom" inns. Such inns offered food, shelter, bathing, and resting rooms as well as stables for horses. These inns were located where many important social gatherings would occur. In France, large buildings began offering rooms to let by the day, week, or longer. These establishments were called HOTEL GARNI.

The Bed and Breakfast Inn concept started in Europe in the 1800s, as overnight stays in private homes, but did not become popular in the United States until nearly a century later.

1818   Black Ball Line in New York was the first shipping company to offer regularly scheduled service from the United States to England and to be concerned with the comfort of their passengers (rather than cargo, which was norm).

1829   The first modern American hotel was the Tremont House, a 170-room property that opened in Boston in 1829. The Tremont House was also the first hotel to have formal public rooms, bell persons, front desk employees, locks on guest room doors, and free soap for guests.

EARLY 1800s: The U. S. parks movement expanded rapidly as a responsibility of government and voluntary organizations.

During the 1800s, legalized lotteries and casinos were initiated, but gambling came under increasing attack and was outlawed. Prohibition, which made the manufacture and sale of alcoholic beverages illegal, also led to the creation of illegal lotteries. The demise of the riverboat gambler also contributed, as did the emergence of railroads and the outbreak of Civil War. Travel by steamboats declined as railroads became the favored method of transportation. Trains were more reliable and were faster than the riverboats.

The Civil War interrupted virtually all river travel and abruptly diminished gambling. The expansion of the western frontier spurred the second wave. As the country moved westward, the frontier spirit continued to spread. Mining booms increased the rush to the Far West. Miners, lured by the promise of easy and abundant riches, personified the frontier spirit better than the explorers before them. Mining was a gamble and, while extremely risky, it was also an opportunity for great wealth. These were restless and ambitious people who had high expectations. Probably nowhere was this more apparent than in California, where laws against gamblers and gambling began to be enacted. Gambling was illegal in Nevada between 1869 and 1910. As a result, gaming activity moved from California to places such as Virginia City, Nevada.

The Great Depression led to a much greater legalization of gambling. The anti-gambling mood changed as tremendous financial distress gripped the country, especially after the stock market crash of 1929. In 1931, The Nevada Legislature was motivated to build additional gaming facilities to take advantage of the tourism boom expected in the wake of the completion of the Hoover Dam. Nevada had a flourishing, albeit illegal, gambling industry prior to the legalization. The move to make gambling legal grew from concerns that illegal gambling was corrupting law enforcement. Gaming in Nevada struggled from its inception until after World War II, when the prosperity of post-war America initiated a boom in the fledging industry. In 1978, New Jersey became the second state to legalize casino gambling in an attempt to revitalize the rundown resort area of Atlantic City.

1830 The first railroad was built in the United States, and by 1869 the transcontinental connection was completed.

1859 The first elevator was installed in New York's Fifth Avenue Hotel.

1841 Thomas Cook, recognized as the first professional travel agent, chartered a train to carry 540 people to a temperance convention in Loughborough, England. In 1872, Cook hosted an around the world trip that took the 10 member group 222 days.

1867 Mark Twain was a passenger on the first cruise originating in America. "Foster," the oldest U.S. travel agency, began in 1888 when Ward Grenelle Foster opened a "travel information office" in St. Augustine, Florida. In the 1890's the legendary agency expanded to all three Sunshine State coasts, New York, and other metropolitan centers.

1891 Automobiles evolved from steam engines in the late 1800's and Karl Benz and Gottlieb Daimler built a factory from internal combustion engines, which is now Mercedes Benz.

Since the hotel opened its doors on June 1, 1898, the Ritz Paris has been a symbol of opulence, luxury and lavish attention to detail. And for more than a century, the hotel has played host to royalty, society mavens, Hollywood stars, literary lions, and fashion giants. Cesar Ritz, the son of a farming family, made his profession out of catering to the tastes of European high society. Ritz devoted his life to defining the deluxe hotel business. When his career began in 1886, the hotel industry was in its infancy. He developed his craft working in the company of some of the industry's great pioneers, including the renowned chef Georges Auguste Escoffier. By making hotels a fashionable and acceptable part of society, Cesar Ritz's reputation was assured. A Ritz hotel syndicate was formed and the London Ritz opened in 1906. Escoffier, the first chef at the Ritz Paris and friend of the hotel's founder, is largely responsible for developing haute gastronomy, an elegantly prepared and served meal. Escoffier, considered by many to be the greatest chef of the 20th century, created some of the most legendary dishes of all time, including the dessert Peach Melba, created to honor the great soprano Nellie Melba.

Across the Atlantic Ocean in America, another icon was blooming—Ellsworth Statler considered to be the finest hotelier of modern times. The hotel business fascinated Statler, and at 15, took a job as a head bellboy at the McClure Hotel, in Wheeling, Ohio; he eventually became clerk, and by the time he was 16, he could manage the hotel books. At 19 he became the untitled manager. Enterprising and innovative, he leased the McLure billiard room and made it a profitable venture. He established a railroad ticket booth in a hotel, essentially the first transportation department located in a hotel. He bought out a company that had been operating the Musee Bowling Lanes. He also opened a lunch room, "The Pie House" in the Musee building and his mother and sister were soon baking there.

Statler's dream was to have his own hotel, which became a reality in 1907. In Buffalo, New York, he opened the Statler and offered "a room and a bath for a dollar and a half." He proceeded to establish a chain of middle-class hotels which set the standard for moderately priced comfort and cleanliness. Seeking a competitive edge, he designed a plumbing shaft that permitted bathrooms to be built back to back, providing two baths for little more than the price of one, and allowing him to offer many private rooms with adjoining baths. He became the first to put telephones and radios in every guest room, along with full-length mirrors, built-in closets and a special faucet for ice water.

Eventually, Statler opened hotels in Boston, Cleveland, Detroit and New York. Emphasizing that "the guest is always right," he demanded top performance from his employees but was also caring about their needs. His program of job and retirement security was unique at the time. Statler's own formal schooling ended with the second grade but he valued education. The terms of his will established the Statler Foundation. The major beneficiary was the School of Hotel Administration at Cornell University, Ithaca, N.Y., but large grants have gone to other colleges and universities as well.

1900–1950

1910   The American Hotel Protective Association (changed in 1917 to the American Hotel Association of the United States and Canada) is founded in Chicago.

1903   The Wright brothers tested their thirteen-horsepower engine.

1904   The widest-reported "first" appearance of the hamburger most commonly cited in the lore of food service appeared at the World's Fair in St. Louis in 1904. The man who gave the hamburger its contemporary look and sought to expand the products appeal through chain operations was Walter J. Anderson, a Wichita, Kansas resident who went on to co-found the White Castle Hamburger system, the oldest continually running hamburger chain. Helped with the marketing savvy of Edgar Waldo "Billy" Ingram, White Castle reached five units by the 1920's, selling a standardized product for five cents.

Later, White Castle would pioneer the concept of chain marketing with the advertising tag line "Buy 'em by the Sack." Another early pioneer in chain development in hamburgers was Wimpy Grills, launched in 1934, in homage to J. Wellington Wimpy, the chubby, mustachioed cartoon character who hung around with Popeye. Wimpy was groundbreaking in two respects: It was the first chain that attempted to court an upscale diner with 10-cent hamburgers, and it was the first to go overseas.

1905   The advent of the railroad led to the founding of Las Vegas on May 15, 1905. The Union Pacific auctioned off 1,200 lots in a single day in an area which today is casino-lined Glitter Gulch.

1907   Air Passenger service began between London and Paris.

1907   Ritz Development Company established the franchising concept (a method of doing business where a franchisor licenses trademarks) when it franchised the Ritz-Carlton name in New York City.

1914   Henry Ford produced one Model-T every twenty-four seconds on the newly created assembly line, as automobiles created a wave of hotel and motel construction in the 1940s, 1950s and 1960s.

1925   Development of a mail transport system by the U.S. Postal Service. The Kelly Airmail Act of 1925 provided airlines the opportunity to function as mail carriers through involvement in a competitive bidding system, which led to cargo and passengers.

1926   The Slater Corporation is founded, which eventually became *ARAMARK Corporation*, the oldest and most experienced firm in the field of food service management. The Slater Corporation initially managed dining service programs in colleges, and eventually expanded to businesses, vending, and hospitals.
In the 1930s and 40s, two other similar companies (which later combined) were founded. Davidson Brothers Inc. and Automatic Retailers Merchandising Company merged and formed Automatic Retailers of America. In 1961, the company, which was doing approximately $65 million in vending sales, was renamed ARA Services, Inc. Since then, ARA has grown to a company managing nearly $5 billion dollars of diversified services. The company now specializes in the management of services in the food and refreshment, health care, environmental and janitorial services, uniform and clothing rental, and magazine and book distribution industries.

1944   In 1994 ARA Services, Inc. officially became ARAMARK. ARAMARK is now owned by its employees.

1927   Charles Lindbergh flew across the Atlantic Ocean, which spurred oceanic flights in the 1930s. In 1944, seventy airlines and forty countries (American and European) ratified an agreement to form the International Air Transportation Association (IATA).

Howard Johnson began franchising his restaurants in 1927, as he was the pioneer of brand leveraging. The financial health of the nation was sound. Economists talked about "an era of prosperity" and the future seemed nothing but bright. However, the outlook for 27-year old Howard Deering Johnson was not so bright. Johnson owed $40,000. He had voluntarily assumed business obligations left by his deceased father and had gone deeper into the debt by borrowing $500 and taking over the operation of a small patent medicine store, soda fountain and newsstand, located in Quincy, Massachusetts.

The store was losing money. Still, Johnson felt he could make it work. The first thing he did was send out delivery boys to sell newspapers in nearby communities. Sales increased and Johnson turned his attention to the soda fountain. The store sold just three flavors of ice cream: vanilla, chocolate, and strawberry. While Johnson believed the number of flavors should be expanded, he was first determined to improve the quality of the ice cream he was selling. Using an old-fashioned freezer in the basement, he began cranking away by hand and experimenting to develop the best product possible. By doubling the butterfat content and using only natural ingredients, Johnson came up with what he thought was a superior ice cream. His customers thought so, too, and soon they were standing in lines outside his establishment. Johnson kept adding new kinds of ice cream until he hit the now-legendary "28 Flavors." The demand led to expansion and soon he was selling his ice cream at stands on nearby beaches and other locations. In three years, his debts were paid and his business was a success. He added frankfurters, hamburgers, and other foods, carefully making sure of the best quality of content and preparation. His little store had become a successful restaurant. In 1929, he opened another restaurant in downtown Quincy, Massachusetts, and began planning further expansion. For most of the twentieth century, the orange roof of Howard Johnson's was a familiar sight along the great American roadside. When the motorist spotted a Howard Johnson's, he knew exactly what to expect: with standardized menus and building designs, a Howard Johnson's miles away felt as familiar and comforting as the one back home.

Meanwhile, many motel operators in the postwar years were finding that a great location was right next door to a Howard Johnson's restaurant. Throughout the automobile age, "Gas-Food-Lodging" have been the three necessities of travelers and it has always made sense to group them together. The success of many of these motels did not go unnoticed by Howard Johnson's. The company decided to enter the lodging business, opening the first Howard Johnson's Motor Lodge in Savannah, Georgia in 1954.

In the mid 1960s, Howard Johnson's was at the top of its game. In 1965, the company's sales exceeded that of McDonald's, Burger King, and Kentucky Fried Chicken combined. However, a few small leaks were beginning to develop in that brilliant orange roof. Social critics of the 1960s were questioning the conformity of the 1950s, and a large chain of look-alike restaurants proved an easy target. In the early days, Howard Johnson's sameness was seen as an improvement over the wildly inconsistent roadside food offerings of the day, but by now it was seen by many as bland and dull. During the next few decades, the impressive chain fell to more progressive chains, until America's once famous nickname, HoJo, was reduced to a distant memory. Only a fraction of the successful chain remains intact.

1919 Conrad Hilton bought his first hotel, The Mobley, in Cisco, Texas. He was a shrewd, cautious bargainer and believed in hiring the best managers available. He built the first Hilton Hotel in 1925 in Dallas, Texas, the Sir Francis Drake in San Francisco in 1938, and Waldorf Astoria in New York City in 1949. In 1982, he owned the largest hotel in the world–The Las Vegas Hilton, which parlayed Conrad Hilton into the gaming business. In 2000, the Hilton Hotels Corporation and Hilton International offer more than 2000 hotels in more than fifty countries.

1927 At age 26, J. Willard Marriott, with his new bride Allie, enters the business world with the opening of a nine-seat root beer stand in Washington, D.C. Hot food was added and the name was changed to The Hot Shoppe. Marriot pioneers in-flight catering at Washington's old Hoover Airfield (current site of Pentagon) serving Eastern, American, and Capital Airlines in 1937.
In 1950, a Belgian Diamond Cutter and water polo champion, Gerard Blitz, conceived the first Club Med Village on the Balearic Islands, Spain. It was created for people from diverse backgrounds, to encourage them to share a good time, and to offer a unique escape from the stress of post World War II Europe.

1931 More than 60 agents formed the American Society of Travel Agents (ASTA), the world's largest travel trade association, which promised to protect and promote the mutual interests of travel agents and the traveling public members.

With the growing affluence of America after World War II and customer demand for automobiles, food service operators turned to the drive-in as the preferred format for serving the hamburger. While drive-ins were conceived as early as the mid-1930s, the concept exploded phenomenally during the war and after. California and Texas were particularly active enclaves for drive-ins, where the hamburger, fries and shakes were the dominant menu offerings, served by a carhop, who often delivered the meal on roller skates.

1939 Colonel Harland Sanders first gave the world a taste of his most famous creation, Original Recipe Kentucky Fried Chicken, featuring the secret blend of 11 herbs and spices in Corbin, Kentucky.

1941 The Travel Industry of America (TIA) became the established national associated for the common interests and concerns of all components of the U.S. travel industry.

Hotel Franchising, partnerships, leasing and management contracts were introduced by Conrad Hilton, Howard Johnson's, and J.W. Marriott. Depression hotel owners defaulted. Hotel building stopped until post war (late) 1940's, when GIs and spouses could relax and travel.

1940s In the 1940s, fast food was introduced to America.
The hamburger craze started with McDonald brothers: Maurice and

Richard. In 1940, the brothers opened a small drive-in restaurant. In its first year, the business made a $40,000 profit. In an effort to improve service, they made some important changes. First, they eliminated the carhops and reduced the menu from 25 items to 9. They also replaced the old grills for larger, more efficient ones. The plates and silverware were replaced by paper, eliminating the need for dishwashers. The size of the hamburgers was reduced, and the workers, not the customers, put the condiments on the burger.

The McDonald brothers ordered 8 milkshake machines that made 5 shakes at the same time, from a man named Ray Kroc. Intrigued by a business that would need so many milkshake machines, Kroc decided to give McDonald's a visit. Liking what he has seen, Ray Kroc offered to run the franchising for McDonald's and, in return, offered a percentage of profits. The brothers eventually sold the business to Ray Kroc.

Starting in 1955, there were 7 McDonald's stores. In 1956, 12 more were added. In 1957, there were 40. By 1958, 79; by 1959, 145; by 1960, 228; by 1970, 1500; and by 1980, 6200. In 1990 a store was opened in Moscow, Russia. There are currently over 7,000 McDonald's restaurants in over 25 countries around the world. McDonald's, a simple restaurant, started by two brothers who had failed in every business they had tried, has set the standard for fast-food restaurants and for franchising.

1949   Hilton becomes the first international hotel chain with the opening of the Caribe Hilton in San Juan, Puerto Rico.

1950s

During this decade, disposable income increased and the society became more mobile (cars, railroad and airlines). As Americans began to travel the countryside, they learned to enjoy the convenience of roadside accommodations. Air transportation also served to entice travelers to resort destinations and urban hotels.

Prior to the 1950s, a few referral chains developed, consisting of all independent owners. The chains (Best Western, for example) helped travelers identify lodging in another town or city and make a reservation through the referral process. Referral chains served a purpose, but they didn't address the inconsistency among motels. The idea for Holiday Inns came to Kemmons Wilson in the early 1950s, when he realized the inconsistency of the mom-and-pop motels.

He decided to create a consistent product in many parts of the country so families could be comfortable when taking trips. This led to franchising in the 1950s and 60s, where a "prepackaged" motel identity was sold to an entrepreneur for a fee. What franchises did better than the referral chains was create consistency in room design and operational standards.

Wilson created Holiday Inns in Memphis, Tennessee. A devoted family man, he introduced Holiday Inn innovations such as children staying free, swimming pools, free ice cream, chaplains on call, and pet kennels. He insisted guests all be treated the same way. In 1962, Wilson made good on his boast by building the 400th Holiday Inn in Vincennes, Indiana.

The cookie-cutter architecture employed by franchises literally enveloped the concept. Holidays Inns created Embassy Suites to handle the upscale suites market for the rapidly growing business traveler in the early 1980, the Holiday Inn Crowne Plaza to handle luxury downtown hotels and Hampton Inns in 1984 to handle the roadside economy business.

One of Wilson's trademarks was his involvement in the business, even flying in his private plane to review proposed Holiday Inn sites. He knew the importance of location to a motel's success. He insisted that new properties be located on the right-hand side of inbound lanes of major commercial highway at a city's gateway. This is well known by commercial property developers as 'the right-turn rule,' allowing motorists easy access from highways.

Holiday Inns International remained based in Memphis until merging with Bass PLC, a British company, in 1990. The company was moved to Atlanta. Bass PLS later purchased Intercontinental Hotels and changed their name to Inter-Continental Hotels Group.

1952 Pete Harman opens in Salt Lake City becomes the first Kentucky Fried Chicken franchise in Salt Lake City, Utah.

1955 Walt Disney opened the first major American Theme Park, Disneyland, in California.

1955 Marriott's Highway Division begins with several shops on the New York State Thruway. That same year, Marriott opens its first hotel, the Twin Bridges Marriott Motor Hotel in Arlington, Virginia. In 1967 Marriott acquires the Big Boy restaurant chain and begins Roy Rogers fast food restaurant division.

1958 The first pizza restaurant appeared in the United States. In Wichita, Kansas, brothers Frank and Dan Carney opened Pizza Hut on June 15, 1958. The Carneys borrowed $600 from their mother, found a pizza cook, purchased some second-hand equipment, and were ready for business. The first night, they gave away pizza to interest potential customers.

1959 In Las Vegas, city and county community leaders realized the need for a Las Vegas convention facility. The initial goal was to fill hotel rooms with conventioneers during slow tourist months. A site was chosen (one block east of the Las Vegas Strip) and a 6,300-seat, silver-domed rotunda with an adjoining 90,000-square-foot exhibit hall opened in April 1959.

1959 Pizza Hut is incorporated and the first franchise unit opened in Topeka, Kansas.

1960s and 1970s

Franchising is rampant with companies such as Motel 6, Days Inn, Sheraton, and Hilton Hotels. Other developmental financing arrangements followed, including partnerships, leasing, syndicates, and management contracts.

This time of improved prosperity resulted in tourists flocking to beaches, hot springs, mountainsides, and other special locations. The net result of the expanded economy and desire to travel within the states was the rapid development of vacation homes and condominiums in popular tourist destinations. The organization now known as the American Resort Development Association (ARDA) began in 1969 as the American Land Development Association. Between 1964–1968, the Société des Grands Travaux de Marseille, a French development company, began offering a time-sharing product. The first resort to benefit from this concept was SuperDevoluy, a ski resort based in the French Alps. Paul Doumier of the Société des Grands Travaux is credited with developing the timeshare industry's first advertising slogan, "No need to rent the room; buy the hotel, it's cheaper!"

Florida was the first state in the continental US to embrace timeshare developments. The 1970s saw condominium developments in Florida and Puerto Rico being transformed into time-sharing resorts. Resort Condominiums International (RCI) was founded in 1974. First based in Indianapolis, Indiana, RCI has grown into the largest exchange company in the world, with offices in the United States and a growing number of countries. RCI presented timeshare owners with the ability to exchange weeks between different resorts, thus offering more flexibility and a variety of vacation options. Vacationers had to reduce vacations costs because of the oil crisis and timeshare continued to gain favor among Americans. Profits from timeshare sales totaled over $50 million by 1976.

The fast-food industry remained a prominent feature, with A&W Restaurants, Steak n' Shake and Sonic Drive-in becoming more popular. While Steak n' Shake later abandoned the carhop format in the early 1970s, Sonic and A&W Restaurants continue to offer this feature. Other popular hamburger establishments included Burger King, Wendy's, and Hardee's, in addition to McDonald's. All four chains experienced tremendous growth during the 1960s and 70s, helped by the now teenagers from the baby boom. At one point in the late 1970s, the four chains together accounted for 37 cents of every dollar Americans spent to eat out.

During this period, Norman Brinker entered the restaurant business, opening Steak and Ale in 1966. In 1976, after building Steak and Ale to 100 restaurants, it was acquired by The Pillsbury Company, and Brinker became a member of the Board and the largest individual shareholder. He continued to develop other casual dining concepts, including Bennigan's. In 1982, he became Chairman of The Pillsbury Restaurant Group, the world's second-largest restaurant organization, which included Burger King and with total sales approaching $4 billion. In 1983, Brinker resigned and bought Chili's, a Dallas-based restaurant company operating 23 units with $35 million in sales. He rechristened the company Brinker International in 1990. It now operates over 1,500 restaurants world-wide with sales exceeding $4 billion annually. Other restaurants in Brinker International include On the Border, Romano's Macaroni Grill, Maggiano's Little Italy, and other chains.

1960 Isadore Sharp opened the first Four Seasons Hotel on Jarvis Street in Toronto, Canada. Four Seasons Hotel has become a multi-million dollar international hotel empire.

1963 The Boeing 727 was built to carry 145 passengers, followed by the 737 in 1967 and the 747 in 1970.

1966 The Robert Mondavi Winery is established, eventually becoming one of the world's top wineries.

1968 Bill Darden founded Red Lobster Restaurant, a key component of what is now Darden Restaurants, and expanded in 1971 with Olive Garden. By 2007, this casual dining restaurant company had more than 1,300 restaurants throughout North America. Along with over 150,000 employees, Darden Restaurants is the world's largest restaurant operator in terms of revenue.

1970 Hilton became the first billion-dollar lodging and food-service company and the first to enter the Las Vegas market. Cecil B. Day opens the first Days Inn on Tybee Island, Ga.

1971 The U.S. government created and subsidized AMTRAK (semi-public) in order to prevent a total collapse of the rail system due to the popularity of the automobile.

1971 Disney World opens in Orlando, Florida, followed by EPCOT, MGM Studios, and Animal Kingdom.

1972 Carlson Properties was founded. In 1973, the name was changed to Carlson Companies and then Carlson Travel Group. In 1994, Carlson Travel Group and Paris Wagonlit Group formed Carlson Wagonlit Travel, one of the world's largest business travel management companies. Other major divisions included Country Inns & Suites By Carlson, Park Plaza and Park Inn hotels in North America, and the T.G.I. Friday's family of restaurants (Friday's American Bar and Friday's Front Row Sports Grill). In addition, other major national partners include Thrifty Car Rental, Radisson Seven Seas Cruises, Ron Jon Surf Shop, and the Flower Club.

1976 Casino-style gaming was legalized in Atlantic City, New Jersey. This initiated the beginnings of the mega resort. Hotel-casinos vied to be destination resorts for travelers, vacationers, gamblers, conventioneers, and all members of the family.

Another important company was founded during the 1970s. In 1971, Starbucks Coffee Company was founded, opening its first location in Seattle's Pike Place Market. Today, Starbucks, named after the first mate in Herman Melville's Moby Dick, is the world's leading retailer, roaster and brand of specialty coffee with coffeehouses worldwide. More than 11 million customers visit a Starbucks coffeehouse each week. Much of their growth can be contributed to Howard Schultz, who joined Starbucks in 1982 as director of retail operations and marketing. That same year, Starbucks also began providing coffee to fine restaurants and espresso bars. In 1984, Schultz convinces the founders of Starbucks to test the coffee bar concept in a new location in downtown Seattle. In 1987, Starbucks open in Chicago and Vancouver, B.C. In 1991, Starbucks opens its first licensed airport location with HMS Host at Sea-Tac International Airport.

In 1992, Starbucks goes public. Common Stock is traded on the NASDAQ National Market under the ticker symbol "SBUX." In 1996, Starbucks Coffee International opens locations in Japan, Hawaii, and Singapore. In 2001, 30 years after it opened, Starbucks opens its first coffeehouse on the European Continent in Zurich, Switzerland. Starbucks Corporation is the largest coffeehouse company in the world, with over 7,500 company-owned and 5,600 licensed stores in over 40 countries. In addition to coffee, Starbucks also includes Starbucks Entertainment, a division with its own brand (Hear Music), which offers books, music, and film.

1980s

The timeshare industry continued to grow during this decade, with Marriot joining the vacation ownership industry in 1984, followed quickly by Disney, and Hilton. These giants added credibility and visibility to the industry, while infusing improved product and service standards.

This decade also included the deregulation of the airline industry, resulting in the growth of smaller carriers and the mergers of larger carriers. The major U.S. airlines expanded, interest rates increased, and price wars followed, resulting in major losses.

Real Estate Investment Trusts (REITS) began to own property outright and focus turned to physical assets like hotels, office buildings, malls, nursing homes, and apartments, which reaped significant tax advantages. At this time, the Japanese economy was robust and their wealthy companies turned to the U.S. to buy real estate in the form of hotels. When the country's economy folded in the early 1990s, these Japanese investors were forced to resell these holdings when prices were low.

1982   Tokyo Disneyland opened, followed by Disneyland Paris in 1992.

1983   Ritz-Carlton Hotel Company was formed under the direction of Horst Schultz, Founding President and CEO. It is the only hospitality organization to be awarded the prestigious Malcolm Baldridge National Quality Award, given by the U.S. Department of Commerce. Schultz's commitment to excellence is based on a trained, fully-empowered workforce, schooled in the company's Gold Standards, which include a credo, motto, three steps to service and twenty Ritz-Carlton basics. The company is also the leader in customer data collection, which is used to ensure the ultimate in consumer relationship building. And finally, Ritz-Carlton sets the standard in the industry for guest recognition programs, luxury amenities, and architectural design.

1987   The Outback Steakhouse Incorporated enterprise was founded in Florida in 1987 by three partners, Tim Gannon, Bob Basham, and Chris Sullivan, all of whom had experience in the restaurant industry. The Outback menu featured items such as "Kookaburra Wings," "Aussie Cheesefries," and "Jackaroo Chops," and the company's signature appetizer, the "Bloomin' Onion." Outback also gave its managers a stake in the company's overall well-being by allowing them to purchase a ten percent interest in their stores, and other employees had the right to purchase stock in the company. In May 1992, Outback was named the third best small company in America by *Business Week* magazine, and opened their 100th restaurant. Outback began to test a second restaurant concept in March 1993, entering into a joint venture with a Houston restaurant group to develop Carrabba's Italian Grill restaurants. By 2006, Outback Steakhouse Inc. had 1300 locations in the U. S. and 20 other countries and continued to develop full-service restaurants under the Outback Steakhouse umbrella: Carrabba's Italian Grill, Fleming's Prime Steakhouse & Wine Bar, Bonefish Grill, Flemings Prime Steakhouse, and Roy's restaurants brand names.

1988   Indian Gaming Regulatory Act was passed to protect both the tribes and the general public. By the year 2000, gaming facilities on reservation lands in thirty-two states and 25 percent of all casino dollars are lost at Native Indian casinos.

During the 1980s, Marriott enjoyed tremendous growth. In 1982, Marriott began to build its travel mega-conglomerate as it acquired Host International, and becomes the country's largest operator of airport terminal food, beverage, and merchandise facilities. That same year, the first Courtyard by Marriott opened near Atlanta, Georgia. The Courtyard offers moderately priced segment hotels. In 1983, Marriott enters the vacation time-sharing business with acquisition of American Resorts Group. Marriott acquires Saga Corporation, a diversified food service management company, in 1986, making Marriott the largest company in food service management in the United States. The following year, Marriott acquires The Residence Inn Company, an all-suite hotel chain targeted toward extended-stay travelers. In that same year, Marriott enters economy lodging segment with the opening of the first Fairfield Inn in Atlanta, Georgia. Marriott's Senior Living Service division announces development plans for assisted living/ personal care complexes called Brighton Gardens, also in 1987. Marriott's growth continues well into the 1990s, with Marriott opening its first TownePlace Suites in Newport News, Virginia, in 1997. Also in 1997, Marriot International acquires Renaissance Hotel Group for approximately $1 billion and adds three brands (Renaissance, Ramada International and New World) and doubles Marriott's presence overseas. Finally, in 1997, Marriott International, Inc. announces its Marriott Rewards program offering frequent flyer miles and more than at nine different brands, representing 1,650 hotels. In 2000 Marriott International celebrates 2,000 properties worldwide.

1990s

In the early 1990s, because of plummeting real-estate values, the high cost of debt service and economic downturn, hotel operating results were poor. Consolidation of the top management companies and branded hotel companies presented a new landscape. Examples of mergers and buyouts included the Hilton Corporation acquiring Embassy Suites, Double Tree Suites, and Homewood Suites. Six Continents (formerly Bass Hotels and Resorts/ Holiday Inns) acquired Intercontinental Hotels and Starwood added Westin to their Sheraton brand.

Despite the plummeting real-estate values, the timeshare industry continued to grow. By 1990, four million timeshare owners worldwide owned property at over 2,300 time-sharing facilities. The 1990s saw widescale expansion in every area of the timeshare industry. Timeshare expanded into new territories in Eastern Europe and Asia. Following Marriott's lead (this hotel chain was arguably the first large corporation to add timeshares to its lodging and hospitality options), big hotel companies realized that there was money to be made with timeshare. Sheraton, Ramada, Hilton, Disney, Four Seasons, Ritz-Carlton, Radisson and Westin all began offering timeshare properties during the late 1980s and early 1990's. This infusion of big-brand respectability boosted consumer confidence and sales of timeshare units reached record highs. By the year 2000, timeshare was a booming multi-million dollar business and by 2006, timeshare resorts worldwide numbered 7,500.

During this time, the hamburger chains found their customers were looking elsewhere for greater value and broader menu diversity, while cash-strapped families began eating at dinner houses where their dollars stretched farther (e.g., Red Lobster, T.G.I. Friday's, and Applebee's).

1990 Pizza Hut delivers more than 1,349,000 pizzas on Superbowl Sunday—about 7,000 pies per minute.

1993 The most ambitious resort project in the history of Las Vegas, the MGM Grand Hotel & Theme Park, opens in 1993. It is the largest resort hotel in the world and the dream of pioneer Las Vegas hotel developer and multimillionaire entrepreneur Kirk Kerkorian. The $1 billion, 112-acre resort hotel, 5,005-room hotel boasts a 171,500-square-foot casino, 12 theme restaurant, a 1,700-seat production showroom, a 630-seat production theatre, three swimming pools, five tennis courts, a child care center and 215,000-square-foot, 15,200-seat special events arena for concerts, sporting events and exhibitions.

1995 Choice Hotels International and Promus become the first companies to offer quests "real-time" access to its central reservations system. Choice and Holiday Inn are the first to introduce online booking capability.

1997 In October of 1997, PepsiCo, owner and franchisor of KFC, Pizza Hut and Taco Bell, spun-off the restaurant brands thereby forming Tricon Global Restaurants, Inc. In 2002, Tricon Global Restaurants, Inc., changed its name to Yum! Brands, Inc., after acquiring the Long John Silver's and A&W All-American Food brands. Yum! Brands Inc. is the world's largest restaurant company in terms of system restaurants with over 34,000 restaurants in more than 100 countries and territories. The company and its franchisees introduced dual branding, and, as of 2007, operated more than 3,600 multibrand restaurants worldwide.

1999   Construction is completed on the world's tallest hotel, the Burj Al Arab, in Dubai, United Arab Emirates. In 2006, also in Dubai, the Rose Rotana Suites surpasses the Burj Al Arab as the world's tallest hotel.

2000s

The electronics "gold rush" of the mid and late 1990s fell out in later 2000 and the terror attacks on New York City and Washington in September, 2001, negatively impacted travel. Business declined by as much as 30% in major metropolitan areas (New York, Orlando, Las Vegas), as international and domestic travel halted.

2001   SUBWAY(R) restaurants, the world's largest submarine sandwich chain made its first NASCAR NEXTEL Cup Series appearance as a team sponsor in 2001.

2003   Papa Murphy's, the world's largest take-and-bake pizza (consumers bake the pizza at their own homes), was voted "Best Pizza Chain in America."

2003   The last flight of the Concorde, the first supersonic transport (SST), was flown on October 23. It had previously flown transatlantic flights for 27 years, flying these routes at record speeds. After its only crash on July 25, 2000, and because of other factors (including the September 11, 2001 attacks) the Concorde ceased operations.

2004   The Queen Mary 2, the largest cruise liner ever built, departs on its maiden voyage from Southampton, in southern England–17 desks, five swimming pools, 2600 passengers

2005   Dubai, United Arab Emirate, finished the year with the world's highest revenue per available hotel room.

2006   Panera Bread was recognized as the top performer in the fast casual restaurant category, opening its 1000th location in the United States.

2006   Macau became the casino city that pocketed the most revenue in the world and, for the first time, outperformed Las Vegas.

2006   The Internet accounted for 38.3 percent of 2006 brand hotel bookings.

2007   Dubailand themepark, two and a half times the size of Walt Disney World Resort in Florida, will become the biggest theme/amusement park in the world. Phase 1 of the Dubailand project will extend from 2007 to 2010 and the final phase of the Dubailand will be completed by 2015.

2007 Dunkin' Donuts is the world's largest coffee and baked goods chain, serving more than two million customers a day.

2007 Airbus A380, the world's largest jet, begins service for 520 passengers.

2008 The World Islands, a collection of 300 small private artificial man-made islands shaped into the continents of the world, located off the coast of Dubai in the United Arab Emirates, will feature four overnight accommodations categories—private homes, estate homes, dream resorts, and community islands.

The items listed above represent but a fraction of the industry highlights that helped shape the hospitality landscape. The list demonstrates the complexity of the industry, and it underlies the constant growth that has been initiated by social, technological, economical, and political changes throughout history.

The Present and Possible Future: Hospitality and Tourism Today and Tomorrow

Today is yet one more advanced dot on the hospitality historical continuum. The emphasis on consolidation, international branding and marketing, global expansion, and overall security and safety drive the priorities of the new millennium. Today's operators are expanding the horizon to include sophisticated approaches to spas as "a way of life" for several and major income levels, upgraded assisted living accommodations, common-campus, multi-brand hotel complexes, sub-segmented time-share and condo-hotel construction, high-tech communications, manufacturing industry's six-sigma quality control programs applied to hospitality, casino mania for each region of the United States, as well as the new giant, Macau, China.

The cruise ship market, having increased 800 percent from 1970–2000, remains a healthy part of the industry (more than 200 ships are providing lake, river and primarily ocean going cruises). With only 5-6 percent of the cruise market tapped and with an estimated market potential of billions, the cruise industry gives all indication of a bright future. Club Med is now worldwide, located in over 28 countries.

International competition and the terrorist attacks on September 11, 2001 became the undoing of several U.S. airlines. The airlines sustained losses in in the billions, which forced global alliances. At the same time, regional carriers in the United States, such as Southwest, Air Tran and Jet Blue, initiated lower operating costs and consequently lower fares. Southwest has become the fourth largest major airline in America, flying more than 64 million passengers a year to over 58 cities. Their success is largely due to their dedication to their employees, a good record of baggage handling, fewest customer complaints, and dependable take-off and landing times.

China's first low-cost airline was launched in July 2005, and many are set to follow. Air Arabia, the largest low-cost carrier in the Middle East, charges some of the lowest fares in the world. Dubai based Emirates Airline is one of the fastest growing airlines in the world and has received more than 200 international awards.

In North America, regional micro-breweries and sports bars are common place, and theme restaurants remain popular. Darden Restaurants continues to thrive in the casual dining sector of the U. S. restaurant industry. Casual dining is forecasted to be the fastest growing segment of the restaurant industry for the next 5–10 years. In this segment are companies such as Outback, Chili's, Macaroni Grill, and Applebee's, as well as with regional companies. Some of their strongest competitors are companies that operate in just one region of the country.

For the years 2006–2010, the Global Entertainment and Media Outlook projects theme and amusement parks spending and growth will grow at a rate of 4.5 percent. It is also projected that the Asia Pacific will be the fastest growing market at 5.9 percent. Worldwide, waterparks are growing in popularity with both leisure travelers and resort developers. Regional indoor waterpark resorts have emerged as a leisure destination for families looking for a convenient weekend getaway. In the United States, the hotel indoor waterpark resort concept quadrupled over the last six years.

Peering into the hospitality and tourism crystal ball, tomorrow's longer term items of interest include the burgeoning travel trade in China and Dubai; Commercial Space Travel; Robotics/Artificial Intelligence; Electronic Travel Agents; and Human Resources Integration (of national and international diversified employees). According to the World Travel and Tourism Council, tourism is forecasted to grow strongly at 40 to 50 percent in real terms in the next ten years. This astronomical growth presents tremendous challenges and career opportunities for today's hospitality and tourism graduates. The famous futurist, John Naisbit, says that the global economy of the twenty-first century will be driven by three superservice industries: Telecommunications, Information Technology, and Travel and Tourism. It is time to take advantage of this, and look beyond the curve regarding the operational and marketing approaches used by our industry. Read on to see if this is the industry for you!

Brief Contents

Chapter 1   Hospitality Spirit   2
Chapter 2   Tourism   28
Chapter 3   Why People Travel   52
Chapter 4   Lodging   74
Chapter 5   Lodging Operations   98
Chapter 6   Cruising   126
Chapter 7   Restaurants   146
Chapter 8   Restaurant Operations   162
Chapter 9   Managed Services   186
Chapter 10   Beverages   210
Chapter 11   Clubs   234
Chapter 12   Theme Parks and Attractions   250
Chapter 13   Gaming Entertainment   268
Chapter 14   Meetings, Conventions, and Expositions   282
Chapter 15   Special Events   304
Chapter 16   The Final Chapter of the Hospitality Story and Your Career Plan   327

Contents

To the Student   xiii
Preface   xxiii
Acknowledgments   xxv
About the Author   xxvi

Chapter 1
HOSPITALITY SPIRIT   2

Welcome to You, the Future Hospitality Industry Leaders!   4
The Pineapple Tradition   5
The Interrelated Nature of Hospitality and Tourism   5
Characteristics of the Hospitality Industry   7
 Careers   8
The Focus on Service   10
Perfecting Service   11
 Success in Service   11
 Moments of Truth   12
 Ways to Perfect Service   13
 Service and Total Quality Management   14
 The Disney Approach to Guest Service   15
 The Disney Service Model   18
Career Paths   20
Career Goals   20
 Is the Hospitality Industry for You?   20
Self-Assessment and Personal Philosophy   21
Professionalism and Etiquette   21
 Now Is the Time to Get Involved   22
 Professional Organizations and Associations   22

Ethics   22
Ethical Dilemmas in Hospitality   24
Trends in Hospitality   25
Career Information   26
Summary   26
Key Words and Concepts   27
Review Questions   27
Internet Exercises   27
Apply Your Knowledge   27
Suggested Activity   27
 Internet Sites   27
Endnotes   27

Chapter 2
TOURISM   28

Tourism   30
Sustainable Cruising   31
 Tourism Defined   31
 Benefits of Tourism   32
 Tourism 2020 Vision   32
Air Travel   33
 The Hub-and-Spoke System   35
Rail, Automobile, and Coach Travel   35
Traveling by Train   35
 Rail Travel Abroad   36
 Does the Train Have a Future?   37
Traveling by Car   37
 Automobile Associations   37
 Rental Cars   38

Traveling by Bus   38
   Types of Bus Service   39
   Motorcoach Associations   39
Paris   39
Tourism Organizations   40
   International Organizations   40
   Domestic Organizations   42
   State Offices of Tourism   43
   City-Level Offices of Tourism and Convention
      Centers   43
The Economic Impact of Tourism   44
   The Multiplier Effect   44
Promoters of Tourism   45
   Tour Operators   45
   Travel Agencies   45
   Travel Corporations   46
   Corporate Travel Manager   47
   Travel and Tour Wholesalers   47
   Certified Travel Counselor (CTC)   47
   National Offices of Tourism (NOT)   48
   Destination Management Companies (DMCs)   48
Trends in Tourism   49
Career Information   49
Summary   50
Key Words and Concepts   50
Review Questions   50
Internet Exercises   51
Apply Your Knowledge   51
Suggested Activity   51
Endnotes   51

What Is Ecotourism?   58
   Environmental Impact of Tourism   61
Cultural Tourism   63
   Impact of Tourism on Culture   63
   Tourism and Art   64
Heritage Tourism   65
   The Benefits of Preservation   66
   Challenges in Heritage Tourism   66
   Find the Fit between Community and Tourism   67
   Four Steps to a Comprehensive Heritage
      Program   67
Nature Tourism   70
Trends in Travel   71
Career Information   71
Summary   72
Key Words and Concepts   73
Review Questions   73
Internet Exercises   73
Apply Your Knowledge   73
Suggested Activity   73
Endnotes   73

Chapter 4
LODGING   74

Hotel Development and Ownership   76
   Franchising   76
Franchised Hotels   76
Franchising Trends   77
   Management Contracts   77
   Real Estate Investment Trust (REIT)   80
Rating and Classification of Hotels   80
Types and Locations of Hotels   84
   City Center Hotels   84
   Airport Hotels   84
   Freeway Hotels and Motels   84
   Casino Hotels   85
   Convention Hotels   85
   Full-Service Hotels   85

Chapter 3
WHY PEOPLE TRAVEL   52

Pleasure Travel   54
   Different Places for Different People   55
Business Travel   56
The Social and Cultural Impact of Tourism   57
Sustainable Tourism and Ecotourism   58

    Economy/Budget Hotels   86
    Extended-Stay Hotels   86
    All-Suite Extended-Stay Hotels   87
    Condotels   87
    Mixed-Use Hotel Development   87
    Bed and Breakfast Inns   87
    Resort Hotels   88
    Vacation Ownership   89
    The Advantages and Disadvantages of Vacation Ownership   90
Best, Biggest, and Most Unusual Hotels and Chains   90
    The Best Hotel Chains   91
    The Most Unusual Hotels   91
International Perspective   92
    Green Lodging   92
Sustainable Lodging   93
    How Fairmont Promises to Fight Climate Changes   93
    Climate Change Impacts the Bottom Line   93
    Examples of Fairmont's Best Practice: 94
    Commitments and Plans   94
Trends in Hotel Development   95
Career Information   96
Summary   96
Key Words and Concepts   96
Review Questions   97
Internet Exercises   97
Apply Your Knowledge   97
Suggested Activity   97
Endnotes   97

Chapter 5
LODGING OPERATIONS   98
Functions and Departments of a Hotel   100
Early Inns   100

Role of the Hotel General Manager   100
Management Structure   101
    The Executive Committee   101
The Departments   102
    Rooms Division   102
    Front Office   102
    Night Auditor   105
Property Management Systems   109
Revenue Management   109
Reservations   111
Communications CBX or PBX   111
Guest Services   111
Concierge   112
Housekeeping   112
Security/Loss Prevention   114
    Security Officers   114
    Equipment   114
    Safety Procedures   114
    Identification Procedures   114
Food and Beverage Management   115
Kitchen   115
Hotel Restaurants   116
Bars   116
Stewarding Department   116
Catering Department   117
    Catering Event Order   117
    Catering Services Manager   117
Room Service/In-Room Dining   119
    Energy Star®   119
    Green Seal   119
    Recycled Content   119
    Hotel Recycling   119
    Water Conservation   119
    Bathroom Amenities   119
    Breakfast   119
Sustainable Lodging Operations   120
    Lounge   121
    Guest Shuttle   121
    Guest Bikes   121
    Coffee Shop   121
    Greening the Guestroom   121
Trends in Lodging Operations   122
Career Information   123
Summary   124
Key Words and Concepts   125
Review Questions   125
Internet Exercises   125

Apply Your Knowledge   125
Suggested Activity   125
Endnotes   125

Chapter 6
CRUISING   126

Cruise Industry Development   128
The First Cruise Ships   128
Cruising Today   129
Key Players in the Cruise Industry   129
The Cruise Market   130
Types of Cruise Markets   133
Types of Cruises   133
Regional Cruises   133
Coastal Cruises   134
River Cruises   134
Barges   134
Steam Boating   134
Expeditions and Natural Cruises   134
Adventure Cruises   134
Sail-Cruises   134
World Cruises   135
Crossings   135
Specialty and Theme Cruises   135
Deluxe Cruising   135
All Aboard—Organization of the Cruise Ship   137
Cruise Destinations   139
Sustainable Cruising   140
Trends in the Cruise Industry   142
Career Information   142
Summary   144
Key Words and Concepts   144
Review Questions   144
Internet Exercises   144
Apply Your Knowledge   145
Suggested Activity   145
Endnotes   145

Chapter 7
RESTAURANTS   146

Restaurants   148
Classification of Restaurants   148
Franchises   149
Fine Dining   149
Casual Dining   152
Quick-Service/Fast-Food Restaurants   153
Sustainable Restaurants   155
Green Restaurant Certification 4.0 Standards   156
Food Trends and Practices   157
Trends in the Restaurant Business   157
Career Information   158
Summary   160
Key Words and Concepts   160
Review Questions   160
Internet Exercises   160
Apply Your Knowledge   160
Suggested Activities   161
Endnotes   161

Chapter 8
RESTAURANT OPERATIONS   162

Front of the House   164
Restaurant Forecasting   165
Service   165
Suggestive Selling   166

viii

Back of the House 167
   Food Production 167
   Kitchen/Food Production 168
   Management Involvement and Follow-Up 170
   Purchasing 170
   Receiving 172
   Storing/Issuing 173
Cost Control 176
   Food and Beverage Cost Percentages 176
   Labor Cost Control 177
Sustainable Restaurant Operations 178
Restaurant Manager Job Analysis 180
   Human Resource Management 180
   Financial Management 180
   Administrative Management 181
   Operations Management 181
Trends in Restaurant Operations 182
Career Information 183
Summary 184
Key Words and Concepts 184
Review Questions 184
Internet Exercises 184
Apply Your Knowledge 185
Suggested Activity 185
Endnotes 185

Leisure and Recreation 203
   Stadium Points of Service 203
   Other Facilities 204
   Advantages and Disadvantages 204
Seniors 204
   Sustainability 204
Sustainable Managed Services 205
Trends in Managed Services 205
   Technology 206
Career Information 207
Summary 208
Key Words and Concepts 208
Review Questions 208
Internet Exercises 208
Apply Your Knowledge 209
Suggested Activity 209
Endnotes 209

Chapter 9
MANAGED SERVICES 186
Overview 188
Airlines and Airports 188
   In-Flight Foodservice 188
Military 190
Elementary and Secondary Schools 191
   Nutrition Education Programs 192
Colleges and Universities 193
   Student Unions 194
   Responsibilities in Managed Services 196
Health Care Facilities 198
Business and Industry 202

Chapter 10
BEVERAGES 210
Wines 212
   Light Beverage Wines 212
   Sparkling Wines 212
   Fortified Wines 213
   Aromatic Wines 213
   The History of Wine 213
Sustainable Wine Production 214
   The Making of Wine 214
   Matching Wine with Food 214
   Major Wine-Producing Countries 217
Beer 218
   The Brewing Process 218
Sustainable Brewing 218
Spirits 222
   Whiskies 222
   White Spirits 222
   Other Spirits 223
   Cocktails 223

Nonalcoholic Beverages 224
  Nonalcoholic Beer 224
  Coffee 224
  Sustainable Coffee 226
  Tea 226
  Carbonated Soft Drinks 226
  Juices 226
  Power Drinks 226
  Bottled Water 227
Types of Bars 227
  Restaurant and Hotel Bars 227
  Nightclubs 227
  Microbreweries 228
  Sports Bars 228
  Coffee Shops 229
Liquor Liability and the Law 229
  Highway Deaths and Alcohol 230
Trends in the Beverage Industry 230
Career Information 231
Summary 232
Key Words and Concepts 232
Review Questions 232
Internet Exercises 233
Apply Your Knowledge 233
Suggested Activities 233
Endnotes 233

Chapter 11
CLUBS 234

Development of Clubs 236
  Size and Scope of the Club Industry 236
Types of Clubs 237
  Country Clubs 237
  City Clubs 237
  Other Clubs 237
Key Players in the Club Industry 238
Club Management 238
  Club Management Structure 240
  Club Food and Beverage Management 242

  The Golf Course Superintendent 244
Sustainable Golf Course Management 246
  The Golf Professional 246
  The Golf Shop 247
Trends in Club Management 247
Career Information 247
Summary 248
Key Words and Concepts 249
Review Questions 249
Internet Exercises 249
Apply Your Knowledge 249
Suggested Activities 249
Endnotes 249

Chapter 12
THEME PARKS AND ATTRACTIONS 250

The Development of Theme Parks 252
Size and Scope of the Theme Park Industry 252
Key Players in the Theme Park Industry 253
  Magic Kingdom 253
  Epcot 254
  Disney–MGM Studios 254
  Universal Studios 254
  SeaWorld Parks and Entertainment 255
  Hershey's 256
Regional Theme Parks 258
  Dollywood 258
  LEGOLAND 259
  Gatorland 259
  Wet 'n Wild 259
Theme Park Management 259
Sustainable Theme Parks 260
Fairs, Festivals, and Events 262
  Oktoberfest 262
  The Carnival in Rio de Janeiro, Brazil 262
  Reggae on the River 262
  Mardi Gras 263
  Grand Ole Opry 263

Employment 263
Trends in the Theme Park Industry 265
Career Information 265
Summary 266
Key Words and Concepts 266
Review Questions 266
Internet Exercises 266
Apply Your Knowledge 266
Suggested Activity 267
Endnotes 267

Chapter 13
GAMING ENTERTAINMENT 268

Gaming Entertainment 270
Historical Review of Gaming Entertainment 272
   Native American Gaming 273
Size and Scope of Gaming Entertainment 274
Key Players in the Industry 275
Positions in Gaming Entertainment 277
   Hotel Operations 277
   Food and Beverage Operations 278
   Casino Operations 278
   Retail Operations 278
   Entertainment Operations 278
Trends in the Gaming Entertainment Industry 278
Career Information 279
Summary 280
Key Words and Concepts 281
Review Questions 281
Internet Exercises 281
Apply Your Knowledge 281
Suggested Activity 281
Endnotes 281

Chapter 14
MEETINGS, CONVENTIONS, AND EXPOSITIONS 282

Development of the Meetings, Conventions, and Expositions Industry 284
Size and Scope of the Industry 284
Key Players in the Industry 284
   Destination Management Companies 286
   Meeting Planners 286
   Service Contractors 287
Types of Meetings, Conventions, and Expositions 289
   Meetings 289
   Association Meetings 290
   Conventions and Expositions 290
   Historical Associations 294
   Meetings, Incentive Travel, Conventions, and Exhibitions (MICE) 294
   Types of Associations 294
   Types of Meetings 294
   Meeting Planning 295
Venues for Meetings, Conventions, and Expositions 298
   City Centers 299
   Convention Centers 299
   Conference Centers 299
   Hotels and Resorts 299
   Cruise Ships 299
   Colleges and Universities 299
Trends in Meetings, Conventions, and Expositions 300
Career Information 301
Summary 302
Key Words and Concepts 302
Review Questions 302
Internet Exercises 302
Apply Your Knowledge 303
Suggested Activity 303
Endnotes 303

Chapter 15
SPECIAL EVENTS 304

What Event Planners Do 306
Event Management 307
- Research 308
- Design 308
- Planning 309
- Coordination 309
- Evaluation 309

Challenges for Event Planners and Managers 309
Classifications of Special Events 310
- Corporate Events 311
- Association Events 311
- Charity Balls and Fund-Raising Events 312
- Social Events 312
- Fairs and Festivals 313
- Concerts and Sporting Events 313
- Mega Events 314

Required Skills and Abilities for Event Management 316
- Leadership Skills 316
- Ability to Communicate with Other Departments 317
- Project Management Skills 317
- Negotiating Skills 317
- Coordinating and Delegating Skills 318
- Budgeting Skills 318
- Ability to Multitask 318
- Enthusiasm 318
- Effective Social Skills 318
- Ability to Form Contacts 319
- Wedding Planning 319

Special Event Organizations 320
- International Festivals & Events Association 320
- Meeting Planners International 321
- Local Convention and Visitors Bureaus 321

Sustainable Special Events 322
The Special Event Job Market 322
Trends in the Special Event Industry 323
Career Information 323
Summary 324
Key Words and Concepts 324
Review Questions 324
Internet Exercises 324
Apply Your Knowledge 325
Suggested Activity 325
Endnotes 325

Chapter 16
THE FINAL CHAPTER OF THE HOSPITALITY STORY AND YOUR CAREER 327

Glossary 335
Index 341
Photo Credits 349

To the Student

Dear Future Hospitality Professional,

This textbook is written to empower you and help you on your way to becoming a future leader of this great industry. ***Exploring the Hospitality Industry*** will give you an overview of the world's largest and fastest-growing industry. Each chapter contains information about the numerous hospitality segments, the many different areas of career opportunities and career paths, as well as profiles of industry practitioners and leaders.

Read the Book

Read and study the text, including the profiles, boxes, Check Your Knowledge questions, industry professionals' advice, career advice, and review questions, and discuss and debate the case studies. Use the many tools throughout this textbook—including bolded key words and concepts and glossary of terms—to facilitate your reading and understanding of the concepts. You will be amazed at how much more you get out of class by preparing ahead of time.

Use the Resources Accompanying This book

Hospitality & Tourism Interactive (HTi) is the first ever comprehensive multimedia resource for Introduction to Hospitality professors and students. HTi combines learning modules that present key topics and objectives across various aspects of the Hospitality Industry, skills-based simulation activities, and assignable & gradable homework and review materials—all within an engaging and interactive graphical interface.

Success in the Classroom

Faculty say that the best students are those who come to class prepared. We know that as a hospitality student, you have many demands on your time—work, a heavy course load, family commitments, and, yes, fun—plus a lot of reading and studying for your other courses. With this in mind, we tried to make this book as visually appealing, easy, and engaging to read as possible—and enjoyable, too.

Wishing you success in your studies and career.

Sincerely,
John and Josielyn Walker

Take some time to review the book's features and tools as described on the following pages; they will facilitate your reading and understanding of the concepts and introduce you to the exciting opportunities in the many, varied segments of the hospitality industry.

TASTES OF THE INDUSTRY

As you read, you'll recognize a hallmark "tastes of the industry" theme that characterizes the text. Because the authors have years of industry operations experience, they include numerous examples to illustrate key topics. This makes for a more engaging read and helps you understand the material presented.

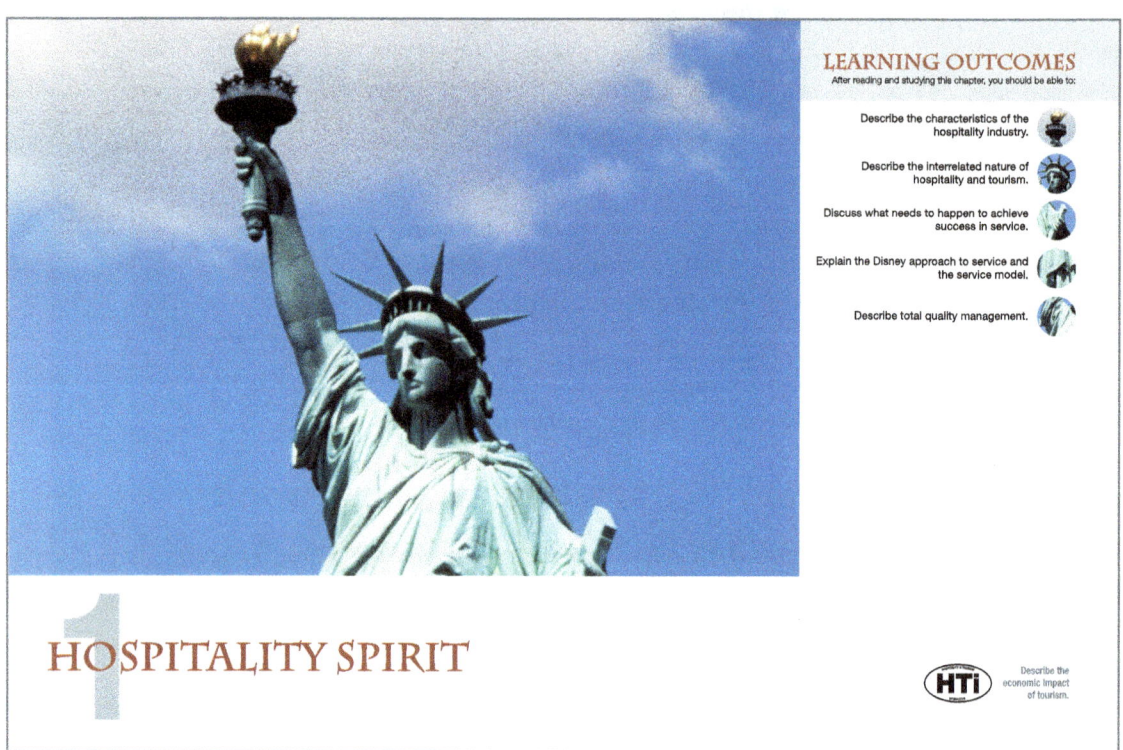

Hospitality–A Service Industry
This introductory chapter describes how and why service is the backbone of the hospitality industry.

FEATURES CONNECTING YOU TO THE REAL WORLD

These segments introduce you to real people and real jobs, with engaging true-to-life scenarios.

Introducing
Patti Roscoe

Patricia L. Roscoe, chairperson of Patti Roscoe and Associates (PRA) and Roscoe/Coltrell Inc. (RCI), landed in California in 1966, charmed by the beautiful San Diego sun (compared to the cold winters in Buffalo, New York, her hometown). She was a young, brilliant middle manager who was to face the challenges of a time when women were expected to become either nurses or teachers. She became involved with the hotel industry, working for a large private resort hotel, the Vacation Village. Those were the years to be remembered. She gained a very thorough knowledge of Southern California tourism, as well as of the inherent mechanisms of the industry. With the unforgettable help and guidance of her manager, she began to lay the foundations of her future career as a very successful leader in the field. The outstanding skills that she learned are, in fact, the very basis of her many accomplishments.

The list of Roscoe's awards and honors is astounding: She earned the prestigious CITE distinction (Certified Incentive Travel Executive), she was named the San Diego Woman of Accomplishment in 1983, and in February, 1990, Roscoe was honored as San Diego's 1989 Allied Member of the Year during the tourism industry's Gold Key Awards. Also in 1990, she was given the Wonder Woman Award by the U.S. Small Business Administration for her outstanding achievements in the field. In 1993, the San Diego Convention and Visitors Bureau conferred on her the prestigious RCA Lubach Award for her contributions to the industry.

She is also extremely involved in civic and tourism organizations, including the Rotary Club, the American Lung Association of San Diego and Imperial Counties, and the San Diego Convention and Visitors Bureau.

The key to Roscoe's success perhaps lies in her remarkable skills of interacting with people. It is the human resources, in fact, that represent the major strength of PRA. Its employees are experienced, dedicated, and service oriented. But what makes them so efficient is their dedication to working together as a team. Roscoe guides, inspires, and motivates these teams. She is a self-admitted "softy," a creative and emotional leader who enjoys training her employees and following their growth step by step, to eventually give them the power of initiative they deserve, as a tool to encourage their creativity and originality. She constantly seeks to balance the concept of teamwork with the individual goals and private lives of her employees. It is through the achievement of such a balance that a profitable, healthy community is preserved. PRA is a bit more than a community, however, it is a family. And just like a mother, Roscoe's formula is discipline and love. At the same time, her leading efforts are aimed at training her employees to "think outside of the box," and "keep one's view as broad as possible," which is the only way to rise above the commonplace, the rhetorical, and the trivial, to escape provincialism, and thus become unique individuals.

That's how the magic is done. PRA excels in creating "something that becomes exclusively yours—that has never been done before." PRA is decentralized into service teams to foster an entrepreneurial environment in which initiative and creativity can be boosted to the fullest. Therefore, PRA staff design personalized unique events to give their customers an unforgettable time.

Since its opening in 1981, PRA has become one of the most successful destination management companies in the country, providing personal, caring service characterized by flexibility and creativity.

Introducing...

This feature highlights selected key hospitality individuals with accounts of their real-life activities. These "Introducing..." boxes give a "from-the-heart" up-close and personal view of their work.

2,000 travel-related businesses, associations, and local, regional, and state travel promotion agencies of the nation's travel industry.

State Offices of Tourism

The next level of organizations concerned with tourism is the state office of tourism. These offices are charged by their legislative bodies with the orderly growth and development of tourism within the state. They promote information programs, advertising, publicity, and research in terms of their relation to the recreation and tourism attractions in the state.

City-Level Offices of Tourism and Convention Centers

Cities have also realized the importance of the "new" that tourism brings. Many cities have established con...

.inc | Corporate Profile

CLUB MED

In 1950, a Belgian diamond cutter and water polo champion conceived of the first Club Med village—funded with army surplus tax money—on the Spanish island of Majorca. The goal of that first resort was to unite people from diverse backgrounds, encourage them to share a good time, and offer them a unique escape from the stress and the tension of the everyday events of post—World War II Europe. The first adventurous vacationers to experience that new environment were mostly young couples or singles, living together in a beautiful natural setting, enjoying the atmosphere of camaraderie and no worries, playing sports, or just simply relaxing on a warm, soft beach.

The following decade was a particularly profitable one because of the overall social climate that characterized the 1960s. The young generation, generally speaking, was wrapped up in a whirl of ideals, such as peace, communion, and the sharing of feelings and experiences—all in the framework of a return to nature. The so-called "flower child" phenomenon saw the young long for a return to primitive purity, innocence, and freedom of expression. It is not surprising, then, that Club Med's clientele rose by 500 percent in that decade. In fact, the features that characterized the resorts made them just the right environment to meet the needs of this target market. Club Med expanded throughout the Mediterranean coastlines and islands, including Greece and Italy. Centers began to spring up on the coasts of Africa and the Middle East. Today Club Med—short for Mediterranean—has more than 120 resorts and vacation villages around the world, hosted by 28 countries in the Mediterranean as well as in the Caribbean, Africa, Mexico, the Bahamas, South Pacific, South America, Asia, and the United States. The little village in Majorca blossomed into a colorful, joyful, sunny, colossal empire: Club Med is the world's largest vacation village organization and the ninth largest hotel chain, with 93,000 beds and 20,000 employees. More than 9 million guests have come to the villages since 1950.

Today's philosophy doesn't differ much from the original one. Club Med intends to provide a spectacular natural setting in which its guests can enjoy life and its amenities, away from the troubles and the worries of the everyday frantic rat race. The theme on the printed advertisements points straight to this: "Club Med: Life as it should be." Sports, various entertaining activities, good food, real concern for guests' needs, and a carefree lifestyle worked wonders. Imagine all of these amenities in the context of white sand beaches and a clear blue sea that seems to stretch out indefinitely to meet a virtually cloudless sky at the horizon.

Club Med's original formula was copied by several other organizations in the travel and tourism industry. The increased competition caused Club Med to revise its management strategies and develop a different product in order to gain and hold market share. Changes in the industry were accompanied by social changes. As the years went by, the baby boomers of the 1960s and 1970s grew up, got married, and began to travel with their families. The target market thus changed again, and the necessity to change along with the market was promptly acknowledged.

The policy that Club Med's managers embraced was one of differentiation and flexibility. Through assiduous market research, studies, and surveys, Club Med identified the continuously changing needs and characteristics of both the market and the clientele. On the basis of their results, they were able to take effective action to keep up with such evolution. Marketing strategies therefore were reelaborated, and the product Club Med offers was repackaged according to the demands of the guests, while still remaining faithful to the original philosophy. The image of Club Med was also reconsidered in order to determine the most appropriate one at all times.

Other significant changes included an entrance into the cruise business—Club Med I is a luxurious cruise ship that offers the excitement of yachting (thanks to a retractable platform that allows activities such as waterskiing, diving, etc.) together with the comforts of the cruise. Activities within the village were also improved and upgraded, following the guests' requests for more in-depth sports teaching, more amenities in the rooms, specialized restaurants, more security, and communication tools.

The clientele target was also widened: Club Med now attempts to attract guests other than the original youth/couples. As a consequence, the individual villages were updated by specializing in a particular area. Although all clubs offer the same basic services, some focus mainly on sports, some on tours and excursions, some on convention and meeting facilities, some on entertainment, and so on. Guests now range from sports enthusiasts to families (mini clubs and baby clubs were recently established), honeymooners, and corporate clients. The new trend at the moment is that of finding ways to attract the older clientele.

Club Med also has had another innovative idea: Wild Card, which offers a bargain rate to vacationers who don't mind gambling on which village they visit. Wild Card confirms participants on a one-week vacation at one of Club Med's Villages in the Bahamas, Caribbean, or Mexico for $999 per

Corporate Profiles

Learn about the practices, growth, and scope of leading corporations and organizations. For example, "the Hawaiian Convention center represents the unique culture of Hawaii and is where business and Aloha meet" (www.hawaiiconventioncenter.com).

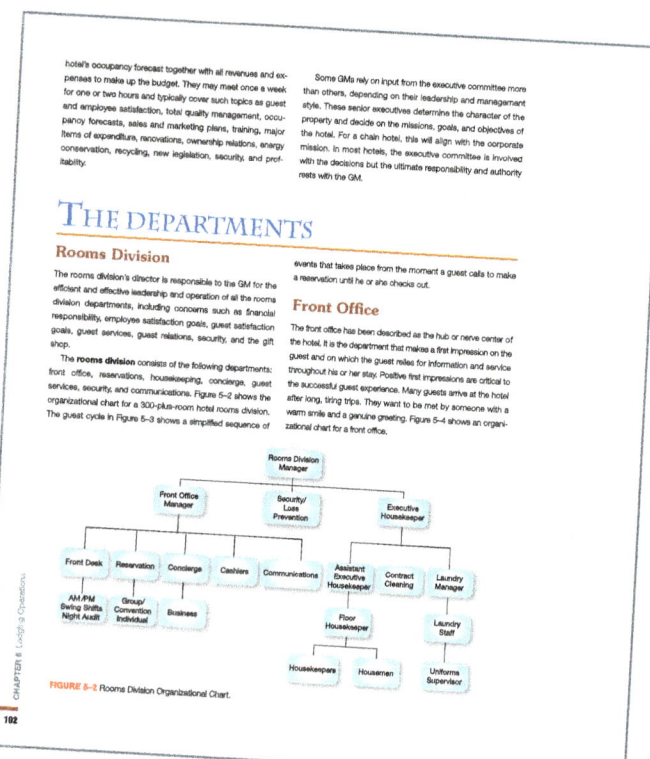

Career Information

This feature describes career opportunities, along with a list of related Web sites. Learn about the skills, challenges, and realities of careers in each segment of the hospitality industry.

Career Paths

Explore potential career paths within each chapter.

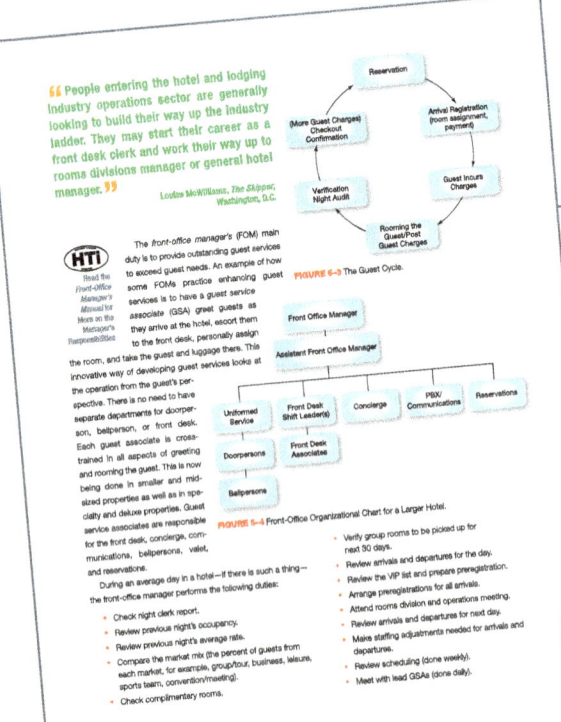

Quotes

In each chapter, comments from students and professionals offer personal perspectives about the industry.

TIMELINESS

the reservation is taken from the embassy of the countries. One Sunday afternoon, you are duty manager and several limos with people from "that part of the world" request rooms for several weeks. You decline even though there are available rooms. They even offer you a personal envelope, which they say contains $1,000. How do you feel about declining their request?

These and other ethical dilemmas are not always simply right or wrong.

Three key categories of questions need to be answered when making decisions:

1. Is it legal? Will I be violating civil law or company policy? Also, will I get fired if I accept it, allow it, or do it?
2. Is it balanced? Is it fair to all concerned in both the short term and the long term? Does it promote win–win relationships?
3. How will it make me feel about myself? Will it make me proud? Would I feel good if my family knew about it?

> The foundation of all principles is that all people's rights are important and should not be violated.

TRENDS in HOSPITALITY

We can identify a number of trends that are having and will continue to have an impact on the hospitality industry. Some, like diversity, are already here and are sure to increase in the future. Here, in no particular order, are some of the major trends that hospitality professionals indicate as having an influence on the industry. You will find these and others discussed in the chapters of this text.

- **Sustainability.** Environmental sustainability has become very important in the marketplace. To be sustainable or "green" means to have no negative environmental impacts (or at least to reduce them down to being as minimal as possible). Sustainable businesses often participate in environmentally friendly activities and advocate their "greenness."
- **Globalization.** We have become the global village that was described a few years ago. We may have the opportunity to work or vacation in other countries, and more people than ever travel freely around the world.
- **Safety and security.** Since September 11, 2001, we have all become more conscious of our personal safety and have experienced increased scrutiny at airports and federal and other buildings. But it goes beyond that: terrorists kidnap tourists from their resorts and hold them for ransom, thugs mug them, and others assault them. Two security experts have made valuable contributions to the chapters that follow by giving us the benefit of their experience and expertise.
- **Diversity.** The hospitality industry is the most diverse of all industries; not only do we have a diverse employee population, but we also have a diverse group of guests. Diversity is increasing as more people with more diverse cultures join the hospitality workforce.
- **Service.** It is no secret that service is at the top of guests' expectations, yet few companies offer exceptional service. World-class service does not just happen; training is important in delivering the service that guests have come to expect.
- **Technology.** Technology is a driving force of change that presents opportunities for greater efficiencies and integration for improved guest service. However, the industry faces great challenges in training employees to use new technology and in standardization of software and hardware design. Some hotels have several systems that do not talk to each other, and some reservation systems bounce between 7 and 10 percent of sales nationally.
- **Legal issues.** Lawsuits are not only more frequent, but they cost more if you lose and more to defend. One company spent several million dollars just to defend one case. Government regulations and the complexities of employee relations create increased challenges for hospitality operators.
- **Changing demographics.** The U.S. population is gradually increasing and the baby boomers are retiring. Many retirees have the time and money to travel and utilize hospitality services.
- **Price and value.** Price and value are important to today's more discerning guests.
- **Sanitation.** Sanitation is critical to the success of any restaurant and foodservice operation. Guests expect to eat healthy foods that have been prepared in a sanitary environment.

Trends

A list of trends gives you an up-to-date and realistic picture of the future of that segment of the industry.

HONE YOUR CRITICAL THINKING SKILLS

Mini Case Studies

Mini case studies dealing with real-world situations in each chapter challenge you to test your skills and knowledge and recommend appropriate actions.

Short Staffed in the Kitchen

Sally is the general manager of one of the best restaurants in town, known as The Pub. As usual, at 6:00 P.M. on a Friday night, there is a 45-minute wait. The kitchen is overloaded and is running behind in check times, the time that elapses between the kitchen getting the order and the guest receiving his or her meal. This is critical, especially if a guest complains about waiting too long for a meal.

Sally is waiting for her two head line cooks to come in for the closing shift. At 6:15 P.M., she receives phone calls from both of them. They are both sick with the flu and are not coming to work.

As Sally gets off the phone, the hostess tells her that a party of 50 is scheduled to arrive at 7:30 P.M. Sally is concerned, knowing that they are currently running a six-person line with only four cooks. The productivity is very high, but the check times are extremely long. How can Sally handle the situation?

DISCUSSION QUESTIONS

1. How would you handle the short-staffing issue?
2. What measures would you take to get the appropriate cooks in to work as soon as possible?
3. What would you do to ensure a smooth, successful transition for the party of 50?
4. How would you manipulate your floor plan to provide exceptional service for the party of 50?
5. How would you immediately make an impact on the long check times?
6. What should you do to ensure that all the guests in the restaurant are happy?

Internet Exercises

Visit informative and varied Web sites to uncover answers to specific hospitality questions. Internet exercises challenge you to learn more and prepare you for a career in this fascinating industry.

Apply Your Knowledge

Apply the knowledge and skills that you have learned in each chapter to real-life industry topics.

IMPORTANT MEMORY TOOLS

LEARNING OUTCOMES
After reading and studying this chapter, you should be able to:

- Describe the characteristics of the hospitality industry.
- Describe the interrelated nature of hospitality and tourism.
- Discuss what needs to happen to achieve success in service.
- Explain the Disney approach to service and the service model.
- Describe total quality management.

Learning Outcomes
At the start of each chapter, this list gives you a "heads up" to what will be discussed, helping you to organize your thoughts. The learning outcomes summarize what you will know after studying the chapter and completing the exercises, cases, questions, and Apply Your Knowledge challenges.

you may want to ask yourself if you are considering a career in the industry:

1. Do you enjoy working with people?
2. Do you enjoy an upbeat work atmosphere?
3. Do you like to travel?
4. Do you value the idea of working in an industry where opportunities for advancement are plentiful?

If you answered yes to these questions, a career in hospitality and tourism may well be for you.

CHARACTERISTICS OF THE HOSPITALITY INDUSTRY

Hospitality businesses are open 365 days a year, 24 hours a day. No, we don't have to work all of that time, but we do tend to work longer hours than some other industries. Those on their way to senior positions in the hospitality industry and many others, for that matter, often work 10 to 12 hours per day. Evenings and weekends are included in the workweek—so we have to accept the fact that we may be working when others are enjoying free time. The hospitality industry depends heavily on shift work. Early in your career, depending on the department, you will likely work one of four shifts. Supervisors and managers often begin at 8 A.M. and work until 6 or 8 P.M. Basically there are four shifts, beginning with the morning shift, so you may be getting up as early as 6 A.M. to get to your 7 A.M. shift. The mid-shift is normally from 10 A.M. to 7 P.M.; the evening shift starts at 3 P.M. and goes until 11:30 P.M.; and finally there is the graveyard shift, which begins at 11 P.M. and ends at 7:30 A.M. Well, success does not come easily.

In the hospitality industry, we constantly strive for outstanding **guest satisfaction**, which leads to guest loyalty and, yes, profit. Our services are mostly **intangible**: the guest cannot "test-drive" a night's stay, "kick the tires" prior to boarding a shuttle, or "squeeze the steak" before dining. Our product is for the guest's use—not possession—only. Even more unique, for us to produce this product, we must get the guest's input. Imagine GE building a refrigerator while the customer is in the factory participating in the actual construction of the product—it would be ridiculous! Yet we do it every single day, numerous times per day, and in a uniquely different way each time. We refer to this as the **inseparability** of production and consumption of the service product and the inherent heterogeneity of the product due to each guest's unique demands. The other unique dimension of our industry is the **perishability** of our product. For example, we have 1,400 rooms in inventory, that is, available to sell, but we sell only 1,200 rooms. What do we do with the 200 unsold rooms? Nothing—we have permanently lost 200 room nights and their revenue.

Restaurants like Coyote Café in Santa Fe are open weekends and holidays.

Check Your Knowledge
1. List and describe the four shifts in the hospitality industry.
2. Explain the pineapple tradition.
3. Discuss how perishability affects hospitality operations.

Each year, the National Restaurant Association (NRA) invites the best and brightest students from universities and colleges to participate in its annual restaurant show in Chicago. The highlight of the show is the "Salute to Excellence" day, when students and faculty attend forums, workshops, and a gala award

Check Your Knowledge
Every few pages, the Check Your Knowledge section helps with a review and reinforcement of material that has just been covered.

Chapter Summary

The chapter summary highlights the most important points in the chapter. This brief review of the chapter reinforces the main terms, concepts, and topics.

Key Words and Concepts

Highlighted in bold, with easy-to-understand definitions in the glossary, the key words and concepts help you to recall the importance and meaning of important terms. Master the key words and concepts of the text and improve your test scores.

Review Questions

By answering these review questions, you will reinforce your mastery of the materials presented in the text and will most likely improve your test scores.

VISUALS

Color format with lively photographs, drawings, and tables will maintain your interest and provide visual aids to learning.

FIGURE 1–2 Scope of the Hospitality and Tourism Industry.

FIGURE 1–3 The Interrelated Nature of Hospitality, Travel, and Tourism.

THE PINEAPPLE TRADITION

The pineapple has enjoyed a rich and romantic heritage as a symbol of welcome, friendship, and hospitality. Pineapples were brought back from the West Indies by early European explorers during the seventeenth century. From that time on, the pineapple was cultivated in Europe and became the favored fruit to serve to royalty and the elite. The pineapple was later introduced into North America and became a part of hospitality there. In the colonial times, sea captains would display a pineapple on their doors or on gateposts giving public notice to friends and acquaintances that they had had a safe trip home. It also symbolized "The ship is in! Come join us. Food and drink for all!" Since its introduction, the pineapple has been internationally recognized as a symbol of hospitality and a sign of friendliness, warmth, and cheer.

Pineapple is the symbol for hospitality.

The **National Restaurant Association (NRA)** forecasts a need for thousands of supervisors and managers for the hospitality and tourism industry. Okay, so you're wondering if there's room in this dynamic industry for you. You bet! There's room for everyone. The best advice is to consider what you love to do and get some experience in that area—to see if you really like it—because our industry has some special characteristics. For starters, we are in the business of giving service. When Kurt Wachtveitl, 30-year veteran general manager of the Oriental Hotel in Bangkok, Thailand—considered by many to be one of the best hotels in the world—is asked, "What is the secret of being the best?" he replies, "Service, service, service!"

THE INTERRELATED NATURE OF HOSPITALITY AND TOURISM

Explore the Tourism Industry— Meet the Island Proprietor

The hospitality and tourism industry is the largest and fastest-growing industry in the world. One of the most exciting aspects of this industry is that it is made up of so many different professions. What picture comes to your mind when you think about a career in hospitality and tourism? Do you picture a chef, general manager, director of marketing, doorman, or server? Hospitality and tourism professions are limitless. They range from positions in restaurants, resorts, cruise lines, theme parks, casinos, and everything in between. Under the umbrella of travel and tourism, countless professions are necessary to meet the needs and wants of people away from home (Figures 1–2 and 1–3). Throughout this book, we discuss some of the career possibilities in hospitality and/or tourism. Here are a few questions

The interrelated nature of hospitality and tourism means that we would fly here and stay in a hotel and eat in a restaurant.

We now invite you to join us and share our enthusiasm for hospitality!

Preface

Exploring the Hospitality Industry was written to fill a vital need: a text that was different in structure and content, and broader in its coverage of the hospitality industry. The introductory course in hospitality serves as a foundation for other courses and is used to attract majors to hospitality management programs. This book is intended for both purposes. The hospitality industry continues to change rapidly, and this text brings you the very latest trends from the broadest array of hospitality industry segments. It is a "need to know" book, vibrant and colorful in design, that is outstanding in its easy-to-use, engaging content.

We thank you if you have used my *Introduction to Hospitality*, which offers an overview of the hospitality industry and has an operational focus; or our *Introduction to Hospitality Management*, which highlights management issues. **Exploring the Hospitality Industry** is different in structure and content and offers a broader coverage of the hospitality sectors. This text is designed for the hospitality professionals of the future. We have strived to create the most accessible intro book on the market—from its easy-to-read conversational writing style to the Hospitality Interactive Web site, we aim to excel. In every chapter, we invite students to share our unique enthusiasm for the hospitality industry.

Goals and Organization of This Text

The primary goal of *Exploring the Hospitality Industry* is to help students advance in their hospitality careers by giving them a foundation of hospitality industry knowledge. The information is presented in a lively and interesting manner, and includes an extensive array of features to facilitate the learning process. Chapters cover all facets and segments of the industry, and present a student-friendly text in an outstanding instructional package.

Exploring the Hospitality Industry is organized into 15 chapters.

1. Hospitality Spirit
2. Tourism
3. Why People Travel
4. Lodging
5. Lodging Operations
6. Cruising
7. Restaurants
8. Restaurant Operations
9. Managed Services
10. Beverages
11. Clubs
12. Theme Parks and Attractions
13. Gaming Entertainment
14. Meetings, Conventions, and Expositions
15. Special Events

Hallmark Chapter Features Include:

- **Learning outcomes** that help the reader focus on the main points of each chapter.
- **Bold key words and concepts** that help the reader hone in on the various topics presented in the chapter.
- **"Introducing..."** features that describe the careers and work of successful industry practitioners.
- **Corporate profiles** that give an overview of leading corporations of excellence.
- **Career information** in each chapter.
- **Check your knowledge** features that encourage students to answer questions relevant to the material covered every few pages.
- **Thorough identification and analysis of trends,** issues, and challenges that will have a significant affect on hospitality in the future.
- **Summaries** that correspond to the chapter learning outcomes.
- **Learning outcome-based and critical thinking review questions related to SCANS (Secretary's Commission on Achieving Necessary Skills)** that review important aspects of the text.
- **Case studies** that challenge students to address real-world situations and recommend appropriate action.
- **Internet exercises** that invite students to visit Web sites to find answers to specific, relevant-to-hospitality questions.
- **Apply Your Knowledge** questions that offer students the chance to apply their knowledge of hospitality industry topics.
- A full **Glossary** that explains the meaning of special words throughout the text.

New to This Edition

Chapter 1.	Three figures on career ladders
	Information on hospitality industry salaries
	New information on career paths and goals
	Is the hospitality industry for you?
	Self-assessment and personal philosophy
	Professionalism and etiquette
	Professional organizations and associations
	Ethics and ethical dilemmas in hospitality
Chapter 2.	A section on sustainable tourism has been added
Chapter 3.	A model of a sustainable ecotourism system
	A framework for ecotourism
	A new section on ecotourism
	A section on the environmental impact of tourism
Chapter 4.	A new section on sustainable lodging and new artwork
Chapter 5.	A new section on sustainable lodging operations and new artwork
Chapter 6.	A new section on sustainable cruising and new artwork
Chapter 7.	A new section on sustainable restaurants and new artwork
Chapter 8.	A new section on sustainable restaurant operations and new artwork
Chapter 9.	A new section on sustainable managed service operations and new artwork

Chapter 10. A new section on sustainable beverages and new artwork

Chapter 11. A new section on sustainable club operations and new artwork

Chapter 12. A new section on sustainable theme parks and attractions and new artwork

Chapter 13. A new section on sustainable gaming and new artwork

Chapter 14. A new section on sustainable meetings and conventions and expositions and new artwork

Chapter 15. A new section on wedding planning and sustainable special events and new artwork

Each chapter has a new section on career advice from industry professionals

ACKNOWLEDGMENTS

Thank you to the professors and students who offered advice and contributions to this text—it is better because of you! Thanks also to the numerous industry professionals who lent their time and expertise to enhance the text. I am especially grateful to Holly Loftus, who did a great research job and helped with all facets of text preparation. Thank you to Karen Harris for her outstanding work on the special events chapter. To Jay Schrock, the best colleague a faculty member could wish for, thanks for your contribution and encouragement.

We are truly grateful to the educators who authored the supplements for this book. Thanks to Eva Smith for the wonderful PowerPoint slides and study guide. John Bandman's work on the companion Web site is deeply appreciated. Thanks to Gary Ward for his fine work on the instructor's manual. And our gratitude goes out to Ken Jarvis for creating the test bank. It was a pleasure working with all of you.

Our thanks also go to Vern Anthony, whose vision inspired this text, and to William Lawrensen, for his guidance.

About the Authors

Dr. John R. Walker, D.B.A., FMP, CHA, is a Fulbright Senior Specialist and the McKibbon Professor of Hotel and Restaurant Management at the University of South Florida, Sarasota–Manatee. John's years of industry experience include management training at the Savoy Hotel London, followed by stints as food and beverage manager, assistant rooms division manager, catering manager, and general manager with Grand Metropolitan Hotels, Selsdon Park Hotel, Rank Hotels, Inter-Continental Hotels, and the Coral Reef Resort, Barbados, West Indies.

He has taught at two- and four-year schools in Canada and the United States. In addition to being a hospitality management consultant and author, he has been published in the *Cornell Hotel Restaurant Administration Quarterly* and the *Hospitality Educators Journal*. He is a 10-time recipient of the President's Award for teaching, scholarship, and service; and he has received the Patnubay Award for exemplary professional performance through teaching and authorship of tourism and hospitality publications.

John is an editorial advisory board member for *Progress in Tourism and Hospitality Research*. He is a past president of the Pacific Chapter of the Council on Hotel, Restaurant, and Institutional Education (CHRIE). He is a certified hotel administrator (CHA) and a certified Foodservice Management Professional (FMP). He and his wife Josielyn T. Walker have twins, Christopher and Selina. The Walkers live in Sarasota, Florida, and Suso Beach, Santa Maria, Ilocos Sur, Philippines.

EXPLORING
the HOSPITALITY INDUSTRY

1 HOSPITALITY SPIRIT

LEARNING OUTCOMES

After reading and studying this chapter, you should be able to:

Describe the characteristics of the hospitality industry.

Describe the interrelated nature of hospitality and tourism.

Discuss what needs to happen to achieve success in service.

Explain the Disney approach to service and the service model.

Describe total quality management.

 Describe the economic impact of tourism.

Welcome to you, the future hospitality industry leaders!

The hospitality industry is one of the most fascinating, fun, and stimulating in which to work, plus you get paid quite well and have excellent advancement opportunities. We often hear from industry professionals that the industry gets in your blood—meaning that we become one with the hospitality industry. On countless class industry visits people who speak to the class say that they wouldn't change their jobs for anything! Only one person has said, "You guys must be nuts if you want to work in this industry." Of course he was joking, but there are some realities that we need to be aware of and which discuss in the section that describes the characteristics of the industry. There are several examples of people graduating and being offered positions that enable them to gain a good foundation of knowledge and experience in the industry. Possible career paths for these graduates are illustrated in Figure 1–1. In most cases, it does not take long for advancement opportunities to come along; however, let's begin our journey with a look at hospitality *service spirit*, which plays a crucial role in the success of our industry, no matter what your position or title is.

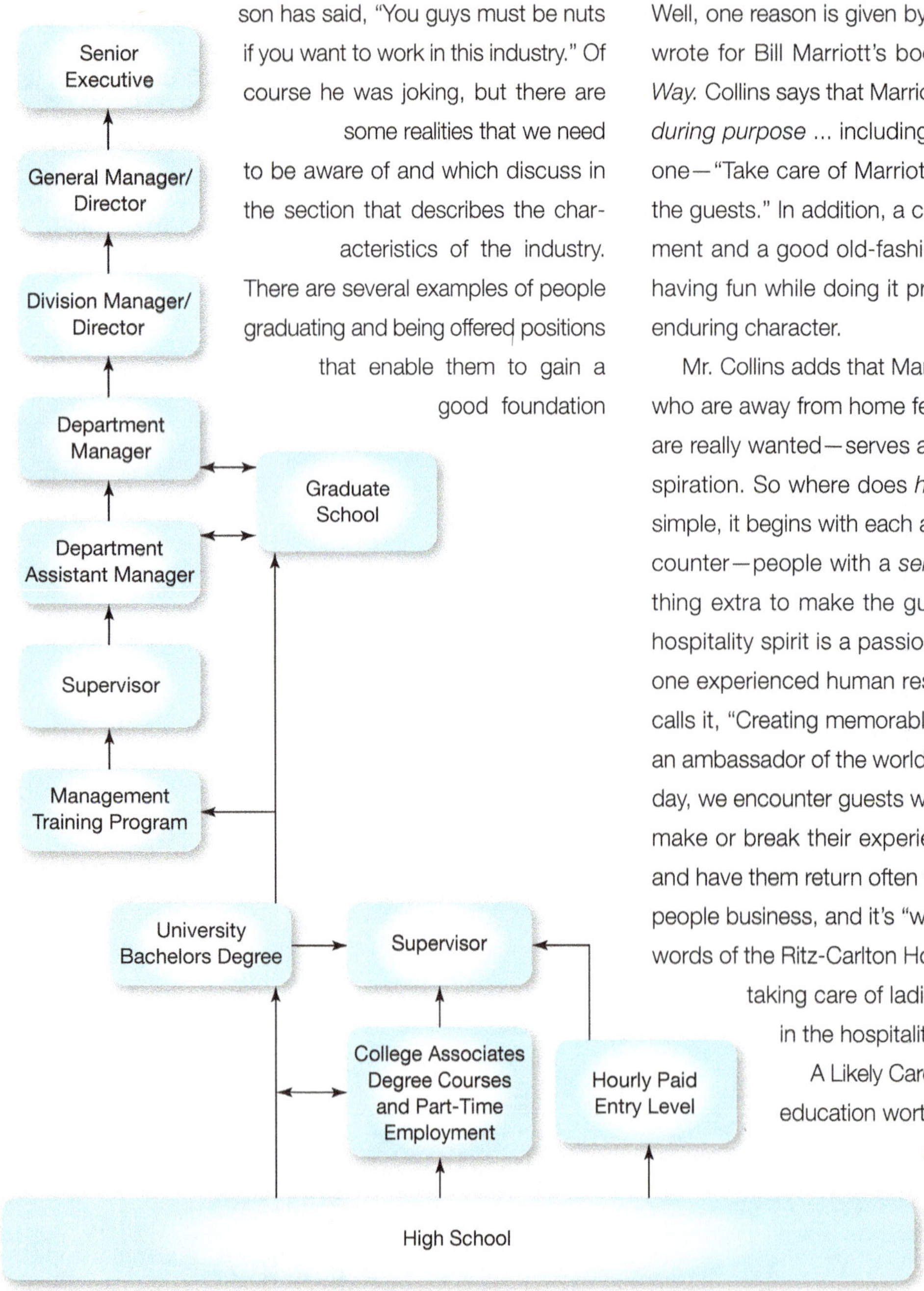

Ever think about why Marriott International is so successful? Well, one reason is given by Jim Collins in the foreword that he wrote for Bill Marriott's book, *The Spirit to Serve: Marriott's Way*. Collins says that Marriott has *timeless core values and enduring purpose* ... including the belief that people are number one—"Take care of Marriott people and they will take care of the guests." In addition, a commitment to continuous improvement and a good old-fashioned dedication to hard work and having fun while doing it provide a foundation of stability and enduring character.

Mr. Collins adds that Marriott's core purpose—make people who are away from home feel that they are among friends and are really wanted—serves as a fixed point of guidance and inspiration. So where does *hospitality spirit* fit in to all this? It's simple, it begins with each and every time we have a guest encounter—people with a *service spirit* are happy to do something extra to make the guest's experience memorable. The hospitality spirit is a passion to give pleasure to others, or, as one experienced human resources director, Charlotte Jordan, calls it, "Creating memorable experiences for others and being an ambassador of the world, adding warmth and caring." Every day, we encounter guests who rely on us for service, which can make or break their experience. We want to wow the guests and have them return often with their friends. Yes, we are in the people business, and it's "we the people" who take pride in the words of the Ritz-Carlton Hotel—"We are ladies and gentlemen taking care of ladies and gentlemen"—who succeed in the hospitality industry.

A Likely Career Path in the Hospitality Industry. Is education worth it? You bet! Just think—the difference in salary between an associate's and a bachelor's degree over the length of a career is $500,000—Yes, that's half a million bucks!

FIGURE 1–1 Probable Career Path in Hospitality.

THE PINEAPPLE TRADITION

The pineapple has enjoyed a rich and romantic heritage as a symbol of welcome, friendship, and hospitality. Pineapples were brought back from the West Indies by early European explorers during the seventeenth century. From that time on, the pineapple was cultivated in Europe and became the favored fruit to serve to royalty and the elite. The pineapple was later introduced into North America and became a part of hospitality there. In the colonial times, sea captains would display a pineapple on their doors or on gateposts giving public notice to friends and acquaintances that they had had a safe trip home. It also symbolized "The ship is in! Come join us. Food and drink for all!" Since its introduction, the pineapple has been internationally recognized as a symbol of hospitality and a sign of friendliness, warmth, and cheer.

Pineapple is the symbol for hospitality.

The **National Restaurant Association (NRA)** forecasts a need for thousands of supervisors and managers for the hospitality and tourism industry. Okay, so you're wondering if there's room in this dynamic industry for you. You bet! There's room for everyone. The best advice is to consider what you love to do and get some experience in that area—to see if you really like it—because our industry has some special characteristics. For starters, we are in the business of giving service. When Kurt Wachtveilt, 30-year veteran general manager of the Oriental Hotel in Bangkok, Thailand—considered by many to be one of the best hotels in the world—is asked, "What is the secret of being the best?" he replies, "Service, service, service!"

THE INTERRELATED NATURE OF HOSPITALITY AND TOURISM

Explore the Tourism Industry- Meet the Island Proprietor

The hospitality and tourism industry is the largest and fastest-growing industry in the world. One of the most exciting aspects of this industry is that it is made up of so many different professions. What picture comes to your mind when you think about a career in hospitality and tourism? Do you picture a chef, general manager, director of marketing, doorman, or server? Hospitality and tourism professions are limitless. They range from positions in restaurants, resorts, cruise lines, theme parks, casinos, and everything in between. Under the umbrella of travel and tourism, countless professions are necessary to meet the needs and wants of people away from home (Figures 1–2 and 1–3).

Throughout this book, we discuss some of the career possibilities in hospitality and/or tourism. Here are a few questions

The interrelated nature of hospitality and tourism means that we would fly here and stay in a hotel and eat in a restaurant.

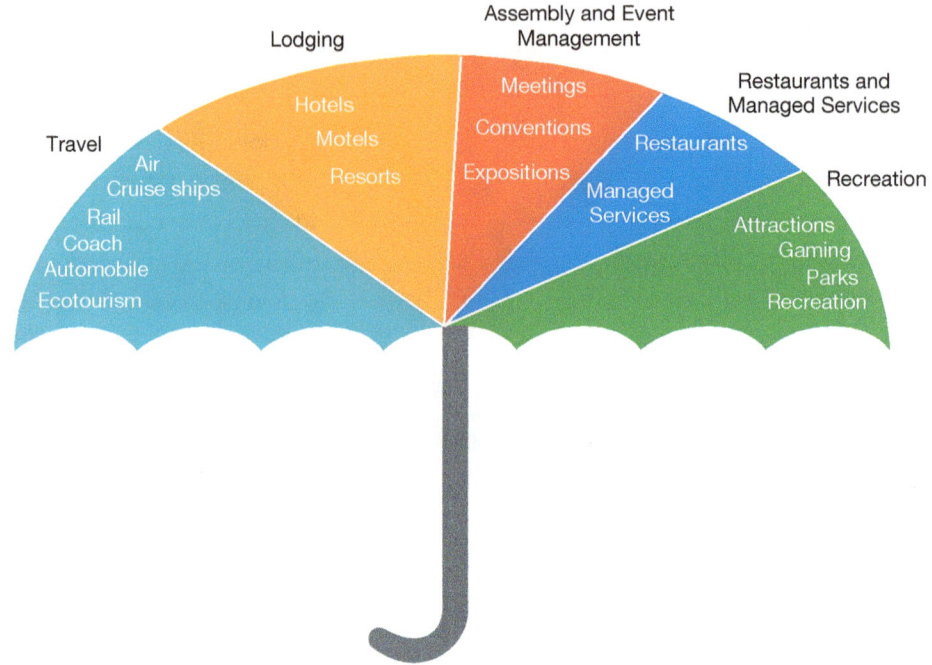

FIGURE 1–2 Scope of the Hospitality and Tourism Industry.

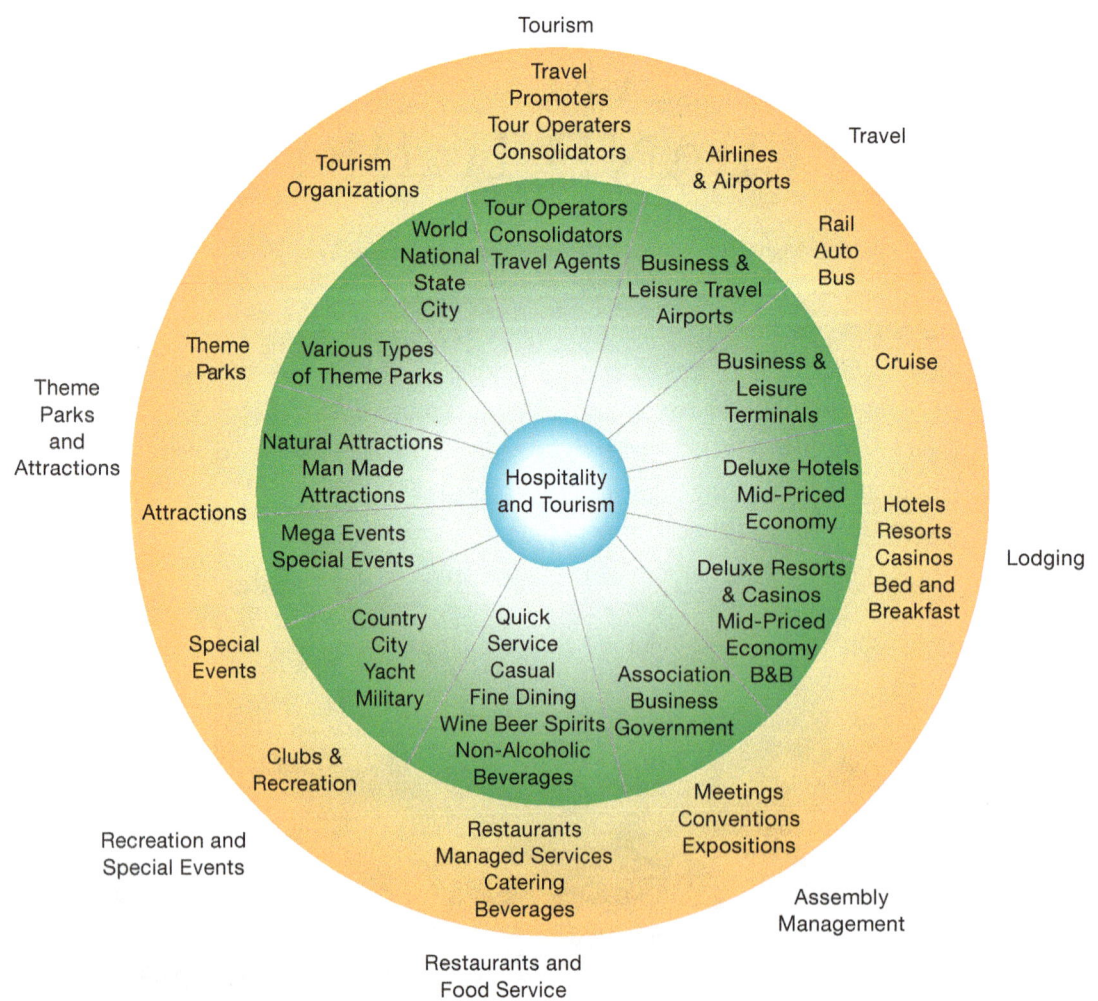

FIGURE 1–3 The Interrelated Nature of Hospitality, Travel, and Tourism.

you may want to ask yourself if you are considering a career in the industry:

1. Do you enjoy working with people?
2. Do you enjoy an upbeat work atmosphere?
3. Do you like to travel?
4. Do you value the idea of working in an industry where opportunities for advancement are plentiful?

If you answered yes to these questions, a career in hospitality and tourism may well be for you.

Characteristics of the Hospitality Industry

Hospitality businesses are open 365 days a year, 24 hours a day. No, we don't have to work all of that time, but we do tend to work longer hours than some other industries. Those on their way to senior positions in the hospitality industry and many others, for that matter, often work 10 to 12 hours per day. Evenings and weekends are included in the workweek—so we have to accept the fact that we may be working when others are enjoying free time. The hospitality industry depends heavily on shift work. Early in your career, depending on the department, you will likely work one of four shifts. Supervisors and managers often begin at 8 A.M. and work until 6 or 8 P.M. Basically there are four shifts, beginning with the morning shift, so you may be getting up as early as 6 A.M. to get to your 7 A.M. shift. The mid-shift is normally from 10 A.M. to 7 P.M.; the evening shift starts at 3 P.M. and goes until 11:30 P.M.; and finally there is the graveyard shift, which begins at 11 P.M. and ends at 7:30 A.M. Well, success does not come easily.

In the hospitality industry, we constantly strive for outstanding **guest satisfaction**, which leads to guest loyalty and, yes, profit. Our services are mostly **intangible**: the guest cannot "test-drive" a night's stay, "kick the tires" prior to boarding a shuttle, or "squeeze the steak" before dining. Our product is for the guest's use—not possession—only. Even more unique, for us to produce this product, we must get the guest's input. Imagine GE building a refrigerator while the customer is in the factory participating in the actual construction of the product—it would be ridiculous! Yet we do it every single day, numerous times per day, and in a uniquely different way each time. We refer to this as the **inseparability** of production and consumption of the service product and the inherent heterogeneity of the product due to each guest's unique demands. The other unique dimension of our industry is the **perishability** of our product. For example, we have 1,400 rooms in inventory, that is, available to sell, but we sell only 1,200 rooms. What do we do with the 200 unsold rooms? Nothing—we have permanently lost 200 room nights and their revenue.

Restaurants like Coyote Café in Santa Fe are open weekends and holidays.

> ## Check Your Knowledge
> 1. **List and describe the four shifts in the hospitality industry.**
> 2. **Explain the pineapple tradition.**
> 3. **Discuss how perishability affects hospitality operations.**

Each year, the National Restaurant Association (NRA) invites the best and brightest students from universities and colleges to participate in its annual restaurant show in Chicago. The highlight of the show is the "Salute to Excellence" day, when students and faculty attend forums, workshops, and a gala award banquet with industry leaders. The event is sponsored by Coca-Cola and several other corporations involved in the industry. During the day, students are invited to write their dreams on a large panel, which is later displayed for all to enjoy reading. Here are a few of the previous year's hopes and dreams:

- To help all people learn and grow. (Jason P.)
- To be the best I can. (NMC)
- To establish a chain of jazz cafés in 6 years and go public in 10 years. (Richard)
- Successfully please my customers. (J. Calicendo)
- To be happy and to make others happy, too.
- To put smiles on all faces.
- To be one of the most creative chefs—I would like to be happy with everything I create.
- To make a difference in the lives of people through food! (Mitz Dardony)
- To be successful professionally, socially, and financially. (Marcy W.)
- To preserve our natural resources by operating a restaurant called "Green." (Kimberley Mauren)
- Anything I do I like to do it in such a way that I can always be meaningful to people. (Christian Ellis-Schmidt)
- To reach the top, because I know there is a lot of space up there. (P. W., Lexington College)
- To use the knowledge that I've gained throughout my career and pass it on to others in hopes of touching their lives in a positive way! To smile and to make smiles. (Armey P. DaCalo)
- I want to be prosperous in my desire to achieve more than $. Happiness and peace are the keys to life. (D. McKinney)
- To teach and be as good as those who have taught me. (Thomas)

So what are your dreams and goals? Take a moment to think about your personal dreams and goals. Keep them in mind and look back on them often. Be prepared to amend them as you develop your career.

Careers

There are thousands of hospitality career options for you to consider, and it's fine if you are not yet sure which is the one for you. In Figure 1–3, you can see the major hospitality and tourism industry segments: lodging, restaurants and foodservice, recreation and special events, assembly management, theme parks and attractions, travel and tourism. For instance, lodging provides career opportunities for many associates who make reservations, greet, assist and serve guests in hospitality operations of varied sizes and in locations all over the world. Among the examples are the operators of a bed and breakfast (B&B) in upstate New York who cater to seasonal guests. Another example is the hundreds of employees necessary to keep the City Center complex in Las Vegas operational. Throughout the chapters of this text we will explore the important segments of the hospitality industry. Enjoy!

Read the Big Book of Tourism to Discover More About These Areas

Figures 1–4, 1–5, and 1–6 show a career ladder for lodging management and food and beverage management, and the rooms division in mid-sized and large hotels. Figure 1–7 shows a career ladder for restaurant management. Remember the U.S. Census Bureau's statistic of lifetime salaries by educational level:

High school graduate: $1.2 million
Associate's degree: $1.6 million
Bachelor's degree: $2.1 million

Consider what this information means—you will likely be $500,000 better off by getting a bachelor's degree. And speaking of salaries, Figure 1–8 is a salary guide for hospitality positions.

FIGURE 1–4 Lodging Management Career Ladder.

MAKE A COMMITMENT to EXCELLENCE

As you begin your career in the hospitality industry, it is important to make a commitment to excellence. You can become whatever you aspire to become—remember, it's your attitude that determines your altitude. Somebody has to be the president of the company. Why not you?

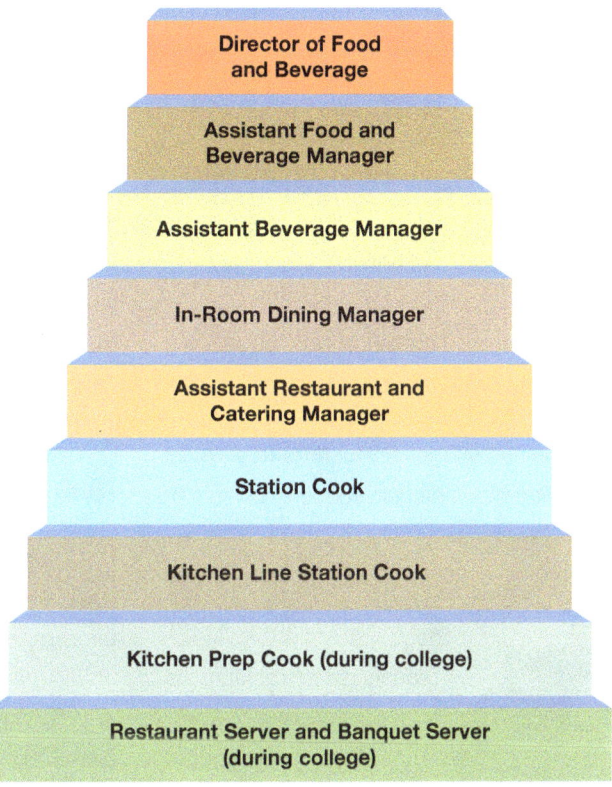

FIGURE 1–5 Lodging Food and Beverage Career Ladder.

FIGURE 1–7 A Restaurant Management Career Ladder.

FIGURE 1–6 Lodging Career Ladder for the Rooms Division.

Hospitality Salaries

President of a Chain Lodging Company	$250,000–500,000
President of a Chain Restaurant Company	$175,000–450,000
Vice President of a Lodging Company	$150,000–250,000
Hotel/Resort General Manager	$75,000–175,000
Country Club General Manager	$100,000–350,000
Vice President of a Restaurant Company	$75,000–150,000
Restaurant General Manager	$40,000–80,000
Hotel or Resort Rooms Division Director	$50–80,000
Hotel/Resort Human Resources Director	$50,000–80,000
Hotel or Resort Food and Beverage Director	$55,000–100,000
Hotel/Resort Catering Manager	$50,000–90,000
Assistant Restaurant Manager	$25,000–40,000
Hotel Front Office Manager	$30,000–60,000
Hotel/Resort Executive Housekeeper	$30,000–75,000
Hotel/Resort Assistant Food and Beverage Manager	$35,000–60,000
Hotel/Resort Executive Chef	$40,000–90,000
Restaurant Chef	$30,000–80,000
Front Desk Agent	$16,000–25,000
Servers	$20,000–40,000
Cooks	$20,000–30,000

FIGURE 1–8 A Guide to Hospitality Salaries.

THE FOCUS ON SERVICE

Watch the Check-In Process in Action with the Front-Desk Agent at Hutchinson Hotel

Why is great service such an essential element in the hospitality industry? The answer is simple, the industry depends on it. Great service results in happy guests. Happy guests provide not only repeated business, but a chain reaction via word of mouth. With so much focus on service, why is it so inconsistent today? Giving good service is a very difficult task; our educational system does not seem to teach service. Few businesses give enough priority to education and training in service. We tend to suffer from an overreliance on technology and service providers are often not motivated to give good service.

For example, when checking a guest into a hotel, the front-desk associate may greet the guest, but then look down at the computer for the rest of the service encounter, even when he or she is asking for the guest's name. Or, consider the reservations associate who says nothing when a guest asks for a specific type of guest room because he or she is waiting for the computer to indicate whether there is availability. An example of outstanding service is one Radisson Hotel associate who noticed that a guest brought in his own brand of soft drink and placed it in the minibar. The housekeeper informed her supervisor, who in turn told guest relations. The next time that guest arrived at the hotel, he was "blown away" when he discovered his favorite drink in the minibar.

In his best-selling book *At America's Service*, Karl Albrecht lists the "Seven Deadly Sins of Service":

1. Apathy
2. Brush-off
3. Coldness
4. Condescension
5. Robotics
6. Rule book
7. Runaround

" Hospitality is important because it determines how the guests feel—and whether or not the business will accomplish its goals. "

Heather Lotts, The Crockpot, Nashville, TN

A *Money Magazine* article titled "The Six Rudest Restaurants in America"[1] detailed a number of characteristically negative experiences guests had with restaurants noted more for their high ordeals than their food and service. The article's author, Michael Williams, identified the most common insults to guests:

1. Grossly overbooked reservations
2. Holding better tables for favorite guests
3. Maître d's who could suddenly conjure up a table for a heavy tip
4. Treating guests with an attitude bordering on arrogance

These are not everyday examples from the thousands of restaurants that offer great service around the country. Danny Meyer, president of the Union Square Hospitality Group, which operates the award-winning Union Square Café, describes his philosophy as enlightened hospitality—if your staff is happy, then your guests will also be happy. Meyer goes the extra mile to keep his employees happy by giving each of them a voucher to dine at his and other restaurants once a month. They must write a report on their experience; Meyer enjoys reading them. As a coach, he says that it's better to have your staff tell you what's wrong than for you to have to tell them.

A restaurant employee (and college student) greets a restaurant guest.

PERFECTING SERVICE

Success in Service

What must happen to achieve success in service? Given that approximately 70 percent of the American and Canadian economies and an increasing percentage of other countries are engaged in **service industries**, it is critical to offer guests exceptional service, but what is exceptional service? Service is defined in *Webster's New World Dictionary* as "the act or means of serving." To serve is to "provide goods and services for" and "be of assistance to."

This is the *age of service,* and the hospitality industry is getting re-vamped because guest expectations have increased and the realization is that *we buy loyalty with service.*[2] With thousands of guest encounters or moments of truth each day, it is critical to incorporate service excellence throughout each hospitality organization. Some corporations adopt the expression, "If you're not serving the guest, you had better be serving someone who is." This is the essence of teamwork; someone in the **back of the house** is serving someone in the **front of the house**, who is serving the guest. Teamwork creates a positive environment in which to work and reduces staff turnover. Most important, it helps to achieve the common goal, guest satisfaction. Without teamwork, success in hospitality is difficult, if not impossible, to achieve.

A *guest* is anyone who receives or benefits from the output of someone's work. The external customer is the customer whom most people think of in the traditional sense. The satisfaction of external customers ultimately measures a company's success, since they are the people who are willing to pay for a company's services. The internal customers are the people inside any company who receive or benefit from the output of work done by others in the company.

For success in service, we need to:

1. Focus on the guest.
2. Understand the role of guest service.
3. Weave a service culture into education and training systems. Remember that we are all serving someone—the dishwasher

Carmen Gonzalez, chef-owner of Carmen the Restaurant, Coral Gables, FL.

> **❝ Great hospitality overrides all elements of the guest's experience. It gives them the most important feeling, the sense that they are important and welcome in the establishment. ❞**
>
> Donald Jones,
> Ocean Side
> Café, Nokomis, FL

has a server as a guest so his or her work is very important. Anticipating guest needs is very important if we want to impress them and win them as frequent guests.

4. Emphasize high touch instead of high tech.
5. Thrive on change—constantly improving the guest experience.

As hospitality professionals, we need to recognize situations and act to relieve them or avoid them. Imagine how an associate can win points by showing empathy, that is, putting herself in someone else's shoes, in the following situation: A party of eight people arrives at a restaurant: Mom, Dad, and the kids, who are running all over the place. Mom and Dad just had a huge fight in the minivan. Obviously, the associate would want to welcome the party to the restaurant and find a way to seat them as quickly

See How the Dishwasher Services the Guest by Keeping the Kitchen Clean at the Sea & Tea Café

as possible, then give the kids something to play with and munch on until the food comes. Also, offer Mom and Dad a margarita, a glass of wine or other cocktail, and so on.

Another key objective in the service equation is to create guest loyalty. We not only need to keep guests happy during their stay, but also to keep them returning—with their friends, we hope! It costs several times more to attract new guests than to retain existing ones. Imagine how much more profit a hospitality business would make if it could retain just 10 percent more of its guests as loyal guests. Losing a guest equates to losing much more than one sale—the potential can be loss of a lifetime guest. Consider a $40 restaurant dinner for two people. If the guests return twice a month over—say, 10 years because they really like the place—the amount quickly becomes huge ($9,600). If they bring some friends, this amount will be even higher. Can you remember your worst service experience? Also, can you recall your best service experience?

We know that service is a complex yet critical component of the hospitality industry. Albrecht and Zemke, in their book *Service America!*, suggest two basic kinds of service: "Help me!" and "Fix it."[3] "Help me!" refers to guests' regular and special needs, such as "Help me find the function room" or "Help me to get a reservation at the best restaurant in town." "Fix it" refers to services such as "Please fix my toilet, it won't flush" or "Please fix the TV so we can watch the World Series." One restaurateur explains that in tough economic times, restaurants are expected to deliver more than your food. "Service used to be an important part of what we do here. Now it's an outrageously important part of what we do," says Jason Babb, general manager of Grill 23 & Bar, a fixture of Boston's dining scene.[4]

Moments of Truth

"Moments of truth" is a phrase credited to Jan Carlson. On becoming president of Scandinavian Airline System (SAS) when it was ranked at the bottom of the European airline market, Carlson realized that he had to spend a lot of time on the frontline coaching SAS associates in how to handle guest encounters or, as he called them, moments of truth. As a result of his efforts, SAS was soon ranked at the top of the European airlines for service. Service commitment is a total organizational approach that makes the quality of service, as perceived by the customer, the number one driving force for the operation of the business.[5]

Learn How Dinner Reservations Are Taken at a Fine Dining Restaurant with Vernon's Maître D'

Every hospitality organization has thousands of moments of truth every day. This leads to tremendous challenges in maintaining expected levels of service. Let's look at just some of the moments of truth in a restaurant dining experience:[6]

1. Guest calls the restaurant for a table reservation.
2. Guest tries to find the restaurant.
3. Guest parks.
4. Guest is welcomed.
5. Guest is informed that the table is not ready.
6. Guest either waits or goes to the lounge for a cocktail.
7. Guest tries to attract the bartender's attention for a cocktail because there are no seats available.
8. Guest is called over a loudspeaker or paged.
9. Guest is seated at the table.
10. Server takes order.
11. Server brings beverages or food.
12. Server clears food or beverages.
13. Server brings check.
14. Guest pays for meal.
15. Guest departs restaurant.

From your own experience, you can imagine just how many moments of truth there are in a restaurant dining experience.

"If you are not serving the guest, then you had better be serving someone who is."

Check Your Knowledge

1. Why is service so important?
2. What is a moment of truth?
3. How does the front-of-the-house and the back-of-the-house staff impact teamwork and also service to the guest?

Introducing Horst Schulze

Horst Schulze is a legendary leader in the hospitality industry and one of the three most influential hospitality industry leaders of our times. His vision helped reshape concepts of guest service throughout the hospitality and service industries.

Schulze grew up in a small village in Germany. At eleven, he told his parents that he wanted to work in a hotel. When he was fourteen, his parents took him to the finest hotel in the region, where they had "an audience" with the general manager. It lasted 10 minutes, and he never spoke to him again during the next two years! Everyone—his mother, the general manager, and the restaurant maître d'—told him how important the guests were, so with knees shaking, he found himself a job busing tables in the restaurant. The maître d' made a favorable impression on the young man because he was respected by both guests and staff alike. So, when Horst had to write an essay for his hotel school (which he attended on Wednesdays), he chose the title of "We Are Ladies and Gentlemen Serving Ladies and Gentlemen." He kept the essay, since it was the only A he received; and that essay became the foundation of his philosophy to create service excellence.

Mr. Schulze now speaks on guest service to thousands every year, graciously sharing his knowledge and experiments with others. He says that there are three aspects of service:

1. Service should be defect free.
2. Service should be timely.
3. People should care.

It is the caring piece that is service. The guest relationship begins when the guest perceives that he or she has contacted you. That human contact should begin with a warm welcome. Schulze adds that all hospitality businesses should be doing four things:

1. Keeping guests = loyalty, meaning guests trust you and are happy to form a relationship with you.
2. Find new guests.
3. Get as much money as you can from guests without losing them.
4. Create efficiencies.

Mr. Schulze spent nine years with Hyatt Hotels Corporation, where he was a hotel general manager, regional VP, and corporate VP. Before his association with Hyatt, he worked for Hilton Hotels. After joining the Ritz-Carlton as a charter member and VP of operations in 1983, Mr. Schulze was instrumental in creating operating and service standards that have become world famous. He was appointed executive vice president in 1987, and president and chief operating officer in 1988. When he left The Ritz-Carlton to form the West Paces Hotel Group, Mr. Schulze was responsible for the $2 billion Ritz-Carlton operations worldwide.

Mr. Schulze served as vice chairman of The Ritz-Carlton Hotel Company from 2001–2002, after serving as president and COO of The Ritz-Carlton Group, starting in 1988. Under his leadership, the Group was awarded the Malcolm Baldrige National Quality Award in both 1992 and 1999, the first and only hotel company to win even one such award. In addition, Ritz-Carlton was continuously voted "Best Hotel Company in the World" by convention and trade publications. Mr. Schulze has been recognized as "Corporate Hotelier of the World" by HOTELS magazine, and he was awarded the Ishikawa Medal for his personal contributions to the quality movement.

In 2002, Schulze and several former Ritz-Carlton executives formed West Paces Hotel Group to create and operate branded hotels in several distinctive market segments. The canon of the company is:

> To create value and unparalleled results for our owners by creating products which fulfill individual customer expectations.
>
> We deliver reliable, genuinely caring and timely service superior to our competition, with respected and empowered employees who work in an environment of belonging and purpose.
>
> We are supportive and contributing members of society, operating with uncompromising values, honor and integrity.

West Paces has hotels and resorts under two brands, Solis and Capella. They can be viewed at www.westpaceshotels.com.

Ways to Perfect Service

To help improve service in the hospitality industry, the Educational Foundation of the National Restaurant Association—one of the hospitality industry's leading associations—developed a number of programs that will enhance your professional development. Further information may be obtained from the NRA's Web site (www.restaurant.org).

Among the NRA's various programs and courses is one on foodservice leadership. Effective leaders are those who make

THE EMPLOYEE PROMISE and RITZ-CARLTON SERVICE VALUES

At The Ritz-Carlton, our Ladies and Gentlemen are the most important resource in our service commitment to our guests.

By applying the principles of trust, honesty, respect, integrity, and commitment, we nurture and maximize talent to the benefit of each individual and the company.

The Ritz-Carlton fosters a work environment where diversity is valued, quality of life is enhanced, individual aspirations are fulfilled, and the Ritz-Carlton mystique is strengthened.

I am proud to be Ritz-Carlton.

1. I build strong relationships and create Ritz-Carlton guests for life.
2. I am always responsive to the expressed and unexpressed wishes and needs of our guests.
3. I am empowered to create unique, memorable, and personal experiences for our guests.
4. I understand my role in achieving the Key Success Factors, embracing Community Footprints, and creating The Ritz-Carlton Mystique.
5. I continuously seek opportunities to innovate and improve The Ritz-Carlton experience.
6. I own and immediately resolve any guest problems.
7. I create a work environment of teamwork and lateral service so that the needs of our guests and each other are met.
8. I have opportunity to continuously learn and grow.
9. I am involved in the planning of the work that affects me.
10. I am proud of my professional appearance, language, and behavior.
11. I protect the privacy and security of our guests, my fellow employees, and the company's confidential information and assets.
12. I am responsible for uncompromising levels of cleanliness and creating a safe and accident-free environment.

© 2009 The Ritz-Carlton Hotel Company, L.L.C. All rights reserved. Reprinted with the permission of The Ritz-Carlton Hotel Company, L.L.C.

---

things happen because they have developed the knowledge, skills, and attitude required to get the most out of the people in their operation.

Leadership involves change; in fact, change is the one thing we can be sure of in the coming years. Our guests are constantly changing; so is technology, product availability, and, of course, our competition. To cope with this constant change, the NRA's group suggests that (1) all change is likely to meet with some resistance, and (2) when implementing change, do the following:

1. State the purpose of the change.
2. Involve all employees in the process.
3. Monitor, update, and follow up.

One way in which leaders involve employees in the process is through total quality management (TQM) and empowerment.

Bill Marriott, Chairman of the Board, Marriott International shakes hands and poses for photographs with the kitchen associates at the Boston Marriott Copley Place.

Service and Total Quality Management

The increasingly open and fiercely competitive marketplace is exerting enormous pressure on service industries to deliver superior service. Inspired by rising guest expectations and competitive necessity, many hospitality companies have jumped on the service-quality bandwagon. The Malcolm Baldrige National Quality Award is the highest level of national recognition for quality that a U.S. company can receive. The award promotes an understanding of quality excellence, greater awareness of quality as a critical competitive element, and the sharing of quality information and strategies.

The Ritz-Carlton Hotel Company, winner of the 1992 and 1999 Malcolm Baldrige National Quality Award, was founded on principles of groundbreaking levels of customer service. The essence of this philosophy was refined into a set of core values collectively called the "Gold Standards." The credo is printed on a small laminated card that all employees must memorize or carry on their person at all times when on duty. The card lists the three steps of service:

1. A warm and sincere greeting; use the guest name, if and when possible.
2. Anticipation and compliance with guests' needs.
3. Fond farewell; give them a warm good-bye and use their names if and when possible.

The quality movement began at the turn of the century as a means of ensuring consistency among parts that were produced in different plants of a single company so that they could be used interchangeably. In the area of service, TQM is a participatory process that empowers all levels of employees to work in groups to establish guest service expectations and determine the best way to meet or exceed these expectations. Notice that the term *guest* is preferred over the term *customer*. The inference here is that if we treat customers like guests, we are more likely to exceed their expectations. One successful hotelier has insisted for a long time that all employees treat guests as they would like to be treated themselves.

Total quality management (TQM) is a continuous process that works best when managers are also good leaders. A successful company will employ leader–managers who create a stimulating work environment in which guests and employees (sometimes called internal guests; one employee serves another employee who in turn serves a guest) become an integral part of the mission by participating in goal and objective setting.

Installing TQM is exciting, because once everyone becomes involved, there is no stopping the creative ways employees will find to solve guest-related problems and improve service. Other benefits include cost reductions and increased guest and employee satisfaction, leading ultimately to increased profits.

Top executives and line managers are responsible for the success of the TQM process; when they commit to ownership of the process, it will be successful. Focused commitment is the foundation of a quality service initiative, and leadership is the critical component in promoting commitment. Achieving TQM is a top-down, bottom-up process that must have the active commitment and participation of all employees from the top executives down to the bottom of the corporate ladder. The expression, "If you are not serving the guest, then you had better be serving someone who is" still holds true today.

The difference between TQM and **quality control (QC)** is that QC focuses on error detection, whereas TQM focuses on error prevention. Quality control is generally based on industrial systems and, because of this, tends to be product oriented rather than service oriented. To the guest, services are experiential; they are felt, lived through, and sensed. The moment of truth is the actual guest contact.

The game of business has changed. Leaders empower employees who welcome change. **Empowerment** is a feeling of partnership in which employees feel responsible for their jobs and have a stake in the organization's success. Empowered employees tend to do the following:

- Speak out about their problems and concerns.
- Take responsibility for their actions.
- Consider themselves a network of professionals.
- Have the authority to make their own decisions when serving guests.

To empower employees, managers must do the following:

1. Take risks.
2. Delegate.
3. Foster a learning environment.
4. Share information and encourage self-expression.
5. Involve employees in defining their own vision.
6. Be thorough and patient with employees.

Check Your Knowledge

1. What is the Malcolm Baldrige National Quality Award?
2. What is the difference between total quality management (TQM) and quality control (QC)?
3. Discuss how empowerment provides the guest with superior service.

The Disney Approach to Guest Service

The Disney mission statement is simple: "We create Happiness." Throughout this text, Disney is regarded as an excellent corporation. The following is adapted from a presentation given by Susan Wilkie to the Pacific CHRIE conference, outlines Disney's approach to guest service.

When conceiving the idea to build Disneyland, Walt Disney established a simple philosophical approach to his theme park

.inc | Corporate Profile

CARLSON COMPANIES

With operations in more than 150 countries, Carlson Companies is one of the largest privately held corporations in the United States and a leader in providing hospitality management, franchising, and direct-to-consumer services.*

Led by Chairperson and Chief Executive Officer Marilyn Carlson Nelson, Carlson Companies continues to build on a cornerstone set by her father, Curt Carlson, nearly 65 years ago: developing long-lasting relationships with clients.

The history of Carlson Companies is one of the classic business success stories in the American free enterprise system. Starting in 1938 with merely an idea and $55 of borrowed capital, entrepreneur Curtis L. Carlson founded the Gold Bond Stamp Company in his home city of Minneapolis, Minnesota. His trading stamp concept, designed to stimulate sales and loyalty for food stores and other merchants, proved to be right for the times and swept the nation in a wave of dramatic growth.

Through the years, Carlson diversified into hotels, travel, and other related businesses. In the 1960s, Carlson and several other partners collectively bought an interest in the original Radisson Hotel in downtown Minneapolis. Eventually, Carlson became sole owner of the hotel brand and expanded it around the globe. Today, there are 400 Radissons in 66 countries.

To reflect the company's growing diversification, its name was changed in 1973 from the Gold Bond Stamp Company to Carlson Companies. Four hotel brands are part of Carlson Hospitality Worldwide, one of Carlson's major business groups. They are Regent International Hotels, Radisson Hotels and Resorts, Country Inns & Suites by Carlson, and Park Plaza and Park Inn hotels. In addition, Carlson hospitality brands include T.G.I. Friday's and Pick Up Stix restaurants and Radisson Seven Seas Cruises.

Carlson Hospitality Worldwide encompasses more than 1,695 hotel, resort, restaurant, and cruise ship operations in 82 countries. Lodging operations include more than 1,000 locations in 74 countries. Restaurant operations include more than 1,000 locations in 60 countries, and cruise operations include six luxury ships with an additional vessel under construction.

These hospitality group brands and services, combined with sister companies, Carlson Marketing Group, Carlson Wagonlit Travel, and other travel industry companies and consumer incentive programs, provide employment for more than 190,000 people around the world.

In addition to global business success, Carlson Companies is also recognized as a top employer. Both *Fortune* and *Working Mother* magazines have rated the company as one of their "100 Best Places to Work in America."

Marilyn Carlson is a regular on *Fortune* magazine's list of the "Most Powerful Women in Business" and has been selected by *Business Week* as one of the "Top 25 Executives in Business." She has been ranked by *Travel Agent* magazine as the "Most Powerful Woman in Travel." She has served as chair of the National Women's Business Council. The council serves as an independent source of advice and counsel to the president, Congress, the U.S. Small Business Administration, and the Interagency Committee on Women's Business.

Carlson has also served as national chair of the Travel Industry Association of America. She is a member of the Council of the World Economic Forum and serves on the forum's board of governors for travel and tourism.

*www.carlson.com/overview/index.cfm, cited April 1, 2009.

---

business, based on quality, service, and show. The design, layout, characters, and magic of Disneyland grew out of Walt's successful experience in the film industry. With Disneyland, he saw an opportunity to create a whole new form of entertainment—a three-dimensional live show. He wanted Disneyland to be a dynamic, ever-changing experience. To reinforce the service concept, Disney has guests, not customers, and cast members, not employees. These terms set the expectations for how guests will be served and cared for while at the park or resort. This commitment to service means:

- Disney clearly understands its product and the meaning of its brand.
- Disney looks at the business from the guests' perspective.

- The company considers it its personal responsibility to create an exceptional experience for every individual who enters its gates.

Management says that "our inventory goes home at night." Disney's ability to create a special brand of magic requires the talents of thousands of people fulfilling many different roles. But the heart of it is the frontline cast members. So what is it that makes the service at Disney so great? The key elements of Disneyland guest services include:

- Hiring, developing, and retaining the right people
- Understanding its product and the meaning of the brand
- Communicating the traditions and standards of service to all cast members
- Training leaders to be service coaches
- Measuring guest satisfaction
- Recognizing and rewarding performance

Disney has used profile modeling, but says it all comes down to a few simple things:

- Interpersonal—relationship building skills
- Communication
- Friendliness

Disney uses a 45-minute team approach to interviewing called peer interviews. In one interview there may be four candidates and one interviewer. The candidates may include a housewife returning to the workforce, a teacher seeking summer work, a retiree hoping for a little extra income, or a teenager looking for a first job. All four candidates are interviewed in the same session. The interviewer is looking for how they individually answer questions, but also how well they interact with each other—a good indicator of their future onstage treatment of guests.

Read About the World of Attractions While You Visit Simmy's Splashtown

The most successful technique used during the 45 minutes is to smile. The interviewer smiles at the people being interviewed to see if they return the smile. If they don't, it doesn't matter how well they interview—they won't get the job. On the first day at work, every new Disney cast member participates in a one-day orientation program at the Disney University, "Welcome to Show Business." The main goal of this experience is to learn the Disney approach to helpful, caring, and friendly guest service.

How does this translate into action? When a guest stops a street sweeper to ask where to pick up a parade schedule and the sweeper not only answers the question, but recites the parade times from memory, suggests the best viewing spots on the parade route, offers advice on where to get a quick meal before parade time, and ends the interaction with a pleasant smile and warm send-off, well, people are impressed. It also makes the sweepers feel their jobs are interesting and important—which they are!

The show is why people go to Disneyland. Each land tells a unique story through its theme and attention to detail, and the cast members each play a role in the Show. The most integral component of the training is the traditions and standards of guest service. The first of these is called the "personal touch." The cast members are encouraged to use their own unique style and personality to provide a personal interaction with each

I AM YOUR GUEST

We can all find inspiration from these anonymous words about people who make our business possible:

- *I am your guest*—Satisfy my needs, add personal attention and a friendly touch, and I will become a "walking advertisement" for your products and services. Ignore my needs, show carelessness, inattention, and poor manners, and I will cease to exist as far as you are concerned.
- *I am sophisticated*—much more so than I was a few years ago. My needs are more complex. It is more important to me that you appreciate my business; when I buy your products and services, I'm saying you are the best.
- *I am a perfectionist*—when I am dissatisfied, take heed. The source of my discontent lies in something you or your products have failed to do. Find that source and eliminate it or you will lose my business and that of my friends as well. For when I criticize your products or services, I will talk to anyone who will listen.
- *I have other choices*—other businesses continually offer me more for my money. You must prove to me again and again that I have made a wise choice in selecting you and your company above all others.

Gain a Better Understanding of a Planned Play Environment at Simmy's Splashtown

guest. One of the primary ways Disney accomplishes this is through name tags. Everyone, regardless of position, goes by his or her first name. This tradition was started by Walt and continues today. It allows cast members to interact on a more personal level with guests. It also assists internally, by creating an informal environment that facilitates the flow of open communication and breaks down some of the traditional barriers.

The Disney Service Model

- *It begins with a smile.* This is the universal language of hospitality and service. Guests recognize and appreciate the cast members' warmth and sincerity.
- *Make eye contact and use body language.* This means stance, approach, and gestures. For instance, cast members are trained to use open gestures for directions, not pointed fingers, because open palms are friendlier and less directive.
- *Respect and welcome all guests.* This means being friendly, helpful, and going out of the way to exceed guests' expectations.
- *Value the magic.* This means that when they're onstage, cast members are totally focused on creating the magic of Disneyland. They don't talk about personal problems or world affairs, and they don't mention that you can find Mickey in more than one place.
- *Initiate guest contact.* Cast members are reminded to actively initiate guest contact. Disney calls this being aggressively friendly. It's not enough to be responsive when approached. Cast members are encouraged to take the first step with guests. They have lots of little tricks for doing this, such as noticing a guest's name on a hat and then using the name in conversation or kneeling to ask a child a question.
- *Creative service solutions.* For example, one Disneyland Hotel cast member recently became aware of a little boy who had come from the Midwest with his parents to enjoy the park and then left early because he was ill. The cast member approached the supervisor with an idea to send the child chicken soup, a character plush toy, and a get-well card from Mickey. The supervisor loved the idea. All cast members are now allowed to set up these arrangements in similar situations, without a supervisor's approval.
- *End with a "thank you."* The phrases that cast members use are important in creating a service environment. They do not have a book of accepted phrases; rather, through training and coaching, cast members are encouraged to use their own personality and style to welcome and approach guests, answer questions, anticipate their needs, thank them, and express with sincerity their desire to make the guest's experience exceptional.

Taken individually, these might sound pretty basic. But, taken together, they help define and reinforce the Disney culture. Once initial cast member training is completed, these concepts must be applied and continually reinforced by leaders who possess strong coaching skills. Disney uses a model called the Five Steps of Leadership to lead the cast member performance.

Each step in the leadership model is equally important in meeting service and business goals. Each leader must:

1. Provide clear expectations and standards.
2. Communicate these expectations through demonstration, information, and examples.
3. Hold cast members accountable for their feedback.
4. Coach through honest and direct feedback.
5. Recognize, reward, and celebrate success.

To supplement and reward the leadership team, Disney provides technical training to every new manager and assistant manager. In addition, the management team also participates

OPENING DISNEYLAND

Disneyland opened on July 17, 1955, to predictions that it would be a failure. And, in truth, everything that could go wrong did:

- Plumbers went on strike.
- Tickets were duplicated.
- Attractions broke down.
- Fantasyland had a gas leak.

- The asphalt on Main Street didn't harden in time, so, in the heat of July, horses' hooves and women's high heels stuck in the street.

As Walt once said, "You may not realize it when it happens, but a kick in the teeth might be good for you." Walt had his fair share of challenges, one of which was obtaining financing to develop Disneyland—he had to deal with more than 300 banks.

THE DISNEY COLLEGE PROGRAM

The Disney Theme Parks and Resorts College Program is an excellent opportunity for those interested in gaining valuable experience while working in frontline positions at the Disneyland resort in Anaheim, California, or Walt Disney World near Orlando, Florida. Participants are able to custom design a learning curriculum that best suits their personal and career development needs and interests by completing education courses and specialized learning activities. Students are able to interact with leaders and other students from around the world, learn transferable skills, and gain real-world experience.

in an acculturation process at the Disney University to learn the culture, values, and the leadership philosophy necessary to be successful in the Disney environment.

Disney measures the systems and reward process by distributing 1,000 surveys to guests as they leave Disneyland and 100 surveys to guests who stay at each of the Disney hotels. The guests are asked to take the surveys home and mail them back to Disney. In return, their names are entered for a drawing to win a family weekend package at the park and hotel.

Feedback from the surveys has been helpful in improving the guest experience. For example, as a result of the surveys, the entertainment division realized that the opportunity to interact with a character was a key driver to guest satisfaction. So the entertainment team designed a brochure, *The Characters Today,* which is distributed at the main entrance daily. This brochure allows guests to maximize their opportunity to see the characters. This initiative has already raised guest satisfaction by 10 percentage points.

Cast members are also empowered to make changes to improve service. These measures are supplemented by financial controls and "mystery shops" that allow Disney to focus resources on increasing guest satisfaction.

The reward system does not consist of just the hard reward system we commonly think of, such as bonuses and incentive plans, important though they are. Recognition is not a one-size-fits-all system. Disney has found that noncash recognition is as powerful if not more powerful a recognition tool in many situations. Some examples are:

- Disney recognizes milestones of years of service. The company uses pins and statues and has a formal dinner for cast members and guests to reinforce and celebrate the value of their experience and expertise at serving Disney's guests.
- Throughout the year, Disney hosts special social and recreational events that involve the cast members and their families in the product.
- Disney invites cast members and their families to family film festivals featuring new Disney releases to ensure that they are knowledgeable about the latest Disney products.
- The Disneyland management team hosts the Family Christmas Party after hours in the park. This allows cast members to enjoy shopping, dining, and riding the attractions. Management dresses in costumes and runs the facilities.

A discussion of ethics, as it pertained to the hospitality industry, follows. Future hospitality and tourism professionals should abide by a code of ethics developed for their industry.

You may work at the Grand Floridian resort at Walt Disney World.

Check Your Knowledge

1. Describe the key elements of Disneyland guest service.
2. Once initial cast member training is completed, what concepts must be applied and continually reinforced by leaders who possess strong coaching skills?
3. What does it mean that " . . . our inventory goes home at night"?
4. Why does Disney call its employees "cast members"?

Career Paths

Now that we know that the hospitality industry is the largest and fastest-growing industry in the world, let's explore some of the many **career paths** available to graduates of hospitality schools.

The concept of career paths describes the career progression available in each segment of the hospitality industry. A career path does not always go in a straight line, as sometimes described in a career ladder. You could liken it to jumping into a swimming pool; you get wet and then swim over to the other side—but not always in a straight line. It's like that in the hospitality industry also. We may begin in one area and later find another that is more attractive. Opportunities come our way and we need to be prepared to take advantage of these. That's fine, because there are plenty of choices available. To illustrate, a few years ago Barbara was a hospitality management major. Because she was not as outgoing as some of the other students, she decided that she would become a hotel accountant. A few years later we visited the hotel where she was working. We were welcomed, from behind the front desk, by a beaming Barbara. She had moved from accounting to become front-office manager. Later, after three years in the sales and marketing department, she became general manager.

Progression means that we can advance from one position to another. In the hospitality industry we don't use straight-line career ladders because we need experience in several areas before becoming, say, a general manager, director of human resources, catering manager, meeting planner, or director of marketing. The career path to general manager may go through food and beverage, rooms division, marketing, human resources, or finance and accounting or, more likely, a combination of these, because it is better to have experience in several areas (cross-training). The same is true with restaurants. A graduate with service experience will need to spend a few years in the kitchen learning each station, then bartend for a few months, before becoming an opening or closing assistant manager, general manager, regional manager, vice president, or president.

> **"A career path does not always go in a straight line."**

Sometimes we want to run before we can walk. We want to progress quickly. But remember to enjoy the journey as much as the destination. If you advance too quickly, you may not be ready for the additional responsibility, and may not have all the skills necessary for the promotion. Be prepared because you never know when an opportunity will present itself. For instance, you cannot expect to become a director of food and beverage in a hotel until you really know "food and beverage": this means spending a few years in the kitchen. Otherwise, how can you expect to relate to an executive chef? You have to know how the food should be prepared and served. You have to set the standards—not have them set for you.

Career Goals

You may already know that you want to be a director of accounting, an event manager, a director of food and beverage, or a restaurant manager. If you are not sure of which career path you want to pursue, that's okay. Now is the time to explore the industry to gain the information you need to decide which career path to follow. A great way to do this is through internships and work experience. Try a variety of jobs rather than sticking with the same one.[1]

If we follow the umbrella scope of hospitality and tourism, we first examine careers in travel; lodging; assembly and event management; restaurants and managed services; and recreation: theme parks and attractions, clubs, gaming, parks, and recreation. Allied industries include suppliers, consultants, party rentals, and related services.

Check Your Knowledge
1. **What is a career path?**
2. **What is a career goal?**

Is the Hospitality Industry for You?

In Chapter 1, we described some characteristics of the hospitality industry. Due to the size and scope of the hospitality industry, career prospects are excellent. We also know that it is an exciting and dynamic industry with growth potential, especially when the economy is strong. In the hospitality industry, we are often working when others are at leisure—think of the evening or weekend shift; however, in some positions and careers, evenings and weekends can be yours to enjoy as you wish.

The hospitality industry is a service industry; this means that we take pride in caring about others as well as ourselves. Ensuring that guests receive outstanding service is a goal of hospitality corporations. This is a business that gets into your blood! It is fun, exciting, and seldom dull, and an industry in which almost everyone can succeed. So what does it take to be successful in the hospitality industry? The personal characteristics, qualities, skills, and abilities that are beneficial for a career in the hospitality industry are honesty, hard work, being a team player, being prepared to work long hours spread over various shifts, the ability to cope with stress, good decision-making skills, good communication skills, being dedicated to exceptional service, and having a desire to exceed guest expectations. Leadership, ambition, and the will to succeed are also important and necessary for career success.

Recruiters look for **service-oriented** people, who "walk their talk," meaning they do what they say they're going to do. Good work experience, involvement in on-campus and professional organizations, a positive attitude, a good grade point average—all show a commitment to an individual's studies. Career-minded individuals who have initiative and are prepared to work hard and make a contribution to the company, which has to make a profit, is what companies look for in their recruits.

Self-Assessment and Personal Philosophy

The purpose of completing a self-assessment is to measure our current strengths and weaknesses and determine what we need to improve on if we are going to reach our goals. Self-assessment helps establish where we are now and shows us the links to where we want to go, our goals. In a self-assessment, we make a list of our positive attributes. For example, we may have experience in a guest service position; this will be helpful in preparing for the goal of becoming a hospitality industry general manager. Other positive attributes include our character and all the other things that recruiters look for, as listed previously.

We also make a list of areas where we might want to make improvements. For example, we may have reached a certain level of culinary expertise, but need more experience and a course in this specialty. Or you may want to improve your Spanish language skills because you intend to work with Spanish-speaking people. Your **philosophy** is your beliefs and the way you treat others and your work. It will determine who you are and what you stand for. You may state that you enjoy giving excellent service by treating others as you would like to be treated and that you believe in honesty and respect.

A great Web resource for self-assessment is www.queendom.com; this site provides several self-assessment quizzes.

Professionalism and Etiquette

Every profession has its norms. In our case, being on time is critical because guests do not want to wait for services. Several companies, including Marriott International, have a policy of requiring associates to clock in 10 minutes before a shift or clock out 10 minutes after a shift. If they fail to do this once, they receive a verbal warning; the second time, it's a written warning. The third time, they're out! So you better opt for the evening shift if you don't like early mornings!

We need to be professional in our appearance, that is, our dress and attire. You may have noticed that several hospitality and tourism associates wear a uniform; this is a part of their profession. Female managers wear a business suit (pants or skirt) with a blouse and polished dress shoes. Male managers wear a business suit with a shirt and tie and polished dress shoes. When going for an interview, you should dress in a business suit. Men should wear powerful color ties—red or blue is best—never yellow. Be discrete; limit rings, no body piercing, and no heavy cologne. Women must not wear too much makeup or jewelry.

Etiquette is about how we behave in a given setting. For example, as children, we are taught to say "please" and "thank you." In a hospitality business setting, we are expected to abide by certain norms. For example, it is important to send a personal, handwritten note of thanks to the person who interviewed us. Not only does it make a good impression; it says that we are courteous. How we behave among others at a business lunch or dinner says a lot about our preparedness for a successful career. Do we have good table manners? Or do we behave inappropriately? Do we treat others with dignity and respect?

> ### Check Your Knowledge
> 1. Name three qualities beneficial for a career in hospitality.
> 2. Define etiquette and explain how it relates to the hospitality industry.

Now Is the Time to Get Involved

For your own enjoyment and personal growth and development, it is important to get involved with on-campus and professional hospitality and tourism organizations. You don't have to take on a leadership role at first; you can just learn how the organization works and participate in the organization of events. Recruiters notice the difference between students who have become involved with the various organizations, and they take that into consideration when assessing candidates for positions within their companies.

Becoming involved will show your commitment to your chosen career and lead you to meet interesting peers and industry professionals who can potentially help you along your chosen career path. You will develop leadership and organizational skills that will help you in your career.

Professional Organizations and Associations

Professional organizations include becoming a student member of the Council on Hotel, Restaurant, and Institutional Education. (CHRIE) (www.chrie.org). You can also access the excellent Webzine *Hosteur*, which is published especially for students. CHRIE offers its members free access. The National Restaurant Association (NRA) (www.restaurant.org) is another organization to join. You will likely find several NRA magazines and publications to be very helpful. The NRA and your state restaurant association are affiliated, and both have trade shows that are worth attending. At the NRA's annual convention, students are invited to attend not only the convention and trade show, but also the Salute to Excellence, a day of activities that culminates with a gala dinner. Only two students from each school are invited to this special event; make sure you're one of them, as it is well worth it.

The American Hotel and Lodging Association (www.ahla.com) is a good organization to belong to if you are interested in a career in the lodging segment of the industry. Benefits of AH&LA membership include access to the organization's career center, which is powered by Hcareers.com, the largest online database of career opportunities in the lodging industry; a subscription to *Lodging Magazine*, a leading industry publication with news, product information, and current articles on industry-related topics; subscriptions to *Lodging News*, *Lodging Law*, and *Lodging H/R* e-newsletters; and use of the AH&LA's information center—helpful for those pesky term papers! And you receive scholarship information, too!

The International Special Events Society (ISES) (www.ises.org) includes over 3,000 professionals representing special event producers, from festivals to trade shows. Membership brings together professionals from a variety of special events disciplines. The mission of the ISES is to educate, advance, and promote the special events industry and its network of professionals, along with related issues.

The Professional Convention Management Association (PCMA) (www.pcma.org) is a great resource for convention management educational offerings and networking opportunities.

The National Society of Minorities in Hospitality (NSMH) (www.nsmh.org) has a membership of several hundred minority hospitality majors who address diversity and multiculturalism, as well as career development via events and programs.

Ethics

Ethics is a set of moral principles and values that people use to answer questions about right and wrong. Because ethics is also about our personal value system, you will understand that there are people with value systems different from ours. Where did the value system originate? What happens if one value system is different from another? Fortunately, certain universal guiding principles are agreed on by virtually all religions, cultures, and societies. The foundation of all principles is that all people's rights are important and should not be violated. This belief is central to civilized societies; without it, chaos would reign.

Today, people have few moral absolutes; they decide situationally whether it is acceptable to steal, lie, or drink and drive.

CAREER INFORMATION

YOUR CAREER IN THE HOSPITALITY INDUSTRY

William Fisher
University of Central Florida

A short while ago, after giving a talk to a hospitality management class, I was approached by a student who asked, "What advice do you have for students who want to progress in a career in the hospitality industry?" It's a thoughtful question and deserves a thoughtful answer. Here is what I said.

1. *Know Yourself.* Come to terms with yourself through an unvarnished assessment of your values, strengths, and areas that need development. Decide that you will always be a person of integrity, exhibit total honesty, live up to your word, and do the right thing for the organization(s) you serve. Live by these values and emblazon them on your total being!

2. *Know Your Immediate Objectives.* You have decades of working years ahead of you, and it is important to have a vision of where you want to be in the future. Today comes before tomorrow, however, and you need to focus on and manage the present if you are ever going to realize your dream for the future. Have a clear view, a firm conviction, and a realistic expectation with respect to the positions you accept. Each position should be one element in a progressive pattern. Recognize that linkages exist. Throughout your career, bring with you the maturity, set of principles, and techniques that you gained from all your prior positions. Build for your future!

3. *Establish a Time Frame.* Set a realistic time period, given the level and complexity of the position. Many young people are impatient and believe they are ready to move on before they really are. A rule of thumb is to multiply the time it took to learn the position—not just the mechanics, but the nuances, relationships, and issues—by two or three. For example, if it takes you a year to be in full command of a position, an appropriate time frame for that position would be two to three years. The timing may be shortened or lengthened depending on circumstances, but there is no magic elixir that will accelerate your management maturity other than hard work and devotion to your assignment!

4. *Remember Names.* Use people's names when addressing them. This applies to everyone—customers, employees, suppliers, and visitors. If name recollection is not one of your strengths, work to improve it. Nothing is so personal to an individual as his or her name. By recognizing and using people's names, you confirm their existence and dignity!

5. *Be an Inside Volunteer.* Your organization will have a number of events, projects, and perhaps crises when employees will be asked to volunteer. Stepping forward demonstrates a good attitude, a cooperative demeanor, and a desire for participation, which can be professionally and developmentally rewarding for you. If appropriate, seek a leadership role, realizing you can be a leader without having a high position!

6. *Be an Outside Volunteer.* Join and participate in at least two outside organizations. One should be related to your industry and/or profession for professional development and networking purposes. The other should contribute to your community in some way, such as a charitable or children's organization.

7. *Follow Up.* Get back to people when you say you will, send thank you notes, send congratulatory messages, compliment good performance, and call people to emphasize appreciation.

8. *Develop a Reputation for Getting Results.* Make good things happen, exceed the expectations of others, demonstrate achievement, and keep a positive future orientation. Read regularly and stay on the cutting edge of your industry and profession!

9. *Maintain a Sense of Humor.* Always be invigorated by life. Never allow yourself to be defeated. You will experience difficult times, but they will pass. You will experience good times, but don't allow them to absorb you. Develop a quick wit, look at the bright side of things, smile frequently, and laugh heartily. It will do wonders for others—and for you!

Overall, be a "can do" person, but also be a "can-did" person!

They seem to think that whatever is right is what works best for the individual. In a country blessed with so many diverse cultures, you might think it is impossible to identify common standards of ethical behavior. However, among sources from many different times and places, such as the Bible, Aristotle's *Ethics*, William Shakespeare's *King Lear,* the Koran, and the *Analects* of Confucius, you'll find the following basic moral values: integrity, respect for human life, self-control, honesty, and courage. Cruelty is wrong. All the world's major religions support a version of the Golden Rule: Do unto others as you would have them do to you.[7]

In the foreword to *Ethics in Hospitality Management,* edited by Stephen S. J. Hall,[8] dean emeritus of Cornell University, Robert A. Beck poses this question: "Is overbooking hotel rooms and airline seats ethical? How does one compare the legal responsibilities of the innkeeper and the airline manager to the moral obligation?" (He also asks, What is a fair or reasonable wage? A fair or reasonable return on investment? Is it fair or ethical to underpay employees for the benefit of investors?)

"English Common Law, on which American law is based, left such decisions to the 'reasonable man,' a judge would ask the jury, 'was this the act of a reasonable man?'" Interestingly, what is considered ethical in one country may not be in another. For instance, in some countries it is considered normal to bargain for room rates; in others, bargaining would be considered bad form.

Ethics and morals have become an integral part of hospitality decisions, from employment (equal opportunity and affirmative action) to truth in menus. Many corporations and businesses have developed a code of ethics that all employees use to make decisions. This became necessary because too many managers were making decisions without regard to the impact of such decisions on others. Stephen Hall is one of the pioneers of ethics in hospitality; he has developed the following code of ethics for the hospitality and tourism industry:[9]

1. We acknowledge ethics and morality as inseparable elements of doing business and will test every decision against the highest standards of honesty, legality, fairness, impunity, and conscience.
2. We will conduct ourselves personally and collectively at all times so as to bring credit to the hospitality and tourism industry.
3. We will concentrate our time, energy, and resources on the improvement of our own products and services and we will not denigrate our competition in the pursuit of our success.
4. We will treat all guests equally regardless of race, religion, nationality, creed, or sex.
5. We will deliver all standards of service and product with total consistency to every guest.
6. We will provide a totally safe and sanitary environment at all times for every guest and employee.
7. We will strive constantly, in words, actions, and deeds, to develop and maintain the highest level of trust, honesty, and understanding among guests, clients, employees, employers, and the public at large.
8. We will provide every employee at every level all the knowledge, training, equipment, and motivation required to perform his or her tasks according to our published standards.
9. We will guarantee that every employee at every level will have the same opportunity to perform, advance, and be evaluated against the same standard as all employees engaged in the same or similar tasks.
10. We will actively and consciously work to protect and preserve our natural environment and natural resources in all that we do.
11. We will seek a fair and honest profit, no more, no less.

As you can see, it is vitally important for future hospitality and tourism professionals to abide by this code. Here are some ethical dilemmas in hospitality. What do you think about them?

Ethical dilemmas in hospitality

Previously, certain actions may not have been considered ethical, but management often looked the other way. A few scenarios follow that are not seen as ethical today and are against most companies' ethical policies.

1. As catering manager of a large banquet operation, the flowers for the hotel are booked through your office. The account is worth $15,000 per month. The florist offers you a 10 percent kickback. Given that your colleague at a sister hotel in the same company receives a good bonus and you do not, despite having a better financial result, do you accept the kickback? If so, whom do you share it with?
2. As purchasing agent for a major hospitality organization, you are responsible for purchasing $5 million worth of perishable and nonperishable items. To get your business, a supplier, whose quality and price are similar to others, offers you a new automobile. Do you accept?
3. An order has come from the corporate office that guests from a certain part of the world may only be accepted if

the reservation is taken from the embassy of the countries. One Sunday afternoon, you are duty manager and several limos with people from "that part of the world" request rooms for several weeks. You decline even though there are available rooms. They even offer you a personal envelope, which they say contains $1,000. How do you feel about declining their request?

These and other ethical dilemmas are not always simply right or wrong.

Three key categories of questions need to be answered when making decisions:

1. Is it legal? Will I be violating civil law or company policy? Also, will I get fired if I accept it, allow it, or do it?
2. Is it balanced? Is it fair to all concerned in both the short term and the long term? Does it promote win–win relationships?
3. How will it make me feel about myself? Will it make me proud? Would I feel good if my family knew about it?

> "The foundation of all principles is that all people's rights are important and should not be violated."

TRENDS in HOSPITALITY

We can identify a number of trends that are having and will continue to have an impact on the hospitality industry. Some, like diversity, are already here and are sure to increase in the future. Here, in no particular order, are some of the major trends that hospitality professionals indicate as having an influence on the industry. You will find these and others discussed in the chapters of this text.

- **Sustainability.** Environmental sustainability has become very important in the marketplace. To be sustainable or "green" means to have no negative environmental impacts (or at least to reduce them down to being as minimal as possible). Sustainable businesses often participate in environmentally friendly activities and advocate their "greenness."
- **Globalization.** We have become the global village that was described a few years ago. We may have the opportunity to work or vacation in other countries, and more people than ever travel freely around the world.
- **Safety and security.** Since September 11, 2001, we have all become more conscious of our personal safety and have experienced increased scrutiny at airports and federal and other buildings. But it goes beyond that: terrorists kidnap tourists from their resorts and hold them for ransom, thugs mug them, and others assault them. Two security experts have made valuable contributions to the chapters that follow by giving us the benefit of their experience and expertise.
- **Diversity.** The hospitality industry is the most diverse of all industries; not only do we have a diverse employee population, but we also have a diverse group of guests. Diversity is increasing as more people with more diverse cultures join the hospitality workforce.
- **Service.** It is no secret that service is at the top of guests' expectations, yet few companies offer exceptional service. World-class service does not just happen; training is important in delivering the service that guests have come to expect.
- **Technology.** Technology is a driving force of change that presents opportunities for greater efficiencies and integration for improved guest service. However, the industry faces great challenges in training employees to use new technology and in standardization of software and hardware design. Some hotels have several systems that do not talk to each other, and some reservation systems bounce between 7 and 10 percent of sales nationally.
- **Legal issues.** Lawsuits are not only more frequent, but they cost more if you lose and more to defend. One company spent several million dollars just to defend one case. Government regulations and the complexities of employee relations create increased challenges for hospitality operators.
- **Changing demographics.** The U.S. population is gradually increasing and the baby boomers are retiring. Many retirees have the time and money to travel and utilize hospitality services.
- **Price and value.** Price and value are important to today's more discerning guests.
- **Sanitation.** Sanitation is critical to the success of any restaurant and foodservice operation. Guests expect to eat healthy foods that have been prepared in a sanitary environment.

CASE STUDY

Being Promoted from Within

One month ago, Tom was promoted from line cook to kitchen manager. It was a significant step up in his life. He felt that his promotion was well deserved, as he had always been a hard worker. Tom never had a second thought about going the extra mile for his employer. He felt that since he had seniority in the kitchen, and was friendly with everyone in the back of the house, he would be sure to get the respect he deserved from everyone he was responsible for. About three weeks into his new position, Tom found that this was not the case. Several back-of-the-house employees had become careless about their responsibilities after Tom was promoted. They were coming to work late, wearing unlaundered uniforms, and were becoming more and more sloppy with their plate presentations. Every day at work Tom was becoming more frustrated and upset. He knows that the employees were never careless about these matters with their previous supervisor.

DISCUSSION QUESTIONS

1. What are some possible reasons for the back-of-the-house employees' carelessness?
2. How should Tom assess the current situation?
3. If you were Tom's supervisor, what advice would you have given him before he started his new position?

CAREER INFORMATION

Do you know exactly where you want to be in 5 or 10 years? The best advice is to follow your interests. Do what you love to do and success will soon come. Often, we assess our own character and personality to determine a suitable path. Some opt for the accounting and control side of the tourism business; others, perhaps with more outgoing personalities, vie for sales and marketing; others prefer operations, which could be either in back or in front of the house. Creating your own career path can be both an exciting and a daunting task. However, the travel and tourism industry is generally characterized as dynamic, fun, and full of challenges and opportunities. And remember, someone has to run Walt Disney World, Holland American Cruise Lines, Marriott Hotels and Resorts, bed and breakfast inns, restaurants, or be the airport manager.

The anticipated growth of tourism over the next few years offers today's students numerous career opportunities in each section of the industry, as well as increasing job stability. Every chapter in this book will list and describe some of the career possibilities for that specific sector. However, there are many general things that can be said about a career in the tourism and hospitality industry. For example, a regular 9-5 job is not the norm for the tourism professional. Nearly all sectors of the industry operate up to 24 hours a day, 365 days a year—including evenings, weekends, and holidays. The good news is that all sectors are experiencing fantastic growth and should continue to do so over the next few years. As we have already mentioned, the number of executive positions is also expected to increase over the next few years, which, if you do some simple calculations, puts *you* in a great position.

SUMMARY

1. The hospitality and tourism industry is the largest and fastest-growing industry in the world.
2. Now is a great time to be considering a career in the hospitality and tourism field because thousands of supervising managers are needed for this dynamic industry.
3. Common dynamics include delivery of services and guest impressions of them.
4. Hospitality businesses are open 365 days a year, 24 hours a day, and are likely to require shift work.
5. One essential difference between the hospitality business and other businesses is that in hospitality we are selling an intangible and perishable product.
6. The pineapple has enjoyed a rich and romantic heritage as a symbol of welcome, friendship, and hospitality.
7. Total quality management (TQM) has helped improve service to guests by empowering employees to give service that exceeds guest expectations.
8. The difference between TQM and quality control (QC) is that QC focuses on error detection, whereas TQM focuses on error prevention.
9. The hospitality industry is a service industry; this means that we take pride in caring about others as well as ourselves. Ensuring that guests receive outstanding service is a goal of hospitality corporations.

KEY WORDS AND CONCEPTS

Back of the house
Empowerment
Ethics
Front of the house
Guest satisfaction
Inseparability
Intangible
National Restaurant Association (NRA)
Perishability
Quality control
Service industry
Total quality management (TQM)

REVIEW QUESTIONS

1. Why is service so critical in the hospitality and tourism industry?
2. Describe and give an example of the following:
   a. The interrelated nature of the hospitality and tourism industry
   b. The characteristics of the hospitality industry
3. What is the Disney service model?
4. Describe why Ritz-Carlton won the Malcolm Baldrige Award.

INTERNET EXERCISES

1. Organization: World Travel and Tourism Council (WTTC)
   Web site: www.wttc.org
   Summary: The World Travel and Tourism Council is the global business leaders' forum for travel and tourism. It includes all sectors of industry—accommodation, catering, entertainment, recreation, transportation, and other travel-related services. Its central goal is to work with governments so that they can realize the full potential economic impact of the world's largest generator of wealth and jobs—travel and tourism.
   a. Find the latest statistics or figures for the global hospitality and tourism economy.
2. Organization: Ritz-Carlton Hotels
   Web site: www.ritzcarlton.com
   Summary: The Ritz-Carlton is renowned for its elegance, sumptuous surroundings, and legendary service. With 58 hotels worldwide, a majority of them award winning, the Ritz-Carlton reflects 100 years of tradition.
   a. What is it about Ritz-Carlton that makes it such a great hotel chain?
3. Organization: Disneyland and Walt Disney World
   Web site: disney.go.com and www.disney.com
   a. Compare and contrast Disneyland's and Walt Disney World's Web sites.

APPLY YOUR KNOWLEDGE

1. Suggest ways to improve service in a hospitality business.
2. Chart out the steps that you will take to get to your career goal.
3. Describe your dream job.

SUGGESTED ACTIVITY

1. Prepare some general hospitality and career-related questions, and interview two supervisors or managers in the hospitality industry. Share and compare the answers with your class.

Internet Sites

American Hotel and Lodging Association (AH&LA) – www.ahla.com
Club Managers Association of America – www.cmaa.org
Council on Hotel, Restaurant, and Institutional Education (CHRIE) – www.chrie.org
Hospitality Career Net – www.hospitalitycareer.com
Hospitality Careers – www.hcareers.com
Hospitality Jobs Online – www.hospitalityonline.com
Hospitality Net – www.hospitalitynet.org
National Restaurant Association – www.restaurant.org

ENDNOTES

1. http://money.cnn.com/magazines/moneymag/moneymag_archive/1987/10/01/84068/index.htm, retrieved April 1, 2009.
2. Mohamed Gravy, General Manager of the Holiday Inn, Sarasota, Florida, address to USF students, February 8, 2010.
3. Karl Albrecht and Ron Zemke, Service America! (Homewood, IL: Dow Jones-Irwin, 1985), pp. 2–18.
4. Andrea Pyenson, "Service First," http://local.msn.com/article.aspx?cp-documentid=23220029&gt1=2400, retrieved February 4, 2010.
5. Karl Albrecht, At America's Service (New York: Warner Books, 1992), p. 13.
6. Ibid., p. 12.
7. Christina Holf Sommers, "Are We Living in a Moral Stone Age?," USA Today, March 1, 1999; and Barbara Frank, "Knowing Yourself Is the First Step," Toronto Sun, April 17, 2000, p. 54.
8. Stephen S. Hall (ed.), Ethics in Hospitality Management: A Book of Readings (East Lansing, MI: American Hotel and Lodging Association Educational Institute, 1992), p. 75.
9. Ibid., p. 108.

2 TOURISM

LEARNING OUTCOMES

After reading and studying this chapter, you should be able to:

Define tourism.

Discuss the long-term prospects for tourism.

Describe the benefits of tourism.

Outline the important international and domestic tourism organizations.

Describe the economic impact of tourism.

Name the major promoters of tourism and describe how they promote tourism.

HTi Describe the economic impact of tourism.

HIGHLIGHTS of TOURISM

Historically, it is hard to say when tourism began because centuries ago very few people traveled for pleasure or business as they do today. We do know that:

- In the 4th century B.C. (before Christ), work started on the Great Wall of China; it continued until the 1600s. Or "Back then, it was not the tourist destination or attraction that it is today."
- In 776 B.C., athletic games were held on the plain of Olympia in Greece (now the Olympic Games). Presumably, people traveled there to participate or to watch.
- The Romans liked to visit the bay of Naples and thus built a road from Rome in A.D. 312 (after Christ). The road was 100 miles long and took four days by litter (a nobleperson sat on a platform and was carried by some unfortunate servants).
- Religious pilgrimages to Rome and the Holy Land (now Israel) began in the 1200s, so inns sprang up to feed and accommodate the pilgrims.
- Marco Polo became the first noted business traveler as he pioneered trade routes from Europe to China from 1275 to 1292. He stayed at primitive inns called khans along the way.
- In the 1600s, during the age of horse-drawn coach travel in England, posthouses were set up every few miles so travelers could eat, take shelter, and change teams of horses. The journey from London to Bristol took three days—it now takes less than three hours by rail.
- In 1841 Thomas Cook organized a group tour for 570 people to a religious meeting in England.
- In the 1850s, Monaco (a principality in the South of France) decided to cure its economic woes by becoming a health resort and casino for the rich.
- Cruising began in the 1840s, with the Cunard Lines crossing the Atlantic between England and America.
- In the 1840s, the Peninsula and Oriental Steam Navigation Company (P & O) cruised the Mediterranean.
- During the age of the Grand Tour, from 1880 through the 1930s, wealthy Europeans toured Europe as a part of their education.
- Rail travel began in the 1800s.
- Auto travel began in the 1900s.
- Air travel began in the 1900s.
- American Airlines' first transcontinental flight between New York and Los Angeles was introduced in 1959.
- In 1970, the Boeing 747 began flying 450 passengers at a time across the Atlantic and Pacific Oceans.
- In the 1970s, ecotourism and sustainable tourism become important topics.
- In the 1980s, cruising became popular.
- In 1986, the United States established the Visa Waiver Program to eliminate unnecessary barriers to travel to the U.S. Currently 27 countries are part of the program.
- In the 2000s, tourism temporarily declined as a result of 9/11, SARS, the avian flu, and war. However, tourism is now increasing at a rate of about 4.6 percent a year, according to the World Travel & Tourism Council.

Tourism

Tourism is a dynamic, evolving, consumer-driven force. It is a system of several of the world's largest industries travel; lodging; conventions, expositions, meetings, and events; restaurants and managed services; and recreation. Tourism plays a foundational role in framing the various roles that hospitality companies perform.

The leading international organization in the field of travel and tourism, the United Nations World Tourism Organization (UNWTO), is vested by the United Nations. This organization has a central and decisive role in promoting the development of responsible, sustainable (environmentally) responsible, and universally accessible tourism, with the aim of contributing to economic development, international understanding, peace, prosperity, and universal respect for, and observance of, human rights and fundamental freedoms. In pursuing this aim, the organization pays particular attention to the interests of the developing countries in the field of tourism.

Acting as the leading organization for world tourism, the UNWTO plays a role in promoting technology transfers and international cooperation, stimulating and developing public-private sector partnerships, and encouraging the implementation of the Global Code of Ethics for Tourism, with a view to ensuring

Sustainable Cruising

The UNWTO strongly suggests that all tourism should be *sustainable* (ecotourism is sustainable tourism). Sustainable tourism is responsible tourism. This concept surfaced as a result of the negative consequences of tourism development on natural resources, ecosystems, and cultural destinations.

The International Ecotourism Society defines ecotourism as "responsible travel to natural areas that conserves the environment and sustains the well-being of local people." The last decades has seen a major increase in the interest and participation in ecotourism. Examples of sustainable (i.e., ecotourism) include using companies who take part in green initiatives, as well as visiting and supporting sustainable areas.

Overall, the past decades have shown an increase not only in the awareness of ecotourism but also in the ways in which to enhance and preserve the natural heritage and culture of a region. Cultural, heritage, and nature tourism are discussed in the next chapter, along with sustainable tourism and ecotourism.

that member countries, tourist destinations, and businesses maximize the positive economic, social, and cultural effects of tourism and fully reap its benefits, while at the same time they minimize its negative social and environmental impacts.

Through tourism, UNWTO aims at stimulating economic growth and job creation, providing incentives for protecting the environment and cultural heritage, and promoting peace, prosperity, and respect for human rights. Membership includes 161 countries and more than 370 affiliate members representing the private sector, educational institutions, tourism associations, and local tourism authorities.[1] Unfortunately, the United States is not a member, but may soon be. The UNWTO and the World Travel and Tourism Council (WTTC) declare the travel and tourism industry to have the following characteristics:[2]

- Accounts for 11.2 percent of world Gross Domestic Product (GDP)
- Employs 8.9 percent of the global workforce
- By 2018 travel and tourism is expected to contribute approximately $14,833 billion in worldwide economic activity (WTTC)
- Leading producer of tax revenues

Given the declining manufacturing and agricultural industries, and in many countries the consequent rise in unemployment, it is to the service industries that world leaders should turn for real strategic employment gains.

Tourism Defined

The United Nations World Tourism Organization's definition of tourism is, "Tourism comprises the activities of persons traveling to and staying in places outside their usual environment for not more than one consecutive year for leisure, business, and other purposes."[3]

For many developing nations, tourism represents a large percentage of gross national product and an easy way of gaining a balance of trade with other nations.

Tourism means different things to different people. To simplify tourism, it is sometimes categorized in terms of the following factors:

Geography—International, regional, national, state, provincial, country, city

Ownership—Government, quasi-government, private

Function—Regulators, suppliers, marketers, developers, consultants, researchers, educators, publishers, professional associations, trade organizations, consumer organizations

Industry—Transportation (air, bus, rail, auto, cruise), travel agents, tour wholesalers, lodging, attractions, recreation

Motive—Profit or nonprofit[4]

Amsterdam in the Netherlands is a popular tourist destination.

Tourism can also be classified as:

Inbound international tourism: visits to a country by nonresidents of that country.

Outbound international tourism: visits by residents of a country to another country.

Internal tourism: visits by tourists of a country to their own country.

Domestic tourism: inbound international plus internal tourists.

National tourism: internal tourists plus outbound international tourists.

Benefits of Tourism

At the start of the new millennium, tourism is firmly established as the number one industry in many countries and the fastest-growing economic sector in terms of foreign exchange earnings and job creation. International tourism is the world's largest export earner and an important factor in the balance of payments of most nations.

Tourism has become one of the world's most important sources of employment. It stimulates enormous investment in infrastructure, most of which helps to improve the living conditions of local people as well as tourists. It provides governments with substantial tax revenues. Most new tourism jobs and businesses are created in the developing countries, helping to equalize economic opportunities and keep rural residents from moving to overcrowded cities. Intercultural awareness and personal friendships fostered through tourism are a powerful force for improving international understanding and contributing to peace among all the nations of the world.

The UNWTO encourages governments, in partnership with the private sector, local authorities and nongovernmental organizations, to play a vital role in tourism. The UNWTO helps countries throughout the world to maximize the positive impacts of tourism, while minimizing its possible negative consequences on the environment and societies. Tourism, the world's largest industry, offers the greatest global employment prospects. This trend is caused by the following factors:

1. The opening of borders; despite security concerns, we can travel to more countries now than we could 10 years ago. The United States has a visa waiver program with 35 countries.
2. An increase in disposable income and vacations.
3. Reasonably priced airfares.
4. An increase in the number of people with more time and money.
5. More people with the urge to travel.

> **Tourism not only provides increased revenues for all types of businesses in the industry, it provides prospective employees and entrepreneurs with an increase in opportunities.**
> John Avery, *American Bar & Bistro,* Stateline, NV

According to the World Travel and Tourism Council—the industry's business leaders' forum—tourism and travel generate, directly and indirectly, 9.4 percent of global gross domestic product (GDP), investment, and employment. Real GDP growth for the travel and tourism economy is expected to decrease 3.5 percent in 2009, down from 1 percent in 2008, but to average 4 percent annually over the coming 10 years.[5]

Tourism 2020 Vision

Despite the increase in terrorist attacks and a weak economic recovery, the long-term prospects for tourism appear to be

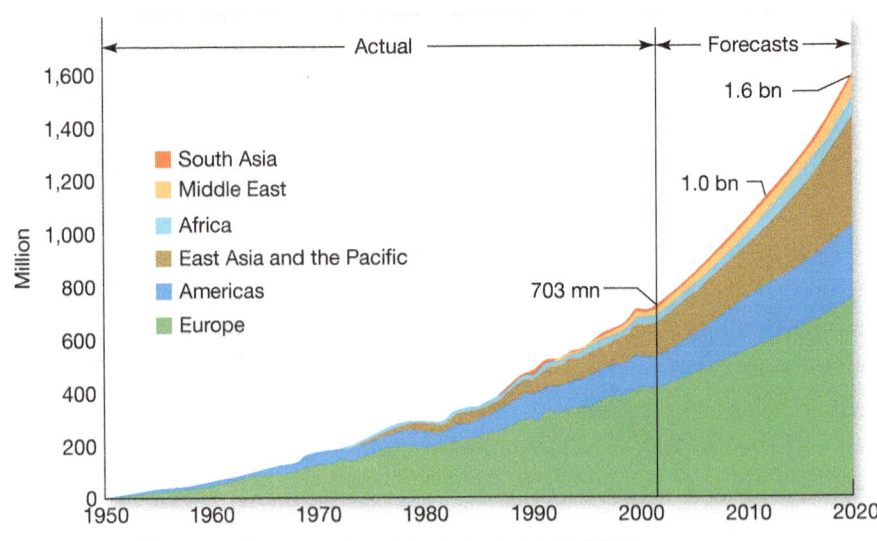

FIGURE 2–1 Actual and Forecast Tourism Arrivals 1950–2020.
(*Source:* World Tourism Organization.)

good. Tourism 2020 Vision is the World Tourism Organization's long-term forecast and assessment of the development of tourism for the first 20 years of the new millennium. An essential outcome of the Tourism 2020 Vision is quantitative forecasts covering a 25-year period, with 1995 as the base year and forecasts for 2000, 2010, and 2020 (Figure 2–1).

Although the evolution of tourism in the last few years has been irregular, WTO maintains its long-term forecast for the moment. The underlying structural trends of the forecast are believed not to have significantly changed. Experience shows that in the short term, periods of faster growth (1995, 1996, and 2000) alternate with periods of slow growth (2001 and 2002). While the pace of growth until 2000 actually exceeded the Tourism 2020 Vision forecast, it is generally expected that the current slowdown will be compensated for in the mid- to long term. WTO's Tourism 2020 Vision forecasts that international arrivals are expected to reach over 1.56 billion by the year 2020. Of these, 1.2 billion will be regional and 0.4 billion will be long-haul travelers.

Total tourist arrivals by region show that by 2020 the top three regions will be Europe (717 million tourists), East Asia and the Pacific (397 million), and the Americas (282 million), followed by Africa, the Middle East, and South Asia.

The Grand Canal, Venice, Italy, is a must-see destination.

❝ Tourism brings growth and opportunities for the economy. Overall, it really helps to keep small business open. ❞

Frank Presby, Dolphin Café, Bradenton, FL

The fact that tourism is expected to grow rapidly presents both tremendous opportunities and challenges. The good news is the variety of exciting career prospects for today's hospitality and tourism graduates. Tourism, although a mature industry, is a young profession. Careful management of tourism and travel will be necessary to avoid repercussions and negativism toward the "pesky" tourist. This is already happening to some extent in Europe, where the sheer number of tourists overwhelms attractions and facilities.

There is **interdependency** between the various segments of tourism: travel, lodging, foodservice, and recreation. Hotel guests need to travel to reach the hotel. They eat in nearby restaurants and visit attractions. Each segment is, to an extent, dependent on another for business. Just think of the interdependency of tourism with travel—likely by air, or ground transportation by car or bus—and with hotels, restaurants, and other related elements that make up the total guest experience.

Check Your Knowledge

1. How does the WTO stimulate growth in international tourism?
2. How would you define the interdependency of tourism segments?

Air Travel

Air travel has made it possible to build great resorts on remote islands, it has fostered multinational enterprises, and it has broadened the horizons of hundreds of millions of people. Without the airplane, most resort destinations would have been virtually impossible to build. The number of international travelers would be far fewer due to the time, money, and difficulty involved in travel. The airplane makes travel easier and more convenient: even the most remote location is just a few hours away by plane and reasonable airfares make it possible for more people to travel by air.

Air transport has become an integral factor in the travel and tourism industry. Hotels, car rental agencies, and even cruise lines depend heavily on airplanes for profits. For instance, lower airfares result in more passengers, and hence a higher occupancy at hotels. Whole towns and cities can and do benefit from this concept by receiving more taxes from tourists, which leads to better public facilities, better schools, and even lower local and property taxes.

To get us started, how many airplanes and air travelers are there? In America, there are about 4,500 airplanes in the skies at peak time. On top of that, by 2012, total passenger traffic between the United States and the rest of the world is projected to reach 1 billion flights annually. The expansion of the airline industry was tremendous in the 1990s, and even though many U.S. airlines are currently facing financial problems, the number of flights is back to pre-September 11, 2001, levels. Industry growth is expected to continue in the future, with additional security measures taken both in the airports and on board. In recent years, the airline has become the preferred means of travel for the long haul. The jet aircraft has made previously inaccessible places like Bali, Indonesia; Boracay, Philippines; and Bangkok, Thailand easily reachable and the travel reasonably priced.

Japan airlines offers excellent service to the U.S., Asia, Australia, Europe, and South America.

Over the past few years—with the exception of Southwest, Spirit, Air Tran, and Jet Blue—major U.S. airlines have lost billions of dollars due to competition from low-cost domestic and international airlines, additional fuel costs, high salaries for the long-term employees, and increasing pension plan and medical and other benefit costs.

Business travelers continue to spend less, and the airlines' pension, fuel, and security costs have risen. The major airlines are laying off employees, delaying delivery of new jets, and closing some hubs, reservations, and maintenance centers in efforts to reduce costs. Some of the major airlines are in or emerging from Chapter 11 bankruptcy protection and are levying an additional fuel surcharge on tickets in an effort to avoid further losses.

The major U.S. airlines have formed strategic alliances with partner airlines to provide their passengers with easier ticketing and transportation access to destinations in other countries not offered by U.S. airlines (e.g., from Tampa, Florida, to Nepal). Alliances of this nature will allow airlines access to each other's feeder markets and to resources that will enable them to flourish in what will ultimately be a worldwide deregulation. A feeder market is a market that provides the source—in this case, passengers for the particular destination. Ultimately, any major European airline without a strategic alliance in the United States will only limit its own horizons and lose market share.

Southwest operates more efficiently than its competition despite the fact that its workforce is unionized. Southwest gets more flight time from its pilots than American Airlines—672 hours a year versus 371—and racks up 60 percent more passenger miles per flight attendant. These efficiencies, along with Southwest's dedication to a low-cost, high-customer-satisfaction strategy, have resulted in annual profits for over 30 consecutive years.

Carriers such as Southwest, Air Tran, Ted (short for United), Song (Delta), and Jet Blue have lower operating costs because they use only one type of aircraft, fly point to point, and offer "no frills" service; consequently, they have lowered fares and forced larger companies to retreat. This has had a positive impact on the efficiency of the airline industry. These carriers charge 6 cents per passenger mile compared to the major airlines' 12 cents per passenger mile.

To reduce losses brought about by deregulation and higher fuel costs, major carriers eliminated unprofitable routes, often those serving smaller cities. New airlines began operating shuttle services between the smaller cities and the nearest larger or hub city. This has created the hub-and-spoke system (see Figure 2–2).

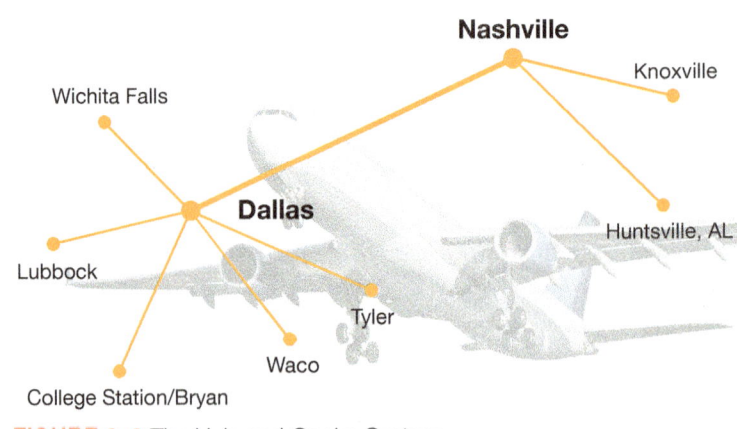

FIGURE 2–2 The Hub-and-Spoke System.

The Hub-and-Spoke System

To remain efficient and cost effective, major U.S. airlines have adopted a **hub-and-spoke system**, which enables passengers to travel from one smaller city to another smaller city via a hub or even two hubs. Similarly, passengers may originate their travel from a small city and use the hub to reach connecting flights to destinations throughout the world.

The hub-and-spoke system has two main benefits: (1) Airlines can service more cities at a lower cost; and (2) airlines can maximize passenger loads from small cities, thereby saving fuel.

Rail, automobile, and coach travel

Change in the technology of travel has had widespread implications for society. Rail travel influenced the building of towns and cities, caused hotels to be built near rail depots, and opened up the West, among other things. Auto travel produced the motel and a network of highways. The commercial jet created destination resorts in formerly remote and exotic locations, made the rental car business a necessity, and changed the way in which we look at geography. Although long-distance travel has always been fairly comfortable for the wealthy, it was not until the development of the railroad in the 1830s that travel became comfortable and cheap enough to be within reach of the masses.

By the 1920s, the automobile and bus began to replace the railroad as the leading common carrier, and the automobile has since become the predominant mode of transportation for short-distance travel. Autos offer the individual the most flexibility and convenience of any travel mode now available. This ease in transportation has in many ways created and unleashed the urge to travel, especially in North America and Europe. How much of automobile travel is properly included in the category of travel/tourism depends upon definition. Yet, however defined, in the industrialized world the auto is the number one transporter of people, carrying many times more people than airplanes, trains, ships, and buses combined. The

> **The choice of travel mode rests upon individuals' preference, budget, and time available.**

auto has become a part of life in the industrialized world, and nothing else in history has so affected people's lives.

The choice of travel mode rests upon individuals' preference, budget, and time available. If cost is an issue, the bus is often a good choice. Auto travel is the most convenient for short distances and less expensive per person when the car is full. The train can be great in heavily trafficked areas, whereas an airplane is the obvious choice for longer distances. Probably the biggest factor is why people are traveling. Is it for pleasure or business? Can they take their time, or do they need to rush to their destination and rush back? Given the choice, people who have the money usually choose speed and convenience over cost. Increases in gasoline prices have had only limited long-term effects on the extent to which people use their cars, and the same can be said of air travel. When fuel costs rise, more attention is generally paid to the efficiency of transportation rather than a reduction in travel.

Traveling by train

Coast to coast, the United States has a lot of land to cross, with a fair share of mountains, canyons, forests, deserts, rivers, and other natural barriers. One of the main factors that led to the development of railroads in the United States was the need to move goods and people from one region of the country to another. Farmed goods needed to be transported to industrial areas, and people wanted a quicker route to the West, especially after the discovery of gold in California. Those who already lived at the frontier wanted the same conveniences as their neighbors in the East, such as efficient postal service.

The train made mass travel possible for everyone. Long-distance travel became both cheaper and faster, making the horse and ship seem like "overpriced snails." The vast rail networks across North America, Asia, and Europe made the train station a central part of nearly every community. Naturally, businesspeople were entrepreneurs even back then, and hotels soon popped up conveniently close to train stations.

Although hugely important and popular for many years, rail travel started to decline as early as the 1920s. Why did people stop using the train? For two main reasons: the bus and the car. In addition, the Great Depression of the 1930s certainly did not help in drawing travelers. Although World War II brought a new surge in passenger numbers, people were seldom traveling for pleasure, and at the close of the war the decline continued. Automobiles were again available, and people had the money to buy them. By 1960, airplanes had taken over much of the long-distance travel market, further reducing the importance of the train.

Facing a possible collapse of passenger rail services, Congress passed the Rail Passenger Service Act in 1970 (amended in 2001). Shortly after, the National Railroad Passenger Corporation began operation as a semipublic corporation established to operate intercity passenger trains, a move in the direction of seminationalization of American railroads. The corporation is known today as Amtrak.

Rail Travel Abroad

While the United States tries to rejuvenate rail travel under the direction of Amtrak, rail service in other parts of the industrialized world is far ahead. Taking the train makes good sense in densely populated areas like those in Western Europe and parts of Asia, and high-speed networks are already well developed, often drawing most of the traffic that formerly went by air. One famous example is the Eurostar, connecting the United Kingdom with mainland Europe via the 31-mile-long underwater Channel Tunnel. France's TGV trains (Train à Grande Vitesse) are perhaps the most famous of them all, serving more than 150 cities in France and beyond, and traveling at about 186 mph (although they have the capacity of running at 250 mph). The TGV's most spectacular feature is the smoothness of the ride, like sitting in your armchair at home. Top that off with the fact that high-speed trains are three times as energy efficient as regional trains, and even the slowest train is 25 percent more energy-efficient than a car.[6] Because of their importance, all trains—high speed or not—run frequently and on time. Fares are generally very reasonable, and service levels are high.

The Eurorail train connects London and Paris in 2 hours, 35 minutes.

Japan's Shinkansen, the bullet train system, makes the 550-mile run between Tokyo and Osaka in 3 hours, 10 minutes (down from 18 hours). In addition, it provides a ride so smooth that a passenger can rest a coffee cup on the windowsill and not a drop will spill, just like the TGV.

Do you dream of exploring Europe? Being a student, you have probably heard of the famous Eurail pass. Several European nations have banded together to offer visitors unlimited first-class rail service for a reduced lump sum. Currently, with the pass you may visit 25 Eurail destinations.[7] However, you must buy the pass before you leave home, as it is only sold outside of Europe. When visiting Europe you can choose to travel in one country, in a few selected ones, or in all (with Eurail); it's up to you to choose between the myriad of different passes available. For example, persons under 26 can use an InterRail card for second-class passage in several European countries. Britain has its own reduced-fare ticket, BritRail, which can be booked by one of the major airline reservation systems. In other parts of the world, Australia offers the Australpass, India the Indrail Pass, Canada the Canrail Pass, and Canada and the United States, the North American Rail Pass. The new rail line in China linking Beijing to Nepal is interesting not only because it is one of the longest and one of the highest rail lines in the world but also because, according to some, it is going to dilute the Tibetan culture. This is one of the dilemmas of tourism: some see a new rail line as economic and social development, while others want to leave things as they are.

Does the Train Have a Future?

For long trips, flying is obviously a lot faster than taking the train. Therefore, long-distance train service is generally used only by those afraid to fly, or those who enjoy train travel as an experience in itself. But as we explored in the case of Amtrak, rail travel may make a comeback in the United States. As airports and roads become more congested, and parking a rare luxury, a train ride becomes more appealing. With the necessary improvements and the development of high-speed links, trains may become more time-efficient.

In addition, the Maglevs are coming. They're not aliens from outer space, but super-fast trains suspended in the air and propelled by magnetic force. Maglevs can travel at speeds of over 300 miles per hour, lifted off the ground on a cushion formed by magnetic forces and pulled forward by magnets. They run more quietly and smoothly and can climb steeper grades than the conventional train. This train is more energy efficient, has lower maintenance costs, and requires fewer staff than comparable transportation; however, given the high cost of construction, it may not prove viable. China, on the other hand, does not seem to worry about the steep cost of the Maglev. The city of Shanghai has chosen Transrapid as its partner to build a 20-mile Maglev link connecting its new airport to Shanghai's business district. If successful, an 800-mile link will be installed from Shanghai to Beijing.

So is the Maglev really feasible? Opponents of the idea claim that the Maglev is far too expensive to be worth the investment, considering that current high-speed trains can travel at speeds exceeding 200 mph if given the right conditions.

TRAVELING BY CAR

The internal combustion engine automobile was invented in Germany, but quickly became America's obsession. In 1895, there were about 300 "horseless carriages" of one kind or another in the United States—gasoline buggies, electric cars, and steam cars. Even during the Great Depression, almost two-thirds of American families had automobiles. Henry Ford's development of the assembly line and construction of good solid roads helped make the automobile the symbol of American life that it is today.

The auto changed the American way of life, especially in the leisure area, creating and satisfying the urge to travel. The automobile remains the most convenient and rapid form of transportation for short and medium distances. Without question, it has made Americans the most mobile people in history and has given them options not otherwise possible. Whereas many Europeans ride their bikes, or use the bus or train to get to school or work, Americans cannot seem to function without their cars. In fact, it is not uncommon for an American to drive 20,000 miles a year.

Road trips are a must for most Americans—college students, families, and retirees alike. Travel by car is by far the largest of all segments in the ground transportation sector of the travel and tourism industry. It is no wonder that the highways and byways of America and Canada play such important roles in tourism. So what are the advantages of car travel? The car brings you to places that are otherwise inaccessible. Mountain resorts, ski destinations, dude ranches, and remote beaches are just a few examples. This travel generates millions of dollars, and in certain places the local economy depends on the car tourist.

Rental cars offer business and leisure travelers the convenience of fly-drive or drive-only to accommodate tourists' needs.

Automobile Associations

If you have a car, and especially if you're thinking of doing a road trip, you might want to join an automobile association. Two main groups are AAA (American Automobile Association) and CAA (Canadian Automobile Association). Both important standards in the industry and lobby political parties to enforce stricter automobile safety laws on behalf of motorists. However, the part that you'll be most interested in is their roadside services. If you should get stuck in the middle of nowhere, with your car broken down, it could be a budget-buster. As a member of an automobile association, you will enjoy benefits ranging from roadside first-aid repairs to battery boosts, fuel delivery, lockout service, flat tire service, extrication, free towing, and emergency financial assistance.

Rental Cars

Some 5,000-rental car companies operate in the United States. Waiting at nearly every sizable airport in the world are several highly competitive rental car agencies, a significant segment of the travel/tourism business. About 75 percent of their sales take place at airport counters that are leased from the airport, the cost of which is passed on to the customer. The larger companies do 50 percent or more of their business with large corporate accounts; these accounts receive sizable discounts under contract. The hurried business traveler is likely to rent a car, speed out of the airport, do his or her business in a day or two, return to the airport, and hop on a plane to return home. The pleasure traveler, however, is more likely to rent a small car for a week or more. This group constitutes about 30 percent of the rental car market.

The top four rent-a-car company agencies in the United States are Hertz, Avis, National, and Budget. The agencies maintain some 625,000-rental cars that are usually new and are sold after six months to reduce maintenance costs and help avoid breakdowns. For some of the large rental car companies, travel agents account for more than 50 percent of reservations.

Car rental companies have a number of practices that don't exactly encourage repeat customers, such as excess charges for dropping off a car at a different place from where it was picked up, or for failing to refill the gas tank before returning the car. You may also have noticed that their advertising often fails to specify extra costs, such as insurance, charges for being under a certain age, taxes, and others. This way, the incredible $19 per day deal can easily become much more expensive. Pressuring or "persuading" customers to buy collision insurance is a criticized practice since many customers are, without knowing it, covered by their own car insurance. A great part of the industry's revenue comes from insurance sales, and it is mostly profit for the rental car companies. Further, travelers who take advantage of express drop-off service often find that their charge card has add-ons they did not anticipate.

Traveling by bus

Although scheduled bus routes aren't as competitive as scheduled service for airlines, buses still play an important role in the travel and tourism industry, especially with regards to their charter and tour services. Some of these companies even offer services such as destination management, incentive programs, and planning of meetings, events, and conferences. Notable bus companies include Gray Line Worldwide, Contiki Tours, and Canadian Tours International.

The major reasons for selecting the bus over other modes of travel are convenience and economy. Many passengers are adventurous college students from the United States and abroad or senior citizens, both with limited funds but plenty of time on their hands. Most people don't choose bus travel for long trips, however, as a flight is much quicker and often just as economical. However, in places such as the heavily populated northeast corridor, regular bus service between most sizable communities in New England and New York often makes it easier and safer for travelers to ride the bus than to drive their cars into the city. Anyone who has experienced New York's traffic will probably agree.

Another reason why buses are popular is that they allow the leisure traveler to sit back, relax, and enjoy the scenery. In addition, they are hassle free and provide riders an opportunity to make new friends and to stop along the way. Long-distance buses offer a variety of amenities similar to an airplane, with an extra benefit of almost door-to-door service! Buses travel to small and large communities, bringing with them tourist dollars and thus a boost to the local economy.

Types of Bus Service

In addition to routes between towns and cities, bus travel includes local route service, charter, tour, and special services, commuter service, airport service, and urban and rapid transit service. The largest and most recognized of all of the specialized travel services is Gray Line. Founded in 1910, Gray Line is a franchise operation based in Colorado. The company assembles package tours and customized tours, arranges rail and air transfers, and even provides meeting and convention services. Its major service, however, is sightseeing trips by bus. When a traveler arrives at a destination and wishes to see the town and the major tourist attractions, Gray Line is usually ready to serve. The 150-member organization carries about 28 million passengers a year to more than 200 destinations, on six continents.[8] Its trips are widely diversified, such as "around-the-town" in Paris and "around-the-country" in Thailand. In the United States, Gray Line's biggest market is Los Angeles, followed by San Francisco, then Manhattan.

The double-decker bus is a great way to see London.

Motorcoach Associations

There are several motorcoach associations in the United States and Canada: the two largest ones are the *American Bus Association* (ABA) and the *National Motorcoach Network* (NMN). The American Bus Association was founded in 1926, and is a trade association of the intercity bus industry in the United States and Canada. A couple of its most important functions are to facilitate "relationships between North American motorcoach and tour companies and all related segments of the travel and supplier industries," as well as promoting bus travel. ABA sponsors several programs including the Certified Travel Industry Specialist Program and the *ABA Scholarship Program*. They also print *Destinations Magazine*, the *Motorcoach Travel Directory* and other publications. ABA's total membership has passed 3,800, approximately 1000 of which are motorcoach and tour companies. Others include organizations working with the North American motorcoach industry, and suppliers of bus products and services.

PARIS

Think of the excitement of planning a trip to a city like Paris, which is, for many, the most fabulous city in the world. Known as the City of Light, it is perhaps the most romantic of cities. Paris is a city of beautiful buildings, boulevards, parks, markets, and restaurants and cafés. Paris has excitement. What to see first is the often-asked question over morning coffee and, of course, a croissant. There are city tours, but the best way to see Paris is on foot, especially if you want to avoid the hoards of tourists hovering around the popular attractions! Take your pick from the many places of interest: We could begin with the Eiffel Tower or the Cathedral of Notre-Dame, the Louvre and the Musée d'Orsay, the Île de la Cité, or simply a stroll down the Champs-Elysées.

Paris began as a small village on an island called Île de la Cité, in the middle of the river Seine. In time, Paris grew onto the Left Bank (Rive Gauche) where the University of the Sorbonne was founded with instruction in Latin—so it became known as the Quartier Latin or Latin Quarter. The Latin Quarter has a Bohemian intellectual character with lots of small cafés and wine bars similar to Greenwich Village and Soho in New York. Nearby is Montparnasse, an area that is popular with today's artists and painters. On the Right Bank (Rive Droit) of the river Seine are many attractions; one favorite is the area of Montmartre, with the diminutive St. Pierre Church, the domes of Sacré-Coeur, and the Place du Tertre. Just walking along the winding streets up to Sacré-Coeur gives one a feel for the special nature of

Paris. To savor the sights of the little markets with an array of fresh fruits, vegetables, and flowers; catch the aromas wafting out from the cafés; and see couples walking arm-in-arm in a way that only lovers in Paris do adds to the ambiance that captivates all who go there, and provides wonderful memories.

Close-up, Sacré-Coeur is a magnificent building in gleaming white. It towers over Paris, with its five bulb-like domes resembling a Byzantine church. The view from here, one of the highest parts of Paris, is spectacular, especially at sunset.

The Cathedral of Notre-Dame is the most famous Gothic cathedral in the world. The thirteenth-century cathedral is adorned with ornate stone carvings depicting the Virgin Mary, the signs of the zodiac, the Last Judgment, Vices and Virtues, Christ and his Apostles, and Christ in Triumph after the Resurrection. A portal above these and other stone carvings are the gargoyles immortalized as Quasimodo's den in Victor Hugo's *The Hunchback of Notre Dame*.

The Eiffel Tower was built over 100 years ago for a World's Fair; it has become one of the most recognizable buildings in the world and a symbol of Paris. On a clear day one can see for up to 40 miles from the tower.

Of the many fashionable boulevards and avenues, the Boulevard des Champs-Elysées, the main boulevard of Paris, stands out as one of the most grand. The Arc de Triomphe, the world's largest war memorial, commemorates Napoleon's victories.

The Louvre, the former residence of King Louis XIV, is the world's largest palace and largest museum. It is here that priceless works of art are displayed for public view. The *Mona Lisa* and *Venus de Milo* are the star attractions of extensive collections of Chinese, Egyptian, Greek, Roman, French, and European art, sculpture, and ceramics. A controversial Plexiglas pyramid stands in the courtyard of the Louvre. It was built to ease overcrowding at the entrance—but perhaps in part because of the pyramid's striking contrast with the palace, the lines are now even longer than before. Other museums in Paris house collections of the best works of art by the greatest painters the world has known. They represent various periods of art throughout the centuries.

The National Motorcoach Network includes over 75 charter and tour affiliates. The network has an established nationwide reservations center and publishes *Byways Magazine* to help consumers plan their leisure vacations. In addition, the NMN also works to promote safety among its affiliate members.

Check Your Knowledge

1. In your own words, define the term *tourism*.
2. What is the hub-and-spoke system?

TOURISM ORGANIZATIONS

Governments are involved in tourism decisions because tourism involves travel across international boundaries. Governments regulate the entrance and exit of foreign nationals. They become involved in the decisions surrounding national parks, heritage, preservation, and environmental protection, as well as the cultural and social aspects of tourism. Tourism is to some extent an international ambassador, fostering goodwill and closer intercultural understanding among the peoples of the world.

International Organizations

Looking first at the macro picture, the **World Tourism Organization (WTO)** is the most widely recognized organization in tourism today. The WTO is the only organization that represents all national and official tourism interests among its allied members. The WTO was described earlier in this chapter.

The International Air Transportation Association (IATA) (www.iata.org) is the global organization that regulates almost all international airlines. The purpose of IATA is to facilitate the movement of people and goods via a network of routes.[9] In addition to tickets, IATA regulations standardize waybills and baggage checks and coordinate and unify handling and accounting procedures to permit rapid interline bookings and connections. The IATA also maintains stability of fares and rates.

The International Civil Aviation Organization (ICAO) (www.icao.int) is made up of 190 contracting states.[10] ICAO coordinates the development of all aspects of civil aviation, specifically with regard to the formulation of international standards and practices.

Several international development organizations share a common purpose that includes tourism development. The better-known organizations include the following:

- The World Bank (WB), which lends substantial sums of money for tourism development. Most of this money is awarded in the form of low-interest loans to developing countries.
- United Nations Development Program (UNDP), which assists countries with a variety of development projects, including tourism.
- Organization for Economic Cooperation and Development (OECD), which was established by an international convention, and signed in Paris in 1960.

.inc Corporate Profile

G. A. P ADVENTURES

If you are tired of the one-week-in-the-Florida-sun vacation and want to do something exciting and off the beaten path, then G. A. P. Adventures is the perfect company to turn to. It provides more than 1,000 different itineraries in over 100 countries, and has given more than 85,000 travelers the adventure of their lifetime. This year, approximately 1.5 million more people are expected to visit the company's Web site, some of them to change their lives forever.

G. A. P Adventure's CEO Bruce Poon Tip has been honored with the Entrepreneur of the Year Award, sponsored by NASDAQ, Ernst & Young, and the National Post. G. A. P Adventures has also been named one of Canada's 50 best managed companies and top 100 employers. Furthermore, it has greatly helped to improve the conditions in the many countries it visits.

Its philosophy, "The Freedom of Independent Travel with the Security of a Group" has been practiced since the start. The company respects its travelers as individuals, and there is no requirement to be athletic to embark on one of its trips. The only requirement is a spirit of adventure and the desire to experience a world totally different from what you are accustomed to.

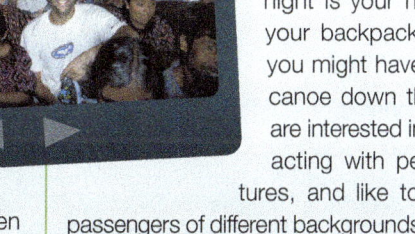

Also, the concept of responsible tourism is very important to G. A. P Adventures; the company comes and goes and interacts with the local populations, leaving behind only footprints. Its commitment is to support local people and communities and to protect the environment they travel in. To that end, G. A. P Adventures developed Planeterra—the G. A. P Adventures Foundation, which gives back to the people and communities their passengers visit on their trips.

G. A. P Adventures employs more than 300 staff worldwide, hiring people in different departments, including Operations, Product, Sales and Marketing, Finance, HR, and Tour Leading. All current postings can be found under the career section of the company's Web site.

Maybe the most obvious choice for you is the position as a G.A.P tour leader. In this position, your main task is to make people's holiday dreams come true and make sure that all passengers have an enjoyable time abroad. Most of the time, the local hostel where you spend the night is your home, and your office is your backpack. On your way to work you might have to hike the Inca Trail or canoe down the Amazon River. If you are interested in meeting and really interacting with people from different cultures, and like to show your passion to passengers of different backgrounds, ages, and interests, this is the perfect job for you.

Some of the requirements in order to work as a G. A. P tour leader include fluency in English and Spanish, a passion for travel, a love for Latin America (which is its main area of operations), and excellent people skills. No

.inc Corporate Profile (Continued)

matter what happens and how bad your day has been, you always have to be the happy and helpful leader. Additional skills needed include awareness of, and commitment to, sustainable tourism, both environmentally and culturally, as well a commitment to an 18-month contract. It takes time to become the perfect adventure tour leader, and once you have learned it, the company may decide to renew your contract. You also need to be resourceful, which means being able to solve any kind of problem that might arise, expected or unexpected. Due to the nature of the work, you also need to have good health, first-aid certification, and an average level of computer literacy (Internet/e-mail/Microsoft Word/Microsoft Excel). If you have seen the world, or want to see it, in a truly interactive way, have leadership skills, and are adventurous and brave, then this might be the perfect job for you. Why not give it a try?

Note: In order to apply to be a tour leader, you will need to complete the online application form found on the G. A. P Adventures Web site.
Source: This draws on G. A. P Adventures Web site: www.gapadventures.com.

Portofino, Italy is a popular town for tourists.

The purpose of the OECD is to do the following:

Support sustainable economic growth
Boost employment
Raise living standards
Maintain financial stability
Assist other countries' economic development
Contribute to growth in world trade[11]

The OECD's tourism committee studies various aspects of tourism, including tourism problems, and makes recommendations to governments. The committee also works on standard definitions and methods of data collection, which are published in an annual report entitled *Tourism Policy and International Tourism in OECD Member Countries.*

Other banks and organizations with similar interests include the Asian Development Bank, Overseas Private Investment Corporation, Inter-American Development Bank, and Agency for International Development.

The **Pacific Area Travel Association (PATA)** represents 34 countries in the Pacific and in Asia that have united behind a common goal: excellence in travel and tourism growth. PATA's accomplishments include shaping the future of travel in the Asia/Pacific region; it has had a remarkable record of success with research, development, education, and marketing.

Domestic Organizations

Many countries have a minister of tourism, which is a cabinet-level position that can advocate tourism development, marketing, and management through the National Tourism Organization (NTO). Unfortunately, the United States does not have even a senior-level government official for tourism. Instead, an organization known as the Travel Industry of America (TIA) is the main body for the promotion and development of tourism in the United States. It speaks for the common interests and concerns of all components of the U.S. travel industry. Its mission is to benefit the whole U.S. travel industry by unifying its goals, coordinating private sector efforts to encourage and promote travel to and within the United States, monitoring government policies that affect travel and tourism, and supporting research and analysis in areas vital to the industry. Established in 1941, TIA's membership represents more than

Introducing Patti Roscoe

Patricia L. Roscoe, chairperson of Patti Roscoe and Associates (PRA) and Roscoe/Coltrell Inc. (RCI), landed in California in 1966, charmed by the beautiful San Diego sun (compared to the cold winters in Buffalo, New York, her hometown). She was a young, brilliant middle manager who was to face the challenges of a time when women were expected to become either nurses or teachers. She became involved with the hotel industry, working for a large private resort hotel, the Vacation Village. Those were the years to be remembered. She gained a very thorough knowledge of Southern California tourism, as well as of the inherent mechanisms of the industry. With the unforgettable help and guidance of her manager, she began to lay the foundations of her future career as a very successful leader in the field. The outstanding skills that she learned are, in fact, the very basis of her many accomplishments.

The list of Roscoe's awards and honors is astounding: She earned the prestigious CITE distinction (Certified Incentive Travel Executive), she was named the San Diego Woman of Accomplishment in 1983, and in February, 1990, Roscoe was honored as San Diego's 1989 Allied Member of the Year during the tourism industry's Gold Key Awards. Also in 1990, she was given the Wonder Woman Award by the U.S. Small Business Administration for her outstanding achievements in the field. In 1993, the San Diego Convention and Visitors Bureau conferred on her the prestigious RCA Lubach Award for her contributions to the industry.

She is also extremely involved in civic and tourism organizations, including the Rotary Club, the American Lung Association of San Diego and Imperial Counties, and the San Diego Convention and Visitors Bureau.

The key to Roscoe's success perhaps lies in her remarkable skills of interacting with people. It is the human resources, in fact, that represent the major strength of PRA. Its employees are experienced, dedicated, and service oriented. But what makes them so efficient is their dedication to working together as a team. Roscoe guides, inspires, and motivates these teams. She is a self-admitted "softy," a creative and emotional leader who enjoys training her employees and following their growth step by step, to eventually give them the power of initiative they deserve, as a tool to encourage their creativity and originality. She constantly seeks to balance the concept of teamwork with the individual goals and private lives of her employees. It is through the achievement of such a balance that a profitable, healthy community is preserved. PRA is a bit more than a community, however, it is a family. And just like a mother, Roscoe's formula is discipline and love. At the same time, her leading efforts are aimed at training her employees to "think outside of the box," and "keep one's view as broad as possible," which is the only way to rise above the commonplace, the rhetorical, and the trivial, to escape provincialism, and thus become unique individuals.

That's how the magic is done. PRA excels in creating "something that becomes exclusively yours—that has never been done before." PRA is decentralized into service teams to foster an entrepreneurial environment in which initiative and creativity can be boosted to the fullest. Therefore, PRA staff design personalized unique events to give their customers an unforgettable time.

Since its opening in 1981, PRA has become one of the most successful destination management companies in the country, providing personal, caring service characterized by flexibility and creativity.

2,000 travel-related businesses, associations, and local, regional, and state travel promotion agencies of the nation's travel industry.

State Offices of Tourism

The next level of organizations concerned with tourism is the state office of tourism. These offices are charged by their legislative bodies with the orderly growth and development of tourism within the state. They promote information programs, advertising, publicity, and research in terms of their relationship to the recreation and tourism attractions in the state.

City-Level Offices of Tourism and Convention Centers

Cities have also realized the importance of the "new money" that tourism brings. Many cities have established **convention**

and visitors bureaus (CVBs) whose main function is to attract and retain visitors to the city. The convention and visitors bureaus comprise representatives of the city's attractions, restaurants, hotels and motels, and transportation. These bureaus are largely funded by the transient occupancy tax (TOT) that is charged to hotel guests. In most cities, the TOT ranges from 8 to 18 percent. The balance of funding comes from membership dues and promotional activities. In recent years, convention centers have sprung up in a number of large and several smaller cities. Spurred on by expectations of economical and social gain, cities operate both convention centers and visitor's bureaus.

The economic impact of tourism

> By employing approximately 1 out of every 10 workers, travel and tourism is the world's largest employer and is the largest industry.

The World Travel and Tourism Council, a Brussels-based organization, commissioned a study[12] from the Wharton Economic Forecasting Association. Their report suggested that the total demand for travel and tourism would be 2,571 billion by 2010, or more than 10 percent of the world's gross national product (GNP). Tourism, says the study, grows about twice as fast as world GNP. Of the industries' total world spending, about 31 percent takes place in the European Community and 30 percent on the North American continent.

International arrivals, according to the WTO, reached 880 million in 2009 and may reach 1.6 billion by 2020, more than triple the 475 million people who traveled abroad in 1992. In 2009 international travel and tourism generated $852 billion in export earnings.[13] Nearly every state publishes its own tourism economic impact study. New York, for example, estimates its tourism revenue to be $38.5 billion; Florida, about $51.7 billion; Texas, $33 billion; and California, just over $53 billion. Tourism is Hawaii's biggest industry with revenues of $23 billion.

The National Travel and Tourism Awareness Council's annual "the Tourism Works for America Report"[14] indicates that travel and tourism is one of the nation's leading sectors. Statistics include the following:

- International travelers spend about $94 billion on travel-related expenses (e.g., lodging, food, and entertainment) in the United States annually.
- At least 20.8 million people are directly employed in the industry, making travel and tourism the nation's second largest employer, after health services.
- Travel generates about $100 billion a year in tax receipts. If it were not for tourism, each U.S. household would need to pay $898 more in taxes.
- International visitors within the United States spend about $21 billion more than do Americans who travel outside the United States.
- Approximately 54.9 million international travelers visit the United States each year.
- Just a 1 percent increase in the world market would mean a 7.6 million increase in visitors, which would create 150,000 jobs and contribute $2 billion in new tax revenue.[15]

By employing approximately 1 out of every 10 workers, travel and tourism is the world's largest employer and is the largest industry. Estimates predict that in the year 2012, there will be 249 million travel and tourism jobs, accounting for 8.6 percent of total employment, or 1 in every 11.7 jobs.

The Multiplier Effect

Tourists bring new money into the economy of the place they are visiting and this has an impact beyond their original expenditures. When a tourist spends money to travel, stay in a hotel, or eat in a restaurant, that money is recycled by those businesses to purchase more goods, thereby generating further use of the money. In addition, employees of businesses who serve tourists spend a higher proportion of their money locally on various goods and services. This chain reaction, called the **multiplier effect**, continues until there is a leakage, meaning that money is used to purchase something from outside the area. Figure 2–3 illustrates the multiplier effect.

Most developed economies have a multiplier effect between 1.5 and 2.0. This means that the original money spent is used again in the community between 1.5 and 2.0 times. If tourism-related businesses spend more money on locally produced goods and services, it will benefit the local economy.

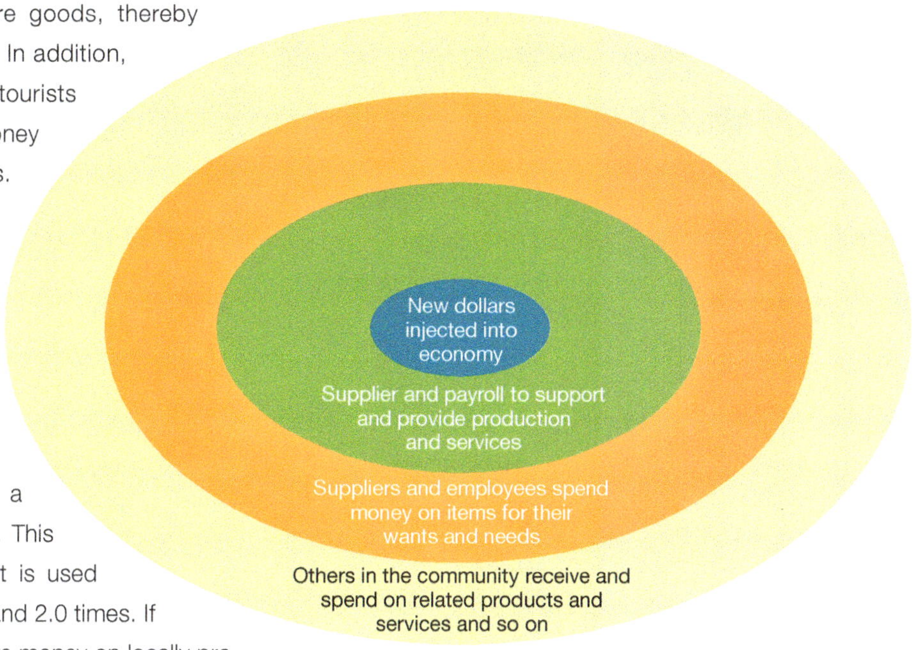

FIGURE 2–3 The Multiplier Effect.

Promoters of Tourism

Tour Operators

The National Tour Association estimates that 1,636 U.S. tour operators conduct nearly 500,000 tours annually. These tours carry 21.2 million passengers, who spend an average of $168 per passenger per day on both one-day and multiday tours. Tour operators promote tours/trips that they plan and organize. A tour/trip is taken by a group of people traveling together, with a professional tour manager/escort, following a preplanned itinerary. Most tours include travel, accommodations, meals, land transportation, and sightseeing, with a markup added before advertising the package. Tour operators also offer *vacation packages* that are for people traveling independently. Vacation packages include a combination of two or more travel services: hotel, car rental, and air transportation, offered at a package price. Most vacation packages offer choice components and options allowing the client to customize *their* package to *their* budget.

Travel Agencies

A travel agent is a middleperson who acts as a travel counselor and sells on behalf of airlines, cruise lines, rail and bus transportation, hotels, and auto rental companies. Agents may sell individual parts of the overall system or several elements, such as air and cruise tickets. The agent acts as a broker, bringing together the client (buyer) and the supplier (seller). An agent has quick access to schedules, fares, and advice for clients about various destinations.

The American Society of Travel Agents (ASTA) is the world's largest travel trade association, with over 20,000 members in more than 165 countries. The Airlines Reporting Corporation (ARC) reports that a travel agency's weekly sales are about $40,000. According to *Travel Weekly Magazine*, the top 50 travel agencies in terms of sales generated (approximately $25 billion in revenue) represent 30 percent of total agency sales.

Agents use computer reservation systems (CRS) to access availability and make bookings. In the United States, the main vendors are Sabre (which also owns Travelocity and, Apollo, Worldspan, System One, and Galileo. Cendant Corporation owns Galileo, which forms the hub of Cendant's travel-related business of hotels, car rental, and vacation ownership. Worldspan is jointly owned by Delta, Northwest, and American Airlines. Worldspan manages 59 percent of all online bookings worldwide, including Internet bookings for Expedia, Hotwire, Orbitz, and Priceline.[16]

According to ASTA, a travel agent is more than a ticket seller. Agents serve their clients in the following ways:

- Arranging transportation by air, sea, rail, bus, car rental, etc.
- Preparing individual itineraries, personally escorted tours, group tours, and prepared package tours
- Arranging for hotel, motel, and resort accommodations; meals; sightseeing tours; transfers of passengers and luggage between terminals and hotels; and special features such as tickets for music festivals, the theater, etc.
- Handling and advising on many details involved with travel, such as insurance, traveler's checks, foreign currency exchange, documentary requirements, and immunizations and other inoculations
- Using professional know-how and experience (e.g., schedules of air, train, and bus connections, rates of hotels, quality of accommodations, etc.)
- Arranging reservations for special-interest activities, such as group tours, conventions, business travel, gourmet tours, sporting trips, etc.[17]

Approximately 9,386, travel agencies are currently operating in 15,761 retail locations in the United States.[18]

Commission Travel agents once gained most of their income from airline and cruise line commissions. However, travel agents have seen air travel commissions, their primary source of income, decline since commission caps were first imposed. The airlines now have eliminated commissions so agencies are charging a fee for their services to offset the costs involved in providing those services.

Out of necessity, travel agents have become more specialized to make up for the loss of commission revenue from the airlines. Some have specialized in the booking of cruises, because cruise lines are still are paying between 10 and 15 percent of the price of the cabin booked. Others have expanded their product offerings by including meeting and event planning and management. Another way of gaining more commission is simply to charge clients an extra amount for their tickets. There are still several business and leisure travelers who do not have the time or inclination to book their trips online. For them, the travel agent can provide a hassle-free service and be there for their clients. However, due to the increasing number of Internet bookings for all types of travel and tourism, the volume of travel agents' bookings has substantially decreased.[19]

Travel Corporations

There are a number of large and successful travel corporations—the largest being American Express Travel Services. American Express (AMEX) is a corporation that has a travel services division with locations worldwide. Each location is licensed and bonded with the International Air Transportation Association (IATA), which provides travel services and tickets through the corporation. The travel services division provides other services, including foreign currencies, AMEX traveler's checks in different currencies, and gift checks. Currently, the travel services division is trying to promote foreign currencies to increase revenues.

The majority of American Express Travel Services' revenues is generated by business travel through corporate accounts. The airlines give the travel agency a discount to share with the corporate client, based on the volume of business the airline gets. The business contract is set up individually, based on annual travel expenses. For example, if IBM's annual travel expenses are $1 million, the airline will give AMEX a 1.4 percent override commission to split with IBM. AMEX chooses its airline vendors according to who gives the largest override percentage and whose negotiated rates are most appealing. The same policy applies to other vendors in the industry, such as cruise lines.

Travel agents offer services like air, cruise, rail, and bus ticketing plus hotel, resort, and car rental reservations.

Travel managers for AMEX function as national account managers. Their pay is based on their grade level, region, and market. Their salary also depends on who they service. A small, local clientele generates a lower salary, and a broader service center provides a higher salary. Depending on whether they are on- or off-site, a travel manager's salary for AMEX is between $60,000 and $95,000 for corporate clients. The salary range for general public leisure travel is between $40,000 and $65,000. Each travel manager is hired internally, and pay is based mostly on seniority.[20]

American Express Travel Services searches the Internet for the best ticket price or the most convenient flights in the same reservations systems used by thousands of travel agents. In a snap, users can check out the price or search for other options and then book their own reservations online. Users can view descriptions of packages to sunny, snow-filled, cultural, or just plain fun destinations, along with full-color photos and a list of amenities. Visitors to the www.americanexpresstravel.com site currently have three options: They can book airline tickets, they can view vacation offers, and they can look up the most convenient American Express Travel office. In addition, card members may take advantage of special travel, retail, restaurant, and entertainment offers and shop for a variety of merchandise on another Internet site called ExpressNet.

Corporate Travel Manager

A corporate travel manager is a type of entrepreneur working within the framework of a large corporation. For example, a few years ago, Mitsubishi Electronics, in Cypress, California, spent about $4 million for travel and entertainment. In addition, 29 field offices operated independently across the United States, Canada, and Mexico. The total expenditure for travel and entertainment was $11 million. Enter John Fazio, recruited by Mitsubishi to improve efficiency and reduce costs. Fazio invited interested agencies to submit proposals based on Mitsubishi's travel needs. The 15 initial proposals were narrowed to 8; finally, 2 were asked to submit their best and final offers. These offers were evaluated based on Mitsubishi's criteria: technological capabilities, locations, and ability to give personal service.

By having travel managers and travel policies companies can literally save thousands of dollars.

An interesting trend in corporate travel is agentless booking via electronic mail (e-mail). Travel is initiated at the keyboard, not at the switchboard. Increasingly, technologically savvy corporations are making travel bookings via e-mail.

Travel and Tour Wholesalers

Tour wholesaling came into prominence in the 1960s because airlines had vacant seats, which, like hotel rooms, are perishable. Airlines naturally wanted to sell as many seats as possible and found that they could sell blocks of seats to wholesalers close to departure dates. These tickets were for specific destinations around which tour wholesalers built a tour. Wholesalers then sold their tours directly through retail agents.

The tour wholesale business is concentrated with about 100 independent tour wholesalers; however, 10 major companies account for about 30 percent of the industry's business. Tour wholesalers offer a wide range of tours at various prices to many destinations. Three key types of wholesalers characterize this segment of the industry:

1. An independent tour wholesaler
2. An airline working in close cooperation with a tour wholesaler
3. A retail travel agent who packages tours for his or her clients

In addition, incentive travel companies (companies that arrange travel for companies who want to motivate their employees with an incentive) and various travel clubs round out the tour wholesale business.

Certified Travel Counselor (CTC)

Leading experts in the travel industry worked together to form the Institute of Certified Travel Agents (ICTA). The ICTA offers specialized professional studies for those seeking higher proficiency in the travel industry. The professional designation of CTC is awarded to individuals who have successfully passed examinations and who have five years' full-time experience in a travel agency or in the marketing and promotion of travel.

> ### Check Your Knowledge
> 1. Name three tourism organizations and describe their purpose.
> 2. What is the mutiplier effect?
> 3. Describe the services offered by a tour operator.

National Offices of Tourism (NOT)

National Offices of Tourism seek to improve the economy of the country they represent by increasing the number of visitors and consequently their spending in the country. Connected to this function is the responsibility to oversee and ensure that hotels, transport systems, tour operators, and tour guides maintain high standards in the care and consideration of the tourist. The key roles of the National Offices of Tourism are supplying information, advising travelers, creating demand for destinations and ensuring they are up to expectations, publicizing, and advertising.

Destination Management Companies (DMCs)

A destination management company is a service organization within the visitor industry that offers a host of programs and services to meet clients' needs. Initially, a destination management sales manager concentrates on selling the destination to meeting planners and performance improvement companies (incentive houses).

The needs of such groups may be as simple as an airport pickup or as involved as an international sales convention with theme parties. DMCs work closely with hotels; sometimes DMCs book rooms, and other times hotels request the DMCs' know-how on organizing theme parties.

Patricia Roscoe, chairperson of Patti Roscoe and Associates (PRA), says that meeting planners often have a choice of several destinations and might ask, "Why should I pick your destination?" The answer is that a DMC does everything, including airport greetings, transportation to the hotel, VIP check-in, theme parties, sponsoring programs, organizing competitive sports events, and so on, depending on budget.

Sales managers associated with DMCs obtain leads, which are potential clients, from the following sources:

- Hotels
- Trade shows
- Convention and visitors bureaus
- Cold calls
- Incentive houses
- Meeting planners

Each sales manager has a staff or team that may include the following:

- Special events manager, who has expertise in sound, lighting, staging, and so on
- Accounts manager, who is an assistant to the sales manager
- Operations manager, who coordinates everything, especially on-site arrangements, to ensure that what is sold actually happens

For example, Roscoe's destination management company organized meetings, accommodations, meals, beverages, and theme parties for 2,000 Ford Motor Company dealers in nine groups over three days.

Roscoe also works closely with incentive houses, such as Carlson Marketing or Maritz Travel. These incentive houses approach a company and offer to evaluate and set up incentive plans for the sales team, including whatever it takes to motivate them. Once approved, Carlson contacts a destination management company and asks for a program.

In conclusion, thousands of companies and associations hold meetings and conventions all over the country. Many of these organizations use the services of professional meeting planners, who in turn seek out suitable destinations for the meetings and conventions. Some larger hotels and resorts now have a destination management department to handle all the arrangements for groups and conventions.

> **Ten major tour wholesaler companies account for about 30 percent of the industry's business.**

TRENDS *in* TOURISM

- Globally, the number of tourist arrivals will continue to increase by about 4 percent per year, topping 1 billion by 2010.
- Overall, the past decades have shown an increase not only in the awareness of ecotourism but also in the ways to enhance and preserve the natural heritage and culture of a region.
- Governments will increasingly recognize the importance of tourism not only as an economic force, but also as a sociocultural force of increasing importance. Please see Figure 2–4 for an example of a career path in tourism.
- Marketing partnerships and corporate alliances will continue to increase.
- Employment prospects will continue to improve.
- Ticketless air travel is rapidly increasing.
- Low-cost, no-frills airlines, such as Jet Blue, ATA, Ted (United), and Southwest are gaining an increased market share at the expense of the six main U.S. airlines their passengers are business and leisure travelers.
- Internet bookings will increase.
- There will be an increase in the number of "boutique" airlines.
- Airlines will try to entice travelers to book their travel using their Web sites rather than Expedia and similar sites.
- One of the main developments over the past few years has been the introduction of more environmentally friendly vehicles and fuels.
- Also on the rise are hybrid vehicles, a cross between a modified gasoline or diesel-powered engine and an electric motor.
- More and more cars and rental cars come equipped with a Global Positioning System (GPS), also known as a car navigation system.
- Many car rental agencies are making it easier for their "regular" customers by letting them bypass check-in lines and use self-service kiosks for rapid service. This trend is also seen at airports, in hotels, and at train stations, saving hurried travelers a great deal of time and adding to their satisfaction with the company.
- An important trend in bus travel is the environmentally friendly vehicles being introduced on the market.
- Partnerships are also on the rise: Greyhound Shore Services have recently started providing meet-and-greet services to Carnival and Holland America cruisers in Los Angeles; Royal Caribbean and Celebrity Cruises contract with Greyhound in various ports in California and Mexico.

CASE STUDY

Overpopulation of National Parks

Our national parks are under serious threat from a number of sources, including congestion resulting from overvisitation, consequent environmental degradation, and pollution.

There are too many people and vehicles in the most popular national parks. Many bring their city lifestyle with them, littering, listening to loud music, and leaving the trails in worse shape than they were.

DISCUSSION QUESTION

1. List your recommendations for how park superintendents can save the parks.

CAREER INFORMATION

CAREER INFORMATION

The field of travel and tourism offers careers that provide information, transportation, accommodations, goods, and other services to travelers. Tourism is established almost everywhere in the world and is the world's largest employer. If restaurant or hotel management career options do not appeal to you, then you may want to consider a career in travel and tourism.

The best advice about the tourism career path is to be proactive during your college years. More than likely, you will have to open your own doors to your first career position in tourism. It is important to start early in your college experience and learn as much about the industry as possible through trade publications, magazines, travel, seminars, course work, volunteer work at convention and visitors bureaus, shadowing at travel agencies, going on tours, and membership in professional organizations. It is beneficial to work in the travel and tourism industry while you are going to school. An internship can provide you with opportunities you may not be able to find on your own.

The travel and tourism business is changing because of the Internet. Many people can access information now that they once had to rely on travel agents and tour guides to provide. However, there will always be a market of individuals who are willing to pay someone else to provide these services.

Opportunities abound in such areas as sales, marketing, public relations, finance, accounting, and human resources. Many companies look for management trainees, starting them out at the bottom and giving them almost unlimited opportunities for growth and advancement when they prove themselves. Common to all these companies is the need for graduates with not only a solid academic background, but also a lot of drive, enthusiasm, and creativity.

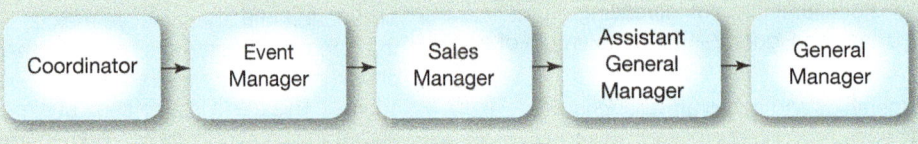

FIGURE 2–4 Example of a Career Path in Travel and Tourism.

SUMMARY

1. Tourism can be defined as the idea of attracting, accommodating, and pleasing groups or individuals traveling for pleasure or business. It is categorized by geography, ownership, function, industry, and travel motive.
2. Tourism involves international interaction and, therefore, government regulation. Several organizations, such as the World Tourism Organization, are responsible for environmental protection, tourism development, immigration, and cultural and social aspects of tourism.
3. Tourism is the world's largest industry and employer. It affects other industry sectors, such as public transportation, foodservice, lodging, entertainment, and recreation. In addition, tourism produces secondary impacts on businesses that are affected indirectly, which is known as the multiplier effect.
4. Travel agencies, tour operators, travel managers, wholesalers, national offices of tourism, and destination management companies serve as intermediaries between a country and its visitors.

KEY WORDS AND CONCEPTS

Convention and visitors bureaus
Hub-and-spoke system
Interdependency

Multiplier effect
Pacific Area Travel Association (PATA)
Tourism

World Tourism Organization (WTO)

REVIEW QUESTIONS

1. Give a broad definition of tourism and explain why people are motivated to travel.
2. Give a brief explanation of the economic impact of tourism. Name two organizations that influence or further the economic impact of tourism.
3. Choose a career in the tourism business and give a brief overview of what your responsibilities would be.
4. Discuss the positive and negative impacts that tourism can have on a country.

INTERNET EXERCISES

1. Organization: World Tourism Organization
   Web site: www.world-tourism.org/
   Summary: The WTO is the only intergovernmental organization that serves in the field of travel and tourism and is a global forum for tourism policy and issues. It has about 138 member countries and territories. Its mission is to promote and develop tourism as a significant means of fostering international peace and understanding, economic development, and international trade.
   a. How much is spent on international tourism?
   b. What does the Tourism 2020 Vision predict?

2. Organization: Air Transport Association
   Web site: www.air-transport.org/
   Summary: The ATA is the first and only trade organization for the principal U.S. airlines. Its purpose is to support and assist its members by promoting the air transport industry and its operations, safety, cost effectiveness, and technological advancement. It has promoted the interest of the commercial airline industry for more than 60 years and now is a key player in the global transportation market.
   a. What were the effects of the Airline Deregulation Act of 1978?
   b. What indirect benefits does the airline industry offer the public?

APPLY YOUR KNOWLEDGE

1. Analyze your family's and friends' recent or upcoming travel plans and compare them to the examples in the text that illustrate the reasons why people travel.

2. How would you promote or improve tourism in your community?

SUGGESTED ACTIVITY

1. Go online and get prices for an airline round trip between two cities for a flight:
   a. more than 60 days out
   b. 7 to 14 days out
   c. leaving tomorrow
   Compare the prices and share the results with your class.

ENDNOTES

1. World Tourism Organization, www.unwto.org/aboutwto/index.php, retrieved May 1, 2009.
2. Ibid.; the World Travel and Tourism Council, www.wttc.org, retrieved May 1, 2009.
3. World Tourism Organization, www.unwto.org, retrieved May 1, 2009.
4. Rosa Songel, "Statistics and Economic Measurement of Tourism," World Tourism Organization, www.unwto.org/statistics/index.htm, retrieved May 1, 2009.
5. World Travel and Tourism Council, www.wttc.org/eng/Tourism_Research/Tourism_Economic_Research/, retrieved May 4, 2009.
6. Rail Europe, www.raileurope.com/about-us/about-us.html, retrieved May 4, 2009.
7. Eurail, www.eurail.com/eurail-where-to-go, retrieved May 4, 2009.
8. Gray Line, www.grayline.com/Grayline/info/aboutus.aspx, retrieved May 4, 2009.
9. International Air Transport Association, www.iata.org/about/mission, retrieved May 4, 2009.
10. International Civil Aviation Organization, www.icao.int/cgi/statesDB4.pl?en, retrieved May 6, 2009.
11. Organization for Economic Co-Operation and Development, www.oecd.org/pages/0,3417,en_36734052_36734103_1_1_1_1_1,00.html, retrieved May 9, 2009.
12. www.wttc.org/economic_research/kystats.htm
13. http://www.unwto.org/index.php, 12, 2010.
14. www.world-tourism.org/market_research/facts@figures/menus.htm, retrieved August 12, 2010.
15. Ibid.
16. Courtesy of the American Society of Travel Agents.
17. American Society of Travel Agents, www.astanet.com/news/releasearchive03/12_23_03.asl.
18. http://www.asta.org/News/content.cfm?ItemNumber=1985&navItemNumber=545, retrieved August 12, 2010.
19. Phone interview with Susan Argon, Minimax Travel, August 16, 2006.
20. Personal conversation with Jay Schrock, May 8, 2009.

3
WHY PEOPLE TRAVEL

LEARNING OUTCOMES

After reading and studying this chapter, you should be able to:

List reasons why people travel.

Describe the sociocultural impact of tourism.

Describe sustainable tourism and ecotourism.

Explain cultural, heritage, and nature tourism.

Describe the economic impact of tourism.

Have you ever been dying for a break? Have you ever caught yourself daydreaming about where you would go if you only had the time, the money, and the opportunity? Are you curious about the world and want to explore it? Well, you are not alone! From the beginning of time, people all over the world have felt the urge to get out there and explore, conquer, and find enlightenment. Though hopefully a little more peaceful, the weary student heading off on spring break, to Europe for the summer, or even for a semester abroad, is not too different from the adventurous Viking seeking greener pastures.

Fantasies aside, why do people travel? Today, there are many reasons (maybe even some excuses) to take to the road. A trip away from home may be for a vacation, to visit friends and family, for work, to attend a conference or a sporting event, even to visit a college campus. Regardless of the purpose of the travel, under the umbrella of travel and tourism, there are many occupations that are necessary to meet the needs and wants of people who are away from home. And this is where you come into the picture!

However, different people have different reasons and motivations for traveling. What type of traveler are *you*?

There are many reasons why people travel; however, they fall under two main headings: "pleasure" and "business." Research shows that when consumers are asked what they associate most with success and accomplishment, the number one response is travel for pleasure.

Among the reasons people travel for pleasure are the following:

Discover the Different Types of Travelers: Visit the Island Proprietor

- Visit friends and relatives
- Health
- Enlightenment, education
- Beauty, nature, and national parks
- Religion
- Indulgence
- Sports
- Festivals
- Shopping
- Fun
- Gaming
- Adventure
- Heritage
- Ecotourism
- Attractions

" There are many reasons why people travel. It could be for business or personal purposes. Regardless, it provides the traveler with an opportunity to encounter somewhere or something new and hopefully exciting! *"*

Joseph Charles, Charles Street Café & Catering, Boston, MA

PLEASURE TRAVEL

Learn about the Different Needs of Travelers at the Front Desk

Eighty-one percent of domestic travel is **Pleasure travel** (leisure, recreation, holidays, and visiting friends and relatives—VFR).[1] Nearly half of all the pleasure travelers visited friends and relatives. When surveyed, people tend to list the following reasons for travel:

- To experience new and different surroundings
- To experience other cultures
- To rest and relax
- To visit friends and family
- To view or participate in sporting/recreational activities

" People travel to get away from everyday life. They want to come in to an establishment, relax and have fun, and create a memorable experience. *"*

Gabriel Alves, A Taste of Maine, South Portland, ME

Travel is likely to increase in the coming years, which will have a significant impact on tourism. Some reasons for the anticipated increases are as follows:

- *Longer life span.* The average person in the United States now has a life expectancy of about 80 years, which allows for more postretirement travel. And baby boomers will be retiring in just a few years, which is expected to swell the population of retirees hitting the road.
- *Flexible working hours.* Today, many people work four 10-hour days and have longer weekends. Of course, many others, especially in the hospitality and tourism industries, work on weekends and have leisure time during the week.
- *Early retirement.* Some people are being given the opportunity to retire between ages 55–65. This is because they generally are earning more than younger workers who replace them.
- *Greater ease of travel.* Today, it is easier to travel on holidays and weekends, for both business and leisure purposes. Each mode of travel affords increasing opportunities to take advantage of the additional leisure time.

- *Tendency to take shorter, more frequent trips.* People now tend to take shorter, but more frequent, mini vacations rather than taking all their vacation time at once. Europeans generally take much longer vacations than do North Americans. For them, four weeks is the normal vacation benefit of new employees, and six weeks is typical after a few years.
- *Increase in the standard of living.* More people in many developing countries have increased their income and wish to travel. China, with its newfound enterprise zones, is producing hundreds of thousands of entrepreneurs who will soon be traveling to foreign countries. Millions of East European residents of the former Soviet Bloc countries now have the capability and the right to travel. And finally, an additional 300 million people from China and India will soon have passports.

Mt. Fuji is a popular destination for many tourists. Courtesy of the Japan National Tourist Office.

Different Places for Different People

Obviously, travelers select destinations for different reasons—climate, history or culture, sports, entertainment, shopping facilities, and so forth. The major appeal of England for Americans seems to be history and culture. American Express surveyed people going to several destinations—Florida, California, Mexico, Hawaii, the Bahamas, Jamaica, Puerto Rico, the Virgin Islands, and Barbados. Almost half of the respondents were professionals, generally middle-aged, and well educated. Many were wealthy travelers who took frequent vacations outside the United States. These respondents ranked the appeals of travel in descending order of importance:

- Scenic beauty
- Pleasant attitudes of local people
- Suitable accommodations
- Rest and relaxation
- Airfare cost
- Historical and cultural interests
- Cuisine
- Water sports
- Entertainment (e.g., nightlife)
- Shopping facilities
- Sports (golf and tennis)

Four basic considerations emerged as factors influencing travel: entertainment, purchase opportunities, climate for comfort, and cost. Even within a group, of course, different factors apply. One individual may select a destination primarily because of opportunities for challenging golf and tennis, another because of the friendly local people, and another because the place offers rest and relaxation. Most of the group would, however, be influenced by airfare costs. Travelers often have culturally based expectations for the travel experience that may or may not be met by international travel. Current research focuses on the impact of the traveler's culture on expectations for service, as well as ways to assess customer expectations and evaluate customer satisfaction. Service providers in destination locations are making efforts to meet the needs of diverse populations of travelers.

Satisfaction, or dissatisfaction, with the travel experience, of course, depends on how it is viewed by the traveler. A glorious sunset may not thrill a gregarious individual traveling alone. The best service in a restaurant with the finest food and decor is meaningless to a person with an upset stomach. One traveler loves the rain, another despises it. Mountains are one person's delight yet make another person dizzy. The anthropologist revels in the remote village; the city dweller finds it dull. So much

The Grand Canyon receives more than 5 million visitors a year.

depends on what the person expects of the experience and how he or she actually experiences it.

Travel is an experience, not a tangible object. It results in psychic reward or punishment. It creates pleasant anticipation or aversion, excitement and challenge, or fatigue and disappointment. The experience and the memory occur in the mind, leaving no concrete evidence as to why travel was undertaken and why the same trip is experienced in so many different ways by different people. Travel literature and films often falsify reality or are shot so selectively that the actual environment is not recognizable by the visitor. The phony shot that makes the pool look longer than it is, the colors that never exist in nature, the lavish buffet that was rigged especially for the photograph, the breathtaking sunset that occurs once a year—all of this creates expectations that cannot be realized, and leads to disappointment.

Business Travel

In recent years, the amount of business travel has declined. The general economic climate, acts of terrorism, and companies' reduced travel budgets have negatively affected business travel.

Yet a high percentage of the guests who check into mid-priced and luxury hotels around the world are traveling for business reasons. A good portion of business travel is, however, mixed with pleasure. Counted as **business travelers** are those who travel for business purposes such as meetings; all kinds of sales, including corporate, regional, product, and others; conventions; trade shows and expositions; and combinations of these. In the United States, meetings and conventions alone attract millions of people annually. Sometimes the distinction between business and leisure travel becomes blurred. If a convention attendee in Atlanta decides to stay on for a few days after the conference, is he a business or leisure traveler? Compared to leisure travelers, business travelers tend to be younger, spend more money, travel farther, and travel in smaller groups. However, they do not stay as long.

Identify the Characteristics of the Business Traveler

Business travel, long the mainstay of airlines and hotels, will likely gradually decline as a percentage of all travel, which includes leisure travel. Leisure travel is forecast to increase due to more people having more disposable income. Many people now have more leisure time and higher levels of education, and the cost of travel has remained constant, or dropped, compared to inflation and other costs combined. These factors indicate a bright future for the travel industry.

An increasing number of business travelers are able to make their own travel arrangements online. For example, in the middle of a client meeting, meeting consultant Suzie Aust realizes that she has forgotten to book the next day's flight. She pulls out her laptop, gets online, and books the flight. Corporate America is worried about travelers like Suzie because they are often able to skirt corporate policies when making their own reservations. Some companies use a product from Microsoft and American Express. Code-named "Rome," the product will allow companies to control their own travelers by insisting that employees buy their own tickets through American Express. American and United Airlines are each rolling out similar products. Ed Gilligan, president of corporate services for American Express, estimates that American companies lose $15 billion a year due to deviations from corporate policy. And the portion of that sum lost to online reservation systems is "ramping up quickly," he says. About 1.8 million business travelers are wired. Soon, almost all airline business travel will be ticketless.

Business travel has changed in recent years due to the increased security at airports and other travel-related places. These security changes include enhanced airport restrictions, time delays, more secure passports and documentation, a "suspect" list, and new software for "recognition" technology, from fingerprint to retina scanning. Add to this flights that are more fully booked, fewer refreshments, and little time to grab a meal during plane changes and we can see why some business travelers prefer not to travel unless absolutely necessary.

We all know about the increased security at airports, cruise line terminals, and rail and bus stations. The traveling public has been very understanding because they realize that the security measures are necessary for our safety.

Check Your Knowledge

1. What four basic considerations have emerged as factors influencing travel?
2. What are the main reasons why people travel?
3. What are the reasons for the increase in travel?

The social and cultural impact of tourism

From a social and cultural perspective, tourism can leave both positive and negative impacts on communities. Undoubtedly, tourism has made significant contributions to international understanding. World tourism organizations recognize that tourism is a means of enhancing international understanding, peace, prosperity, and universal respect for, and observance of, human rights and fundamental freedom for all without distinction as to race, sex, language, or religion. Tourism is a very interesting sociocultural phenomenon. Seeing how others live is an interest of many tourists, and the exchange of sociocultural values and activities is rewarding.

Provided that the number of tourists is manageable and that they respect the host community's sociocultural norms and values, tourism provides an opportunity for a number of social interactions. A London pub or a New York café are examples of good places for social interaction. Similarly, depending on the reason for the visit, myriad opportunities are available for tourists to interact both socially and culturally. Even a visit to another part of the United States would be both socially and culturally stimulating. For example, New Orleans has a very diverse social and cultural heritage. Over the years, the city has been occupied by the Spanish, French, British, and Americans. The food, music, dance, and social norms are unique to the area.

Courtesy of Joanne di Bona and the San Diego Convention and Visitors Bureau.

The competitiveness of international destinations is based on such attributes as service quality, as well as the value for the price, safety, security, entertainment, weather, infrastructure, and natural environment. Political stability is also important in determining the desirability of a destination for international tourism. Imagine the feelings of an employee in a developing country who earns perhaps $4.50 per day when she sees wealthy tourists flaunting their money, jewelry, and a lifestyle that is out of her reach.

Just imagine what will happen when another 300 million people become tourists by virtue of higher standards of living and an increase in the number of people who can obtain passports. Currently, only 21.7 percent of the U.S. population has passports. The population of Eastern Europe

A mariachi band playing in Old Town San Diego, California.
Courtesy of the San Diego Convention and Visitor's Bureau.

and the nouveau riche of the Pacific Rim countries will substantially add to the potential number of tourists. So, it's no surprise that travel tourism is expected to double by 2015.

Machu Picchu is a popular ecotourism destination

Sustainable Tourism and Ecotourism

The increased number of tourists visiting destinations has heightened concern for the environment, physical resources, and sociocultural degradation. The response of tourism officials has been to propose that all tourism be sustainable. The concept of **sustainable tourism** places a broad-based obligation on society—especially those involved with tourism policy, planning, and development—and on federal, state, and local governments to harmonize tourism and tourism development by improving the quality of its environment and resources—physical and sociocultural. Sustainable tourism includes **infrastructure** (roads, water, sewage, communications, and stores which meet local needs). **Superstructure** is the facilities built to accommodate tourists, such as airports, cruise terminals, convention centers, hotels, and restaurants. The facilities should be appropriate for the number of tourists visiting the area; otherwise, if the area has too many tourists the experience becomes unpleasant for all, including the host community.

WHAT IS ECOTOURISM?

The roots of **ecotourism** can be traced to the "responsible tourism" movement of the 1970s. This concept emerged as a reaction to the negative consequences of tourism development on natural resources, ecosystems, and cultural destinations. The movement toward responsible tourism helped spawn "environmental tourism" in the early 1980s, which in turn led to the birth of ecotourism.

Héctor Caballos-Lascuráin, head of the Ecotourism Consulting program for the World Conservation Union and co-author, with Elizabeth Boo, of the book *Ecotourism: The Potential and Pitfalls*, coined the term in July 1983. He offers one of the most comprehensive descriptions of ecotourism: "Environmentally responsible travel and visitation to relatively undisturbed natural areas, in order to enjoy and appreciate nature (and any accompanying cultural features—both past and present) that promotes conservation, has low negative visitor impact, and provides beneficially active socioeconomic involvement of local populations."[1] The Ecotourism Society in Bennington, Vermont, suggests a simplified (and widely used) definition of ecotourism: "Responsible travel to

FIGURE 3–1 A Model of a Sustainable Ecotourism System.

natural areas that conserves the environment and sustains the well-being of the host people." Dr. David Weaver, a respected ecotourism author and scholar, defines ecotourism as: "A form of tourism that fosters learning experiences and appreciation of the natural environment, or some component thereof, within its associated cultural context. It is managed in accordance with industry best practice to attain environmentally and socioculturally sustainable outcomes as well as financial viability."[2] To illustrate the conceptualization of an ecotourism system, Figure 3–1 shows a model. Notice how this is like a flower: it needs all parts of the system to harmonize to flourish.

Interactions between hosts and tourists entail more than simple transactions of money for goods or services. They also involve the exchange of expectations, stereotypes, and expressions of ethnicity and culture.[3] For example, the Infierno and Posada Amazonas in the province of Tambopata, Peru, are located several hours by motorized boat from the provincial capital. The community covers almost 10,000 hectares (24,700 acres) on both sides of the Tambopata River and has a mixed economy based on fishing, hunting, and gathering some horticulture. Community members travel to the market in Puerto Maldonado to sell produce and manufactured goods. Three different ethnic groups came together to form a community that signed a joint venture agreement with Rainforest Expeditions, a Peruvian ecotourism company with the purpose of combining tourism with environmental education, research, and local sustainable development to support conservation in the areas in which they operate.[4] Over time, a lodge was built to accommodate ecotourists and several studies were conducted on various aspects of life in the community. These studies examined complex issues of ethnic identity of the three groups and their relationships with the ecotourists. Some said that there was little identity to lose, but others said that they wanted to save something about their identity from the Westernizing influences of tourism. Interestingly, it was the ecotourists who prompted a revival of the ethnic cultures.[5]

Complementing the model of a sustainable ecotourism system (Figure 3–1) is a framework for an ecotourism system, which is shown in Figure 3–2. It illustrates the stakeholders and other parts of the ecotourism system, including carrying capacity and limits of acceptable change; sustainable activity and impact assessment; social and economic impact; and site management, certification, geotourism, and carbon footprints.

Explore the Role of Ecotourism on the Local Environment

Ecotourism is more focused on individual values; it is tourism with a conscience, sharing many of the same aspirations of sustainable tourism—the terms are often used interchangeably. The International Ecotourism Society (TIES) defines ecotourism as "responsible travel to natural areas that conserves the environment and improves the well-being of local people." Those who want to participate in ecotourism activities should follow these principles:

- Minimize impact.
- Build environmental and cultural awareness and respect.
- Provide positive experiences for both visitors and hosts.
- Provide direct financial benefits for conservation.
- Provide financial benefits and empowerment for local people.
- Raise sensitivity to host countries' political, environmental, and social climate.
- Support international human rights and labor agreements.[2]

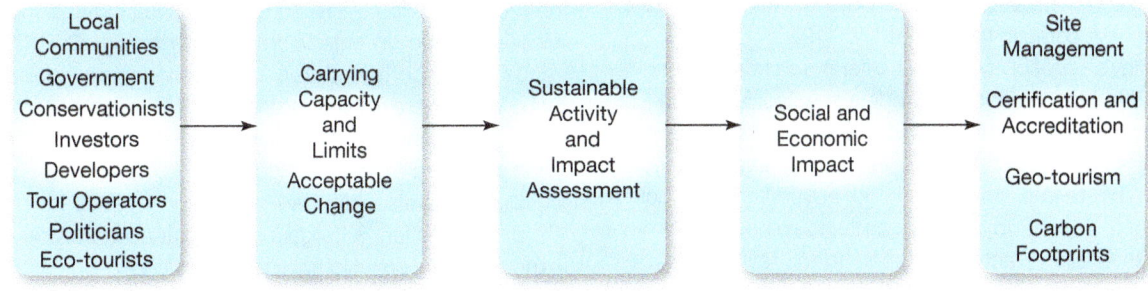

FIGURE 3–2 A Framework for Ecotourism.

.inc Corporate Profile

CLUB MED

In 1950, a Belgian diamond cutter and water polo champion conceived of the first Club Med village—funded with army surplus tax money—on the Spanish island of Majorca. The goal of that first resort was to unite people from diverse backgrounds, encourage them to share a good time, and offer them a unique escape from the stress and the tension of the everyday events of post—World War II Europe. The first adventurous vacationers to experience that new environment were mostly young couples or singles, living together in a beautiful natural setting, enjoying the atmosphere of camaraderie and no worries, playing sports, or just simply relaxing on a warm, soft beach.

The following decade was a particularly profitable one because of the overall social climate that characterized the 1960s. The young generation, generally speaking, was wrapped up in a whirl of ideals, such as peace, communion, and the sharing of feelings and experiences—all in the framework of a return to nature. The so-called "flower child" phenomenon saw the young long for a return to primitive purity, innocence, and freedom of expression. It is not surprising, then, that Club Med's clientele rose by 500 percent in that decade. In fact, the features that characterized the resorts made them just the right environment to meet the needs of this target market. Club Med expanded throughout the Mediterranean coastlines and islands, including Greece and Italy. Centers began to spring up on the coasts of Africa and the Middle East. Today Club Med—short for Mediterranean—has more than 120 resorts and vacation villages around the world, hosted by 28 countries in the Mediterranean as well as in the Caribbean, Africa, Mexico, the Bahamas, South Pacific, South America, Asia, and the United States. The little village in Majorca blossomed into a colorful, joyful, sunny, colossal empire: Club Med is the world's largest vacation village organization and the ninth largest hotel chain, with 93,000 beds and 20,000 employees. More than 9 million guests have come to the villages since 1950.

Today's philosophy doesn't differ much from the original one. Club Med intends to provide a spectacular natural setting in which its guests can enjoy life and its amenities, away from the troubles and the worries of the everyday frantic rat race. The theme on the printed advertisements points straight to this: "Club Med: Life as it should be." Sports, various entertaining activities, good food, real concern for guests' needs, and a carefree lifestyle worked wonders. Imagine all of these amenities in the context of white sand beaches and a clear blue sea that seems to stretch out indefinitely to meet a virtually cloudless sky at the horizon.

Club Med's original formula was copied by several other organizations in the travel and tourism industry. The increased competition caused Club Med to revise its management strategies and develop a different product in order to gain and hold market share. Changes in the industry were accompanied by social changes. As the years went by, the baby boomers of the 1960s and 1970s grew up, got married, and began to travel with their families. The target market thus changed again, and the necessity to change along with the market was promptly acknowledged.

The policy that Club Med's managers embraced was one of differentiation and flexibility. Through assiduous market research, studies, and surveys, Club Med identified the continuously changing needs and characteristics of both the market and the clientele. On the basis of their results, they were able to take effective action to keep up with such evolution. Marketing strategies therefore were reelaborated, and the product Club Med offers was repackaged according to the demands of the guests, while still remaining faithful to the original philosophy. The image of Club Med was also reconsidered in order to determine the most appropriate one at all times.

Other significant changes included an entrance into the cruise business—Club Med I is a luxurious cruise ship that offers the excitement of yachting (thanks to a retractable platform that allows activities such as waterskiing, diving, etc.) together with the comforts of the cruise. Activities within the village were also improved and upgraded, following the guests' requests for more in-depth sports teaching, more amenities in the rooms, specialized restaurants, more security, and communication tools.

The clientele target was also widened: Club Med now attempts to attract guests other than the original youth/couples. As a consequence, the individual villages were updated by specializing in a particular area. Although all clubs offer the same basic services, some focus mainly on sports, some on tours and excursions, some on convention and meeting facilities, some on entertainment, and so on. Guests now range from sports enthusiasts to families (mini clubs and baby clubs were recently established), honeymooners, and corporate clients. The new trend at the moment is that of finding ways to attract the older clientele.

Club Med also has had another innovative idea: Wild Card, which offers a bargain rate to vacationers who don't mind gambling on which village they visit. Wild Card confirms participants on a one-week vacation at one of Club Med's Villages in the Bahamas, Caribbean, or Mexico for $999 per person, double occupancy; this is a savings of up to $500 over the weekly standard rate. Included is the price of the airfare from specified gateway cities. Wild Card presents a win—win situation. Club Med wins because it can utilize vacant space on air charters and accommodations; guests win because they get a great vacation at a bargain price.

To cope with the changes and implementations in the global structure of the Club Med villages, human resources staff (also called GOs—"gentle organizers") have been selected and trained more thoroughly. GOs come from all over the world; they must have some foreign language proficiency (to keep up with an extremely cosmopolitan clientele), skills in sports or entertainment, and, most of all, be extremely enthusiastic and very people oriented. In fact, the spirit of the village depends almost entirely on the creative ideas and contact generated by the staff.

Overall, Club Med has shown a very remarkable ability to reinvent itself according to the continuous evolution of the market and society. The genuine commitment to excellence that Club Med has demonstrated should help it retain its status as the ultimate destination resort organization. www.clubmed.com

---

Most ecotourism destinations can be found in developing countries with vast natural surroundings and plentiful flora and fauna. Places like deserts, tropical rain forests, coral reefs, and ice glaciers are prime locations. The presence of a culture that is unique to the visitor is also important in ecotourism. The focus of ecotourism is to provide tourists with new knowledge about a certain natural area and the culture that is found within, along with a little bit of adventure. As for the natives, ecotourism is meant to help improve the local economy and conservation efforts. All parties are to gain a new appreciation for nature and people.

Thus far, ecotourism projects tend to be developed on a small scale. It is much easier to control such sites, particularly because of limits that are normally set on the community, the local tourism business, and the tourists. Limitations may include strict control of the amount of water and electricity being used, tougher recycling measures, regulating park and market hours, and, more importantly, limiting the number of visitors to a certain location at one time and restricting the size of the business. Another reason ecotourism projects are kept small is to allow more in-depth tours and educational opportunities.

Generally, most of the more popular ecotourism destinations are located in underdeveloped and developing countries. As vacationers become more adventurous and visit remote, exotic places, they participate in activities that should have a positive impact on nature, the host communities, and themselves. It is because of the growing interests of travelers that many developed countries are following the trend. This is apparent from Yellowstone National Park in the United States to the Mayan Ruins of Tikal in Guatemala; from the Amazon River in Brazil to the vast safari lands of Kenya; from the snowcapped Himalayas in Nepal to the sultry jungles of Thailand; and from the Great Barrier Reef in Australia to the massive ice glaciers in Antarctica. There is no doubt that this is an attractive trend in many parts of the world. Sustainable tourism, especially ecotourism, can be a main source of worldwide promotion of sustainable development geared toward tourists and communities in all countries.

Ecotourists can enjoy viewing the National Parks.

Environmental Impact of Tourism[3]

Tourism can and does affect the environment in a number of ways. As mentioned earlier, "over visitation" of a particular resort, attraction, or city can have an adverse impact on ecology. Natural resources may be threatened or seriously disturbed by poorly managed tourism. In the Caribbean, for example, tourist demand for seafood is the primary cause of the increasing pressure on lobster, conch, and fish populations.

Read about Conducting Safe Tours in the Tour Operator's Guide

Tourism development also puts pressure on local resources. The superstructure (airports, convention centers, hotels, bridges, roads, railways) and the infrastructure (electric, water, sewage, communications, government services—including police and fire departments and transportation) frequently are overused in a way that they become harmful to the natural environment. Nature's delicate balance has often been disturbed by the rapid and seemingly unrestricted growth of some tourist areas. In Mexico and parts of the Mediterranean, for example, tourist demands have led to an often disorderly urbanization of large stretches of the coastline.

Tourists also cause pollution in the form of sewage and solid waste, litter, noise, and air pollution. For residents, tourism can disrupt an otherwise blissful lifestyle. Unfortunately, these forms of tourist pollution are on the rise in many developing countries, which often lack the technological or financial capacity to handle these problems.

The big question is how to balance tourism growth in such a way as to protect the environment and residents' lifestyle and culture. The answer largely centers on partnership and cooperation within the tourism industry and between businesses, governments, and tourists. Regulation, both voluntary self-regulation and government legislation, can work in practice. A good example is Pattaya, Thailand. After years of neglect, the beach and ocean became so polluted that the tourists stayed away. This forced a collection of hoteliers, city officials, the Tourism Authority of Thailand, and a handful of tour operators to step in. The goal was to stop sewage and waste pollution from going directly into the ocean untreated. The outcome is that the sewage treatment plants now modify the waste. The beaches and ocean are again welcoming tourists. This example illustrates the need for cooperation between central and local governments.

Governments can sponsor, with the use of tourism and other taxes, environmental studies that identify valuable fragile habitats and protect them by monitoring them. Governments have a major role to play in minimizing the environmental impact of tourism. Federal, state, and city governments can pass legislation to limit the number of visiting tourists. Generally, this is done in an indirect manner. For example, placing a height restriction on new buildings will limit the number of high-rise buildings in an area, which in turn will affect the number of hotel rooms that are created. Governments may either increase or restrict access to destinations or attractions by manipulating air, railroad, and cruise capacity. By refusing to build or expand the access to destinations and attractions, the number of tourists will automatically be limited.

In the early 1970s, several remote areas of the world saw that tourism could be profitable; however, they did not want to destroy the exotic environment that surrounded them. One such place was Cancun, Mexico. Cancun was a prime beach location, but the number of tourists was quite low. Developers recognized Cancun's potential and drew up a master plan that placed priority on environmental protection. Unfortunately, Mexico began to experience political and economical instability. The recession caused the government and business leaders to scramble, trying to find a way to bring money into the economy—specifically, U.S. dollars. Tourism in Mexico was one of the few industries that showed signs of growth. However, in an effort to make a quick profit, Cancun's environmentally friendly attractions have been sacrificed to make room for large-scale development. As a result, the few natives who were living in the assigned resort area were relocated to the mountains, to live in cardboard shacks without plumbing. The beaches surrounding Cancun have become cluttered with garbage, and the reef off of the coastline is damaged by ships coming into the wharf. Water treatment is insufficient. Further, it is practically impossible to meet the growing **capacity requirement** of the tourists.

Cancun, Mexico, is not the only place to experience such disruption and environmental hardships because of tourism. We might surmise that rampant and damaging overdevelopment is present only in less developed destinations, but that is not true. Sometimes much pollution—air, water, or land pollution—and overpopulation occur in areas that are well developed.

As similar stories surface, ecologists and tourism leaders have come to realize how important it is to preserve the environment so that generations to come can continue to enjoy the earth's natural beauty. Because of this idea, most ecotourism destinations can be found in areas with vast natural surroundings and plentiful flora and fauna. Places such as deserts, tropical rainforests, coral reefs, and ice glaciers are prime locations. Also important in ecotourism is the presence of a culture that is different from that of the visitor. The focus of ecotourism is to provide tourists with new knowledge about a certain natural area and the culture that is found there, along with a little bit of adventure.

Footprints in the sand exemplify ecotourism: a wave will soon wipe away the footprints left by tourists.

Check Your Knowledge

1. What is the competitiveness of international destinations based on?
2. What is the social and cultural impact of tourism?
3. What does ecotourism focus on?

Cultural Tourism

Cultural tourism is defined as tourist visits "motivated wholly or in part by interest in the historical, artistic, scientific, or lifestyle/heritage offerings of a community, region, group, or institution."[4] It is a recognized form of tourism that has been around for a long time and one that has gained in popularity and importance during the last decades. The older civilizations in Asia, Europe, Africa, North America, and Latin America hold a special fascination for many travelers who appreciate the wealth of culture found in these parts of the world. Few tourists can resist being attracted to one or more aspects of cultural tourism: architecture, anthropology, art, local food and beverages, music, dance, museums, scenic tours, gardens, and festivals.

Both culture and heritage tourism benefit from the **United Nations Educational, Scientific, and Cultural Organizations (UNESCO)**, which has designated a number of World Heritage Sites worthy of protection and preservation due to the outstanding value to humanity of the natural and cultural heritage. There are 20 U.S. sites on the World Heritage List; among them are the Statue of Liberty and the Grand Canyon. Around the world there are 878 heritage sites deemed worthy of protection and preservation, including some of the world's treasures like the Imperial Palaces of the Ming and Qing Dynasties and the Great Wall in China; the Acropolis in Athens, Greece; the Taj Mahal in India; the center of Rome, Italy; and the Tower of London.[5]

Impact of Tourism on Culture

The general public and tourism experts around the globe do not seem to agree on whether tourism has a positive or negative impact on culture. Take a moment to think about it. What is your opinion?

Dr. Philip McKean, an anthropologist who studied the impact of tourism on cultural patterns in Bali, concluded in 1972 that the culture change brought

CASE STUDY

Ecotourism at a Glance

- Promotes biodiversity
- Promotes conservation
- Minimizes the environmental impact of tourism
- Increases knowledge of culture and the environment
- Sustains the livelihood of locals

Introducing Holly Carvalho
Destination Manager

I work for a national tour operator company selling air and vacation packages and customized tours within the U.S. and to Europe. I spend most of my day selling to prospective buyers, servicing client inquiries, staffing and training the operations department. I also maintain contact with and negotiate contracts for hotels, airlines, and ground transportation for our individual and group clients. The most important skills for my position are communication and organization. I need to communicate with clients and vendors as well as approve advertisements.

As a destination manager, I must also be responsible for managing destinations that are popular for conventions and corporations for major events. The client frequently needs the help of someone with local knowledge and the ability to orchestrate a successful event, including hotel site selection, convention planning and organizing, entertainment selection, airport greeting, ground transportation, theme parties, spousal programs, and custom design of programs for clients. It's a fun career that allows me to use all my creative talents.

about by tourism actually strengthened several of the folk traditions. Beginning in 1969, when an airport was opened in Bali, tens of thousands of tourists arrived to enjoy the island and to be entertained by Balinese temple performances of dancing and religious rites. They purchased handicrafts, paintings, and carvings. Interactions between tourists and the Balinese were, for the most part, structured via hotel staff and tour agencies. These people may be considered "culture brokers." Although tour guides are the most common "culture brokers," there are many different types of brokers. At the local level, guides and interpreters are culture brokers, but because tourism has grown from a business to an industry, others—including travel agents, accommodation providers, government at all levels, and international agencies—have assumed leadership.[6] In exchange for their money, the tourists were allowed to enter the mythic reality of the Balinese cosmos. They were welcomed as spectators at well-staged aesthetic events.

A lot has changed over the past three decades, and acculturation has occurred at a fast pace. An increasing number of Balinese people have taken on the Western lifestyle, discarding their traditional values and lifestyles. Popular paintings, carvings, and antiques are mass-produced, their quality steadily declining, and temples are pillaged for artifacts to satisfy naïve tourists. Religious ceremonies, dances, and traditional crafts are all being changed and in some cases subverted to fit tourist tastes. Whereas a lot of locals are profiting from tourism, jealousy and envy has sprung up alongside and, among other things, many people have begun to curse the tourists for dressing inappropriately.[7] These are just a few of the impacts that tourism has had on Bali and its rich cultural heritage. What other impacts do you think have occurred? What, for example, do you think has happened to the environment and residents' quality of life?

Tourism and Art

The effects of tourism on the arts of developing regions have been debated, with pros and cons taken into account. The impacts have been favorable in a number of places. Pottery making, weaving, embroidery, jewelry making, and other crafts have been revived in Tunisia and Cyprus. In Malta, tourism has encouraged craftwork in knitwear, textiles, and glass making. Peasant music and folk dancing have been revitalized, and new dances have been developed. West African carving, originally closely related to ritual, had been gradually disappearing until tourist purchases gave it new stimulus. African artisans responded by developing new forms and styles based on traditional models. In the Bahamas, a couple developed a style of batik printing on cotton, and have made it into a profitable business that sells largely to tourists. In Fiji, woodcarving was a lost art. An artist from Hawaii reintroduced woodcarving techniques so indigenous that carvers could create the works needed for a new hotel. The carvers then set up a shop on the hotel grounds where they sell their products to visitors.

> **Tourism enhances the arts and crafts of a destination by providing new markets for artisans, often reviving a fading art or craft and fostering the development of traditional forms!**

In general, placing local arts and crafts in hotel lobbies, guest-rooms, and restaurants increases the demand for them and at the same time creates a desirable local ambiance in the hotels. Inevitably, plastic objects appear in the form of shell beads, for example, made in Manila or Hong Kong and sold in Hawaii. Machinery replaces the hand in making cheap imitations, and plastic copies of art substitute for the authentic. Though many people see this development as something solely detrimental and negative, markets actually exist for both the authentic and the copy.

Several anthropologists take the view that artists in developing countries have consciously responded to the souvenir market and in doing so have actually improved indigenous art in many cases. New art forms have evolved and can continue to evolve. For example, Eskimo art that uses ivory from Arctic animals has changed drastically from its earlier form. Some Eskimo artists do market their products just as other businesspeople do, by making what people want. A number of developing nations have established state-run craft shops that tend to "authenticate" the product and ensure its quality. The range in quality, however, is great. In Apia, Western Samoa, state-operated craft shops display all sizes and designs of tap a cloth (a bark cloth), kava bowls, and eating utensils. The state-operated craft shop in the Acapulco Convention Center enhances the objects for sale with dramatic displays and by its prestigious setting. Other craft centers, however, seem to do little but provide for middle-income functionaries.

Overall, it is safe to say that tourism enhances the arts and crafts of a destination by providing new markets for artisans, often reviving a fading art or craft and fostering the development

Investigate Different Types of Tourism on the Island

of traditional forms. In a number of instances, tourism has encouraged new art forms or adaptations of traditional ones. But the question of all the plastic souvenirs and the imitations and copies passed off as the real thing still remains relevant. Not to mention the new dances and ceremonies developed solely for the amusement of tourists and sold as "the real thing." Are they also desirable and positive, or are they rather detrimental cultural developments and clever exploitations of gullible tourists?

What effect will tourism have on this young girl in Peru?

Heritage tourism

Tourism that respects natural and built environments, in short, the heritage of the people and place, is called **heritage tourism**. Renewed appreciation for historical milestones and the development of "heritage trails" linking cultural landmarks produce new tourism services and products that can assist local economies.[8] Heritage in relation to tourism is a growing phenomenon in America. This is in part due to greater interest in our roots, especially among more senior travelers. It can also provide travelers with unique experiences, such as getting the feel of a very particular place or time.

Heritage was for years a forgotten element in tourism planning and policy. However, with the awakening of the social conscience that has taken place during the recent decades, it has now become a key element in the decision-making process in countries like the United Kingdom and others. Central to the heritage issue is how irreplaceable resources are to be used by people of the present and conserved for the future generation in a fast-changing world.[9]

One of the most popular historic sites in America is the Alamo in Texas, a battlefield site that attracts over 2.5 million visitors a year.[10] There are many other popular historical sites, mainly related to Revolutionary War and Civil War battlefields. Native American cultural sites are also significant heritage attractions. The main problem with conserving heritage is that the sheer volume of tourism may, if not properly managed, come into conflict with and defeat the conservation of the tourism heritage. Conservation and tourism need to be complementary and in harmony.

American Express, in a unique partnership with the National Trust for Historic Preservation, has sponsored an excellent workbook, *Getting Started: How to Succeed in Heritage Tourism*. The workbook suggests that tourism and preservation are very likely to overlap. It claims, "Linking tourism and preservation can do more for local economies and for tourism and preservation than promoting them separately. That's the core idea in heritage tourism: save your heritage, share it with visitors, and reap the economic benefits of tourism." Indeed, some state tourism offices now help develop heritage resources, and a number of preservation organizations are marketing their sites to tourists.[11]

As we will discuss in the following chapters, tourism development follows the creation of tourism policies and planning. Any development should comply with the mission and objectives of the nation/region's tourism plan. Tourism development usually involves interactions between several governmental and private organizations. Requiring a company to secure land-use permits before building an attraction is one example. This was the case with Disney World just outside Orlando, Florida. The land Disney wanted to develop was originally designated for agriculture. The Disney Corporation, which had wanted to expand for years, was granted the necessary permissions only after lengthy negotiations with the city government.

The Benefits of Preservation

But why do we place so much importance on preservation? Well, the wealth of buildings, traditions, and natural beauty that one generation leaves to the next are inherited assets. The purpose of preservation is to protect those assets for the enjoyment of present and future generations. How appealing do you think the Grand Canyon would be if it, 20 years from now, were completely destroyed by tourism, and all that the pollution and wear and tear that tourism brings with it?

The facade of the Alamo Mission is a significant heritage tourist attraction.

The preservation movement first gathered momentum in this country when Ann Pamela Cunningham initiated efforts to save Mount Vernon in 1853 followed by the chartering of the Mount Vernon Ladies Association in 1856 and the start of its restoration in 1859. A century later, the passage of the National Historic Preservation Act of 1966 motivated many supporters to continue the early preservationists' mission of saving America's heritage resources. People are now starting to recognize the need to preserve heritage, in addition to the economic benefits it brings. Put simply, preservation pays. A building torn down is an asset destroyed, whereas a building that is restored continues its useful life. Also, rehabilitating an existing building is often cheaper than building a new structure. A storytelling festival that perpetuates an area's oral tradition attracts listeners, and a river left wild attracts fee-paying fishermen and rafters. All these examples of preservation help establish and maintain the "sense of place" that gives a community its distinct character, and we all know that a rich historic and cultural heritage attracts visitors.

The economic potential of preservation benefits cities as well as rural areas. Outside metropolitan centers, economic growth has not always been easy to build and maintain. By putting their inherited assets to work, however, small towns, groups of small towns, and even entire regions can generate new prosperity, and attract other forms of economic development along with tourism.

Check Your Knowledge

1. Apart from creating an ambiance in the hotels what purpose does the display of local arts and crafts achieve?
2. Describe heritage tourism.
3. Why is heritage tourism important?

Challenges in Heritage Tourism

When a community's heritage is the substance of what it offers visitors, protecting that heritage is essential. Therefore, a major challenge in heritage tourism programs is ensuring that increased visitation does not destroy the very qualities that attract tourists in the first place. As you can imagine, this can be a very complicated task.

Because tourism is a highly competitive, sophisticated, and fast-changing industry, it presents its own challenges. Tourism is generally a "clean" industry; no smokestacks or dangerous chemicals. But it does put demands on infrastructure—on roads, airports, water supplies, and public services like police and fire protection. It also has an impact on resources.

These problems, the increase in the number of travelers, and the added stress and strain to infrastructure and heritage sites, are only the beginning. Thankfully, the travel industry is already addressing them. The challenge results not only from visitor impact, but also from visitor expectation of quality products and services. Tourism is essentially a service industry, which means that it depends on the competence of people in many different jobs and locations. While there is no universal remedy, tourism can indeed provide an attractive form of economic development.

As a good look around almost any city or town will show, people are often tempted to provide quick fix or "Band-aid" solutions, for example, to cover up an old storefront inexpensively rather than restoring it. But when your historic and cultural assets are at the heart of your plans to develop tourism, it is essential to protect them for the long term. A good example of this is the now famous Gaslamp Quarter in San Diego, California. The restored downtown area, with its 16 blocks of beautiful Victorian architecture, is now one of San Diego's main attractions. This is a designated National Historic District doubling as an entertainment mecca. This incredibly popular entertainment, shopping, and dining district features many of Southern California's hottest restaurants, bars, clubs, theaters, and galleries.

However, not all stories are success stories. The history of the preservation movement is a history of high hopes met and sometimes of heartbreak. Many hearts break when irreplaceable structures are destroyed or damaged beyond repair instead of preserved and protected, as they deserve. Once a historic train station has been demolished, the visual story it could have told about the present and about the past is silenced forever. A plaque pointing out that "On this site a great building once stood" can't tell that story. Equally tragic to many is the loss of traditions: a way of crafting wood or farming, of celebrating holidays or feasting on "old-world" cuisine. The preservation and continuation of traditions is important to tell the story of the people who once settled the land and to keep the spirit of the past alive. By protecting the buildings or special places and qualities that attract visitors, you also safeguard the future.

Quincy Market in Boston is an example of a good fit between the community and tourism—the market benefits both residents and tourists alike.

Find the Fit between Community and Tourism

Local priorities and capabilities, in other words local circumstances that determine what your area needs to do and can do in heritage tourism, vary. Successful programs have widespread local acceptance and meet recognized local needs. They are also realistic, based on the talents of specific people as well as on specific attractions, accommodations, and sources of support and enthusiasm. One of the reasons that heritage tourism is on the rise in the United States is that travelers seek experiences that are distinctive, not homogenized. They want to get the feel of a very particular place or time. You can supply that experience, and benefit in the process—but only if your heritage tourism program is firmly grounded in the local environment.

Agritourism has become a good fit for tourists and the local community. For the tourists who have an interest in agriculture, a visit or stay on a farm can be very rewarding. After experiencing the hard work of farmers and perhaps milking a cow or two, or helping with the harvest, we will respect and appreciate them all the more.

Check Your Knowledge

1. What challenges does the travel and tourism industry face?
2. Why is the fit between the community and tourism important?

Four Steps to a Comprehensive Heritage Program

Groups that succeed in heritage tourism pay close attention to all parts of an integrated process. They take four basic steps:[13]

- Assessing the potential
- Planning and organizing
- Preparing, protecting, and managing
- Marketing for success

Each of these steps gives results. The biggest payoff, however, comes when each separate action ties in to the other actions in a genuinely comprehensive program. Below we will give you a brief summary of each of the steps in the process.

Step One: Assessing the Potential

What do you think would draw tourists to your area? Beaches? Huge theme parks and resorts? When assessing an area's potential, don't make the mistake of underestimating the drawing power of cultural resources such as art museums, theaters, or local cuisine. Partnerships between heritage sites and parks, sports facilities, as well as recreational facilities, are beneficial to a community and attractive to the visitor. From a humble beginning as a group of storytellers swapping tales, the festival in Jonesborough, Tennessee, has grown to attract thousands of visitors, and has spun off many other profit-related activities as well.[14]

Keep in mind that natural resources such as local, state, and national parks do not need to be right next door to serve as a resource for your community. If a major natural resource is within a day's drive, it can bring tourists your way. In this case, scenic byways make the journey as rewarding as the destination. Another suggestion is to check out parks and sports and recreational facilities that already attract visitors. You can partner heritage sites and events with attractions like these to keep visitors in your area for a longer stay.

Such awareness of a community and its resources may uncover hidden treasures, as was the case in Fort Scott, Kansas. In 1973, plans were made to tear down an old church. A resident of the community saw that the church was a valuable resource. Her efforts to halt demolition of the church initiated a prospering heritage tourism program, bringing nearly 100,000 visitors a year to the town. Since the program's start, 98 percent of downtown Fort Scott has been refurbished. The fort is now a National Historic Site and the state highway that runs through town has been designated as the "Frontier Military Scenic Highway."[15]

Once key landmarks and destinations are chosen, community planners should prioritize the resources. A site may be the actual reason why an individual or a group will travel to a place—a destination in its own right. Tourists will likely add other sites or events as part of the itinerary when they plan trips to a particular destination. Other visitors will learn about some sites once they are in the community. Simply because they are there.

But the community must also keep in mind that some sites may be important to local residents, but not attract particular interest from tourists. The purpose of the community's assessment of its potential for heritage tourism is to scout the possibilities and potential support from local organizations that can focus energies on specific projects. This way, the best service and quality can be provided to all parties involved, residents and tourists alike.

Some key questions to answer during the assessment include:

- What is the local preservation organization's view of tourism?
- Do local businesses support the preservation of heritage?
- Are people enthusiastic about developing heritage sites and willing to make a long-term financial commitment?
- Do organizations actively seek funds from individuals and/or companies?

Perhaps the biggest concern of the lead organization will be protecting the area's assets. Protecting in this context means the full array of measures needed to protect the value of historic, cultural, and natural assets. This includes finding out what protection local governments already offer.

Step Two: Planning and Organizing

A community united can accomplish a lot; a community divided is not ready for heritage tourism. Thus, building a local consensus that supports heritage tourism is crucial. The process begins by gaining support from local business people, including bankers, travel professionals, owners of restaurants and shops, and operators of hotels and motels. Their expertise and enthusiasm can help build a stronger foundation for a successful program. Others in the community who may help are prominent families, religious leaders, and individuals with influence and credibility. The heritage group should seek to unite local government behind its efforts. From the government can come leadership, preservation ordinances, review boards, and landmark commissions. This offers protection of the resources that attract tourists. Last, but not least, the group should seek the assistance of service organizations and local historic and preservation associations. Such groups with strong membership bases and good track records on community projects will fortify efforts of planning a heritage program.

> "Begin by gaining support from local business people and community leaders"

Once the consensus comes together, the next step is to formalize the action plan. This outlines the group's mission and how it expects to carry it out. Goal by goal, and objective by objective, a good action plan specifies responsibility and accountability. The following process is a suggested model of how to construct the plan:[16]

- Establish the Mission
- Review the Assessment and Determine the Appropriate Goals
- Develop "Results-Oriented" Objectives for Each Goal
- List Specific Projects for Each Goal
- Prepare an Action Plan That Includes for Each Project
- Date of Completion
- Specific Tasks to Accomplish in Order to Complete the Project
- A Budget and How It Will Be Funded
- The Person Responsible for the Project
- Appoint Committees with Designated Chairs to Implement Components of the Action Plan
- Monitor Progress against the Timeline and Mission
- This Is Also a Good Time to Plan Any Fundraising Efforts the Group Wants to Undertake

Step Three: Preparing, Protecting, and Managing

When taking this step, the community must look to the future as well as to the present. As it prepares for visitors, it must make choices that will improve the community in the long term.

The choices being made should consider the quality of service the community provides its tourists and the lasting impression tourists take home with them. Much of the pleasure of a trip comes from how well visitors are treated. A short-tempered agent, an uninformed tour guide, a rude bus driver—these unfortunate experiences often stay with the traveler the longest. The obvious goal for a community is to avoid giving tourists such bad impressions. The travel industry depends on many different people doing different jobs, so the challenge is to build community pride and understanding of the visitor's needs.

In order to achieve this, it may be necessary to implement a community-wide hospitality training program. For example, the State Division of Tourism for Wisconsin and the National Trust sponsored "Celebrating Our Heritage: A Community Pride and Hospitality Training Program," a three-day seminar held at Wisconsin's four heritage tourism pilot areas. The goal was to teach participants key concepts in hospitality and encourage a better understanding of heritage tourism. When developing a training program, it is important to share with the community how the heritage program is planned to protect the area's resources, ensuring a long and productive life. The community should consider the following:[17]

- Develop a comprehensive preservation plan, which gives participants a way to view and protect its historic resources overall, and not just one by one. This also helps the community to look ahead, not just react to emergencies.
- Use the designation of historic significance to protect historic resources. National designation occurs when resources are listed on the National Register of Historic Places. Benefits of a National Register listing include the recognition of the property's significance, consideration in planning for federal or federally funded projects, eligibility for certain federal tax benefits, and qualification for federal preservation grants. The National Register provides no controls over private demolition or unsuitable alteration. Many states and municipalities also have designation programs. Federal, state, and local designation programs differ in the degree of protection they provide.
- Create zoning, which specifies where particular land uses and densities are appropriate to keep excessive development away from sensitive historic sites.
- Set up a design review board to administer the guidelines that should be followed.
- Require demolition review so property owners cannot abruptly tear down buildings that have historic significance.
- Develop a sign ordinance that regulates such matters as size, materials, illumination, and placement of signs.
- Set up an easement program to allow owners of historic or natural areas to receive a tax deduction by donating the development rights of their property to a tax-exempt organization.
- Establish a revolving loan fund to recycle the money from completed preservation projects into loans on subsequent projects.
- Create local incentives to encourage preservation.
- Integrate tourism with other forms of economic development through a growth management plan.

Check Your Knowledge

1. What is the purpose of the community's assessment of its potential for heritage tourism?
2. How many key steps are involved in the model to construct the plan for heritage tourism?
3. Apart from the quality of service, what else should the community look into regarding its visitors?

Step Four: Marketing for Success

Consider the Importance of Marketing in Bringing Guests to Your City

Having made your plans, how do you then get visitors to come to your area? In order to draw new people and money into the community, a multiyear, many-tiered marketing plan must be developed. The goal is to reach the target market and to seize opportunities to partner with local, regional, state, or national groups. The four components that should be included in the marketing plan are:

- Public relations
- Advertising
- Graphic materials
- Promotions

Public relations include many ventures, such as short spots on radio and television to publicize sites and events. Another valuable source of public relations is documented success stories. These could include any written article or presentation featuring the community. Organizing a photo/slide library is also important and can be used for a number of projects. Setting up a speaker's bureau to respond to requests for information about the area's heritage tourism program with the names, addresses, and phone numbers of people who are willing to make public presentations is of great assistance to both the community and the visitors. Within this group should be a spokesperson to deliver important information concerning major events.

Advertising, although costly, can be very beneficial to the community in targeting audiences and attracting visitors to heritage sites. Advertising requires creating convincing messages and supporting visuals, appropriate media placement, responding to inquiries, and measuring effectiveness. When advertising, it is important to match the message with the site and the budget allotted, keeping in mind that messages do tend to get across if given frequently. Such announcements can be put in newspapers and magazines, on radio and television and of course, on the Internet. Print advertising is generally less expensive than the electronic methods. Therefore, it is often best for heritage groups with limited budgets to start in newspapers and magazines.

"Co-op" advertising is a good way to share the costs of an ad campaign. In co-op advertising, multiple partners cooperate to produce advertisements or special sections dedicated to their area or destination. Magazines and newspapers provide special rates for advertising participants. Using co-op ads are effective, for example when targeting a new market or entering an expensive venue like a national magazine.

Another good idea is to develop various graphic materials communicating information about the program and its resources to potential visitors. Graphic materials present the image the community is trying to portray to targeted audiences. A color scheme or unique design element (logo) that appears throughout all the graphic materials created by the area helps to define the image of the region and establishes identification for the visitor. Once a logo has been chosen, it should be used widely and consistently so that it becomes closely associated with the heritage tourism program in the community.

Brochures introduce visitors to the area's attractions, but can be used for other purposes as well, such as during trade shows or special events. Brochures should be displayed at key locations where they can be easily seen and picked up, for example, at visitor centers, airports, hotels, as well as historic, cultural, and natural sites. If the community is targeting a specific group or if it wishes to promote a specific site or event, then specialized brochures should be developed. Also, a visitor and group services directory should be developed, offering information for tourists and groups about where to stay, where to eat, and what tours are available. The directory may even include suggested itineraries for groups. As you can imagine, as with co-op advertising, this is great for promoting local businesses.

Signs should be created and placed where visitors will see them. They should be legible and informative. If possible, investing in professionally made signs is a smart move. All signs should also be made with international symbols to help guide visitors to restrooms, information centers, museums, gas stations, lodging, and dining establishments. Signs with graphic symbols such as logos help designate sites and roadways. Maps are sometimes more effective, highlighting key attractions or major features of a single attraction. These maps should be attractive, accurate, and easy to read.

Nature tourism

Nature tourism is motivated by nature, such as a visit to a national park. In recent years, the aging baby boomers have increasingly become interested in nature tourism and include nature as a part of their vacation or reason for their trip. Notice that there are some similarities among these tourism areas of special interest.

These residents seem to accept nature tourists.
Courtesy of Mark Green.

TRENDS in TRAVEL

- Ecotourism, sustainable tourism, and heritage tourism will continue to grow in importance.
- Globally, the number of tourist arrivals will continue to increase by about 4 percent per year, topping 1 billion by 2010 (www.wttc.org).
- Governments will increasingly recognize the importance of tourism not only as an economic force, but also as a sociocultural force of increasing significance.
- Internet bookings will increase.
- More bilateral treaties are being signed, which will make it easier for tourists to obtain visas to visit other countries.
- Low-cost airlines like Jet Blue, ATA, Ted, Song, and Southwest will continue to gain market share at the expense of the larger airlines.
- Ticketless travel will increase.
- There will be an increase in the use of technology for security at entry points of countries to prevent terrorists from entering the country.
- The promotion and development of tourism is moving from the public sector (government) to the private sector (involved industry segments).
- Technology will continue to advance, allowing even more information to be available more quickly to more places around the world.
- As an ever-increasing number of tourists visit destinations, managing these destinations is becoming a challenge.
- The cruise industry will continue to expand.
- Companies are offering different kinds of cruises, such as single, gay, adventure, and nature cruises.
- There is increased concern for the health and safety of travelers and tourists.
- There is an increase in nature tourism.

CASE STUDY

Building a Convention Center

Congratulations! You have just been appointed to your city council. You discover that a hot topic soon to be brought before the council is the construction of a convention center. Your initial research shows that several midsized cities are considering the construction of a convention center as a way of increasing economic activity including job creation. The challenge that these cities face is how to finance the convention center—projected costs are $100 million. Voters may resist a ballot to increase local taxes (either property or sales); however, there is the transient occupancy tax (TOT)—that consists of taxes paid by people at local hotels. However, that tax is already earmarked for various local charities—and as we know all good politicians want to get reelected. Therefore, voting against several worthy causes would not be popular.

DISCUSSION QUESTIONS

1. How can the center be financed and built? The city could float a bond on the market, or could raise the TOT tax, but that might dissuade some groups from coming to your city because other cities have lower TOTs.
2. What would you do in this situation?
3. What information would you need in order to make the best decision if faced with deciding to support or oppose the convention center?

CAREER INFORMATION

Travel can serve as an important step toward global understanding, cultural appreciation, and tolerance. "To travel is to live," according to the Danish writer Hans Christian Andersen. Clearly, the travel industry can provide the opportunity for personal travel, professional accomplishment, and a rewarding career. Travel includes air, sea, rail, and automobile, and tourism includes the attractions and

Discover a Variety of Cruise Ship Careers

places that people visit. The airline industry offers a number of career opportunities for college graduates including work as a flight attendant or at the flight deck, or in operations, marketing, accounting, and finance.

The cruise industry offers a limited number of onboard positions, such as cruise director and hotel manager. Most ships have foreign crews because they can avoid American laws on things like overtime. Americans would not tolerate the conditions, the long hours, and the length of time away. There are numerous onshore careers in marketing and sales, human resources, accounting, and finance.

The car rental business has opportunities in the areas of sales, marketing, public relations, finance, accounting, and human resources. Many companies look for management trainees, starting them at the bottom and then giving them almost unlimited opportunities for growth and advancement when they prove themselves. All these companies share a need for graduates with not only a solid academic background, but also a lot of drive, enthusiasm, and creativity.

Have you considered going into the rental car business? As you might remember from our profile of Enterprise, there is a great demand for qualified graduates, and in regard to opportunities, the sky's the limit! Positions and responsibilities are varied, but here's a brief guide to what you might encounter in a car-rental career. An *account manager* is responsible for acquiring new and maintaining existing corporate accounts, as well as promoting company products and services to travel managers, travel agents, and corporate executives at home office locations in their assigned area. The position demands that you have sales experience in a business-to-business environment, and prior experience in managing an area or "territory." A possible step on the way might be working as a *rental sales agent*. You will be required to work different shifts as well as evenings, and will be responsible for selling the company's products and services while providing excellent customer service in accordance with company policies and procedures. You will handle and reconcile cash transactions, and occasionally drive vehicles and/or escort customers. To do well in this position and have the opportunity for advancement, you must be a team player, possess the ability to effectively sell your company's products and services, have good judgment and problem-solving skills, and exhibit excellent oral and written communication skills. Naturally, it is also important that you are computer literate and have a current driver's license.

Iso-Ahola presents the notion that there are two motivational forces that become determinants of tourism behavior: 1) the desire to leave the everyday environment behind—escaping personal and/or interpersonal environments; and 2) the desire to obtain psychological or intrinsic rewards through travel in a contrasting environment—seeking personal and/or interpersonal intrinsic rewards.[18]

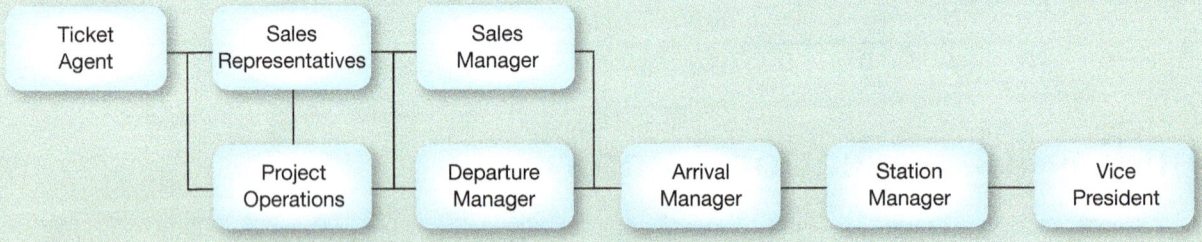

FIGURE 3–3 A Career Ladder for becoming a Convention Center Manager.

SUMMARY

1. There are many reasons why people travel; however, they fall under two main headings: pleasure and business.
2. Eighty-two percent of domestic travel is pleasure travel (leisure, recreation, holidays, and visiting friends and relatives—VFR).
3. Travelers select destinations for different reasons—climate, history or culture, sports, entertainment, and shopping facilities. Four basic considerations have emerged as factors influencing travel: entertainment, purchase opportunities, climate for comfort, and cost.
4. In recent years, business travel has been on the decline.
5. From a social and cultural perspective, tourism can further international understanding and economically improve a poor country. However, it can also disturb a culture by confronting it with mass tourism, causing the destruction of natural sites. A trend in avoiding tourism pollution is ecotourism.
6. The concept of sustainable tourism places a broad-based obligation on society—especially those involved with tourism policy, planning, and development—and on federal, state, and local governments to harmonize tourism and tourism development by improving the quality of its physical and sociocultural environment and resources.
7. Ecotourism is focused on individual values. It is tourism with a conscience, and shares many of the same aspirations of sustainable tourism. The terms "ecotourism" and "sustainable tourism" are often used interchangeably.

KEY WORDS AND CONCEPTS

Business travelers
Cultural tourism
Capacity requirement
Ecotourism
Heritage tourism
Infrastructure
Nature tourism
Pleasure travel
Superstructure
Sustainable tourism
United Nations Educational, Scientific, and Cultural Organizations (UNESCO)

REVIEW QUESTIONS

1. How is ecotourism defined by The International Ecotourism Society (TIES)?
2. Where are most ecotourism destinations found?
3. What is the goal of the United Nations Educational, Scientific, and Cultural Organizations?

INTERNET EXERCISES

1. Organization: Club Med Web site: www.clubmed.com (a) Go to the Club Med Web site and follow the Club Med job prompts. As you will soon see, Club Med offers a wealth of positions. Which of these positions are you most interested in?

APPLY YOUR KNOWLEDGE

1. Analyze your family's and friends' recent or upcoming travel plans. How do they compare to the examples in the text for reasons why people travel?
2. Suggest some ecotourism activities for your community.

SUGGESTED ACTIVITIES

1. Go online and map out a plan to visit your dream pleasure travel destination. Be sure to include all expenses (i.e., flight, rental car/car service, hotel/lodge, etc.).
2. In groups, create an outline plan for a resort that follows the rules for both sustainable and ecotourism.

ENDNOTES

1. U.S. Travel Association, www.ustravel.org/pressmedia/domestic_activities.html, retrieved May 5, 2009.
2. The International Ecotourism Society, www.ecotourism.org, retrieved May 9, 2009.
3. John R. Walker and Josielyn T. Walker, *Tourism: Concepts and Practices* (Upper Saddle River, NJ: Pearson, 2011), pp. 380–382.
4. Gary McCain and Nina M. Ray, "Legacy Tourism: The Search for Personal Meaning in Heritage Travel," www.rpts.tamu.edu, retrieved May 6, 2009.
5. World Heritage, whc.unesco.org/en/list, retrieved May 5, 2009.
6. Noel B. Salzar, "Developmental Tourist vs. Development Tourism: A Case Study." www.sas.upenn.edu/~nsalazar/DevelopmentalTourists.pdf, retrieved May 6, 2009.
7. Tour de Bali, "A Complete Reference," http://tourdebali.net/33/history-of-tourism/, retrieved May 6, 2009.
8. R. Mader, "Exploring Ecotourism," Definitions, www.planeta.com/ecotravel/tour/definitions.html, retrieved May 6, 2009.
9. Ibid., p. 115.
10. The Alamo, www.thealamo.org/, retrieved. May 6, 2009.
11. Information for this section is drawn from the American Express booklet produced in partnership with the National Trust for Historic Preservation.
12. *60 Minutes*, CBS News, January 13th, 1992.
13. Texas Historical Commission, *Heritage Tourism Guidebook*, www.thc.state.tx.us/publications/booklets/HTGuidebook.pdf, retrieved May 9, 2009.
14. Historic Jonesborough Web site, www.jonesboroughtn.org/, retrieved May 5, 2009.
15. Fort Scott Online Community, http://www.fortscott.com/cityinfo/history.htm, retrieved August 19, 2010.
16. *Heritage Tourism Guidebook*.
17. Travel Wisconsin, www.tourism.state.wi.us/, retrieved May 6, 2009.
18. Iso-Ahola, as cited in John R. Walker and Josielyn T. Walker, *Tourism: Concepts and Practices* (Upper Saddle River, NJ: Pearson, 2011); and in Uysal and Hagan, "Motivation of Pleasure Travel and Tourism," in VNR's *Encyclopedia of Hospitality and Tourism*, ed. Mahmood A. Kahn, Michael D. Olsen, and Turgut Var (New York: Van Nostrand Reinhold, 1993), p. 799.

4 LODGING

LEARNING OUTCOMES

After reading and studying this chapter, you should be able to:

Explain the concepts of hotel franchising and management contracts.

Classify hotels by type, location, and price.

Name some prestigious and unusual hotels.

Describe the effects of a global economy on the hotel industry.

HTi Describe the economic impact of tourism.

Hotel development and ownership

Read *A GM's Guide to Hotel Properties* to Learn about Ownership Opportunities

Franchising and management contracts are the two main driving forces in the development and operation of the hotel business. Once the potential of franchising caught on, there was no stopping American ingenuity. In about a half century, the hotel business had been changed forever. Here is how it happened.

Franchising

Franchising in the hospitality industry is a concept that allows a company to quickly expand by using other people's money rather than its own financing. For a fee, the company or franchisor grants certain rights, for example, to use its trademark, signs, proven operating systems, operating procedures and reservations system, marketing know-how, and purchasing discounts. In return, the franchisee agrees (under contract) to operate the restaurant and/or hotel in accordance with the franchisor's guidelines. Franchising is a way of doing business that benefits both the franchisor—who wants to expand the business rapidly—and the franchisee—who has financial backing but lacks specific expertise and recognition. Some corporation's franchise by individual outlets, others by territory.

> **"** Giving positive feedback to your staff is important as a hotel manager. If your staff feels like they are part of a team—working on the same goals—they are more likely to perform their tasks at an optimal level. **"**
>
> Margaret Price, Mountain View Resort, Asheville, NC

Franchising hotels in the United States began in 1907, when the Ritz Development Company franchised The Ritz-Carlton name in New York City.[1] Howard Johnson began franchising his restaurants in 1927 and built their first motor lodge in 1954. This allowed for rapid expansion, first on the East Coast, then in the Midwest, and finally in the mid-1960s into California.

Holiday Inns, now a part of Intercontinental Hotel Corporation (the largest lodging enterprise in the world), also grew through franchising. In 1952, Kemmons Wilson, a developer, had a disappointing experience while on a family vacation when he had to pay for an extra room for his children. Therefore, Wilson decided to build moderately priced, family-style hotels and motels. Each room was comfortably sized and had two double beds; this enabled children to stay for free in their parents' rooms. In the 1950s and early 1960s, as the economy thrived, Holiday Inns grew in size and popularity, adding restaurants, meeting rooms, and recreational facilities. They upgraded the furnishings and fixtures in the bedrooms and almost completely abandoned the original concept of being a moderately priced lodging operation.

Franchised hotels

North America is host to more than 180 hotel brand extensions and franchised hotel brands. Franchising remains a mostly North American activity, with limited opportunities in international markets. This is because what was once plentiful—the capital needed to drive hotel franchising—is now less accessible. Brand strategies for hotel franchisors in the new millennium seem to be influenced by mergers and a peaking market. Despite the constant progress, one area remains tense, the relationship between hotel companies and franchisees. There is tension for varying reasons, including fees, services, reservations inspections, and maintenance of standards.

One of the key factors in the successful development of Holiday Corporation is that it was one of the first companies to enter the midpriced range of the market. These inns or motor hotels were often located away from the expensive downtown sites, near important freeway intersections and the more reasonably priced suburbs. Another reason for their success was the value they offered: comfort at a reasonable price, without the expensive trimmings of luxury hotels. Today, midpriced hotels or motels include Courtyard Inn, Days Inn, Radisson Inn, Ramada Inn, Sheraton Inn, Four Points, Quality Inn, Hilton Inn, and Holiday Inn.

About this time, a new group of budget motels emerged. California's Motel 6 (so named because the original cost of a room was $6 a night) slowly spread across the country, as did Days Inn and others. Cecil B. Day was in the construction business and found Holiday Inns too expensive when traveling on vacation with his family. He bought cheap land and constructed buildings of no more than two stories to keep the costs down. These hotels and motels were primarily for commercial travelers and vacationing families, located close to major highways, and built to provide low-cost lodging without frills. Some of these buildings were modular constructions. Entire rooms were built elsewhere, transported to the site, and placed side by side.

It was not until the 1960s that Hilton and Sheraton began to franchise their names. Franchising was the primary growth and development strategy of hotels and motels during the 1960s, 1970s, and 1980s. However, franchising presents two major challenges for the franchisor: the maintenance of quality standards and avoidance of financial failure on the part of the franchisee.

FRANCHISING TRENDS

Factors propelling franchise growth include:

- Fresh looks (curb appeal)
- Location—near highways, airports, and suburbs
- Expansion in smaller cities throughout the United States
- New markets—located in proximity to golf courses and other attractions
- Foreign expansion—a move to increase brand awareness

It is difficult for the franchise company to state in writing all the contingencies that will ensure that quality standards are met. Recent franchise agreements are more specific in terms of the exterior maintenance and guest service levels. Franchise fees vary according to the agreements worked out between the franchisor and the franchisee; however, an average agreement is based on 3 or 4 percent of room revenue.

The world's largest franchisor of hotels, with nearly 7,000 hotels, is Wyndham Worldwide.[2] Choice Hotels International (a subsidiary of the Blackstone Group, New York) ranks second, with over 5,000 franchised hotels.[3] Intercontinental Hotels Group is now the third largest franchisor with 4,200 hotels.[4] Figure 4–1 shows franchise and management contract hotels among the top corporate chains.

Franchising provides both benefits and drawbacks to the franchisee and franchisor. The benefits to the franchisee include:

- A set of plans and specifications from which to build
- National advertising
- Centralized reservation system
- Participation in volume discounts for purchasing furnishings, fixtures, and equipment
- Listing in the franchisor's directory
- Low-fee percentage charged by credit card companies

The drawbacks to the franchisee are as follows:

- High fees, both to join and ongoing
- Central reservations generally producing between 17 and 26 percent of reservations
- Franchisees must conform to the franchisor's agreement
- Franchisees must maintain all standards set by the franchisor

The benefits to the franchise company are as follows:

- Increased market share and recognition
- Up-front fees

The drawbacks to the franchise company are as follows:

- The need to be very careful in the selection of franchisees
- Difficulty in maintaining control of standards

Franchising continues to be a popular form of expansion both in North America and the rest of the world.

Management Contracts

Management contracts have been responsible for the hotel industry's rapid boom since the 1970s. They became popular among hotel corporations because they involved little or no

Company	Number of Guest Rooms	Management Contract Hotels or Franchised	Total Hotels
Wyndham Worldwide (Wyndham, Day's Inn, Howard Johnson, Ramada, Knights Inn, Super 8, Travel Lodge, Villager Lodge, Wingate Inn, Hawthorn Suites, Microtel Inns & Suites)	588,000	6,500	6,509
Choice Hotels International (Clarion, Quality Inn, Comfort Inn, Econolodge, Friendship Inn, Mainstay, Roadway Inn)	485,000	6,000	6,250
Intercontinental Hotels Corp. (Inter-Continental Hotels & Resorts, Crowne Plaza Hotels & Resorts, Hotel Indigo, Holiday Inn Hotels & Resorts, Holiday Inn Express, Staybridge Suites, Candlewood Suites)	645,000	4,400	4,976
Hilton World Wide (World of Astoria, Home 2 suites, Hilton Hotel, Hilton Garden Inn, Doubletree, Embassy Suites, Hampton Inn, Homewood Suites, Conrad Hotels, Hilton grand vacations)	624,139	3,175	3,500
Marriott International (JW Marriott, Marriott Hotels & Resorts, Renaissance Hotels & Resorts, Courtyard by Marriott, Residence Inn, Fairfield Inn, TownePlace Suites, SpringHill Suites Horizons, The Ritz-Carlton Hotel Company, L.L.C., The Ritz-Carlton Club)	532,476	3,400	3,400
Carlson Hospitality Worldwide (Regent International, Raddison, Country Inn & Suites, Park Plaza, Park Inn Hotels)	169,427	926	1,060
AccorIbis (All seasons Suite, a diago, Hotel F1, Novotel, Mercure, Red Roof, Motel 6, Studio 6, etc.)	495,433	1,096	4,100
Le Meriden (Element, Aloft, Kyriad Prestige, Kyriad, Hotel du Crillon, Concord Hotels & Resorts)	55,538	566	887
Starwood Hotels & Resorts Worldwide (St. Regis, The Luxury Collection, W Hotels, Sheraton, Four Points Sheraton, Westin)	305,000	678	1,032

FIGURE 4–1 The Largest Chains in Franchised and Managed Contract Hotels.

Explore the Difference in Ownership Types: Read *A GM's Guide to Hotel Properties*

up-front financing or equity. Even if the hotel corporation was involved in the construction of the hotel, ownership generally reverted to a large insurance company. This was the case with the La Jolla Marriott Hotel in California. Marriott Corporation built the hotel for about $34 million, and then sold it to Paine Webber, a major investment-banking firm, for about $52 million on completion. Not a bad return on investment!

The management contract usually allows for the hotel company to manage the property for a period of 5, 10, or 20 years. For this, the company receives as a management fee, often a percentage of gross and/or net operating profit, usually about 2 to 4.5 percent of gross revenues. Lower fees in the 2 percent range are more prevalent today, with an increase in the incentive fee based on profitability. Some contracts begin at 2 percent for the first year, 2.5 the second, and 3.5 the third and remainder of the contract. Today, many contracts are for a percentage of total sales and a percentage of operating profit. This is normally 2 plus 2 percent. Increased competition among management companies has decreased the management contract fees in the past few years. Hotel companies have increasingly opted for management contracts because considerably less capital is tied up in managing as compared with owning properties. This has allowed for a more rapid expansion of both the U.S. and international markets.

The Marriott's Ocean Club Ka'anapali Beach Resort. Resort is a Marriott Management Contract property.

Corporate Profile

AVIS BUDGET GROUP, INC.

The Avis Budget Group (formerly Cendant) is an empire consisting of businesses and brands under three major names: Wyndham Worldwide, Realogy (the real estate branch), and Avis Budget Group (vehicle rentals). Wyndham Worldwide includes Wyndham, Days Inn, Howard Johnson, Ramada, Knights Inn, Super 8, Travelodge, Villager Lodge, and Wingate Inn. Realogy includes Century 21, ERA (Electronic Realty Associates), Coldwell Banker, Avis Rent-a-Car, and PHH Corp. Combined, these businesses account for approximately half a million hotel rooms in the United States, Canada, Latin America, and Europe, and more than 11,500 franchised real estate offices with more than 190,000 brokers in the United States, Mexico, Canada, Puerto Rico, Europe, Africa, and the Asia-Pacific region.

Although clearly in the consumer services industry, Avis Budget Group's clients include other businesses and corporations—not individual consumers. As a franchisor, the company licenses the owners and operators of independent businesses to use brand names, without taking on big business risks and expenses. The company does not operate hotels or real estate brokerage offices, but instead provides coordination and services that allow franchisees to retain local control of their activities. At the same time, franchisees benefit from the economies of scale of widely promoted brand names and well-established standards of service, national and regional direct marketing, co-marketing programs, and volume purchasing discounts. By monitoring quality control and extensively promoting the brand names, the company offers its independent franchise owners franchise fees that are relatively low compared to the increased profitability they gain.

Through franchising, the company limits its own risks and is able to keep overhead costs low. A further advantage of being a franchiser of such dimension is that the company is even more protected from the cyclical nature of the economy than are other franchise ventures.

The critical mass created by all the businesses working together makes them more valuable as a whole than as the sum of its parts, gives it outstanding purchasing power and market control, and makes it extremely effective in selling to a wide audience.

Seventy-six million baby boomers are beginning to retire; this trend will continue for several more years. This clientele consumes primarily two things: travel and residential real estate. In light of this trend, diversification from the hotel market to real estate, mortgage companies, and timeshare operators makes sense.

The synergy is recognized by offering travel, accommodation, and related services. Services like Cheap Tickets, Lodging.com, Rates to Go, HotelClub.com, Cendant Travel, and Galileo, a travel distribution service, are used by 44,000 travel agencies. WizCom supplies its customers with electronic distribution and e-commerce solutions for Internet global distribution services (GDS) and travel reservations systems.

Hotel management companies often form a partnership of convenience with developers and owners who generally do not have the desire or ability to operate the hotel. The management company provides operational expertise, marketing, and sales clout, often in the form of a centralized reservation system (CRS).

Some companies manage a portfolio of properties on a cluster, regional, or national basis. Most of these companies manage hotels in the same classifications. This enables them to focus their efforts on managing properties of a similar nature rather than properties in different classifications. Recent contracts have called for an increase in the equity commitment on the part of the management company. In addition, owners increased their operational decision-making options, something they had seldom done in the past.

With international expansion, a hotel company entering the market might actively seek a local partner or owner to work within a form of joint venture. Today, hotel management companies exist in an extremely competitive environment. They have discovered that the hotel business, like most others, has changed and they are adapting accordingly. Today's hotel owners are demanding better bottom-line results and reduced fees. Management companies are seeking sustainability and a bigger share of the business.

> **Check Your Knowledge**
>
> 1. What main factor changed the nature of the hotel industry? What impact does it have today?
> 2. In your own words, define *franchising* and *management contracts*.

Real Estate Investment Trust (REIT)

Real estate investment trusts (REITs) have existed since the 1960s. In those early days, they were mostly mortgage holders. But in the 1980s, they began to own property outright, often focusing on specific sectors like hotels, office buildings, apartments, malls, and nursing homes. Today, about 300 REITs, with a combined market value of $70 billion, are publicly traded. Investors like them because they do not pay corporate income tax and instead are required to distribute at least 95 percent of net income to shareholders. In addition, because they trade as stocks, they are much easier to get into or out of than limited partnerships or direct ownership of properties. In the hotel industry, REITs are clearly where the action is.

The Sheraton Moana Surfrider, in O'ahu, Hawaii, is a part of the Starwood REIT.

The two leading REIT corporations are Patriot American Hospitality and Starwood Lodging Trust. Patriot American Hospitality acquired Wyndham Hotels, which has become its operating company and given it a well-regarded brand name. Starwood Lodging Trust acquired Westin Hotels and Resorts for $1.4 billion and outbid Hilton for ITT Sheraton. Patriot and Starwood are the only REITs allowed to both manage and own properties.

Rating and Classification of Hotels

According to the American Hotel and Lodging Association, the U.S. lodging industry consists of 48,062 properties, with a total of 4.5 million rooms. The gross volume of business generated from these rooms is $139.4 billion.[5] Unlike many other countries, the United States has no formal government classification of hotels. However, the American Automobile Association (AAA) rates hotels by diamond award, and the Mobile Travel Guide offers a five-star award.

The AAA inspects and rates the nation's hotels, and only 27 percent of the 60,000 properties inspected annually throughout the United States, Canada, and Mexico have earned the five-diamond award, which is the association's highest award for excellence.[6] The AAA uses descriptive criteria to evaluate the hotels that it rates annually in the United States, Canada, Mexico, and the Caribbean (see Figure 4–2).

- One-diamond properties have simple roadside appeal and the basic lodging needs.
- Two-diamond properties have average roadside appeal, with some landscaping and a noticeable enhancement in interior decor.

A guest relaxing in a Homewood Suites property on Chicago's East Grand Avenue.

	◇	◇◇	◇◇◇	◇◇◇◇	◇◇◇◇◇
General	Simple roadside appeal Limited landscaping	Average roadside appeal Some landscaping	Very good roadside appeal Attractive landscaping	Excellent roadside appeal Professionally planned landscaping	Outstanding roadside appeal Professional landscaping with a variety of foliage and stunning architecture
Lobby	Adequate size with registration, front desk, limited seating, and budget art, if any	Medium size with registration, front desk, limited seating, carpeted floors, budget art, and some plants	Spacious with front desk, carpeted seating area arranged in conversation groupings, good-quality framed art, live plants, luggage carts, and bellstation	Spacious or consistent with historical attributes; registration and front desk above average with solid wood or marble; ample seating area with conversation groupings and upscale appointments including tile, carpet, or wood floors; impressive lighting fixtures; upscale framed art and art objects; abundant live plants; background music; separate check-in/-out; bellstation	Comfortably spacious or consistent with historical attributes; registration and front desk above average; ample seating with conversation groupings and upscale appointments; impressive lighting fixtures; variety of fine art; abundant plants and fresh floral arrangements; background music; separate check-in/-out; bellstation that may be part of concierge area; concierge desk
Guestrooms	May not reflect current industry standards	Generally reflect current industry standards	Reflect current industry standards	Reflect current industry standards and provide upscale appearance	Reflect current standards and provide luxury appearance
Service	Basic attentive service	More attentive service	Upgraded service levels	High service levels and hospitality	Guests are pampered by flawless service executed by professional staff

FIGURE 4–2 Summary of AAA Diamond-Rating Guidelines.
(*Source:* Courtesy of Hotel and Lodging Management.)

- Three-diamond properties carry a degree of sophistication through higher service and comfort.
- Four-diamond properties have excellent roadside appeal and service levels that give guests what they need before they even ask for it.
- Five-diamond properties have the highest service levels, sophistication, and offerings.

Examine How Hotels Are Classified

Hotels may be classified according to location, price, and type of services offered. This allows guests to make a selection on these as well as personal criteria. A list of hotel classifications follows:

By location—City center—luxury, first class, midscale, economy, suites

Resort—Luxury, midscale, economy suites, condominium, time-share, convention

Airport—Luxury, midscale, economy, suites

Freeway—Midscale, economy suites

By price—Luxury, all-suites, upscale, midpriced, economy, budget

By level of service—Luxury, full-service, midscale, extended-stay, limited service, economy

By guest type—Convention, leisure, business, extended-stay, condotel, vacation ownership, family

By type of service—Spa, families, couples, resort, convention, business

Casino—Luxury, midscale, economy

Bed & breakfast

Figure 4-3 gives an example of a national or major regional brand-name hotel chain in each price segment.

Budget $35–$49	Economy $49–$69	Midprice $69–$125	Up Scale $125–$225	Luxury $150–$450	All-Suites $125–$225
	Holiday Inn Express	Holiday Inn	Holiday Inn	Crown Plaza	
	Fairfield Inn	Courtyard Inn Residence Inn	Marriott	Marriott Marquis Ritz-Carlton	Marriott Suites
		Days Inn	Omni	Renaissance	
		Radisson Inn	Radisson		Radisson Suites
	Ramada Limited	Ramada Inn	Ramada		Ramada Suites
	Sheraton Inn	Sheraton Inn Four Points	Sheraton	Sheraton Grande	Sheraton Suites
			Hyatt	Hyatt Regency Hyatt Park	Hyatt Suites
Sleep Inns	Comfort Inn	Quality Inn	Clarion Hotels		Quality Suites Comfort Suites
		Hilton Inn	Hilton	Hilton Towers	Hilton Suites
		Doubletree Club	Doubletree		Doubletree Suites
Thrift Lodge	Travelodge Hotels	Travelodge Hotels	Forte Hotels	Forte Hotels	
			Westin	Westin	
Sixpence Inn	La Quinta				
E-Z-8	Red Roof Inn				
	Best Western				
	Hampton Inn				Embassy Suites

FIGURE 4-3 Hotels by Price Segment.

Introducing Valerie Ferguson

Past Chair of the American Hotel & Lodging Association and Regional Vice-President of Loews Hotels.

To most, "making it big" seems like a regular statement and a task easily achieved. To Valerie Ferguson, it comes with a lot of work, dedication, and heart. She speaks often about seizing opportunities and incorporating self-interest into your career. For this African-American female, life wasn't always easy. As the managing director of Loews Philadelphia Hotel and regional vice-president of Loews Hotels, Ferguson has a lot to say about what got her to where she is now. One of her most important role models was her father, Sam Ferguson. She says, "My father and I had a great relationship in which he supported me, but in which he never put any images in front of me about what I should shoot for." Ferguson's father was a chairman of the Life Sciences Department at a small California school that she herself attended as a little girl.

Ferguson earned a degree in government from the University of San Francisco, but eventually realized that her heart wasn't in a career in law. She decided to move to Atlanta, and found a job as a nighttime desk clerk at the Hyatt Regency. She fell in love with the hotel industry and saw it as a challenge. Soon enough though, she realized that the challenges she faced were issues of race and gender. She explains, "I was raw in my approach to the business world, but I soon came to realize that it takes more than working hard. To succeed, a person must be able to proclaim his or her goals."

She calls her career in hospitality "the opportunity of a lifetime." She believes that lodging is a vital force in the national economy. She visits key industries and attends association events to encourage hoteliers to seek out young men and women who represent the new and upcoming generation of hoteliers. She urges hoteliers to strive to create a diverse work force that reflects the real-world marketplace.

Ferguson's success comes from being connecting with people and society. Valerie is past chair of the American Hotel & Lodging Association (AH&LA) board and still serves on the association's Diversity Committee. Valerie was nominated general manager of the year for the Hyatt Hotels Corporation. Through the years, she has held management positions at the Hyatt Regency Atlanta, the Lodge in Chicago, the Hyatt Regency Flint, Michigan, and the Hyatt Atlanta Airport Hotel. Her outstanding work and devotion to the hospitality and lodging industry has not gone unrewarded. She was named one of the Top 100 Black Women in Corporate America by *Ebony* magazine. She received the Atlanta Business League Pioneer Award and the Network of Executive Women in Hospitality's Woman of the Year award. She was named one of the Top 100 Black Women of Influence by the Atlanta Business League Pioneer and the Turner Broadcasting Trumpet Award, which salutes achievement by African-Americans.

After 23 years of working with The Ritz-Carlton Hotel Company and the Hyatt Hotels—including a stint as general manager at The Ritz-Carlton, Atlanta, in 1995 and general manager at the Hyatt Regency Atlanta—Ferguson left to become a regional Vice president for Loews Hotels and managing director for the Loews Philadelphia Hotel. Regional Vice-President Bill Rhodes says, "her drive to grow and learn" was what impressed him most about Ferguson. He continues, "She is obsessed with continuing her education in the industry and is not intimidated by any situation or any opportunity. She has a lot of self-confidence and jumps in with both feet, providing a tremendous amount of leadership." She worked her way up from being director of rooms, to rooms executive, to assistant director of housekeeping, and to front office manager. Ed Rabin, executive vice president of Hyatt and an early Ferguson mentor says, "From the get-go she demonstrated an ability and willingness to understand and learn the business and win over guests, colleagues, and peers in the process."

When Loews opened, Ferguson was excited by the adventure of working for a company that was still to grow. Loews President and CEO Jonathan Tisch and Ferguson became close friends when they served together on the board of the AH&LA. Ferguson ran for a seat on AH&LA's executive committee and eventually succeeded Tisch as chair. She was the first African-American and second woman to serve in this role. Regarding her industry, she says, "The hospitality industry is one of the last vestiges of the American dream, where you can enter from very humble beginnings and end up a success."

The great relationship that Ferguson has with people has been a great contribution to her well-deserved success. She relates well with her employees and always wants to be the person to help them aim high in

(Continued)

their careers and achieve their goals. Ed Rubin remarks, "She has remarkable empathy for all people in all walks of life, and that is the main reason for her success." Ferguson believes in promoting diversity in the workplace and marketplace and will go to great lengths to do so. She is involved in issues involving legislation and regulation, making use of her degree in government from the University of San Francisco. She supports local initiatives by hotel associations against occupancy taxes that hurt business.

Ferguson has come a long way in her career. She is proud of what she is doing and doesn't believe that she has stopped climbing the ladder of success. She is fighting to make other women and minority members realize that there is a whole world of opportunities out there and that they should set their goals high. She believes that equality of opportunity "should not come as the result of a mandate for the federal government or pressure from groups outside this industry. The impetus for change must come from within the hearts and souls of each of us."

Sources: *Lodging*, 23, 5, January 1998; www.loewshotels.com; www.ahma.com; www.hotel-online.com.

Types and Locations of Hotels

City Center Hotels

City center hotels, by virtue of their location, meet the needs of the traveling public for business or leisure reasons. These hotels could be luxury, midscale, business, suites, economy, or residential. They offer a range of accommodations and services. Luxury hotels might offer the ultimate in decor, butler service, concierge and special concierge floors, secretarial services, computers, fax machines, beauty salons, spas, 24-hour room service, swimming pools, valet service, ticket office, airline office, car rental, and doctor/nurse on duty or on call. Generally, they offer a signature restaurant, coffee shop, or an equivalent name restaurant; a lounge; a name bar; meeting and convention rooms; a ballroom; and possibly a fancy night spot. The Drake Hotel in Chicago is an example of a city center luxury hotel. An example of a midscale hotel in New York is the Ramada Hotel; an economy hotel is the Days Inn; and a suites property is the Embassy Suites.

Airport Hotels

Many airport hotels enjoy a high occupancy because of the large number of travelers arriving and departing from major airports. The guest mix in airport hotels consists of business, group, and leisure travelers. Passengers with early or late flights may stay over at the airport hotel, while others rest while waiting for connecting flights.

Airport hotels are generally in the 200- to 600-room size and are full service. To care for the needs of guests who may still feel as if they are in different time zones, room service and restaurant hours may be extended, even offered 24 hours. More moderately priced hotels have vending machines.

As competition at airport hotels has intensified, some have added meeting space to cater to businesspeople who want to fly in, meet, and fly out. Here, the airport hotel has the advantage of saving the guests from having to go downtown. Almost all airport hotels provide courtesy van transportation to and from the airport.

Convenient locations, economical prices, easy and less costly transportation costs to and from the airport are some reasons why airport hotels are becoming intelligent choices for business travelers. Airport hotels can mean a bargain for groups, especially considering that the transportation to the hotel and back from the airport is usually free or very inexpensive, according to Brian Booth, director of sales and marketing at the Dallas Hyatt Regency Airport Hotel. One of the most conveniently located hotels in the country is the Miami International Airport Hotel, which is located within the airport itself. The BWI corridor (Baltimore, Washington International) is another example of huge growth in hotels.

Freeway Hotels and Motels

Freeway hotels and motels came into prominence in the 1950s and 1960s. As Americans took to the open road, they needed a convenient place to stay that was reasonably priced with few frills. Guests could simply drive up, park outside the office, register, rent a room, and park outside the room. Over the years, more facilities were added: lounges, restaurants, pools, soft-drink machines, game rooms, and satellite TV.

Motels or motor hotels are often clustered near freeway off-ramps on the outskirts of towns and cities. Today, some are made of modular construction and have as few as 11 employees per hundred rooms. These savings in land, construction, and operating costs are passed on to the guest in the form of lower rates.

Casino Hotels

Canada Place in Vancouver, British Columbia, Canada, has a hotel, two convention centers, and a cruise terminal.

Investigate the Exciting World of Casino Properties

The casino hotel industry is now coming into the financial mainstream, to the point that, as a significant segment of the entertainment industry, it is helping to reshape the U.S. economy. Casino hotels are different from other hotels in that they make more money from the gaming than from the rooms. The entertainment and recreation sector has become a very important engine for U.S. economic growth, providing a boost to consumer spending and creating tremendous prosperity for the industry. The fastest-growing sector of the entertainment field is gaming, which is discussed in Chapter 13.

The Wynn Hotel and Resort Las Vegas, Creating a New Level of Luxury in the Gaming Market.

Casino hotels are leaning toward turning their hotels into "family friendly" hotels. The gaming business is strictly for adults; however, these hotels realize that making their hotels family friendly will entice more families to spend a day or two in their hotels. Circus Circus in Las Vegas pioneered the concept more than a decade ago, and now various other casino hotels have followed suit. They have babysitters available at any time of the day, children's attractions ranging from parks to circuses and museums, and kid's menus in their restaurants. In addition to gaming, a multinational cuisine for dining, health spas for relaxation, dance clubs, and dazzling shows are available for the adults.

Casino hotels now market themselves as business hotels. They include work space, a fax machine, a copier, and computer data ports in their rooms. Other amenities include a full-service business center, travel bureau, and room service. Larger casino hotels also attract conventions, which represent a lucrative business.

Convention Hotels

Convention hotels provide facilities to meet the needs of groups attending and holding conventions. They also attract seasonal leisure travelers. These hotels typically exceed 500 guest rooms, with larger public areas to accommodate hundreds of people at any given time. Convention hotels have many banquet areas within and around the hotel complex. These hotels have a high percentage of double occupancies, and rooms have double queen-sized beds. Convention hotels may also offer a concierge floor to cater to individual guest needs. Other amenities include round-the-clock room service, an in-house laundry, a business center, a travel desk, and an airport shuttle service.

Full-Service Hotels

Another way to classify hotels is by the degree of service offered: full-service, economy, extended-stay, and all-suite hotels. Full-service hotels offer a wide range of facilities, services, and amenities, including many that were mentioned under the luxury hotel category: multiple food and beverage outlets including bars, lounges, and restaurants; both formal and casual dining; and meeting, convention, and catering services. Some hotels are offering smart or partially smart guest rooms. Increasingly, luxury and full service hotels and resorts are offering smart rooms whose features include:[7]

1. Nintendo Wii
2. The Guestroom Digital Assistant by INNCOM International Inc.

3. Compact Concealed Emergency Lights by Sentry Light (http://sentrylight.com/) (Download Brochure-PDF)
4. Energy Management System by INNCOM International Inc. (http://www.inncom.com/products/energy-management/)
5. Guestroom Status Control System by INNCOM International, Inc. (http://www.inncom.com/products/guestroom-status/)
6. Lighting Control System by INNCOM International, Inc. (http://www.inncom.com/products/lighting-controls/)
7. The Digital Door Viewer by First View Security (http://firstviewsecurity.com/about.htm)
8. The AnyFill by TeleAdapt (http://www.teleadapt.com/hotels/anyfill.php)
9. Clocky by Nanda (http://www.nandahome.com)
10. Digital Frame by Edge Tech Corporation (http://www.edgetechcorp.com/accessories/digital-picture-frame.asp)
11. Remote Control Luminary Pillars©™ by Flame Free Candles, Inc. (http://www.flamefreecandles.com/index.php)
12. Quiet Ionic Lighted Hair Dryer©™ by Andis (http://www.andis.com/)
13. The Tri Spa Showerhead by Oxygenics (www.oxygenics.com)
14. The Media Center by Microsoft
15. A Stain-Resistant Mattress Cover by WL Gore &. Associates, Inc.
16. SmartLine Waethermatic: Smart watering system

Most of the major North American cities have hotel chain representation, such as Doubletree, Four Seasons, Hilton, Holiday Inn, Hyatt, Marriott, Omni, Ramada, Radisson, Ritz-Carlton, Loews, Le Meridian, Sheraton, and Westin. Some of these chains are positioning themselves as basic full-service properties. An example of this strategy is Marriott's Courtyard hotels, which have small lobbies and very limited food and beverage offerings. The resulting savings are passed on to the guests in the form of more competitive rates. Thus, the full-service market may also be subdivided into upscale and midpriced hotels.

Economy/Budget Hotels

An economy or budget hotel offers clean, reasonably sized, and furnished rooms without the frills of full-service hotels. Chains like Travelodge, Motel 6, Microtel, Days Inn, and La Quinta became popular by focusing on selling beds rather than meals or meetings. This enables them to offer rates that are about 30 percent lower than the midpriced hotels. Economy properties, which represent about 15 percent of total hotel rooms, have experienced tremendous growth.

Promus' Hampton Inns, Marriott's Fairfield, and Choice's Comfort Inns are more recent entrants to this market sector. These properties do not have restaurants or offer substantial food and beverages, but they do offer guests a continental breakfast in the lobby.

Formule 1 is an Accor hotel economy property.

After enjoying a wave of growth for much of the past 20 years, the economy hotel segment may be close to the saturation point. There are about 25,000 properties in this segment, with many markets. The economic law of supply and demand rules; if an area has too many similar properties, price wars usually break out as hotels try to attract guests. Some will attempt to differentiate themselves and stress value rather than discounts. This adds to the fascination of the business.

Extended-Stay Hotels

Other hotels cater to guests who stay for an extended period. They will, of course, take guests for a shorter time when space is available. However, the majority of guests are long term. Guests take advantage of a reduction in the rates based on the length of their stay. The mix of guests is mainly business and professional/technical, or relocating families.

Residence Inns, Candlewood, and Homewood Suites are market leaders in this segment of the lodging industry. These properties offer full kitchen facilities and shopping services or a convenience store on the premises. Complimentary continental breakfast and evening cocktails are served in the lobby. Some properties offer a business center and recreational facilities.

All-Suite Extended-Stay Hotels

All-suite extended-stay hotels typically offer approximately 25 percent more space for the same cost as will a regular hotel in the same price range. The additional space is usually in the form of a lounge and possibly a kitchenette area.

Embassy Suites, owned and operated by the Hilton Corporation; Residence Inns, Fairfield Suites, and Town-Place Suites, all by Marriott; Extended Stay America; Homewood Suites; and Guest Quarters are the market leaders in the all-suite, extended-stay segment of the lodging industry. Candlewood has some all-suite extended-stay rooms in its properties and full kitchens, whereas Embassy Suites does not have full kitchens. The additional space of a suite property plus a full kitchen is an advantage for some guests. Several of the major hotel chains have all-suite extended-stay subsidiaries, including Radisson, Choice Hotels (which dominates the economy all-suite segment with Comfort and Quality Suites), Sheraton Suites, Hilton Suites, Homegate Studios, and Suites by Wyndham Hotels. These properties provide a closer-to-home feeling for guests who may be relocating or attending seminars or who are on work-related projects that necessitate a stay of greater than about five days.

There are now over 2,500 extended-stay properties. Many of these properties have business centers and offer services like grocery shopping and laundry/dry cleaning. The designers of extended-stay properties realize that guests prefer a homelike atmosphere. Accordingly, many properties are built to encourage a community feeling, which allows guests to informally interact.

Condotels

As the word suggests, a condotel is a combination of hotel and condominium. Developers build a hotel and sell it as condo units, which the owners can pool for use as hotel rooms and suites. The hotel operating company gets a cut of the money from renting the units and so does the owner. The owner of the condo unit may have exclusive right to the use of the unit for a fixed period of time (usually one month); other than that, the hotel operating company knows that it can rent out the condos.

Mixed-Use Hotel Development

Some new hotels are developed as mixed-use properties. This means that a hotel may also have "residences"—actual condos that are used by people rather than let like condotels; a spa, and sports facilities. Mixed-use hotels can also be a part of a major urban or resort development, which may include office buildings, convention centers, sporting facilities, or shopping malls.

Bed and Breakfast Inns

Bed and breakfast inns, or B&Bs as they are familiarly known, offer an alternative lodging experience to the typical hotel or motel. According to *Travel Assist Magazine*, the B&B is a concept that began in Europe and started as overnight lodging in a private home. A true B&B is an accommodation with the owner, who lives on the premises or nearby, providing a clean, attractive accommodation and breakfast, usually a memorable one. The host also offers to help the guest with directions, restaurants, and suggestions for local entertainment or sightseeing.

There are many different styles of B&Bs with prices ranging from about $30 to $300 or more per night. A B&B may be a quaint cottage with a white-picket fence leading to a gingerbread house, tiny and homey, with two or three rooms available. On the other hand, some B&Bs sprawling, ranch-style homes in the Rockies; multistoried town homes in large cities;

> **"** Bed and breakfasts try to provide a personal experience during the guest's stay. They are a simple, quiet way for people to just get away and usually offer more affordable costs than big corporate chains. **"**
>
> Rebecca Boulay,
> The Oxford Bed and Breakfast,
> Marlborough, MA

A bed and breakfast in Lavenham, Suffolk, England.

farms; adobe villas; log cabins; lighthouses; or stately mansions. The variety is part of the thrill, romance, and charm of the B&B experience.[8]

There are an estimated 25,000 B&Bs in the United States. These inns have flourished for many reasons. Some business travelers have grown weary of the complexities of the check-in/check-out processes at some commercial hotels. The high transient rates at hotels has created an opportunity to serve a segment of travelers who are more price-sensitive. Also, many leisure travelers are looking for accommodation somewhere between a large, formal hotel and staying with friends. B&Bs offer a homelike atmosphere. They are aptly called "a home away from home." A community breakfast with other lodgers and hosts enhances this feeling. Each B&B is as unique as its owner. Décor varies according to the region of the location and the owner's tastes. B&B owners often provide all the necessary labor, but some employ full- or part-time labor.

Resort Hotels

Resort hotels came of age with the advent of rail travel. Increasingly, city dwellers and others had the urge to vacation in locations that they found appealing. Traveling to these often more exotic locations became a part of the pleasure experience. In the late 1800s, luxury resort hotels were developed to accommodate the clientele that the railways brought.

Such hotels include the famous Greenbrier at White Sulphur Springs, West Virginia; the Hotel del Coronado in Coronado (near San Diego), California; and the Homestead at Hot Springs, Virginia. In Canada, the Banff Springs Hotel and Chateau Lake Louise drew the rich and famous of the day to picturesque locations in the Canadian Rocky Mountains.

The leisure and pleasure travelers of those days were drawn by resorts, beaches, or spectacular mountain scenery. At first, many of these grand resorts were seasonal. However, as automobile and air travel made even the remote resorts more accessible and an increasing number of people could afford to visit, many resorts became year-round properties.

Resort communities sprang up in the sunshine belt from Palm Springs to Palm Beach. Some resorts focused on major sporting activities such as skiing, golf, or fishing; others offered family vacations. Further improvements in both air and automobile travel brought exotic locations within the reach of the population. Europe, the Caribbean, and Mexico became more accessible. As the years passed, some of the resorts declined causing guests to seek other locations.

The traditional month-long, family resort vacation gave way to shorter, more frequent getaways of four to seven days. The regular resort visitors became older; in general, younger guests preferred the mobility of the automobile and the more informal atmosphere provided by the newer and more informal resorts.

To survive, the resort hotels became more astute in marketing to different types of guests. For example, certain resorts do not allow children in the high season because some adult guests prefer a quiet ambiance. Other resort hotels go out of their way to encourage families: Camp Hyatt is a prominent example. Hyatt hotels have organized a program with a variety of activities for children, which gives parents an opportunity to either enjoy some free time or join in the fun with their children. Many resort hotels began to attract conventions, conferences, and meetings. This enables them to maintain or increase occupancy, particularly during the low and shoulder (between high and low travel) seasons.

A resort in Johor, Malaysia, attracts guests from around the world.

Guests go to resorts for leisure and recreation. They want a good climate—summer or winter—in which they can relax or engage in recreational activities. Due to the remoteness of many resorts, guests are a "captured clientele"; they may be on the property for days at a time. This presents resort managers with some unique operating challenges. Another operating hurdle concerns seasonality—some resorts either do not operate year-round or have periods of very low occupancy. Both can make it difficult to attract, train, and retain competent staff.

Many guests travel to resorts from considerable distances. Consequently, they tend to stay longer than they would at transient hotels. The food and beverage manager must then provide varied, quality menus that are served in an attractive, attentive manner. To achieve this, resorts often use a cyclical menu that repeats itself every 14 to 21 days. Also, they provide a wide variety and number of dishes to stimulate interest. Menus are now more health conscious—lighter and low in saturated fats, cholesterol, salt, and calories.

The food needs to be presented in a variety of different ways. Buffets are popular because they give guests the opportunity to make choices from an array of foods. Barbecues, display cooking, poolside, specialty restaurants, and reciprocal dining arrangements with nearby hotels give guests more options.

With increased global competition, not only from other resorts but also from cruise lines, resort managers must first attract guests and then turn them into repeat business, which traditionally has been the foundation of the resort's viability.

To increase occupancy rates resorts have diversified their marketing mix to include conventions, business meetings, sales meetings, incentive groups, sporting events, additional sporting and recreational facilities, spas, adventure tourism, ecotourism, and so on. Because guests are captive in the resort, they expect to be pampered. This requires an attentive, well-trained staff and that is a challenge in some remote areas and in developing countries.

There are a number of benefits to operating resorts. The guests are much more relaxed compared to those at transient hotels, and the resorts are located in scenically beautiful areas. This frequently enables staff to enjoy a better quality of life than do their transient hotel counterparts. Returning guests tend to treat associates like friends. This adds to the overall partylike atmosphere, which is prevalent at many of the established resorts.

Check Your Knowledge

1. How are hotels rated and classified?
2. Name and describe the different types of hotels and lodging.

Vacation Ownership

From its beginnings in the French Alps in the late 1960s, vacation ownership has become the fastest-growing segment of the U.S. travel and tourism industry, increasing in popularity at the rate of about 15 percent each year. Vacation ownership offers consumers the opportunity to purchase fully furnished vacation accommodations in a variety of forms, such as weekly intervals or points in points-based systems, for a percentage of the cost of full ownership. For a one-time purchase price and payment of a yearly maintenance fee, purchasers own their vacation either in perpetuity or for a predetermined number of years. Owners share both the use and the costs of upkeep of their unit and the common grounds of the resort property. Vacation ownership purchases are typically financed through consumer loans of 5 to 10 years' duration, with terms dependent on the purchase price and the amount of the buyer's down payment. The average cost of a vacation ownership ranges from about $7,000 for a studio to about $15,000 for a two bedroom unit.

> **About 4.0 percent of all U.S. households own vacation ownership.**

Yearly maintenance fees are paid each year to a homeowners' association for the maintenance of the resort. Just like taking care of a home, resort maintenance fees help retain the quality and future value of the resort property.

Vacation clubs, or point-based programs, provide the flexible use of accommodations in multiple resort locations. With these products, club members purchase points that represent either a travel and use membership or a deeded real estate product. These points are then used like currency to purchase accommodations of various sizes, during a certain season, for a set number of days at a participating resort. The number of points needed to access the resort accommodations will vary by the members' demand for unit size, season, resort location, and amenities. A vacation club may have a specific term of ownership or be deeded in perpetuity.

Vacation ownership is the politically correct way of saying time-share. Essentially, vacation ownership means that a person purchases the use of a unit similar to a condominium for blocks of times, usually in weeks. Henry Silverman of Cendant, which owns the Indianapolis, Indiana-based Resort Condominiums International (RCI), says that a time-share is really a two-bedroom suite that is owned, rather than a hotel room that is rented for a transient night. A vacation club, on the other hand, is a "travel-and-use" product. Consumers do not buy a vacation with a fixed week, unit size, season, location, or length each year. Instead, they purchase points that represent currency, which is used to access the club's vacation benefits. An important advantage to this is the product's flexibility, especially when it is tied to a point system. Vacation clubs are not involved with real estate, so this type of system works well with the hotel marketing programs, such as rewards programs.

The Advantages and Disadvantages of Vacation Ownership

Unlike a hotel room or rental cottage that requires payment for each use according to rates that usually increase each year, ownership at a time-share property enables vacationers to enjoy a resort, year after year, for the duration of their ownership for a one-time purchase price and the payment of yearly maintenance fees. Time-share ownership offers vacationers an opportunity to save on the escalating costs of vacation accommodations over the long term, while enjoying all the comforts of home in a resort setting.

Truly a home away from home, vacation ownership provides the space and flexibility to meet the needs of any size family or group. While most vacation ownership condominiums have two bedrooms and two baths, unit sizes range from studios to three or more bedrooms. Unlike hotel rooms, there are no charges for additional guests. Also unlike hotels, most units include a fully equipped kitchen with dining area, washer and dryer, stereo, DVD players, and more.

Time-share resort amenities rival those of other top-rated resort properties and may include swimming pools, tennis, Jacuzzi, golf, bicycles, and exercise facilities. Others feature boating, ski lifts, restaurants, and equestrian facilities. Most time-share resorts offer a full schedule of on-site or nearby sporting, recreational, and social activities for adults and children. The resorts are staffed with well-trained hospitality professionals, and many offer concierge services for assistance in visiting area attractions.

The World Tourism Organization has called time-shares one of the fastest-growing sectors of the travel and tourism industry. Hospitality companies are adding brand power to the concept with the participation of corporations such as Marriott Vacation Club International, the Walt Disney Company, Hilton Hotels, Hyatt Hotels, Promus' Embassy Suites, Inter-Continental, and even Four Seasons in an industry that has grown rapidly in recent years. Still, only about 4 percent of all U.S. households own vacation ownership. RCI estimates that the figure could rise to 10 percent within the next decade for households with incomes of more than $50,000. No wonder hotel companies have found this to be a lucrative business.

RCI, the largest vacation ownership exchange (allowing members to exchange vacations with other locations), has more than 3 million members. Some 3,700 participating resorts and members can exchange vacation intervals for vacations at any participating resort.[9] Vacation ownership is popular at U.S. resorts from Key West in Florida to Kona in Hawaii, and from New York City and Las Vegas to Colorado ski resorts.

The disadvantages of vacation ownership are that you may be "locked in" to the same time frame each year; swapping to another time can be difficult. Maintenance fees increase with time and must be paid. Furthermore, if you want out, it can be hard to sell the unit.

Check Your Knowledge

1. What is vacation ownership?
2. What are the most frequent reasons for purchasing time-shares?
3. What characteristics do the following hotel segments encompass?
   a. City center hotels
   b. Resort hotels
   c. Airport hotels
   d. Freeway hotels and motels
   e. Full-service hotels
   f. Economy/budget hotels
   g. Extended-stay hotels
   h. Bed and breakfast inns

Best, biggest, and most unusual hotels and chains

So which is the best hotel in the world? The answer may depend on whether you watch the Travel Channel or read polls taken by a business investment or travel magazine. The Oriental Hotel in Bangkok, Thailand, has been rated number one in the world; so too has the Regent of Hong Kong, the Mandarin Oriental of Hong Kong, and the Connaught of London. Each "list" includes different hotels. The largest hotel in the world is the Venetian Hotel, in Las Vegas, with 6,172 rooms.

The Best Hotel Chains

The Ritz-Carlton and the Canadian-owned and -operated Four Seasons are generally rated the highest quality chain hotels. The Ritz-Carlton Hotel Company has received all the major awards that the hospitality industry and leading consumer organizations can bestow, including the Malcolm Baldrige National Quality Award, from the United States Department of Commerce—the first and only hotel company to win the award, not just once but twice. 1992 and 1999. Ritz-Carlton has long been recognized as one of the best luxury hotel chains in the industry. Its approach to quality centers on a number of basic but complex principles, many drawn from traditional total quality management theory.

Experience Some of the World's Most Unusual Hotels: View *A GM's Guide to Hotel Properties*

The Most Unusual Hotels

Among the world's most unusual hotels include the Treetops Hotel in a wild animal park in Kenya—it is literally in the treetops, built on the tops of trees overlooking a wild animal watering hole.

Another magnificent spectacle is the Ice Hotel, situated on the shores of the Torne River in the historic village of Jukkasjäsvi in Swedish Lapland. The Ice Hotel is built from scratch on an annual basis with a completely new design, new suites, new departments, and even an "Absolut Ice Bar," a bar carved in ice with ice glasses and ice plates. The Ice Hotel can accommodate over 100 guests, and each room has its own distinct style. The hotel also has an Ice Chapel, an ice art exhibition hall, and, believe it or not, an ice cinema.

Australia boasts an underwater hotel at the Great Barrier Reef, where guests enjoy wonderful subterranean views from their rooms. Japan has several unusual hotels. One is a cocoon-like hotel, called Capsule Hotel, in which guests do not have a "room." Instead, they have a space of about 7 feet by 7 feet that contains a bed and television. (The space is so small that from the bed, you almost have to operate the TV with your toes!) Such hotels are popular with people who get caught up in the obligatory late-night drinking with the boss and with visiting professors, who find them the only affordable place to stay in expensive Tokyo.

The hotel built at the highest altitude in the world (13,000 feet) is nestled in the Himalayan Mountains. Weather permitting, there is a marvelous view of Mount Everest. As many as 80 percent of the guests suffer from nausea, headaches, or sleeplessness caused by the altitude. It is no wonder that the hottest-selling item on the room-service menu is oxygen—at $1 a minute.[10]

The lobby of an ice hotel in Arctic Lapland, Sweden.

INTERNATIONAL PERSPECTIVE

We are all part of a huge global economy that is splintered into massive trading blocks—such as the European Union (EU) and the North American Free Trade Agreement (NAFTA)—among Canada, the United States, and Mexico, and comprising a total population of 350 million consumers.

The EU, with a population of over 400 million people in 25 nations, is an economic union that has removed national restrictions not only on trade but also on the movement of capital and labor. The synergy developed between these member nations is beneficial to all and is a form of self-perpetuating development. As travel, tourism, commerce, and industry have increased within the EEC, so has the need for hotel accommodations.

NAFTA will likely be a similar catalyst for hotel development in response to increased trade and tourism among the three countries involved. But Argentina, Brazil, Chile, and Venezuela may also join an expanded NAFTA, which would become known as the Americas Trading Block.

It is easy to understand the international development of hotels, given the increase in international tourism trade and commerce. The growth in tourism in Pacific Rim countries is expected to continue at the same rate as in recent years. Several resorts are planned in Indonesia, Malaysia, Thailand, Mexico, and Vietnam. Further international hotel development opportunities exist in Eastern Europe, Russia, and the other republics of the former Soviet Union, where some companies have changed their growth strategy from building new hotels to acquiring existing properties.

In Asia, Hong Kong's growth has been encouraged by a booming Chinese economy along with several other Asian countries and the kind of tax system for which supply-siders hunger. The Hong Kong government levies a flat 16.5 percent corporate tax, a 15 percent individual income tax, and no tax on capital gains or dividends. Several hotel corporations have their headquarters in Hong Kong. Among them are Mandarin Oriental, Peninsula, and Shangri-La, all world-renowned for their five-star status. They are based in Hong Kong because of low corporate taxation and their ability to bring in senior expatriate executives with minimum bureaucratic difficulty.

In developing countries, once political stability has been sustained, hotel development quickly follows as part of an overall economic and social progression. An example of this would be the former Eastern European countries and former Soviet republics, who for the past few years have offered development opportunities for hotel corporations.

> **As travel, tourism, commerce, and industry have increased within the EEC, so has the need for hotel accommodations.**

Green Lodging

Fairmont Hotels and Resorts are among the leading sustainable lodging companies. The main focus of the company's Green Partnership program is sustainable, responsible practices—both at a corporate and individual properties level—achieved through initiatives such as recycling, kitchen-waste diversion, retrofitting energy-efficient lighting, conducting community-outreach programs, and buying green power.

Fairmont's projects fall into three key areas: 1) to minimize the company's impact on the environment by making ongoing operational improvements, mainly in waste management and energy and water conservation; 2) to work at a corporate level to foster high-profile partnerships and accreditations that help promote environmental issues, and to share its stewardship message; and 3) to follow best practices, which include working at individual properties to develop innovative community-outreach programs involving and respecting local groups. Fairmont also works to ensure that local ecosystemse are protected and preserved.

In all areas of the Green Partnership, Fairmont Hotels and Resorts aim to help educate and, in many cases, to involve guests, because its program truly is a partnership: everyone

# Sustainable Lodging

Discover the Benefits of Going Green at Hutchinson Hotel

Within the past few years, the tourism industry has witnessed a phenomenon that continues to intrigue tourists and industry leaders alike. Sustainable tourism (often dubbed ecotourism or responsible tourism) has become one of the fastest-growing segments within the world's largest industry. For the lodging sector, sustainability is a potentially prosperous business.

How can hotels, motels, lodges, and resorts become sustainable? Reducing (and eliminating) waste can produce the biggest positive environmental impact. This can be accomplished through a number of practices including sustainable lighting and water conservation. A property with 350 guest rooms can spend $300,000 per year on electricity, $50,000 on natural gas, and another $60,000 annually on water and sewer.[11]

Lighting can account for 30 to 40 percent of commercial electricity consumption. This can be reduced by:

- Using lighting only when necessary (employ motion detectors).
- Using energy efficient fixtures and lamps.
- Using low wattage lighting for signs and décor.
- Avoiding overlighting wherever possible.[12]

Water conservation is another method that can greatly reduce waste. Today many hotels are replacing showerheads, toilets, and faucets with new low-flow water devices. Low-flow showerheads can save 10 gallons of water for every five minutes of showering. That means a savings of over $3,600 annually if 100 people shower each day, and water and sewer costs are 1¢ per gallon.[13] Other water conservation methods include only washing full loads of dishes and laundry, serving drinking water by request only, asking guests to consider reusing their towels, and restricted lawn watering.

involved in the tourism industry—hotel management, colleagues, guests and local communities—shares responsibility for taking care of the environment.

How Fairmont Promises to Fight Climate Change

Fairmont Hotels & Resorts' Climate Savers commitment includes:

- Reducing operational CO_2 emissions from its existing portfolio of hotels by 20 percent below 2006 levels by 2013
- Ensuring that new properties participate in its Energy and Carbon Management Program and striving to reduce their CO_2 emissions; updating existing design and construction standards to incorporate and reflect LEED standards by the end of 2011
- Educating and encouraging emissions reductions from its supply chain through the development of a "Green Procurement Policy and Supplier Code of Conduct" to be implemented by the end of 2009

Fairmont Hotels & Resorts is a global hospitality leader with an exceptional collection of luxury hotels, including numerous iconic landmarks. Fairmont's portfolio presently includes distinctive hotels in 16 countries with services delivered by over 30,000 employees.

Climate Change Impacts the Bottom Line

As a leading travel provider, Fairmont is reliant on destination health to be profitable and is committed to preserving the places where its guests and colleagues, work, live, and play. Fairmont is resolutely aware of the business impacts associated with environmental damage, such as diminishing snowfall at ski resorts and other extreme weather events, and is taking proactive steps to reduce its CO_2 output and help mitigate the effects of climate change.

Fairmont has implemented an energy and carbon management program to provide a framework so that information associated with CO_2 producing activities can be tracked and monitored on a consistent and measurable basis by all Fairmont properties.

Fairmont has designed a comprehensive strategy for reducing operational emissions, having recently completed a number of energy demand reduction projects across its portfolio. Fairmont will use these best practices to guide the development of energy reduction strategies in the future and will focus on implementing greater conversion to renewable energy supply.

Examples of Fairmont's Best Practice:

- Three properties (The Fairmont Chateau Lake Louise, The Fairmont Washington D.C. and Fairmont Hotel Vier Jahreszeiten) currently reduce their carbon footprint by contracting part of their electricity consumption from renewable sources such as wind. Presently, half of the Chateau Lake Louise's electricity needs are met by a blend of wind and run-of-river electricity generation.
- Nine of the 13 chalets at Fairmont Kenauk at Fairmont Le Chateau Montebello (Quebec, Canada), situated on a remote lake, are not connected to the electrical grid, using instead solar power systems to supply about half of their power demand.
- Currently three Fairmont properties (The Fairmont San Jose, The Fairmont Newport Beach, and Fairmont St Andrew's, Scotland) use co-generation in their facilities, which captures excess heat for hotel building use as well as produce electricity on site.
- The Fairmont Orchid, Hawaii, has completed a lighting retrofit, replacing 8,035 incandescent bulbs with energy-efficient fluorescents. This retrofit has resulted in an annual savings of 532,000 kWh of electricity, representing a cost savings in excess of $130,000.

" Lighting can account for 30 to 40 percent of commercial electricity consumption. "

Commitments and Plans

In addition to adopting best practice examples from renewable energy and retrofit strategies to reduce operational emissions, Fairmont will address sustainable design and construction. This will be achieved by updating existing design and construction standards to incorporate and reflect LEED (Leadership in Energy and Environmental Design) standards by 2011, and educating hotel development partners to site, design, and construct hotels to follow internationally recognized green building standards, including the U.S. Green Building Council Leadership in Energy and Environmental Design (LEED) and the International Tourism Partnership Sustainable Hotel Manual. Fairmont will also endeavor to include sustainable and LEED-certified hotels across the brand, and relocate its corporate offices in Toronto, Canada, to a building with a LEED NC Gold target by 2011.

Fairmont will endeavor to educate and engage its top suppliers (representing 25 percent of its supply chain) to provide products in accordance with its updated Green Procurement policy and Supplier Code of Conduct by 2010, and work with its suppliers to improve the energy efficiency of their manufacturing operations and product design, and to minimize shipping frequency and packaging waste. In addition to this, Fairmont will engage guests by offering carbon offsets meeting Gold Standard requirements, and share best practices with other organizations committed to the protection of the environment. Fairmont will also strive to work with WWF to raise awareness of the need for business and industry to lower absolute emissions among policy makers, guests, employees and suppliers, to stimulate market transformation. The Fairmont approach is holistic: addressing climate change by capturing emissions abatement opportunities from operational activities associated with existing and new properties, while enabling further CO_2 footprint reductions through the supply chain. Moreover, given that Fairmont's portfolio consists exclusively of managed (not owned) luxury and heritage properties, this positions Fairmont as a global leader in emission reduction efforts in the hospitality sector.

TRENDS in HOTEL DEVELOPMENT

- **Capacity control:** This refers to who will control the sale of inventories of hotel rooms, airline seats, auto rentals, and tickets to attractions. Presently, owners of these assets are in control of their sale and distribution, but increasingly control is falling into the hands of those who own and manage global reservation systems and/or negotiate for large buying groups. Factors involved in the outcome will be telecommunications, software, available satellite capacity, governmental regulations, limited capital, and the travel distribution network.
- **Safety and security:** Important aspects of safety and security include terrorism, the growing disparity between the "haves" and "have nots" in the world, diminishing financial resources, infrastructure problems, health issues, the stability of governments, and personal security.
- **Assets and capital:** The issues concerning assets and capital include rationing of private capital and rationing of funds deployed by governments.
- **Technology:** An example of the growing use of expert systems (a basic form of artificial intelligence) would be making standard operating procedures available online, 24 hours a day, and establishing yield management systems designed to make pricing decisions. Other examples include the smart hotel room and communications ports to make virtual office environments for business travelers; and the impact of technology on the structure of corporate offices and individual hotels.
- **New management:** The complex forces of capacity control, safety and security, capital movement, and technology issues will require a future management that can adapt to rapid-paced change across all the traditional functions of management.
- **Globalization:** A number of U.S. and Canadian chains have developed and are continuing to develop hotels around the world. International companies are also investing in the North American hotel industry.
- **Consolidation:** As the industry matures, corporations are either acquiring or merging with each other.
- **Diversification within segments of the lodging industry:** The economy segment now has low-, medium-, and high-end properties. The extended-stay market has a similar spread of properties, as do all the other hotel classifications.
- **Rapid growth in vacation ownership:** Vacation ownership is the fastest-growing segment of the lodging industry and is likely to continue growing as the baby boomers enter their fifties and sixties.
- **An increase in the number of spas and the treatments offered:** Wellness is in increasing demand as guests seek release from the stresses of a fast-paced lifestyle.
- **Gaming:** Several new casino hotels are opening.
- An increasing number of condotels and hotels are being developed as multiuse, meaning hotels with residences (condominiums), spas, and recreational facilities.
- There are increasing sustainable practices in the lodging sector.

CASE STUDY

To Flag or Not to Flag—and if So, Which Flag?

Amanda and Jason Smith are contemplating turning their inn into a franchise. The 75-room Cozy Inn is located in a picturesque New England town, clearly accessible from the turnpike. The inn has just been refurbished, and the fresh paint and attractive landscaping adds to its presentation.

The Cozy Inn's year-round occupancy is 58 percent, which is about 10 percentage points below the national average. The average daily rate is $78. The Cozy Inn's guests are a mix of business travelers, who are mostly from companies at a nearby business park; a few retirees traveling for pleasure; an occasional bus tour; and some sports teams.

The Smiths have asked several franchise corporations to submit their best offers. The best one indicates that the cost of a franchise application fee is $20,000, there is a 2 percent revenue-marketing fee, and a reservation fee of $4 per room booked by the Central Reservation System (CRS).

DISCUSSION QUESTIONS

1. What would you do in the Smiths' situation? Make assumptions if needed.
2. What terms and conditions of a franchise agreement would be acceptable to you?
3. What additional information would you need to know if you were in the Smiths' situation?

CAREER INFORMATION

A variety of career opportunities are directly and indirectly related to hotel development and classification. Some examples include: Working in the corporate offices to develop hotels or searching out locations, negotiating the deals, and organizing the construction or alterations. This involves knowledge of operations plus expertise in marketing, feasibility studies (to find out if the planned hotel will be profitable), finance, and planning. Similarly, consulting firms like Pannel Kew Foster (PKF) have interesting positions for consultants who provide specialized services in feasibility studies, marketing expertise, human resources, accounting, and finance due diligence (a check to ensure that the proposed cost of a property is reasonable). Working for a consulting firm usually requires a master's degree plus operational experience and an area of specialty.

AAA and Mobile both have inspectors who check hotel standards. Inspectors are required to travel and write detailed reports on the properties at which they stay.

Suppliers to the industry: These companies manufacture or distribute and sell all the furnishings, furniture, and equipment (FF&E). A visit to a trade show may be an eye-opener as to the number of suppliers in the hospitality industry. It is a good idea to explore, as many career paths as possible. Ask questions about lifestyle, career challenges and, yes, salaries. Map out your path to see where you want to be in 5, 10, 15, and even 20 years from now.

Good advice comes from Jim McManemon, general manager, The Ritz Carlton, Sarasota, Florida: "It is important to have a love of people, as there is so much interaction with them. I also suggest working in the industry to gain experience. Actually, it is a good idea to work in various departments while going to school so you can either join a management training program or take a supervisory or assistant management position upon graduation. Work hard, be a leader, and set an example for the people working with you.

Chris Bryant, Guest Services Manager, Grand Hyatt Tampa Bay, Florida.

SUMMARY

1. Improved transportation has changed the nature of the hotel industry from small, independently owned inns to big hotel and lodging chains, operated by using concepts such as franchising and management contracts.
2. Hotels can be classified according to location (city center, resort, airport, freeway), types of services offered (casino, convention), and price (luxury, midscale, budget, and economy). Hotels are rated by Mobil and AAA awards (five-star or five-diamond rankings).
3. Vacation ownership offers consumers the opportunity to purchase fully furnished vacation accommodations, similar to condominiums, sold in a variety of forms, such as weekly intervals or point-based systems, for only a percentage of the cost of full ownership. According to the WTO, time-shares are one of the fastest-growing sectors of the travel and tourism industry.
4. Every part of the world offers leisure and business travelers a choice of unusual or conservative accommodations that cater to the personal ideas of vacation or business trips.
5. The future of tourism involves international expansion and foreign investment, often in combination with airlines and with the goal of improving economic conditions in developing countries. It is further influenced by increased globalization, as evidenced by such agreements as NAFTA.

KEY WORDS AND CONCEPTS

Franchising
Management contracts
Real estate investment trust (REIT)
Vacation ownership

REVIEW QUESTIONS

1. What are the advantages of (a) management contracts and (b) franchising? Discuss their impacts on the development of the hotel industry.

2. Explain how hotels cater to the needs of business and leisure travelers in reference to the following concepts: (a) resorts and (b) airport hotels.

3. Explain what vacation ownership is. What are the different types of time-share programs available for purchase?

INTERNET EXERCISES

1. Organization: Hilton Hotels
   Web site: www.hilton.com
   Summary: Hilton Hotels Corporation and Hilton International, a subsidiary of Hilton Group PLC, have a worldwide alliance to market Hilton. Hilton is recognized as one of the world's best-known hotel brands. Collectively, Hilton offers more than 2,500 hotels in more than 50 countries, truly a major player in the hospitality industry.

   a. What are the different hotel brands that can be franchised through Hilton Hotels Corporation?
   b. What are your views on Hilton's portfolio and franchising options?

   Click on the "Franchise Development" icon. Now click on "All HHC Franchise Brands."

2. Organization: *HOTELS* Magazine
   Web site: www.hotelsmag.com
   Summary: *HOTELS* magazine is a publication that offers vast amounts of information on the hospitality industry with up-to-date industry news, corporate trends, and nationwide developments.

   a. What are some of the top headlines currently being reported in the industry?
   b. Click on the "Hotels Giants" icon. Browse through the Corporate Rankings and Industry Leaders. List the top five hotel corporations and note how many rooms each one has.

APPLY YOUR KNOWLEDGE

1. From a career perspective, what are the advantages and disadvantages of each type of hotel?

SUGGESTED ACTIVITY

1. Identify which kind of hotel you would like to work at and give some reasons why.

2. Go to Eco Guru at http://ecoguru.panda.org/#calculator/comparison and calculate your footprint. What other things can we do to decrease our footprint?

ENDNOTES

1. Tom Fletcher's New York Architecture, www.nyc-architecture.com, retrieved March 7, 2010.
2. Wyndham Worldwide, www.wyndhamworldwide.com/about/, retrieved March 9, 2010.
3. Choice Hotels International, www.choicehotels.com/ires/en-US/html/AboutChoiceHotels?sid=F4dTM.0Jp6Sg5CQ.3, retrieved March 9, 2010.
4. Intercontinental Hotels Group, www.ihgplc.com, retrieved March 10, 2010.
5. American Hotel and Lodging Association, www.ahla.com/content.aspx?id=3448, retrieved March 12, 2010.
6. American Automobile Association Newsroom, www.aaanewsroom.net/Main/Default.asp?CategoryID=9&SubCategoryID=22&ContentID=88, retrieved March 12, 2010.
7. Personal correspondence with Dr. Cihan Cobanoglu, August 21, 2010.
8. Travel Assist, http://travelassist.com/mag/a88.html, retrieved March 12, 2010.
9. RCI, www.rci.com/RCI/RCIW/RCIW_index?body=RCIW_AboutUs, retrieved March 9, 2010.
10. Jeannie Realston, "Inn of Thin Air," *American Way,* October 15, 1992.
11. N.C. Division of Pollution Prevention and Environmental Assistance (DPPEA), Hotel/Motel Waste Reduction: Facilities Management, www.p2pays.org/ref/14/13910.pdf retrieved March 12, 2010.
12. Ibid.
13. Ibid.

LODGING OPERATIONS
5

LEARNING OUTCOMES

After reading and studying this chapter, you should be able to:

Outline the duties and responsibilities of key executives and department heads.

Draw an organizational chart of the rooms and food and beverage divisions of a hotel and identify the executive committee members.

Describe the main functions of the hotel departments.

Explain property management systems and discuss revenue management.

Calculate occupancy percentages, average daily rates, and actual percentage of potential rooms revenue.

List the duties and responsibilities of a food and beverage director and other department heads.

HTi — Describe the economic impact of tourism.

This chapter describes the functions of a hotel and the many departments that make up a hotel. It also helps to explain why and how the departments are interdependent in successfully running a hotel.

Functions and departments of a hotel

The main function of a hotel is to provide an outstanding lodging experience. A large hotel is run by a general manager and an **executive committee** that includes the key associates who head major departments: rooms division director, food and beverage director, marketing and sales director, human resources director, chief accountant or controller, and chief engineer or facility manager.

A hotel is made up of several businesses or revenue centers and cost centers. A few thousand products and services are sold every day. Each area of specialty requires dedication and a quality commitment for each department to get many little things right all of the time. Hotels need the cooperation of a large and diverse group of people to perform well. Godfrey Bler, the *general manager* (GM) of the elegant 800-room General Eisenhower Hotel, calls it a "business of details."

Check Out the Role of the Executive Committee: Ask the GM

Hotels are places of glamour; even the experienced hotel person is impressed by a beautiful hotel like a Ritz-Carlton. The atmosphere of a hotel is stimulating to a hospitality student. Let's step into an imaginary hotel to feel the excitement and the rush that is similar to show business, for a hotel is live theater and the GM is the director of the cast of players. Hotels, whether they are chain affiliated or independent properties, all exist to serve and offer a great lodging experience while making a profit for the owners. Hotels are meant to provide all the comforts of home to those who are away from home.

Early inns

Increased travel and trade made some form of overnight accommodations an absolute necessity. Because travel was slow and journeys long and arduous, many travelers depended solely on the hospitality of private citizens.

In the Greek and Roman empires, inns and taverns sprang up everywhere. The Romans constructed elaborate and well-appointed inns on all the main roads. Marco Polo later proclaimed these inns as "fit for a king." They were located about 25 miles apart to provide "fresh houses" for officials and couriers of the Roman government. They could only be used with special government documents granting permission. These documents became revered as status symbols and were subject to numerous thefts and forgeries. By the time Marco Polo traveled to the Far East, there were 10,000 inns.

Role of the hotel general manager

Hotel and resort general managers have a lot of responsibilities. They must keep guests satisfied and returning, keep employees happy, and provide owners with a reasonable return on investment. This may seem easy, but because there are so many interpersonal transactions and because hotels are open all day every day, the complexities of operating become challenges that the general manager and his or her team must face and overcome.

Larger hotels can be more impersonal. Here, the general manager may only meet and greet a few VIPs. In the smaller property, it is easier—though no less important—for the GM to get to know guests, to make sure their stay is memorable, and

The Grand Hall of the Willard Inter-Continental Hotel in Washington, D.C. The term *lobbyist* was coined here when President Grant would retire after dinner to an armchair in the lobby. People would approach him and try to gain his support for their causes.

Learn about the Art of Delegation: Ask the GM

to get them to return. One way that experienced GMs can meet guests, even in large hotels, is to be visible in the lobby and F&B (food and beverage) outlets at peak times (check-out, lunch, check-in, and dinner time). Guests like to feel that the GM takes a personal interest in their well-being. To be successful, GMs need to have a broad range of personal qualities. The positive qualities most often quoted by GMs include leadership, attention to detail, follow-through (getting the job done), people skills, patience, and the ability to delegate effectively.

A successful GM selects and trains the best people. A former GM of Chicago's Four Seasons Hotel deliberately hired division heads who had more experience in their role than he did. The GM sets the tone—a structure of excellence—and others try to match it. Once the structure is in place, each employee works to define the hotel commitment to excellence.

Management structure

Management structure differs among larger, midsized, and smaller properties. The midsize and smaller properties are less complex in their management structures than are the larger ones. However, someone must be responsible for each of the key areas that make the operation successful. For example, a small property may not have a director of human resources, but each department head will have general day-to-day operating responsibilities for the human resources function. The manager will have the ultimate responsibility for all human resources decisions. The same is possible with engineering and maintenance, accounting and finance, marketing and sales, and food and beverage management.

The Executive Committee

The general manager, using input from the *executive committee* (Figure 5–1), makes all the major decisions affecting the hotel. These executives, who include the directors of human resources, food and beverage, rooms division, security, marketing and sales, engineering, and accounting, compile the

Executive Committee Chart for a 300 Plus - Room Hotel

General Manager

| Director of Human Resources | Director of Food and Beverage | Director of Rooms Division | Director of Marketing and Sales | Director of Engineering | Director of Accounting |

FIGURE 5–1 Executive Committee Chart of a 300-Plus-Room Full-Service Hotel.

hotel's occupancy forecast together with all revenues and expenses to make up the budget. They may meet once a week for one or two hours and typically cover such topics as guest and employee satisfaction, total quality management, occupancy forecasts, sales and marketing plans, training, major items of expenditure, renovations, ownership relations, energy conservation, recycling, new legislation, security, and profitability.

Some GMs rely on input from the executive committee more than others, depending on their leadership and management style. These senior executives determine the character of the property and decide on the missions, goals, and objectives of the hotel. For a chain hotel, this will align with the corporate mission. In most hotels, the executive committee is involved with the decisions but the ultimate responsibility and authority rests with the GM.

THE DEPARTMENTS

Rooms Division

The rooms division's director is responsible to the GM for the efficient and effective leadership and operation of all the rooms division departments, including concerns such as financial responsibility, employee satisfaction goals, guest satisfaction goals, guest services, guest relations, security, and the gift shop.

The **rooms division** consists of the following departments: front office, reservations, housekeeping, concierge, guest services, security, and communications. Figure 5–2 shows the organizational chart for a 300-plus-room hotel rooms division. The guest cycle in Figure 5–3 shows a simplified sequence of events that takes place from the moment a guest calls to make a reservation until he or she checks out.

Front Office

The front office has been described as the hub or nerve center of the hotel. It is the department that makes a first impression on the guest and on which the guest relies for information and service throughout his or her stay. Positive first impressions are critical to the successful guest experience. Many guests arrive at the hotel after long, tiring trips. They want to be met by someone with a warm smile and a genuine greeting. Figure 5–4 shows an organizational chart for a front office.

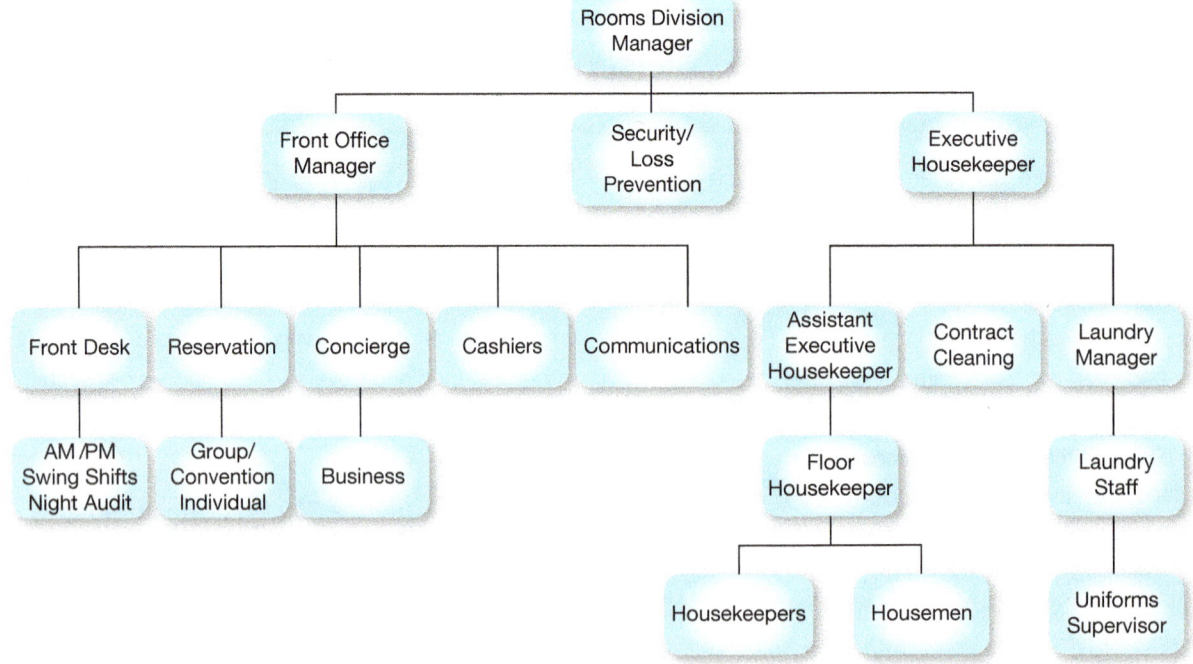

FIGURE 5–2 Rooms Division Organizational Chart.

> **People entering the hotel and lodging industry operations sector are generally looking to build their way up the industry ladder. They may start their career as a front desk clerk and work their way up to rooms divisions manager or general hotel manager.**
>
> Louise McWilliams, *The Skipper*, Washington, D.C.

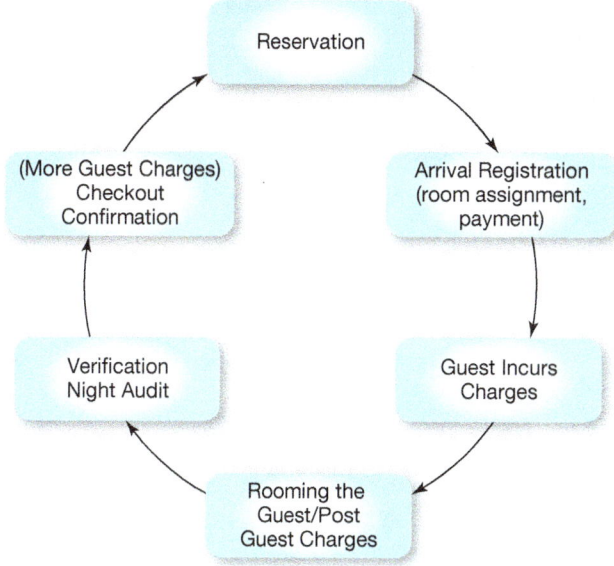

FIGURE 5–3 The Guest Cycle.

Read the *Front-Office Manager's Manual* for More on the Manager's Responsibilities

The *front-office manager's* (FOM) main duty is to provide outstanding guest services to exceed guest needs. An example of how some FOMs practice enhancing guest services is to have a *guest service associate* (GSA) greet guests as they arrive at the hotel, escort them to the front desk, personally assign the room, and take the guest and luggage there. This innovative way of developing guest services looks at the operation from the guest's perspective. There is no need to have separate departments for doorperson, bellperson, or front desk. Each guest associate is cross-trained in all aspects of greeting and rooming the guest. This is now being done in smaller and mid-sized properties as well as in specialty and deluxe properties. Guest service associates are responsible for the front desk, concierge, communications, bellpersons, valet, and reservations.

During an average day in a hotel—if there is such a thing—the front-office manager performs the following duties:

- Check night clerk report.
- Review previous night's occupancy.
- Review previous night's average rate.
- Compare the market mix (the percent of guests from each market, for example, group/tour, business, leisure, sports team, convention/meeting).
- Check complimentary rooms.

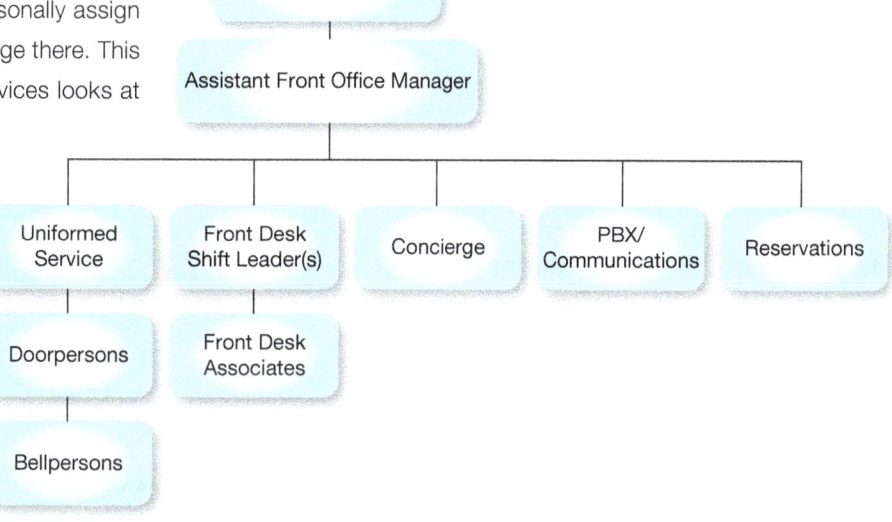

FIGURE 5–4 Front-Office Organizational Chart for a Larger Hotel.

- Verify group rooms to be picked up for next 30 days.
- Review arrivals and departures for the day.
- Review the VIP list and prepare preregistration.
- Arrange preregistrations for all arrivals.
- Attend rooms division and operations meeting.
- Review arrivals and departures for next day.
- Make staffing adjustments needed for arrivals and departures.
- Review scheduling (done weekly).
- Meet with lead GSAs (done daily).

The Departments

103

Front-office associates taking care of guest requests.

The guest service agents take reservations, register guests, allocate rooms, answer guest inquiries, provide information on restaurants and attractions, and check out guests.

The position's description for a guest service agent details the work performed. Position descriptions for the three main functions of the front office are as follows:

1. *To sell rooms.* All front-desk associates sell rooms—today, chain hotels have reservations centers—but some guests prefer to call the hotel directly. Front-desk associates also *upsell* guest rooms; upselling occurs when the guest service agent/front-desk clerk suggestively sells the features of a larger room, a higher floor, or perhaps a better view.

Explore the Guest Check-in Process: Follow a Front-Office Clerk

2. *To maintain balanced guest accounts.* This begins with advance deposits, opening the guest folio (account), and posting all charges from the various departments. Most hotels now have property management systems (PMS) (property management systems are explained in more detail later in this chapter) and point-of-sale (POS) terminals, which are online to the front office. This means that guest charges from the various outlets are directly debited to the guest's folio. Payment is either received on guest checkout, or transferred to the **city ledger** (a special account for a company that has established credit with the hotel). The account will be charged to the guest and paid within a specified time period. Figure 5–5 shows the types of rates offered by hotels.

3. *To offer services such as handling mail, faxes, messages, and local and hotel information.* People constantly approach the front desk with questions. Front-desk employees need to be knowledgeable about the various activities offered by the hotel. The size, layout, and staffing of the front desk will vary with the size of the hotel. A busy, 800-room city center property will naturally differ from a country inn. The front desk is staffed throughout the 24 hours by three shifts.

The morning shift duties mostly consist of:

1. Checking out guests.
2. Responding to guest requests.
3. Preallocating all VIP and special request rooms.
4. Coordinating with housekeeping over VIP, special requests, and room status.

Major hotel chains offer a number of different room rates, including the following:

rack rate
corporate
association rate
government
encore
cititravel
entertainment cards
AAA
AARP (American Association of Retired Persons)
wholesale
group rates
promotional special

The rack rate is the rate that is used as a benchmark quotation of a hotel's room rate. Let us assume that the Hotel California had a rack rate of $135. Any discounted rate may be offered at a percentage deduction from the rack rate. An example would be a corporate rate of $110, an association rate of $105, and AARP rate of $95—certain restrictions may apply. Group rates may range from $95 to $125 according to how much the hotel needs the business.

Throughout the world there are three main plans on which room rates are based:

AP/American Plan—room and three meals a day
MAP/Modified American Plan—room plus two meals
EP/European Plan—room only, meals extra

FIGURE 5–5 Types of Rates.

The evening shift duties include:

1. Check the log book for special items. (The log book, which may be electronic is kept by guest contact associates at the front office to note specific and important guest requests and occurrences such as requests for room switches or baby cribs, etc.)
2. Check on room status, outstanding check-outs, and arrivals by double-checking registration cards and the computer in order to update the forecast of the night's occupancy. This will determine the number of rooms left to sell. Nowadays, this is all part of the capability of the PMS.
3. Handle guest check-ins. This means notifying the appropriate staff of any special requests guests may have made (e.g., nonsmoking room or a long bed for an extra-tall guest).
4. Take reservations for that evening and the future after the reservations staff has left for the day.

See the Reservation Process in Action with the Front-Office Manager

Night Auditor

A hotel is one of the few businesses that balance their accounts at the end of each business day. Because a hotel is open 24 hours every day, it is difficult to stop transactions at any given moment. The **night auditor** waits until the hotel quiets down at about 1:00 A.M. and then begins the task of balancing the guests' accounts receivable.

Explore the Night Audit Process

Other duties include the following:

1. Post any charges that the evening shift was not able to post.
2. Pass discrepancies to shift managers in the morning. The room and tax charges are then posted to each folio and a new balance shown.
3. Run backup reports so if the computer system fails, the hotel will have up-to-date information to operate a manual system.
4. Reconcile point-of-sale and PMS to guest accounts. If this does not balance, then the auditor must investigate errors or omissions. He or she does this by checking that every departmental charge shows up on guest folios.
5. Complete and distribute the daily report. This report details the previous day's activities and includes vital information about the performance of the hotel.
6. Be on the lookout for security issues, including areas of the hotel where theft could potentially occur.

.inc | Corporate Profile

HYATT HOTELS

When Nicholas Pritzker emigrated with his family from Ukraine to the United States, he began his career by opening a small law firm. His outstanding management skills led to the expansion of the law firm, turning it into a management company. The Pritzkers gained considerable financial support, which allowed them to pursue their goals of expansion and development. These dreams came into reality when the Pritzkers opened the first Hyatt Hotel, inaugurated on September 27, 1957.

Today, Hyatt Hotel Corporation is a multibillion-dollar hotel management and development company; together with Hyatt International, they are among the leading chains in the hotel industry. Hyatt has earned worldwide fame as the leader in providing luxury accommodations and high-quality service, targeting especially the business traveler, but strategically differentiating its properties and services to identify and market to a very diverse clientele. This differentiation has resulted in the establishment of four basic types of hotels:

1. *The Hyatt Regency Hotels* represent the company's core product. They are usually

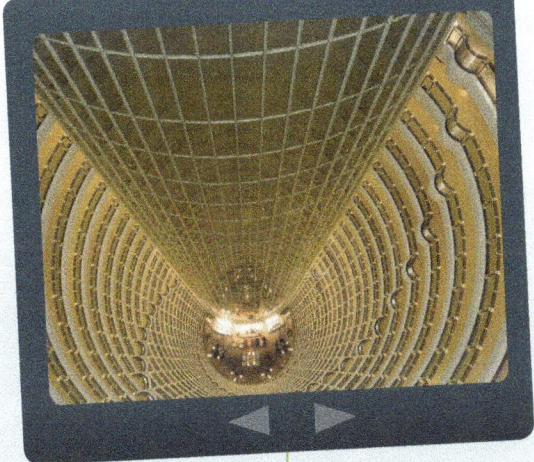

Corporate Profile (Continued)

located in city business centers and are regarded as five-star hotels.

2. *Hyatt Resorts* are vacation retreats. They are located in the world's most desirable leisure destinations, offering the "ultimate escape from everyday stresses."
3. *The Park Hyatt Hotels* are smaller, European-style, luxury hotels. They target the individual traveler who prefers the privacy, personalized service, and discreet elegance of a small European hotel.
4. *The Grand Hyatt Hotels* serve culturally rich destinations that attract leisure business as well as large-scale meetings and conventions. They reflect refinement and grandeur, and they feature state-of-the-art technology and banquet and conference facilities of world-class standard.
5. *Hyatt Place* is an upscale, limited-service property.
6. *Hyatt Vacation Ownership* is a time-share operation.

Hyatt Hotels Corporation has been recognized by the *Wall Street Journal* as one of 66 firms around the world poised to make a difference in the industries and markets. As a matter of fact, the effective management that characterized the company in its early years with the Pritzker family has continued through time. Hyatt Hotels Corporation is characterized by a decentralized management approach, which gives the individual general manager a great deal of decision-making power, as well as the opportunity to stimulate personal creativity and, therefore, differentiation and innovation. The development of novel concepts and products is perhaps the key to Hyatt's outstanding success. For example, the opening of the Hyatt Regency Atlanta, Georgia, gave the company instant recognition throughout the world. Customers were likely to stare in awe at the 21-story atrium lobby, the glass elevators, and the revolving roof-top restaurant. The property's innovative architecture, designed by John Portman, revolutionized the common standards of design and spacing, thus changing the course of the lodging industry. Its atrium concept represented a universal challenge to hotel architects to face the new trend of grand, wide-open public spaces.

A further positive aspect of the decentralized management structure is the individual manager's ability to be extremely customer responsive by developing a thorough knowledge of the guest's needs and thereby providing personalized service—fundamental to achieving customer satisfaction. This is, in fact, the ultimate innkeeping purpose, which Hyatt attains at high levels. Perhaps the most striking result of this forecasting is, again, the introduction of innovative and diversified products and services. For business travelers, for example, Hyatt introduced the Hyatt Business Plan, which includes fax machines in every room, 24-hour access to copiers and printers, and other features designed to address the needs of the targeted clientele. Hyatt has also been on the forefront in developing faster, more efficient check-in options, including a phone number, 1-800-CHECK-IN, that allows guests to check in to their hotel rooms by telephone. In addition, the needs of families have been considered as well. The company offers Camp Hyatt, the hotel industry's most extensive children's program.

The other side of Hyatt's success is the emphasis on human resources management. Employee satisfaction, in fact, is considered to be a prerequisite to external satisfaction. Hyatt devotes enormous attention to employee training and selection. What is most significant, however, is the interaction among top managers and operating employees.

The company operates 243 hotels and resorts worldwide in 43 countries. Several of the hotels and resorts are now implementing green initiatives to minimize their carbon footprint. Hyatt's program focuses on water savings, energy savings, waste reduction/recycling, and staff environmental education.[1]

Read about Key Operating Ratios in the Front-Office Manager's Manual

The **daily report** contains some key operating ratios such as **room occupancy percentage (ROP)**, which is rooms occupied, divided by rooms available. Thus, if a hotel has 850 rooms and 622 are occupied, the occupancy percentage is 622 ÷ 850 = 73.17 percent. The **average daily rate (ADR)** is, together with the occupancy percentage, one of the key operating ratios that indicates the hotel's performance.

The average daily rate is calculated by dividing the rooms revenue by the number of rooms sold. If the rooms revenue was $75,884 and the number of rooms sold was 662, then the ADR would be $114.63. See Figure 5–6 for an example of a daily report.

Clarion Hotel Bayview

Daily Management Report Supplement
January 2007

Daily Report
January 2007

Occupancy %	Today	Avg or %	M–T–D	Avg or %	Y–T–D	Avg or %
Rack Rooms	9	2.9%	189	3.37	189	3.37
Corporate Rooms	0	0.0%	103	1.83	103	1.83
Group Rooms	274	87.8%	2,379	42.36	2,379	42.36
Leisure Rooms	3	1.0%	395	7.03	395	7.03
Base Rooms	23	7.4%	348	6.14	345	6.14
Government Rooms	2	0.6%	32	.57	32	.57
Wholesale Rooms	1	0.3%	121	2.15	121	2.15
No-Show Rooms		0.0%	0	.00	0	.00
Comp Rooms	0	0.0%	37	.66	37	.66
Total Occ Rooms & Occ %	312	100%	3,601	64.12	3,601	64.12
Rack	$1,011	$112.33	17,207	91.04	17,207	91.04
Corporate	$0	ERR	8,478	82.31	8,478	82.31
Group	$22,510	$82.15	178,066	74.85	178,066	74.85
Leisure	$207	$69.00	24,985	63.25	24,985	63.25
Base	$805	$35.00	12,063	34.97	12,063	34.97
Govt	$141	$70.59	2,379	74.34	2,379	74.34
Wholesale	$43	$43.00	5,201	42.98	5,201	42.98
No-Show/Comp/Allowance	$0		−914	−24.69	−914	−24.69
Total Rev & Avg Rate	$24,717	$79.22	247,466	68.72	247,466	68.72
Hotel Revenue						
Rooms	$24,717		247,466	77.46	247,466	77.46
Food	$1,400		37,983	11.89	37,983	11.89
Beverage	$539		9,679	3.03	9,679	3.03
Telephone	$547		5,849	1.83	5,849	1.83
Parking	$854		11,103	3.48	11,103	3.48
Room Svc II	$70		1,441	.45	1,441	.45
Other Revenue	$1,437		963	1.87	963	1.87
Total Revenue	$29,563		319,484	100.00	319,484	100.00

FIGURE 5–6 Daily Report.

Room Occupancy Percentage (ROP):

If total available rooms are 850
And total rooms occupied are 622

Then:

Occupancy percentage: $= (622/850) \times 100 = 73.17\%$

Average Daily Rate:

If rooms revenue is $75,884
And total number of rooms sold is 662

Then:

Average daily rate $= \dfrac{75{,}884}{662} = \mathbf{\$114.63}$

Introducing Ryan Adams

Guest Services Manager, Hotel del Coronado, San Diego, California.

From what I gather, there is supposed to be some sort of magical formula for how everything works out. You should have a plan with some kind of divine guidance; if you are spiritual, then you are on your way. However, I cannot rightly say that this has become known to me. I have been lucky enough to develop a plan and to make some rather good decisions to get where I am.

I have been in the industry now for 11 years and am still amazed at the magnetic draw it has on people. I always say, "It's not that the job that is hard, that is rudimentary. It is the people that really make the challenge worth undertaking."

I wake up at 5.30 A.M. every morning before work to prepare myself mentally for tackling the day. I take a shower, pour myself a cup of coffee, and then watch a little CNN to catch up on politics and headline news—there may something of interest to me in my isolated world.

My suit always reflects my mood, so I take time to select the right color and style. I will choose blue if I feel like communicating well; brown if I am feeling emotional and warm-hearted. If I am working a night shift, I usually wear black with a tie, most often red. I am a big fan of ties. I believe they are like someone's eyes—windows to the soul, expressing our mood or persona. As I dress, I think of what I have to accomplish for the day in terms of meetings or just pure operational work.

I usually roll into work at about 7 A.M. so I can see the graveyard bellman, morning valet, and cashiers. You learn a lot from the night crew. They witness a lot of the nonsense that happens during the midnight hours. I touch base with the front desk and the concierge to see if there any challenges with which to start the day. I then retreat to my office.

It never fails: I will have at least five voice mails and 10 e-mails. I listen to my voice mails and print my e-mails and look at my calendar to see a list of meetings. I then make a list of what I need to respond to and work on the pile of papers on my desk. I look at my 14-day forecast to see what events or groups we have in house, and touch base with my bell phone receptionist, who usually has good insight into the day's events.

My responsibilities include overseeing the functions of the bellman, elevator operators, doorman, valet runners, kiosk cashiers, mass transportation, parking control, and the concierge. I have two assistant guest services managers who arrive at 11 A.M. and 2.30 P.M. to cover the other shifts. I also have a parking operations supervisor and a cashier supervisor. We hold a weekly meeting so I can share the vision of the company, and my own. After all, I am not just a manager, I am a leader who must take people somewhere they would not otherwise go.

I spend most of my day in meetings. On Tuesday, I attend operations meetings. Our managing director and general manager speak to us about our financial position and goals for the quarter. They also bring up special highlights or events. We hear from sales and convention management about groups and catering for events. Room reservations personnel update us on their budget and on the number of rooms that will be occupied for the next two weeks in comparison to the forecasted occupancy. We then hear from accounting facilities, recreation, retail, guest services, and signature services. It is a very informative meeting, and gives me a good read on the mood of upper management.

I try to spend as much face time with my associates as possible, getting feedback and safety suggestions, and letting them vent frustrations. I try to win them over to the big picture. I spend a little time "schmoozing" clients who have porterages and deliveries to ensure that my team is doing their best to impress them. I attend preconvention meetings to discover what our clients are about. We identify their needs and provide them with the kind of guest service that makes their jaws drop.

The funny thing about modern technology is how dependent you become on it. Gone are the days of the good ol' boy network, when all you had to do was ask. Now you have to set up a meeting in Microsoft Outlook, send e-mails, fill out tons of paperwork, and constantly check your voice mail and e-mail inbox. The company has made it a little easier by supplying me with a Nextel phone, or "the leash," as we call it. This phone has walkie-talkie capability and allows the executive team to communicate on a network.

I know what you're thinking: It sounds tedious and problematic. Well, it is. The challenge of making it all come together is what is so appealing to me. I usually get so involved that I forget to eat lunch, unless one of my teammates pulls me away for a bite and engages me in some endless banter about work. I stock my office refrigerator with candy bars and various beverages because I usually don't make the time to eat. It just gets too busy.

My days typically end about 5 P.M. or 6 P.M. By then, I have passed on all information the night crews will need and delegated responsibilities to the two assistant guest services managers. I still have a big stack of papers to go through and file for tomorrow. I hop on my bicycle, ride by security to drop off my keys, and then I am off to go home and see my lovely wife. This is a day in a life of a guest services manager.

A more recent ratio to gauge a hotel rooms division's performance is the percentage of potential rooms revenue, which is calculated by determining potential rooms revenue and dividing the actual revenue by the potential revenue.

Larger hotels may have more than one night auditor; however, in smaller properties, these duties may be combined with night manager, desk, or night watchperson duties.

> ### Check Your Knowledge
> 1. Name the functions performed by the general manager.
> 2. What does an executive committee for a hotel of 300+ rooms look like?
> 3. What are the subdepartments that fall under the rooms division? What is each department's main function?

PROPERTY MANAGEMENT SYSTEMS

Property management systems (PMS) help hotels to accept, store, and retrieve guest reservations, guest history, requests, and billing arrangements electronically. The reservations part of the property management system also provides the reservations associates with information on the types of rooms available, features, views, and room rates. A list of expected arrivals can be easily generated. Before the advent of PMS, it took reservation associates much longer to learn the features and rates of each room and to make up the arrivals list.

A property management system contains a set of computer software packages capable of supporting a variety of activities in front- and back-office areas. The three most common front-office software packages are designed to assist front-office employees in performing functions related to the following tasks:

- Reservations management
- Rooms management
- Guest account management

Medium- to large-sized hotels typically have a computer with front- and back-office (accounting, control, purchasing, and conference and catering scheduling) applications. Smaller hotels use a microcomputer either as a standalone system or with a local area network to support the applications.

REVENUE MANAGEMENT

Revenue management is a demand-forecasting technique used to maximize room revenue that the hotel industry borrowed from the airlines. It is based on the economics of supply and demand, which means that prices rise when demand is strong and drop when demand is weak. Thus, the purpose of revenue management is to increase profitability. Naturally, management would like to sell every room at the highest **rack rate** (the "published" rate that the hotel would like to get for the room). However, this is not reality, and rooms are sold at discounts on the rack rate. Some examples would be the corporate or group rate, AAA rate, AARP rate, or government rate. In most hotels, only a small percentage of rooms are sold at rack rate. This is because of conventions and group rates and other promotional discounts that are necessary to stimulate demand. What revenue management does is to allocate the right type of capacity to the right guest at the right price so as to maximize revenue or yield per available room.

> **In most hotels, only a small percentage of rooms are sold at rack rate.**

Generally, the demand for room reservations follows the pattern of group bookings being made months or even years in advance of arrival and individual bookings, which mostly are made a few days before arrival. Figures 5–7 and 5–8 show the pattern of group and individual room reservations. Group reservations are booked months or years in advance, as Figure 5–8 shows. Revenue management will monitor reservations and, based on previous trends and current demand, determine the number and type of rooms to sell at what price to obtain the maximum revenue.

HTi — Discover the Methods of Setting Room Rates at the Front Office

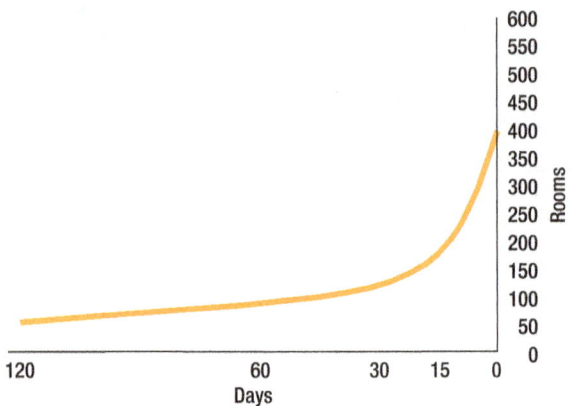

FIGURE 5–7 Individual Room Booking Reservations Curve.
(*Source:* Jay R. Schrock, personal correspondence, February 22, 2006.)

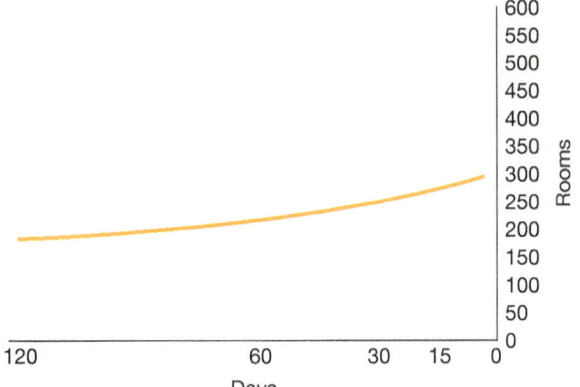

FIGURE 5–8 Group Booking Curve.

The curve in Figure 5–7 indicates the pattern of few reservations being made 120 days prior to arrival. Most of the individual room bookings are made in the last few days before arrival at the hotel. The revenue management program will monitor the demand and supply and recommend the number and type of rooms to sell for any given day, and the price for which to sell each room.

With revenue management, not only will the time before arrival be an important consideration in the pricing of guest rooms, but also the type of room to be occupied. For example, there could be a different price for a double, queen, or king room when used for single occupancy. This rate could be above the single rack rate. Similarly, double and multiple room occupancy would yield higher room rates. It works as follows:

Study the Importance of Yield Management at the Front Desk

Suppose a hotel has 300 rooms and a rack rate of $150. The average number of rooms sold is 200 per night at an average rate of $125. The yield for this property would be:

Room occupancy percentage = 200/300 = 66.6%
The rate achievement factor is:
$$\$125/\$150 = 0.833$$
and the yield would be:
$$0.666 \times 0.833 = 55.4\%$$

The application of revenue management in hotels is still being refined to take into consideration such factors as multiple nights' reservations and incremental food and beverage revenue. If the guest wants to arrive on a high-demand night and stay through several low-demand nights, what should the charge be?

Revenue management has some disadvantages. For instance, if a businessperson attempts to make a reservation at a hotel three days before arrival and the rate quoted in order to maximize revenue is considered too high, this person may decide to select another hotel and not even consider the first hotel when making future reservations.

Revenue per available room, or **rev par**, was developed by Smith Travel Research. It is calculated by dividing room revenue by the number of rooms available. For example, if room sales are $50,000 in one day for a hotel with 400 available rooms, then the formula would be $50,000 divided by 400, or $125. Hotels use rev par to see how they are doing compared to their competitive set of hotels.

According to Dr. Gabor Forgacs, the following are the top five revenue management mistakes hotels can make:

1. Believing that discounting is an efficient means of increasing revenue.
2. Believing that the correct price to charge for a room night is established costs and ROI expectations.
3. Believing that artificial intelligence is better than human intelligence.
4. Thinking that short-term goals are always higher in priority than long-term goals.
5. Counting revenue dollars as equal, regardless of the distribution channel they came through.[2]

Check Your Knowledge

1. What does PMS stand for? What functions does this system perform?
2. What is revenue management? How is revenue management applied in the hotel industry?

Reservations

Today, many hotels, especially chain hotels, have reservation centers that take guest calls or online reservations, and the individual properties have a reservations person who constantly interacts with the central reservations office to adjust the rates to be charged. Reservations are the first contact for the guest or person making the reservation for the guest. Although the contact may be by telephone, a distinct impression of the hotel is registered with the guest. This calls for exceptional telephone manners and telemarketing skills. Because some guests may be shopping for the best value, it is essential to sell the hotel by emphasizing its advantages over the competition.

Communications CBX or PBX

The communications CBX or PBX (the telecommunications department) includes in-house communications; guest communications, such as pagers and radios; voice mail; faxes; messages; and emergency center. Guests often have their first contact with the hotel by telephone. This underlines the importance of prompt and courteous attention to all calls, because first impressions last.

The communications department is a vital part of the smooth running of the hotel. It is also a profit center, because hotels generally add a 50 percent charge to all long-distance calls placed from guest rooms. Local calls cost about $0.75 to $1.25, plus tax.

> **❝ The Internet has created a major impact on lodging operations as online booking continues to increase. You have a major advantage in today's world of lodging if you have the capacity to provide online booking. ❞**
>
> James Wright, *Wrights Place Inn*, Providence, RI

Communications operates 24 hours a day, in much the same way as the front office does, in three shifts. It is essential that this department be staffed with people who are trained to be calm under pressure and who follow emergency procedures.

Guest services

Because first impressions are very important to the guest, the guest service or uniformed staff has a special responsibility. The *guest services* department is headed by a guest services manager, who may also happen to be the bell captain. The staff consists of door attendants and bellpersons and the concierge, although in some hotels the concierge reports directly to the front-office manager.

Door attendants are the hotel's unofficial greeters. Dressed in impressive uniforms, they greet guests at the hotel front door, assist in opening/closing automobile doors, removing luggage from the trunk, hailing taxis, keeping the hotel entrance clear of vehicles, and giving guests information about the hotel and the local area in a courteous and friendly way. People in this position generally receive many gratuities (tips); in fact, years ago, the position was handed down from father to son or sold for several thousand dollars. Rumor has it that this is one of the most lucrative positions in the hotel, even more than the general manager's.

The bellperson's main function is to escort guests and transport luggage to their rooms. Bellpersons also need to be knowledgeable about the local area and all facets of the hotel and its services. Because they have so much guest contact, they need a pleasant, outgoing personality. The bellperson explains the services of the hotel and points out the features of the room (lighting, TV, air conditioning, telephone, wake-up calls, laundry and valet service, room service and restaurants, and the pool and health spa).

Concierge

The concierge is a uniformed employee of the hotel who has her or his own separate desk in the lobby or on special concierge floors. The concierge is a separate department from the front-office associates and cashiers. Until 1936, a concierge was not an employee of the hotel but an independent entrepreneur who purchased a position from the hotel and paid the salaries, if any, of his or her uniformed subordinates.

Luxury hotels in most cities have concierges who assist guests with a broad range of services that include:

- Tickets to the hottest shows in town, even for the very evening on the day they are requested. Naturally, the guest pays up to about $250 per ticket.
- A table at a restaurant that has no reservations available.
- Advice on local restaurants, activities, attractions, amenities, and facilities.
- VIP's messages and special requests, such as shopping.

Concierges assist guests with a variety of services.

HTi Learn about the Responsibilities of the Concierge at the Lighthouse Hotel

What will a concierge do for a guest? Almost anything, *Condé Nast Traveler* learned from concierges at hotels around the world. The most unusual requests included:

1. Some Japanese tourists staying at the Palace Hotel in Madrid decided to bring bullfighting home. Their concierge found bulls for sale, negotiated the bulls' purchase, and had them shipped to Tokyo.

2. After watching a guest pace the lobby, the concierge of a London hotel asked the pacer if he could help. The guest was to be married within the hour, but his best man had been detained. Because he was dressed up anyway, the concierge volunteered to stand in.

The concierge needs in-depth knowledge of the hotel, its services, the city, and even international details. Many concierges speak several languages; most important of all, they must want to help people and have a pleasant, outgoing personality. The concierges' organization, which promotes high professional and ethical standards, is the UPPGH (Union Professionelle des Portiers des Grand Hotels). This is commonly called the *Clefs d'Or* (Golden Keys) because of the crossed gold-key insignia concierges usually wear on the lapels of their uniforms.

Housekeeping

The department with the greatest number of employees is housekeeping. Some 50 percent of hotel employees work in this department. According to Sudhir Andrews, author of *Hotel Housekeeping*:

> A hotel survives on the sale of rooms, food, and beverage, and other minor operating services, such as laundry, health clubs, etc. Of these, the sale of rooms constitutes a minimum of 50 percent. In other words, the hotel's largest margin of profit comes from room sales because a room, once made, can be sold over and over

again. A good hotel operation ensures optimal room sales to the maximum profit.[3]

The executive housekeeper or director of services is the person in charge. Duties and responsibilities call for exceptional leadership, organization, motivation, and commitment to maintaining high standards. The logistics of servicing large numbers of rooms on a daily basis can be challenging.

HTi Experience a Typical Day in Housekeeping

The importance of the housekeeping department is underlined by guest surveys that consistently rank the cleanliness of rooms as number one.

The four major areas of responsibilities for the executive housekeeper are:

1. Leadership of people, equipment, and supplies
2. Cleanliness and servicing the guest rooms and public areas
3. Operating the department according to financial guidelines prescribed by the general manager
4. Keeping records

Perhaps the biggest challenge of an executive housekeeper is the leadership of all the employees in the department. Further, these employees are often of different nationalities. Depending on the size of the hotel, the executive housekeeper is assisted by a housekeeping manager and one or more housekeeping supervisors,

Learn How to Create a Housekeeping Schedule

who in turn supervise a number of room attendants (see Figure 5–9). The housekeeping manager manages the housekeeping office. The first important daily task of this position is to break out the hotel into sections for allocation to the room attendants' schedules.

The rooms of the hotel are listed on the floor master. If the room is vacant, nothing is written next to the room number. If the guest is expected to check out, then SC will be written next to the room number. A stayover will have SS, on hold is AH, out of order is OO, and VIPs are highlighted in colors according to the amenities required.

If 258 rooms are occupied and 10 of these are suites (which count as two rooms), then the total number of rooms to be allocated to room attendants is 268 (minus any no-shows). The remaining total is then divided by 17, the number of rooms that each attendant is expected to make up.

Total number of rooms occupied	258
Add 10 for the suites	10
Total number of rooms and suites occupied	268
Less any no-shows	3
	265

Divide 265 by 17 (the number of rooms each attendant services) = 16 (the number of attendants required for that day)

> **The importance of the housekeeping department is underlined by guest surveys that consistently rank cleanliness of rooms number one.**

The housekeeping associates clean and service between 15 and 20 rooms per day depending on the individual hotel's characteristics. Servicing a room takes longer in older hotels than it does in newer properties. Also, service time depends on the number of check-out rooms versus stayovers, because servicing check-outs takes longer. Housekeeping associates begin their day at 8:00 A.M., reporting to the executive or assistant executive housekeeper. They are assigned a block of rooms and given room keys, for which they must sign and then return before going off duty.

The executive housekeeper is responsible for a substantial amount of record keeping. In addition to the scheduling and evaluation of employees, an inventory of all guest rooms and public area furnishings must be accurately maintained with the record of refurbishment. Most of the hotel's maintenance work orders are initiated by the housekeepers, who report the maintenance work order. Many hotels now have a computer link-up between housekeeping and engineering and maintenance to speed the process. Guests expect their rooms to be fully functional, especially at today's prices. Housekeeping maintains a perpetual inventory of guest room amenities, cleaning supplies, and linens.

Amazingly, after only about 2,000 years, hotels have realized that we spend most of our time on a bed. So, they are introducing wonder beds that will let us sleep in—and even

FIGURE 5–9 Housekeeping Personnel Organization Chart.

miss our wake-up call (now, there's another lawsuit!). Around the country, guest rooms are getting a makeover that includes new mattresses with devices that allow one side to be set firmer than the other or on an incline. Other room amenities include new high-definition flat screen TVs, Wi-Fi services, and room cards that activate elevators.

> **Check Your Knowledge**
> 1. What is a PBX or CBX?
> 2. What departments are included in guest services?
> 3. Name the characteristics that an executive housekeeper should possess.

Security/loss prevention

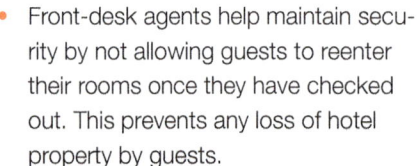

Providing guest protection and loss prevention is essential for any lodging establishment, regardless of size. Violent crime is a growing problem, and protecting guests from bodily harm has been defined by the courts as a reasonable expectation from hotels. The security/loss division is responsible for maintaining security alarm systems and implementing procedures aimed at protecting the personal property of guests and employees and the hotel itself. A comprehensive security plan must include the following elements:

Explore the Responsibilities of the Security Officer at the Lighthouse Hotel

Security Officers

- Make regular rounds of the hotel premises, including guest floors, corridors, public and private function rooms, parking areas, and offices.
- Observe suspicious behavior and take appropriate action, investigate incidents, and cooperate with local law enforcement agencies.

Equipment

- Two-way radios between security staff are common.
- Closed-circuit television cameras are used in out-of-the-way corridors and doorways, as well as in food, liquor, and storage areas.
- Smoke detectors and fire alarms, which increase the safety of the guests, are a requirement in every part of the hotel by law.
- Electronic key cards offer superior room security. Key cards typically do not list the name of the hotel or the room number. So if lost or stolen, the key is not easily traceable. In addition, most key card systems record every entry in and out of the room on the computer for any further reference.

Safety Procedures

- Front-desk agents help maintain security by not allowing guests to reenter their rooms once they have checked out. This prevents any loss of hotel property by guests.
- Security officers should be able to gain access to guest rooms, store rooms, and offices at all times.
- Security staff develop catastrophe plans to ensure staff and guest safety and to minimize direct and indirect costs from disaster. The catastrophe plan reviews insurance policies, analyzes physical facilities, and evaluates possible disaster scenarios, including whether they have a high or low probability of occurring. Possible disaster scenarios may include fires, bomb threats, earthquakes, floods, hurricanes, and blizzards. The well-prepared hotel will develop formal policies to deal with any possible scenario and will train employees to implement chosen procedures should they become necessary.

For More on Disaster Recovery, Read the Security Department Training Manual

Identification Procedures

- Identification cards with photographs should be issued to all employees.
- Name tags for employees who are likely to have contact with guests not only project a friendly image for the property, but are also useful for security reasons.

Food and beverage management

Discover the Diverse World of Food and Beverage Operations

In the hospitality industry, the food and beverage division is led by the *director of food and beverage*, who reports to the general manager and is responsible for the efficient and effective operation of the following departments:

- Kitchen/Catering/Banquet
- Restaurants/Room Service/Minibars
- Lounges/Bars/Stewarding

A typical food and beverage director's day might include the following:

8:00 A.M. Check messages and read logs from outlets and security. Tour outlets, especially the family restaurant (a quick inspection).
Check breakfast buffet, reservations, and shift manager.
Check daily specials.
Check room service.
Check breakfast service and staffing.
Visit executive chef and purchasing director.
Visit executive steward's office to ensure that all equipment is ready.
Visit banquet service office to check on daily events and coffee break sequence.

10:00 A.M. Work on current projects: new summer menu, pool outlet opening, conversion of a current restaurant with a new concept, remodeling of ballroom foyer, installation of new walk-in freezer, analysis of current profit-and-loss (P&L) statements. Plan weekly food and beverage department meetings.

11:45 A.M. Visit kitchen to observe lunch service and check the "12:00 line," including banquets.
Confer with executive chef.
Check restaurants and banquet luncheon service.
Have working lunch in employee cafeteria with executive chef, director of purchasing, or director of catering.

1:30 P.M. Visit human resources to discuss current incidents.

2:30 P.M. Check messages and return calls. Telemarket to attract catering and convention business.
Conduct hotel daily menu meeting.

3:00 P.M. Go to special projects/meetings.
Tour cocktail lounges.
Check for staffing.
Review any current promotions.
Check entertainment lineup.

6:00 P.M. Check special food and beverage requests/requirements of any VIPs staying at the hotel.
Tour kitchen.
Review and taste.

8:00 P.M. Review dinner specials.
Check the restaurant and lounges.

A food and beverage director's typical day—if there is such a thing!—starts at 8:00 A.M. and ends between 6 and 8:00 P.M., unless early or very late events are scheduled, in which case the working day is even longer. Usually, the food and beverage director works Monday through Saturday. If there are special events on Sunday, then she or he works on Sunday and takes Monday off. In a typical week, Saturdays are used to catch up on reading or specific projects.

Kitchen

A hotel kitchen is under the charge of the *executive chef* or chef in smaller or medium-sized properties. This person, in turn, is responsible to the director of food and beverage for the efficient and effective operation of kitchen food production. The desired outcome is to exceed guest expectations in the quality and quantity of food, its presentation, taste, and portion size, and to ensure that hot food is served hot and cold food is served cold. The executive chef operates the kitchen in accordance with company policy and desired financial results.

Hotel restaurants

A hotel may have several restaurants or no restaurant at all; the number and type of restaurants varies as well. A major chain hotel generally has two restaurants: a signature or upscale formal restaurant and a casual coffee-shop type of restaurant. These restaurants cater to both hotel guests and the general public. In recent years, because of increased guest expectations, hotels have placed greater emphasis on food and beverage preparation and service. As a result, there is an increasing need for professionalism on the part of hotel personnel. Hotel restaurants are run by restaurant managers in much the same way as other restaurants.

A hotel restaurant ready for guests.

Bars

Visit the Tiki Bar to Learn about Safe Beverage Service

Hotel bars allow guests to relax while sipping a cocktail after a hectic day. This opportunity to socialize for business or pleasure is advantageous for both guests and the hotel. Because the profit percentage on all beverages is higher than on food items, bars are an important revenue source for the food and beverage departments. The cycle of beverages from ordering, receiving, storing, issuing, bar stocking, serving, and guest billing is complex; however, unlike restaurant meals, a beverage can be held over if not sold.

Stewarding department

The *chief steward* is responsible to the director of food and beverage for the following functions:

- Cleaning the back of the house (all the backstage areas that hotel guests do not see)
- Maintaining clean glassware, china, and serviceware for the food and beverage outlets
- Maintaining strict inventory control and monthly stock check
- Maintaining dishwashing machines
- Taking inventory of chemical stock
- Sanitizing the kitchen, banquet isles, storerooms, walk-ins/freezers, and all equipment
- Undertaking pest control and coordinating with exterminating company
- Forecasting labor and cleaning supplies

In some hotels, the steward's department is responsible for keeping the kitchen(s) clean. This is generally done at night to prevent disruption of the food production operation. A more limited cleaning is done in the afternoon between the lunch and dinner services. The chief steward's job can be an enormous and thankless task. In hotels, this involves cleaning up for several hundred people three times a day. Just trying to keep track of everything can be a headache. Some hotels have different patterns of glasses, china, and cutlery for each outlet. The casual dining room frequently has an informal theme, catering and banqueting a more formal one, and the signature restaurant very formal place settings. It is difficult to ensure that all the pieces are returned to the correct places. It is also difficult to prevent both guests and employees from taking souvenirs. Strict inventory control and constant vigilance help keep pilferage to a minimum.

If you were working in the development office of a major hotel corporation, what information would you need to obtain in order to consider the development of a AAA three-diamond property in a town near you?

Catering Department

Throughout the world's cultural and social evolution, numerous references have been made to "breaking of bread" together. Feasts or banquets are one way to show one's hospitality. Frequently, hosts attempted to outdo one another with the extravagance of their feasts. Today, occasions for celebrations, banquets, and catering include the following:

Explore a Career in Event Planning: Visit the Nunaley Meeting Room

- State banquets, when countries' leaders honor visiting royalty and heads of state
- National days
- Embassy receptions and banquets
- Business and association conventions and banquets
- Gala charity balls
- Company dinner dances
- Weddings

Catering has a broader scope than banquets. Banquets refer to groups of people who eat together at one time and in one place. Catering includes a variety of occasions when people may eat at varying times. However, the terms are often used interchangeably.

For example, catering departments in large, city center hotels may service the following events in just one day:

- A *Fortune* 500 company's annual shareholders meeting
- An international loan-signing ceremony
- A fashion show
- A product launch—like a new automobile
- A convention
- Several sales and board meetings
- Private luncheons and dinner parties
- Weddings

Naturally, each of these requires different and special treatment. Hotels in smaller cities may cater the local chamber of commerce meeting, a high school prom, a local company party, a regional sales meeting, a professional workshop, and a small exhibition. Catering may be subdivided into on-premise and off-premise. In off-premise catering, the event is catered away from the hotel. The food may be prepared either in the hotel or at the event.

Hotels generally have specialized catering salespeople who may operate independently from the rooms sales but obviously in cooperation with the hotel's sales team. Over the years, catering sales specialists gather lots of clients and contacts that are vital to bringing in business to fill the function space.

Catering Event Order

A *catering event order* (CEO), which may also be called a banquet event order (BEO), is prepared/completed for each function to inform not only the client but also the hotel personnel about essential information (what needs to happen and when) to ensure a successful event.

The CEO is prepared based on correspondence with the client and notes taken during the property visits. Figure 5–10 shows a CEO and lists the room's layout and decor; times of arrival; if there are any VIPs and what special attention is required for them, such as reception; bar times; types of beverages and service; cash or credit bar; time of meal service; the menu; wines; and service details. The catering manager or director confirms the details with the client. Usually, two copies are sent, one for the client to sign and return and one for the client to keep.

Catering Services Manager

The *catering services manager* (CSM) has the enormous responsibility of delivering higher-than-expected service levels to guests. The CSM is in charge of the function from the time the client is introduced to the CSM by the director of catering or catering manager. This job is very demanding: not only do the functions have to be set up, served and cleared, but several functions frequently occur simultaneously. Timing and logistics are crucial to the success of

A catering manager and chef ready for a function.

SHERATON GRANDE TORREY PINES
BANQUET EVENT ORDER

POST AS: WELCOME BREAKFAST
EVENT NAME: MEETING
GROUP: CROCKER AND ASSOCIATES
ADDRESS: 41 MAIN ST
BOWLING GREEN, OHIO 43218
PHONE: (619) 635-4627
FAX: (619) 635-4528
GROUP CONTACT: Dr. Ken Crocker
ON-SITE-CONTACT: same

CHERI WALTER

BILLING: DIRECT BILL

Amount Received:

DAY	DATE	TIME	FUNCTION	ROOM	EXP	GTE	SET	RENT
Wed	January 25, 2007	7:30 A.M. – 12:00 P.M.	Meeting	Palm Garden	50			250.00

BAR SET UP:

N/A

MENU:

7:30 A.M. CONTINENTAL BREAKFAST

Freshly Squeezed Orange Juice, Grapefruit Juice, and Tomato Juice
Assortment of Bagels, Muffins, and Mini Brioche
Cream Cheese, Butter, and Preserves
Display of Sliced Seasonal Fruits
Individual Fruit Yogurt
Coffee, Tea, and Decaffeinated Coffee

PRICE: $9.95

11:00 A.M. BREAK

Refresh Beverages as needed

WINE:

FLORAL:

MUSIC:

AUDIO VISUAL:
–OVERHEAD PROJECTOR/SCREEN
–FLIPCHART/MARKERS
–VCR/MONITORS

PARKING:

HOSTING PARKING, PLEASE PROVIDE VOUCHERS

LINEN:
HOUSE

SETUP:
–CLASSROOM-STYLE SEATING
–HEAD TABLE FOR 2 PEOPLE
–APPROPRIATE COFFEE BREAK SETUP
–(1) 6' TABLE FOR REGISTRATION AT ENTRANCE WITH 2 CHAIRS, 1 WASTEBASKET

All food and beverage prices are subject to an 18% service charge and 7% state tax. Guarantee figures, cancellations, changes must be given 72 hours prior or the number of guests expected will be considered the guarantee. To confirm the above arrangements, this contract must be signed and returned.

ENGAGOR SIGNATURE _____ DATE _____

BEO # 003069

FIGURE 5–10 CEO and Special Details.

the operation. Sometimes, there are only a few minutes between the end of a day meeting and the beginning of the reception for a dinner dance. The job of a CSM can include hiring, training and motivating staff, organizing staff rotas, overseeing the budget, and ordering supplies for forthcoming menus. The most important part of the job is achieving good quality at low cost and maintaining high standards of hygiene and customer satisfaction.[4]

Room Service/In-Room Dining

The term *room service* has for some time referred to all service to hotel guest rooms. Recently, some hotels have changed the phrase "room service" to "in-room dining" to present the service as more upscale. The intention is to bring the dining experience to the room with quality food and beverage service. Generally, the larger the hotel and the higher the room rate, the more likely it is that a hotel will offer room service. Economy and several midpriced hotels avoid the costs of operating room service by having vending machines on each floor and food items like pizza or Chinese food delivered by local restaurants.

Watch Room Service in Action: Visit the Hutchinson Hotel

Energy Star®

Energy Star is a joint program of the U.S. Environmental Protection Agency and the U.S. Department of Energy. The "energy star" reflects an innovative energy rating system and provides a trustworthy label on thousands of products that use less energy. Fluorescent bulbs and digital guestroom thermostats ensure energy efficiency.

Green Seal

Founded in 1989, Green Seal is a nonprofit organization that provides science-based environmental certification standards that are credible, transparent, and essential in an increasingly educated and competitive marketplace. It identifies and promotes products and services that cause less toxic pollution and waste, conserve resources and habitats, and minimize ozone effects. Green Seal–approved cleaning chemicals are used in the laundry room and on housekeeping carts. The pest control program has switched to bio-friendly chemicals.

Recycled Content

The U.S. Environmental Protection Agency's comprehensive procurement guidelines (CPG) encourages the use of materials recovered through recycling with the goal to reduce the amount of disposed waste. One hundred percent postconsumable recycled products are used for all toilet paper, tissues, paper towels, office printing paper, paper coffee cups, and paper napkins.

Hotel Recycling

Recycling is encouraged by providing an additional receptacle in guest rooms for glass, paper, aluminum, and plastic. A local elementary school takes the paper; the hotel transports the rest of the items to a local recycling center.

Water Conservation

Available fresh water amounts to .5 percent of all water on earth. Global water consumption doubles every 20 years, and the current demand for water exceeds supply by 17 percent. Hotels go through lots of water, so aerators are installed on every device that moves water and on low-flow shower heads and toilets. Laundry washers employ a system that combines the detergent with water before being pumped into the washers. This device reduces water use by 30 percent for the washers. Guests are encouraged to reuse their towels; linens are not changed during normal length stays unless requested by the guest.

> **Eco-efficiency helps hotels provide better service while using fewer resources.**

Bathroom Amenities

A partnership with Aveda provides ecofriendly individual amenities. Bulk shower dispensers have been installed in each shower to avoid the use the individual products. All unused, leftover amenities are donated to a community center.

Breakfast

Leftover food is collected and given to a local organic farmer for composting. Ceramic plates and glassware (verses plastic) are

Sustainable Lodging Operations

Ecoefficiency, also generally termed "green," is based on the concept of creating more goods and services while using fewer resources and creating less waste and pollution. In other words, it means doing more with less. So what does this have to do with your bottom line? It helps hotels provide better service with fewer resources: reducing the materials and energy intensity of goods and services lowers the hotel's ecological impact and improves the bottom line. It's a key driver for overall business performance.[5] Figure 5–11 shows a model for the implementation of sustainable lodging practices.

Triple bottom line, sometimes called the TBL or 3P approach (people, planet and profits), requires thinking in three dimensions, not one. It takes into account ecological and societal performance in addition to financial. Today, quantifiable environmental impacts include consumption of finite resources, energy usage, water quality and availability, and pollution emitted. Social impacts include community health, employee and guest safety, education quality and diversity.[6]

Sustainable lodging, also known as green hotels, has become a powerful movement. The American Hotel and Lodging Association (AH&LA) and various state associations are leading the way with operational suggestions for best practices that lead to a green certification. Both corporations and independent properties are increasingly becoming greener in their operating practices. Sustainable Lodging & Restaurant–certified facilities develop goals and identify people in their organizations to find new opportunities to improve their operations through education, employee ideas, and guest feedback.

J. D. Power and Associates' 2009 North America Hotel Guest Satisfaction Index Study, which surveyed over 66,000 guests who stayed in North American hotels between May 2008 and June 2009, found that guests' awareness of their hotel's green programs increased significantly in 2009. Sixty-six percent of guests said they were aware of their hotel's conservation efforts, up from 57 percent the previous year.[7]

Ray Hobbs, a member of EcoRooms & EcoSuites' board of advisors and a certified auditor for Green Globe International, said, "In the hospitality industry, we're seeing a wave of new government mandates stating that employees can only stay in or host meetings in green hotels. But there are only 23 states with official green certification programs, and the industry is still attempting to find the certification process that best serves its needs."[8]

Being green is also financially good for certified properties. By saving energy and water, reducing waste and eliminating toxic chemicals, green properties lower their operating costs, which allows them to provide enhanced services to their guests and a healthier environment for both their guests and employees.

Sustainable properties are doing the following to become more sustainable in their operating practices:[9]

Reducing energy needs by:

Installing motion sensors in public areas and occupancy sensors in guestrooms

Installing energy efficient lighting, dimmers, and timers to reduce energy consumption

Installing LED exit signs

Installing Energy Star appliances

Increasing building insulation

Using natural day lighting whenever possible

Tightening the property shell, with added/better insulation, eliminating leaks, replacing windows

Conserving water by:

Installing aerators on faucets

Installing water diverters on existing toilets or low-flow toilets

Installing low-flow showerheads

Implementing towel and linen reuse programs

Landscaping with native plants

Using timers/moisture sensors in landscape watering

Changing lawn watering to encourage deeper root growth

Reducing waste by:

Providing recycling areas for guests and staff

Purchasing postconsumer recycled paper and buying in bulk

Serving meals with cloth napkins and reusable china and dinnerware

Using refillable soap/shampoo dispensers in bathrooms

Recycling usable furniture, etc. at "dump stores" or through charity

Reusing old towels and linens as cleaning rags

Asking vendors to minimize packaging

Recycling cooking grease

Composting food and lawn waste

Reducing hazardous waste by:

Properly disposing of fluorescent lighting, computers, and other electronic equipment

Participating in local hazardous waste collection days

Using low VOC (volatile organic compound) paints, carpets, and glues

Using rechargeable batteries

Using energy-efficient shuttle vans

Using environmentally friendly cleaning products

Another hotel company has a plan for its sustainability:[10]

Our "Eco-Plan," broken down by specific components

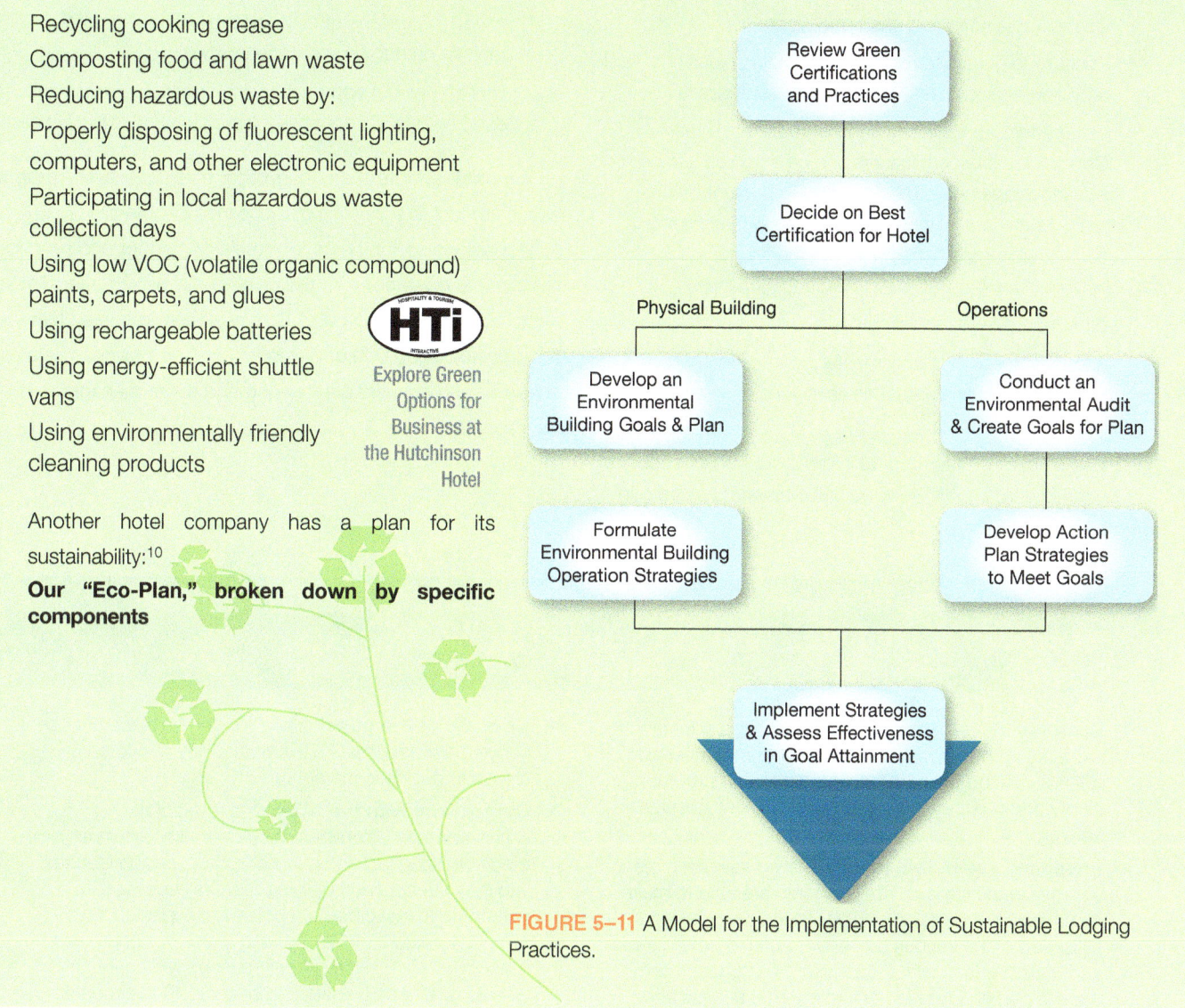

FIGURE 5–11 A Model for the Implementation of Sustainable Lodging Practices.

used; all food condiments are purchased and presented in bulk instead of individual packaging. Organic options are presented when the seasons allow.

Lounge

Organic wine choices are offered at the lobby bar.

Guest Shuttle

Free shuttle service to area attractions is provided; the vehicle is either a hybrid car or a 15-passenger van for bigger groups.

Guest Bikes

Bicycles are available for guest use in warm weather. Excellent bike route maps are provided for those who want to explore the city on two wheels.

Coffee Shop

All coffee drinks made in the lobby coffee bar use organic, fair-trade certified, and Rainforest Alliance–approved coffee.

Greening the Guestroom

Guest rooms offer an opportunity for greening. Sustainable hotels do the following:[11]

- Give guests an option to have the towels and linens changed every other day, or less frequently, rather than every day. Surveys have shown that more than 90 percent of guests like the option.
- Encourage staff to close drapes and turn off lights and air conditioning when rooms are unoccupied.
- Install water-efficient fixtures, such as showerheads, aerators, and low-flow toilets in each room.

- Use refillable soap and shampoo dispensers.
- Encourage guests to recycle by providing clearly marked recycling bins for cans, bottles, and newspapers.
- Install energy-efficient lighting fixtures in each room. Compact fluorescent fixtures can be screwed into many existing lamps and ceiling fixtures. To prevent theft, many hotels are installing new fixtures with compact fluorescent lamps hard-wired into the fixture.
- Consider purchasing Energy Star®–labeled TVs and other energy-efficient appliances.
- Clean rooms with environmental cleaners to improve indoor air quality and reduce emissions of volatile organic chemicals.
- Use placards in the room to inform your guests about your "green" efforts. (Why not tell them that a hotel can save 13.5 gallons of freshwater by choosing not to replace bath towels and linen daily?)
- Use an opt-out approach to linen and towel reuse (this can save a 250-room hotel more than $15,000 per year).

If a hotel adopts these and other measures every year, it would amount to a savings of thousands of dollars.

Consider also the gains for hotels that adopt and practice sustainable operations. In the case of the Willard Inter-Continental hotel in Washington, D.C., it has been estimated that the hotel gained $800,000 of incremental group business as a result of having sustainable meeting and event management at the property.[12]

TRENDS in LODGING OPERATIONS

- **Diversity of workforce:** Experts project a substantial increase in the number of women and minorities who will not only be taking hourly paid positions, but will also work in supervisory and management positions as well.
- **Increased use of technology:** Individuals make reservations via the Internet. Travel agents are able to make reservations at more properties. There is increasing simplification of the various property management systems and their interface with POS systems. In guest room, there is demand for high-speed Internet access and Wi-Fi services.
- Technology enhances guest services and control costs in all areas of the hotel, including guest ordering and payment, food production, refrigeration, marketing, management, control, and communication.
- **Continued quest for increases in productivity:** As pressure mounts from owners and management companies, hotel managers are looking for innovative ways to increase productivity and to measure productivity by sales per employee.
- Revenue management increases profit by effective pricing of room inventory.
- **Greening of hotels and guest rooms:** This includes an increase in recycling and the use of environmentally friendly products, amenities, and biodegradable detergents and other topics discussed in the chapter.
- **Security:** A survey by the International Hotel Association indicated that guests continue to be concerned about personal security. Hotels are constantly working to improve guest security. For example, one hotel has instituted a women-only floor with concierge and security.
- **Diversity of the guest:** More women travelers are occupying hotel rooms. This is particularly due to an increase in business travel.
- **Compliance with the ADA:** As a result of the Americans with Disabilities Act (ADA), all hotels must modify existing facilities and incorporate design features into new construction that make areas accessible to persons with disabilities. All hotels are expected to have at least 4 percent of their parking space designated as "handicapped." These spaces must be wide enough for wheelchairs to be unloaded from a van. Guest rooms must be fitted with equipment that can be manipulated by persons with disabilities. Restrooms must be wide enough to accommodate wheelchairs. Ramps should be equipped with handrails, and meeting rooms must be equipped with special listening systems for those with hearing impairments.
- Hotel companies are trying to persuade guests to book rooms via the company Web site. When guests use an Internet site like hotels.com, the hotel must pay about $20 for each booking.
- Hotels are using branded restaurants instead of operating their own restaurants.
- Hotel restaurants are using system-wide, standardized, casual menus with some regional variations.
- Hotel restaurants are adopting themes (for example, Northern Italian).
- Many hotels are converting one of their beverage outlets into a sports-themed bar.
- Technology is being used to enhance guest services and control costs in all areas, including guest ordering and payment, food production, refrigeration, marketing, management control, and communication.

CASE STUDY

Overbooked: The Housekeeping Perspective

It is no secret that in all hotels, the director of housekeeping must be able to react quickly and efficiently to any unexpected circumstances that arise. Jamie Gibson, executive housekeeper at The Regency, usually starts his workday at 8:00 A.M. with a departmental meeting. These meetings help him and other employees visualize their goals for the day. On a particularly busy day, Gibson arrives at work and is told that four of the housekeepers have called in sick. This presents a serious challenge for the hotel because it is overbooked and has all of its 400 rooms to service.

DISCUSSION QUESTION

1. What should Jamie do to maintain the hotel's standards and ensure that all guest rooms are serviced?

CAREER INFORMATION

HOTEL OPERATIONS

Hotel management is probably the most popular career choice among seniors who are graduating from hospitality educational programs. The reason for this popularity is tied to the elegant image of hotels and the prestige associated with being a general manager or vice president of a major lodging chain. Managing a hotel is a complex balancing act that involves keeping employees, guests, and owners satisfied while overseeing a myriad of departments, including reservations, front desk, housekeeping, maintenance, accounting, food and beverage, security, concierge, and sales.

To be a GM, a person must understand all of the various functions of a hotel and how their interrelationship makes up the lodging environment. The first step down this career path is to get a job in a hotel while you are in college. Once you become proficient in one area, volunteer to work in another. A solid foundation of broad-based experience in the hotel will be priceless when you start your lodging career. Some excellent areas to consider are the front desk, night audit, food and beverage, and maintenance. Another challenging but very important place to gain experience is in housekeeping. It has been said that if you can manage the housekeeping department, the rest of lodging management is easy. An internship with a large hotel chain property can also be a powerful learning experience. There is simply no substitute for being part of a team that operates a lodging property with several hundred rooms.

You may hear about graduates being offered "direct placement" or "manager in training" (MIT) positions. (There are several name variations for these programs.) Direct placement means that when you graduate, you are offered a specific position at a property. An MIT program exposes you to several areas of the hotel over a period of time. Then you are given an assignment based on your performance during training. Neither one is better than the other from a career standpoint.

Another important consideration of a lodging career is your wardrobe. In a hotel environment, people are judged based on their appearance. A conservative, professional image is a key to success. Clothes are the tools of the lodging professional's trade and they are not inexpensive. Begin investing in clothes while you are in school. Buy what you can afford, but buy items of quality. Stay away from trendy or flashy clothes that will quickly be out of fashion.

When you take a position, you can expect to work around 50 hours per week. The times you work may vary. You can expect to have a starting salary of between $30,000 and $34,000. Some hotel chains will assist with moving expenses and may even offer a one-time signing bonus. However, try not to focus too much on the money; instead try to find a company that you feel comfortable with and will allow you opportunities for advancement. Figure 5–12 shows a career path in lodging management.

Bob Weil, director of food and beverage, Longboat Key Club and Resort, Sarasota, Florida, offers the following advice: "Be passionate about what you do and be in touch with the people you work with. I tour the property every day to get a feeling for the challenges our team may have—it's important to be in tune with what's going on". Another piece of advice is to never stop cooking and to maintain your fitness so that you can be a high-energy person. Students can expect many rewards in the hospitality business, but remember, it's a long journey, a process. You need to experience all levels in order to become a complete leader.

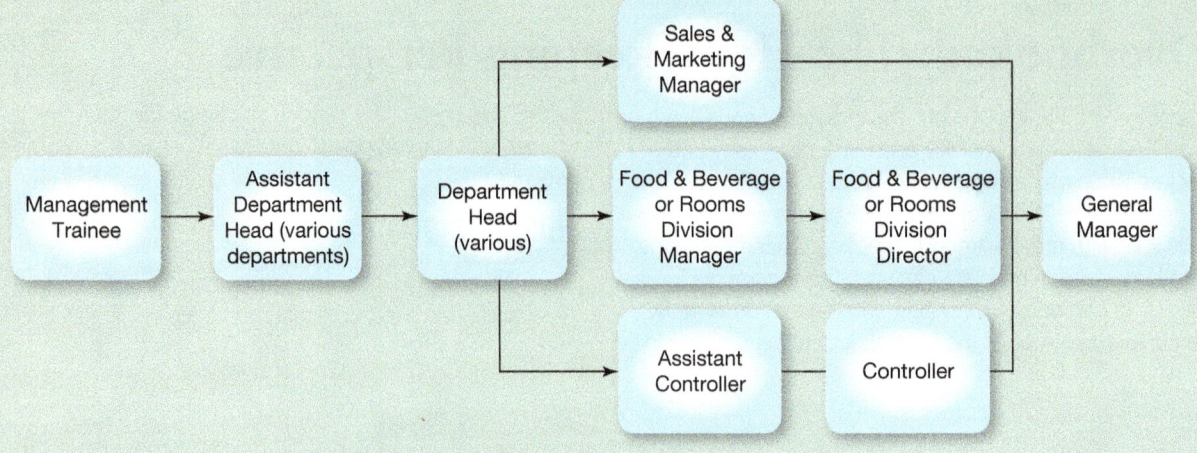

FIGURE 5–12 A Career Path in Lodging Management.

Related Web Sites

www.hoteljobs.com/—Careers in lodging
www.hyatt.com/—Hyatt Hotels
www.marriott.com/—Marriott International

Courtesy of Charlie Adams.

SUMMARY

1. A big hotel is run by a general manager and an executive committee, which includes the key executives of all the major departments, such as rooms division, food and beverage, marketing, sales, engineering, and human resources.
2. The general manager represents the hotel and is responsible for its profitability and performance. Because of increased job consolidation, he or she also is expected to attract business and to empathize with the cultures of both guests and employees.
3. The rooms division department consists of front office, reservations, housekeeping, concierge, guest services, and communications.
4. The front desk, as the center of the hotel, sells rooms and maintains balanced guest accounts, which are completed daily by the night auditor. The front desk constantly must meet guests' needs by offering services such as mailing, faxing, and messages.
5. The property management system, centralized reservations, and revenue management have enabled a hotel to work more efficiently and to increase profitability and guest satisfaction.
6. The communications department, room service, and guest services (such as door attendants, bellpersons, and the concierge) are vital parts of the personality of a hotel.
7. Housekeeping is the largest department of the hotel. The executive housekeeper is in charge of inventory, cleaning, employees, and accident and loss prevention. The laundry may be cleaned directly in the hotel or by a hired laundry service.
8. The electric room key and closed-circuit television cameras are basic measures provided to protect the guests and their property.
9. The food and beverage division is led by the director of food and beverage, who is responsible for the efficient and effective operation of all departments: kitchen, catering, restaurants, bars, stewarding, and room service.
10. A hotel kitchen is the responsibility of the executive chef, who is in charge of the quality and quantity of food, organization of the kitchen and his or her sous chefs, administrative duties, and careful calculation of financial results.
11. The chief steward has the often unrewarded job of cleaning the kitchen—including cutlery, plates, glasses—and backstage of the hotel and is in charge of pest control and inventory.
12. Catering is subdivided into on-premise and off-premise occasions, which may include meetings, conventions, dinners, luncheons, and weddings. According to the occasion, the type of service and room setup may vary. It involves careful planning and the interaction and cooperation of many people.
13. Room service offers the convenience of dining in the room, with quality food and beverage service, at a price acceptable to both the guest and the hotel.

KEY WORDS AND CONCEPTS

Average daily rate (ADR)
City ledger
Daily report
Executive committee
Night auditor
Property management systems (PMS)
Rack rate
Rev par
Room occupancy percentage (ROP)
Rooms division

REVIEW QUESTIONS

1. Briefly define the purpose of a hotel. Why is it important to empathize with the culture of guests?
2. List the main responsibilities of the front-office manager.
3. Describe the role of the general manager.
4. What are the advantages and disadvantages of revenue management?
5. Why is the concierge an essential part of the personality of a hotel?
6. Explain the importance of accident and loss prevention. What security measures are taken in order to protect guests and their property?

INTERNET EXERCISES

1. Organization: Hyatt Hotel Corporation
   Web site: www.hyatt.com
   Summary: Hyatt Hotel Corporation is a multibillion-dollar hotel management and development company. Together with Hyatt International, the company has close to 10 percent of the hotel industry market share. Hyatt is recognized for its decentralized management approach, in which general managers are given a great deal of the management decision-making process.
   Click on the "Careers" icon and take a look at Hyatt's management training program.
   a. What is Hyatt's management training program?
   b. What requisites must applicants meet in order to qualify for Hyatt's management training program?

2. Organization: Hotel Jobs
   Web site: www.hoteljobs.com
   Summary: Hoteljobs.com is a Web site that offers information to recruiters, employers, and job seekers in the hospitality industry.
   a. What different jobs are being offered under "Job Search" and which one, if any, interests you?
   b. Post your résumé online.

APPLY YOUR KNOWLEDGE

1. If you were on the executive committee of a hotel, what kinds of things would you do to ensure the hotel's success?
2. Your hotel has 275 rooms. Last night 198 were occupied. What was the occupancy percentage?

SUGGESTED ACTIVITY

1. Go to a hotel's Web site and find the price of booking a room for a date of your choice. Then go to one of the Web sites (Hotels.com, Expedia, Travelocity, etc.) that "sell" hotel rooms and see how the price compares.

ENDNOTES

1. *HOTELS* Magazine, "Hyatt Regency Denver Implements Green Initiatives," http://www.hotelsmag.com/article/CA6573285.html, retrieved June 3, 2009.
2. Gabor Forgacs, *Hoteliers Hospitality, Hotel, & Travel News*, "Top Ten Revenue Management Mistakes Hotels Can Make," www.4hoteliers.com/4hots_fshw.php?mwi=357, July 15, 2004.
3. Sudhir Andrews, *Hotel Housekeeping Training Manual* (New Delhi: Tata McGraw-Hill, 2008).
4. Courses and Careers, "Catering Manager," www.ca.courses-careers.com/articles/catering_manager.htm, retrieved June 3, 2009.
5. http://www.ecogreenhotel.com/green_hotel_news_Triple-Bottom-Line-and-Eco-Efficiency.php, retrieved February 26, 2010.
6. Ibid.
7. http://blog.sustainabletravel.com/green_hotel_certification_prog_1.html, retrieved February 26, 2010.
8. Ibid.
9. http://www.nhslrp.org/, retrieved February 26, 2010.
10. http://www.theqhotel.com/content.php?content_id=1, retrieved February 26, 2010.
11. http://www.dep.state.pa.us/dep/deputate/pollprev/industry/hotels/operations.htm, retrieved February 26, 2010.
12. http://hotelier.typead.com/hotelier/2009/11/sustainable-fb-operations-can-create-valuable, retrieved February 26, 2010.

6 CRUISING

LEARNING OUTCOMES

After reading and studying this chapter, you should be able to:

Describe how the cruise industry developed.

Know the key players in the cruise industry.

Identify the different segments in the cruise market.

Describe the different types of cruises.

Explain the organization of a cruise ship.

Describe the economic impact of tourism.

Cruising . . . the mere word conjures up images of lazy days by the pool, romantic evenings with fine dining, entertainment, moonlight promenades, and exciting excursions at distant exotic ports. Does this sound like a dream? It doesn't have to be! The best part of the story is that in recent years, cruising has become increasingly varied and affordable, giving virtually everyone the opportunity to share the fun. As we will see later in this chapter, more and more people are making their dream a reality, and an overwhelming majority are completely blown away by the experience. Welcome to the magical world of cruising!

More than 200 cruise lines offer a variety of wonderful vacations, from the "Fun Ships" of Carnival, to the "Love Boat," to freighters that carry only a few passengers. Travelers associate a certain romance with cruising to exotic locations and all-day pampering. Being on a cruise ship is like being on a floating resort. Accommodations range from luxurious suites to cabins that are even smaller than most jail cells or faculty offices. Attractions and distractions range from early morning workouts to fabulous meals, with nightlife consisting of dancing, cabarets, and possibly gambling. Day life might involve relaxation, visits to the spa or beauty parlor (or both), organized games, or simply reclining in a deck chair by the pool reading a novel. Nonstop entertainment includes language lessons, charm classes, port-of-call briefings, cooking, dances, bridge, table tennis, shuffleboard, and more.

CRUISE INDUSTRY DEVELOPMENT

Explore the History of the Cruise Industry: Read the *Guide to Cruises*

Cruising has not always been a popular vacation choice. For centuries, a seaworthy vessel was simply considered a mode of transportation, especially for those who inhabited coastal communities on oceans, rivers, and lakes. Even after Columbus's historic voyage in 1492, cruising the high seas was merely a way to establish new colonies and bring glory to a country. Ship travel was uncomfortable and unsanitary—a far cry from the luxury lines that sail today. For some unfortunate few, however, it was a necessity. Until about the 1830s, the principal reasons for undertaking water travel were immigration, trade, and war. So how did ship travel develop into an important part of the world's largest industry?

The First Cruise Ships

The Peninsula and Oriental Steam Navigation Company (P&O) is recognized as the inventor of cruising. The company's first cruise is thought to have occurred in 1844 when novelist William Makepeace Thackeray sailed around the Mediterranean.[1] By 1880, one of P&O's ships had been upgraded to the status of a cruising yacht, and sailed around the world. The first American cruise ship didn't set sail until 1867. The *Quaker City* left port from New York City and traveled to Europe and the Middle East.[2] However, passengers aboard the P&O cruise line and the *Quaker City* represented a very small minority in transatlantic travel. Most ocean travel still consisted of poor immigrants looking for a better life overseas.

In the early 1900s, even more passengers took to the sea. By this time, wealthy landowners and merchants also felt the need to travel by sea, which resulted in the eventual evolution of luxurious ocean liners. The elite were fitted into first-class accommodations, while other passengers were crowded into unsanitary conditions and cramped living quarters.

This aspect of sea travel was well portrayed in Hollywood's blockbuster hit movie, *Titanic*. The original *Titanic* was one of three new ships built in the early 1900s by the White Star Line, in an effort to compete against Cunard, the world-famous luxury cruise line. White Star's goals were to make its new ships—the *Olympic*, *Titanic*, and *Britannic*—the quietest, most luxurious, and most stable ships afloat. This was made possible, in part, because White Star only installed as many lifeboats as maritime regulations called for (enough to carry half the people aboard).[3] In 1911, the *Olympic* made its maiden voyage. It was a huge success and so its sister ship, the *Titanic*, made its first trip one year later on April 10, 1912. It carried 2,225 passengers, most of whom traveled in second and third class. On April 15, the *Titanic* collided with an iceberg, and we all know the rest of the story. The poorer passengers were locked below deck while the first-class passengers boarded the lifeboats. Only 705 passengers survived, and Captain Smith, who is blamed for the *Titanic* disaster, went down with the ship. The only good thing that came out of the accident was the realization of the need to increase safety regulations—particularly sufficient lifeboats.[4]

World War I dramatically changed the ship travel industry. Many factors played a part in this, including the United States change in immigration policies and the new attraction that

Europe came to hold for the Americans. All in all, cruising became the fashionable thing to do, leading to an increase in the number of cruise ships built and operated. Despite a slight decline during World War II, the popularity of cruising continued and transatlantic passenger cruises reached an all-time high in the mid 1950s. Later, passenger numbers momentarily declined with the increasing popularity of air travel. Today, most cruises are Caribbean or Mediterranean cruises that underscore the ease of being aboard. Ports of call add interest to the cruise. Transatlantic voyages are few—regularly offered only by the *Queen Elizabeth II*. Around-the-world cruises are also rare.

Interestingly, the airplane, which caused the demise of most transoceanic passenger service, actually helped stimulate the cruise business. In fact, as early as the 1950s, most of the passengers on some Mediterranean-based cruise ships arrived at the embarkation point by plane. These **air-cruise packages** made cruising an option for millions of potential new passengers, and to this date they are still a popular means for inland passengers to make their way to the coast. For many years, the packages meant savings for the cruise passenger. This trend has turned, however, as cruise lines have found themselves at odds with the airlines, to the point where it sometimes may be cheaper for customers to make their own travel arrangements.

> **Interestingly, the airplane, which caused the demise of most transoceanic passenger service, actually helped stimulate the cruise business.**

major cruise lines have launched 62 new cruise ships. In the past decade, there has been an increase in embarkations from North American ports, and there are currently no signs that this growth will stop. The past couple of years have resulted in a port expansion program for the U.S. cruise industry.

The cruise industry has experienced a steady growth over the last 10 years. Cruise lines are spending billions on new and refurbished ships, all with the intention of adding capacity. Yet significant growth opportunities still exist for the industry. With only about 10 percent of the potential cruise market tapped and with an estimated market of millions, the cruise industry is assured of a bright future. Over the next three years, 51 million North Americans say they plan to cruise. To date, approximately 19.9 percent of the U.S. population has ever cruised.[6] About 50 percent of these itineraries will be heading for the Caribbean and 1.5 million of these cruisers will be passengers from Europe. Multiply 51 million passengers by a low estimate of $500 a ticket and then add on all the extras (drinks, gaming, entertainment, shopping, spa treatments, and shore excursions, etc.) and we can realize the economic impact of the cruise industry!

Cruising Today

Today, cruising is on the rise. The cruise business is reported to be an over 30-billion-dollar industry.[5] In the past few years, the

Check Your Knowledge

1. Who is considered the inventor of cruising, and in what year did this happen?
2. What was the name of the first American cruise ship and where and when did it sail?
3. Name some of the factors contributing to the growth of cruising.

KEY PLAYERS IN THE CRUISE INDUSTRY

The three top key players in the cruise industry are Carnival Cruise Lines, Royal Caribbean Cruises, and Norwegian Cruise Line. Carnival is the most successful financially, netting about 20 percent of sales. It targets adults between the ages of 25 and 54, and expects to attract close to 3 million passengers with its awesome atriums and round-the-clock activities. Its largest income, other than the fare itself, is from beverage service. Casino income

Discover More about Cruise Lines in the *Guide to Cruises*

is also high, and its casinos are the largest afloat. Carnival hopes that passengers will enjoy buying drinks and putting quarters, or preferably dollars, into the shipboard slot machines or better yet, gaming tables. It also hopes that their passengers will not mind its small cabins, since the activities on the ship occupy all their waking hours and much of the night. Carnival Corporation & PLC includes Carnival Cruise Lines, Holland America Line, Cunard Line, Princess Cruises, Seabourn Cruise Line, and Costa Cruises.[7]

The second largest cruise line is Royal Caribbean Cruises, which operates two cruise brands, Royal Caribbean International and Celebrity Cruises. Combined, the two cruise brands carry over 3 million passengers a year. The fleet consists of 20 ships, which offer 280 destinations worldwide.[8] Royal Caribbean Cruises has a target market of 35-plus with a

Cruise ships have a significant economic impact on their ports of call. Courtesy of Bel Kambach.

relatively high income, and welcomes families.

The third largest is Star Cruises, which now operates Norwegian Cruise Line (NCL). The company has received the "Leading Cruise Line in Asia-Pacific" award. Star Cruises Limited continues to grow, with new ships on the way. Star Cruises Limited is currently employing what it calls the "freestyle cruising" concept, in which all passengers are allowed to dress as they wish, and eat when and where they like. They operate both an Asian fleet and an American fleet, with a combined fleet of 16 ships cruising to over 200 destinations in the world.[9]

The cruise market

Who goes cruising? Well, as we already know, cruising is now more affordable than ever, and appeal to a broad market—from silver-haired seniors to young couples getting married, or families celebrating a graduation (now there's a thought!). The growth of cruising has been phenomenal, with passenger growth exceeding growth in capacity (ships). According to the **Cruise Lines International Association (CLIA)**, the average cruise passenger is about 46 years old, is married, has no children in the household, and has a household income of $79,000. However, cruisers are not a homogeneous group, and take a wide variety of vacations of which cruising is a part. They usually travel with family members, in particular their spouse.[10]

> **I think people go away on cruises because of ease-ability. When you book a cruise, you basically book your hotel, food, entertainment, and transportation—all in one shot.**
>
> Ralph Smith, Cruiser, Tampa, FL

Cruises offer me an easy way to go on all-inclusive vacations. By booking a cruise for my family vacation, I can plan a getaway in just one step. And that one step takes care of our automobile, airfare, lodging, and, of course, the fantastic cuisine!

—Perpetual Cruiser

Most of the cruise market is for trips of seven days or less, regardless of the fact that cruise passengers spend more per day on a short cruise than they do on longer ones. While the short-cruise passenger gets younger each year, middle-aged passengers prefer to take cruises of two to three weeks. Round-the-world cruises are usually for the elderly, who have the leisure and the money needed for such a long trip. However, people of all ages find that if they work hard enough during the year, they can save enough to take one week out of the year to board a cruise ship. They see the ship as a relaxing and safe venture, where they don't need to plan a day of activities. Passengers may prefer an afternoon nap or tea, gambling, sunbathing, or participating in a number of shows and events offered on board.

Then there are the perpetual cruisers. They spend three, four, even five months aboard different cruise ships each year. For these enthusiasts, cruising is an escape from the realities and stresses of the world. As might be expected, a majority of these are well-to-do. Privileged voyagers segregate themselves on the 12 to 15 mostly smaller, elite ships like *Seabourn*, *Sea Goddess I*, and *Sea Goddess II*, which cater to those with annual incomes of about $200,000 and up. Sometimes this group takes world cruises and is found occupying the deluxe suites of elite ships. These travelers are more likely to be repeat travelers. They are older, wealthier, and more discerning than the megaship cruise-goers.

Introducing Richard Spacey

Cruise Director, Royal Caribbean International

Voyager of the Seas, one of the largest and most innovative cruise ships ever built, was introduced by Royal Caribbean International in November 1999. At 142,000 gross tons, she has a total guest capacity of 3,700 with 1,200 crew members. *Voyager of the Seas* is truly a revolution in the cruising industry. A virtual city in itself, she features the world's first floating ice skating rink, a rock climbing wall, an inline skating track, and the largest and most technically advanced theater afloat. There is a four-story Royal Promenade shopping and entertainment boulevard spanning the length of the ship that acts as a hub for the ship's vast array of activities and entertainment. Cruise Director Richard Spacey joined Royal Caribbean International as cruise director's staff in 1997. As a cruise director for the past five years (and with 18 years of experience in the field of entertainment), he was instrumental in implementing the unique entertainment and activities program aboard with a support staff of 130 people. What follows is an account of a day in the life of the cruise director of one of the largest ships in the world.

Monday—First Day at Sea

7:30–8:30 A.M. The plan. Yesterday we embarked 3,650 guests in Miami and headed for our first port of call, Labadee, our own private island on the coast of Hispaniola. Before most of the guests are up for the day, I plan and submit our daily activities schedule for the entire voyage to our hotel director for his approval. All of the cruise director's staff management team submitted their reports after our staff meeting at embarkation yesterday. Scheduling of the 12 activities staff for the week is handled by the assistant cruise director, who also submits the payroll and overtime hours for my approval. Our cruise programs administrator says that three couples were married in the wedding chapel yesterday and they are included in the 108 couples that have chosen to spend their honeymoon with us. A special party will be held later on in the week to celebrate this happy occasion. The youth activities manager reports that there are over 600 children aboard, ranging in age from three to seventeen. The youth activities manager and her team of 13 are responsible for providing age-appropriate activities for our junior cruisers. We offer a special deck and pool area/arcade for children in addition to our extensive youth facilities, which include a teen disco.

Fourteen hundred international guests are aboard, consisting of 60 different nationalities. The international ambassador (who speaks five languages) provides translations of our daily program and acts as the cruise director's liaison for all of our international guests. Daily announcements and publications are translated in the most predominant languages. For this voyage, those happen to be Spanish and Portuguese.

A large part of our business is group and incentive business. The group coordinator appropriates lounges and facilities for these special group events under the auspices of the cruise director. This week we have 25 groups, which include 800 people. There will be seminars, group meetings, presentations, and cocktail parties. We have a state-of-the-art conference center/executive boardroom/screening room in addition to a large convention facility named "Studio B," which doubles as the ice rink. A retractable floor over the ice rink makes this a great space for large conventions. The shore excursion manager reports that tour sales are good for this voyage among the 50 land-based excursions that we offer. All of this information is consolidated into a daily report submitted to the hotel director.

8:45–9:30 A.M. Hotel director's meeting. All of the division heads in the hotel department meet to discuss the daily operation of this floating hotel. Today's agenda includes a monthly safety meeting. Each division head presents his or her monthly report on safety and environmental protection. Hospitality and the safety of our guests and crew are our top priorities. Following this meeting, the captain introduces the senior officers to the new crew members, who are just beginning their 40 hours of training.

9:45 A.M. The start of my public duties. I give a daily announcement and rundown of all the activities and entertainment happenings around the ship.

10:00 A.M. Morning walkaround. Time to kick off the first session of Jackpot Bingo for the week. On my way through the promenade, I see our interactive performers hamming it up with our guests. This is a troupe of two highly skilled performers (including former Ringling Brothers' clowns.) They play different characters throughout the voyage and add quite a lot to the guest experience. I also stop by the Royal Caribbean Online Internet center, which is quite busy. We also offer an in-stateroom hook-up of personal computers for unlimited Internet access (for a fee). The loyalty ambassador is in charge of offering these services as well as booking future cruises for our

(Continued)

traveling guests. (We have a weekly average of 40 percent repeat guests.)

10:30 A.M. The Studio B ice rink is busy with guests skating at our first all-skate session. There are several sessions throughout the day. The ice skating cast (10 individuals) is responsible for running the sessions as well as skating in our ice show. The show is featured four times throughout the voyage and even has a competition segment that is judged by five audience members. The team consists of an international cast of skaters, some of whom are former national amateur champions in their native countries (and a few former Olympic team members).

11:00 A.M. Change out of my day uniform into a business suit, and put on stage makeup for the taping of our onboard talk and information show, *Voyager Live*. I produce this segment from the Royal Promenade. We have three video programmers and an interactive television technician. Interactive TV allows our guests to order room service, excursions, and movies with the click of a button in the privacy of their staterooms.

On today's show, I have the pleasure of interviewing the Osmonds. Royal Caribbean International is one of the few cruise lines that offers a celebrity entertainment program. There is an extensive shoreside entertainment network responsible for the booking of our acts as well as our in-house production shows. In conjunction with the stage and production manager, I make sure that the entertainers are well taken care of once they come on board. Luckily, the Osmonds are as nice in person as they appear on stage. In the past, I have encountered a few difficult and challenging celebrity entertainers. Also featured on today's show are two members of the ice skating cast and our Discover Shopping guide, the person who dispenses shopping tips for the islands. Commercials for our onboard services run between segments. I am one of the main sources for revenue promotion on board. The television programming is a great asset in a small floating city of this size. Thirty-seven channels offer safety information, music, shopping tips, CNBC, CNN, ESPN, and free movies in several languages.

Noon Lunch with the staff in the Officers and Staff Dining Room.

1:00 P.M. Change out of my suit into shorts and a Polo shirt to emcee the 1:30 Belly Flop Competition poolside. This is always a "big" event among our guests, with quite a few laughs. This is followed by horse racing, cruising style. We pick six jockeys who move six wooden horses by a roll of the dice. The betting is fierce as the guests cheer their favorite horses on. I become the track announcer for three races and horse auctioneer. Today we auction off the six horses for our Voyager Derby later in the week. The horses go to the highest bidder and then the "owners" run them in a race later on in the week for all the money. The six horses go for $2,100. A nice pot for one lucky winner.

2:30 P.M. Stop by the sports court to check out the action. The sports court is full of families enjoying our family hour activities with the youth staff. Four sports and fitness supervisors run the sports program. We offer a nine-hole miniature golf course, golf driving simulator, full-court basketball/volleyball, inline skating, Ping Pong, and a rock climbing wall that rises up the smokestack 200 feet above sea level—the best view in the Caribbean. By the end of the day, 125 people will have climbed the wall.

3:00–4:30 P.M. POWER NAP TIME. My day won't end until about 12:30 A.M. Being "on stage" and available practically 24 hours a day can take its toll. This nap will carry me through until the end of the evening.

6:00 P.M. Back to the office to catch up on e-mail and general administrative business. It is also time to work on budget and revenue forecasting for the upcoming year.

7:30 P.M. Off to the Royal Promenade deck to mingle with the guests at the Welcome Aboard reception. The captain gives his welcome speech and then we send them off to their dinner or the show at 8:30.

8:30 P.M. Meet in the Champagne Bar with the hotel director before dinner. Tonight we will entertain guests who are on their fiftieth cruise and also with a representative from an insurance company who is thinking of booking 700 guests on a future cruise with us.

9:00 P.M. Introduce our production show in the La Scala Theater for the main seating guests on my way to dinner. The three-tiered theater has a capacity of 1,350 guests. It features state-of-the-art production facilities that include fly space, video support, Surround Sound, movable scenery, hydraulics, pyrotechnics, and an orchestra pit. Tonight's show is a collection of Broadway hits entitled *Broadway's Rhythm and Rhyme*. The cast consists of 14 singers and dancers and a 10-piece orchestra as well as full technical support. A production manager is in charge of six stage staff, a rigger, and sound and light technicians. The show will last an hour. (Just enough time for me to get through my entrée before I have to come back and close the show at 10:00 P.M.)

10:45 P.M. Introduce the show for second seating guests and watch for quality control.

11:45 P.M. Final walk around the lounges on the ship with my assistant. Karaoke has just finished in one of the secondary lounges and we have music playing everywhere. We have 35 musicians in several bands featuring all varieties of music (string quartet, jazz ensemble, piano bar, Calypso, Latin, Top 40). The disco is lively with singles' night tonight and there are a few couples enjoying light jazz in the Jazz Club.

12:30 A.M. A full day. Definitely a far cry from Julie, on the "Love Boat"! It's time for bed, as I have to be on the gangway at 8:00 A.M. to welcome our guests to Labadee.

Courtesy of Richard Spacey and Royal Caribbean International.

About 11 million passengers take a cruise each year and many passengers are remarkably loyal to their particular ship; as many as half of the passengers on a cruise may be repeat guests. Rates vary from a starting point of about $100 per person per day on Carnival Cruise Lines to $800 on the *Radisson Diamond* and similar luxury ships. Rates typically are quoted per diem (per day) and are cruise-only figures, based on double occupancy. Beverages, gaming, spa treatments, and shore trips are extra.

Types of Cruise Markets

There are marked differences between the segments of the cruise industry. The three types of cruise industry markets are the mass, middle, and luxury markets. The **mass market** generally consists of people with incomes in the $30,000 to $60,000 range. Discounts are common in this market; however, these cruisers are interested in an average cost per person of between $100 and $300 per day, depending on the location and size of the cabin. On mass-market cruise ships there are plenty of activities and food is abundant, but it is far from fine dining. A few cruise lines in the mass market are Carnival Cruise Line, Disney Cruises, Princess Cruises, Norwegian Cruise Lines, and Royal Caribbean.

The **middle market** includes people with incomes in the $60,000 to $80,000 range. These passengers are interested in an average cost per person of $250 to $500 per day. On a middle-market cruise ship, passengers can expect superior meals and attentive service. The middle-market ships are stylish and comfortable: each vessel has its own personality that caters to a variety of different guests. These ships can accommodate 750 to 1,000 passengers. Cruise lines in the middle market include Holland America Lines, Windstar Cruises, Cunard Lines, and Celebrity Cruises.

The **luxury market** generally consists of people with incomes higher than $80,000. They are interested in an average cost per person of more than $500 per day. In this market, the ships tend to be smaller, averaging about 700 passengers, with superior appointments and service. What constitutes a luxury cruise is a matter of individual judgment, advertising, and public relations. The

The World is a cruise ship that literally cruises around the world, stopping at exotic ports. Courtesy of Mark Green.

ships that receive the top accolades from travel industry writers and others who assign such ranks cater only to the top 5 percent of North American income groups. Currently, the ships considered to be in the very top category are *Sea Goddess I*, *Sea Goddess II*, *Seabourn Spirit*, *Seabourn Legend*, *Seabourn Pride*, *Crystal Harmony*, *Crystal Hanseatic*, *Radisson Diamond*, *Silver Wind*, and *Song of Flower*. These six-star vessels have sophisticated cuisine, excellent service, far-reaching and imaginative itineraries, and highly satisfying overall cruise experiences.

> **People go on dinner cruises because it is a nice, quick way to get away for an evening. It requires no advance preparation, and you can go home that evening!**
>
> Andrew Webber, *Fisherman Drew's Dinner Cruise*, Portland, OR

Check Your Knowledge
1. Who goes on cruises?
2. How is the cruise market segmented?

TYPES OF CRUISES

Regional Cruises

Regional cruises are the most popular, sailing in the Caribbean, the Mediterranean, and to a lesser extent, the Baltic Sea and other small seas. The majority of cruise lines offer regional cruises, and many specialize in one area, such as the Caribbean, or switch between the Mediterranean during summer and the Caribbean during winter.

Read about Several Types of Cruises on the S.S. Haywood

Coastal Cruises

Coastal cruises are offered in Northern Europe, the United States, and Mexico. Significantly smaller than the average floating resort, they sail closer to land, seeking out areas not accessible to larger ships. This way, the passenger gets to see more than a destination's main ports. While onboard entertainment is usually limited to a piano, passengers get the opportunity to visit their ports during the evenings, and experience the local culture and cuisine. Other amenities are usually also sparse, so don't expect an Olympic-sized swimming pool, shopping malls, or a choice of fine dining!

River Cruises

European river cruise ships have a friendly and international atmosphere, which offsets the fact that they often lack in size and luxury. The newer, more modern ships often have the feel of a small hotel, with features like public rooms, a large dining room, three to four decks, air-conditioning, an observation lounge, a bar, heated pool, sauna, gym, massage therapists, and salons. Cabins are small but comfortable, and meals are of high quality. River cruises are not only found in Europe, however. Russia, China (the Yangtze), Egypt (the Nile), and Australia (River Murray) are some other exciting destinations.

A Danube River cruise ship in Budapest, Hungry, takes passengers on river cruises for several days.

Barges

Another option is to take a barge, which is an even smaller vessel than the river cruise ships. Barges cruise Europe's inland waterways and canals, from April to November when the weather permits. They offer a close-knit, personal, and completely informal atmosphere, the largest vessels taking up to 24 people. Each barge is equipped with a dining room and bar, serving local foods. At night, passengers can go ashore to explore the local villages. Do you have a special occasion coming up? Barges may also be chartered for small parties.

Steam Boating

Steam boating is a concept unique to the United States, and travels along Mark Twain's favorite destination, the Mississippi River, as well as other major rivers, offering passengers a unique chance to see America's Heartland. Steamboat cruises are a wonderful way to experience American folklore, and partake in "real" American foods, such as steak, shrimp, Creole sauces, and fried foods. The steamboats also feature theme cruises, such as sports, music, and health and fitness—very popular among tourists as well as locals.

Expeditions and Natural Cruises

Many cruise lines offer **expeditions** and **natural cruises** to exotic and exciting places. Passengers play an active part in every aspect of the trip, which tends to be oriented toward visiting interesting destinations, exploring and studying nature. Rather than employing ritzy entertainment, these cruise lines hire special lecturers, naturalists, and historians. A personal logbook illustrated and written by renowned artists and specialists is included in the package.

Adventure Cruises

Adventure cruises explore a number of areas, including Alaska, the Amazon River, the Orinoco River, Antarctica, Greenland, the Galápagos Islands, the South Pacific, and the Northwest Passage. One of the most well-known adventure cruisers is Abercrombie and Kent. Others include, for example, Quark Expeditions, which is owned by NYK of Japan; Oceanic Society Expeditions; and Lindblad Expeditions, which cruise coastal areas of both the continental United States and Alaska.

Sail-Cruises

This is what cruising was traditionally all about; traveling under white sails, letting the wind propel you to your ports of call, and enjoying the feeling of being one with nature. Apart from mealtimes, your day has no rigid structure and is yours to enjoy. There are two types of **sail-cruise** vessels—those that rely on their sails at least 80 percent of the time—and those that don't. If you are looking for the ultimate authentic experience, go for a sail-powered ship. If not, there are plenty of high-tech, sail-assisted ships to choose from. A large crew takes care of all the ship's needs. However, if you'd like, you certainly have the opportunity to help out and share in the sailing experience. Sail-cruises in small boats enable you to reach places that large ships could not get close to, such as the small island group of the Marshall Islands.

World Cruises

For those with time and money to spare, a world cruise is the ultimate opportunity. These cruises generally last from three to six months, and are for many people the travel experience of a lifetime. The accommodations are luxurious, the food is delicious, the entertainment is great, and passengers get the best of sightseeing and excursions. Are there any drawbacks? Well, the world cruise can be very expensive, sometimes up to $3,000 per day per person, with suites costing up to $300,000. Some ships, however, are more reasonable. Ukrainian vessels, for instance, sometimes charge less than $100 a day per person, and that includes gratuities! There is also the option of booking just a part of the trip. So, what are you waiting for?

For such long cruises, planning and preparation is vital. World cruise ships must be totally self-sufficient; fuel, foods, and other supplies must last until the next port. Once the ship has left port, it may not see land for several weeks. Therefore, there is a large storeroom where all sorts of odds and ends and spare parts are stowed, just in case. Cruise entertainment is also an issue, and includes hundreds of entertainers, lecturers, musicians, and bands who must be booked a year in advance.

Crossings

The term **crossing** implies sailing across the northern Atlantic Ocean either to or from the Americas, although it can take place across any major ocean. The five-day Europe–America crossing is seen by most people as romantic and magical, reminiscent of the pilgrims' hazardous voyages, or maybe of one of the great ocean liners of the past. Other cruise ships sometimes offer crossings as one-way trips in order to make a profit while repositioning their vessels. In spring, they sail from the Caribbean to the Mediterranean to catch the European summer season and vice versa in the fall. These crossings may last anywhere from one to two weeks.

Specialty and Theme Cruises

For those who wish to enjoy the relaxing and luxurious life aboard a cruise ship while expanding their knowledge, there are countless specialty and **theme cruises** options available. These are often culture-rich, off-the-beaten-path itineraries based on passengers' special interests and hobbies, and high on enrichment and adventure. The target customers are experienced cruisers who are looking for something more than the conventional cruise experience.

Popular themes over the past couple of years have been nature, art, theater, literature, history and heritage, all kinds of music, sports and fitness, food and wine, education, and lifestyle. Other cultural and enrichment trends are destination-intensive cruises, ecotourism and natural history, enrichment seminars and demonstrations, special performances by artists and musicians, even singles and gay and lesbian cruises—if you can think of it, it probably exists! Figure 6–1 has a limited sample of cruise lingo.

Deluxe Cruising

Larger ships with resort-like design, numerous activities, and amenities such as "virtual golf," pizzerias, and caviar bars will continue to change with time. On the "caviar and champagne"

Aft:	Toward the rear of the ship
Beam:	Ship's width at the widest point
Bridge:	Part of the ship where the navigation is done
Cabin:	Name given to a passenger's room
Forward:	Toward the bow or front of the ship
Galley:	Seagoing word for kitchen
Knot:	Nautical speed (about 1 1/16 of a land mile per hour)
Port side:	Left-hand side of the ship as you face forward
Starboard side:	Right-hand side of the ship as you face forward
Stern:	Aft of the ship
Tonnage:	A customary measure of a ship's size
Wake:	Waves behind a ship

FIGURE 6–1 Cruise Lingo.

ships, the slogan is "no matter what you want, the company will get it for you." Chefs will prepare items following recipes that the passengers bring with them. The wine steward gives tastings and lectures on the wines being served. The chefs brief the waitstaff on menu items and discuss such things as the procedure for making sabayon sauce.

The ritual of food and its service is so central to luxury cruising that digestion is the principal pastime aboard luxury cruise ships. Tastes, textures, and prestige in foods are a matter of concern to both passengers and cruise operators. The assumption is made that all passengers will be fed as much and as often as they wish. Some passengers do not constrain themselves and have been known to gain three pounds a day while cruising.

Food cost as such is not as much as one might guess—maybe $40 a day per passenger for elite ships compared to $15 to $20 for the mass-market ships. Elite cruisers may breakfast in their cabin, take another meal on deck, and a third in the dining room. Foodservice is impeccable: silver, table linen, glass, and stemware. An eight-course dinner prepared by highly skilled chefs can be served in one's cabin—there is room service around the clock. Waitstaff are expected to know such niceties as the source of turbot and three kinds of caviar.

The *Seabourn Cruise Line*, which is actually owned by Carnival, has a trio of ships—the *Pride*, the *Spirit*, and the *Legend*—motor ships of 10,000 tons. Compare that to some megaships, which can weigh over 142,000 tons. Seabourn ships host only 200 guests in 100 suites. Each ship has a few larger suites as well. The after part of each ship has a foldout marina from which guests may swim and participate in a variety of water sports. An enclosed steel mesh pool allows passengers to swim directly into the ocean. The ships fly the Norwegian flag and are officered by Norwegians; the hotel staff is also European.

There are optional shore excursions such as a visit to the Yusupov Palace or the Hermitage Museum in Russia, a family chateau visit in the Bordeaux region continuing on to the Dordogne Valley, or a visit to France's lovely Loire Valley.

Seabourn is a "Preferred Partner" with Preferred Hotels and Resorts Worldwide. Under this partnership, arrangement for a free day can be earned on selected cruises for every five nights stayed at a participating preferred hotel or resort. And every time a passenger cruises for 10 days with Seabourn, a free night is available at participating hotels and resorts. Precruise and post-cruise room reservations are arranged with such hotels as the Cipriani or Gritti Palace in Venice, the Hassler in Rome, or the Four Seasons in Singapore. After each cruise, Seabourn clients receive a dozen roses in a crystal vase delivered to their homes.

One of the ways in which the luxury ships delineate themselves is by the crew-to-passenger ratio. On Seabourn ships, there are 296 guests for 148 suites, or one crewmember for every 1.51 passengers. Private verandas are another selling point. Seventy-five percent of the *Silversea* suites have private verandas. *Seabourn and Silversea* fares are pretty much inclusive, except for premiums paid for premium drinks. Fares include round-trip economy air, and hotel accommodations prior to embarkation. It all comes to about $800 per day for each passenger on all of the top ships.

The Crystal Cruise Line comprises the *Crystal Cruises* sister ships—*Crystal Harmony* and *Crystal Symphony*. On these ships, penthouse decks get European trained, white-gloved butlers and room stewards who coordinate, among other things, intimate dinners. Penthouse suites are large, the largest being 982 square feet, the same size as a small condominium. All staterooms come with goose down pillows, French twin beds, bathtubs and showers, fresh flowers, and fruit. The public spaces include a two-story atrium lobby accented by hand-cut sculptures and a waterfall. Shoppers are treated to an "Avenue of the Stars" shopping arcade. Gamblers get a 2,500 square foot "Caesar's Palace at Sea Casino," which is operated by the Las Vegas casino. A "bistro" wine bar serves international coffees, cheeses, and wine by the glass.

Radisson Seven Seas Cruises is part of the huge conglomerate of travel agencies, hotels, motels, restaurants, tour wholesalers, and rental car sales under the aegis of Carlson Travel, based in Minneapolis, Minnesota. Each part of the group can sell the others. Radisson Seven Seas Cruises is based in Ft. Lauderdale, Florida. It has five ships under its banner: the *Bremen*, *Hanseatic*, *Radisson Diamond*, *Song of Flower*, and *Paul Gauguin*. The *Paul Gauguin* seems particularly suited for its sailing area, Hawaii and the Islands of French Polynesia. It is "the most deluxe ship ever to sail the South Seas," with 160 outside staterooms and suites and 80 balconies. Most cruises on the *Paul Gauguin* start and end in Tahiti, the only sizeable town (and the laid-back capital) of French Polynesia. French-built and French-owned, the ship was designed for casual elegance. Its restaurants are alive with French gastronomy.

Check Your Knowledge

1. What is the most popular kind of cruise?
2. Where can you go on a coastal cruise?
3. What does the term *crossing* mean?

All aboard—organization of the cruise ship

Meet the Ship's Captain to Learn about Cruise Ship Careers

Captain is the highest ranking position on a cruise ship, receiving most of the perks. The captain position comes with a lot of responsibility, including caring for all of the staff and passengers. The captain also makes virtually every executive decision dealing with the ship. These decisions include navigation, operations, and company policies. To obtain this position one must possess a captain's license and all applicable certifications by a recognized maritime government body. Captains have also earned a diploma from maritime training school. Generally, the captain of a cruise ship has moved up the ladder by having held subordinate positions on cruise ships for five to eight years and experience in navigational electronic and computerized equipment.

The **hotel manager** is in charge of all hotel operations on board the ship, which consist of administration, staff, entertainment, food and beverage, dining room, and housekeeping. The hotel manager is also in charge of training the hotel staff and overseeing financial operations. Because a hotel manager has direct contact with the guests, he or she must be courteous and accommodating. A hotel manager must also be able to communicate well with the ship's captain. Generally, the position requires a bachelor's degree and five years in a management position, and at least eight years' cruise ship experience.

The hotel manager and the management team have to deal with the unexpected, like guests who have disputes, and with medical services (larger ships even have operating rooms and a morgue on board). Lately, there have been incidents of norovirus and other shipboard illnesses. Ships' officers have increased the supervision of hygiene and cleanliness on board and even screened staff and crew for illnesses.

.inc Corporate Profile

CARNIVAL CRUISE LINES

The name Carnival Cruise Lines is a good indication of what the company is all about. Festive yet casual, and affordable to all, Carnival brings the fun into cruising. Starting in 1972 with only one ship, the *Mardi Gras,* entrepreneur Ted Arison realized his vision of making cruising available to the masses, not only to the very rich. Fifteen years later, with seven ships in service, Carnival had become the first cruise line to advertise on network TV (1984), earned its distinction as "Most Popular Cruise Line in the World," carried more passengers than any other cruise line, and undertook its initial public offering on Wall Street to raise capital for future expansion.

So how is the situation today? Not surprisingly, Carnival is still the largest and most popular cruise line in the world. Carnival Cruise Lines is only one part of the huge Carnival Corporation. It also operates Holland America and Windstar, and has interests in Cunard Line, Costa Cruises, and Seabourn. A merger with P&O Princess Cruises PLC (now called Carnival PLC) made the company even larger. Carnival Corporation and Carnival PLC function as a single economic entity through contractual agreements between two separate legal entities. Together, these brands operate 90 ships totaling more than 171,000 lower berths. Carnival Corporation & PLC also operate the leading tour companies in Alaska and the Canadian Yukon, Holland America Tours, and Princess Tours.

So what is it like to cruise with Carnival? The key word is fun—for all ages. What sets Carnival apart from the competition is its commitment to enhance all aspects of the vacation experience and stay ahead of the industry,

Corporate Profile (Continued)

as expressed by its slogan, "Today's Carnival." All ships have a diverse and always-improving selection of amenities, activities, and facilities. Each vessel has at least three swimming pools, a full casino, duty-free shopping, the "Nautica Spa" health club, Internet cafés, and a complimentary "Camp Carnival" children's program, top rated in the industry. Some ships even have a wedding chapel! Activities span every age group's interests, and include multigenerational games for the whole family to enjoy. Entertainment ranges from Las Vegas–style shows to high-tech revues with the latest in video projections, laser techniques, and pyrotechnics, comedy shows, big band music, and much more. Shore excursions offer traditional city tours and nature walks as well as kayaking, scuba diving and "flightseeing" (airal tours) for the more active cruiser. As if this weren't enough, Carnival has the most comprehensive food offered in the cruise industry, ranging from elegant multicourse meals to casual bistros for alternative dinner services, specialty areas, and 24-hour pizzerias and room service.

Carnival is the only cruise line (at the time of writing) to offer a vacation guarantee. Confident that you will have a great time, Carnival offers a refund and a chance to disembark should you for some reason not be satisfied with your cruise experience. For first-time cruisers, this gives a sense of comfort, and increases their likelihood of trying a cruise despite any doubts they might have.

If you smell awards in the air, you're absolutely right. Carnival's list is endless. Some of the more prestigious awards include:

- The "Fun Ships" of Carnival Cruise Lines have been voted the number one cruise choice in *Southern Living Magazine*'s annual readers' poll.
- Carnival's group reservations and sales service departments were named the "Best of the Best" by *Cruise One,* a national travel consortium that comprises some of the top travel agencies in the United States and Canada.
- Carnival received the "Gold Award of Excellence" based on the responses of more than 2,000 American Express Travel Network company owners and representatives who were asked to rank various components of service, including sales assistance, reservations, product, and to make an overall evaluation of the company.
- Carnival received Cruise Line of the Year, Best Group Department, and Best District Sales Managers awards based on a survey of more than 700 NACOA members who were asked to rate cruise operators in a variety of service- and marketing-related categories.

Source: www.carnival.com.

The **food and beverage manager** is in charge of—you guessed it—all of the areas that serve food and beverages on board the ship. He or she is in charge of food costs and the overall quality of the food and beverages on board the ship. Since one of the primary reasons people take cruises is for the never-ending flow of food, as long as the ship is at sea, the food and beverage manager's job is never complete. This position generally requires six years in a food and beverage department or management school, and three years in a management position or four years ship's experience.

The **chief purser** is a part of the hotel operations department on a cruise ship. He or she is responsible for supervising all other departments on board, with the exception of deck and engine. The chief purser has extensive hotel experience, at least five years as a hotel manager, a degree in hotel management, and/or prior cruise ship experience. Of course, he or she must be fluent in the English language.

The **cruise director** is in charge of all onboard entertainment and activities. He or she creates, coordinates, and implements all daily activities, and acts as master of ceremonies at all social activities and evening shows. The cruise director also does a lot of public speaking, as well as delegate responsibilities among the staff. Direct reports include the assistant cruise director, social hostess, cruise staff, and activities coordinators. The job requires strong organizational abilities and fluency in the English language. A background in professional entertainment is preferred, or two to five years on board working one's way up from an entry-level cruise staff position. Typical salaries range from $3,800 to $7,500 U.S. per month, depending on the cruise line.

The **chief steward** (or **director of housekeeping**) supervises the housekeeping department. The chief steward also regulates and accounts for cleaning supplies, equipment used, cabin services, room services, bell services, and passenger baggage. The chief steward must be a good organizer and communicator. Usually this department promotes from within. This position reports to the hotel manager.

A great way to enhance your cruise experience is to take part in shore excursions. Depending on the port of call, cruise shore excursions may include:

- Snorkeling
- Scuba diving
- Swimming with dolphins
- Tubing and rafting
- Tours
- Canoeing
- Hiking/climbing
- Nature walks
- Shopping
- Flightseeing

Cruise destinations

The Caribbean is one of the most popular cruise destinations in the world. This region stretches from South Florida to South America. The three regions one may choose from in the Caribbean include the Western, Southern, and Eastern Caribbean. Western Caribbean cruises take passengers on a journey to Mexico's Yucatán coast, Belize, or to Grand Cayman. Southern Caribbean cruises sail to places including Aruba, Martinique, or St. Thomas. Eastern Caribbean cruises include popular destinations such as the Bahamas, San Juan, the Virgin Islands, and the Turks and Caicos Islands. The Caribbean offers an array of ports, a number of the world's greatest beaches, duty (tax)-free shopping, and the most choices for itineraries and cruise lengths.

Mediterranean cruises are the only type of cruise that puts passengers within just a few hours' sailing of another country and/or continent. Western Mediterranean cruises travel to places in Southern Europe that include Naples, Italy; France; and Spain. Eastern Mediterranean cruises take passengers to places such as Turkey, Greece, and the Nile (Egypt). Eastern Mediterranean cruises may also travel to countries that have just recently opened their doors to cruise tourism such as Syria, Lebanon, and Libya. Another popular cruise destination in the area is the cruises from Piraeus (the port of Athens) to former Soviet countries along the Black Sea. Cruisers that prefer these types of destinations are generally interested in history and have experience with a variety of cultures.

Cruise destinations include some of the most exotic places in the world.

Discover the Appeal of Shore Excursions

Cruises have become the most popular way to visit Alaska and are offered by most of the major cruise lines. Cruises typically sail along the Inside Passage and travel to Glacier Bay National Park or Hubbard Glacier. For sunlight (and temperature) purposes, Alaska cruises are only offered in the summer months (May to September). June, July, and August are the peak season when the daily average temperatures actually reach 75 degrees Fahrenheit! Alaska cruises feature vast pine forests, snowy ridges, glaciers, wildlife, interesting ports of call, and captivating tours.

Cruises have also become one of the most popular ways to visit Hawaii. The most popular type of Hawaiian cruise sails entirely within the Hawaiian Islands. The seven Hawaiian Islands spread out across the area are Hawaii, Kauai, Lanai, Maui, Molokai, Niihau, and Oahu. Ports of call include Honolulu, Nawiliwili, Kauai, Lahaina, Maui, Kona, and Hilo. Hawaii features breathtaking mountains, volcanoes, tropical forests, waterfalls, coral reefs, sunken lava flows, and underwater caves. It is one of the world's best places to experience snorkeling, scuba diving, deep-sea fishing, and glass-bottom boat tours.

Check Your Knowledge

1. Who are the key staff on board ship?
2. Name some of the popular cruise destinations.
3. What are the reasons why people travel to Hawaii?

♻ Sustainable Cruising

While cruising is not the most ecofriendly mode of travel, due to increases consumer interest and developing technologies, the industry is making efforts at becoming greener. Hydrogen-powered ships may become the future of the cruise industry. It's important to know that all cruise lines do follow their own set of environmental policies; major components of these include recycling, as well as incinerating and processing waste on board.[11] Members of the Cruise Lines International Association have agreed to follow strict voluntary environmental standards for wastewater and recycling. Some of them have gone a step further, offering additional ecoamenities and conservation practices.[12] While technologies are continuing to develop, there are also things that cruisers themselves may ask passengers to do in the meantime to make the cruise vacations more sustainable:

- Conserve, conserve, conserve!
  Take short showers
  Reuse towels
  Eat in moderation (don't overindulge in the buffet)

- When you are in port:
  Travel by foot or bike
  Support the local cultures

- Look into alternatives
  Try sailing
  Look into smaller cruises

Cruise only with Members of the Cruise Lines International Association

Cruise industry experts estimate that despite the current state of the economy, a record 13.5 million people took a cruise in 2009. Those kinds of numbers represent a potentially huge impact on the environment.[13]

According to the environmental group Ocena, cruise ships daily dump into the ocean 168,000 gallons of liquid waste and sewage from toilets, sinks, showers, and kitchens. Add to this seven tons of solid waste, seven thousand gallons of bilge water contaminated with oil, and fifteen gallons of toxic chemicals.[14] Realizing that they have an image problem, and after being fined for illegal discharges, cruise lines are beginning to go green. In the past six years they have cut their waste in half. Some are employing new gas turbines that drastically reduce nitrogen and sulfur emissions. Another will turn off its engines while in port in Juneau, Alaska, plugging into local hydroelectric power instead. Yet another has installed scrubbers that use seawater to remove smokestack pollutants. One cruise line is buying carbon offsets in order to promote carbon-neutral cruises.[15]

One of the newest cruise ships, the Orphalese, recycles all onboard waste; treat its wastewater; use GPS to prevent dropping anchor on coral and other fragile sites; desalinates its water without chlorine; uses LED lighting, biodegradable cleaning items, and water-efficient washing machines; and uses golf balls that dissolve into fish food should a shot go overboard!

HAWAII: LAND of ALOHA!

Alooooooha! is the outrageously enthusiastic greeting that scantily clad Polynesian dinner show emcees roar into microphones, urging audience members to repeat with the same elation. It's centered in bright yellow cartoon letters dancing above the escalator that takes arrivals to baggage claim at Honolulu International Airport. A hotel front-desk receptionist greets guests with this salutation; it has replaced "Hello" in all hospitality operations. Naturally, it is even the policy of many establishments to answer the telephone with "Aloha, my name is _____ How can I be of help to you today?"

Pronounced ä-'lō-hä (not the word with a silent "h"), its literal translation is hello, goodbye, and I love you. Aloha, with its many beautiful meanings, is analogous to the many traditions and people of Hawaii. This uniqueness is the result of sugar cane plantation laborers being imported from Asia to the islands in the late 1800s to early 1900s. With a rich blend of Pacific Basin nationalities, the state became a "melting pot" of the various cultures that have influenced its being. Besides stunning sunsets and balmy tropical weather year-round, the people and their Aloha are reasons why tourists continue to return.

Tourism is Hawaii's largest and most important industry and is expected to continue to grow in the next 10 years. Essentially the lifeline to Hawaii, the industry directly accounts for approximately one-third of the jobs, so the value of tourism is not underestimated.

The Hawaii Tourism Authority is authorized to: create a vision and develop a long-range plan for tourism; develop, coordinate and implement state policies and directions for tourism and related activities; have a permanent, strong focus on marketing and promotion; and coordinate the development of new product lines with public and private sectors, including the development of sports, culture, health, education, business, and ecotourism.

- *Sports tourism:* The majority of sporting events are held during the winter months; such activities are not possible in most areas of the continental U.S. Televised events have helped to boost tourism, including the National Football League Pro Bowl and the Professional Golfers Association's Sony Open and Mercedes Championships. Billfish tournaments held off the Kona Coast and the Honolulu Marathon show draw increasing crowds. Visitors can participate in water sports and golf year-round. The Big Island of Hawaii claims to be the only place in the U.S. where one can surf and ski in the same day.
- *Cultural tourism:* Hawaii's history of Polynesian ancestry and monarchial rule have not been forgotten. Since Hawaii was annexed to the U.S. in 1898 and attained statehood in 1959, native Hawaiian traditions still endure. The Polynesian Cultural Center is dedicated to sharing insights into the culmination of cultures that make up the islands.
- *Health tourism:* The Big Island of Hawaii is home to world-class health and wellness facilities. One of these was pioneered by Earl Bakken, the inventor of the cardiac pacemaker.
- *Education tourism:* Short-term continuing education classes at the University of Hawaii and its community colleges draw visitors from all parts of the globe for studies ranging from English as a second language to marine biology to professional pastry design.
- *Business tourism:* With a brand-new convention center, this niche is the primary focus of the Hawaii Visitors and Conventions Bureau. The Meetings, Conventions and Incentives Department assists meeting planners with programs ranging from 10 to 30,000 people.
- *Ecotourism:* Molokai Ranch is an ecologically responsible resort on an island still rooted in nature. Taking a sure-footed mule ride down the side of a mountain is another distinguishing experience.

The tourism industry is relatively young to the islands, given that it is dependent upon the transportation industry. Its foundations lie in biweekly ocean voyages across the Pacific on Matson liners in the mid-1900s. Today, there are 700 trans-Pacific flights per week, and 200 flights per week to and from Japan, making it the world's busiest international route after London–Paris. However, the emerging cruise segment is making a reappearance with "boat days" glory. American Hawaii Cruises offers seven-day inter-island cruises, and Norwegian Cruise Lines is looking to expand to Hawaii.

Ironically, Hawaii has become a target for Japanese visitors in a very different way as compared to the events of December 7, 1941. During the latter half of the 1980s, an increase in tourism from Japan resulted from an increase in the value of yen, in addition to a policy by the Japanese government to lower its foreign trade surplus. Japanese were welcomed with open arms, changing the face of Waikiki. In order to accommodate these visitors' needs, brand-name stores sprung up along Kalakaua Avenue, and Japanese restaurants found new life in *yen*. Retail stores enjoyed prosperity in light of the obligatory tradition of buying *omiyage* (presents brought back home for friends and family). Today, Japanese-English bilingual speaking ability is a factor in the hiring of hospitality industry employees. Despite a drop in eastbound visitors to Hawaii due to the Asian economic crisis of the late 1990s, Japanese continue to return, perhaps because of the strong Asian heritage that exists within the islands. Their presence remains an integral part of Hawaii's tourism industry.

Westbound tourism has also been aggressively marketed via television. Hawaii's mild weather throughout the year, with sunshine, clear skies, and an average of 78 degrees Fahrenheit distinguishes it as a year-round vacation destination. Hawaii offers the leisure of the tropics, accommodations to suit any budget, all political advantages of the United States (including currency and language), and a living, breathing view of Diamond Head with Waikiki Beach sand between the toes.

Geographically, Hawaii links the East and West. The islands have proven to be a strategic commercial and military location through the whaling industry of early to mid-1800s and Pearl Harbor's eminent strength as a prime military position. Hawaii has established its location as ideal for business relations linking Asia with the United States. Materialization of a state-of-the-art convention center on Oahu came with a $350 million price tag, but will undoubtedly reaffirm Hawaii's exclusivity in the center of the Pacific Rim.

The cuisine of Hawaii is another incomparable fascination. Similar to the multicultured people, "local food" has grown to include a mélange of ethnicities. A local menu can include everything from Japanese teriyaki beef to Korean kalbi, Filipino pork adobo, American fried chicken with brown gravy, and Chinese chow mein. With a sophisticated sense, Hyde Park and internationally trained chefs of Hawaii developed Hawaii Regional Cuisine. With the goal of utilizing local products and flavors, dishes such as Chef Roy

(Continued)

Yamaguchi's blackened ahi with soy mustard sauce epitomizes the Euro-Asian style of this new age cuisine. In a world where a cuisine showcases its respective culture, Hawaii is surely a "mixed plate."

With eight major islands, the state of Hawaii is home to 1.2 million people. The state capital, Honolulu, is located on Oahu, the "Gathering Place." Kauai, known as the "Garden Isle" for its lush tropical gardens, is where *Jurassic Park* was filmed. Molokai, the "Friendly Isle," features ecotourism and naturalism. Lanai, the "Pineapple Island," is the most secluded and is recognized by its two world-renowned luxury hotels. Maui, the "Valley Isle," is the second most popular destination in Hawaii and is crowned by a high altitude observatory atop Haleakala. Hawaii, the "Big Island," is still growing, with its active volcanoes and energy research lab among prominent resorts. Hawaii is the all-encompassing "Land of Aloha," where all are embraced and the Aloha Spirit keeps it alive.

Source: Courtesy of Tobie Cancino, alumna of Kapiolani Community College, Culinary Institute of the Pacific.

TRENDS *in* THE CRUISE INDUSTRY

- A rapid expansion in the number of cruise ships.
- New accommodations and entertainment to distinguish themselves from other cruises.
- An increase in the number of North American ports.
- An increase in the number of embarkations, destinations, and itineraries offered through North American ports.
- An increase in the number of refurbished ships, with the intention of adding capacity.
- Expansion of the passengers within the cruise market.
- Continual development in the different types of cruises offered.
- A sizable growth in the number of job opportunities in the cruise industry.
- An increase in actions taken towards making cruises more sustainable.

CASE STUDY

Becoming Captain

Tom is currently the hotel manager of a very successful cruise ship. He has a bachelor's degree and has been a hotel manager for five years. Before becoming hotel manager, Tom worked his way up the ladder from several entry-level positions, which he held for a total of four years. Tom has now decided that he would like to become a cruise captain.

DISCUSSION QUESTION

1. What steps should Tom take to meet the requirements necessary for becoming a cruise captain?

CAREER INFORMATION

Since the cruise industry is one of the fastest-growing sectors in the world, it comes as no surprise that the job outlook is very good. An estimated 5 to 10 ships are built each year. This greatly increases the number of employment positions that are offered yearly. As mentioned earlier in the text, employment opportunities for Americans are mainly in sales, marketing, and U.S. shore-based activities (i.e., reservations and supplies). There are also positions such as cruise director, purser, chief steward, and hotel manager. There are many other careers in the diverse tourism industry, including travel manager, destination management, tour operator, and a position at convention and visitors bureaus. With its rapid expansion and various job opportunities, the travel industry is, without a doubt, one of the best industries in which to work at the present time. Figure 6–2 shows a career path in the cruise industry.

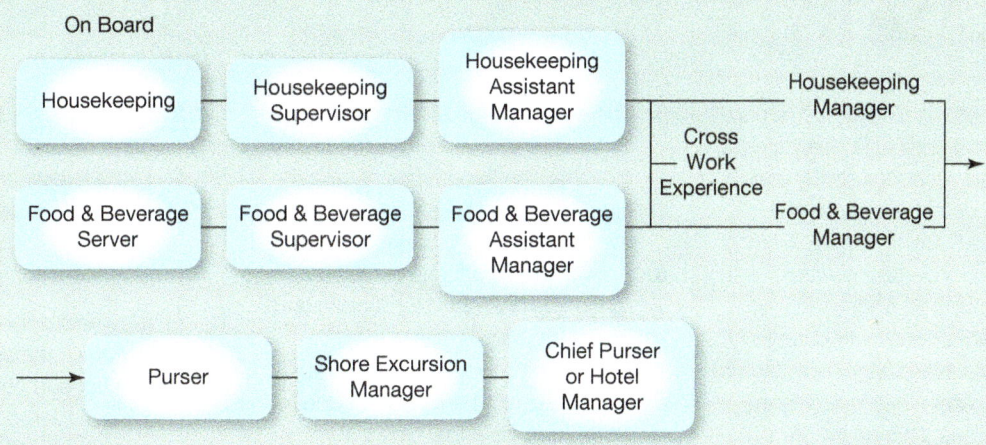

FIGURE 6–2 A Career Path in the Cruise Industry.

Cruise Industry Employment

No two ships are alike: each has its own personality and character. The nationality of the ship's officers and staff contributes greatly to the ship's ambiance. For example, the ships under the Holland America flag have Dutch officers and Indonesian/Filipino crew, and those belonging to the Epirotiki flag have Greek officers and crew. Most cruise ships sail under foreign flags because they were built abroad for the following reasons:

1. U.S. labor costs for ships, officers, and crew, in addition to maritime unions, are too high to compete in the world market.
2. U.S. ships are not permitted to operate casino-type gambling.
3. Many foreign shipyards are government subsidized to keep workers employed, thereby lowering construction costs.

In addition, cruise ships sail under foreign flags (called flags of convenience) because registering these ships in countries such as Panama, the Bahamas, and Liberia means fewer and more lax regulations and little or no taxation.

Land-based jobs within the cruising industry are much like those of any tour operator, and are found in areas such as administration, sales, reservations, marketing/public relations, human resources, accounting, finance, and customer service. Jobs on board a cruise ship are a bit different, ranging from food and beverage, catering, hotel, and concierge-type jobs to entertainment and activities to the traditional shipboard jobs that keep the vessel safely afloat.

On board, Americans sometimes occupy certain positions such as cruise director and purser. The reasons that few Americans work on board cruise ships are that the ships are at sea for months at a time with just a few hours in port. The hours are long and the conditions for crew are not likely to be acceptable to most Americans. (No, you don't get your own cabin!) Still interested? One good place to start your search is the Web site www.cruiseshipjob.com. Here you can browse the qualifications needed, the job descriptions, and the salary ranges for all positions in the industry.

Cruise ships have a limited number of high-ranking onboard positions such as cruise director and hotel manager. Most ships also have foreign crews because they can avoid American laws on things like overtime. As we mentioned above, cruising offers numerous onshore careers in marketing and sales, human resources, accounting, and finance. Cruise directors arrange all the onboard activities and entertainment. This sounds exciting, and it is as long as you're organized and can work under pressure. The career path to a cruise director begins with a position as an activities staff member or a sports and fitness specialist. Then, after a year or more at each of these positions, the employee is promoted to a supervisor in one department and then another, until he or she reaches the level of assistant cruise director.

Cruise Director Bill Johnson offers this advice: "The actual number of career positions on a cruise ship is limited since most ships are registered in foreign countries in order to avoid U.S. labor laws. Remember, most crews come from developing countries and work breakfast, lunch and dinner for days on end. The hotel manager and cruise director are generally from America or Europe. However, there are several land-based positions in marketing and sales and passenger service that are available to Americans. Holland America does employ more Americans than most other cruise lines and they cruise to some interesting places. If you have a flair for organizing onboard entertainment, then consider going for an assistant's position to learn the fundamentals of this important department. To become a hotel manager, you would need experience in housekeeping, food and beverage preparation and service, and supervision and management for several years."

Related Web Sites

www.cruiseshipjob.com
www.cruisejobfinder.com

SUMMARY

1. Cruising has not always been a popular vacation choice. For centuries, a seaworthy vessel was simply considered a mode of transportation. Until about the 1830s, the principal reasons for undertaking water travel were immigration, trade, and war.
2. World War I dramatically changed the ship travel industry. Many factors played a part in this, including the United States' change in immigration policies and the new attraction that Europe came to hold for Americans. All in all, cruising became the fashionable thing to do, leading to an increase in the number of cruise ships built and operated.
3. Today, cruising is on the rise. In the past decade, there has been an increase in embarkations from North American ports, and there are currently no signs that this growth will stop.
4. The three top key players in the cruise industry are Carnival, Royal Caribbean Cruises, and Norwegian Cruise Line.
5. There are marked differences between the segments of the cruise industry. The three types of cruise industry markets are the mass, middle, and luxury markets.
6. Several different types of cruises range from regional to specialty and theme cruises.
7. The term *crossing* implies sailing across the Northern Atlantic Ocean either to or from the Americas, although it can take place across any major ocean.
8. Five of the essential positions on a cruise ship are the captain, hotel manager, chief purser, cruise director, and the chief steward (or director of housekeeping).
9. Most cruise ships sail under foreign flags because they were built abroad for the following reasons:
    1. U.S. labor costs for ships, officers, and crew, in addition to maritime unions, are too high to compete in the world market.
    2. U.S. ships are not permitted to operate casino-type gambling.
    3. Many foreign shipyards are government subsidized to keep workers employed, thereby lowering construction costs.
10. Employment opportunities for Americans are mainly in sales, marketing, and other U.S. shore-based activities, such as reservations and supplies. Land-based jobs are much like those of any tour operator, in areas such as administration, sales, reservations, marketing/public relations, human resources, accounting, finance, and customer service.
11. The most popular cruise destinations are the Caribbean, Mediterranean, Alaska, and Hawaii.
12. While cruising is not the most ecofriendly mode of travel, due to increases consumer interest and developing technologies, the industry is making efforts at becoming greener.

KEY WORDS AND CONCEPTS

Adventure cruise
Air-cruise packages
Captain
Chief purser
Chief steward (or director of housekeeping)
Coastal cruises
Crossings
Cruise director
Cruise Lines International Association (CLIA)
Expeditions and natural cruises
Food and beverage manager
Hotel manager
Luxury market
Mass market
Middle market
Regional cruises
Sail-cruises
Specialty and theme cruises
Steam boating

REVIEW QUESTIONS

1. Why did the World War I dramatically change the ship travel industry?
2. How did the airplane affect the cruise industry?
3. What is the status of cruising today?
4. Who are the key players in the cruise industry?
5. What are the three segments of the cruise industry?
6. How does the career path to a cruise director begin?

INTERNET EXERCISES

1. Search the Internet to find the ports of call nearest to your location. How far is it from your location? Where do ships leaving from this port sail to? What itinerary options would you have leaving from this port (total length, length in port, where to)?
2. Using three types of cruises, search the Internet to find out which interests you most.

APPLY YOUR KNOWLEDGE

1. Brainstorm examples of who is likely to be a cruise passenger.
2. Using the examples above, apply your likely cruise passengers to the three segments of the cruise industry.
3. Map out a plan of action that you would take to become a captain of a cruise ship.
4. Map out a plan of action that you would take to become a hotel manager of a cruise ship.

SUGGESTED ACTIVITIES

1. How do you feel about most cruise ships sailing under foreign flags? Discuss your position on the current U.S. stipulations for cruise ships.
2. Discuss your position on one cruise line dominating the industry, such as Carnival.

ENDNOTES

1. P&O Cruises, www.pocruises.com.au/html/po-invents-cruising.cfm, retrieved October 2009.
2. Bob Dickinson and Andy Vladimir, *Selling the Sea* (New York: John Wiley & Sons, 1997), p. 3.
3. William H. Miller, Jr., "A History of Luxury Cruising," Seabourn Cruise Line's *Club Herald* (Spring 1996).
4. Ibid.
5. CNBC, "The Ultimate Getaway," www.cnbc.com/id/29139914/, retrieved October 2009.
6. Cruise Line International Association, www.cruising.org/Press/overview2008/#ExecSummary, retrieved October 2009.
7. Carnival Cruise Lines, www.carnival.com/cms/fun/vacation_interchange_privileges.aspx, retrieved October, 2009.
8. Royal Caribbean International, www.royalcaribbean.com/ourCompany/messageFromPresident.do, retrieved October 2009.
9. Star Cruises, www.starcruises.com/newweb/about_starcruises/default.aspx, retrieved October 2009.
10. Cruise Line International Association, www.cruising.org/Press/research/Market_Profile_2008.pdf, retrieved October 2009.
11. Cruise Critic, "Green Cruising," www.cruisecritic.com/articles.cfm?ID=528, retrieved October 2009.
12. Green Your, www.greenyour.com/transportation/travel/vacation/tips/choose-an-eco-friendly-cruise, retrieved October 2009.
13. "How Sustainable Is the Cruise Industry?," Seattle Examiner.com, http://www.examiner.com/international-travel-in-seattle/how-sustainable-is-the-cruise-industry, retrieved March 4, 2010.
14. "Eco-Tips from Sustainable Lawrence," http://sustainablelawrence.org/green_everyday.html, retrieved March 4, 2010.
15. Ibid.

7 RESTAURANTS

LEARNING OUTCOMES

After reading and studying this chapter, you should be able to:

Describe the different characteristics of chain and independent restaurants.

Identify some of the top chain and independent restaurants.

List the classifications of restaurants.

Describe characteristics of the restaurant market.

Describe the economic impact of tourism.

Restaurants

Restaurants are a vital part of our everyday lifestyles; because we are a society on the go, we patronize them several times a week to socialize, as well as eat and drink. Restaurants offer a place to relax and enjoy the company of family, friends, colleagues, and business associates, to restore our energy level before heading off to the next class or activity. Actually, the word restaurant comes from the French word meaning *restore.* Today, there are more than 945,000 restaurants in the United States with sales of $566 billion and 13 million employees. The restaurant industry is the largest employer outside of government, and its share of the food dollar has risen to 47.5 percent. On a typical day, more than 130 million people in the U.S. are guests in restaurants and foodservice operations.[1]

As a society, we spend an increasing amount—approaching 50 percent—of our food dollar away from home. Restaurants are a multibillion-dollar business that employ about 11.5 million people and contribute to our social and economic well-being.

> **Today there are more than 945,000 restaurants with sales of $566 billion and 13 million employees.**

This chapter looks at the different types of restaurants and classifies them into recognizable segments.

There is an interesting story behind the word *restaurant*. Monsieur Boulanger set up what many consider to be the first European restaurant of modern times in 1765 when he placed a sign above his Paris restaurant saying, "Boulanger sells restoratives fit for the gods." One of his featured dishes, a restorative made of sheep's feet in a wine sauce, caused a commotion when the Caters' Guild found out what he was offering and took him to court (at that time only members of the guild had the right to sell whole pieces of meat—or so they thought), but the Parliament of Paris decided in Monsieur Boulanger's favor, thus ensuring his restaurant a place in history.

Classification of Restaurants

Read the *Restaurant Ownership Handbook*: Learn about Franchising vs. Independent Operations

There is no single definition of the various classifications of restaurants, perhaps because the restaurant industry is an evolving business. Most experts would agree, however, that there are two main categories: **independent restaurants ("indies")** and **chain restaurants**. Other categories include designations as *fine dining, casual restaurants,* and *quick-service restaurants*. Some restaurants may even fall into more than one category; for instance, a restaurant can be both ethnic and quick service, such as Taco Bell.

The National Restaurant Association's figures indicate that Americans are spending an increasing number of food dollars away from home in various foodservice operations. Americans are eating out more than ever—up to five times a week, including special occasions like birthdays, anniversaries, Mother's Day, and Valentine's Day. The most popular meal eaten away from home is lunch, which brings in approximately 50 percent of fast-food restaurant sales.

Individual restaurants (also called *indies*) are typically owned by one or more proprietors, who are usually involved in the day-to-day operation of the business. Even if the owners have more than one store ("store" is restaurantspeak for "restaurant"), each functions independently. These restaurants are not affiliated with any national brand or name. They offer the owner independence, creativity, and flexibility. However, they are accompanied by some risk: the restaurant may not be as popular as the owners hoped it would be, the owners lack the knowledge and expertise necessary for success in the restaurant business; or the owners do not have the cash flow to last several months before a profit can be made. One example is a Southern-style restaurant in California—it was not appropriate for the market. You have only to look around your neighborhood to find examples of restaurants that failed for one reason or another.

Chain restaurants, on the other hand, are a group of restaurants, each identical in market, concept, design, service, food, and name. Part of the marketing strategy of a chain restaurant is to remove uncertainty from the dining experience. The same menu, food quality, level of service, and atmosphere can be found in any one of the restaurants in a chain, regardless of location. Chain restaurants can be owned by large companies or entrepreneurs, they can be franchised, or several may be owned by one person or a group of people. One example of a restaurant chain is Applebee's. Some Applebee's restaurants are company owned, but the majority are franchised by territory.

CLASSICAL CUISINE

North America gained most of its culinary legacy from France. Two main events were responsible for this culinary legacy. First was the French Revolution in 1793, during which the best chefs of the day lost their employment when their bosses lost their heads! Many chefs came to North America as a result, bringing their culinary talents. The second was Thomas Jefferson, who was envoy to France from 1784–1789 and brought a French chef to the White House when he became president. This act stimulated interest in French cuisine and enticed U.S. tavern owners to offer better quality and more interesting food.

Explore a Bit of Culinary History at Vernon's

No mention of classical cuisine can be made without talking about the founders. Marie-Antoine Carême (1784–1833), known as the "Chef of Kings and King of Chefs," is credited as the founder of classical cuisine and menu making. Carême was abandoned on the streets of Paris as a child, and worked his way up from cook's helper to become chef to Prince de Talleyrand, who was the prince regent of England. He also served as head chef to the future King George IV of England, Tsar Alexander I of Russia, and Baron de Rothschild. His goal was to achieve "lightness," "grace," "order," and "perspicuity" of food.[2]

The other great contributor to classical cuisine was Auguste Escoffier (1846–1935) who, unlike Carême, never worked in an aristocratic household. Instead, he held forth in the finest hotels of the time: the Place Vendôme in Paris, and the Savoy and Carlton Hotels in London. Escoffier is noted for his many contributions to cuisine, including simplifying Carême's *grande cuisine* by reducing the number of flavors and garnishes used in a dish, and even simplifying the number of sauces to five "mother" or leading sauces. Escoffier brought simplicity and harmony to refine the *grande cuisine*. His many cookbooks are still in use today: *La Guide Culinaire* (1903), a collection of over 5,000 classic cuisine recipes; *Le Livre des Menus* (1912), in which he compares a great meal to a symphony; and *Ma Cuisine* (1934). All of his books emphasize the importance of mastering the techniques of cooking.[1]

Meet Some Famous Chefs in *Culinary History*

Sarah R. Labensky and Alan M. Hause, *On Cooking*, 4th ed. (Upper Saddle River, NJ: Prentice Hall, 2007), pp. 6–7.

Franchises

Franchises are a major driving force in the restaurant industry. With a franchise, successful restaurant operators can expand more rapidly than if they used their own capital or financing. By using other people's money, they can save their own and still make money in the process. A person who wants a franchise must pay an initial royalty fee of several thousand dollars, plus an average of 3 to 6 percent of sales for marketing and other support. The main benefit of a franchise is that the concept is proven and unlikely to fail, so there is less risk involved compared to opening a standalone restaurant. Franchise owners also receive help marketing and preopening help, as well as operating assistance in the form of procedures and training.

The drawbacks of franchising are:

1. The initial franchise fee can cost from $20,000 to $40,000, or more.
2. An average restaurant's construction will cost about $100,000 plus.
3. Royalty payments, which must be paid for as long as the proprietor owns the franchise, are a percentage of sales (usually 4 percent).
4. There is a charge for marketing and advertising (usually about 2 percent of sales).
5. A franchise offers limited flexibility and creativity because the owner must comply with the terms of the franchise.

Having said all that, many successful restaurant operators have become wealthy by franchising their restaurants; many more franchisees are millionaires because they have purchased and successfully operate a franchise.

Fine Dining

A **fine dining restaurant** offers a good selection of menu items: generally, at least 15 or more different entrees are cooked to order, with nearly all the food being made on the premises from scratch, using raw or fresh ingredients. Full-service restaurants may be formal or casual, and may be further categorized by price, decor/atmosphere, level of formality, and menu.

Experience Fine Dining Firsthand at Vernon's Restaurant

The level of service in fine dining restaurants is generally high. A greeter welcomes and seats guests. Captains and food servers advise guests of special items and assist with the description and selection of dishes during order taking. If there is no separate sommelier (wine expert and server), the captain or food server may offer a description of the wine that will complement the meal and help take the order. The decor is generally compatible with the overall ambiance and theme that the restaurant seeks to create. These elements of food, service, and decor create a memorable experience for the restaurant guest.

Most fine dining restaurants are independently owned and operated by an entrepreneur or a partnership. These restaurants are in almost every city. In recent years, fine dining has become more fun. as creative chefs offer guests fine cuisine as an art. At places like Union Square Café and Gramercy Tavern in New York, owner Danny Meyer looks for guests who want spectacular meals without the fuss. Many cities have independent fine dining restaurants that offer fine dining for an occasion—a birthday, an "expense account" (business entertaining), or other celebration.

Fine dining offers many different kind of experiences: the steak house, or ethnic, celebrity, and theme restaurants. The upscale steak dinner houses, such as Morton's of Chicago, Ruth Chris's, and Houston's, continue to attract the expense account and "occasion" diners. Naturally, they are located near their guests, in cities with large convention centers or attractions that draw big crowds.

A few ethnic restaurants are considered fine dining—most cities have a sampling of Italian, French, and other European, Latin, or Asian restaurants. Some even have a **fusion** (a blend of two cuisines, such as Italian and Japanese).

Notable celebrity chef–owned fine dining restaurants include Spago in Los Angeles and Chinois in Santa Monica, California (co-owned by Wolfgang Puck); Charlie Trotter's in Chicago (owned by Charlie Trotter); and Chez Panisse in Berkeley, California (owned by Alice Waters), have done much to inspire a new generation of talented chefs. Alice Waters has been a role model for many female chefs; she has received numerous awards and published several cookbooks, including one for children.

Discover the Art of Menu Development with the Chef of Vernon's

Fusion restaurants must pay particular attention when blending two unique ethnic flavors. If successful, the dish could turn out to be the latest craze; if unsuccessful, it could be disastrous!

Check Your Knowledge

1. Describe the differences between a chain and an independent restaurant.
2. Describe some characteristics of a fine dining restaurant.
3. Explain the term fusion cuisine.

Theme Restaurants

Charlie Trotter, King of Fusion and one of America's finest chef-owners.

Many **theme restaurants** combine a sophisticated specialty with another type of restaurants. They aim to wow the guest with a total experience: a particular decor and atmosphere, and a limited menu that blends with the theme. Of the many popular theme restaurants, two stand out. The first highlights the nostalgia of the 1950s, serving all-American food like meatloaf in a fun atmosphere (maybe a T-Bird or Corvette diner) that is a throwback to the seemingly more carefree 1950s. The food servers wear short polka-dot skirts with saddle shoes and bobby socks. Other popular themes found in the United States and across the globe include the airplane, railway, or dining car; rock and roll; 1960s' nostalgia; and many others.

The second is the dinner house category: some of the better-known national and regional chains include TGI Friday's, Houlihan's, and Bennigan's. These casual, American bistro-type restaurants offer a lively atmosphere created in part by assorted bric-a-brac on shelves and walls. Popular during the past 20 years, these restaurants can do extremely well in a prime location.

A vintage car and other memorabilia create the theme at this restaurant.

.inc | Corporate Profile

OUTBACK STEAKHOUSE

The founders of Outback Steakhouse, a pioneer in the steak house sector of the restaurant business, have proved that unconventional methods can lead to profitable results. Such methods include opening solely for dinner, sacrificing dining-room seats for back-of-the-house efficiency, limiting servers to three tables each, and giving 10 percent of cash flow to the restaurants' general managers (as an incentive to manage all the way to the bottom line).

March 1988 saw the opening of the first Outback Steakhouse. Outback's founders, Chris Sullivan, Robert Basham, and Senior Vice President Tim Gannon, know plenty about the philosophy of "No rules, just right", because they were already living it. And their venture to launch a casual steak place came when many pundits were pronouncing red meat consumption dead in America.

It was evident that the three founders were piloting one of the country's hottest restaurant concepts when they found themselves with 230 restaurants instead of the 5 they had originally envisioned.

Robert Basham, cofounder, president, and chief operating officer, received the Operator of the Year award at MUFSO '96 (Multi-Unit Foodservice Operators Conference). He has helped expand the chain and earn some of the highest sales per unit in the industry in spite of the fact that it serves only dinner.

Perhaps the strongest indication of what this company is about lies in its corporate structure, or lack thereof. Despite its rapid growth, the company has no public relations department, no human resources department, and no recruiting apparatus. In addition, the Outback Steakhouse headquarters is very different from that of a typical restaurant company. There is no lavish tower—only modest office space in an average suburban complex. Instead of settling into a conservative chair and browsing through a magazine-lined coffee table (as is the case in most reception areas), at Outback you must belly up to an actual bar, brass foot rail and all, to announce your arrival.

Also, Outback's dining experience—large, highly seasoned portions of food for moderate prices—is so in tune with today's dining experience that patrons in many of its restaurants experience hour-long dinner waits seven nights a week. The friendly service is notable, from the host who opens the door and greets guests, to the well-trained servers, who casually sit down next to patrons in the booths and explain the house specialties featured on the menu.

Using such tactics and their "No rules, just right" philosophy, they have accomplished two main goals: discipline and solid growth. Good profits and excellent marketing potentials show just how successful the business has become. Outback also owns and operates Bonefish Grill, Fleming's Prime Steakhouse, Caraba's Italian Grill, Roy's, and Cheeseburger in Paradise.

Celebrity Restaurants

Celebrity-owned restaurants are popular. Some celebrities came from a culinary background, such as Wolfgang Puck. Others have not, such as supermodels Naomi Campbell, Claudia Schiffer, and Elle Macpherson (Fashion Café); Peter Fonda (Thunder Roadhouse); Kevin Costner (The Clubhouse); Arnold Schwarzenegger (Schazi); and Jennifer Lopez (Madre's). A number of sports celebrities also have restaurants, including are Michael Jordan, Dan Marino, Junior Seau, and Wayne Gretzky. Television and movie stars have also gotten into the act: Oprah Winfrey was part owner of The Eccentric in Chicago for a number of years; Dustin Hoffman and Henry Winkler are investors in Campanile, a popular Los Angeles restaurant; and Denzel Washington and Dan Ackroyd are involved in House of Blues. Musicians Kenny Rogers and Gloria Estefan are also restaurant owners. Celebrity restaurants generally have an extra zing to them—a winning combination of design, atmosphere, food, and perhaps the thrill of an occasional visit by the owner(s).

Steakhouses

Some steak restaurants add value-priced items like chicken and fish to their menus in order to attract more customers. Steak restaurant operators admit that they are not expecting to see the same customers every week, but hopefully every two or three weeks. The Chart House chain is careful to market its menu as seafood and chicken, but steak is at the heart of the business, with most of its sales from red meat.

The Longhorn Steakhouse chain has 323 units and is owned by Darden Restaurants. Other steak house chains include Outback Steakhouse, the number one volume steak sales restaurant. Stewart Anderson's Black Angus, Golden Corral, Western Sizzlin', and Ryan's Family Steak Houses all have sales in the millions of dollars. In this segment, chains have the biggest share of the market.

Casual Dining

Restaurants that fall into the casual dining category include:

Midscale casual restaurants	Romano's Macaroni Grill, The Olive Garden
Family restaurants	Cracker Barrel, Coco's, Carrow's
Ethnic restaurants	Flavor Thai, Cantina Latina, Panda Express

As implied, **casual dining** is relaxed. It may include restaurants from several classifications: chain or independent, ethnic, or theme. Hard Rock Cafe, TGI Friday's, The Olive Garden, Houston's, Romano's Macaroni Grill, and Red Lobster are good examples of casual dining.

Houston's is a leader in the casual restaurant segment with about $5.5 million in average per unit sales in its 43 restaurants (most other casual restaurants do between $2 and $3.5 million in sales). The menu is limited to about 40 items and focuses on American cuisine, with a $16 average per-person ticket for lunch and a cost of $35 to $45 for dinner. While encouraging local individuality in its restaurants and maintaining exceptional executive and unit general manager stability, it succeeds with no franchising and virtually no external advertising.³

Over the past few years, the trend in **dinner house restaurants** has been toward more casual dining. This trend merely reflects the mode of society. A variety of restaurant chains call themselves "dinner house restaurants." Some of them could fit into the theme category. Many dinner house restaurants have a casual, eclectic decor that may promote a theme.

Friday's is an American bistro dinner house chain with a full menu and bric-a-brac decor that contributes to the fun atmosphere. Friday's has been in operation for nearly 40 years, so the concept has stood the test of time. (See Chapter 8 for a feature on Friday's as a corporation of excellence.)

A casual restaurant offers guests a chance to enjoy each other's company and good food and drinks.

Family Restaurants

Family restaurants have evolved from the coffee-shop style of restaurant. Most of these restaurants are individually or family operated and are generally located in or with easy access to the suburbs. Most offer an informal setting with a simple menu and service designed to please the entire family. Some family restaurants offer alcoholic beverages, consisting mostly of beer, wine, and perhaps a cocktail special. There is often a greeter/cashier standing near the entrance to welcome and seat guests while food servers take the orders and bring the plated food from the kitchen. Some family restaurants have incorporated salad and dessert bars to offer more variety and increase the average check.

The lines separating the various restaurants and chains in the family segment are blurring as operators upscale their concepts. Coco's and Carrow's family restaurant brands have created the high-end niche of family dining—somewhere between traditional coffee shops and the casual dining segment. Denny's is an example of the value-oriented family dining restaurant. The more upscale family concepts include Perkins, Marie Callender's, and Cracker Barrel, all of which are sometimes referred to as the "relaxed" segment. These chains tend to have higher check averages than do traditional and value-oriented family chains, and compete not only with them, but also with moderately priced, casual-themed operators, such as Applebee's and TGI Friday's.

Karen Brennan, former vice president of marketing for the Coco's concept, says that people's use of restaurants is very different from just five years ago. Consumers now think in terms of "meal solutions." The operators in this segment seek to capitalize on two trends affecting the industry as a whole: the tendency of families to dine out together more often, and the quest among adults for higher-quality, more flavorful food offerings.

Ethnic Restaurants

The majority of **ethnic restaurants** are independently owned and operated. The owners and their families provide something different for the adventurous diner or a taste of home for those of the same ethnic background as the restaurant. Historically, the traditional ethnic restaurants sprang up to cater to the taste of the various immigrant groups—Italian, Chinese, and so on.

Read about the Different Types of Menus Offered to Guests at the Sea & Tea Café

Perhaps the fastest-growing segment of ethnic restaurants in the United States, popularity-wise, is Mexican. Mexican food has a heavy representation in the Southwestern states, although, because of near-market saturation, the chains are spreading east. Taco Bell is the Mexican quick-service market leader, with a 60 percent share. This *Fortune* 500 company has achieved this incredible result with a value-pricing policy that has increased traffic in all units. Taco Bell has more than 7,000 units with sales of about $5 billion, 70 percent of which is via the drive-thru.[4] Other large Mexican food chains are Del Taco, Chi-Chi's, and El Torito. These Mexican-food chains can offer a variety of items on a value menu, starting at 69 cents.

U.S. major cities offer a great variety of ethnic restaurants, and their popularity is increasing. Just consider the growth of recent ethnic restaurants in your community. How many ethnic restaurants do you have and what kinds of food are they serving?

Quick-Service/Fast-Food Restaurants

Quick-service restaurants consist of diverse operating facilities whose slogan is "quick food." Types of operations in this category include hamburger, pizza, chicken, pancakes, sandwich shops, and delivery services.

The quick-service sector really drives the industry. Recently, the home-meal replacement and fast casual concepts have gained momentum.

Quick-service or fast-food restaurants offer limited menus, featuring food such as hamburgers, fries, hot dogs, chicken (in all forms), tacos, burritos, gyros, teriyaki bowls, various finger foods, and other items for the convenience of people on the go. Customers order their food at a counter under a brightly lit menu featuring color photographs of food items. Customers are even encouraged to clear their own trays, which helps reduce costs.

The following are examples of the different types of quick-service/fast-food restaurants:

Hamburger—McDonald's, Burger King, Wendy's
Pizza—Pizza Hut, Domino's, Godfather's, Papa John's
Seafood—Long John Silver's
Chicken—KFC, Church's, Boston Market, Kenny Roger's, Popeye's
Sandwich—Subway
Mexican—Taco Bell, El Torito
Italian—Sbarro's

A floating restaurant in Hong Kong provides an interesting dining alternative.

Chinese—Panda Express
Delivery—Domino's, Pizza Hut

See Suggestive Selling in Action: Visit the Sea & Tea Café

Quick-service restaurants have increased in popularity because of their location strategies. They are found in very convenient locations in every possible area. Their menus are limited, which makes it easy for customers to make quick decisions on what to eat. The world equates time with money these days, and most people do not want to spend time trying to look through long menus to make an eating decision. These restaurants deliver fast service and usually include self-service facilities, too. They also use cheaper, processed ingredients, which allow them to have extremely low, competitive prices. Quick-service restaurants also require minimum use of both skilled and unskilled labor, which increases profit margins. Figure 7–1 shows the market shares by restaurant segment.

In an attempt to raise flat sales figures, more quick-service restaurant (QSR) chains are using co-branding at stores and nontraditional locations, including highway plazas and shopping cen-

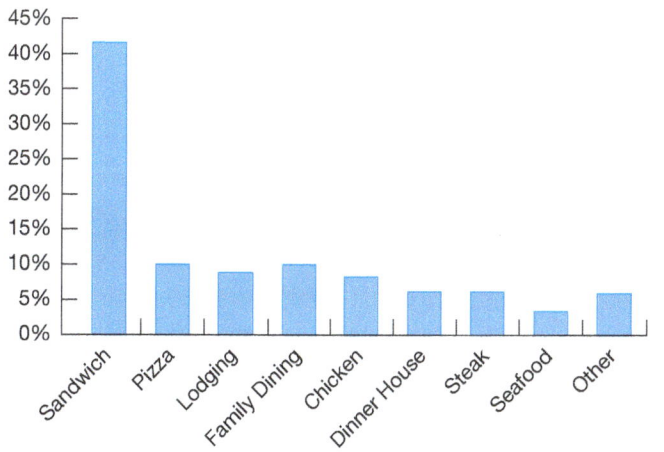

FIGURE 7–1 Top 100 Market Shares by Restaurant Segment.

ters. Taco Bell and Long John Silver are a good example. It is hoped that the traffic-building combos will increase sales among the separate brands, such as Carl's Jr. and Green Burrito, as well as concepts like Triarc Co.'s Arby's, Zu Zu, P. T. Noodles, and T. J. Cinnamon brands. Many QSR chains are targeting international growth, mostly in the larger cities in a variety of countries.

Hamburger

McDonald's is the giant of the quick-service/fast-food segment, with worldwide sales in the billions. This total is amazing because it is more than the next three megachains combined—Burger King, KFC, and Pizza Hut. McDonald's has individual product items other than the traditional burger—for example, chicken McNuggets, burritos, salads, and fish, which all aim to broaden customer appeal. Customer appeal has also been extended by the introduction of breakfast and by targeting not only kids but also seniors. Innovative menu introductions have helped stimulate an increase in per-store traffic. McDonald's Bistro is an innovative concept that is receiving great guest reviews.

A pizza being cooked in a special pizza oven.

In recent years, because traditional markets have become saturated, McDonald's has adopted a strategy of expanding overseas. It has embarked on a rapid expansion in the world's most populous nation, China, with more than 12,000 restaurants nationwide. The country's rapidly developing middle class with a growing appetite for Western culture and food is driving this expansion. McDonald's is now in 118 countries and has a potential audience of 3.2 billion people. Of the company's roughly 31,000 restaurants, some 8,600 are outside the United States, serving 58 million people each day.[5]

More than two-thirds of new restaurants added by McDonald's are outside of the United States. It is interesting to note that about 50 percent of McDonald's total profits come from outside of the United States. McDonald's also seeks out nontraditional locations in the U.S. market, such as military bases or smaller-sized units in high-rent districts.

McDonald's is taking another step toward being the most convenient foodservice operation in the world by striking deals with gasoline companies Chevron, U.S. Petroleum Star Enterprise, and Mobil Oil Corporation to co-develop sites.

It is very difficult to obtain a McDonald's franchise in the United States because the company has virtually saturated the primary markets. It often costs between $1 million and $2 million to open a major brand fast-food restaurant. Franchises for lesser known chains are available for less money (about $35,000 and a 4 percent of sales royalty fee and 4 percent for advertising).

Each of the major hamburger restaurant chains has a unique positioning strategy to attract its target markets. Burger King hamburgers are flame broiled, Wendy's uses fresh patties. Some smaller regional chains are succeeding in gaining market share from the big-three burger chains because they provide an excellent burger at a reasonable price. In-N-Out Burger, Sonic, and Rally's are good examples of this.

Pizza

The pizza segment continues to grow. By some estimates, it is now a $21 billion market, with much of the growth fueled by the convenience of delivery. Chains include Pizza Hut, Domino's, Godfather's, Papa John's, and Little Caesar's. Pizza Hut, with 7,500 system-wide sales of $5 billion, has broken into the delivery part of the business over which, until recently, Domino's had a virtual monopoly. Pizza Hut has now developed system-wide delivery units that also offer two pizzas at a reduced price.

In response to the success of Pizza Hut's Stuffed Crust Pizza, Domino's highlights its Ultimate Deep Dish Pizza and Pesto Crust Pizza. With 12 toppings to choose from, people can have fun designing their own pizza.

Chicken

Chicken has always been a popular menu item and is likely to remain so because it is relatively cheap to produce, readily available, and adaptable to a variety of preparations. It also is perceived as a healthier alternative to burgers (but, depending on the item, it may contain more calories!).

Kentucky Fried Chicken (KFC) has a worldwide total of more than 15,000 units in the U.S. and 36,000 around the world. KFC is a part of Yum Brands, Inc., the world's largest restaurant company. With sales of $11 billion, KFC dominates the chicken segment. Even though KFC is a market leader, the company continues to explore new ways to get its products to consumers. More units now offer home delivery, and in many cities KFC is teaming up with sister restaurant Taco Bell to sell products from both chains in one convenient location. KFC continues to build menu variety as it focuses on providing complete meals to families, with new products such as Tender Roast® chicken pieces,

Sustainable Restaurants

The average American meal has a shockingly large carbon footprint, usually traveling 1,500 miles to the plate and emitting large amounts of CO_2 in the process, according to the Leopold Center for Sustainable Agriculture. Each meal created produces 275 pounds of waste a day, making restaurants the worst aggressors of greenhouse gas emissions in retail industry, says the Boston-based Green Restaurant Association [GRA], a nonprofit organization that works to create an ecologically sustainable restaurant industry.[7]

A recent NRA [National Restaurant Association] study shows that utility costs are a big line item for restaurateurs, accounting for a median of between 2.3 percent and 3.6 percent of sales, depending on the type of operation. According to *Zagat's America's Top Restaurants*, 65 percent of surveyors said they would pay more for food that has been sustainably raised or procured. According to National Restaurant Association research, 62 percent of adults said they would likely choose a restaurant based on its environmental friendliness.[8]

Does greenings restaurant sound challenging, time-consuming, and costly? According to the Green Restaurant Association (GRA), it doesn't have to be any of those things. The GRA was founded almost 20 years ago with the mission of creating an ecologically sustainable restaurant industry, and it has the world's largest database of environmental solutions for the restaurant industry.[9] The GRA strives to simplify things because it realizes that restaurateurs have enough on their plates without worrying what kind of paper towel to order, or where they'll get next month's supply of ecofriendly dish soap.[10]

Chunky Chicken Pot Pie, and Colonel's Crispy Strips. There are now more than 1,000 KFC restaurants in China.[6]

Church's Chicken, the 1,500-unit division of AFC Enterprises, is the second-largest chicken chain. Its value menu features Southern-style chicken, spicy chicken wings, okra, corn on the cob, coleslaw, biscuits, and other items. Church's has focused on becoming a low-cost provider and the fastest to market. To give customers the value they expect day in and day out, it is necessary to have system-wide unit economies in order.

Popeye's is now the third-largest chain in the chicken segment with 1,700 units. It is owned by AFC, the same parent company as Church's. Popeye's is a New Orleans–inspired, "spicy chicken" chain operating more than 300 restaurants in Texas and Louisiana that is expanding into 11 markets around the country. The chain hopes to increase average-unit sales to $1 million.

There are a number of up-and-coming regional chains, such as El Pollo Loco, of Irvine, California. El Pollo Loco focuses on a marinated, flame-broiled chicken that is a unique, high-quality product. Kenny Rogers and Cluckers are also expanding rotisserie chains.

Sandwich Restaurants

Indicative of America's obsession with the quick and convenient, sandwiches have achieved star status. Recently, menu debuts in the sandwich segment have outpaced all others. Classics, like melts and club sandwiches, have returned with a vengeance—and now there are also wraps.

Au Bon Pain of Boston is currently rolling out a line of eight new sourdough bagels designed to boost breakfast sales and keep regulars engaged. The bagels, which include such signature flavors as Asiago cheese and wild blueberry, are also available as a sandwich option. The company has also introduced a chicken salad sandwich made from all natural chicken with almonds and dried cranberries.

A sandwich restaurant is a popular way for a young entrepreneur to enter the restaurant business. The leader in this segment is Subway, which operates more than 20,000 units in 75 countries. Cofounder Fred Deluca parlayed an initial investment of $1,000 into one of the largest and fastest-growing chains in the world. Franchise fees are $10,000 with a second store fee of $2,500. Average unit sales are about $270,000 annually, with yearly costs of about $75,000.

The Subway strategy is to invest half of the chain's advertising dollars in national advertising. Franchise owners pay 2.5 percent of sales to the marketing fund. As with other chains, Subway is attempting to widen its core 18- to 34-year-old customer base by adding kids' meals and "value 4-inch round" $5 foot long sandwiches. Sandwich restaurants stress the health value of their restaurants.

> **"** Subway average unit sales are about $270,000 annually, with yearly costs of about $75,000. **"**

Delivery Services

Delivery services take prepared foods to customers' homes. Delivery service describes meals-on-wheels programs, as well as urban restaurants that deliver to a neighborhood. A customer calls the operation to place an order after looking at restaurant menus from home. The delivery service processes the order and delivers it. These services can be connected to an existing

Introducing Richard Melman

Chairman of the Board and Founder, Lettuce Entertain You Enterprises, Inc.

Richard Melman is founder and chairman of Lettuce Entertain You Enterprises, Inc., a Chicago-based corporation that owns and licenses nearly 50 restaurants nationwide and in Japan.

The restaurant business has been Melman's life work, beginning with his early days in a family-owned restaurant, later as a teenager working in fast-food eateries and a soda fountain, and then selling restaurant supplies. After realizing that he wasn't cut out to be a college student and failing to convince his father that he should be made a partner in the family business, Melman met Jerry A. Orzoff, a man who immediately and unconditionally believed in Melman's ability to create and run restaurants. In 1971, the two opened R. J. Grunts, a hip burger joint that soon became one of the hottest restaurants in Chicago. Here, Melman and Orzoff presented food differently and with a sense of humor, creating the youthful and fun restaurant that was a forerunner in the trend toward dining out as entertainment that swept this country in the early 1970s.

Melman and Orzoff continued to develop restaurant concepts together until Orzoff's death in 1981. Through his relationship with Orzoff, Melman formulated a philosophy based on the importance of partners, of sharing responsibilities and profits with them, and of developing and growing together.[1]

To operate so many restaurants well, Lettuce must hire, train, and develop its employees, and then keep them happy and focused on excellence. Melman's guiding philosophy is that he is not interested in being the biggest or the best known—only in being the best he can be. He places enormous value on the people who work for Lettuce Entertain You Enterprises and feels tremendous responsibility for their continued success. Today, he has 40 working partners, most of whom came up through the organization, and 5,000 people working for him. Over the years, Melman has stayed close to the guests by using **focus groups** (groups of "typical" guests who give an opinion on topics presented to them—companies use these groups to see how well an idea would be accepted by guests) and frequent diner programs. The group's training programs are rated among the best in the business. Melman's own management style is clearly influenced by team sports. He says, "There are many similarities between running a restaurant and a team sport. However, it's not a good idea to have 10 all-stars; everybody can't bat first. You need people with similar goals—people who want to win and play hard."[2]

[1] Marilyn Alva, "Does He Still Have It?" *Restaurant Business*, 93, 4, March 1, 1994, pp. 104–111.
[2] Personal communication with Richard Melman, June 8, 2004.

---

restaurant or operate on their own. Domino's Pizza is a primary example of this kind of operation. Many restaurants followed Domino's lead, and other popular delivery services in the United States now include Papa John's and Pizza Hut.

Some delivery services function differently. They offer a limited menu from various participating neighborhood restaurants. The customer places an order with the delivery service, and then the service places the order with the restaurant, picks it up, and delivers it to the customer.

Check Your Knowledge

1. Describe the different types of restaurants and give examples of each. Highlight some of the characteristics that make up the specific restaurant types.
2. What are some characteristics of casual dining?

GREEN RESTAURANT CERTIFICATION 4.0 STANDARDS[11]

The GRA has been certifying restaurants for the past two decades. Green Restaurant® 4.0 provides a comprehensive and user-friendly method of rewarding existing restaurants and foodservice operations, new builds, and events with points in each of the GRA's "Seven Environmental Categories."

1. Water efficiency
2. Waste reduction and recycling
3. Sustainable furnishings and building materials
4. Sustainable food
5. Energy

6. Disposables
7. Chemical and pollution reduction

Certified Green Restaurants accumulate points and are awarded two, three, or four stars, according to the number of points they have. As more restaurants join the Green Restaurant Association and become certified, the greater the impact on reducing their environmental footprint will be.

Food Trends and Practices

Discover New Food Trends: Visit the Sea & Tea Café

As the level of professionalism rises for the chef of the twenty-first century, chefs will need a strong culinary foundation of multicultural cooking skills and strong employability traits, such as passion, dependability, cooperation, and initiative. Additional management skills include strong supervisory training; a sense of urgency; and training in accounting, sanitation/safety, nutritional awareness, and marketing/merchandising.

The term *back-to-basics cooking* has been redefined to mean infusing modern technology and science into classical cooking methods to create healthy and flavorful dishes. Some examples include:

- Thickening soups and sauces by processing and using the food item's natural starches instead of traditional thickening methods
- Redefining the basic mother sauces to omit the béchamel and egg-based sauces and add or replace with coulis, salsas, or chutneys
- Pursuing cultural culinary fusion to develop bold and aggressive flavors
- Experimenting with sweet and hot flavors
- Taking advantage of the shrinking globe and the disappearance of national borders to bring new ideas and flavors to restaurants
- Evaluating recipes and substituting ingredients for better flavor; that is, flavored liquid instead of water, infused oils and vinegars instead of nonflavored oils and vinegars
- Substituting herbs and spices for salt
- Returning to one-pot cooking to capture flavors

This is truly an exciting time to enter the hospitality industry and in particular the culinary arts. Today, being a chef is considered a profession that offers a variety of opportunities in every segment of the hospitality industry and anywhere in the world.

TRENDS in THE RESTAURANT BUSINESS

- **Demographics:** Almost one-third of the American population, the 78 million baby boomers, are beginning to retire, many of whom are wealthy. Simply put, the largest demographic group has the most money. The boomers are seeking attention, and if we make them feel special and give them what they like, they will become loyal guests. So, look for more early bird specials!
- **Branding**: Restaurant operators are using the power of branding, both in terms of brand-name recognition from a franchising viewpoint and in the products they use. People associate a level of quality with branding and often feel more comfortable purchasing a recognized brand.
- **Alternative outlets:** There will be increased competition from convenience "c-stores" and home meal replacement outlets. More and more, we are a society on the move with time constraints, so there will continue to be increased use of alternative outlets.
- **Globalization:** Look for continued transnational development. Restaurant chains are now increasing their operations in several other countries. There is increased interest in food from other countries, and people are trying different cuisines with greater frequency.
- **Continued diversification within the various dining segments:** An example is the quick, casual restaurant—people want better but still quick-service food. More chain and independent restaurants are likely to open up to satisfy the market demands.
- **More twin and multiple locations:** Due to the high costs of land and of opening up a restaurant, operators will continue to open twin and multiple restaurants. This also ties in with giving guests what they want, where they want it, and when they want it.
- **More points of service (e.g., Taco Bell at gas stations):** More points of service mean more convenience for guests and opportunities for expansion for operators.
- **Sustainability:** The greening of restaurants is increasing as more guests and restaurateurs' realize the importance of sustainability and the fact that it helps improve bottom lines.

CASE STUDY

Short Staffed in the Kitchen

Sally is the general manager of one of the best restaurants in town, known as The Pub. As usual, at 6:00 P.M. on a Friday night, there is a 45-minute wait. The kitchen is overloaded and is running behind in check times, the time that elapses between the kitchen getting the order and the guest receiving his or her meal. This is critical, especially if a guest complains about waiting too long for a meal.

Sally is waiting for her two head line cooks to come in for the closing shift. At 6:15 P.M., she receives phone calls from both of them. They are both sick with the flu and are not coming to work.

As Sally gets off the phone, the hostess tells her that a party of 50 is scheduled to arrive at 7:30 P.M. Sally is concerned, knowing that they are currently running a six-person line with only four cooks. The productivity is very high, but the check times are extremely long. How can Sally handle the situation?

DISCUSSION QUESTIONS

1. How would you handle the short-staffing issue?
2. What measures would you take to get the appropriate cooks in to work as soon as possible?
3. What would you do to ensure a smooth, successful transition for the party of 50?
4. How would you manipulate your floor plan to provide execptional service for the party of 50?
5. How would you immediately make an impact on the long check times?
6. What should you do to ensure that all the guests in the restaurant are happy?

CAREER INFORMATION

The restaurant industry employs over 12 million people in 878,000 locations and continues to grow. In the year 2010, the industry is projected to have one million locations and employ 13 million people.[12] Due to the number of restaurants, careers are readily available. The key is determining which aspect of the restaurant is most favorable to you. The typical restaurant career leads to kitchen manager, bar manager, restaurant manager, general manager, vice president, president, and owner.

During the college years, it is best to gain experience in as many areas of the restaurant as possible. Because most food and beverage service jobs are part time, it is easy to fit them around your school schedule. You may start out as a food runner, primarily delivering meals to guests, or a busser, clearing tables of used dishes. Sticking with the job can result in advancement to a food server. A food server's primary job is to be sure that the guest has a pleasurable dining experience. Servers greet guests, take orders, refill drinks, serve guests, and clean up tables to prepare for new guests. The job of a food server is often fast paced and requires patience and a good attitude when dealing with guests.

Tips make up the majority of a food server's wages. Competition among employees often arises at fine dining restaurants where potential earnings from tips are greatest. It is usually not the server with the most seniority who is given the best tables but instead the server who has the best people skills and gives guest turnover priority. Once a food server is fully competent in his or her area, he or she may advance to shift leader. A shift leader has the same responsibilities as a food server but is also often responsible for training new staff, opening and closing the restaurant, and scheduling sections for the day. After being a shift leader, you will need to gain experience as a bar-back (the person who stocks and preps the bar prior to service), then bartender. Being bartender can be challenging, but is mostly great fun and is well-paid work.

Because servers work primarily for tips, it is difficult to determine an average salary. The average hourly earnings of food servers, not including tips, is $6.42. For most servers, higher earnings are primarily the result of receiving more money in tips rather than a higher hourly wage. Tips usually average between 10 and 20 percent of a guest check, so servers working in busy, expensive restaurants earn the most.[13] Another aspect of the restaurant industry that appeals to many is the career of kitchen manager or chef.

Since the food is the primary reason guests continue to patronize a restaurant, it is up to the chef to be sure that the guests receive a meal that meets or exceeds their expectations. In chain-operated restaurants, menus are prepared at the corporate office; in independent restaurants, chefs prepare menus, measure and mix ingredients, and use a variety of pots, blenders, etc., to prepare meals. The kitchen

HTi Learn about Great Customer Service at the Sea & Tea Café

HTi Discover What It Takes to Be a Chef

usually consists of a kitchen manager or chef and at least one prep cook who performs preliminary tasks, such as gathering ingredients and preparing them for use. Large operations employ several chefs who specialize in one area of cooking. For example, a pastry cook may be hired to make desserts, a pantry cook to prepare cold dishes for lunch and dinner, and a grill cook to take care of that station.

Most chefs start out as prep cooks to gain experience. Cooking not only requires education; it is also about experience. After acquiring basic skills and a college degree in culinary arts, it is not hard to advance to higher positions.

However, to achieve the level of skill required of an executive chef or cook in a fine restaurant, several years of training and experience are necessary. More and more chefs are choosing to obtain formal training through vocational programs, colleges and universities, or at culinary institutes.

The salary of a chef depends greatly on the location and type of restaurant he or she works in. Chefs in high-end restaurants can make as much as $58,000; executive chefs in very famous restaurants earn much more, up to and over $100,000 if they are superstars. Some chefs go on to own their own restaurants.

Restaurant managers have a variety of tasks to perform. Not only do they oversee the daily activities in the restaurant, but they must also be proficient in all areas of the establishment, from the kitchen to the host stand to the tables. They select menu items, predict daily food and beverage consumption totals, and place orders based on these predictions. Managers also act as the human resources department, recruiting, hiring, firing, and keeping peace among the employees. One of a manager's toughest tasks is employee retention, as turnover in the industry is incredibly high.

Because peak restaurant times are nights and weekends, managers often work long shifts at these times. It is not uncommon for a manager to work 12- to 15-hour days, six or seven days a week, logging more than 50 hours of work. However, most restaurant companies have adjusted to a five-day week.

Some restaurants recruit managers from two- or four-year college hospitality programs. Although others hire those with a degree of any sort, the hospitality degree with work experience in the industry is preferred. Advancement in management will come with experience over time. Willingness to relocate is also a big factor in advancement because opportunities often arise in regional management positions within restaurant chains.

Restaurant managers and general managers can earn from about $55,000 to $150,000, depending on the size, volume, and amount of their bonus. In addition to typical benefits, managers also receive free meals and continued education and training, depending on the length of their employment. Restaurant general managers can advance to regional manager or director with salaries of about $60,000 to $175,000. Vice presidents and presidents can earn from $75,000 to over $300,000.

Opening your own restaurant as an entrepreneur can be an exciting prospect. For the winners, the restaurant business is fun—lots of people coming and going. The business is always challenging because other restaurant owners are striving to attract your guests—but with the right location, menu, atmosphere, and management, the winners continue to attract the market. The successful restaurant offers a high return on investment. One restaurant, then two, perhaps a small chain. Retire wealthy. It happens.

In addition to ownership in the restaurant business, there are a number of career paths in the supply sector of the industry. Someone has to consult, plan, design, construct, and outfit each restaurant. The larger chain restaurants all have marketing, human resources, financial, and accounting positions.

For those interested in a career in the restaurant business, it is a good idea to gain experience in all facets of restaurant operations. As one famous restaurateur once said to me, "You must know how to steal the chicken first before you can stop someone else from stealing the chicken." Culinary experience is a must in order to protect yourself in case your chef/cook walks out. Obviously, front-of-the-house experience is a must and is also a good way of financing college.

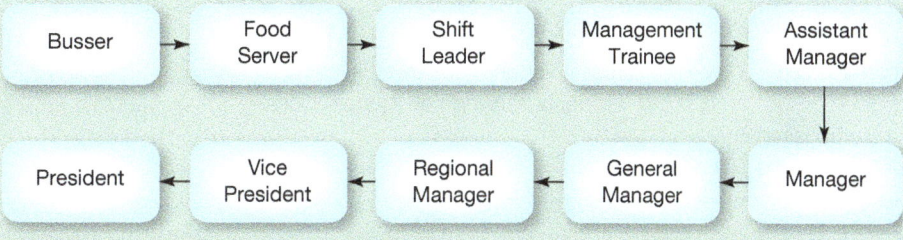

FIGURE 7–2 A Career Path in the Restaurant Industry.

John Mayers SVP of Bonefish Grill and chef Gary Colpitts have this advice to offer: "The restaurant industry has changed: quality-of-life issues are now very important. Consequently, the hours that employees work are monitored. Most restaurant managers work a 50-hour-week. Try to work with the best companies, one that will allow you to grow and make an impact, or perhaps one with a long track record. Employment selection is based on energy, knowledge, job performance. Anybody can operate a popular restaurant, and many people want to own one, but it's best to go through the trials and tribulations of learning about a restaurant—learn both sides of the coin—working as a server and bartender, plus learning how to prepare food.

For chefs, the place you work is very important: it's an investment in your future. The type of job and the type of chef you are working with can add to your value. It takes years of experience to become a chef or kitchen manager—perhaps 10 years. Gain exposure to different types of environments, restaurants, and cooking methods. Finally, be professional and dedicated . . . and success will come."

SUMMARY

1. Restaurants offer the possibility of excellent food and social interaction. In general, restaurants strive for an operating philosophy that includes quality food, good value, and gracious service.
2. To succeed, a restaurant needs the right location, food, atmosphere, and service to attract a substantial market. The concept of a restaurant has to fit the market it is trying to attract.
3. The menu and pricing of a restaurant must match the market it wants to attract, the capabilities of the cooks, and the existing kitchen equipment.
4. The main categories of restaurants are fine dining, specialty, independent, and chain. Further distinctions can be made: quick-service, ethnic, dinner house, occasion, and casual. In general, most restaurants fall into more than one category.

KEY WORDS AND CONCEPTS

Casual dining
Chain restaurant
Dinner house restaurant
Ethnic restaurant
Fine dining restaurant
Focus groups
Fusion
Independent restaurant ("indies")
Quick-service restaurant
Theme restaurant

REVIEW QUESTIONS

1. Name some of America's finest chefs.
2. How are restaurants classified?
3. Explain why there is no single definition of the various classifications of restaurants; give examples.

INTERNET EXERCISES

1. Organization: Charlie Trotter
   Web site: charlietrotters.com/restaurant
   Summary: Charlie Trotter is regarded as one of the finest chefs in the world. Chef Trotter's restaurant has received numerous awards, yet Chef Trotter is seeking new opportunities.

   a. What are Chef Trotter's recent activities?

APPLY YOUR KNOWLEDGE

1. In groups, evaluate a restaurant and write out a list of its weaknesses. Use the headings outlined in the restaurant chapters. Then, for each weakness, decide on what actions you would take to exceed guest expectations.

SUGGESTED ACTIVITIES

1. Choose a restaurant in your neighborhood and identify its catchment area (the area around the restaurant that guests come from—usually a few miles). How many potential guests live and work in the catchment area?

2. List the things you like about your favorite restaurant. Compare your answers with your class.

ENDNOTES

1. National Restaurant Association, *Restaurant Industry Fact Sheet*, 2006.
2. Sarah R. Labensky, Alan M. Hause and Priscilla A. Martel, *On Cooking* 5th ed., Pearson, Upper Saddle River NJ. 1001. P.5.
3. http://www.hillstone.com/#/restaurants/houstons/, retrieved March 9, 2010.
4. http://www.tacobell.com, retrieved March 9, 2010.
5. www.aboutmcdonalds.com/mcd/our_company.html, retrieved March 9, 2010.
6. http://www.kfc.com/about, retrieved March 9, 2010.
7. http://www.restaurantreformer.com/, retrieved March 8, 2010.
8. Ibid.
9. http://www.dinegreen.com/restaurants/standards.asp, retrieved March 8, 2010.
10. Ibid.
11. Ibid.
12. http://www.restaurant.org/research/ind-glance.cfm, retrieved March 8, 2010.
13. U.S. Department of Labor, Bureau of Labor Statistics, www.bls.gov, retrieved March 8, 2010.

RESTAURANT OPERATIONS

LEARNING OUTCOMES

After reading and studying this chapter, you should be able to:

Describe restaurant operations for the front of the house.

Explain the important aspects of food production.

Outline back-of-the-house operations.

Calculate basic food cost percentages.

Identify the key areas and tasks of a restaurant manager's job.

HTi

Describe the economic impact of tourism.

FRONT OF THE HOUSE

Restaurant operations are generally divided between what is commonly called **front of the house** and back of the house. The front of the house includes anyone with guest contact from the hostess to the busperson. The sample organization chart in Figure 8–1 shows the differences between the front and back of the house areas.

The general manager or restaurant manager runs the restaurant. Depending on the size and sales volume of the restaurant, there may be more managers with special responsibilities, such as kitchen manager, bar manager, and dining room manager. These managers are usually cross-trained in order to relieve each other.

In the front of the house, restaurant operation begins with creating and maintaining what is called *curbside appeal,* or keeping the restaurant looking attractive and welcoming. Ray Kroc, of McDonald's, once spent a couple of hours in a good suit with one of his restaurant managers cleaning up the parking lot of one of his restaurants. Word soon got around to the other stores that management begins in the parking lot and ends in the bathrooms. Most restaurant chains have checklists that each manager uses. In the front of the house, the parking lot, including the flower gardens, needs to be maintained in good order. As guests approach the restaurant, greeters may hold the door open and welcome them to the restaurant. At the 15th Street Fisheries Restaurant in Ft. Lauderdale, greeters welcome the guests by assuring them that "we're glad you're here!"

Once inside, the greeter, or as T.G.I. Friday's calls them, a "smiling people greeter" (SPG), greets guests appropriately and, if seating is available, escorts them to a table. If there is a wait, the hostess will take the guests' names and ask for their table preference.

Aside from greeting the guests, one critical function of the hostess is to rotate arriving guests among the sections or stations. This ensures an even and timely distribution of guests—otherwise one section may get overloaded. Guests are sometimes asked to wait a few minutes even if tables are available. This is done to help manage the kitchen's workload—because most kitchens have limited space and cannot cope with too much volume at one time.

> **Working together is the key to success in the restaurant business.**
>
> Bruce Folkins, Marina Jacks, Sarasota, FL

The greeters maintain a book, or chart, showing the sections and tables so they know which tables are occupied. Greeters escort guests to the tables, present menus, and may explain special sales promotions. Some may also remove excess place settings from the table.

In some restaurants, servers are allocated a certain number of tables, which may vary depending on the size of the tables and the volume of the restaurant. Normally, five is the maximum. In other restaurants, servers rotate within their section to cover three or four tables.

Servers introduce themselves and offer a variety of beverages and/or specials, or invite guests to select from the menu. This is known as **suggestive selling**. The server then takes the entree orders. Often, when taking orders, the server begins at a designated point and takes the orders clockwise from that point. In this way, the server will automatically know which person is having a particular dish. When the entrees are ready, the

> **Management involvement is vital to the success of a restaurant.**

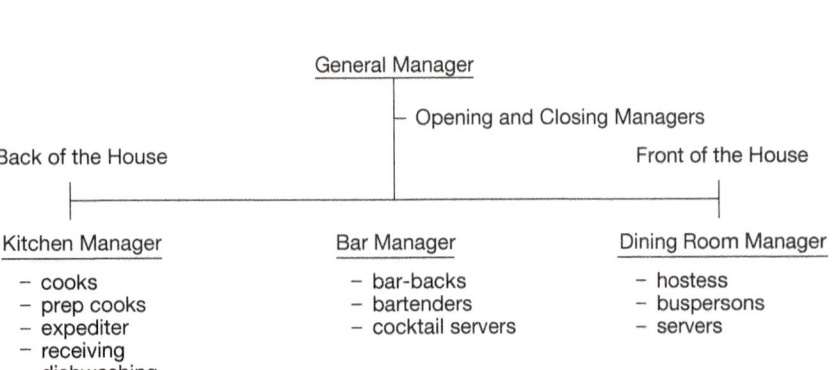

FIGURE 8–1 Restaurant Organization Chart.

server brings them to the table. He or she checks a few minutes later to see if everything is to the guests' liking and perhaps asks if they would like another beverage. Good servers are also encouraged, when possible, to pre-bus tables.

Bussers and servers may clear the entree plates, while servers suggestively sell desserts by describing, recommending, or showing the desserts. Coffee and after-dinner cocktails are also offered. Suggestions for steps to take in table service include the following:

- Greet the guests.
- Introduce and suggestively sell beverages.
- Suggest appetizers.
- Take orders.
- Check to see that everything is to the guests' liking within two bites of the entrees.
- Ask if the guests would like another drink.
- Bring out dessert tray and suggest after-dinner drinks and coffee.

A sushi chef ready for an order.

In addition to the seven steps of the table service, servers are expected to be NCO—neat, clean, and organized—and to help ensure that hot food is served hot, and cold food is served cold.

For example, during the lunch hour, servers may be scheduled to start at 11:00 A.M. The opening group of two or three people is joined by the closing group of the same number at around 11:45 P.M. If the restaurant is quiet, servers may be phased out early. When the closing group comes in, there is a quick shift meeting, or "alley rally." This provides an opportunity to review recent sales figures, discuss any promotions, and acknowledge any items that are "86'ed"—the restaurant term for a menu item that is not available. Recognition is also given to the servers during the meetings, serving as morale boosters.

Restaurant Forecasting

Most businesses, including restaurants, operate by formulating a budget that projects sales and costs for a year on a weekly and monthly basis. Financial viability is predicted on sales, and sales budgets are forecasts of expected business.

Forecasting restaurant sales has two components: **guest counts or covers** and the **average guest check**. Guest counts or covers are the number of guests patronizing the restaurant over a given time period—a week, month, or year. To forecast the number of guests for a year, the year is divided into twelve 28- and one 29-day accounting periods. The accounting periods then are broken down into four 7-day weeks. Restaurant forecasting is done by taking into consideration meal period, day of week, special holidays, and previous forecast materializations.

In terms of number of guests, Mondays usually are quiet; business gradually builds to Friday, which is often the busiest day. Friday, Saturday, and Sunday frequently provide up to 50 percent of revenue. This, however, can vary according to type of restaurant and its location.

The *average guest check* is calculated by dividing total sales by the number of guests. Most restaurants keep such figures for each meal. The number of guests forecast for each day is multiplied by the amount of the average food and beverage check for each meal to calculate the total forecast sales. Each day, actual totals are compared with the forecasts. Four weekly forecasts are combined to form one accounting period; the 13 accounting periods, when totaled, become the annual total.

Restaurant forecasting is used not only to calculate sales projections but also to predict staffing levels and labor cost percentages. Much depends on the accuracy of forecasting. Once sales figures are determined, all expenditures, fixed and variable, have to be deducted to calculate profit or loss.[1]

Service

More than ever, what American diners really want to order when eating out is good service. All too often, this is not on the menu. With increased competition, however, bad service will not be tolerated in American restaurants. Great service adds tremendous value to the dining experience; something most guests are willing to pay for.

American service is a method in which the food is prepared and decoratively placed onto plates in the kitchen, carried into the dining room, and served to guests. American service is a less formal—yet professional—approach preferred by today's restaurant guests. The restaurants' commitment to service is evidenced by the fact that most have increased training for new employees. For example, at Splendido in San Francisco's Embarcadero, the amount of time new servers spend in training has increased from 40 to 100 hours. Servers are not merely order takers; they are the salespeople of the restaurant. A server who is undereducated about the menu can seriously hurt business. One would not be likely to buy a car from a salesperson who knew nothing about the car; likewise, guests feel uneasy ordering from an unknowledgeable waiter. Restaurants in the United States and Canada and many other parts of the world all use American service.

With American service, the food is more likely to come out hot and is beautifully presented on the plate.

Other types of service used less often in the United States are:

French Service: This service is used in very formal restaurants where the food is attractively arranged on platters in the kitchen and brought to the table by servers and presented to guests, after which the preparation of the food is completed on a *gueridon* table beside the guest's seat. A *gueridon* is a trolley-like table with a gas burner for tableside cooking. This is the most impressive and expensive form of service. Due to the higher cost of training and employing servers who can do French service, and given that sometimes the food is cold by the time the guest gets to eat, this form of service is rarely used today except in very formal service situations.

Russian Service: The food is cooked in the kitchen, cut, placed onto a serving dish, and beautifully garnished. The dish is then presented to the guests and served individually by lifting the food onto the guest's plate with a serving spoon and fork. Russian service can be used at a formal restaurant where the servers use white gloves. Russian and French service share the same challenges: to get the food to the guests quickly so it is still hot, and to keep it priced reasonably. Russian service is also only used at very formal restaurants; it also costs much more than American service.

At Posterio, in Las Vegas, servers are invited to attend a one-and-a-half-hour wine class in the restaurant; about three-quarters of the 40-member staff routinely benefit from this additional training. The best employees are also rewarded with monthly, semiannual, and/or annual prizes, which could be $100 cash, a limousine ride, dinner at Posterio, a night's lodging at the Prescott Hotel, or a week in Hawaii. Servers at some San Francisco restaurants role-play the various elements of service such as greeting and seating guests, suggestive selling, correct methods of service, and guest relations to ensure a positive dining experience. A good food server in a top restaurant in many cities can earn about $50,000 a year.

Good servers quickly learn to gauge guests' satisfaction levels and needs; they check to ensure guests have everything they need as their entree is placed before them. Even better, they anticipate guests' needs. For example, if the guest had used the entree knife to eat the appetizer, then a clean one should automatically be placed to the guest's right side. In other words, the guest should not receive the entree and then realize that he or she needs another knife.

Another example of good service is when the server does not have to ask everyone at the table who is eating what. The server should either remember or make a seating plan so that the correct dishes are automatically placed in front of guests.

Danny Meyer, owner of New York City's celebrated Union Square Café and recipient of both the Restaurant of the Year and Outstanding Service Awards from the James Beard Foundation, gives each of the restaurant's 95 employees—from busperson to chef—a $600 annual allowance ($50 each a month) to eat in the restaurant and critique the experience.[2]

At the critically acclaimed Inn at Little Washington in Washington, Virginia, servers are required to gauge the mood of every table and jot a number (1 to 10) and sometimes a description ("elated, grumpy, or edgy") on each ticket. Anything below a seven requires a diagnosis. Servers and kitchen staff work together to try to elevate the number to at least a nine by the time dessert is ordered.

Suggestive Selling

Suggestive selling can be a potent weapon in the effort to increase food and beverage sales. Many restaurateurs cannot think of a better, more effective, and easier way to boost profit margins. Most guests are not offended or uncomfortable with suggestive selling techniques, provided servers are properly

A server is a salesperson, explaining a dish on the menu to guests. *Courtesy of the San Diego Convention and Visitors Bureau.*

On a hot day, for example, servers can suggest frozen margaritas or daiquiris before going on to describe the drink specials. Likewise, servers who suggest a bottle of fumé blanc to complement a fish dish or a pinot noir or cabernet sauvignon to go with red meat are likely to increase their restaurant's beverage sales. Upselling takes place when a guest orders a "well" drink like a vodka and tonic. In this case, the server asks if the guest would like a Stoli and tonic. (Stoli is short for Stolichnaya, a popular brand of vodka.)

Check Your Knowledge

1. What is considered the front of the house?
2. Define curbside appeal.
3. Explain the suggestions for steps to take in table service.
4. Explain the purpose of forecasting.
5. Briefly explain American service.

For a restaurant to be successful, there must be clear lines of communication between the front and back of the house.

trained not to overdo it! In fact, guests may feel special that the server is in tune with their needs and desires. It may be that the server suggests something to the guest that he or she has never considered before. The object here is to turn servers into sellers. Guests will almost certainly be receptive to suggestions from competent servers.

BACK OF THE HOUSE

The **back of the house** is generally run by the kitchen manager and refers to all the areas that guests do not normally come in contact with. This includes purchasing, receiving, storing/issuing, food production, stewarding, budgeting, accounting, and control.

One of the most important aspects to running a successful restaurant is having a strong back-of-the-house operation, particularly in the kitchen. The kitchen is the backbone of every full-service restaurant, so it must be well managed and organized. Some of the main considerations in efficiently operating the back of the house include staffing, scheduling, training, food cost analysis (internal controls), production, management involvement, management follow-up, and employee recognition.

Food Production

Planning, organizing, and producing food of a consistently high quality is no easy task. The kitchen manager, cook, or chef begins the production process by determining the expected volume of business for the next few days. Sales during the same period in the previous year give a good indication of the expected volume and the breakdown of the number of sales of each menu item. As described earlier, ordering and receiving will have already been done for the day's production schedule.

The kitchen manager checks the head line cook's order, which will bring the prep (preparation) area up to the par stock of prepared items. Most of the prep work is done in the early part of the morning and afternoon. Taking advantage of slower times allows the line cooks to do the final preparation just prior to and during the actual meal service. The kitchen layout is set up according to the business projected as well as the menu design. Most full-service restaurants have similar layouts and designs for their kitchens. The layout consists of the receiving area, walk-ins, the freezer, dry storage, prep line, salad bar, cooking line, expediter, dessert station, and service bar area.

The cooking line is the most important part of the kitchen layout. It might consist of a broiler station, pickup area, fry station, salad station, sauté station, and pizza station—just a few

Chefs working on "the line."

Kitchen/Food Production

Staffing and Scheduling

Practicing proper staffing is absolutely crucial for the successful running of a kitchen. It is important to have enough employees on the schedule to enable the restaurant, as a whole, to handle the volume on any given shift. Often it is better to overstaff the kitchen, rather than understaff it, for two reasons. First, it is much easier to send an employee home than it is to call someone in. Second, having extra employees on hand allows for cross-training and development, which is becoming a widely used method.

Problems can also be eliminated if a staffing plan is created to set needed levels. These levels should be adjusted according to sales trends on a monthly basis. Also crucial to the smooth running of the kitchen is having a competent staff. This means putting the best cooks in the appropriate stations on the line, which will assist in the speed of service, the food quality, and the quality of the operations.

Training and Development

Due to a high turnover rate, implementing a comprehensive training program is vital in the kitchen. Trainers should, of course, be qualified and experienced in the kitchen. Often, the most competent chefs are used to train new hires. Such trainings are usually done on the job and may include study material. Some restaurants may even require new hires to complete a written test, evaluating the skills acquired through the training process.

Ensuring adequate training is necessary because the success of the business lies in the hands of the trainer and the trainee. If employees are properly trained when they begin their employment, little time and money will need to be spent on correcting errors. Thorough training also helps in retaining employees for longer periods of time.

Training, however, does not stop after passing a test. Developing the skills of all the employees is critical to the growth and success of the kitchen and, ultimately, the restaurant. A development program may consist of delegating duties or projects to the staff, allowing them to expand their horizons within the kitchen and the restaurant business. Such duties include projections of sales, inventory, ordering, schedule writing, and training. This will help management get feedback on the running of the kitchen and on how well the development program works in their particular operation. Also, this allows for internal growth and promotion. Having "trainers" and people who train the trainers is important to the restaurant's goal of offering exceptional quality and service.

of the intricate parts that go into the setup of the back of the house. The size of the kitchen and its equipment are all designed according to the sales forecast for the restaurant and by the menu. The menu dictates the equipment needed as well as the experience level of the cooks.

The kitchen will also be set up according to what the customers prefer and order most frequently. For example, if guests eat more broiled or sautéed items, the size of the broiler and sauté must be larger to cope with the demand.

Teamwork, a prerequisite for success in all areas of the hospitality and tourism industry, is especially important in the kitchen. Due to the hectic pace, pressure builds, and unless each member of the team excels, the result will be food that is delayed, not up to standard, or both.

While organization and performance standards are necessary, it is helping each other with the prepping and the cooking that creates teamwork. "It's just like a relay race; we can't afford to drop the baton," says Amy Lu, kitchen manager of China Coast restaurant in Los Angeles. Teamwork in the back of the house is like an orchestra playing in tune, each player adding to the harmony.

Another example of organization and teamwork is T.G.I. Friday's five rules of control for running a kitchen:

1. Order it well.
2. Receive it well.
3. Store it well.
4. Make it to the recipe.
5. Don't let it die in the window.

It is amazing to see a kitchen line being overloaded, yet everyone is gratified when the team succeeds in preparing and serving quality food on time.

Introducing **James Lorenz**

Kitchen Manager, T.G.I. Friday's, La Jolla, California

7:00 A.M.–Arrive. Check the work of cleaning crew (such as clogs in burners, stoves/ovens, etc.) for overall cleanliness.

7:15–7:40–Set production levels for all stations (broiler/hot sauce/expediter, cold sauce, vegetable preparation, baker preparation, line preparation: sauté/noodles, pantry, fry/seafood portioning).

8:00–The first cooks begin arriving; greet them and allocate production sheets with priority items circled.

9:00–On a good day, the produce arrives at 9:00 A.M. Check for quality, quantity, accuracy (making sure the prices match the quotation sheet) and that the produce is stored properly.

9:30–11:00–Follow up on production. The sauté cook, who is last to come in, arrives. He or she is the closing person for the morning shift.

- Follow up on cleanliness, recipe adherence (using standardized recipes), and production accuracy.
- Check the stations to ensure the storage of prepped items (e.g., plastic draining inserts under poultry and seafood), the shelf life of products, general cleanliness, and that what is in the station is prepared correctly (e.g., turkey diced to the right size and portioned and dated correctly).

10:45–Final check of the line and production to ensure readiness. Did everyone prepare enough?

11:00–2:30–All hands on deck. Jump on the first ticket. Pretoast buns for burgers and hold in heated drawers. Precook some chicken breasts for salads. Monitor lunch until 2:30 P.M.

- Be responsible for cleanliness.
- Determine who needs to get off the clock.
- Decide what production is left for the remainder of the day.
- Focus on changing over the line, change the food pan inserts (BBQ sauce, etc.).

2:30–3:15–Complete changeover of the line and check the stocking for the P.M. crew.

- Final prep portioning.
- Check the dishwasher area and prep line for cleanliness.
- Check that the product is replaced in the store walk-in or refrigerator.
- Reorganize the produce walk-in. Check the storage of food, labels, and day dots, lids on.
- Thank the A.M. crew and send them home.

4:00–4:15–Welcome the P.M. crew.

- Place produce order (as a double-check, ask the P.M. crew what they might need).

5:00–Hand over to P.M. manager.

Production Procedures

Production in the kitchen is key to the success of a restaurant since it relates directly to the recipes on the menu and how much product is on hand to produce the menu. Thus, controlling the production process is crucial. To undertake such a task, **production control sheets** are created for each station, for example, broiler, sauté, fry, pantry, window, prep, dish, and dessert. With the control sheets, levels are set up for each day according to sales.

The first step in creating the production sheets is to count the products on hand for each station. Once the production levels are determined, the amount of product required to reach the level for each recipe is decided. Once these calculations are completed, the sheets are handed to the cooks. It is important to make these calculations before the cooks arrive, considering the amount of prep time that is needed before the restaurant opens. For instance, if a restaurant is open only for lunch and dinner, enough product should be on hand by 11:00 A.M. to ensure that the cooks are prepared to handle the lunch crowd.

When determining production, par levels should be changed weekly according to sales trends. This will help control and minimize waste levels. Waste is a large contributor to increasing food cost; therefore, the kitchen should determine the product levels necessary to make it through only one day. Products have a particular shelf life, and if the kitchen overproduces and does not sell the product within its shelf life, it must be thrown away. More importantly, this practice allows for the freshest product to reach the customers on a daily basis.

After the lunch rush, the kitchen checks to see how much product was sold and how much is left for the night shift. (Running out of a product is unacceptable and should not happen. If proper production procedures are followed, a restaurant will not have to "86" anything on the menu.) After all production is completed on all stations, the cooks may be checked out. It is essential to check out the cooks and hold them accountable for production levels. If

Checking the temperature of a roasting chicken to ensure that it is properly cooked.

they are not checked out, they might slide on their production, negatively impacting the restaurant and the customer.

The use of production sheets is also critical in controlling how the cooks use the products, since production plays a key role in food cost. Every recipe has a particular "spec" (specification) to follow. When one deviates from the recipe, quality goes down, consistency is lost, and food cost goes up. That is why it is important to follow the recipe at all times. Standardized recipes are developed for each menu item to maintain consistency and minimize waste. It is very important to use them; otherwise, a dish will taste one way today but be quite different tomorrow. And fluctuation in standards leads to guest complaints.

Management Involvement and Follow-Up

As in any business, management involvement is vital to the success of a restaurant. Management should know firsthand what is going on in the back of the house. It is also important that they be "on the line," assisting the staff in the preparation of the menu and in the other operations of the kitchen, just as they should be helping when things are rushed. When management is visible to the staff, they are prone to do what they need to be doing at all times, and food quality is more apparent and consistent. Managers should constantly be walking and talking food cost, cleanliness, sanitation, and quality. This shows the staff how serious and committed they are to the successful running of the back of the house. Figure 8–2 is a job description for a typical assistant restaurant manager.

As management spends more time in the kitchen, more knowledge is gained, more confidence is acquired,

and more respect is earned. Employee–management interaction produces a sense of stability and a strong work ethic among employees, resulting in higher morale and promoting a positive working environment. To ensure that policies and standards are being upheld, management follow-up should happen on a continual basis. This is especially important when cooks are held accountable to specifications and production and when other staff members are given duties to perform. Without follow-up, the restaurant may fold.

Check Your Knowledge

1. Who runs the back of the house and what areas does back of the house refer to?
2. List T.G.I. Friday's five rules of control and explain why they are important.
3. Explain the importance of training and development.

It happens all too often: Supervisors only notice when a mistake is made or something is going wrong. It is important for management to recognize the good things and give praise when it is deserved. Employees appreciate positive reinforcement and recognition.

Purchasing

Purchasing for restaurants involves procuring the products and services that the restaurant needs in order to serve its guests. Restaurant operators set up purchasing systems that determine the following:

- Standards for each item (product specification)
- Systems that minimize effort and maximize control of loss from within the restaurant (theft, pilferage, or spoilage) and losses from other sources
- The amount of each item that should be on hand (par stock and reorder point)
- Who will do the buying and keep the purchasing system in motion
- Who will do the receiving, storage, and issuing of items[3]

> **A restaurant owner must oversee all of the operations going on in the business, from the front of the house, to back of the house, to all of the administrative aspects.**
>
> Jonathan W. Seigal,
> *Gulf Seafood Plus*, St. Petersburg, FL.

It is desirable for restaurants to establish standards for each product, called **product specification**. When ordering meat, for example, the cut, weight, size, percentage of fat content, and number of days aged are all factors that are specified by the purchaser.

Establishing systems that minimize effort and maximize control of loss

POSITION TITLE: Assistant Manager
REPORTS TO: Manager

POSITION OVERVIEW:
Under the general supervision of the manager, subject to the Service Policy and Procedure Manual, assures constantly and consistently the creation of maximal guest satisfaction and dining pleasure.

RESPONSIBILITIES AND DUTIES:
A. Planning and organizing
  1. Studies past sales experience records, confers with manager, keeps alert to holidays and special events, and so on; forecasts loads and prepares work schedules for service employees in advance to meet requirements.
  2. Observes guest reactions and confers frequently with servers to determine guest satisfactions, dissatisfactions, relative popularity of menu items, and so on and reports such information with recommendations to the manager.
  3. Observes daily the condition of all physical facilities and equipment in the dining room, making recommendations to the manager for correction and improvements needed.
  4. Anticipates all material needs and supplies and assures availability of same.
  5. Inspects, plans, and assures that all personnel, facilities, and materials are in complete readiness to provide excellent service before each meal period.
  6. Anticipates employment needs, recommending to the manager plans for recruitment and selection to meet needs as they arise.
  7. Discusses menu changes with servers in advance to assure full understanding of new items.
  8. Conducts meetings of service employees at appropriate times.
  9. Defines and explains clearly for servers and buspersons their responsibilities for relationships
     ✔ with each other
     ✔ with guests
     ✔ with the hostess/host
     ✔ with the manager
     ✔ with the cashier
     ✔ with the kitchen personnel
B. Coordinating
  1. Ensures that servers are fully informed as to all menu items—how they are prepared, what they contain, number of ounces per portion.
  2. Periodically discusses and reviews with employees company objectives, and guest and personnel policies.
  3. Keeps manager informed at all times about service activities, progress, and major problems.
C. Supervising
  1. Actively participates in employment of new servers and buspersons, suggests recruitment sources, studies applications, checks references, and conducts interviews.
  2. Following an orientation outline, introduces new employees to the restaurant, restaurant policies, and fellow employees.
  3. Using a training plan, trains new employees and current employees in need of additional training.
  4. Promptly corrects any deviations from established service standards.
  5. Counsels employees on job issues and personal problems.
  6. Follows established policy in making station assignments for servers.
  7. Establishes, with approval of manager, standards of conduct, grooming, personal hygiene, and dress.
  8. Prepares, in consultation and with approval of the manager, applied standards of performance for servers and buspersons.
  9. Recommends deserving employees for promotion, and outstanding performers for special recognition and award.
  10. Strives at all times through the practice of good human relations and leadership to establish esprit de corps—teamwork, unity of effort, and individual and group pride.
  11. Remains constantly alert to the entire dining room situation—is sensitive to any deviation or problem and assists quickly and quietly in its correction, alleviating guests' complaints.
  12. Greets and seats guests cordially and courteously, to assure a sincere welcome and to express a genuine interest in their dining pleasure.
D. Controlling
  1. Controls performance, conduct, dress, hygiene, sanitation, and personal appearance of employees according to established policies, standards, and procedures.
  2. Studies all evidence of waste of time and materials, and makes recommendations for preventing further waste.
E. Other
  1. In emergency situations, may serve guests, act as cashier, or perform specifically assigned duties of the manager.
  2. Personifies graciousness and offers hospitality to guests and employees by showing "we're glad you're here" and "we're proud to serve you."

FIGURE 8–2 Job Description for an Assistant Restaurant Manager.

may be done manually or by computer or a combination. However, merely computerizing a system does not make it theft-proof. Instead, employing honest workers is a top priority because temptation is everywhere in the restaurant industry. One story about stealing happened at a restaurant the author worked at. It was a nice old place with wrought iron gates as a door to the bar. The thieves got a fishing pole and inserted it between the iron posts of the gate and took several bottles out. They removed some of the alcohol, then added water or colored liquid. Eventually, external auditors checked the proof content of the spirits and found them diluted. It was later discovered that several servers at the restaurant had incurred gambling debts at the new casino and were paying them off with the restaurant's liquor. This was discovered when the police "interviewed" some of the suspects. Would you believe that some of the bottles at the casino had the stamp of the restaurant on them?

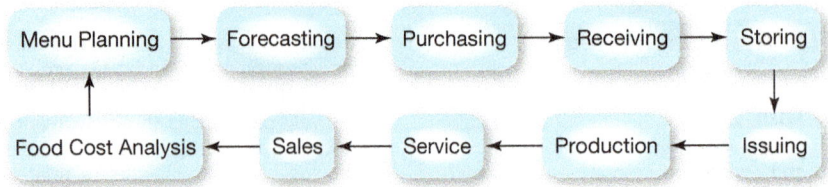

FIGURE 8–3 Food Cost Control Process.

An efficient and effective system establishes a stock level that must be on hand at all times. This is called a **par stock**. If the stock on hand falls below a specified reorder point, the computer system automatically reorders a predetermined quantity of the item.

In identifying who will do the buying, it is most important to separate task and responsibility between the person placing the order and the person receiving the goods. This avoids possible theft. The best way to avoid losses is to have the chef prepare the order, the manager or the manager's designee place the order, and a third person responsible for the stores receive the goods together with the chef (or the chef's designee).

Commercial (for-profit) restaurant and foodservice operators who are part of a chain may have the menu items and order specifications determined at the corporate office. This saves the unit manager from having to order individually; specialists at the corporate office not only develop the menu but also write the specifications for the ingredients to ensure consistency. Both chain and independent restaurants and foodservice operators use similar prepurchase functions (Figure 8–3).

- Plan menus.
- Determine quality and quantity needed to produce menus.
- Write specifications and develop market orders for purchases.
- Determine inventory stock levels.
- Identify items to purchase by subtracting stock levels from the quantity required to produce menus.

Professor Stefanelli at the University of Nevada, Las Vegas, suggests a formal and an informal method of purchasing that includes the following steps.[4]

Formal	Informal
Develop purchase order	Develop purchase order
Establish bid schedule	Quote price
Issue invitation to bid	Select vendor and place order
Tabulate and evaluate bids	
Award contract and issue delivery order	
Inspect/receive deliveries, inventory stores, and record transactions in inventory	Receive and inspect deliveries, store, and record transaction
Evaluate and follow up	Evaluate and follow up
Issue food supplies for food production and service	Issue food supplies for food production and service

The formal method is generally used by chain restaurant operators and the informal one by independent restaurant operators.

A **purchase order** comes as a result of the *product specification*. As it sounds, a purchase order is an order to purchase a certain quantity of an item at a specific price. Many restaurants develop purchase orders for items they need on a regular basis. These are then sent to suppliers for quotations, and samples are sent in for product evaluations. For example, canned items have varying amounts of liquid. Normally, it is the drained weight of the product that matters to the restaurant operator. After comparing samples from several vendors, the operator can choose the supplier that best suits the restaurant's needs.

Receiving

When placing an order, the restaurant operator specifies the day and time for the delivery to be made (for example, Friday, 10:00 A.M. to 12:00 noon). This prevents deliveries from being made at inconvenient times.

Receiving is a point of control in the restaurant operation. The purpose of receiving is to ensure that the quantity, quality, and price are exactly as ordered. The quantity and quality relate to the **order specification** and the **standardized recipe**. Depending on the restaurant and the type of food and beverage control system, some perishable items are issued directly to the kitchen, and most of the nonperishable items go into storage.

Storing/Issuing

Control of the stores is often a problem. Records must be kept of all items going into or out of the stores. If more than one person has access to the stores, it is difficult to know where to attach responsibility in case of losses.

Items should only be issued from the stores on an authorized requisition signed by the appropriate person. One restaurateur who has been in business for many years issues stores to the kitchen on a daily basis. No inventory is kept in the production area and there is no access to the stores. To some, this may be overdoing control, but it is hard to fault the results: a good food cost percentage. All items that enter the stores should have a date stamp and be rotated using the **first in–first out (FIFO) system**.

First in–first out is a simple but effective system of ensuring stock rotation. This is achieved by placing the most recent purchases, in rotation, behind previous purchases. Failure to do this can result in spoilage.

Obviously, restaurants should maintain strict controls. Better-known controls include taking inventory regularly; and calculating food, beverage, and labor cost percentages. For a restaurant to be successful, management must "manage" by controlling food, beverage, and labor costs and keeping them in line with company expectations based on budget.

Restaurant managers need to spend time coaching associates.

A tight control is maintained on food costs by having the receiving done by a person other than the person who orders the food—this lessens the chance of overordering. At one restaurant where I worked as a food and beverage manager, it was discovered that the chef was doing the ordering and receiving; however, some of the receiving was done at "another" restaurant owned by the chef's brother! Needless to say, the chef was let go. Other strict controls include using a "par stock" reordering system; using one entrance/exit for employees and not permitting employees to bring bags into the restaurant with them; employing a good accountant; and, yes, checking the garbage! You'll be amazed what you will find in the garbage—some dishonest people use the garbage as a constant way to remove valuable items from the restaurant and collect them later from the garbage area.

.inc Corporate Profile

T.G.I. FRIDAY'S® RESTAURANT

In the spring of 1965, Alan Stillman, a New York perfume salesman, opened a restaurant located at First Avenue and 63rd Street. The restaurant boasted striped awnings, a blue exterior, and a large yellow sign reading T.G.I. Friday's. Inside were wooden floors covered with sawdust, Tiffany-style lamps, Bentwood chairs, red-and-white tablecloths, and a bar area complete with brass rails and stained glass.

T.G.I. Friday's was an immediate success. The restaurant on Manhattan's Upper East Side became the meeting place for single adults. In fact, *Newsweek* and the *Saturday Evening Post* called the opening of T.G.I. Friday's "the dawn of the singles' age."

T.G.I. Friday's goal was to create a comfortable, relaxing environment where guests could enjoy food and drink. Stained glass windows, wooden airplane propellers, racing sculls, and metal advertising signs comprised the elegant

.inc Corporate Profile (Continued)

clutter that greeted guests when they entered a T.G.I. Friday's. Nothing was left to chance. Music, lights, air conditioning, decor, and housekeeping were all designed to keep guests comfortable. Employees were encouraged to display their own personalities and to treat customers as they would guests in their own homes.

As guests demanded more, T.G.I. Friday's provided more—soon becoming the industry leader in menu and drink selection. The menu expanded from a slate chalkboard to an award-winning collection of items representing every taste and mood.

T.G.I. Friday's also became the industry leader in innovation—creating the now-famous Jack Daniel's® Grill. This was the first restaurant chain to offer stone ground whole-wheat bread, avocados, bean sprouts, and Mexican appetizers across the country.

America owes the popularization of frozen and ice cream drinks to T.G.I. Friday's, where smooth, alcoholic and nonalcoholic drinks were made with fresh fruit, juices, ice cream, and yogurt. These recipes were so precise that T.G.I. Friday's drink glasses were scientifically designed for the correct ratio of each ingredient. These specially designed glasses have since become popular throughout the industry.

Through the years, T.G.I. Friday's success has been phenomenal. More than 750 restaurants have opened in 49 states and 55 countries, with average gross revenues of $3.75 million per year at each location.

T.G.I. Friday's is privately owned by Carlson Companies, Inc., of Minneapolis—one of the largest privately held companies in the country. Today, T.G.I. Friday's has come to be known as a casual restaurant where family and friends meet for great food, fun, and conversation. Everyone looks forward to T.G.I. Friday's!

What does it take to be successful in the restaurant business, and what does it take to be a leader? The answers to these questions are crucial to success as a restaurant company. The essentials of success in business are as follows:

1. Treat everyone with respect for their dignity.
2. Treat all customers as if they are honored guests in your home.
3. Remember that all problems result from either poor hiring, lack of training, unclear performance expectations, or accepting less than excellence.
4. Remember that management tools are methods, not objectives.

As you can see, these are principles to guide decision making as opposed to step-by-step actions that form a base on which you can easily decide which specific actions are necessary in any given situation.

The basics of leadership are as follows:

1. Hire the right people.
2. Train everyone thoroughly and completely.
3. Be sure that everyone clearly understands the performance expectations.
4. Accept only excellence.

Here we are dealing with the very basics of how to provide strong, clear leadership. However, once again we are talking about only the minimum requirements, not all the qualities necessary to be a good leader. Individual success and that of the company, T.G.I. Friday's Inc., are predicated on understanding and following the essentials of success in business and the basics of leadership. Whether you are an hourly employee or a manager, it is critical that you manage your part of the business using these philosophies.

One thing that makes T.G.I. Friday's unique is the philosophies and theories. These are principles that each employee understands to ensure everyone stays focused on the same goals. T.G.I. Friday's philosophies and theories were first conceived in the mid-1970s. They are used to solve existing problems and enable management to be proactive to problems experienced in the past.

THE GUEST FOCUS

At most companies, it appears that senior management runs the company. The employees consider senior management to be the most important people with whom they interact. As a result, decisions are made in an effort to please senior management, and decisions that affect people lower in the hierarchy are viewed as less important. T.G.I. Friday's success is dependent on inverting the typical management pyramid. Guests are the most important element in the organization; immediately following them are the employees who are closest to the guests—those people who have the greatest impact on the guests' experience. The livelihood of each employee depends on one group of people: guests. It is critical to determine what guests' needs are and fill those needs. To the extent that this objective is accomplished, the needs of each person in the pyramid will be fulfilled. Every decision at T.G.I. Friday's is made with guests in mind.

The "Five Easy Pieces Theory" stresses T.G.I. Friday's deep concern for the guests' satisfaction. T.G.I. Friday's will always cheerfully go out of its way to serve a quality product prepared to individual tastes.

T.G.I. Friday's managers and employees are responsible for honoring any guest request within realistic possibilities. Many managers take a guest's request even further and get them exactly what they want—even if the ingredients are not in the restaurant.

The "Triangle Theory" explains the need to balance and expand upon the goals of the guest, employee, and company, and maximize the results to each. Managers make many decisions and must always consider the effect of those decisions on all three sides of the triangle—the guest, the employee, and the company. Some decisions can cause one side of the triangle to prosper (temporarily) at the expense of the other two. For example, if a company overprices its menu items, it can greatly improve the bottom line. However, guests will object to being cheated and will not return. This will ultimately result in lower staffing and will eventually kill the company. Management's responsibility is to balance the results among the three sides so all sides thrive. But this is only the first step. To grow and expand the business, decisions must be made that maximize or expand all three sides of the triangle at the same time.

These are just a few of the philosophies and theories on which T.G.I. Friday's is based.

BENEFITS

Starting compensation for managers is an individual issue, based on background and experience. In addition to a competitive base salary, T.G.I. Friday's also offers a bonus based on sales and/or profits to all managers.

Management staffing is designed to meet volume needs and may number four to seven per store. Management generally works a five-day work week.

T.G.I. Friday's offers a complete benefits program for both hourly and management personnel. Among its features are health and dental coverage (dependent coverage is also available), vision care, life insurance, paid vacations, tuition assistance, scholarships, disability coverage, credit union, education assistance program, and a 401(k) plan. At T.G.I. Friday's, the company also believes that recognizing employees for their outstanding effort is its opportunity to acknowledge and reinforce the behavior it wants to encourage.

T.G.I. Friday's values are summed up in the Carlson Credo, shown below.

The Carlson Credo

Whatever you do, do it with INTEGRITY.
Wherever you go, go as a LEADER.
Whomever you serve, serve with CARING.
Whenever you dream, dream with your ALL.
And never, ever give up.

—Curt Carlson

In the movie *Five Easy Pieces*, star Jack Nicholson goes to a restaurant and orders a side order of whole-wheat toast. The waitress makes it clear that they do not serve whole-wheat toast. Nicholson notes on the menu that the chicken salad sandwich comes on whole-wheat bread. The annoyed waitress points to a sign in the restaurant that reads "No substitutions" and "We reserve the right to refuse service to anyone." Jack Nicholson orders a chicken salad sandwich on

Introducing The REstaurant General Manager
Chris Robinson

Chain Restaurant General Manager

Chris works a combination of open (typically 7 A.M.–6 P.M.), swing (11 A.M.–10 P.M.), and close (5 P.M.–3 A.M.) shifts, depending on the needs of the business and her goals for the week. Regardless of when Chris works, she is ultimately responsible for food safety and quality, employee staffing and training, guest satisfaction, and restaurant profitability. Chris's responsibilities are accomplished throughout the day by conducting food line checks, employee shift meetings, and guest table visits. As the general manager, Chris is expected to be a role model for all the employees and managers and is responsible for upholding the company credo.

Expectations of the General Manager
The expectations of the general manager are different in each restaurant; however, there are certain commonalities as well. Some of these include:

- General managers answer directly to the owner or to regional directors in major corporations.
- General managers are expected to run good numbers for the periods. The numbers analyzed are food cost, labor cost, and beverage cost. These areas are controlled in order to produce sufficient profit for the restaurant.
- General managers promote good morale and teamwork in the restaurant. Having a positive environment in the restaurant is of utmost importance. This will not only keep the employees happy, but it will also contribute to providing better service to the guests.

Duties and Responsibilities
The general manager of a restaurant is directly responsible for all the operations in the restaurant. General managers are also in charge of the floor managers, the kitchen manager, and the other employees of the restaurant.

The general manager should always check on the floor managers to ensure

(Continued)

that all policies and regulations are being met. This will keep operations running smoothly.

Another important duty is to organize and control the staffing of the restaurant. The floor managers usually write the employee schedule; however, the general manager is still directly responsible for proper staffing for the period. This will help keep labor costs to about 20 percent of sales. The general manager also conducts employee reviews and training.

Qualifications for a General Manager
A general manager has the following qualifications:

- He or she should be very knowledgeable about the restaurant business.
- He or she should have worked all the stations in a restaurant and be very familiar with them.
- The general manager should be able to get along with all people, be fair with all employees, and not discriminate.

Budgeted Costs in a Restaurant
Running a good pace in the restaurant is of absolute importance. Every restaurant has different numbers to make. The following results came from a chain restaurant. These results reflect their goals versus actual numbers run for a given week.

As can be seen, this restaurant did well with the beverage cost; however, the food cost and the labor cost are two areas to focus on for the upcoming week. Making good percentages for the restaurant is the top priority because this is where the restaurant makes or does not make a profit. When the general manager runs good numbers, he or she receives a large bonus check for contributing to the profit of the restaurant. This is why it is so important to focus on these three key areas.

Scheduling the Restaurant
Appropriate scheduling plays a key role in the success of the restaurant. For one thing, overscheduling and underscheduling have a direct effect on the labor cost. If there are too many employees working on a shift for the business that is done, then the labor cost will be high. In contrast, if there are not enough employees working, then the service will suffer and overtime will increase the labor cost.

	Goal	Actual	Variance
Food Cost	27.0	27.2	+0.2
Labor Cost	19.9	20.8	+0.9
Beverage Cost	19.0	18.2	−0.8

whole-wheat toast, but tells the waitress to hold the mayo, hold the lettuce, hold the chicken salad, and just bring him the whole-wheat toast. Unwisely, she asks where she should hold the chicken salad. Nicholson sarcastically responds, "Between your knees!" On that note he leaves, a very dissatisfied guest.

Check Your Knowledge

1. Why do restaurant operators set up purchasing systems?
2. What is the purpose and importance of receiving?
3. What is par stock?

COST CONTROL

Food and Beverage Cost Percentages

Managing restaurants is a complex operation. There are many variables that need to be in line if the operation is to be successful. One way that managers keep tabs on the operation's performance is by checking the food, beverage, and labor costs. These costs, more than any other, need to be carefully monitored on a daily, sometimes hourly, basis. Calculating a food, beverage, or labor cost is like taking the temperature of the operation. We can find out how we are doing on a regular basis. The **food cost percentage** is calculated as the cost of food sold divided by food sales for a specific period, such as a week, 14 days, a month, or a year to date. The result is compared to the budgeted percentage for the period. An example is of a casual restaurant:

Total Food Sales	$95,400
Total Beverage Sales	$46,000
Cost of Food Sold	$22,896
Cost of Beverage Sold	$ 8,892
Labor Costs	$35,350

The food cost percentage is (remember the simple formula, cost over sales times 100):

$$\frac{\text{Cost of food sold}}{\text{Total food sales}} = \frac{\$22,896}{\$95,400} = 0.24 \text{ or } 24\% \text{ food cost}$$

A food cost of 24 percent shows us that $0.24 of each $1.00 of food sales is spent on the cost of food prepared. Most chain restaurants calculate the cost of ingredients and use standardized recipes so that they expect a menu item to have a $0.24 food cost percentage. As you progress in your career, you will realize that some menu items have a higher or lower food cost percentage and that the restaurant company must decide what results it expects. For example, 24 percent is too low for some restaurants and means that guests may find the prices too high. Restaurants generally average about 28 percent food cost; however, high-end steak houses run a 34 percent food cost—they make up for that with a lower labor cost in the kitchen.

The **beverage cost percentage** is calculated in the same way as the food cost: cost of beverages sold divided by the total beverage sales for a period. Like the food cost percentage, it is best utilized as a tool for cost control when compared to the budgeted percentage for the same period. Any significant variances from the budgeted amount should be investigated. The beverage cost in the casual restaurant above is:

$$\frac{\text{Cost of beverage sold}}{\text{Total beverage sales}} = \frac{\$8,892}{\$46,000} = 0.19 \text{ or } 19\%$$

So, for every beverage dollar earned, the cost was 19 percent. Restaurants vary in their beverage cost percentage from a low of 18 on up to 30 percent, with an average around 22 to 26 percent beverage cost. Of course, there are different percentages for beer, wine, spirits, and cocktails—just to make the job more interesting!

Labor Cost Control

Like other service industries, labor is the highest cost in operating a restaurant. Labor costs range from about 24 to 30 percent of total sales. One of the challenges of restaurant operations is scheduling the right amount of staff for each shift. As the number of guests and sales increases, more staff are needed but, when sales drop so should the number of staff.

In the above example, the food and beverages sales are $95,400 and $46,000, making the total sales $141,400. Given a labor cost of $35,350, by using the formula of labor costs over sales we have

$$\frac{\$35,350}{\$141,400} = 0.25 \text{ or } 25\%$$

A labor cost of 25 percent means that for every dollar of sales, 25 percent goes to cover labor costs. Other operating costs include nonfood or labor costs like office supplies, china, glassware, knives, forks, spoons, table napkins, heat, light and power, cleaning, rent, lease or mortgage, music, menus, accounting and legal fees, licenses, uniforms, and so on. Total other operating costs range from 14 to 20 percent of sales.

Given that total sales are 100 percent, and each cost has to be deducted from it, an example of restaurant costs would look like this:

Total Sales   100%
Food Cost   16.19% cost (as a percentage of total sales, not just food sales)

$$\$22,896 \div 141,400 \times 100 = 16.19\%$$

Beverage Cost 6.28% cost

$$\$8,892 \div 141,400 \times 100 = 6.28\%$$

Labor Cost 25% cost

$$\$35,350 \div 141,400 \times 100 = 25\%$$

Other Costs $\frac{20\%}{67.47}$

Leaving 32.53% for any other costs, taxes, and profit.

Another important part of restaurant control is stopping employee theft. As one experienced operator put it, "In each of the restaurants that I worked at, someone was stealing."[5] Here are a few of the many ways employees can steal from restaurants. Some restaurant employees underring sales and tear up the order ticket. For example, if an order for a round of drinks comes to $16.95, the employee rings up $6.95 and puts a swizzle stick in the till as a reminder that the draw is over by $10. If there are eight swizzle sticks in the draw at the end of the shift, the employee pockets $80. Or, when the guest pays the check, the server tears up the order and pockets the cash instead of putting the money and a completed order ticket in the register. In order to avoid this, restaurants use *spotters* (people who sit in a bar or restaurant and watch everything that goes on). Restaurants also require sequentially numbered checks and insist that the servers return all checks at the end of the shift.

Sustainable Restaurant Operations[6]

Sustainability is not just a philosophy about food—it's about people, attitudes, communities, and lifestyles. In the spirit of the theme of this year's International Chefs Congress—"The Responsibility of a Chef"—the ideas below come from chefs across the country. There's an idea to inspire you each day of the next month; even picking one to look into, or act on, per week is a good way to start. Almost everywhere one goes, we hear the same message: small changes and efforts can make a big difference!

1. **Go local.** It's not possible for everyone all the time. But when it *is* possible, support your local farmers.
2. **Take your team to visit a farmer.** This is good practice for remembering that each piece of food has a story and a person behind it. (And you can bring back extra produce for a special family meal.)
3. **Know your seafood.** The criteria for evaluating the sustainability of seafood differ from those for agriculture. Inform yourself using resources like California's Monterey Bay Aquarium's *Seafood Watch Guide*, and demand that your purveyors are informed too. If they can't tell you where a fish is from and how and when it was caught, you probably don't want to be serving it.
4. **Not all bottled water is created equal.** Some companies are working to reduce and offset their carbon footprint through a number of innovative measures. And some of the biggest names in the restaurant world (like *The French Laundry*) are moving away from water bottled out of house. In-house filtration systems offer a number of options—including in-house sparkling water!
5. **Ditch the Styrofoam.** Replace cooks' drinking cups with reusable plastic ones, and replace Styrofoam take-out containers with containers made of recycled paper. BioPac packaging is one option.
6. **Support organic, biodynamic viniculture.** There are incredible, top-rating biodynamic or organic wines from around the world.
7. **Support organic bar products.** All-natural and organic spirits, beers, and mixers are growing in popularity and availability.
8. **Even your kitchen and bar mats can be responsible.** Waterhog's EcoLine is made from 100 percent recycled PET postconsumer recycled fiber reclaimed from drink bottles and recycled tires.
9. **Devote one morning per quarter or one morning per month to community service.** Send staff to a soup kitchen, bring local kids into the kitchen, teach the kitchen staff of the local elementary school a few tricks, or spend a few hours working in the sun at a community garden.
10. **The kitchen equipment of the future is green!** Major equipment producers, like Hobart and Unified Brands, are developing special initiatives to investigate and develop greener, cleaner, energy-smart machines (that also save you money in the long run).
11. **Shut down the computer and POS systems when you leave at night.** When the computer system is on, the juice keeps flowing—shutting it down can save significant energy bill dollars over the course of a year.
12. **Check the seals on your walk-in.** If they're not kept clean and tight, warm air can seep in, making the fridge work harder to stay cool.
13. **Compact fluorescent light bulbs (CFLs) use 75 percent less energy than incandescent bulbs.** CFLs also last 10 times longer, giving them the environmental *and* economic advantage.
14. **Consider wind power.** Ask your energy provider about options—ConEd, for example, offers a wind power option. Though it tends to cost 10 percent more than regular energy, there's an incentive to bring the bill down by implementing other energy-saving techniques to offset the higher cost of wind power.
15. **Look into solar thermal panels to heat your water.** Solar Services, one of the oldest and biggest companies, will walk you through the process—from paperwork to tax credits. With the money saved on a water heater, the system will have paid for itself in two to three years.
16. **Green your cleaning routine.** Trade astringent, nonbiodegradable, potentially carcinogenic chemical kitchen cleaners for biodegradable, eco-safe products.
17. **Use nontoxic pest control.** The options are increasing, and even some of the major companies have green options.

18. **Consider purchasing locally built furniture.** See if there are any artisans in your state working with reclaimed wood (from trees that have fallen naturally because of storms or age).
19. **Recycle your fryer oil.** Biofuel companies across the country will pick it up and convert it.
20. **Grow your own.** Consider a roof-top garden or interior/exterior window boxes for small plants and herbs. EarthBoxes are one low-maintenance solution.
21. **Cut down on shipping materials.** Request that purveyors send goods with the least amount of packing materials possible. Request that Styrofoam packaging not be used.
22. **Trade in white toilet paper, c-folds, and restroom paper towels.** Instead, use products made of chlorine-free unbleached, recycled paper.
23. **Need new toilets?** There are a number of water-saving options that save anywhere from half a gallon to more than a gallon per flush. The old-fashioned brick technique is a good start too: place a brick in the tank of your toilet—the space that it takes up is water saved each time the toilet is flushed.
24. **Compost garbage.** Even high-volume establishments can make this happen. Keep separate cans for all food-based waste, and dump it in a compost bin out back. A common misconception about compost is that it smells bad—this is not true!
25. **Recycle!** Be strict about kitchen and bar staff recycling glass and plastic receptacles. Recycle cardboard and wood boxes used for produce, and any newspapers or magazines sent to the restaurant.
26. **Cut down on linens.** Tablecloths and napkins require a large amount of chemical cleaners, bleaches, and starches. Stay away from white, if possible. If it's not imperative, consider eliminating tablecloths all together. Go for soft cloth napkins instead of starched.
27. **Ice = water + energy.** Don't waste it! Don't automatically refill ice bins—wait until they truly get low, and only add as much as you need to get through the crush. Ice is expensive to produce, both in terms of money and resources.
28. **If you're a small restaurant or café, without huge needs or storage space, look into joining (or forming) a local co-op for purchasing green items.** Cleaning supplies, paper products, etc are all cheaper in bulk.
29. **Educate yourself!** From agricultural philosophy to the specifics of restaurant operations, the number of resources for green issues and practices is ever-growing. Pick up *The Omnivore's Dilemma* by Michael Pollan, the Green Restaurant Association's *Dining Green: A Guide to Creating Environmentally Sustainable Restaurants and Kitchens,* and *Sourcing Seafood, a Resource Guide for Chefs* by Seafood Choices Alliance.
30. **Last but not least, educate your staff!** They need to know *why* you're doing what you're doing, so that they can spread the word—to the diners, and beyond!

> *Small changes and efforts can make a big difference.*

Restaurant manager job analysis

The National Restaurant Association (NRA) has formulated an analysis of the foodservice manager's job by functional areas and tasks, which follows a natural sequence of functional areas from human resources to sanitation and safety.

Human Resource Management

Recruiting/Training

1. Recruit new employees by seeking referrals.
2. Recruit new employees by advertising.
3. Recruit new employees by seeking help from district manager/supervisor.
4. Interview applicants for employment.

Orientation/Training

1. Conduct on-site orientation for new employees.
2. Explain employee benefits and compensation programs.
3. Plan training programs for employees.
4. Conduct on-site training for employees.
5. Evaluate progress of employees during training.
6. Supervise on-site training of employees that is conducted by another manager, employee leader, trainer, and so on.
7. Conduct payroll signup.
8. Complete reports or other written documentation on successful completion of training by employees.

Scheduling for Shifts

1. Review employee work schedule for shift.
2. Determine staffing needs for each shift.
3. Make work assignments for dining room, kitchen staff, and maintenance person(s).
4. Make changes to employee work schedule.
5. Assign employees to work stations to optimize employee effectiveness.
6. Call in, reassign, or send home employees in reaction to sales and other needs.
7. Approve requests for schedule changes, vacation, days off, and so on.

Supervision and Employee Development

1. Observe employees and give immediate feedback on unsatisfactory employee performance.
2. Observe employees and give immediate feedback on satisfactory employee performance.
3. Discuss unsatisfactory performance with an employee.
4. Develop and deliver incentive for above-satisfactory performance of employees.
5. Observe employee behavior for compliance with safety and security.
6. Counsel employees on work-related problems.
7. Counsel employees on nonwork-related problems.
8. Talk with employees who have frequent absences.
9. Observe employees to ensure compliance with fair labor standards and equal opportunity guidelines.
10. Discipline employees by issuing oral and/or written warnings for poor performance.
11. Conduct employee and staff meetings.
12. Identify and develop candidates for management programs.
13. Put results of observation of employee performance in writing.
14. Develop action plans for employees to help them in their performance.
15. Authorize promotion and/or wage increases for staff.
16. Terminate employment of an employee for unsatisfactory performance.

Financial Management

Accounting

1. Authorize payment on vendor invoices.
2. Verify payroll.
3. Count cash drawers.
4. Prepare bank deposits.
5. Assist in establishment audits by management or outside auditors.

6. Balance cash at end of shift.
7. Analyze profit and loss reports for establishment.

Cost Control
1. Discuss factors that impact profitability with district manager/supervisor.
2. Check establishment figures for sales, labor costs, waste, inventory, and so on.

Administrative Management
Scheduling/Coordinating
1. Establish objectives for shift based on needs of establishment.
2. Coordinate work performed by different shifts, for example, cleanup, routine maintenance, and so on.
3. Complete special projects assigned by district manager/supervisor.
4. Complete shift readiness checklist.

Planning
1. Develop and implement action plans to meet financial goals.
2. Attend off-site workshops and training sessions.

Communication
1. Communicate with management team by reading and making entries in daily communication log.
2. Prepare written reports on cleanliness, food quality, personnel, inventory, sales, food waste, labor costs, and so on.
3. Review reports prepared by other establishment managers.
4. Review memos, reports, and letters from company headquarters/main office.
5. Inform district manager/supervisor of problems or developments that affect operation and performance of the establishment.

6. Initiate and answer correspondence with company, vendors, and so on.
7. File correspondence, reports, personnel records, and so on.

Marketing Management
1. Create and execute local establishment marketing activities.
2. Develop opportunities for the establishment to provide community services.
3. Carry out special product promotions.

Operations Management
Facility Maintenance
1. Conduct routine maintenance checks on facility and equipment.
2. Direct routine maintenance checks on facility and equipment.
3. Repair or supervise the repair of equipment.
4. Review establishment evaluations with district manager/supervisor.
5. Authorize the repair of equipment by outside contractor.
6. Recommend upgrades in facility and equipment.

Food and Beverage Operations Management
1. Direct activities for opening establishment.
2. Direct activities for closing establishment.
3. Talk with other managers at beginning and end of shift to relay information about ongoing problems and activities.
4. Count, verify, and report inventory.
5. Receive, inspect, and verify vendor deliveries.

> " Ray Kroc, of McDonald's, once spent a couple of hours in a good suit with one of his restaurant managers cleaning up the parking lot of one of his restaurants. Word soon got around to the other stores that management begins in the parking lot and ends in the bathrooms. "

6. Check stock levels and submit orders as necessary.
7. Talk with vendors concerning quality of product delivered.
8. Interview vendors who wish to sell products to establishment.
9. Check finished product quality and act to correct problems.
10. Work as expediter to get meals served effectively.
11. Inspect dining area, kitchen, rest rooms, food lockers, storage, and parking lot.
12. Check daily reports for indications of internal theft.
13. Instruct employees regarding the control of waste, portion sizes, and so on.
14. Prepare forecast for daily or shift food preparation.

Service

1. Receive and record table reservations.
2. Greet familiar customers by name.
3. Seat customers.
4. Talk with customers while they are dining.
5. Monitor service times and procedures in the dining area.
6. Observe customers being served in order to correct problems.
7. Ask customers about quality of service.
8. Ask customers about quality of the food product.
9. Listen to and resolve customer complaints.
10. Authorize complementary meals or beverages.
11. Write letters in response to customer complaints.
12. Telephone customers in response to customer complaints.
13. Secure and return items left by customers.

Sanitation and Safety

1. Accompany local officials on health inspections on premise.
2. Administer first aid to employees and customers.
3. Submit accident, incident, and OSHA reports.
4. Report incidents to police.
5. Observe employee behavior and establishment conditions for compliance with safety and security procedures.

TRENDS in RESTAURANT OPERATIONS

- More flavorful food
- Increased take-out meals, especially at lunch and more home meal replacement (for dinner)
- Increased food safety and sanitation
- Increasingly sophisticated guests need more exciting offerings
- More food court restaurants in malls, movie theater complexes, and colleges and universities where guests line up (similar to a cafeteria), select their food (which a server places on a tray), and pay a cashier
- Steak houses are becoming more popular
- With more restaurants in each segment, the segments are splitting into upper, middle, and lower tiers
- Twin and multirestaurant locations
- Quick-service restaurants (QSRs) in convenience stores
- Difficulty in finding good employees
- Increase in casual dining, especially fast casual

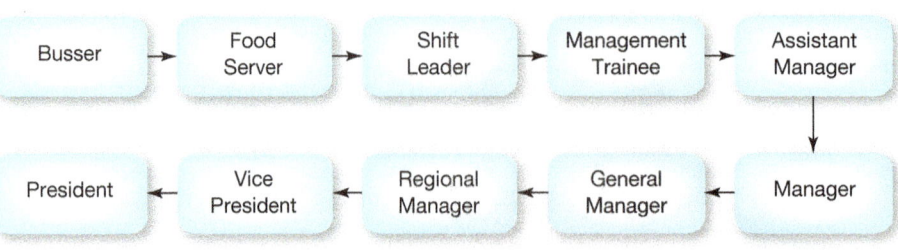

FIGURE 8–4 Career Pattern in the Restaurant Industry.

Shortage in Stock

It's 9:30 on a Friday morning at The Pub. Product is scheduled to be delivered at 10:00. Sally specifically ordered an exceptional amount of food for the upcoming holiday weekend because she is projecting it to be busy. Sally receives a phone call at 10:30 from J&G groceries, stating that it cannot deliver the product until 10:00 A.M. on Saturday morning. She explains to the driver that it is crucial that she receives the product as soon as possible. He apologizes; however, it is impossible to have delivery made until Saturday morning.

By 1:00 P.M., The Pub is beginning to run out of product, including absolute necessities such as steaks, chicken, fish, and produce. The guests are getting frustrated because the staff are beginning to "86" a great deal of product. In addition, if they do not begin production for the P.M. shift soon, the restaurant will be in deep trouble. On Friday nights, The Pub does in excess of $12,000 in sales. However, if the problem is not immediately alleviated, it will lose many guests and a great amount of profits.

DISCUSSION QUESTIONS

1. What immediate measures would you take to resolve the problem?
2. How would you produce the appropriate product as soon as possible?
3. Who should you call first, if anyone, to alleviate the problem?
4. What can you do to always have enough product on hand?
5. Is it important to have a backup plan for a situation like this? If so, what would it be?

CAREER INFORMATION

RESTAURANT OPERATIONS

Choosing a management career in restaurant operations means that you have just selected the area of hospitality that offers college graduates enormous opportunity, the highest starting salaries in the hospitality industry, and the best opportunities for advancement. Opportunities range from fast-food to five-star dining. Salaries range from $32,000 to over $40,000 for assistant management positions (this may be slightly lower or higher depending on the location in the U.S.). Where you will be on that continuum depends on the skills you acquired while in the restaurant industry during college and your ability to sell yourself. (The type of operation, sales volume, and location of the establishment also affect salaries.)

Higher salaries mean a more competitive environment for jobs. In the last few years, salaries have started to increase, reflecting the restaurant industry's willingness to hire experienced young talent. Recruiters refer to these graduates sometimes as grade A candidates or thoroughbreds. Recruiters want graduates who are confident in their skills and have a work record that shows a genuine interest in restaurant management.

Possessing confidence and skill is necessary to complete the management training programs and to get through your first year as a manager. Typically, restaurant managers work 50 to 60 hours a week, including weekends and holidays. It is a physically demanding job that requires being constantly on your feet and working under pressure in a fast-paced environment.

However, this kind of challenge has tremendous rewards. As a manager, you will work in an atmosphere that offers endless opportunities to delight customers and motivate employees. Few things are more gratifying than a genuinely satisfied customer or sharing in the pleasure of the restaurant crew's successfully completed shift. Restaurant operations typically pay people based strictly on performance. It is not uncommon for restaurant general managers to make six-figure incomes from restaurants that generate $5 million plus in sales.

Related Web Sites

http://www.nraef.org/—NRA educational foundation
www.restaurant-careers.com/—Career Bulletin Board
www.darden.coml—Darden Restaurants employment opportunities

SUMMARY

1. Most restaurants forecast a budget on a weekly and monthly basis that projects sales and costs for a year in consideration of guest counts and the average guest check.
2. To operate a restaurant, products need to be purchased, received, and properly stored.
3. Food production is determined by the expected business for the next few days. The kitchen layout is designed according to the sales forecasted.
4. Good service is very important. In addition to taking orders, servers act as salespersons for the restaurant.
5. The front of the house deals with the part of the restaurant that has direct contact with guests, in other words, what the guests see—grounds maintenance, hosts/hostesses, dining and bar areas, bartenders, bussers, etc.
6. The back of the house is generally run by the kitchen manager and refers to all areas that guests normally do not come in contact with. This includes purchasing, receiving, storing/issuing, food production, stewarding, budgeting, accounting, and control.

KEY WORDS AND CONCEPTS

American service
Average guest check
Back of the house
Beverage cost percentage
First in–first out (FIFO)
Food cost percentage
Front of the house
Guest counts or covers
Order specification
Par stock
Product specification
Production control sheets
Purchase order
Receiving
Restaurant forecasting
Standardized recipe
Suggestive selling

REVIEW QUESTIONS

1. Briefly describe the two components of restaurant forecasting.
2. Explain the key points in purchasing, receiving, and storing.
3. Why is the kitchen layout an important aspect of food production?
4. Explain the purpose of suggestive selling. What characteristics make up a good server?
5. What are the differences between the back of the house and the front of the house?
6. What steps must one take in preparing production sheets?
7. What are standardized recipes and why are they important?

INTERNET EXERCISES

1. Organization: National Restaurant Association (NRA)
   Web site: www.restaurant.org/
   Summary: The NRA is the business association of the food industry. It consists of 400,000 members and over 170,000 restaurants. Member restaurants represent table service and quick-service operators, chains, and franchises. The NRA helps international restaurants receive the benefits of the association and gives guidance for success to nonprofit members.

   a. List the food-borne diseases presented on the NRA site. Read about each disease and what the National Restaurant Association says about how to prevent it.
   b. What kinds of careers are available in the restaurant and hospitality industry?
   c. Check the top stories at the NRA'S Web site www.restaurant.org

2. Organization: Chili's Grill and Bar
   Web site: www.chilis.com
   Summary: Chili's is a fun and exciting place to have burgers, fajitas, margaritas, and chili. Established in 1975 in Dallas, the chain now has more than 637 restaurants in the United States and 20 other countries.

   a. What requirements must you meet to open a Chili's franchise? From what you have learned about the issues involved in starting your own business, how is setting up your own business different from having a franchise?
   b. What is the "Chilihead culture"?

APPLY YOUR KNOWLEDGE

1. In a casual Italian restaurant, sales for the week of September 15 are as follows:
   Food sales: $10,000
   Beverage sales: $ 2,500
   Total $12,500
   a. If the food cost is 30 percent, how much did the food actually cost?
   b. If the beverage cost is 25 percent of beverage sales, how much did the beverages cost?
   c. If the labor cost is 28 percent, how much money does that represent and how much is left over for other costs and profit?
2. If a 33 percent food cost is required and a menu item sells for $16.95, what is its cost supposed to be?
3. Sales at your restaurant for the month of October are $685,324. If a 25 percent labor cost is expected, what would that be in dollars?

SUGGESTED ACTIVITIES

1. In groups, interview a restaurant manager and check how his or her duties and responsibilities compare with those in the text.
2. In groups, look at the example of results in the chapter and decide what you would do to improve the labor cost percentage for the next week.

ENDNOTES

1. This section draws on John R. Walker, *The Restaurant from Concept to Operation,* 5th ed. (New York: John Wiley and Sons, 2009), pp. 86–87.
2. Personal conversation with Danny Meyer, January 14, 2006.
3. This section draws on John R. Walker, *The Restaurant from Concept to Operation,* p. 275.
4. Ibid.
5. Personal conversation with Joe Riley, July 12, 2006.
6. This section is adapted from http://www.starchefs.com/features/trends/30_sustainability_tips/index.shtml, retrieved March 10, 2010.

9 MANAGED SERVICES

LEARNING OUTCOMES

After reading and studying this chapter, you should be able to:

Outline the different managed services segments.

Describe the five factors that distinguish managed services operations from commercial ones.

Explain the need for and trends in elementary and secondary school foodservice.

Describe the complexities in college and university foodservice.

Identify characteristics and trends in health care, business and industry, and leisure and recreation foodservices.

Describe the economic impact of tourism.

Overview

Read the *Guide to Managed Services: Explore the scope of This Segment*

Managed services consists of all foodservice operations as follows:

- Airlines
- Military
- Elementary and secondary schools
- Colleges and universities
- Health care facilities
- Business and industry
- Leisure and recreation
- Seniors
- Conference centers
- Airports
- Travel plazas
- National parks

Several features distinguish managed services operations from **commercial foodservices**:

1. In a restaurant, the challenge is to please the guest. In managed services, it is necessary to meet both the needs of the guest and the client (the institution itself).
2. In some operations, the guests may or may not have alternative dining options available to them and are a captive clientele. These guests may be eating at the foodservice operation only once or on a daily basis.
3. Many managed operations are housed in host organizations that do not have foodservice as their primary business.
4. Most managed services operations produce food in large-quantity batches for service and consumption within fixed time periods. (**Batch cooking** means to produce a batch of food to serve at 11:30 A.M., another batch to serve at 12:15 P.M., and a third batch to serve at 12:45 P.M., rather than putting out all the food for the whole lunch period at 11:30 A.M. This gives the guests who come to eat later in the serving period as good a quality meal as those who came to eat earlier.)
5. The volume of business is more consistent and therefore easier to cater. Because it is easier to predict the number of meals and portion sizes, it is easier to plan, organize, produce, and serve meals; therefore, the atmosphere is less hurried than that of a restaurant. Weekends tend to be quieter than weekdays in managed services and, overall, the hours and benefits may be better than those of commercial restaurants.

A company or organization might contract its foodservice operations or other services for the following reasons: financial; quality of program; recruitment of management and staff; expertise in management and of service operations; resources available: people, programs, management systems, information systems; labor relations and other support; outsourcing of administrative functions.[1]

Airlines and Airports

In-Flight Foodservice

Airlines are constantly striving to be more efficient, demanding better food at the same or lower costs. Airlines may either provide meals from their own *in-flight* business or have the service provided by a contractor. In-flight food may be prepared in a factory mode at a facility close to but outside of the airport. In these cases, the food is prepared and packaged; it then is transported to the departure gates for the appropriate flights. Once the food is loaded onto the aircraft, flight attendants take over serving the food and beverages to passengers.

In-flight foodservice is a complex logistical operation: The food must be able to tolerate the conditions of an extended hot

A sample airline meal available on long-haul flights.

or cold holding period from the time it is prepared until the time it is served. If a food item is to be served hot, it must be able to rethermalize well on the plate. In addition, the meal needs to look appealing, be tasty, fit on the tray, and be microwavable. Finally, all food and beverage items must be delivered on time and correctly to each departing aircraft.

LSG Sky Chefs is the largest airline catering company, with 300 international airline partners—in the air, and on the ground at 200 service centers. At its main production center near Frankfurt, Germany, it can produce 130,000 meals in just 16 hours.[2] Gate Gourmet International is another major player in the in-flight foodservices sector, operating in 49 countries on six continents, with 200 flight kitchen facilities producing over 427 million meals and annually supported by more than 30,000 employees.[3]

The in-flight foodservice management operators plan the menus, develop the product specifications, and arrange the purchasing contracts. Each airline has a representative who oversees one or more locations and checks on the quality, quantity, and delivery times of all food and beverage items. Airlines regard in-flight foodservice as an expense that needs to be controlled. The cost for the average in-flight meal is just over $7. The cost had been higher, but in order to trim costs, airlines now offer just pretzels with a beverage on short flights and flights that do not span main meal times. Airlines are experimenting with optional meals paid for by the passenger (buy-on-board).

International airlines try to stand out by offering superior food and beverages in hopes of attracting more passengers. Others reduce or eliminate foodservice as a strategic decision to sup-

.inc | Corporate Profile

SODEXHO

Sodexho is a leading North American food and facilities management services company. This company is also a member of the international Sodexho Alliance, which was founded in 1966 by Frenchman Pierre Bellon with its first service provider in Marseille, France. Primarily serving schools, restaurants, and hospitals, the company soon became internationally successful by signing deals with Belgian foodservice contractors. After considerable success in Europe, Africa, and the Middle East, in 1980 Sodexho Alliance decided to expand its reach into North and South America. In 1997, the company joined with Universal Ogden Services, a leading U.S. remote-site service provider. The empire grew a year later, when Sodexho Alliance and Marriott Management Services merged. The merger created a new company called Sodexho Marriott Services. Listed on the New York Stock Exchange, the new company became the market leader in food and management services in the United States. At that time, Sodexho Alliance was the biggest shareholder, holding 48.4 percent of shares of the company's capital. In 2001, however, Sodexho Alliance acquired 53 percent of the shares in Sodexho Marriott Services, which changed its name to simply Sodexho.

Today, Sodexho Alliance has over 270,000 employees at 6,000 sites in 70 countries. In the United States there are 110,000 employees. Sodexho's goal is to improve the quality and life of customers and clients all over the United States and Canada. It offers outsourcing solutions to the health care, corporate, and education markets, including housekeeping, groundskeeping, foodservice, plant operation and maintenance, and integrated facilities management.

Sodexho's mission is to create and offer services that contribute to a more pleasant way of life for people wherever and whenever they come together. Its challenge is to make its mission and values come alive through the way in which employees work together to serve clients and customers. The values of Sodexho are service spirit, team spirit, and spirit of progress.

A leading provider of food and facilities management services in North America, Sodexho serves corporations, colleges and universities, health care organizations, and school districts. It is always looking to develop talent. Sodexho offers internships in foodservice and facilities management businesses as well as in staff positions such as finance, human resources, marketing, and sales. Sodexho believes that workforce diversity is essential to the company's growth and long-term success. By valuing and managing diversity at work, Sodexho can leverage the skills, knowledge, and abilities of all employees to increase employee, client, and customer satisfaction.

This draws from www.sodexhousa.com/about_us.html and www.sodexousa.com/.

port lower fares. Generally, international flights have better quality food and beverage service. On board, each aircraft has two or three categories of service, usually economy/coach, business, and first class. First- and business-class passengers usually receive free beverages and upgraded meal items and service. These meals may consist of items like fresh salmon or filet mignon; those traveling in coach receive "carry-on doggie-bags" if they're lucky! Passengers eat any meal that is served with plastic knives, forks, and spoons.

A number of smaller regional and local foodservice operators contract to a variety of airlines at hundreds of airports. Most airports have caterers or foodservice contractors who compete for airline contracts. With several international and U.S. airlines using U.S. airports, each must decide whether to use its own foodservice (if it has one) or to contract with one of several independent operators.

As airlines have decreased their in-flight foodservice, airport restaurants have picked up the business. Popular chain restaurants like T.G.I. Friday's and Chili's are in several terminals, along with quick-service restaurants like Pizza Hut. These restaurants supplement airport foodservice offered by contractors like Sodexho, ARAMARK, and Host International, a division of Marriott International. Menus may be more limited to offer quicker service for those with connecting flights.

Check Your Knowledge

1. What are managed services?
2. Why would companies use contract management?

Military

Military foodservice is a large and important component of managed services. There are about 1.5 million soldiers, sailors, and pilots in active duty in the United States. Even with the downsizing of the military, foodservice sales top $6 billion per year. Base closings have prompted many military foodservice organizations to reassess services and concepts in order to better meet the needs of their personnel.

Recent trends in military foodservice call for services such as officers' clubs to be contracted out to foodservice management companies. This change has reduced military costs because many of the officers' clubs lost money. The clubs now have moved the emphasis from fine dining to a more casual approach with family appeal. Many clubs are renovating their base concept even further, restyling according to theme concepts, such as sports or country western, for example. Other cost-saving measures include menu management, such as the use of a single menu for lunch and dinner (guests seldom eat both meals at the clubs). With proper plating techniques and portion-size manipulation, one menu can be created for lunch and dinner, meaning one inventory for both meals and less stock in general. To make this technique work successfully, the menu features several choices for appetizers, entrees, and desserts.

Another trend is the testing of prepared foods that can be reheated and served without much labor. Technological advances mean that field troops do not eat out of tin cans anymore; instead, they receive their food portions in plastic-and-foil pouches called meals ready-to-eat (MREs). Today, mobile field kitchens can be run by just two people, and bulk food supplies have been replaced by preportioned, precooked food packed in trays, which then are reheated in boiling water.

> **Feeding military personnel includes feeding troops and officers in clubs, dining halls, and military hospitals, as well as in the field.**

Feeding military personnel includes feeding troops and officers in clubs, dining halls, and military hospitals, as well as in the field. As both the budget and the numbers of personnel decrease, fewer cooks are required.

A model for such downsizing is the U.S. Marine Corps, which contracts out foodservice. With smaller numbers, they could not afford to take a marine away from training to work in the dining facilities without affecting military operations. Sodexho has the contract for the U.S. Marine Corps, serving on seven bases in 55 barracks, plus clubs and other related services. In addition, fast-food restaurants like McDonald's and Burger King have opened on well over 150 bases; they are now installing "expressway" kiosks on more bases. The fast-food restaurants on base offer further alternatives for military personnel on the move.

One problem that may arise as a result of the downsizing and contracting out of military foodservice is the improbability that McDonald's could set up on the front line in a combat situation. The military will still have to do their own foodservice when it comes to mobilization.

Elementary and Secondary Schools

The United States government enacted the National School Lunch Act of 1946 in response to concern about malnourishment in military recruits. The rationale was that if students received good meals, the military would have healthier recruits. In addition, such a program would make use of the surplus food that farmers produced. Today, about 29.6 million children are fed breakfast or lunch, or both, each day in approximately 98,000 schools, at a cost of about $7 billion annually.[4]

Elementary and secondary school foodservice currently face many concerns, including the major challenge of balancing salability with good nutrition. Apart from cost and nutritional value, there is the broader social issue of the universal free meal. Proponents of the program maintain that children who are better nourished have a greater attention span, are less likely to be absent from school, and will stay in school longer. Offering free meals to all students also removes the poor kid stigma from school lunch. Detractors from the universal program say that, if we learned anything from the social programs that were implemented during the 1960s, it was that throwing money at problems is not always the best answer.

Both sides agree that there is serious concern about what young students are eating. The news about the fat and cholesterol in the popcorn served at movie theaters shocked many adults. More shocking, though, is what schoolchildren are eating, as one survey illustrates.[5] A U.S. Department of Agriculture survey found that school lunches, on average, exceeded dietary guidelines for fat by 25 percent, for saturated fat by 50 percent, and for sodium by 85 percent. Equally shocking is the percentage of children who eat one serving or less of fruits and vegetables each day (excluding french fries), as shown in Figure 9–1.

The preparation and service of school foodservice meals varies. Some schools have on-site kitchens where the food is prepared, and dining rooms where the food is served. Many large school districts operate a central commissary that prepares the meals and then distributes them among the schools in that district. Or, some schools purchase ready-to-serve meals that require only assembly at the school.

Schools may decide to participate in the **National School Lunch Program (NSLP)** or operate on their own. In reality, most schools have little choice: by participating in the program, they receive federal funding to the tune of about $2.73 per meal per student. Contract companies such as Sodexho are introducing more flexibility in choices for students.

Meeting dietary guidelines is also an important issue. Much work has gone into establishing standard nutritional requirements for children. It is difficult to achieve a balance between healthy food and costs while taking children's eating habits into account. Under the NSLP regulations, students must eat from what is commonly known as the "type A" menu. Children must be offered all the items on the type A menu at every meal; they must select at least three of the five meal components in order for the school to qualify for

Getting kids to eat healthy food is a challenge.

HTi — Discover the Challenges of Menu Planning for Managed Services Operations

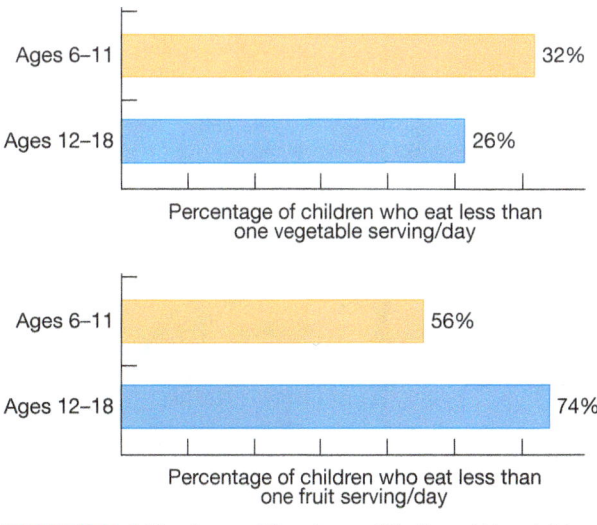

FIGURE 9–1 Numbers of Servings of Fruit and Vegetables That Children Eat.
(**Source:** National Cancer Institute.)

funding. However, USDA regulations have established limits on the amount of fat and saturated fat that can be offered. Fat should not exceed 30 percent of calories per week, and just 10 percent of calories may come from saturated fat per week.

The government-funded NSLP, which pays over $7 billion per year for the meals given or sold at a discount to schoolchildren, is a huge potential market for fast-food chains. Chains are extremely eager to penetrate into the elementary and secondary school markets, even if it means a decrease in revenues. "We do reduce the price of our product, and we do make less margin than in our normal operations," says Joy Wallace, national sales director/nontraditional sales for Pizza Hut. However, the company believes that it is to its benefit to introduce Pizza Hut to young people very early—in other words, the aim is to build brand loyalty. As a matter of fact, in Duluth, Minnesota, James Bruner, foodservice director for the city schools, was forced into offering branded pizza in several junior high and high schools. The local principals, hungry for new revenue, began offering Little Caesar's in direct competition to the cafeteria's frozen pizzas. Taco Bell is in nearly 3,000 schools, Pizza Hut in 4,500, Subway in 650; Domino's, McDonald's, Arby's, and others are well established in the market as well.

Despite the positives, although it is not hard to convince the children, chains need to convince the adults. There has been much debate as to whether chains should be allowed into schools or not. Many parents feel that the school environment should provide a standard example of what sound nutrition should be, and they believe that with fast food as an option, that will not be the case.

At a school lunch challenge at the American Culinary Federation (ACF) conference, chefs from around the country developed nutritious menus geared to wean children away from junk food and toward healthy foods. An 80-cent limit on the cost of raw ingredients was placed on the 11 finalists. Innovation and taste, as well as healthfulness, were the main criteria used to evaluate the winning entry: turkey taco salad, sausage pizza bagel, and stuffed potatoes.

Nutrition Education Programs

Nutrition education programs are now a required part of the nation's school lunch program. As a result of this program, children are learning to improve their eating habits, which, it is hoped, will continue for the rest of their lives. To support the program, nutritional education materials are used to decorate the dining room halls and tables. Perhaps the best example of this is the food pyramid developed by the Food and Nutrition Service of the U.S. Department of Agriculture. Figure 9–2 shows this food pyramid, which shows what to eat each day for a healthy diet.

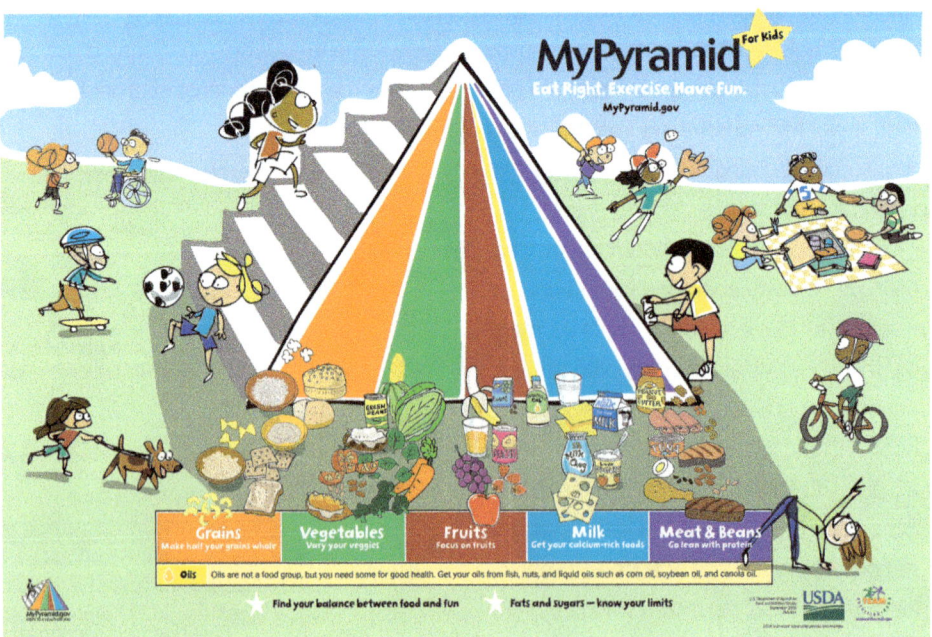

FIGURE 9–2 Food Pyramid.
(*Source:* U.S. Department of Agriculture and U.S. Department of Health and Human Services.)

COLLEGES AND UNIVERSITIES

College and university foodservice operations are complex and diverse. Among the various constituents of foodservice management are residence halls, sports concessions, conferences, cafeterias/student unions, faculty clubs, convenience stores, administrative catering, and outside catering.

On-campus dining is a challenge for foodservice managers because the clientele live on campus and eat most of their meals at one of the campus dining facilities. If the manager or contractor is not creative, students, staff, and faculty may quickly become bored with the "sameness" of the surroundings and menu offerings. Most campus dining is cafeteria style and offers cyclical menus that rotate on a predetermined schedule—usually every 14 or 21 days.

College students getting a meal in the cafeteria.

However, a college foodservice manager does have some advantages when compared with a restaurant manager. Budgeting is made easier because the on-campus students have already paid for their meals and their numbers are easier to forecast. When the payment is guaranteed and the guest count is fairly predictable, planning and organizing staffing levels and food quantities are relatively easy and should ensure a reasonable profit margin. For instance, the **daily rate** is the amount of money required per day from each person to pay for the foodservice. Thus, if foodservice expenses for one semester of 98 days amount to $650,000 for an operation with 1,000 students eating, the daily rate will be:

$$\frac{\$750{,}000 / 98 \text{ (days)}}{1000} = \$7.65$$

College foodservice operations now offer a variety of meal plans for students. Under the old board plan, when students paid one fee for all meals each day—whether they ate them or not—the foodservice operator literally made a profit from the students who did not actually eat the meals they had paid for. More typically now, students match their payments to the number of meals eaten: Monday–Friday, breakfast, lunch, dinner; dinner only; and prepaid credit cards that allow a student to use the card at any campus outlet and have the value of the food and beverage items deducted from his or her credit balance.

Leaders of the National Associations of College Auxiliary Services (NACAS), who represent 1,200 member institutes, have noticed that on-campus services and activities are undergoing continuous change. The environment has become a critical part of policy and implementation that transcends parochial interests for those that best meet the needs of the institution and, ultimately, its students.

The driving forces of change on campuses are the advent and growth of branded concepts, privatization, campus cards, and computer use. There is a strong shift toward the acceptance of student meal cards as branded or alternative concepts on campus, even with local commercial eateries off campus. Many universities and colleges have adopted a food court offering students more choice in their dining.

Students are expressing an interest not only in the recipes, flavor profiles, and ingredients, but also where products come from and how they are made. Campus kitchens are using more local and organic produce and proteins where available. A small but growing number of students look for items like range-free chicken breasts and cage-free eggs. Healthful dining is here to stay as operators use trans fat–free oils, whole grains, and a boarder range of vegetarian and vegan recipes.[6]

ADVANTAGES AND DISADVANTAGES OF CONTRACT MANAGEMENT FROM A CLIENT PERSPECTIVE

Advantages
- Experience in size and types of operations
- Use contracted department as a model for rest of institution
- Variety of services
- Resource and support available
- Hold contractor to a higher level of performance

Disadvantages
- Some segments perceived as institutionalized
- Potential for lost contracts

Courtesy of Susan Pillmeier, Manager of College Relations, ARAMARK, and John Lee, Director of Staffing Services, Sodexho.

Student Unions

Explore a Variety of Cafeteria Set-Ups at Dimmick Hall

The college student union offers a variety of managed services that caters to the needs of a diverse student body. Among the services offered are cafeteria foodservice, beverage services, branded quick-service restaurants, and take-out foodservice.

The cafeteria foodservice operation is often the "happening" place in the student union, where students meet to socialize as well as to eat and drink. The cafeteria is generally open for breakfast, lunch, and dinner. Depending on the volume of business, the cafeteria may be closed during the nonmeal periods and weekends, and the cafeteria menu may or may not be the same as the residence foodservice facility. Offering a menu with a good price value is crucial to the successful operation of a campus cafeteria.

On campuses at which alcoholic beverage service is permitted, beverage services mainly focus on some form of a student pub where beer and perhaps wine and spirits may be offered. Not to be outdone, the faculty will undoubtedly have a lounge that also offers alcoholic beverages. Other beverages may be served at various outlets such as a food court or convenience store. Campus beverage service provides opportunities for foodservice operators to enhance profits.

"On-campus dining is a challenge for foodservice managers because the clientele live on campus and eat most of their meals at one of the campus dining facilities."

In addition, many college campuses have welcomed branded, quick-service restaurants as a convenient way to satisfy the needs of a community on the go. Such an approach offers a win–win situation for colleges. The experience and brand recognition of chain restaurants like Pizza Hut, McDonald's, Subway, and Wendy's attract customers; the restaurants pay a fee, either to the foodservice management company or the university directly. Obviously, there is a danger that the quick-service restaurant may attract customers that the cafeteria might then lose, but competition tends to be good for all concerned.

Take-out foodservice is another convenience for the campus community. At times, students—and staff—do not want to prepare meals and are thankful for the opportunity to take meals with them. And it is not just during exam time that students, friends, and staff have a need for the take-out option. For example, tailgate parties prior to football and basketball games or concerts and other recreational/sporting events allow entrepreneurial foodservice operators to increase revenue and profits.

The type of contract that a managed services operator signs varies depending on the size of the account. If the account is small, a fee generally is charged. With larger accounts, operators contract for a set percentage (usually about 5 percent) or a combination of a percentage and a bonus split. Figure 9–3 shows a typical college menu for the dining hall, where students usually eat on campus.

Dining INNOVATIONS

WEEK 1

	MONDAY	TUESDAY	WEDNESDAY	THURSDAY	FRIDAY
Breakfast—Cold cereal, fruit and yogurt bar, toast, juices, milks, coffee, tea, hot chocolate and fresh fruit					
Bakery:	Quick Coffee Cake	Assorted Danish	Cinnamon Coffee Cake	Sticky Top Roll	Banana Nut Muffins
Hot Cereal:	Oatmeal	Malt-O-Meal	Cream of Wheat	Grits	Oatmeal
Entrees:	Buttermilk Pancakes Scrambled Eggs Sausage Gravy & Biscuits Cottage Fries	Waffles Scrambled Eggs Egg O'Muffin w/Bacon Hearty Fried Potatoes Bacon	French Toast Scrambled Eggs Ham & Cheese Omelette Hash Browns	Oatmeal Pancakes Scrambled Eggs Chorizo & Eggs Cottage Fries Sausage Links	Waffles w/Peaches Scrambled Eggs Egg Burrito Home Fries
Lunch—Salad Bar, Rice & Chili Bar, Cereal, Build-Your-Own-Sandwich Bar & Fresh Fruit					
Soup:	Beef Barley	Italian Minestrone	Chicken Gumbo	Chicken Noodle	New England Clam Chowder
Entrees:	Baked Seafood & Rice Grilled Ham & Cheese Potato Salad Wax Beans Mixed Vegetables	Chicken Tortilla Casserole Patty Melt French Fries Hominy Spinach	Fishwich Spanish Macaroni Ranch Beans Italian Green Beans Braised Carrots & Celery	Cheesy Mushroom Burger Hamburger Grilled Cheese Onion Rings Carrots Oriental Veg. Blend	BBQ Ham Sandwich Ground Beef & Potato Pie Whipped Potatoes Italian Green Beans Beets
Dessert:	Chocolate Pudding Soft Serve Ice Cream	Applesauce Cake Soft Serve Ice Cream	Peanut Butter Cookies	Coconut Cake	Vanilla Pudding
Dinner—Salad Bar, Cereal, & Fresh Fruit (Tortillas served at Breakfast & Dinner)					
Soup:	Beef Barley	Italian Minestrone	Chicken Gumbo	Chicken Noodle	New England Clam Chowder
Entrees:	Oven Broiled Chicken Grilled Liver & Onions Parsley Potatoes Corn Zucchini	Beef Fajitas Fried Perch Spanish Rice Asparagus Carrots	Roast Turkey w/Gravy Old Fashion Beef Stew Whipped Potatoes Corn Cobbettes Brussel Sprouts	Egg Roll Over Rice Grilled Pork Chop Rice Beets Cauliflower au Gratin	Pizza! Pizza! Pizza! Curly Fries Broccoli Mixed Vegetables
Dessert:	Chocolate Chip Cookies	Spicy Whole Wheat Bar	Chocolate Mayo Cake	Peach Cobbler	Best Ever Cake

FIGURE 9–3 Sample College Menu.
(*Courtesy:* Sodexho Foodservice Management.)

Introducing Cherry Cerminia

Dietitian and General Manager, Sodexho.

I am a registered dietitian and the general manager of a K–12 Sodexho school foodservice program. Sodexho has been contracted to manage the food and nutrition program for the school I serve. It is a five-building, 4,000-student operation. Sodexho School Services leads the nation in providing food and facilities management solutions that support the educational process. From nutrition education to monitoring air quality, our efforts enable students and faculty to consistently perform at a high level. Every day, Sodexho serves the needs of more than 400 school districts. Our expertise allows school administrators to focus on education leadership activities. Best of all, our partnering approach always saves money. Our programs have been tested, and the results are conclusive: Sodexho's food service and facilities management solutions improve the quality of life for students, faculty, and the communities we serve.

As the general manager for this operation, a day in my life includes hiring, training, and managing of employees, ordering foods, inventory, managing budgets, financial reporting, menu preparation, production, and nutrition. School meals operations are regulated by the USDA nutrition according to age-specific needs. Both breakfast and lunch are served. We even provide nutrition education both in the classroom and in the lunchroom.

Other areas of concentration include food safety (following HACCP) and physical safety for the employees and our customers. We are audited every year by the National School Foodservice and at least twice per year by the county health department. As a manager, customer service is extremely important in my day-to-day operations. Although the audience is captive, they are still our customers. We look at the student, staff, parents, and administration as our customers. If I cannot train my employees to respect this aspect of their performance, we will lose revenue, and perhaps lose the business to someone perceived to provide a better service. Providing management services to Pine-Richland School District in Gibsonia, Pennsylvania, is really a pleasure. Students are interested in what they eat. They enjoy their meal periods and expect great service. Well-managed, trained, and enthusiastic employees work at Pine-Richland. All of these elements contribute to the company being successful.

Responsibilities in Managed Services

Identify Priorities of Managed Services Managers

A foodservice manager's responsibilities in a small or midsized operation are frequently more extensive than those of managers of the larger operations. This is because larger units have more people to whom to delegate certain functions, such as human resources. For example, following are some of the responsibilities that the foodservice manager in a small or midsized operation might have in addition to strictly foodservice responsibilities:

Employee Relations

- Team development
- Rewards/recognition
- Drug alcohol abuse/prevention
- Positive work environment
- Coaching/facilitating vs. directing

" As in-house kitchens are getting smaller (or in offices are nonexistent), there is a greater need for managed services companies to provide readily available solutions. "

Ana Souza,
Souza's Managed Services,
Wilmington, DE

Human Resource Management

- Recruitment/training/evaluating
- Wage/salary administration
- Benefits administration
- Compliance with federal/state laws/EEO/Senate Bill 198
- Harassment/OSHA
- Disciplinary actions/terminations
- Unemployment/wrongful disclosure

Financial/Budgeting

- Project budgets
- Actual vs. budget monitoring (weekly)
- Controlling food cost, labor, expenses, and so on
- Record keeping requirements/audit
- Monitoring accounts payable/receivable
- Billing/collecting
- Compliance to contracts
- Cash procedures/banking

Safety Administration

- Equipment training/orientation
- Controlling workers' compensation
- Monthly inspections/audits (federal/state/OSHA requirements/Senate Bill 198)

Safety Budget

- Work on the expensive injuries

Food Production/Service

- Menu/recipe development
- Menu mix vs. competition
- Food waste/leftovers utilization
- Production records
- Production control
- Presentation/merchandising

Sanitation/FBI Prevention

- FBI (food-borne illness) prevention
- Sanitation/cleaning schedule
- Proper food handling/storage

- Daily prevention/monitoring
- Monthly inspection
- Health department compliance

Purchasing/Recruiting

- Ordering/receiving/storage
- Food and beverage specifications/quality
- Inventory control
- Vendor relation/problems

Staff Training/Development

- On-the-job vs. structured
- Safety/sanitation/food handling and so on
- Food preparation/presentation

A number of staff support positions offer career opportunities not only within managed services but also in all areas of hospitality operations. They include sales, marketing, controller/audit, financial analysis, human resources, training and development, affirmative action/EEO compliance, safety administration, procurement/distribution, technical services (recipes, menus, product testing), labor relations, and legal aspects. A sample operating statement is shown in Figure 9–4. It shows a monthly statement for a college food-service operation.

> **Managed services are a large component of the hospitality industry. We provide companies such as educational institutions, healthcare facilities, and offices with on-site food service.**
>
> Jessica Turner,
> Restaurant Associates Managed Services,
> Sacramento, CA

Check Your Knowledge

1. In your own words, define in-flight foodservice.
2. What are some of the challenges faced by in-flight foodservice operators? What can be done to solve these problems?
3. Name the foodservice operations that constitute managed services.
4. How is each foodservice operation characterized?
5. In small groups, discuss the differences between the foodservice operations; then share with the class.

DESCRIPTION		%	STUDENT UNION	%	TOTAL	%
SALES						
FOOD REGULAR	$ 951,178				$ 951,178	
FOOD SPECIAL FUNCTIONS	40,000				40,000	
PIZZA HUT EXPRESS			$ 100,000		100,000	
BANQUET & CATERING	200,000				200,000	
CONFERENCE	160,000				160,000	
BEER			80,000		80,000	
SNACK BAR			300,000		30,000	
A LA CARTE CAFE	60,000				60,000	
** TOTAL SALES	$1,411,178		$ 480,000	100.0%	$1,891,178	100.0%
PRODUCT COST						
BAKED GOODS	$ 9,420		$ 4,700		$ 14,120	
BEVERAGE	10,000		8,000		18,000	
MILK & ICE CREAM	11,982		2,819		14,801	
GROCERIES	131,000		49,420		180,420	
FROZEN FOOD	76,045		37,221		113,266	
MEAT, SEAFOOD, EGGS, & CHEESE	129,017		48,000		177,017	
PRODUCE	65,500		26,000		91,500	
MISCELLANEOUS					0	
COLD DRINK	0		0		0	
** TOTAL PRODUCT COST	$ 432,964		$ 176,160	36.7%	$ 609,124	32.2%
LABOR COST						
WAGES	$ 581,000		$ 154,000		$ 735,000	
LABOR—OTHER EMPLOYEES	101,500		545,000		156,000	
BENEFITS + PAYROLL TAXES	124,794		50,657		175,451	
MANAGEMENT BENEFITS	58,320		6,000		64,320	
WAGE ACCRUALS	0				0	
** TOTAL LABOR COST	$ 865,614		$ 265,157	55.2%	$1,130,771	59.8%
FOOD OPERATING COST— CONTROLLABLE						
CLEANING SUPPLIES	$ 24,000		$ 6,000		$ 30,000	
PAPER SUPPLIES	9,000		46,000		55,000	
EQUIPMENT RENTAL					0	
GUEST SUPPLIES					7,000	
PROMOTIONS	4,500		2,500		40,000	
SMALL EQUIPMENT	35,000		5,000		0	
BUSINESS DUES & MEMBERSHIP					3,000	
VEHICLE EXPENSE	3,000				4,300	
TELEPHONE	3,600		700		$ 22,000	
	$ 17,000		$ 5,000			

FIGURE 9–4 Sample Operating Statement.

HEALTH CARE FACILITIES

Health care managed services operations are remarkably complex because of the necessity of meeting the diverse needs of a delicate clientele. Health care managed services are provided to hospital patients, long-term care and assisted-living residents, visitors, and employees. The service is given by tray, cafeteria, dining room, coffee shop, catering, and vending.

The challenge of health care managed services is to provide many special meal requirements to patients with very specific dietary requirements. Determining which meals need to go to which patients and ensuring that they reach their destinations employs especially challenging logistics. In addition to the patients, health care employees need to enjoy a nutritious meal in pleasant surroundings in a limited time (usually 30 minutes). Because employees typically work five days in a row, managers must be creative in the development of menus and meal themes.

DESCRIPTION		%	STUDENT UNION	%	TOTAL	%
LAUNDRY & UNIFORMS					0	
MAINTENANCE & REPAIRS	$ 1,200		$ 200		$ 1,400	
FLOWERS	10,000		4,000		140,000	
TRAINING					0	
SPECIAL SERVICES	18,000		3,000		21,000	
MISCELLANEOUS						
** TOTAL CONTROLLABLE SUPPLIES	$ 125,300	8.9%	$ 72,400	15.1%	$ 197,700	10.5%
OPERATING COSTS— NONCONTROLLABLE						
AMORTIZATION & DEPRECIATION	$ 13,500		$ 7,000		$ 20,500	
INSURANCE	55,717		14,768		70,485	
MISCELLANEOUS EXPENSE	12,400		4,100		16,500	
ASSET RETIREMENTS					0	
RENT/COMMISSIONS	48,000		40,000		88,000	
PIZZA HUT ROYALTIES			7,000		7,000	
PIZZA HUT — LICENSING MARKETING			7,000		7,000	
TAXES, LICENSE & FEES	5,000		500		5,500	
VEHICLE — DEPRECIATION & EXPENSE	4,000				4,000	
ADMINISTRATION & SUPERVISION						
** TOTAL NONCONTROLLABLE COST	$ 138,617	9.8%	$ 80,368	16.7%	$ 218,985	11.6%
** TOTAL COST OF OPERATIONS	$ 1,562,495	110.7%	$ 594,085	123.8%	$2,156,580	114.0%
EXCESS OR (DEFICIT)	(151,317)	(10.7%)	(114,085)	(23.8)	(265,402)	(14.0%)
PARTICIPATION-CONTRACTOR						
*** NET EXCESS OR (DEFICIT)						
STATISTICS						
CUSTOMER COUNT						
HOURS WORKED						
AVERAGE FOOD-SALES/CUSTOMER						

FIGURE 9–4 (*Continued*)

The main focus of hospital foodservice is the **tray line**. Once all the requirements for special meals have been prepared by a registered dietitian, the line is set up and menus color coded for the various diets. The line begins with the tray, a mat, cutlery, napkin, salt and pepper, and perhaps a flower. As the tray moves along the line, various menu items are added according to the color code for the particular patient's diet. Naturally, each tray is double- and triple-checked, first at the end of the tray line and then on the hospital floor. The line generally goes floor by floor at a rate of about five trays a minute; at this rate, a large hospital with 600 beds can be served within a couple of hours. This is time consuming for the employees, because three meals a day represent up to six hours of line time. Clearly, health care foodservice is very labor intensive, with labor accounting for about 55 to 66 percent of operating dollars. In an effort to keep costs down, many operators have increased the number of help-yourself food stations, buffets, salads, desserts, and topping bars. They also focus on increasing revenues through catering and retail innovations. In some markets, patient counts and lengths of stay are declining, which emphasizes the importance of finding new ways of generating revenues. According to the 10 largest self-operated hospitals, one of the basic service areas, the cafeteria, is generating the biggest revenue-producing opportunities.[7]

Find Out Why Menu Planning Is Important to Managed Services

.inc | Corporate Profile

ARAMARK

In the 1950s, Dave Davidson and Bill Fishman, both in the vending business, realized that they shared the same dreams of turning vending into a service and combining it with foodservice. The two entrepreneurs joined forces to become the first truly national vending and foodservice company. Automatic Retailers of America (ARA) was born in 1959. Fishman and Davidson had the management skills, the capital, and the expertise to expand. And this they did—ARAMARK is the world's leading provider of quality managed services. It operates in all 50 states and in 18 foreign countries, offering a very diversified and broad range of services to businesses of all sizes, and to thousands of universities, hospitals, and municipal, state, and federal government facilities. Every day, the company serves millions of people at more than 500,000 locations worldwide. ARAMARK's emphasis on the quality of service management was evident from the very beginning of its operations. ARAMARK entered new markets by researching the best-managed local companies, acquiring them, and persuading key managers to stay with the company.

ARAMARK's business purpose states: "We are a professional services organization dedicated to excellence."

- We develop and sustain our leadership position by engaging and supporting our most valuable differentiated asset; the competence, commitment, and creativity of *our people*.
- We provide world-class *experiences, environments* and *outcomes* for our clients and customers by developing relationships based on service excellence, partnership, and mutual understanding.
- We enable our clients to realize their *core mission*, and we will anticipate the needs and exceed the expectations of customers by dedicating our skills in professional services—hospitality, food, facilities, and uniforms—to the goals and priorities of their institution.
- We create long-term value and capture the greatest opportunity for all ARAMARK shareholders—our people, clients, customers, communities and shareholders—by delivering sustainable profitable growth in sales, earnings and cash flow in a global company built on pride, integrity, and respect.

ARAMARK began the diversification process and continued to amplify its portfolio of services. The focus on management skills at every level, especially the local one, gave ARAMARK an invaluable resource. In fact, with every acquisition, local managers were encouraged and rewarded for becoming multiskilled entrepreneurs. This approach to outsourcing is, put more simply, the ability of the company to take the best management skills and apply them to all the lines of business the company uses to diversify.

ARAMARK operations include the following:

Food, leisure, and support services: The company provides food, specialized refreshments, dietary services, and operation support to businesses, educational facilities, government, and medical institutions. ARAMARK also manages food, lodging, hospitality, and support services at national parks and other recreational facilities that serve the general public.

Health services: ARAMARK provides specialized management services for hospitals and medical services. It maintains hospital equipment valued at $5 billion and services 1,300 hospitals and senior living centers with 400,000 beds.

Education services: ARAMARK specializes in providing early childhood and school-age education services. It partners with more than 1,400 educational institutions to provide services to more than 7 million students.

Business and industry services: ARAMARK services thousands of industry accounts, including office refreshments for 50,000 locations.

Uniform services: ARAMARK is America's largest provider of uniform services and work apparel for virtually all types of institutions. At least 3 million customers use uniforms and work clothing services by ARAMARK.

ARAMARK has created an Innovation Center for corporate research, design, and product development resources. One interesting outcome is the design of a "cool" place for students to eat, which is different from the old days of dining in the gym.

ARAMARK successfully manages the diversity of segment concepts under the guideline of one single purpose: to be the world leader in managed services. With annual revenues in excess of $11 billion, the company is among the market leaders in all of its businesses, and is in an ideal position for further market growth. Joseph Neubauer, chairman and CEO, realizes this: "I am energized by the bright prospects for the journey ahead."

Source: Courtesy of ARAMARK.

Hospital foodservice has evolved to the point where the need for new revenue sources has changed the traditional patient and nonpatient meal-service ratios at many institutions. This situation was imposed by the federal government when it narrowed the treatment-reimbursement criteria; originally 66 percent of a typical acute-care facility's foodservice budget went toward patients' meals, with the remainder allocated for feeding the employees and visitors. In the past few years, as cash sales have become more important, the 66/33 percent ratio has reversed.

Ever resourceful, managers of health care operations, like Dolly Strenko of Southwestern General Hospital in Middleburg Heights, Ohio, have created such concepts as a medical mall with a retail pharmacy; flower and gift shops; boutique; a retail bakery, with an exhibition conveyor oven; and a 112-seat restaurant deli with take-out services for adjacent medical offices and outside catering for weddings, bar mitzvahs, and other functions. Strenko has also been instrumental in elevating culinary standards, the result of hiring an executive chef who was a graduate of the Culinary Institute of America.

Experts agree that because economic pressures will increase, foodservice managers will need to use a more high-tech approach, incorporating laborsaving sous-vide and cook–chill methods. This segment of the industry, which currently is dominated by self-operated managed services, will continue to see contract specialists (such as Sodexho, Compass, and ARAMARK Services) increase their market share at the expense of self-operated health care managed services. One reason for this is that the larger contract companies have the economy of scale and a more sophisticated approach to quantity purchasing, menu management, and operating systems that help to reduce food and labor costs. A skilled independent foodservice operator has the advantage of being able to introduce changes immediately without having to support layers of regional and corporate employees.

Another trend in health care managed services is the arrival of the major quick-service chains. McDonald's, Pizza Hut Express, Burger King, and Dunkin' Donuts are just a few of the large companies that have joined forces with the contract managed services operators. Using branded quick-service leaders is a win–win situation for both the contract foodservice operator and the quick-service chain. As one operator put it, "The new McDonald's can be a training facility for future employees—in effect, a potential resource for our staff needs. Our union scale of $7.22 per hour could entice some 'cross-overs.' The branded image also helps the overall retail side of the foodservice operation."

The chains benefit from long-term leases at very attractive rates compared with a restaurant site. Chains assess the staff size and patient and visitor count to determine the size of unit to install. Thus far, they have found that weekday lunches and dinners are good, but the numbers on weekends are disappointing.

In contrast, several hospitals are entering the pizza-delivery business: They hook up phone and fax ordering lines, and they hire part-time employees to deliver pizzas made on the premises. This ties in with the increasing emphasis on customer service. Patients' meals now feature "comfort foods," based on the concept that the simpler the food is, the better. Hence, there has been a resurgence of meat loaf, pot pies, meat and potatoes, and tuna salad, which contributes to customer satisfaction, and makes them feel at home and comfortable.

Foodservice hospitality associates deliver food to patients.

.inc | Corporate Profile

THE COMPASS GROUP

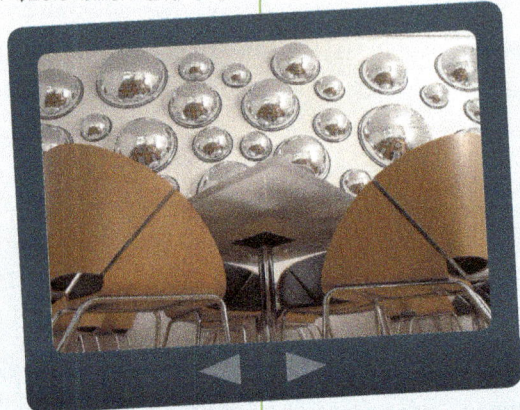

Compass Group is a leading foodservice company with annual revenues of $23.5 billion and over 400,000 employees working in more than 90 countries around the world. Compass develops and delivers original food and service solutions to the workplace, schools and colleges, and hospitals; and to people at leisure, on the move, or in remote environments. Compass provides a portfolio of foodservice brands—offering consistency, recognition, quality, and value. Its strategy is that the greater attraction of brands generates more customers, thus improving the commercial returns on foodservice. Brands include World Marche, Profiles, and Steamplicity—a new concept that uses a simple valve mechanism to steam cook prepared fresh ingredients within minutes to meet individual patient orders. Steamplicity improves nutritional content, choice, and service, and reduces costs. These brands sit alongside franchised brands such as Caffe Ritazza, Upper Crust, and Harry Ramsden's. The brands operate across all sectors of the market and are offered in fully flexible formats to suit different requirements.

Compass Group divisions in the U.S. include corporate catering, vending, health care, sports and entertainment, education, restaurants, remote sites, and strategic partners.

BUSINESS AND INDUSTRY

Discover the Roles of Contract Management Companies and Self-Operators

Business and industry (B&I) is one of the most dynamic segments of the managed services industry. In recent years, B&I foodservice has improved its image by becoming more colorful, with menus as interesting as commercial restaurants.

There are important terms to understand in B&I foodservice:[8]

1. **Contractors:** Companies that operate foodservice for the client on a contractual basis. Most corporations contract with managed services companies because they are in manufacturing or some other service industry. Therefore, they engage professional managed services corporations to run their employee dining facilities.

2. **Self-operators:** Companies that operate their own foodservice operations. In some cases, this is done because it is easier to control one's own operation; for example, it is easier to make changes to comply with special nutritional or other dietary requests.

3. **Liaison personnel:** A liaison is responsible for translating corporate philosophy to the contractor and for overseeing the contractor to make certain that he or she abides by the terms of the contract.

A Sodexho business and industry account.

Contractors have approximately 80 percent of the B&I market. The remaining 20 percent is self-operated, but the trend is for more foodservice operations to be contracted out. The size of the B&I sector is approximately 30,000 units. To adapt to corporate downsizing and relocations, the B&I segment has offered foodservice in smaller units rather than huge, full-sized cafeterias. Another trend is the necessity for B&I foodservice to break even or, in some cases, make a profit. An interesting twist is the emergence of multitenant buildings, the occupants of which may all use a central facility. However, in today's turbulent business environment, there is a high vacancy rate in commercial office space. This translates into fewer guests for B&I operators in multitenant office buildings. As a result, some office buildings have leased space to commercial branded restaurants.

B&I managed services operators have responded to requests from corporate employees to offer more than fast-food standards like pizza and hamburgers; they want healthier foods, such as make-your-own sandwiches, salad bars, fresh fruit stations, and ethnic dishes. Most B&I managed services operators offer a number of types of service. The type of service is determined by the resources available, including money, space, time, and expertise. Usually these resources are quite limited, which means that most operations use some form of cafeteria service.

B&I foodservice is characterized as full-service cafeterias with straight line, scatter, or mobile systems; or limited-service cafeterias offering parts of the full-service cafeteria, fast-food service, cart and mobile service, fewer dining rooms, and executive dining rooms.

An ARAMARK business and industry foodservice account.

Check Your Knowledge

1. What roles other than those strictly related to foodservice does the foodservice manager perform?
2. Briefly explain some of the tasks the foodservice manager performs. What makes each task so important?

LEISURE AND RECREATION

The leisure and recreation segment of managed services may be the most unique and fun part of the foodservice industry in which to work. Leisure and recreation foodservice operations include stadiums, arenas, theme parks, national parks, state parks, zoos, aquariums, and other venues where food and beverage are provided for large numbers of people. The customers are usually in a hurry, so the big challenge of the foodservice segment is to offer its product in a very short period of time. For example, the average professional sporting event only lasts for two to three hours of actual playing time.

What makes this segment unique and fun is the opportunity to be part of a professional sporting event, a rock concert, a circus, or other event in a typical stadium or arena. There is also the choice of working in a national or state park and being part of the great outdoors (if that is to your liking). The roar of the crowd and the excitement of the event make this a very stimulating place to work. Imagine getting paid to see the Super Bowl versus paying to see the Super Bowl.[9]

Stadium Points of Service

Leisure and recreation facilities usually have several points of service where food and beverage are provided. In the typical stadium, a vendor yells, "Here, get your hot dog here!" to the fans in the stands, while on the concourse other fans get their food and beverage from concession stands. These stands offer everything from hot dogs and hamburgers to local cuisine (cheese steak sandwiches in Philadelphia, crab cake sandwiches in Baltimore). Another place for people to get food is a restaurant, which most stadiums have as a special area. In some cases, fans must be members of the restaurant; in other cases, they can buy special tickets that provide them with access to this facility. These restaurants are like any other except that they provide unobstructed views of the playing area.

The other major point of service is the food and beverage offered in the premium seating areas known as superboxes, suites, and skyboxes. These premium seating areas are usually leased by corporations to entertain corporate guests and customers. In each of these areas, food and beverage service is provided for the guests. These facilities are capable of holding 30 to 40 guests. They usually have an area where the food is set up buffet style and a seating area where the guest can see the sporting or other event. In a large, outdoor stadium, there could be as many as 60 to 70 of these superbox-type facilities.

A large stadium/arena could have vendors in the stands, concession outlets, restaurants, and superboxes together serving upward of 60,000 to 70,000 fans. To feed all these people takes tremendous planning and organization on the part of the foodservice department. The companies that have many of the contracts for these stadiums and arenas are ARAMARK, Fine Host, Sodexho, Compass Group, Wood Company, and Delaware North.

Other Facilities

Besides stadiums and arenas, food and beverage service is provided in several other types of facilities by the same major managed service companies that service stadiums. Most of the U.S. national parks are contracted to these companies. These parks have hotels, restaurants, snack bars, gift shops, and a myriad of other service outlets where tourists can spend their money. In addition to these parks, other venues where food and beverage is offered include zoos, aquariums, tennis tournaments (such as the U.S. Open in New York), and PGA golf tournaments. All these events involve large numbers of people. For example, a PGA event, which lasts a week including practice time, will have upward of 25,000 spectators per day watching the pros play. These tournament events are similar to stadiums and arenas because they also include concession stands, food and beverage areas for the fans, and "corporate tents" for special catering and company guests.

Advantages and Disadvantages

A foodservice career in this segment has several advantages, including the unique opportunity to see professional and amateur sporting events to your heart's delight, to hear the "roar of the crowd," to be in rural, scenic areas and enjoy the great outdoors, to provide a diverse set of services for the guests or fans, and to have a set work schedule.

Review the Guide to Managed Services: Explore Career Options

The disadvantages of this segment include very large crowds of people to serve in a short time; a work schedule of weekends, holidays, and nights; impersonal service; less creativity with food; seasonal employees; and an on-season/off-season work schedule.

Leisure and recreation foodservice is a very exciting and unique part of the hospitality industry that offers employees very different opportunities from standard hotel and restaurant jobs. With the current trend toward building new stadiums and arenas around the country, this segment offers many new career openings.

Seniors

With more than 70 million people in retirement and soon to retire, the major service providers have a strong presence in the seniors market, offering building, nutritional, and dining services. An example is Sodexho's resident dining program, which is regarded as an ongoing opportunity to create enjoyable, rewarding social situations for residents.

Options include: "To the Table," is a concept that features a moving buffet cart, which provides visualization of good food, as well as enjoyment of food aromas that enhance the meal experience; New Menu Tasting Parties; Hands-On Creation; Village Merchant; Home Sweet Home; Chef Stage Center; Every Bite Counts; Recipes from Home; Spirit of Choice; Sensations; Dining with the Chef; and On the Town.

Sustainability

Restaurant Associates, a division of the Compass Group, recently implemented its "green dining practices." These

Sustainable Managed Services

Hospital foodservice directors often say that offering healthy choices in their cafeterias is a key department mission. But many operators are quick to add that they still offer the so-called unhealthy options to prevent a drop in participation and revenues. However, Raquel Frazier, food service director at La Rabida Children's Hospital in Chicago, did not have that luxury. She was mandated by the hospital's administration to make the cafeteria 100 percent healthy.[10] To meet new nutritional guidelines, food items could not exceed 450 calories, with 10 grams of fat or three grams of saturated fat, and had to contain at least three grams of fiber. In addition, nutritional information for all items had to be posted on the menu and at the point of service. The outcome has been that most employees reported losing weight and to keeping it off and leading to a more healthy lifestyle.[11]

practices—developed in partnership with the Environmental Defense Fund—are science-based recommendations for an environmentally friendly foodservice option and include tips for sustainable food purchasing.[12] Early results were annualized, and it is estimated that the green dining best practices for just two locations will save more than $85,000 each year, cut 275 tons of carbon pollution, and reduce landfill waste by 60 tons. Buying organic food does cost more, but with savings in other areas more than making up the difference, these green dining restaurants are still ahead on budget. One way to save money is for managers to make sure that staff doesn't cut too much away from the vegetables. And an anaerobic digester can cut down on waste: it mixes the food waste with wood chips that contain a certain enzyme that breaks the material down to a mush. After a day or so, all food turns to water and goes down the drainpipe.[13]

> **Green Dining Best Practices will save more than $85,000 each year, cut 275 tons of carbon pollution and reduce landfill waste by 60 tons for jus two locations.**

At the University of Indianapolis, the "Green Team" recommended going trayless, a move that has saved thousands of gallons of water a day—and has probably saved on food costs, too. The university installed purified water fountains so that students can refill water bottles. The campus now orders just 25 cases of bottled water a week, down from an average of 300 cases a week.[14]

TRENDS in MANAGED SERVICES

Listen to the Dimmick Hall Kitchen Manager Discuss Trends

Restaurants and Institutions magazine asked several managers to identify some of the challenges that college and university foodservice managers face. In general, managers mentioned trying to balance rising costs with fewer dollars.

- Bill Rigan, foodservice center manager at Oklahoma State University, Stillwater, pointed out two main challenges: a reduction of revenues from board-plan sales combined with increased costs, such as food and utilities. He dealt with these challenges by recognizing that, inasmuch as he could not change the utilities or hourly rates for employees, he would have to maximize purchasing potential. He also made optimal usage of from "scratch" cooking, convenience foods, and more efficient labor scheduling.
- Martha Willis, foodservice director at Tennessee Technological University, Cookesville, sees declining enrollment and a reduction in state funding as challenges. This translates to a cutback in services and more pressure to produce a bigger bottom line. She intends to achieve this by filling vacant full-time positions with part-time and student employees. The savings made by not paying full-time employee benefits can amount to 30 percent of a person's wage.
- Increased use of campus cards (declining balance or debit cards)
- Increased use of food-to-go, for instance before sporting events
- Increased use of carts at vantage points
- Dueling demands for foodservice managers—from students who want more freshly prepared foods in convenient locations and from administrators who want more revenue from existing sources
- Twenty-four-hour foodservice
- Increased business in health care and nursing homes
- Proliferation of branded concepts in all segments of managed services, including military, school and college, business and industry, health care, and airport
- Development of home meal replacement options in each segment of the managed services sector, as a way to increase revenue
- Increasing use of fresh product

The two cafeterias that service the 8,000 employee Indiana Government Center, recently switched to bioplastic containers made from compostable resins. The cafeterias now also use biodegradable and compostable cold drink cups and takeout containers.[15]

Technology

Foodservice operators now use Facebook and Twitter to inform guests/students about campus offerings. Social media now plays a role in meal preparation, menus, special offerings, and culinary trends on many campuses. At Washington State University, campus dining uses Facebook and Twitter to highlight limited time offerings; upcoming pace changes, such as strawberry shortcake bar; and an ongoing monthly promotional series, a Culinary Adventure to Cuisine, where a different culture's cuisine is featured each month. They use this avenue of communication because it is of no cost and is the way students want to be connected.[16]

CASE STUDY

Gas Leak

The kitchen at a major corporation's managed service business account includes several gas and electric stoves, ovens, broilers, steamers, and BBQs. On average, the kitchen serves 500 lunches. At 10:15 A.M., on a Tuesday in December, a gas leak prompts the gas company to cut off the gas supply.

DISCUSSION QUESTION

1. What can be done to offer the best possible lunch food and service?

CASE STUDY

Chaos in the Kitchen

Jane is the foodservice director at an on-campus dining service that feeds 800 students per meal for breakfast, lunch, and dinner. Jane arrives at her office at 7:00 A.M. (half an hour before breakfast begins) only to find many problems.

After listening to her phone messages, she finds that her breakfast cashier and one of her two breakfast dishroom employees have called in sick. The cashier position is essential and the second dishroom person is necessary at 8:15 A.M. when the students leave to go to their 8:30 A.M. classes.

Shortly after listening to the messages, the executive chef tells Jane that one of their two walk-in refrigerators is not working properly, thus some of the food is above the safe temperature of 40°F. The lead salad person comes to her later, saying that one of the three ice machines is not working. Hence, there will not be enough ice to ice down the salad bars and to use for cold beverages at lunch.

Lastly, the catering supervisor tells Jane that he has just found out that there was a misunderstanding with the bakery that supplies their upscale desserts. The desserts were requested by the president of the university for a luncheon he is having that day; however, because the employee at the bakery wrote the wrong delivery date, the desserts would not be delivered. This president will be angry.

DISCUSSION QUESTIONS

1. How should Jane handle being short a cashier and a dishroom person at breakfast?
2. What should Jane do with the food in the defective refrigerator? Should the food that is measured to be above 40°F be saved?
3. What are Jane's options concerning the ice shortage?
4. How should Jane handle the president's function, knowing that the requested desserts have not been delivered?
5. If the special dessert cannot be purchased in time, how should the catering supervisor approach this situation when speaking with the president's office?
6. What can be done to ensure that mistakes, such as the one made by the bakery employee, do not happen again?

CAREER INFORMATION

Management careers in the field of managed services offer college graduates a vast array of opportunities. A tremendous advantage to this type of career is that as a manager, you have more control over your time because of the structured nature of the environment. Airlines, schools, and health care foodservice, as well as college and university dining, usually work on a set schedule that is based on a menu rotation. There are no late nights unless you are supervising a catering event or special function. Within the educational environment, summers and school breaks allow managers time to get caught up on projects and/or take vacations.

If you are looking for a managed services career, these areas offer a rare opportunity for a quality of life that is often not available in foodservice. One drawback to this type of career is that there is often little or no interpersonal relationships with your customers. Reduced customer contact means that there is often limited recognition and acknowledgment by patrons.

Military dining operations can offer a more restaurant or club-oriented career path. Working as a civilian for the military means competitive salaries, excellent benefits, and the opportunity to travel.

Business and industry dining is the most diverse career segment of institutional foodservice. It draws from all aspects of the industry. Hours are usually longer but still defined, and there is a greater potential for bonuses and advancement.

Institutional foodservice is enjoying unprecedented growth as a multibillion dollar industry. It has expanded to include services outside the hospitality industry, such as groundskeeping, maintenance, janitorial services, and vending machine sales. Figure 9–5 illustrates a possible career path in managed services.

Managed Services Career Path

- Assistant foodservice director: Salary range of $32,000 to $39,000 plus benefits, which can be about 30 percent of salary and include a pension plan. If you already have experience in a variety of foodservice operations/positions, it is possible to gain this type of position upon graduation. It is possible that you would move to a larger operation or a different type of account to broaden your experience and knowledge before moving up to the next level.

- Foodservice director: $40,000 to $60,000 plus benefits. It is likely that you would begin at one account and then move to a larger one after a few years.

- General manager: $60,000 to $80,000 plus benefits. After spending a few years at one location it is likely that you would move to another, possibly larger one. For example, you may be GM of a $4million account and go to a $10 million account.

- District manager: $85,000 to $100,000 plus benefits. The district manager is responsible for several accounts; other responsibilities include making proposals to gain new accounts and negotiating contracts with clients.

> **Health care foodservice is very labor intensive, with labor accounting for about 55 to 66 percent of operating dollars.**

Adena Osika, Director of Nutrition and Hospitality Services at Sarasota Memorial Hospital offers this advice: "Work in a field that you have interest in and a passion for. You have to do what you like and want to do. I look for a person with a smile, high level of service, and engagement that will enable him or her to connect with patients. Have an open mind and be flexible, be willing to take charge, and look for the good in other people. There are good growth and advancement opportunities in the managed services sector of the hospitality industry."

Related Web Sites

www.sodexhousa.com/—Sodexho
www.aramark.com/—ARAMARK foodservice

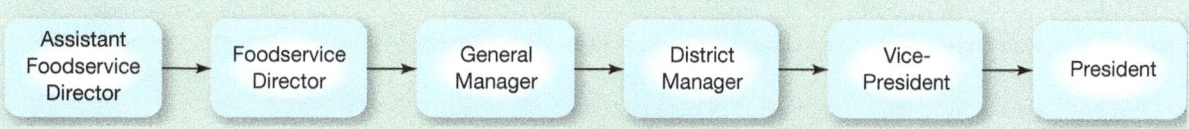

FIGURE 9–5 A Career Path in the Managed Services Sector of the Hospitality Industry.

SUMMARY

1. Managed services operations include segments such as airlines, military, schools and colleges, health care facilities, and businesses.
2. Quality food has become a major competitive factor among airlines, which either provide meals from their own in-flight business or have it prepared by a contractor, such as Dobbs International or Sky Chefs.
3. Service to the military includes feeding troops and officers in clubs, dining halls, and hospitals as well as out in the field. Direct vendor delivery, menu management, prepared foods, and fast-food chains located on the base have met new trends in military foodservice.
4. Schools are either equipped with on-site kitchens and dining rooms or receive food from a central commissary. They try to balance salability with good nutrition. Today, nutrition education is a required subject in school.
5. College and university managed services operations include residence halls, cafeterias, student unions, faculty clubs, convenience stores, and catering.
6. The responsibilities of a foodservice manager are very complex. He or she is in charge of employee relations, human resource management, budgeting, safety administration, sanitation, and inventory.
7. Health care managed services operations need to provide numerous special meals to patients with very specific dietary requirements and nutritious meals in a limited time period for employees. The main areas of concern for health care managed services operations are tray lines and help-yourself food stations.
8. Business and industry managed services operations either operate with a full-service cafeteria or limited-service cafeteria. The type of service is determined by money, space, and time available.
9. Leisure and recreation foodservice offers yet more career opportunities. It is often available at several points of service.
10. Given the 70 million aging baby boomers, senior services will soon be a booming business.

KEY WORDS AND CONCEPTS

Batch cooking
Commercial foodservice
Contractors
Daily rate
Liaison personnel
Managed services
National School Lunch Program (NSLP)
Nutrition education programs
Self-operators
Tray line

REVIEW QUESTIONS

1. What are managed services operations?
2. List and explain features that distinguish managed services operations from commercial ones.
3. Describe the issues that schools are currently facing concerning school food service.
4. Explain the term *National School Lunch Program (NSLP)*.
5. Identify recent trends in college foodservice management.
6. What are the pros and cons concerning fast-food chains on campus?
7. Briefly explain the complex challenges for health care managed services operations.

INTERNET EXERCISES

1. Organization: ARAMARK
   Web site: www.aramark.com
   Summary: According to its Web site, ARAMARK is "a global leader in managed services." ARAMARK is an outsourcing company that provides services ranging from everyday catering to corporate apparel.
   a. Click on "Careers." Who is ARAMARK's star of the month? What is his or her position and responsibilities?
   b. What are some of the characteristics that make a star of the month?
2. Organization: SODEXHO
   Web site: www.sodexhousa.com
   Summary: Sodexho offers a full range of outsourcing solutions and is a leading food and facilities management services company in North America.
   a. What corporate services does Sodexho offer?
   b. Look at the current opportunities (at Sodexho or ARAMARK) within your area.

APPLY YOUR KNOWLEDGE

1. From the sample operating statement (Figure 9–4), calculate the labor cost percentage by taking total labor cost and dividing by total sales × 100. Remember the formula:

$$\frac{\text{Cost}}{\text{Sales} \times 100}$$

2. Consider a retail operation at a local college that offers a grilled chicken combo (a grilled chicken breast, fries, and a 20-oz. soda) on the menu. Cost out the ingredients by writing out everything needed for the combo, including its service. What is your cost price? How much would you sell it for to make a reasonable profit?

SUGGESTED ACTIVITY

1. Create a sample menu for a day at an elementary or high school. Then compare your items to the food guide pyramid and the recommended daily servings. How does your menu measure up?

ENDNOTES

1. Personal correspondence with John Lee, Sodexho, March 23, 2006.
2. Personal correspondence with John Lee, Sodexho, March 23, 2006. www.skychefs.com.
3. lgskychefs.com/en/about-us.html, retrieved March 11, 2010.
4. NSLP, www.fns.usda.gov, retrieved March 17, 2006.
5. Allison Perlink, *Best in Class, Restaurants and Institutions*, 116, 15, August 1, 2006, p. 22.
6. Ibid., John Lee.
7. This beginning section is courtesy of David Tucker.
8. Ibid., John lee.
9. Ibid., David Tucker.
10. Becky Schilling, "Healthy's Hero," *FoodService Director* 22(8), August 15, 2009, p. 44.
11. Ibid.
12. FSD Staff, "Environmental Awareness," *FoodService Director* 22(8), August 15, 2009, p. 58.
13. Ibid.
14. FSD Staff, "University of Indianapolis Green Team to the Rescue," *FoodService Director*, 22(8), August 15, 2009, p. 59.
15. FSD Staff, "Government Center Cafeteria to Use Bio-Plastic Containers," *FoodService Director* 22(1), January 15, 2009, p. 12.
16. Lindsey Ramsey, "The Online Revolution," *FoodService Director* 22(7), July 15, 2009, p. 18.

10 BEVERAGES

LEARNING OUTCOMES

After reading and studying this chapter, you should be able to:

List and describe the main grape varieties.

Suggest appropriate pairings of wine with food.

Identify the various types of beer.

List the types of spirits and their main ingredients.

Explain a restaurant's liability in terms of serving alcoholic beverages.

HTi Describe the economic impact of tourism.

This chapter offers an overview of alcoholic and nonalcoholic beverages in the hospitality industry. Beverages are a good source of income and profit in the hospitality industry. Most restaurants that serve beverages, especially alcoholic ones, make about 25 percent of total sales on beverages, any more would invite close attention from local law enforcement. The profit margins are good, but the responsibilities are many. Several legal issues need to be addressed—these are discussed later in the chapter.

Serving beverages is traditional throughout the world. According to the particular culture, a person might welcome a visitor with coffee or tea—or other beverage. Beverages in moderation are enjoyable, whether to quench a thirst after a workout or to drink with friends during a restaurant meal. Beverages are generally categorized into two main groups: alcoholic and nonalcoholic. Alcoholic beverages are further categorized as wines, beer, and spirits. Figure 10–1 shows these three categories.

WINES

Wine is the fermented juice of freshly gathered ripe grapes. Wine may also be made from other sugar-containing fruits, such as blackberries, cherries, or elderberries. In this chapter, however, we will confine our discussion to grape wines. Wine may be classified first by color: *red, white,* or *rosé*. Wines are further classified as *light beverage wines, still wines, sparkling wines, fortified wines,* and *aromatic wines.*

Wine	Beer	Spirits
Still	Top fermenting	Grapes/fruit
Natural	Lager	Grains
Fortified	Bottom fermenting	Cactus
Aromatic	Ale	Sugar cane/molasses
Sparkling	Stout	
	Lager	
	Pilsner	
	Porter	

FIGURE 10–1 Alcoholic Beverages.

Light Beverage Wines

Read the Wine Reference Book from Vernon's

White, red, or rosé table wines are "still" (no carbonation) light beverage wines; such still table wines come from a variety of growing regions around the world. In the United States, the premium wines are named after the grape variety, such as *chardonnay* and *cabernet sauvignon*. This has proved so successful that European winemakers are now also naming their wines after the grape variety and their region of origin, such as Pouilly Fuissé and Chablis.

Sparkling Wines

Champagne, sparkling white wine, and sparkling rosé wine are called the **sparkling wines**. Sparkling wines sparkle because they contain carbon dioxide. The carbon dioxide may be either naturally produced or mechanically infused into the wine. The best-known sparkling wine is champagne, which has become synonymous with celebrations and happiness.

Champagne became the drink of fashion in France and England in the seventeenth century. Originating in the Champagne region of France, the wine owed its unique sparkling quality to a second fermentation—originally unintentional—in the bottle itself. This process became known as *méthode champenoise.*

Champagne may, by law, only come from the Champagne region of France. Sparkling wines from other countries have *méthode champenoise* written on their labels to designate that a similar method was used to make that particular sparkling wine.

Champagne is served chilled in fluted glasses, which help keeps the bouquet and effervescence longer.

Champagne should be stored horizontally at a temperature between fifty and fifty-five degrees Fahrenheit. However, it should be served at a temperature between forty-three and forty-seven degrees Fahrenheit. This is best achieved by placing the bottle in an ice bucket.

When serving champagne, there are some recommended steps to take to achieve the best results, as listed below.

1. If the bottle is presented in a champagne cooler, it should be placed upright in the cooler, with fine ice tightly packed around the bottle.
2. The bottle should be wrapped in a cloth napkin. Remove the foil or metal capsule to a point just below the wire, which holds the cork securely.
3. Hold the bottle firmly in one hand at a forty-five degree angle. Unwind and remove the wiring. With a clean napkin, wipe the neck of the bottle and around the cork.
4. With the other hand, grasp the cork so that it will not fly out. Twist the bottle and ease the cork out.
5. When the cork is out, retain the bottle at an angle for about five seconds. The gas will rush out and carry with it some of the champagne if the bottle is held upright.
6. Champagne should be served in two motions: pour until the froth almost reaches the brim of the glass. Stop and wait for the foam to subside. Then finish filling the glass to about three-quarters full.

FIGURE 10–2 Handling and Serving Champagne.

Check Your Knowledge

1. Why is champagne served in fluted glasses?
2. How are alcoholic beverages categorized?

Fortified Wines

Sherries, ports, Madeiras, and Marsalas are fortified wines, meaning that they have had brandy or wine alcohol added to them. The brandy or wine alcohol imparts a unique taste and increases the alcohol content to about 20 percent. Most **fortified wines** are sweeter, with different tastes and aromas, than regular wines.

Aromatic Wines

Aromatized wines are fortified and flavored with herbs, roots, flowers, and barks. These wines may be sweet or dry. Aromatic wines are also known as aperitifs, which generally are consumed before meals as digestive stimulants. Among the better known brands of aperitif wines are Dubonnet red (sweet), Dubonnet white (dry), vermouth red (sweet), vermouth white (dry), Byrrh (sweet), Lillet (sweet), Punt e Mes (dry), St. Raphael Red (sweet), and St. Raphael White (dry).

The History of Wine

Wine has been produced for centuries. The ancient Egyptians and Babylonians recorded the fermentation process. The very first records about wine making date back about 7,000 years. The Greeks received the vine from the Egyptians, and later the Romans contributed to the popularization of wine in Europe by planting vines in the territories they conquered.

The wine produced during these times was not the cabernet or chardonnay of today. The wines of yesteryear were drunk when they were young and likely to be highly acidic; they would have tasted awful by today's standards. To help offset these deficiencies, people added different spices and honey, which made the wine at least drinkable. To this day, some Greek and German wines have flavoring added.

The making of good wine is dependent on the quality of the grape variety, type of soil, climate, preparation of vineyards, and method of wine making. Thousands of grape varieties exist, thriving in a variety of soil and climatic conditions. Different plants thrive on clay, chalky, gravelly, or sandy soil. The most important wine-making grape variety is the *vitis vinifera*, which yields cabernet sauvignon, gamay, pinot noir, pinot chardonnay, and riesling.

Port wines are generally red, fortified, and sweet. Vintage port is the most prized by port lovers. Port is normally served with cheese and biscuits at the end of a meal.

Sustainable Wine Production[1]

Environmentally and socially responsible grape growing and wine making is not new, but what was once labeled a trend is now becoming an industry standard. Organic is a term given to environmentally friendly methods that use no chemicals or pesticides. Sustainability is defined as a holistic approach to growing and food production that respects the environment, the ecosystem, and even society.

The California Association of Wine Grape Growers has prepared a "Code of Sustainable Winegrowing Practices"; this is a 490-page voluntary self-assessment workbook covering everything from pest management to wine quality to water conservation to environmental stewardship. This tool allows growers and vintners to gauge how they are doing, and then to design and implement their own action plans.

A good example of sustainable wine making is the Viansa Winery in California. It has long boasted a natural antipest team of bats, barn owls, and insectaries to keep its bug populations under control. The winery uses organic fungicide and has eliminated all herbicides.

red grape skins. After fermentation has ceased, the wine is transferred to racking containers, where it settles before being poured into oak barrels or large stainless steel containers for the maturing process. Some of the better wines are aged in oak barrels, from which they acquire additional flavor and character during the barrel aging. Throughout the aging process, red wine extracts tannin from the wood, which gives longevity to the wine. Some white wine and most of the better red wine is barrel-aged for periods ranging from months to more than two years. Other white wines that are kept in stainless steel containers are crisp, with a youthful flavor; they are bottled after a few months for immediate consumption.

After maturing, the wine is filtered to help stabilize it and remove any solid particles still in the wine. This process is called **fining**. The wine is then **clarified** by adding either egg white or bentonite, which sinks to the bottom of the vat. The wine then is bottled.

Fine **vintage** wines are best drunk at their peak, which may be a few years—or even several years later. Red wines take a few more years to reach their peak than do white wines. In Europe, where the climate is more variable, the good years are rated as vintage. The judgment of experts determines the relative merits of each wine-growing district and awards merit points on a scale of 1 to 10.

Matching Wine with Food

The combination of food and wine is one of life's great pleasures. We eat every day, so a gourmet will seek out not only exotic foods and vintage wines, but also simple food that is well prepared and accompanied by an unpretentious, but quality, wine.

Observe a Server Pairing Food and Wine at Vernon's

Over the years, traditions have developed a how-to approach to the marrying of wines and food. Generally, the following traditions apply:

- White wine is best served with white meat (chicken, pork, or veal), shellfish, and fish.
- Red wine is best served with red meat (beef, lamb, duck, or game).

The Making of Wine

Discover Some Wine Basics at Vernon's

Wine is made in six steps: *crushing, fermenting, racking, maturing, filtering,* and *bottling.* Grapes are harvested in the fall, after they have been scientifically tested for maturity, acidity, and sugar concentration. The freshly harvested grapes are taken to pressing houses where the grapes are de-stemmed and crushed.

Red wine gains its color during the fermentation process from the coloring pigments of the

Wine maturing in oak barrels.

- The heavier the food, the heavier and more robust the wine should be.
- Champagne can be served throughout the meal.
- Port and red wine go well with cheese.
- Dessert wines best complement desserts and fresh fruits that are not highly acidic.
- When a dish is cooked with wine, it is best served with that wine.
- Regional food is best complemented by wines of the region.
- Wines are best not served with salads because the vinegar in the dressing will spoil the taste of the wine.
- Sweet wines should be served with foods that are not too sweet.

Figure 10–3 matches some of the better known varietal wines with food.

Food and wine are described by *texture* and *flavor*. Textures are the qualities in food and wine that we feel in the mouth, such as *softness, smoothness, roundness, richness, thickness, thinness, creaminess, chewiness, oiliness, harshness, silkiness, coarseness*, and so on. Textures correspond to sensations of touch and temperature, which can be easy to identify—for example, hot, cold, rough, smooth, thick, or thin. Regarding the marrying of food and wine, light food with light wine is always a reliable combination. Rich food with rich wine can be wonderful as long as the match is not too rich. The two most important qualities to consider when choosing the appropriate wine are richness and lightness.

Flavors are food and wine elements perceived by the olfactory nerve as fruity, minty, herbal, nutty, cheesy, smoky, flowery, earthy, and so on. A person often determines flavors by using the nose as well as the tongue. The combination of texture and flavor is what makes food and wine a pleasure to enjoy; a good match between the food and wine can make occasions even more memorable. Figure 10–4 suggests the steps to be taken in wine tasting.

Wine and cheese is a good pairing.

Check Your Knowledge

1. What are the names of the main white and red grape varieties used to make wine?
2. Cabernet sauvignon is best served with _____.
3. Chardonnay is best served with _____.
4. Why does a wine taster swirl the wine around the glass before tasting it?
5. What is the general guideline of serving wine with food?

WINE	SMELL AND TASTE ASSOCIATED WITH WINE	FOOD PAIRING
Gewurztraminer (Alsace in France)	grapefruit, apple, nectarine, peach, nutmeg, clove, cinnamon	Thai, Indian, Tex-Mex, Szechwan, ham, sausage, curry, garlic
Chardonnay Chablis (Burgundy in France)	citrus fruit, apple, pear, pineapple, other tropical fruit	pork, salmon, chicken, pheasant, rabbit
Sauvignon Blanc Sancerre (Loire in France)	citrus fruit, gooseberry, bell pepper, black pepper, green olives, herbs	goat cheese, oysters, fish, chicken, pork, garlic
Pinot Blanc	citrus fruit, apple, pear, melon	shrimp, shellfish, fish, chicken
Pinot Noir Cote d' Or (Burgundy in France)	strawberry, cherry, raspberry, clove, mint, vanilla, cinnamon	duck, chicken, turkey, mushrooms, grilled meats, fish and vegetables, pork
Merlot Gamay (Beaujolais in France)	cherry, raspberry, plum, pepper, herbs, mint	beef, lamb, duck, barbecued meats, pork ribs
Cabernet Sauvignon Medoc (Bordeaux in France)	cherry, plum, pepper, bell pepper, herbs, mint, tea, chocolate	beef, lamb, braised, barbecued and grilled meats, aged cheddar, chocolate
Late harvest white wines	citrus fruit, apple, pear, apricot, peach, mango, honey	custard, vanilla, ginger, carrot cake, cheesecake, cream puffs, apricot cobbler

FIGURE 10–3 Matching Wine with Food.

> Many restaurants have introduced wine tastings as special marketing events to promote the restaurant itself, or a particular type or label of wine. Wine tasting is more than just a process—it is an artful ritual. Wine offers a threefold sensory appeal: color, aroma, and taste. Wine tasting, thus, consists of three essential steps.
> 1. Hold the glass to the light. The color of the wine gives the first indication of the wine's body. The deeper the color, the fuller the wine will be. Generally, wines should be clear and brilliant.
> 2. Smell the wine. Hold the glass between the middle and the ring finger in a "cup-like" fashion and gently roll the glass. This will bring the aroma and the bouquet of the wine to the edge of the glass. The bouquet should be pleasant. This will tell much about what the taste will be.
> 3. Finally, taste the wine by rolling the wine around the mouth and by sucking in a little air—this helps release the complexities of the flavors.

FIGURE 10–4 Wine Tasting.

WINE AND FOOD PAIRING

Jay R. Schrock *University of South Florida*

The combination of food and wine is as old as the making of wine. It is truly one of the great pleasures in life. Food and wine are natural accompaniments and enhance the flavor and enjoyment of each other. The flavor of a wine consumed by itself will taste different than when it is imbibed with food. Much of the wine taste experience is actually perceived from the nose; hence you will hear that "the wine has a good nose." In fact, wine experts, called sommeliers, say that 80 percent of the taste comes from the nose. The nose is where the flavors described as nuts, oak, fruits, herbs, spices, and all the others that describe wine come from. To improve the smell and taste of wine, we often decant it and serve it in stemware with large openings. The wine taster often swirls the wine to increase the aromas entering the nose.

Over the years, traditions have developed as to how to approach wine and food pairing. Remember these are traditions and that food and wine pairing is a highly subjective and an inexact process. The traditional rules basically state that red wines are served with red meat and white wines are served with fish and poultry. These are rules that are still generally valid; but they don't take into consideration the complexity of today's multiethnic fusion cuisines, with their wide range of flavors, and the corresponding wide range of wines from around the world that are now readily available to everyone. They also do not take into account that more than one wine may be served with a meal.

Today you are more likely to hear of food and wine pairing suggestions, rather than the hard and fast traditional rules of the past. There is considerably more room for experimentation and self-expression in the pairing of food and wine than there was just a couple of decades ago. Always remember that the goal in food and wine pairing is the enjoyment of the food and wine. You and your guests will be the judge of this experience.

The traditional rules developed over the years are still general guides to selecting a wine that will not overpower the accompanying food. Just as having your morning grapefruit after eating your toast with jelly changes the flavor of the fruit, drinking a full-bodied red wine before a delicately flavored food alters its flavor.

The new tradition has begun:

1. When serving more than one wine at a meal, it's best to serve lighter wines before full-bodied ones. The dryer wines should be served before sweeter wines. The exception is if a sweet flavored food is served early in the meal. Serve wines with lower alcohol content before wines with higher alcohol content.

2. Pair light-bodied wines with lighter food and fuller-bodied wines with heavier or richer food.

3. Match flavors. A pinot noir goes well with duck, prosciutto, and mushrooms and gewürztraminer is a well-suited accompaniment for ham, sausage, curry, and Thai and Indian food. Beware of pairing a wine with food that is sweeter than the wine. Most people agree that chocolate is the one exception: it seems to go with almost anything.

4. Delicately flavored foods that are poached or steamed should be paired with delicate wines.

5. Match regional wines with regional foods; they have been developed together and have a natural affinity for each other. The red sauces of Tuscany and the Chianti wines of the Tuscany region in Italy are an unbeatable combination.

6. Soft cheese like Camembert and Brie pair well with a variety of red wine, including cabernet sauvignon, zinfandel, and red burgundy. Cabernet sauvignon

WINE AND FOOD PAIRING (CONTINUED)

also goes well with sharp, aged cheddar cheese. Pungent and intensely flavored cheeses, such as a blue cheese, are better with the sweeter *eis* wine or late harvest dessert wines. Sheep and goat cheeses pair well with dry white wines, while red wine with fruit flavors goes best with milder cheeses.

Many of your restaurant guests may want to have wine with their dinner but are intimidated by the process or are afraid of the price. Set your guests' minds at ease when they are ordering wine. The know-it-all attitude will not work here; you are not trying to sell a car or life insurance. You are trying to improve your guests' experience, the check average, and your tip. Make an honest suggestion and try to explain the differences in wine choices. If guests are pondering two wines by the glass, do not just suggest the more expensive one; bring two glasses and let them taste. They will decide for themselves.

CASE STUDY

Wine and Health

A glass of wine may be beneficial to health. This perspective was featured in the CBS news magazine program *60 Minutes*, which focused on a phenomenon called the French paradox. The French eat 30 percent more fat than Americans, smoke more, and exercise less, yet they suffer fewer heart attacks—about one-third as many as Americans. Ironically, the French drink more wine than people of any other nationality—about 75 liters per person a year. Research indicates that wine attacks platelets, which are the smallest of the blood cells and which cause the blood to clot, preventing excess bleeding. However, platelets also cling to the rough, fatty deposits on arterial walls, clogging and finally blocking arteries and causing heart attacks. Wine's flushing effect removes platelets from the artery wall. After the *60 Minutes* program was broadcast, sales of wine, particularly red wine, in the United States increased dramatically.

Major Wine-Producing Countries

Identify Wine Traits Read the Wine Guide at Vernon's

United States

In California, viticulture began in 1769 when Junipero Serra, a Spanish friar, began to produce wine for the missions he founded. At one time, the French considered California wines to be inferior. However, California is blessed with a near perfect climate and excellent vine-growing soil. In the United States, the name of the grape variety is used to name the wine, not the village or chateau used by the French. The better-known varietal white wines in the United States are chardonnay, sauvignon blanc, riesling, and chenin blanc; varietal red wines are cabernet sauvignon, pinot noir, merlot, syrah, and zinfandel.

California viticulture areas are generally divided into three regions:

1. North and central coastal region
2. Great central valley region
3. Southern California region

The north and central coastal region produces the best wines in California. A high degree of use of mechanical methods allows for efficient, large-scale production of quality wines. The two best-known areas within this region are the *Napa and Sonoma valleys.* The wines of the Napa and Sonoma valleys resemble those of Bordeaux and Burgundy. In recent years, the wines from the Napa and Sonoma valleys have rivaled and even exceeded the French and other European wines. The chardonnays and cabernets are particularly outstanding. The Napa and Sonoma valleys are the symbols as well as the centers of the top-quality wine industry in California.

Several other states and Canadian provinces provide quality wines. New York, Oregon, and Washington are the other major U.S. wine-producing states. In Canada, the best wineries are in British Columbia's Okanagan Valley and southern Ontario's Niagara peninsula. Both of these regions produce excellent wines. Wine also is produced in many other temperate parts of the world, most notably Australia, France, Germany, Italy, New Zealand, Chile, Argentina, and South Africa.

Europe

Germany, Italy, Spain, Portugal, and France are the main European wine-producing countries. Germany is noted for the outstanding Riesling wines from the Rhine and Moselle river valleys. Italy produces the world-famous Chianti. Spain makes good wine, but is best known for sherry. Portugal also makes good wine, but is better known for its port.

France is the most notable of the European countries, producing not only the finest wines but also champagne and cognac. The two most famous wine-producing areas in France are the Bordeaux and Burgundy regions. The vineyards, villages, and towns are steeped in the history of centuries devoted to the production of the finest quality wines. They represent some of the most beautiful countryside in Europe and are well worth visiting.

In France, wine is named after the village in which the wine is produced. In recent years, the name of the grape variety is also used. The name of the wine grower is also important; because the quality may vary, reputation understandably is very important. A vineyard might also include a chateau in which wine is made.

Within the Bordeaux region, wine growing is divided into five major districts: Medoc, Graves, St. Emilion, Pomerol, and Sauternes. The wine from each district has its own characteristics.

There are several other well-known wine-producing regions of France, such as the Loire Valley, Alsace, and Côtes du Rhône. French people regard wine as an important part of their culture and heritage.

> **The very first records about wine making date back about 7,000 years.**

Australian Wines

Australia has been producing wines for about 150 years, but it is only in the last half-century that they have achieved the prominence and recognition that they rightly deserve. Australian winemakers traveled to Europe and California to perfect their wine-making craft. Unlike France, with many rigid laws controlling wine growth and production, Australian winemakers use high technology to produce excellent wines, many of which are blended to offer the best characteristics of each wine.

Australia has about 60 wine-growing regions, with diverse climates and spit types. These regions are mostly in the southeastern part of the continent, in New South Wales, Victoria, and South Australia, all within easy reach of the major cities of Sydney, Melbourne, and Adelaide. There are about 1,120 wineries in Australia. One of the larger and more popular wineries is Lindeman's, which regularly receives accolades for its consistent quality and value. The leading wines are red, cabernet sauvignon, cabernet-shiraz blends, cabernet-merlot blends, merlot, shiraz, white, chardonnay, sémillon, sauvignon blanc, and sémillon chardonnay. Among the better-known wine-growing areas is Hunter Valley in New South Wales, which produces sémillon. When mature, this wine has a honey, nut, and butter flavor. The chardonnay is complex with a peaches-and-cream character. In recent years, Australian wines have shown exceptional quality and value, leading to increased sales in Europe, the United States, and Asia.

BEER

Discover More about the Brewing Process in the Book of Beverages at the Tiki Bar

Beer is a brewed and fermented beverage made from malted barley and other starchy cereals, and flavored with hops. Beer is a generic term for a variety of mash-based, yeast-fermented, brewed malt beverages with an alcohol content varying from 3 to 16 percent.[2]

The term **beer** includes the following:

- Lager, the beverage that is normally referred to as beer, is a clear light-bodied refreshing beer.
- Ale is fuller bodied and more bitter than lager.
- Stout is a dark ale with a sweet, strong, malt flavor.
- Pilsner is not really a beer. The term *pilsner* means that the beer is made in the style of the famous beer brewed in Pilsen, Czech Republic.

The Brewing Process

Beer is brewed from water, **malt, yeast**, and **hops**. The brewing process begins with water, an important ingredient in the making of beer. The mineral content and purity of the water largely determine the quality of the final product. Water accounts for 85 to 89 percent of the finished beer.

Next, grain is added in the form of malt, which is barley that has been ground to a course grit. The grain is germinated,

Introducing Rob Westfall

Bar Manager, The Speakeasy, Siesta Key, Florida

The Speakeasy has been a staple in Siesta Key Village for over five years. Known for its exceptional variety of live music, it is also a place where locals feel right at home. The Speakeasy offers its patrons premium cigar service, a pool table, specialty drinks, and a menu that is loaded with innovative cocktails that are hard to find at other establishments. Along with our extensive list of wines by the glass, the Speakeasy offers many premium single-malt scotches, cognacs, bourbons, and a host of fine liqueurs. The Speakeasy is owned and operated by Café Gardens, which also owns the Daiquiri Deck located next door. For more information on The Speakeasy or the Daiquiri Deck, visit www.daiquirideck.com.

A typical day for a manager at The Speakeasy goes like this:

9:45 A.M. – Arrive for managers' meeting at the Daiquiri Deck. All Daiquiri Deck managers, the owners, and I are present at this meeting. The meeting consists of a variety of issues. Typically, the first order of business is reviewing the numbers from the previous week, including net sales, cost of labor, cost of goods, and promotional costs. Budgets are also a major concern every week. They are based on sales projections from the previous year and are very important to the success of the business. Next, we discuss any issues from the previous week. In the bar business, an "issue" could be just about anything from fights to vandalism. We find it extremely important to discuss all of these issues so that the management team is all on the same page. The meeting is adjourned after everyone around the table is given a chance to raise any other issues. After everything has been discussed, it's time to go to work.

11:00 A.M. – Mondays are very important in the bar business. Inventory is taken to ensure that costs are in line, and a list is made of the all needed products. First, I take an inventory of all beverage products at The Speakeasy. Liquor, beer, wine, cigarettes, cigars, and mixers must all be counted.

12:00 P.M. – Upon completion of the inventory, it is time to put my orders together for the week. Knowing my usage is extremely important when placing an order. Buying in bulk is always superior to simply filling holes from week to week. Simply, it allows me more buying power and, essentially, more free goods. Bar supplies also need to be monitored. Straws, olive picks, stir sticks, bar glass cleaner and sanitizer, and bar napkins all need to be kept in stock. The absence of one item can often make or break a busy night at the bar.

1:00 P.M. – Confirm band schedule. Booking bands and maintaining an entertainment schedule can sometimes be one of the most frustrating areas of the bar business. However, it can also be the most rewarding. The experience I gain from working with so many different types of entertainment is difficult to replace. The majority of bands show up on time and treat their job professionally, but there are a significant amount of them that do not. I call my bands to confirm their schedule on a weekly basis for this very reason. There is no worst feeling than walking into a potentially busy night and having your entertainment cancel.

2:00 P.M. – Typically there is a bar maintenance issue that needs to be addressed. I always take a walk around and check everything out to make sure that everything is working properly. Smoke eaters, bathrooms, light bulbs, and bar cleanliness are all part of this maintenance.

3:00 P.M. – Work on any upcoming promotions and ensure their success. Spirit tastings, holidays, Full Moon parties, and private parties are examples of these types of events. Planning is extremely important for the ultimate success of these events. I find that no matter how much I plan, I will have to improvise somewhere along the line, so the more planning you do, the less improvisation that is necessary.

4:00 P.M. – Send memo to corporate office regarding what checks need to be written for entertainment that week. Ensure that each band has proper paperwork filled out for tax purposes.

5:00 P.M. – Every day the staff needs to be reminded to step it up. Motivation comes from the top down. The bar business is a stage, and the bartenders are on a stage. The staff will typically need to be reminded of this on a consistent basis. Open lines of communication are very important and allow you to apply constructive criticism or accolades, as they are appropriate.

6:00 P.M. – It's time to have a drink.

That's the management side of the bar. The nighttime is another animal entirely!

In the process of making beer, hops are added to the wort in the brew-kettle.

producing an enzyme that converts starch into fermentable sugar. The yeast is the fermenting agent. Breweries typically have their own cultured yeasts, which, to a large extent, determine the type and taste of the beer. **Mashing** is the term for grinding the malt and screening out any bits of dirt. The malt then goes through a hopper into a mash tub, which is a large stainless steel or copper container. Here the water and grains are mixed and heated.

The liquid is now called **wort** and is filtered through a mash filter or lauter tub. This liquid then flows into a brewing kettle, where hops are added and the mixture is boiled for several hours. After the brewing operation, the hop wort is filtered through the hop separator or hop jack. The filtered liquid then is pumped through a wort cooler and flows into a fermenting vat, where pure-culture yeast is added for fermentation.[3] The brew is aged for a few days prior to being barreled for draught beer or pasteurized for bottled or canned beer.

In the process of making beer, hops are added to the wort in the brew-kettle.

Sustainable Brewing

Breweries use a lot of resources yet have the potential to significantly reduce their environmental footprint. Here is how some brewers are reducing their footprint:[4]

- Efficient brewhouse: The brewery is as sustainable and efficient as possible, starting with the parts of the building that were reclaimed and recycled when the Full Sail brewery first opened in the old Diamond Fruit cannery in Oregon. Full Sail utilizes measures such as energy-efficient lighting and air compressors, and compresses the work week into four very productive days, which helps reduce water and energy consumption by 20 percent.
- Sustainable brew process: Pure water literally flows from the peaks that surround the brewery, so Full Sail takes care to conserve this precious resource. While average breweries consume six to eight gallons of water for every gallon of beer produced, Full Sail has reduced its consumption to a mere 3.45 gallons, and operates its own on-site wastewater treatment facility. Local farms supply the other essential ingredients for award-winning brews: 85 percent of hops and 95 percent of barley come straight from Northwest farms.
- Reduce-Reuse-Recycle: Full Sail uses 100 percent recycled paperboard on all its packaging (and was one of the first in the industry to commit to long-term purchasing of recycled paper products). Everything from office paper to glass to stretch wrap to wooden pallets is recycled. Even dairy cows are beneficiaries of brewery waste: 4,160 tons of spent grain and 1,248 tons of spent yeast are sent back to farmers every year to use as feed for cows.
- Community-wide practices: Full Sail purchases 140 blocks of Pacific Power Blue Sky renewable energy per month. This practice results in the reduction of 168 tons of carbon dioxide emissions, the equivalent of planting 33,000 trees. Full Sail also supports over 300 events and charities each year, with a focus on those in Oregon. Employees at the company have inspired environmental change among other businesses in the Hood River area as well. Full Sail was a founding member of the Hood River Chamber of Commerce's "Green Smart" program, an initiative that helps businesses and organizations within the Hood River watershed increase their productivity and profitability by improving resource efficiency and by reducing waste and pollution.

As the push for sustainability gains momentum, one only need to look down at the pint or mug he or she is holding to see how breweries are joining the growing green movement! Beer is the third most-consumed beverage in the world behind water and tea. Upon surveying a number of breweries, and sustainable brewing documents, BlueMap Inc. has determined 10 green steps every brewery should consider.[5]

Utilize Biochar Processing to Re-Use Spent Grains

Processing spent grains through pyrolisis (a process that burns grains to create Biochar, a valuable soil amendment), is a carbon-negative process: it creates heat and syngas while sequestering carbon. By doing so, pyrolisis decreases a brewery's carbon footprint.

Implement Water Use Reduction Measures

Water is one of the largest inputs in brewing. A brewery can conserve water by reducing lost steam, increasing the efficiency of wort production, increasing the life of water in boiler systems, and altogether preventing waste.

Implement Variable-Speed Fans or Motors

Many brewery processes have variable loads that are more efficiently served by variable-speed motors, fans, and drives. Where applicable, an upgrade in a brewery's fans and motors can offer substantial savings and have favorable pay back periods. Savings are only observed if loads vary.

Ensure a Regular Maintenance Regime

A regular maintenance regimen is a great way to cut down on energy inefficiencies. Regularly schedule maintenance allows breweries to catch problems sooner and address them before excess energy is wasted. Also, keeping a system tuned up means that motors and pumps run at optimum speeds, controls are set properly, and control systems are turned on.

Capture Methane at On-Site Water Treatment Facilities

For breweries that process wastewater on-site, methane capture is a great way to re-gain value from a waste stream. Currently, closed systems and pond cover methane capture exist. These systems purify and burn methane onsite, which typically offsets the brewery's fuel costs while cutting costs.

Recapture CO_2 during Fermentation

Fermentation releases CO_2. Savvy breweries can capture this CO_2 and use it (instead of purchased CO_2) in the bottling process to carbonate their beer. This reduces both CO_2 released to the air and CO_2 purchasing costs.

Optimize Thermal Resources within the Brewing Process

Much of the brewing process consists of thermal processes: boiling and cooling liquids. Auditing the entire process can reveal ways to capture thermal resources and apply them to other brewing processes, thereby reducing energy and fuel costs of heating and cooling.

Implement Alternatives to Diatomaceous Earth (DE) Filtering

Though DE is a long-standing industry standard as a filter medium, health risks associated with DE (and potential problems regulating its use and disposal) are prompting some to seek alternatives. Where applicable, sheet filtering, cross flow filtration systems, and DE recycling systems can be used to avoid some of these flaws.

Optimize Refrigeration, Lighting, Construction, and Other Building Controls

Sustainable building is potentially one of the largest opportunities for a brewery to reduce energy consumption and curtail demand spikes (thereby minimizing fines). Management systems can be installed to green the lighting of spaces, maximize building functions, optimize chill systems, and stagger cooling loads.

Utilize Renewable Energy Technologies

Beer is made with hops, grain, water and yeast. What could be a more natural way to complement these natural ingredients than using sun or wind to power the beer brewing process? Renewable energy sources include geothermal, syngas, or biogas. When sized correctly, these technologies greatly reduce purchased electricity and fuel and can have very attractive payback periods.

By considering these 10 recommendations, the third-largest beverage industry in the world can reduce its overall ecological impact while in many cases save money.

Further examples of breweries around the country that are finding creative ways to reduce their carbon footprint are by installing wind and solar power. Colorado's New Belgium Brewery has an 870 panel solar array from which it gets 13 percent of its energy needs; Odell Brewing Company gets 39 percent of its energy needs.[6]

> **Beer is the third most consumed beverage in the world behind water and tea.**

Spirits

Learn to Recognize Different Types of Spirits from the Book of Beverages

A **spirit** (liquor) is made from a liquid that has been fermented and distilled. Consequently, a spirit has a high percentage of alcohol, gauged in the United States by its proof content. **Proof** is equal to twice the percentage of alcohol in the beverage; therefore, a spirit that is 80 proof is 40 percent alcohol. Spirits traditionally are enjoyed before or after a meal, rather than with the meal. Many spirits can be consumed straight or neat, or they may be enjoyed with water, soda water, juices, or cocktail mixes.

Whiskies

Among the better-known spirits is whisky, which is a generic name for the spirit first distilled in Scotland and Ireland centuries ago. The word *whisky* comes from the Celtic word *visgebaugh* meaning "water of life." Whisky is made from a fermented mash of grain to which malt, in the form of barley, is added. The barley contains an enzyme called diastase that converts starch to sugars. After fermentation, the liquid is distilled. Spirits naturally are white or pale in color, but raw whisky is stored in oak barrels that have been charred (burnt). This gives whisky its caramel color. The whisky is stored for a period of time, up to a maximum of 12 to 15 years. However, several good whiskies reach the market after three to five years.

Most whiskies are blended to produce a flavor and quality that is characteristic of the brand. Not surprisingly, the blending process at each distillery is a closely guarded secret. There are four distinct whisky types that have gained a worldwide acknowledgment throughout the centuries: Scotch whisky, Irish whisky, bourbon whisky, and Canadian whisky.

Scotch Whisky

Scotch whisky, or Scotch, has been distilled in Scotland for centuries and has been a distinctive part of the Scots' way of life. From its origins in remote and romantic Highland glens, Scotch whisky has become a popular and international drink, its flavor appreciated throughout the world. Scotch became popular in the United States during the days of **Prohibition** (1919–1933), when it was smuggled into the country from Canada. It is produced like other whiskies, except that the malt is dried in special kilns that give it a smoky flavor. Only whisky made with this process can be called Scotch whisky. Some of the better-known quality blended Scotch whiskies are Chivas Regal and Johnnie Walker Black, Gold, Blue, and Green Labels.[7]

Other Whiskies

Irish whisky is produced from malted or unmalted barley, corn, rye, and other grains. The malt is not dried like Scotch whisky, which gives it a milder character, yet great flavor. The well-known Irish whiskies are Old Bushmill's and Jameson's 1780.[8] Bourbon whisky is produced mainly from corn; other grains are also used, but they are of secondary importance. The distillation processes are similar to those of other types of whisky. Charred barrels provide bourbon with its distinctive taste. It is curious to note that barrels can only be used once in the United States to age liquor. Aging, therefore, occurs in new barrels after each distillation process. Bourbon may be aged up to six years to improve its mellowness. Among the better-known bourbon whiskies are Jack Daniels, Makers Mark, and George Dickle.

Like bourbon, Canadian whisky is produced mainly from corn. It is characterized by a delicate flavor that nonetheless pleases the palate. Canadian whisky must be at least four years old before it can be bottled and marketed. It is distilled at 70 to 90 percent alcohol by volume. Among the better-known Canadian whiskies are Seagram's and Canadian Club.

White Spirits

Gin, rum, vodka, and tequila are the most common of the spirits that are called **white spirits**. Gin, first known as Geneva, is a neutral spirit made from juniper berries. Although gin originated in Holland, it was in London that the word *Geneva* was shortened to gin, and almost anything was used to make it. Often gin was made in the bathtub in the morning and sold in hole-in-the-wall dram shops all over London at night. Obviously, the quality left a lot to be desired, but the poor drank it to the point of national disaster.[9] Gin also was widely produced in the United States during Prohibition. In fact, the habit of mixing something else with it led to the creation of the cocktail. Over the years, gin became the foundation of many popular cocktails (e.g., martini, gin and tonic, gin and juice, and Tom Collins).

Rum can be light or dark in color. Light rum is distilled from the fermented juice of sugarcane, and dark rum is distilled from molasses. Rum comes mainly from the Caribbean Islands of Barbados (Mount Gay), Puerto Rico (Bacardi), and Jamaica (Myers). Rums are mostly used in mixed frozen and specialty drinks such as rum and Coke, rum punches, daiquiris, and piña coladas.

Tequila is distilled from the agave tequilana (a type of cactus), which is called *mezcal* in Mexico. Official Mexican regulations require that tequila be made in the area around the town of Tequila, because the soil contains volcanic ash, which is especially suitable for growing the blue agave cactus. Tequila may be white, silver, or golden in color. The white is shipped unaged, silver is aged up to three years, and golden is aged in oak from two to four years. Tequila is mainly used in the popular margarita cocktail or in a tequila sunrise (made popular in a song by the Eagles rock group).

Vodka can be made from many sources, including barley, corn, wheat, rye, or potatoes. Because it lacks color, odor, and flavor, vodka generally is combined with juices or other mixers whose flavors will predominate.

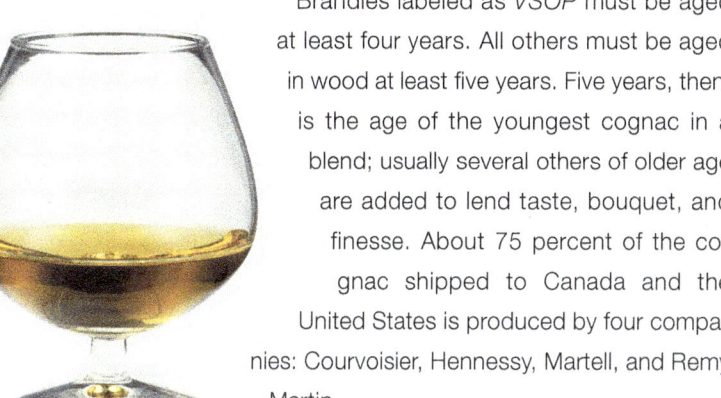

A glass of Cognac.

Other Spirits

Brandy is distilled from wine in a fashion similar to that of other spirits. American brandy comes primarily from California, where it is made in column stills and aged in white-oak barrels for at least two years. The best-known American brandies are made by Christian Brothers and Ernest and Julio Gallo. Their brandies are smooth and fruity with a touch of sweetness. The best brandies are served as after-dinner drinks, and ordinary brandies are used in the well for mixed drinks.

Cognac is regarded by connoisseurs as the best brandy in the world. It is only made in the Cognac region of France, where the chalky soil and humid climate combine with special distillation techniques to produce the finest brandy. Only brandy from this region may be called cognac. Most cognac is aged in oak casks from two to four years or more. Because cognacs are blends of brandies of various ages, no age is allowed on the label; instead, letters signify the relative age and quality.

Brandies labeled as *VSOP* must be aged at least four years. All others must be aged in wood at least five years. Five years, then, is the age of the youngest cognac in a blend; usually several others of older age are added to lend taste, bouquet, and finesse. About 75 percent of the cognac shipped to Canada and the United States is produced by four companies: Courvoisier, Hennessy, Martell, and Remy Martin.

Cocktails

Learn the Language of Bartending at the Tiki Bar

Cocktails are usually drinks made by mixing two or more ingredients (wines, liquors, fruit juices), resulting in a blend that is pleasant to the palate, with no single ingredient overpowering the others. Cocktails are mixed by stirring, shaking, or blending. The mixing technique is particularly important to achieve the perfect cocktail. Cocktails are commonly divided into two categories according to volume: short drinks (up to 3.5 ounces) and tall drinks (generally up to 8.5 ounces).

The secret of a good cocktail lies in several factors:

- The balance of the ingredients.
- The quality of the ingredients. As a general rule, cocktails should be made from a maximum of three ingredients.
- The skill of the bartender. The bartender's experience, knowledge, and inspiration are key factors in a perfect cocktail.

A good bartender should understand the effect and the "timing" of a cocktail. It is not a coincidence that many cocktails are categorized by when they are best served. There are aperitifs, digestifs, corpse-revivers, pick-me-ups, and so on. Cocktails can stimulate an appetite or provide the perfect conclusion to a fine meal. Cocktails are "in" again, with some hot names like sex-on-the-beach, woo woo, Jaeger bomb, etc.

Check Your Knowledge

1. Describe the different types of beer.
2. Describe the various spirits.

Nonalcoholic Beverages

Nonalcoholic beverages are increasing in popularity. In the 1990s and into the 2000s there has been a radical shift from the free love 1960s and the singles bars of the 1970s and early 1980s. People are, in general, more cautious about the consumption of alcohol. Lifestyles have become healthier, and organizations like MADD (Mothers Against Drunk Driving) have raised the social conscience about responsible alcohol consumption. Overall consumption of alcohol has decreased in recent years, with spirits declining the most. In recent years, several new beverages have been added to the nonalcoholic beverage list.

Nonalcoholic Beer

Guinness, Anheuser-Busch, Miller, and many other brewers have developed beer products that have the same appearance as regular beer, but have a lower calorie content and approximately 95 to 99 percent of the alcohol removed, either after processing or after fermentation. The taste, therefore, is somewhat different from regular beer.

Coffee

Coffee is *the* drink today. People once frequented bars, now they patronize coffeehouses. Sales of specialty coffees annually exceed $4 billion. The Specialty Coffee Association of America estimates that there are more than 17,800 coffee cafés nationwide.[10]

Explore a Bit of Coffee Lore in the Book of Beverages

Coffee first came from Ethiopia and Mocha, which is in the Yemen Republic. Legends say that Kaldi, a young Abyssinian goatherd, accustomed to his sleepy goats, noticed that after chewing certain berries, the goats began to prance about excitedly. He tried the berries himself, forgot his troubles, lost his heavy heart, and became the happiest person in "happy Arabia." A monk from a nearby monastery surprised Kaldi in this state, decided to try the berries too, and invited the brothers to join him. They all felt more alert that night during prayers![11]

In the Middle Ages, coffee found its way to Europe via Turkey. In 1637, the first European coffeehouse opened in England; within 30 years, coffeehouses had replaced taverns as the country's social, commercial, and political melting pots.[12] The coffee houses were nicknamed *penny universities*, where any topic could be discussed and learned for the price of a pot of coffee. The men of the period not only discussed business but actually conducted business. Banks, newspapers, and the Lloyd's of London insurance company began at Edward Lloyd's coffeehouse.

A casual coffeehouse offers coffee and related beverages and snacks. (Dave King © Dorling Kindersley, Courtesy of Big Cup, New York.)

Coffeehouses were also popular in Europe. In Paris, Café Procope, which opened in 1689 and still operates today, has been the meeting place of many a famous artist and philosopher, including Rousseau and Voltaire (who are reputed to have drunk 40 cups of coffee a day).

The Dutch introduced coffee to the United States during the colonial period. Coffeehouses soon became the haunts of the revolutionary activists plotting against King George of England and his tea tax. John Adams and Paul Revere planned the Boston Tea Party and the fight for freedom at a coffeehouse. This helped establish coffee as the traditional democratic drink of Americans.

Coffee may be roasted from light to dark according to preference. Light roasts

The Infidels' Drink

During the sixteenth century, travelers to Constantinople (now known as Istanbul, Turkey) enjoyed coffee there and brought it back to Europe. By the end of the sixteenth century, coffee had become noticed enough to bring about the censure of the Roman Catholic Church, which called it the wine of Islam, an infidel drink. When Pope Clement VIII tasted the drink, he is reputed to have remarked that the Satan's drink was too delicious to leave to the heathens so he made a Christian beverage of it.

CASE STUDY

.inc | Corporate Profile

STARBUCKS COFFEE COMPANY

Operations

Starbucks Coffee Company (named after the first mate in Herman Melville's *Moby-Dick*) is the leading retailer, roaster, and brand of specialty coffee in North America. More than 7 million people visit Starbucks stores each week. In addition to thousands of retail locations, the company supplies fine dining, food-service, travel, and hotel accounts with coffee and coffee-making equipment and operates a national mail-order division.

Locations and Alliances

Starbucks currently has multiple locations in all 50 states and in 34 countries. In addition, Starbucks has about 100 licensed locations that serve customers in unique areas such as airports, university campuses, hospitals, and business dining facilities. Marriott Management Services operates most of these locations.

Starbucks fresh roasted coffee and related products are distributed through U.S. Office Products' extensive North American distributorship. Starbucks is the exclusive supplier of coffee on every United Airlines flight. In addition, Starbucks specialty sales and marketing supplies coffee to the health care, business and industry, college and university, and hotel and resort segments of the food service industry; to many fine restaurants throughout North America; and to companies such as Costco, Nordstrom, Barnes & Noble, Inc., Hilton Hotels, Westin Hotels, ARAMARK, Sodexho, Sysco, Radisson, Safeway, Albertsons, PepsiCo, and Marriott International.

Product Line

Starbucks roasts more than 30 varieties of the world's finest Arabica coffee beans. The company's retail locations also feature a variety of espresso beverages and locally made fresh pastries. Starbucks specialty merchandise includes Starbucks private-label espresso makers, mugs, plunger pots, grinders, storage jars, water filters, thermal carafes, and coffeemakers. An extensive selection of packaged goods, including unique confections, gift baskets, and coffee-related items, are available in stores, through mail order, and online.

Starbucks offers Frappuccino® blended beverages, a line of low-fat, creamy, iced coffee drinks. This product launch was the most successful in Starbucks history. In January 1996, the North American Coffee Partnership between Starbucks New Venture Company, a wholly owned subsidiary of Starbucks Corporation, and Pepsi Cola began marketing a bottled version of Frappuccino®. The product, a low-fat, creamy blend of Starbucks brewed coffee and milk, is distributed on a national basis and available in grocery stores and in many Starbucks retail locations.

Community Involvement

Starbucks contributes to a variety of organizations that benefit AIDS research, child welfare, environmental awareness, literacy, and the arts. The company encourages its partners (employees) to take an active role in their own neighborhoods.

Starbucks fulfills its corporate social responsibility mission by reducing its environmental footprint on the planet. The company addresses three high-impact areas: sourcing of coffee, tea, and paper; transportation of people and products; and design and operations (energy, water, waste reduction, and recycling). Starbucks has developed relations with organizations that support the people and places that grow their coffee and tea, such as Conservation International, CARE, Save the Children, and the African Wildlife Foundation. Starbucks works with the U.S. Agency for International Development and Conservation International to improve the livelihoods of small-scale farmers by initiatives that are environmentally sensitive, socially responsible, and economically viable. Starbucks has received numerous awards for quality innovation, service and giving, including the World Environment Center's Gold Medal for Corporate Achievement in Sustainable Development.

are generally used in canned and institutional roasts, and medium is the all-purpose roast most people prefer. Medium beans are medium brown in color, and their surface is dry. Although this brew may have snappy, acidic qualities, its flavor tends to be flat. Full, high, or Viennese roast is the roast preferred by specialty stores, where balance is achieved between sweetness and sharpness. Dark roasts have a fancy rich flavor, with espresso the darkest of all roasts. Its almost black beans have shiny, oily surfaces. All the acidic qualities and specific coffee flavor are gone from espresso, but its pungent flavor is a favorite of espresso lovers.

Decaffeinating coffee removes the caffeine with either a solvent or water process. In contrast, things are added to many specialty coffees. Among the better-known specialty coffees are café au lait or caffe latte. In these cases, milk is steamed until it becomes frothy and is poured into the cup together with the coffee. Cappuccino is made by adding steamed and frothed hot milk to an espresso; it may then be sprinkled with cinnamon, chocolate, or nutmeg for extra flavor.

Sustainable Coffee

Coffee is grown in over 60 tropical countries, with most still being produced on small family farms. One of the main challenges for sustainable coffee growth is the fact that in the last decade, a huge worldwide surge in demand for coffee has led to an increase in production. This has caused a shift away from traditional sustainable coffee-growing methods to intense monocultures that require large amounts of fertilizer and pesticides, which bring about a loss in biodiversity, which depletes the land.[13]

The indicators of sustainable coffee are:[14]

- Was the coffee grown in the shade?
- Certification—is the coffee certified as bird friendly by the Smithsonian Migratory Bird Center, and is it grown under the most stringent environmental standards of any certification system?
- Does it have organic certification by the USDA?
- Is it certified by the rainforest alliance?

Countries that are more likely to grow shade coffee are Mexico, El Salvador, Nicaragua, Honduras, and Bolivia.

Tea

Tea is a beverage made by steeping in boiling water the leaves of the tea plant, an evergreen shrub, or a small tree native to Asia. Tea is consumed as either a hot or cold beverage by approximately half of the world's population, yet it is second to coffee in commercial importance because most of the world's tea crop is consumed in the tea-growing regions. The following list shows where the different types of tea originate:

China—Oolong, Orange pekoe
India—Darjeeling, Assams, Dooars
Indonesia—Java, Sumatra

Carbonated Soft Drinks

Coca-Cola and Pepsi have long dominated the carbonated soft drink market. Diet Coke and Diet Pepsi were introduced in the early 1970s. Both quickly gained in popularity and now command about a 15 percent market share. Caffeine-free colas offer an alternative, but they have not, as yet, become as popular as diet colas. Due to an increase in our taste for more health-conscious drinks, sales of carbonated beverages have declined. The U.S. market sales grow at about 2 percent, so companies have expanded internationally with a 5 percent growth; now almost 66 percent of Coca-Cola's sales come from international sales.[15]

Juices

Popular juice flavors include orange, cranberry, grapefruit, mango, papaya, and apple. Nonalcoholic versions of popular cocktails made with juices have been popular for years and are known as virgin cocktails.

Juice bars have established themselves as places for quick, healthy drinks. Lately, "smart drinks" that are supposed to boost energy and improve concentration have become popular. The smart drinks are made up of a blend of juices, herbs, amino acids, caffeine, and sugar and are sold under names such as Energy Plasma Blast and IQ Booster.

Other drinks have jumped on the healthy drink bandwagon, playing on the consumer's desire to drink something refreshing, light, and healthful. Often, these drinks are fruit flavored, giving consumers the impression that they are drinking something healthier than sugar-filled sodas. Unfortunately, these drinks usually just add the flavor of the fruit and rarely have any nutritional value. Some drinks are created by mixing different fruit flavors to arrive at new, exotic flavors, such as Passion-Kiwi-Strawberry and Mango-Banana Delight. Some examples of such drinks are Snapple and Tropicana Twister.

Sport enthusiasts also find drinks available in stores that professional athletes use and advertise. These specially formulated isotonic beverages help the body regain the vital fluids and minerals that are lost during heavy physical exertion. The National Football League sponsors Gatorade and encourages its use among its athletes. The appeal of being able to drink what the professionals drink is undoubtedly one of the major reasons for the success of Gatorade's sales and marketing. Other brands of isotonic beverages include Powerade and All Sport, which is sponsored by the National Collegiate Athletics Association.

Power Drinks

Recently power drinks (or energy drinks) have been increasing in popularity. They contain a variety of legal stimulants and claim to give consumers a boost of energy. Ingredients in power drinks include caffeine, vitamins, sugar, glucose, guarana, taurine, and various types of herbs (i.e., ginseng and ginkgo biloba). Some energy drinks contain up to 80 mg of caffeine, the same amount as a regular cup of coffee. These drinks are most commonly targeted toward the student population and people on the go. The most popular brands of energy drink are Red Bull, SoBe, Monster, Rockstar, Full Throttle, and Hype.

Power drinks claim to increase alertness, endurance, and improve brain functions (such as memory and concentration). While some consumers may benefit from the boost of energy these drinks provide, they are not for everyone. In some cases, energy drinks can cause increased heart rate, blood pressure, and even palpitations.

Bottled Water

Bottled water was popular in Europe years ago when it was not safe to drink tap water. In North America, the increased popularity of bottled water has coincided with the trend toward healthier lifestyles. Domestic bottled water is equally as good as imported and is now available in various flavors that offer the consumer a greater selection. Bottled waters are available as sparkling, mineral, and spring waters. Bottled water is a refreshing, clean-tasting, low-calorie beverage that will likely increase in popularity as a beverage on its own or to accompany another beverage such as wine or whisky.

TYPES OF BARS

Restaurant and Hotel Bars

In restaurants, the bar is often used as a holding area to allow guests to enjoy a cocktail or aperitif before sitting down to dinner. This allows the restaurant to space out the guests' orders so that the kitchen can cope more effectively; it also increases beverage sales. The profit margin from beverages is higher than the food profit margin.

In some restaurants, the bar is the focal point or main feature. Guests feel drawn to having a beverage because the atmosphere and layout of the restaurant encourages them to have a drink. Beverages generally account for about 25 to 30 percent of total sales. Many restaurants used to have a higher percentage of beverage sales, but the trend toward responsible consumption of alcoholic beverages has influenced people to decrease their consumption.

A popular method of costing each of the spirits poured is calculated according to the following example:

A premium brand of vodka such as Grey Goose costs $32.00 per liter and yields twenty-five 1 1/4-oz. shots that each sell for $5.50. So the bottle brings in $137.50. The profit margins produced by bars may be categorized as follows:

Liquor Pouring Cost % (approx.)	12
Beer	25
Wine	38

When combined, the sales mix may have an average pouring cost of 16 to 24 percent.

Most bars operate on some form of par stock level, which means that for every spirit bottle in use, there is a minimum par stock level of one, two, or more bottles available as a backup. As soon as the stock level falls to a level below the par level, more is automatically purchased.

Nightclubs

Discover the Importance of Safe Alcohol Service at the Tiki Bar

Nightclubs have long been a popular place to go to get away from the stresses of everyday life. From the small club in a suburban neighborhood to the world famous clubs of New York, Las Vegas, and Miami's South Beach, all clubs have one thing in common: people frequent them to kick back, relax, and, more often than not, enjoy a wild night of dancing and partying with friends and strangers alike.

Nightclubs can be satisfying experiences for both patrons and owners (revenues can be very high). However, it is important to remember the risks involved and work to minimize them. Owners should know all the legal issues that come with running a nightclub. For example, many laws exist for the sale and distribution of alcohol. In many instances, if a problem occurs involving a patron who was last drinking at the club, the problem can be considered the fault of the operation's management. Be sure to know lawsuits can arise fairly easily, and it is highly important to be aware of such possibilities.

Nightclubs offer fun, excitement, and socialization.

As with all business endeavors, the more one knows about the industry that he or she is getting involved with, the better off the business will be. With the right education and proper planning, nightclub ownership can be a very profitable endeavor. As with most businesses in the hospitality industry, many believe that experience is more important than education and that you can learn as you go. However, when embarking on a journey as involved as owning a nightclub, a person with a degree and a high level of experience is well ahead of the game. For more information regarding the nightclub industry, go to www.nightclub.com or www.nightclubbiz.com.

Microbreweries

In recent years, the advent of microbreweries and brewpubs (a combination brewery and pub or restaurant that brews its own fresh beer on-site to meet the taste of local customers) has changed the trend of homogenization that had characterized the brewing industry since the 1950s. Microbreweries are defined as craft breweries that produce up to 15,000 barrels (or 30,000 kegs) of beer a year. The North American microbrewery industry trend began in the 1990s, reviving the concept of small breweries serving fresh, all-malt beer. Although regional breweries, microbreweries, and brewpubs account for only a small part of the North American brewing industry in terms of total beer production (less than 5 percent).

One reason for the success of microbreweries and brewpubs is the wide variety of styles and flavors of beer they produce. On one hand, this educates the public about beer styles that have been out of production for decades; on the other hand, it helps brewpubs and restaurants meet the individual tastes and preferences of their local clientele. Starting a brewpub is a fairly expensive venture. Although brewing systems come in a wide range of configurations, the cost of the equipment ranges from $200,000 to $800,000. Costs are affected by factors such as annual production capacity, beer types, and packaging. The investment in microbreweries and brewpubs is well justified by the enormous potential for returns. To quote the *Wall Street Journal*, "With profit margins as high as 70%, a $250,000 microbrewery can triple the bottom line for a 200-seat restaurant and pay for itself in two years."

Microbreweries can produce a wide variety of ales, lagers, and other beers, the quality of which depends largely on the quality of the raw materials and the skill of the brewer.

Sports Bars

Sports bars have always been popular but have become more so with the decline of disco and singles bars. Here, people relax in a sporting atmosphere: bar/restaurants like Trophies or Characters at Marriott hotels have become popular "watering holes."

However, sports bars have evolved over the years into much more than a corner bar that features the game of the week. In the past, sports bars were frequented by die-hard sports fans and rarely visited by other clientele. Today the original sports bar is more of an entertainment concept and is geared toward a more diverse base of patrons. Now such places have been transformed into mega-sports adventures, featuring musical entertainment, interactive games, and hundreds of TVs tuned in to just about every sport imaginable.

Sports bars were once a destination for mainly male sports fans. Now more women and families are frequenting these venues. This provides a new prospect for revenue for bar owners. Recognizing this, owners are making adjustments, such as changing masculine themes to be nongender-specific. Sports bars are also making changes in their establishments to become more family oriented. Many families go into sports bars requesting a room with no TVs, so more owners choose to set aside a special place where families can eat quietly. Another method of attracting bar patrons on slower nights is to offer games and family friendly menus. Frankie's Food, Sports, and Spirits in Atlanta attracts families by hosting a sports-trivia game for teens. For the younger crowd, the restaurant provides pint-sized meals from the kids' menu on upside-down Frisbees, which children can take home as souvenirs.

Sports bars have also become the latest version of the traditional arcade. Many bars offer interactive video games where friends and families can compete against one another. Virtual reality games such as Indy 500 and other sports games are available at many establishments. Some venues have even gone a step farther and offer batting cages, bowling alleys, and basketball courts for their patrons to enjoy.

Sports bars have a reputation for serving spicy chicken wings, hamburgers, and other typical bar fare. But just as sports bars have evolved in their entertainment offerings, so too have their menus. People's tastes have changed, causing sports bars to offer a more diverse menu. Today guests can dine on a variety of foods, from filet mignon to fresh fish to gourmet sandwiches and pizza. People now frequent sports bars as much for the great meal they will have as for the entertainment.

In the past, sports bars usually had a few TVs that showcased games that would appeal to the area and big games such as the Super Bowl. The sudden increase in technology and TV programming available have made game viewing very different. The popularity of satellites and digital receivers has allowed bars to tune in to virtually dozens of events at any given time. Bars now have hundreds of televisions, and fans can watch games featuring every sport, team, and level of play around the world at any time of the day or night.

Burbank, California-based ESPN Zone has about 200 televisions in each of its locations so that fans can catch all the action. A handful of televisions are even placed in the restaurant's bathrooms, because "we don't want you to miss a second," says Nina Roth, marketing manager for ESPN Zone in New York City. "If you have to go at the last minute, you're not going to miss the end of the game."

Coffee Shops

Another fairly recent trend in the beverage industry in the United States and Canada is the establishment of coffeehouses, or coffee shops. Coffeehouses were originally based on the model of Italian bars, which reflected the deeply rooted espresso tradition in Italy. The winning concept of Italian bars lies in the ambiance they create, which is suitable for conversations of a personal, social, and business nature. A talk over a cup of coffee with soft background music and maybe a pastry is a typical scenario for Italians. Much of the same concept was re-created in the United States and Canada, where there was a niche in the beverage industry that was yet to be acknowledged and filled. The original concept was modified, however, to include a much wider variety of beverages and styles of coffee to meet the tastes of consumers, who have a tendency to prefer a greater selection of products. Consequently, the typical espresso/cappuccino offered by Italian bars has been expanded in North America to include items such as iced mocha, caramel macchiato, iced cappuccino, even a gingerbread latte.

Students as well as businesspeople find coffeehouses a place to relax, converse, socialize, and study. The success of coffeehouses is reflected in the establishment of chains, such as Starbucks, as well as family-owned, independent shops.

Cyber and Wi-Fi cafés are a recent trend in the coffeehouse sector. Cyber cafés offer the use of computers, with Internet capability, for about $6 per hour. Guests can enjoy coffee, snacks, or even a meal while online. Reasonable rates allow regular guests to have e-mail addresses.

> ### Check Your Knowledge
> 1. Describe the bar setup.
> 2. What is the average beverage pouring cost percentage?
> 3. What is a trend in sports bars?

LIQUOR LIABILITY AND THE LAW

Owners, managers, bartenders, and servers may be liable under the law if they serve alcohol to minors or to persons who are intoxicated. The extent of the liability can be very severe. The legislation that governs the sale of alcoholic beverages is called **dram shop legislation**. The dram shop laws, or civil damage acts, were enacted in the 1850s and dictated that owners and operators of drinking establishments are liable for injuries caused by intoxicated customers.[16]

Some states have reverted back to the eighteenth-century common law, removing liability from vendors except in cases involving minors. Nonetheless, most people recognize that as a society we are faced with major problems of underage drinking and drunk driving.

Observe Signs of Possible Drinking Problems at the Tiki Bar

To combat underage drinking in restaurants, bars, and lounges, a major brewery distributed a booklet showing the authentic design and layout of each state's driver's licenses. Trade associations, like the National Restaurant Association and the American Hotel and Motel Association, have, together with other major corporations, produced a number of preventive measures and programs aimed at responsible alcohol beverage service. The major thrust of these initiatives is awareness programs and mandatory training programs like ServSafe, which is a certification program sponsored by the National Restaurant Association that teaches participants about alcohol and its effects on people, the common signs of intoxication, and how to help customers avoid drinking too much.

Other programs include designated drivers, who only drink nonalcoholic beverages to ensure that friends return home safely. Some operators give free nonalcoholic beverages to the designated driver as a courtesy. One positive outcome of the responsible alcohol service programs for operators is a reduction in the insurance premiums and legal fees that had skyrocketed in previous years.

Learn about the Stoplight System of Safe Alcohol Service at the Tiki Bar

Be sure that you realize the utmost importance of responsible beverage consumption and service. Arrange for a designated driver if you intend to have a drink. If you do drink alcoholic beverages, then stay with the same drink—don't mix them (two different types are grape and grain, that is, wine and spirits). That's when trouble really begins and hangovers are bad. Remember that moderation is the key to enjoying beverages, whether it is a get-together with friends at a local restaurant or a spring break getaway. Examine the tragic alcohol-related auto and other accidents that too many people are involved in each year. Enjoy but do not overindulge.

Highway Deaths and Alcohol

Each year, thousands of people are killed on the highways in the United States. Many of these accidents can be prevented, as they are a result of carelessness and bad decision making while drinking. The National Highway Traffic Safety Administration is committed to decreasing the number of alcohol-related highway deaths. "You Drink & Drive, You Lose" and "Friends Don't Let Friends Drive Drunk" are national slogans created to discourage impaired driving and are familiar to millions of Americans. On the positive side, the message is getting through to the public. However, the battle with drunk driving is far from over.

In 2005, 16,885 people died in motor vehicle crashes in the U.S. in which alcohol was a factor. This on average is 1 fatality every 31 minutes.[17] Keep in mind that thousands more are injured due to alcohol-related vehicle crashes. Alcohol-related crashes are painful and expensive. Costs to treat the injured are passed on to taxpayers in the form of increased public health costs and higher insurance premiums. When it comes to impaired driving, everyone loses.

Because of recent increases in underage drinking, bars have been greatly encouraged to crack down on such practices. Bouncers are expected to know the signs of a fake ID and must confiscate such. In many areas, the establishment will be fined if underage patrons are found to have been let in the door with a fake ID. It is also common practice to reward bar owners for confiscating fake IDs. Many places in the United States have a system of undercover police who monitor and stop underage drinking in bars. For example, in Tallahassee, Florida, the Alcohol, Tobacco, and Firearms unit of the police department travels to bars and parties disguised as regular partygoers. When underage drinking is spotted, teens can be fined, have their driver's licenses revoked, and even be arrested.

The key to stemming underage drinking is to take a preventive approach. Many schools have such programs in place, starting while children are very young, to discourage negative behavior in the future. Strong family relationships that enforce healthy lifestyles also greatly reduce the probability that a teenager will drink in the first place.

Check Your Knowledge

1. How many people die each year in the United States as a result of alcohol-related auto accidents?
2. Why is early intervention important to prevent underage drinking?
3. Discuss the problems relating to alcohol abuse and underage drinking.

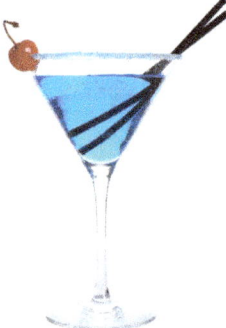

TRENDS in THE BEVERAGE INDUSTRY

- The comeback of cocktails
- Designer bottled water
- Microbreweries
- More wine consumption
- Increase in coffeehouses and coffee intake
- Increased awareness and action to avoid irresponsible alcoholic beverage consumption

CASE STUDY

Java Coffee House

Michelle Wong is manager of the Java Coffee House at a busy location on Union Street in San Francisco. Wong says that there are several challenges in operating a busy coffeehouse, such as training staff to handle unusual circumstances. For example, one guest consumed a cup of coffee and ate two-thirds of a piece of cake and then said he didn't like the cake. Another problem is suppliers who quote good prices to get her business and then, two weeks later, raise the price of some of the items.

Wong says that the young employees she has at the Java Coffee House are her greatest challenge of all. According to her, there are four kinds of employees—lazy; good, but not responsible; those who steal; and great ones who are no trouble.

DISCUSSION QUESTIONS

1. What are some suggestions for training staff to handle unusual circumstances?
2. How do you ensure that suppliers are delivering the product at the price quoted?
3. What do you do with lazy employees?
4. What do you do with irresponsible employees?
5. How do you deal with employees who steal?

CAREER INFORMATION

A career in beverage management includes everything from coffee shops and restaurants to bars and nightclubs to wineries and breweries. Careers can involve production of the product or selling and marketing it to customers.

Winery or brewery careers are very specialized. A great way to explore this career option is to work at a winery or brewpub in your area while you are attending college. If you discover that this is what you want to do, try taking some related courses at a college or university in your area. Taking courses in viticulture and enology can help develop your knowledge about grapes and wine making in order to help you decide if this is a career path you wish to pursue. Viticulture is the science of growing grapes and enology is the science of making wine. Knowledge in these areas is becoming so important that some universities are offering specialized degrees in both areas. Brewery schools offer brewer certification programs and associate degrees in malting and brewing science or brewing technology.

Selling wine or spirits for a distributor can also be a very lucrative and interesting career. If you enjoy meeting people and like the idea of working on a commission, this may be an option you want to consider. As with any type of selling you need to be a person who is motivated, organized, and outgoing. You will also be selling a product that requires you to have very specialized knowledge. When you are hired your employer will spend time and money training you; however, it is advantageous to develop your knowledge of "adult beverages" while you are in college. Beverage management courses, seminars, and working for liquor distributors are great ways to develop this expertise.

Beverage management in nightclubs and restaurants involves late nights and sometimes long hours. Establishments can keep their bars open until well into the morning hours. Serving alcohol requires an understanding of hospitality law and of how to deal with your customers responsibly. While you are in school, you should take courses in beverage management and hospitality law and also work as a barback, bartender, or part-time manager. Upon becoming a manager you will experience late nights, intoxicated people, and face the constant temptation of substance abuse. It takes self-control to work such long, irregular hours and not join your customers for a good time. If you are a disciplined person, who likes being where the action is and can handle the late hours, then this could be your type of hospitality career.

Coffee shops emerged during the 1990s and have become a separate segment of the hospitality business. Well-managed coffee bars offer a relaxed environment where customers can enjoy themselves with a good cup of coffee while reading a book or talking with friends. Coffee shops foster close relationships between customers and managers. It is not uncommon for people to visit a coffee bar several times each month. If you enjoy personal relationships and a low-stress environment, this career is worth checking out. Figure 10–5 shows a likely career path in the beverage industry.

John Saputo, president of Gold Coast Eagle distributors offers this advice: "I look for an honest people who will look me in the eye and tell me what they are going to do and actually do it. I look for enthusiasm, dedication, and 'fire in the belly.' You can't be a 'C' or 'B' player we need everyone to be on their 'A' game. In the beverage industry, there are positions like inside sales, restaurant sales, hotel sales, wine representatives, logistics, warehousing, marketing, deliveries, and promotions. Cross-training and advancement opportunities are good,

Related Web Sites

www.americanwineries.org/—National Associations of American Wineries

winery education information and links to other sites

www.realbeer.com/—great Web site for information on beer

hbd.org/brewery/—information and links to brewing

www.abgbrew.com/—American Brewers Guild brewing school

www.siebelinstitute.com/—Siebel Institute of Technology and World Brewing Academy

www.republicbeverage.com/—career information and links to other sites

Courtesy of Charlie Adams.

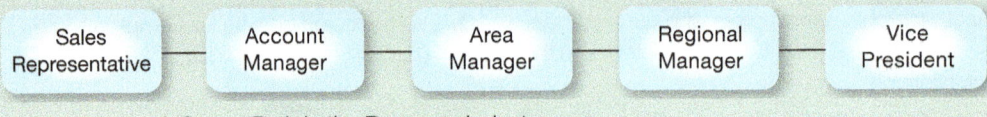

FIGURE 10–5 A Career Path in the Beverage Industry.

SUMMARY

1. Beverages are categorized into alcoholic and nonalcoholic beverages. Alcoholic beverages are further categorized into spirits, wines, and beer.
2. Wine is the fermented juice of ripe grapes. It is classified as red, white, and rosé, and we distinguish between light beverage wines, sparkling wines, and aromatic wines.
3. The six steps in making wine are crushing, fermenting, racking, maturing, filtering, and battling. France, Germany, Italy, Spain, and Portugal are the main European wine-producing areas, and California is the main American wine-producing area.
4. Beer is a brewed and fermented beverage made from malt. Different types of beer include ale, stout, lager, and pilsner.
5. Spirits have a high percentage of alcohol and are served before or after a meal. Processing includes fermentation and distillation. The most popular white spirits are rum, gin, vodka, and tequila.
6. Today, people have become more health conscious about their consumption of alcohol; nonalcoholic beverages such as coffee, tea, soft drinks, juices, and bottled water are increasing in popularity.
7. Beverages make up 20 to 30 percent of total sales in a restaurant, but managers are liable if they serve alcohol to minors. Programs such as designated driver and the serving of virgin cocktails have increased.
8. Close to 17,000 people die each year in the United States in alcohol-related auto accidents.
9. Underage drinking leads to significant personal and social problems.

KEY WORDS AND CONCEPTS

Beer
Brandy
Champagne
Clarified
Cognac
Dram shop legislation
Fining

Fortified wines
Hops
Malt
Mashing
Nonalcoholic beverages
Prohibition
Proof

Sparkling wine
Spirits (liquor)
Vintage
White spirits
Wort
Yeast

REVIEW QUESTIONS

1. What is the difference between fortified and aromatic wines? In what combination is it suggested to serve food and wine and why?
2. What is the difference between a stout and a pilsner?
3. Name and describe the main types of spirits.
4. Why have nonalcoholic drinks increased in popularity?
5. What difficulties do bar managers face when serving alcohol?
6. Describe the origin of coffee.
7. Describe the proper procedure for handling and serving champagne.
8. Describe a typical bar setup.
9. What are the problems relating to alcoholic beverage drinking and how can they be avoided?

INTERNET EXERCISES

1. Organization: Clos Du Bois
   Web site: www.closdubois.com
   Summary: Clos Du Bois is one of America's well-known and loved wineries and is the premier producer of wines from Sonoma County, California. The winery was started in 1974, and has since acquired many more vineyards and made a name for itself. It now sells about a million cases of premium wine annually.
   a. Take a look at the detailed food and wine pairings. What can you serve with the Clos Du Bois Sonoma County sauvignon blanc? Compare it to what you already know about what to eat with sauvignon blanc.
   b. The Clos Du Bois has been named Wine of the Year for nine years by *Wine & Spirits* magazine. What is it about this wine that makes it so different from others?

2. Organization: Siebel Institute of Technology
   Web site: www.siebelinstitute.com
   Summary: Siebel Institute of Technology is recognized for its training and educational programs in brewing technology.
   a. What are some of the services that the Institute of Technology offers its students?
   b. List the career path options available through Siebel Institute of Technology.

APPLY YOUR KNOWLEDGE

1. In groups, do a blindfold taste test with cans of Coke and Pepsi. See if your group can identify which is which and who likes Coke or Pepsi the most.
2. Complete the class survey and share the results with your classmates.
3. Demonstrate the correct way of opening and serving a bottle of non-alcoholic wine.
4. What type of wine would be recommended with the following?
   a. Pork
   b. Cheese
   c. Lamb
   d. Chocolate cake
   e. Chicken
5. Mothers Against Drunk Drivers (MADD) is a nonprofit organization working to stop drunk drivers and support victims of drunk drivers. Find out what impact MADD has had on society.

SUGGESTED ACTIVITIES

1. Search the Internet for underage drinking statistics and related highway deaths in your state.
2. Create an outline for a sports bar concept.

ENDNOTES

1. This section draws on Sarah Berkley, "Organic and Sustainable Wine Production Expanding Rapidly in California," Organic Consumers Association, http://www.organicconsumers.org/organic/wine012104.cfm, retrieved March 12, 2010.
2. www.cookingvillage.com, retrieved March 10, 2006.
3. Budweiser Brewing Company Presentation, University of South Florida, September 7, 2004.
4. Walker_ExpHosp_Chapter10cb[1].doc http://thefullpint.com/beer-news/oregon-honors-full-sail-brewing-for-sustainability, retrieved March 14, 2010.
5. Josh Amaris, "**10 Steps toward Sustainability Every Brewery Should Consider,**" www.bluemap-inc.com/articles/article_12_brewing.html and www.checkthemarkets.com/index.php?option=com_content&task=view&id=688&Itemid=98, retrieved March 15, 2010.
6. http://biggreenboulder.com/energy/sustainable- and http://biggreenboulder.com/energy/sustainable-brewing-in-colorado-not-done-impressing-you-yet/, retrieved March 15, 2010.
7. www.wikipedia.org, retrieved March 10, 2006.
8. Ibid.
9. C. Katsigris, M. Porter, and C. Thomas, *The Bar and Beverage Book,* 3rd ed. (New York: John Wiley & Sons, 2002).
10. Personal conversations with Susan Davis of the Specialty Association of America, August 26, 2005.
11. www.anocora-coffee.com, retrieved March 10, 2006.
12. www.thebeanshop.com, retrieved March 10, 2006.
13. http://coffee_habitat.com, retrieved March 16, 2010.
14. Ibid.
15. Coca-Cola's 2005 annual report.
16. www.3.madd.org, retrieved March 10, 2006.
17. www.nrd.nhtsa.gov/pdf/nrd-30/NCSA/RNotes/2006/810686.pdf.

11 CLUBS

LEARNING OUTCOMES

After reading and studying this chapter, you should be able to:

Distinguish between different types of clubs.

Know the key players in the club industry.

Define club management.

Know the crucial roles in the club management structure.

Describe the economic impact of tourism.

In this chapter, we will explore the world of clubs, including country clubs; city clubs; and other clubs such as professional, social, athletic (such as tennis), dining, university, military, yachting, fraternal, and proprietary.

DEVELOPMENT OF CLUBS

Private clubs are places where members gather for social, recreational, professional, or fraternal reasons. Members enjoy bringing friends, family, and business guests to their club. Their club is like a second home, but with diverse facilities and staff to accommodate the occasion. It can be more impressive than inviting them to their homes, and there is still a level of the same personal atmosphere as there would be if they were invited home. Many of today's clubs are adaptations of their predecessors, mostly from England and Scotland. For example, the North American country club is largely patterned after the Royal and Ancient Golf Club of St. Andrews, Scotland, founded in 1758 and recognized as the birthplace of golf. Many business deals are negotiated on the golf course.

> **Clubs provide a place that members and guests are always welcome. They are generally well-rounded establishments that offer members a venue for a simple luncheon, perhaps a business affair, or larger personal functions and banquets.**
>
> Debbie Smith, *Clearwater Country Club, Clearwater, FL*

Historically, the ambiance of these clubs attracted affluent individuals frequently referred to as "blue bloods," "old money," or "crackers." Their character transcended generations. Their etiquette and mannerisms were developed over the years to a definable point by which they could recognize each other through subtleties; those not possessing the desired qualities were not admitted.

Today there are more affluent people than ever and their number continues to grow. The new rich are now targeted and recruited for a variety of new hybrids that also call themselves clubs. At the newer clubs, the cost of initiation and membership may be considerably less than at some of the more established clubs. The stringent screening process and lengthy membership applications are now simplified, and cash is the key to admittance. People join clubs for social and business reasons and for use of the recreational facilities.

New clubs are born when a developer purchases a tract of land and builds a golf course with a clubhouse surrounded by homes or condominiums. Whoever buys the homes receives a membership to the club. Once all the homes are sold, the developer announces that he will be selling the golf course and clubhouse to an investor who wishes to open it up to the public. The homeowners rush to purchase the clubhouse and golf course to protect their investment. A board is formed, and the employees of the developer and all operations are usually transferred to and become the responsibility of the new owners or members.

HTi Read the Club Management and Member Guide to Discover More about Club Operations

Size and Scope of the Club Industry

There are approximately 14,000 private clubs in America, including both country and city clubs. About 6,000 of these clubs are country clubs. When the total resources of all the clubs are considered (such as land, buildings, equipment, along with thousands of employees), it creates an economic impact worth billions of dollars.

The Old Golf Course at St Andrews, the home of golf.

Types of Clubs

Country Clubs

Nearly all **country clubs** have one or more golf courses (some have swimming pool and tennis courts), a clubhouse, locker rooms, lounges, bars and restaurants, and most have banquet facilities. Members and their guests enjoy these services and are billed monthly—if they use the facility or not! These **monthly dues** range from $100 to $1,500, with the average at about $250 to $350. The club's banquet facilities are used for formal and informal parties, dinners, dances, and weddings by members and their personal guests, but some clubs prefer that there are no disruptions to the club—they prefer not to be disturbed by parties for others, mostly nonmembers. Some country clubs charge what might seem to be an excessive amount for the **initiation fee**—as much as $250,000 in some cases. However, this fee is usually several thousand dollars, which may be refundable when the member resigns.[1] Needless to say, country club members are the movers and shakers of society and they regard membership as a reward for their success in life.

A bunker shot—a player's ball is emerging from a bunker.

> **Country clubs offer recreation for their members. Many of them have a place to dine, and play golf and tennis. Members like to go there to get away for the day or even hold functions, like weddings!**
>
> Joe Calhoun, *Sarasota Country Club*, Sarasota, FL

Country clubs have two or more types of membership. Full membership enables members to use all the facilities all the time. Social membership only allows members to use the social facilities, including lounges, bars, and restaurants, and perhaps the pool and tennis courts. Other forms of membership can include weekday and weekend memberships. The more exclusive the club, the fewer the types of membership.

City Clubs

City clubs are predominantly business oriented, although some have rules prohibiting the discussion of business and the reviewing of business-related documents in dining rooms. They vary in size, location, type of facility, and services offered. Some of the older, established clubs own their own buildings; others lease space. Clubs exist to cater to the wants and needs of members.

Other Clubs

Other clubs include a variety of clubs in the following categories:

Professional clubs, as the name implies, are clubs for people in the same profession. The National Press Club in Washington, D.C., the Lawyer's Club in New York City, and the Friars Club for actors and other theatrical people in Manhattan are good examples.

Social clubs allow members to enjoy one another's company; members represent many different professions, yet they have similar socioeconomic backgrounds. Social clubs are modeled after the famous men's social clubs in London, such as Boodles, St. James's, and White's. At these clubs, it is considered bad form to discuss business. Therefore, conversation and social interaction focus on companionship or entertainment. The oldest social club in America is thought to be the Fish House in Philadelphia, founded in 1832. To ensure that the Fish House would always be socially oriented rather than business oriented, it was formed as a men's cooking club, with each member taking turns preparing meals for the membership. Other social clubs exist in several major cities. The common denominator is that they all have upscale food and beverage offerings and club managers to manage them.[2]

Athletic clubs give city workers and residents an opportunity to work out, swim, play squash and/or racquetball, and so on. Some of the downtown athletic clubs provide tennis courts and running tracks on the roof. Athletic clubs also have lounges, bars, and restaurants at which members may relax and interact socially. Some athletic clubs also have meeting rooms and even sleeping accommodations. The newest feature is known as the executive workout. This begins with a visit to the steam room, followed by a trip to the Jacuzzi, then sauna, a massage, and nap in the resting room before showering and returning to work.

Dining clubs are generally located in large city office buildings. Memberships are often given as an inducement to tenants who lease space in the office building. These clubs are always open for lunch and occasionally for dinner.

University clubs are private clubs for alumni or alumnae. University clubs are generally located in the high-rent district and offer a variety of facilities and attractions focusing on food and beverage service.

Military clubs cater to both NCOs (noncommissioned officers) and enlisted officers. Military clubs offer similar facilities as other clubs for recreation and entertainment and food and beverage offerings. Some military clubs are located on base. The largest membership club in the country is the Army Navy Country Club in Arlington, Virginia. The club has over 6,000 members, 54 holes of golf, two clubhouses, and a host of other facilities. In recent years, many of these clubs have given over their club management to civilians.

Yacht clubs provide members with moorage slips, where their boats are kept secure. In addition to moorage facilities, yacht clubs have lounge, bar, and dining facilities similar to other clubs. Yacht clubs are based on a sailing theme and attract members with various backgrounds who have sailing as a common interest.

Fraternal clubs include many special organizations, such as the Veterans of Foreign Wars, Elks, and Shriners. These organizations foster camaraderie and often assist charitable causes. They generally are less elaborate than other clubs, but have bars and banquet rooms that can be used for various activities.

Proprietary clubs operate on a for-profit basis. They are owned by corporations or individuals; individuals wanting to become members purchase a membership, not a share in the club. Proprietary clubs became popular with the real estate boom in the 1970s and 1980s. As new housing developments were planned, clubs were included in several of the projects. Households paid a small initiation fee and monthly dues between $30 and $50, allowing the whole family to participate in a wide variety of recreational activities.

Clearly, the opportunities for recreation and leisure abound. The goal must be to achieve a harmony between work and leisure activities and to become truly professional in both giving and receiving these services. The next few years will see a substantial increase in the leisure and recreational industries.

Check Your Knowledge

1. What are two types of membership country clubs have?
2. Approximately how many private clubs are in America?
3. What type of clientele are city clubs oriented toward?

Key players in the club industry

Key players in the club industry include ClubCorp, WCI Communities, and American Golf. They are profiled and described next.

Club management

Club management is similar in many ways to hotel management: both have evolved in recent years. The general managers of clubs now assume the role of chief operating officer, and in some cases chief executive officer of the corporation. They may also have responsibility for management of the homeowners' association (if there are homes around the golf course) and all athletic facilities, including the golf courses. In addition, they are responsible for planning, forecasting and budgeting, human resources, food and beverage operations, facility management, and maintenance.

.inc Corporate Profile

CLUBCORP

Founded in 1957, Dallas-based ClubCorp is the world leader in delivering premier golf, private club, and resort experiences. Internationally, ClubCorp's affiliates own or operate nearly 170 golf courses, country clubs, private business and sports clubs, and resorts. ClubCorp has approximately $1.5 billion in assets. Among the company's nationally recognized golf properties are Pinehurst in the Village of Pinehurst, North Carolina (the largest golf resort in North America and site of the 1999 and 2005 U.S. Opens); Firestone Country Club in Akron, Ohio (site of the 2003–2005 World Golf Championships—Bridgestone Invitational); The Homestead in Hot Springs, Virginia (America's first resort, founded in 1766); and Mission Hills Country Club in Rancho Mirage, California (home of the Kraft Nabisco Championship).

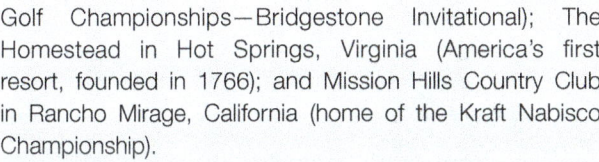

The more than 60 business clubs and business and sports clubs include the Boston College Club; City Club on Bunker Hill in Los Angeles; Citrus Club in Orlando, Florida; Columbia Tower Club in Seattle; Metropolitan Club in Chicago; Tower Club in Dallas; and the City Club of Washington, D.C. The company's 18,000 employees serve the nearly 200,000 member households and 200,000 guests who visit ClubCorp properties each year.

ClubCorp is in the business of building relationships and enriching lives. Its extraordinary private club environments nourish relationships old and new, as well as create a world of privacy, luxury, and relaxation where every need is anticipated and every expectation exceeded. Crafting fine, private club traditions for more than 50 years, ClubCorp has developed a signature philosophy of service that resonates with every encounter, every warm welcome, and every magic moment, joining to form the bedrock of all we do.

Each club has its own distinctive personality and takes pride in creating the perfect settings for casual gatherings with friends to business meetings to formal celebrations. The clubs provide safe havens, where its members and their guests always are welcome. Whether looking for a country club experience or a professional retreat from which to conduct business affairs, our members are the beneficiaries of the ultimate in private club service and tradition.

ClubCorp clubs provide a variety of membership options and experiences for a range of lifestyle pursuits. In more than 170 private business and sports clubs, country clubs, golf courses, and golf resorts around the world, from Seattle to Mexico and from Boston to Beijing.

Source: www.clubcorp.com.

.inc Corporate Profile

WCI COMMUNITIES

For almost 60 years, WCI Communities has been an industry leader in building lifestyles, not just homes and communities. More than 160,000 people have experienced the WCI lifestyle in some 50 master-planned communities and 60-plus luxury high-rise towers in Florida, New York, New Jersey, Connecticut, and the Washington, D.C., area. With a focus on building primary move-up, retirement, and second homes, WCI is a recognized leader in its commitment to green building and sustainable practices; building luxury high-rise towers; and creating highly amenitized master-planned communities. We have formed strategic partnerships with some of the most recognized names in the hospitality industry and sports world, including Starwood Hotels and Resorts Worldwide, Regency International Hotels, Greg Norman, Pete Dye, Raymond Floyd, and Peter Jacobsen. Named America's Best Builder in 2004 by the National Association of Homebuilders, WCI's 4,000-plus employees are dedicated to providing the best customer service possible, turning the purchase of a home into the experience of a lifetime.

Source: wcicommunities.com.

.inc Corporate Profile

AMERICAN GOLF

American Golf manages over 170 premier private, resort, and daily fee golf courses in the United States designed by some of the world's most renowned course architects. American Golf is responsible for more than 35,000 events each year and employs over 10,000 people. It caters weddings, corporate events, and private parties and is committed to giving back to the community through sponsorship of several charities.

American Golf and the Tiger Woods Foundation formed an alliance to foster opportunities for underprivileged youths to learn and play golf. The program stages junior golf clinics for inner-city youths ages 8 to 18 and is hosted by golf superstar Tiger Woods.

Source: www.americangolf.com/about.cfm

Uncover the Traits of a Successful Club Manager at the Gessell Country Club

The main difference between club management and hotel management is that with clubs, the guests *feel* as if they are the owners (in many cases they are) and thus frequently *behave* as if they are the owners. Their emotional attachment is stronger than that of hotel guests who do not use hotels with the same frequency that members use clubs. Another difference is that most clubs do not offer sleeping accommodations. Club members pay an initiation fee to belong to the club and annual membership dues thereafter. Some clubs also charge a set utilization fee, usually related to food and beverages, which is charged whether or not those services are used.

The **Club Managers Association of America (CMAA)** is the professional organization to which many of the club managers of the 6,000 private country clubs belong. The association's goal is to advance the profession of club management by fulfilling the educational and related needs of the club managers. The association provides networking opportunities and fosters camaraderie among its member managers through meetings and conferences held locally and nationally. These gatherings keep managers abreast of current practices and procedures and new legislation. The general managers who join CMAA subscribe to a code of ethics.[3]

The CMAA has reexamined the role of club managers and, due to ever-increasing expectations, the role of the general manager has changed from the traditional managerial model to a leadership model. The new CMAA model is based on the premise that general managers or COOs are more than chief operating officers responsible for operating assets and investments and club culture.

Figure 11–1 shows the **core competencies** of a general manager or COO to be private club management, food and beverage, accounting and financial management, human and professional resources, building and facilities management, external and governmental influences, management, marketing, and sports and recreation.

The second tier of the model is mastering the skills of asset management. Today's general manager or COO must be able to manage the physical property, the financial well-being, and the human resources of the club. These facets of the manager's responsibility are equally as important as managing the operations of the club.

The third and final tier of the new model is preserving and fostering the culture of the club, which can be defined as the club's traditions, history, and vision. Many managers or COOs intrinsically perform this function; however, it is often an overlooked and underdeveloped quality. A job description for club manager is given in Figure 11–2. The Club Management Competencies are shown in Figure 11–3.

Discover the Role of the Club Managers Association: Read the Club Management Manual

Check Your Knowledge

1. Who are the three key players in the club industry?
2. Describe American Golf.
3. What is the Club Managers Association of America?

Club Management Structure

The internal management structure of a club is governed by the corporation's articles of incorporation and bylaws. These establish election procedures, officer positions, a board of directors, and standing committees. Guidance and direction also are provided

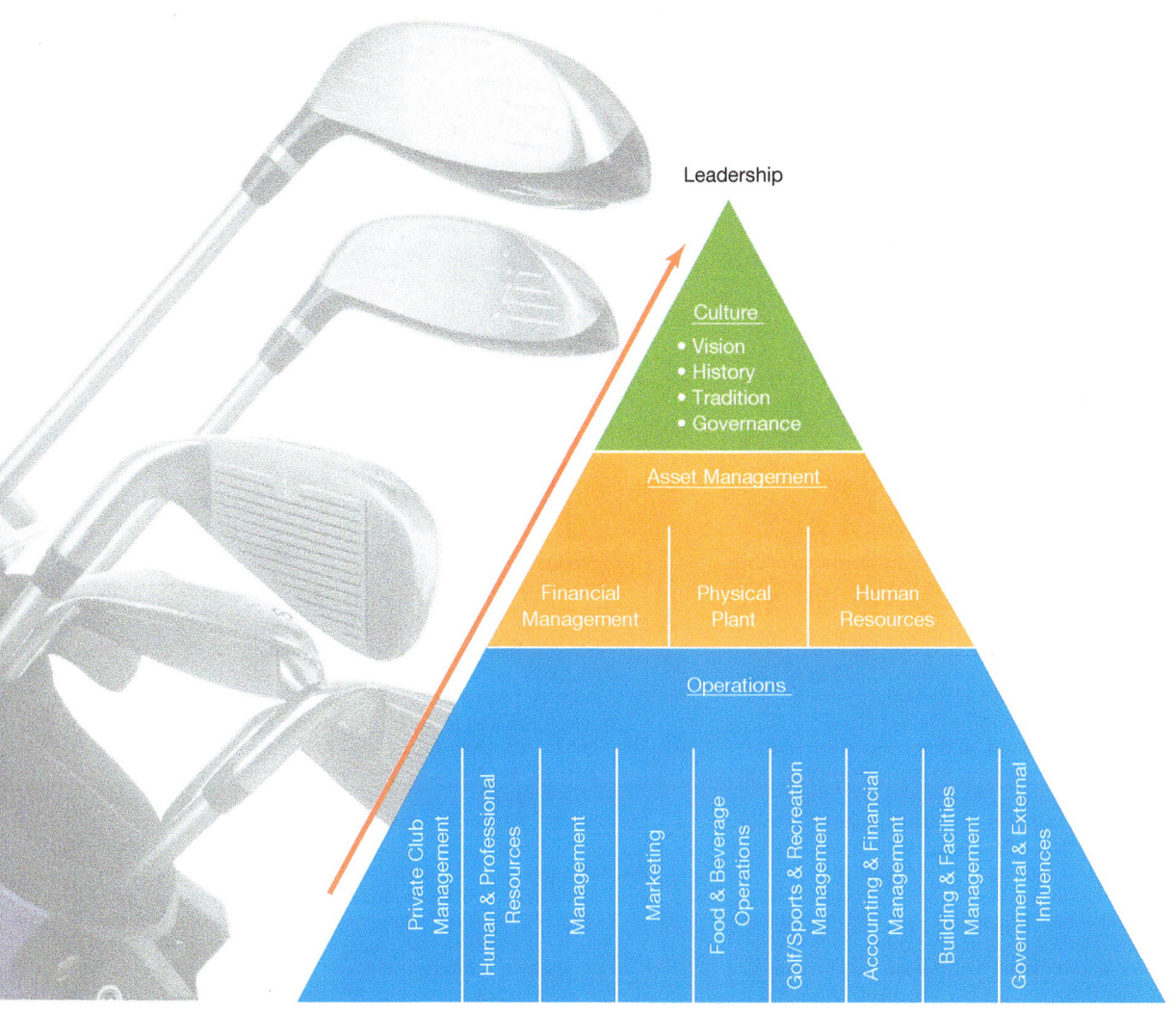

FIGURE 11–1 Core Competencies for Management to Leadership.
(*Source:* Courtesy of the Club Managers Association of America.)

for each office and committee and how it will function. The general manager will usually provide an orientation for the new directors and information to help them in their new role. The members elect the officers and directors of the club.

The officers represent the membership by establishing policies by which the club will operate. Many clubs and other organizations maintain continuity by having a succession of officers. The secretary becomes the vice president and the vice president becomes the president. In other cases the person elected president is simply the person believed to be the most qualified person to lead the club for that year. Regardless of who is elected president, the club's general manager must be able to work with that person and the other officers. Figure 11–4 shows an organization chart for a country club.

The president heads up all official meetings and is a leader in policy making. The vice president is groomed for the role of president, which is usually eminent, and will in the absence of the president perform the presidential duties. If the club has more than one vice president, the title first, second, third, and so on, may be used. Alternatively, vice presidents may be assigned to chair certain committees, such as membership. Board members usually chair one or more committees.

> **If the committees are effective, the operation of the club is more efficient.**

Committees play an important part in the club's activities. If the committees are effective, the operation of the club is more efficient. The term of committee membership is specified, and committee meetings are conducted in accordance with Robert's Rules of Order, which are procedural guidelines on the correct way to conduct meetings. Standing committees include house, membership, finance/budget, entertainment, golf, greens, tennis, pool, and long-range planning. The president may appoint additional committees to serve specific functions commonly referred to as ad hoc.

The treasurer obviously must have some financial and accounting background, because an integral part of his or her

I. **Position:** General Manager
II. **Related Titles:** Club Manager; Club House Manager
III. **Job Summary:** Serves as chief operating officer of the club; manages all aspects of the club including its activities and the relationships between the club and its board of directors, members, guests, employees, community, government, and industry; coordinates and administers the club's policies as defined by its board of directors. Develops operating policies and procedures and directs the work of all department managers. Implements and monitors the budget, monitors the quality of the club's products and services, and ensures maximum member and guest satisfaction. Secures and protects the club's assets, including facilities and equipment
IV. **Job Tasks (Duties):**
   1. Implements general policies established by the board of directors; directs their administration and execution
   2. Plans, develops, and approves specific operational policies, programs, procedures, and methods in concert with general policies
   3. Coordinates the development of the club's longrange and annual (business) plans
   4. Develops, maintains, and administers a sound organizational plan; initiates improvements as necessary
   5. Establishes a basic personnel policy; initiates and monitors policies relating to personnel actions and training and professional development programs
   6. Maintains membership with the Club Managers Association of America and other professional associations. Attends conferences, workshops, and meetings to keep abreast of current information and developments in the field
   7. Coordinates development of operating and capital budgets according to the budget calendar; monitors monthly and other financial statements for the club; takes effective corrective action as required
   8. Coordinates and serves as ex-officio member of appropriate club committees
   9. Welcomes new club members; meets and greets all club members as practical during their visits to the club
   10. Provides advice and recommendations to the president and committees about construction, alterations, maintenance, materials, supplies, equipment, and services not provided in approved plans and/or budgets
   11. Consistently ensures that the club is operated in accordance with all applicable local, state, and federal laws
   12. Oversees the care and maintenance of all the club's physical assets and facilities
   13. Coordinates the marketing and membership relations programs to promote the club's services and facilities to potential and present members
   14. Ensures the highest standards for food, beverage, sports and recreation, entertainment, and other club services
   15. Establishes and monitors compliance with purchasing policies and procedures
   16. Reviews and initiates programs to provide members with a variety of popular events
   17. Analyzes financial statements, manages cash flow, and establishes controls to safeguard funds; reviews income and costs relative to goals; takes corrective action as necessary
   18. Works with subordinate department heads to schedule, supervise, and direct the work of all club employees
   19. Attends meetings of the club's executive committee and board of directors
   20. Participates in outside activities that are judged as appropriate and approved by the board of directors to enhance the prestige of the club; broadens the scope of the club's operation by fulfilling the public obligations of the club as a participating member of the community
V. **Reports to:** Club President and Board of Directors
VI. **Supervises:** Assistant General Manager (Club House Manager); Food and Beverage Director; Controller; Membership Director; Director of Human Resources; Director of Purchasing; Golf Professional (Director of Golf); Golf Course Superintendent; Tennis Professional; Athletic Director; Executive Secretary

FIGURE 11–2 A Club Manager's Job Description.
(**Source:** Club Managers Association of America).

duties is to give advice on financial matters, such as employing external auditors, preparing budgets, and installing control systems. The general manager is responsible for all financial matters and usually signs or co-signs all checks.

It is the duty of the secretary to record the minutes of meetings and to take care of club-related correspondence. In most cases, the general manager prepares the document for the secretary's signature. This position can be combined with that of treasurer, in which case the position is titled secretary–treasurer. The secretary may also serve on or chair certain committees.

Club Food and Beverage Management

Learn the Basics of Club Food and Beverage in the F&B in Clubs Manual

Food and beverage management in a club is similar to that in a hotel except that the guests actually own—or think they own—the club. (Remember that each member pays an initiation fee and so much per month for food and beverages regardless of whether they are consumed.) The food and beverage director reports to the general manager and

Private Club Management
History of Private Clubs
Types of Private Clubs
Membership Types
Bylaws
Policy Formulation
Board Relations
Chief Operating Officer Concept
Committees
Club Job Descriptions
Career Development
Golf Operations Management
Golf Course Management
Tennis Operations Management
Swimming Pool Management
Yacht Facilities Management
Fitness Center Management
Locker Room Management
Other Recreational Activities

Food and Beverage Operations
Sanitation
Menu Development
Nutrition
Pricing Concepts
Ordering/Receiving/Controls/Inventory
Food and Beverage Trends
Quality Service
Creativity in Theme Functions
Design and Equipment
Food and Beverage Personnel
Wine List Development

Accounting and Finance in the Private Club
Accounting and Finance Principles
Uniform System of Accounts
Financial Analysis
Budgeting
Cash Flow Forecasting
Compensation and Benefit Administration
Financing Capital Projects
Audits
Internal Revenue Service
Computers
Business Office Organization
Long-Range Financial Planning

Human and Professional Resources
Employee Relations
Management Styles
Organizational Development
Balancing Job and Family Responsibilities
Time Management
Stress Management
Labor Issues
Leadership vs. Management

Building and Facilities Management
Preventive Maintenance
Insurance and Risk Management
Clubhouse Remodeling and Renovation
Contractors
Energy and Water Resource Management
Housekeeping
Security
Laundry
Lodging Operations

External and Governmental Influences
Legislative Influences
Regulatory Agencies
Economic Theory
Labor Law
Internal Revenue Service
Privacy
Club Law
Liquor Liability
Labor Unions

Management and Marketing
Communication Skills
Marketing Through In-House Publications
Professional Image and Dress
Effective Negotiation
Member Contact Skills
Working with the Media
Marketing Strategies in a Private Club Environment

FIGURE 11–3 Club Management Competencies.
Club Managers Association of America.

CMAA CODE *of* ETHICS

We believe the management of clubs is an honorable calling. It shall be incumbent upon club managers to be knowledgeable in the application of sound principles in the management of clubs, with ample opportunity to keep abreast of current practices and procedures. We are convinced that the Club Managers Association of America best represents these interests and, as members thereof subscribe to the following:

We will uphold the best traditions of club management through adherence to sound business principles. By our behavior and demeanor, we shall set an example for our employees and will assist our club officers to secure the utmost in efficient and successful club operations.

We will consistently promote the recognition and esteem of club management as a profession and conduct our personal and business affairs in a manner to reflect capability and integrity. We will always honor our contractual employment obligations.

We shall promote community and civic affairs by maintaining good relations with the public sector to the extent possible within the limits of our club's demands.

We will strive to advance our knowledge and abilities as club managers, and willingly share with other Association members the lessons of our experience and knowledge gained by supporting and participating in our local chapter and the National Association's educational meetings and seminars.

We will not permit ourselves to be subsidized or compromised by any interest doing business with our clubs.

We will refrain from initiating, directly or through an agent, any communications with a director, member, or employee of another club regarding its affairs without the prior knowledge of the manager thereof, if it has a manager.

We will advise the National Headquarters, whenever possible, regarding managerial openings at clubs that come to our attention. We will do all within our power to assist our fellow club managers in pursuit of their professional goals.

We shall not be deterred from compliance with the law, as it applies to our clubs. We shall provide our club officers and trustees with specifics of federal, state and local laws, statutes, and regulations to avoid punitive action and costly litigation.

We deem it our duty to report to local or national officers any willful violations of the CMAA CODE OF ETHICS.

Source: Courtesy of the Club Managers Association of America.

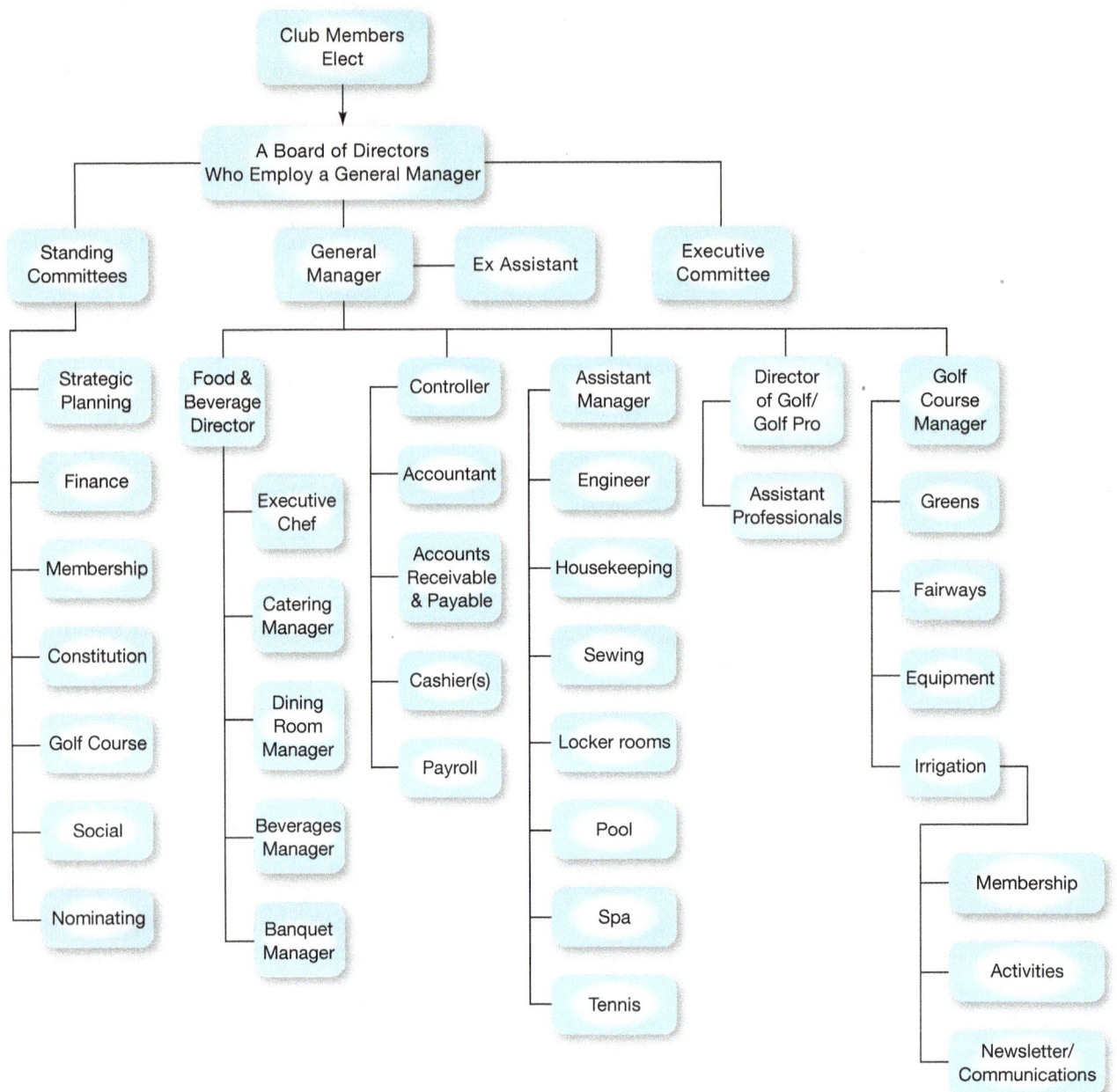

FIGURE 11–4 The Organization Chart of a Country Club.

is responsible for the entire food and beverage operation. Clubs generally have a formal or semiformal restaurant and a casual dining facility. Other food outlets may be at the pool or at the ninth hole (halfway around the golf course). Some clubs have a mobile trolley that brings refreshments around the course.

Clubs may also have a function room for catering for banquets, weddings, and other private parties such as a wedding anniversary. These parties bring in additional revenue and help maintain employees' hours. However, some clubs do not allow these events to disturb members who feel that they pay a lot not to be disrupted.

The Golf Course Superintendent

The golf course superintendent is the key to the success of the quality and condition of the golf course and the main reason that members join a club. The superintendent is responsible for the things that make a golf course great, and is evaluated by the condition of five critical aspects of the course:

- *Greens:* The area surrounding the hole that the golf ball is knocked into. Greens are measured by how fast they are:

Introducing Edward J. Shaughnessy CCM, MBA, CHE

For Ed Shaughnessy, working in a country club is not just a job but a passion. Clubs feature great recreational facilities, including fabulous golf courses, plus gourmet dining, the finest entertainment, and clientele who are more like family than customers. Shaughnessy has worked for three prestigious clubs in his career. He began working in clubs at the tender age of 14 as a busboy. Shortly after graduating from high school, he accepted a full-time evening bar manager position at Sleepy Hollow Country Club in New York. He worked full time at night while attending college full time until he received his AAS degree. Upon graduation, he was promoted to food and beverage manager. He continued his education, taking two or three courses every semester until he earned and received his BBA. He was subsequently promoted to assistant general manager.

After 14 years at the same club (and on his twenty-ninth birthday), he was offered and accepted the general manager's position at Belle Haven Country Club in Alexandria, Virginia. He began an active role in the National Capital Club Managers Association and was elected president. He continued his education and earned his certified club manager (CCM) designation through the Club Managers Association of America and his certified hospitality educator (CHE). He stayed at Belle Haven Country Club for eight years, but wanted to live closer to sunny beaches in a warmer climate.

An opportunity at the prestigious Belleair Country Club was brought to Shaughnessy's attention by John Sibbald, a top recruiter in the club industry; in 1997, Ed Shaughnessy accepted a position there as general manager/chief operating officer. He continued his education, earning his MBA in international hotel and tourism management from Schiller International University, where he now teaches a variety of hospitality-related courses. Shaughnessy is still active with the Club Managers Association and serves on the Club Foundation Allocation Committee. This committee reviews scholarship and grant applications and recommends the awarding of funds to promote education. He also serves as the ethics chair for the Florida's Chapter Club Managers Association.

Shaughnessy believes that there are two stages in life, growth and decay, and that we are all in one of these stages. He prefers the growth stage! He believes that we are all given the choice to change our environment, and he enjoys catering to those with the highest expectations. It appears that people will always recognize and be willing to pay for great value and quality. Meticulous attention to detail and proactively giving customers what they want before they have to ask are the keys to success.

Explore the Importance of Service

No two days are the same or predictable for a general manager. One day you could be developing a strategic plan, the next you may be invited to fly on a private Lear jet to see the Super Bowl. You have to make a conscious effort to balance work and family life. A general manager should remember that, although you enjoy many of the same privileges as the elite, you are still an employee and must always set an exemplary role as a professional. A general manager's people skills are very important, as is a comprehensive understanding of financial statements.

The challenge for the future is finding talented and service-oriented people who can handle the constantly increasing expectations of sophisticated and discriminating club members. Shaughnessy discovered some time ago that it may be necessary to grow one's own talent among his employees, and this gives him the confidence that he will be ready to serve his guests well. Shaughnessy has a high concern for the welfare of his loyal and dedicated employees. They and their families count on him to operate the club efficiently: they could lose their jobs if the club is mismanaged. He also recognizes that he must be proactive to ensure the growth and success of his club. With two waterfront golf courses, a marina, and the amenities of a full-service country club, Ed Shaughnessy is working to position the club for continued success.

---

a stint meter is used to measure the ball's ability to travel across the green (known as the quickness of the green).

- *Bunkers or Traps:* Bunkers or traps are sandbox-like areas on the course (where the author's ball always ends up).
- *Teeing Surfaces:* The area where players tee-off (hit their ball from).
- *Fairways:* The long stretch of grass between the tee-off area and the hole that players are supposed to hit the ball into.
- *Rough:* The area on each side of the fairway leading to the green (another area where my ball spends a lot of time).

Sustainable Golf Course Management

The golf course industry recognizes sustainability as it is referenced by the Environmental Protection Agency and the United Nations, which indicates that it is "meeting the needs of the present without compromising the ability of future generations to meet their own needs."[4] In an effort to appear sustainable, some courses call themselves "green." This is vague. However, it is not vague to say that a course engages in water quality protection through the responsible use of all inputs, such as nutrients and pesticides.

The Environmental Agency (EPA) gives a basic run-down of sustainability (www.epa.gov/sustainability/basicinfo.htm). The Environmental Institute for Golf lists basic golf management practices (www.eifg.org). Sustainable practices include:[5]

- Reducing energy use especially during the peak times (a utility company's bill is much higher for consumption during peak times).
- Holding departments accountable for their energy consumption budgets by breaking down the bills by departments.
- Recycling: from aluminum cans in the clubhouse to grass clippings on the course to motor oil from the golf carts.

Golf course facilities are prime candidates for reducing or reusing waste: as landfill disposal costs rise, recycling becomes even more important. Golf courses can improve their sustainability by grass and plant selection, and by using well water and organic fertilization.

The golf superintendent works with the greens committee and the golf committee to ensure that all the goals of the club are met and maintained.

Check Your Knowledge

1. What role do the officers play in the club management structure?
2. What role do committees play in the club management structure?
3. What is a golf course superintendent responsible for?

The Golf Professional

The golf professional handles all tournaments, such as a club-sponsored fund-raisers for cancer research; championship club and outside tournaments; or local area fund-raisers such as the Boy Scouts or local charities. The golf pro is responsible for caddies (people who carry the golf bags and advise players on what clubs to use along the course), the driving range where golfers practice, ball cleaning, and the markers that are moved back and forth on the tees. The golf pro used to be on contract

Golf practice can be enjoyed by the whole family.

and would also run the pro shop; however, today, the golf pro is on staff and receives a six-figure income.

The Golf Shop

The golf shop used to be run by the golf pro; however, in recent years, clubs realized that they needed to upgrade their shops and extend the range of merchandise. Many shops have revenues in excess of $1 million; with a margin of 15 percent, that means that the club takes in $150,000 to use as it likes. Golf shops stock a range of golfing equipment, from balls to clubs to clothing.

TRENDS in CLUB MANAGEMENT

- Some country clubs are part of an estate development that includes a golf course (or two) with houses surrounding the course. The general manager is very involved with the real estate package's overall operation.
- A few clubs are beginning to introduce spas as an additional amenity for members.
- The golf professional is now more likely to be a member of staff rather than a contract for hire.
- Golf shops are run by the club, not by the golf pro.

An Ethical Dilemma

An Ethical Dilemma (Courtesy of Ian Fetigan, General Manager, the Founders Club, Sarasota, Florida.)

You are the general manager of a prestigious club. The club president comes into your office with some important items to discuss: your annual salary and benefits package, his daughter's wedding, and his wife's charity golf event. Once your generous salary and benefits package have been finalized, the president begins to talk about the requirements for his daughter's wedding. The conversation is going in the direction of substantial discounts for the food and beverages to be offered. This goes against club policy. What are you to do? He is the club president. Then to add to the dilemma, he tells you that his wife is planning a charity golf event, and that he wants the usual fee of $75 per person waived. What would you say to the president of the club?

DISCUSSION QUESTIONS

1. In your opinion, should the fees be waived?
2. What would you say or do?

CAREER INFORMATION

CLUB MANAGEMENT

Club managers and hotel managers share many of the same responsibilities. They are in charge of preparing budgets and forecasting future sales; monitoring restaurants on the property and various internal departments, such as human resources; and making sure maintenance work is done properly. They are responsible for the overall well-being of the club. the Club Managers Association of America (www.cmaa.org) gives club managers certification and other membership benefits, such as professional development and networking. Its Web site is worth a visit.

Club management is different from hotel management, in that the guests at a club are members and typically pay for their memberships. Because of this, many feel a much stronger tie to the club and therefore expect a higher level of service.

Of the many types of clubs within the club management industry, the most predominant are golf, country, city, athletic, and yacht. Country clubs are the most common. They are typically based on outdoor activities. Golf is the main draw, but other sports such as tennis and swimming are also popular. Some country clubs also offer their members a variety of classes and social activities. They typically have a lounge and/or restaurant on the property as well. Country clubs can be private or semiprivate. If a club is private, its facilities are only available to members; a semiprivate club offers some services to nonmembers.

There is no one definite career path when it comes to club management. However, most people make the transition to club manager from positions in kitchen or bar management (see Figure 11–5). It is rare that employees move from areas such as accounting to become club managers.

Depending on the level of experience, one might start out as an assistant banquet or dining room manager and then progress to a position as catering manager or assistant clubhouse manager. The next step occurs according to the amount of time spent in these positions, as well as to the quality of the experience. For example, four to six years in a club that has a gross income of $1.5 million in food and beverages would most likely lead to a club management position.

Club managers do not keep regular hours. They work long hours when the club is busy, and fewer hours when the club is slow. Club managers usually create their own schedules according to fluctuations in activity. On average, they typically work five or six days a week, 10 hours a day.

Most entry-level club management positions have set salaries that range from $27,000 to $33,000. Entry-level positions are usually not subject to negotiation. Midlevel position salaries, however, can often be negotiated until an agreeable sum is met. The actual salary depends on the amount of experience the employee has and the strength of his or her references. The best aspect of working as a club manager is that the environment and facilities are usually top notch. Managers typically have access to the club's facilities and receive meals.

ClubCorp is one of the largest corporate owners of clubs, operating more than 220 country clubs, business clubs, and golf resorts.[6] Recent expansions in corporate ownership have made it slightly easier to enter the club management profession. If you are serious about a career in club management, you should join a local student chapter of the Club Managers Association of America (CMAA). CMAA meetings are a great place for networking to find a summer job or internship. The experience you gain during your college tenure will provide you with the knowledge you need to begin your career in the recreation and leisure industries.

Excellent opportunities for advancement come frequently. Club managers also often receive bonuses based on performance. These bonuses range from 5 to 15 percent of the manager's base salary of more than $100,000 annually. The highest-paid country club general manager makes $350,000 annually. (Yes, $350,000!)

John Costello, country club general manager, offers this advice: "If you have an interest in country clubs, get a job in a club, and then do an internship in one. The most likely area of initial employment is in the food and beverage department with opportunities in the dining rooms/restaurants, catering, bars and beverage service and culinary. The job and internship experiences will help you determine if the country club environment is for you. There is one big possible advantage over other types of hospitality employment: you have an opportunity to interact with club members over time rather than with transient guests. The general manager's six-figure income maybe of interest, too. Good luck!"

Related Web Sites

www.clubcorp.com—ClubCorp
www.cmaa.org—Club Managers Association of America
http://www.naylornetwork.com/mam-nxt/—Club Management Online: The Virtual Clubhouse
www.nps.gov—National Parks Service
www.natlclub.org—National Club Association

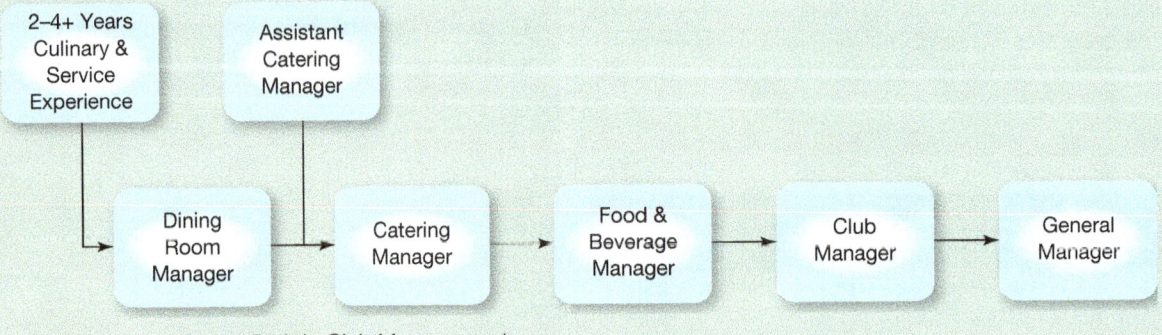

FIGURE 11–5 A Career Path in Club Management.

SUMMARY

1. Private clubs are places where members gather for social, recreational, professional, or fraternal reasons.
2. There are approximately 14,000 private clubs in America, including both country and city clubs. About 6,000 of these clubs are country clubs.
3. Country clubs have two or more types of membership: they include full membership and social membership.
4. City clubs are predominantly business oriented, although some have rules prohibiting the discussion of business and the reviewing of business-related documents in dining rooms.

5. Key players in the club industry include ClubCorp, WCI Communities, and American Golf.
6. The general manager of a club now assumes the role of chief operating officer and, in some cases, chief executive officer of the corporation.
7. The Club Managers Association of America (CMAA) is the professional organization to which many of the club managers of the 6,000 private country clubs belong.
8. The internal management structure of a club is governed by the corporation's articles of incorporation and bylaws.
9. The golf course superintendent is the key to the success of the quality and condition of the golf course and the main reason that members join a club.

KEY WORDS AND CONCEPTS

Club management
Club Managers Association of America (CMAA)
Committees
Core competencies
Country club
Initiation fee
Monthly dues
Private clubs

REVIEW QUESTIONS

1. Describe the development of clubs.
2. Name the different types of clubs.
3. What is the difference between club and hotel management?
4. How are clubs mostly being developed today?
5. What areas does a club general manager need to know about?

INTERNET EXERCISES

1. Go to the Web site for the Club Managers Association of America (www.cmaa.org) and see what benefits members are offered.
2. Go to the Web site for ClubCorp at www.clubcorp.com and see if you agree with its company philosophy. If you're really interested, request that a list of opportunities be e-mailed to you.
3. Organization: Prestonwood Country Club
Web site: www.prestonwoodcc.com
Summary: Prestonwood is a full-service country club that offers activities and fine food.
   a. What kinds of activities are offered at the Prestonwood Country Club?
   b. Parents may wish to take their children on vacations. In these situations, what might this country club offer kids?

APPLY YOUR KNOWLEDGE

1. Which of the club manager's core competencies would you find the most difficult to accomplish?

SUGGESTED ACTIVITIES

1. Plan the steps in your career toward a club manager's position.
2. In groups of four, interview a club manager and write up a "day in the life" of your manager. Ask what challenges she or he faces.

ENDNOTES

1. Personal conversation with Edward J. Shaughnessy, November 4, 2006.
2. Ibid.
3. www.cmaa.org.
4. www.nxtbook.com/nxtbooks/naylor/MAMS0110/index.php?startpage=43&qs=sustainability#/42.
5. www.nxtbook.com/nxtbooks/naylor/MAMS0609/index.php?startpage=29&qs=sustainability#/28.
6. www.clubcorp.com.

12 THEME PARKS AND ATTRACTIONS

LEARNING OUTCOMES

After reading and studying this chapter, you should be able to:

Discuss how theme parks developed.

Recognize the key players in the theme park industry.

Discuss the structure of theme park management and operations.

Distinguish between different types of employment in the theme park industry.

Describe different types of fairs, festivals, and events.

HTi Describe the economic impact of tourism.

The development of theme parks

It all began in the 1920s in Buena Park, California, with a small berry farm and tea room. As Knott's restaurant business grew, different attractions were added to the site to keep waiting customers amused. After a gradual expansion, more than 80 years after its humble beginnings, Knott's Berry Farm has become the largest independent theme park in the United States.

Today, Knott's Berry Farm offers 150 acres of rides, attractions, live entertainment, historical exhibits, dining, and specialty shops. The park features six themes—Ghost Town, Indian Trails, Fiesta Village, the Boardwalk, Wild Water Wilderness, and Camp Snoopy, which is the official home of Snoopy and the Peanuts characters. In addition, the California Marketplace is located right outside the park, and offers 14 unique shops and restaurants.

Explore the Variety of Regional Attractions at Simmy's Splashtown

> *Roller coaster rides give thrill seekers a sense of adventure without consequence!*
> — Martha Carvalho, *Universal Studios,* Orlando, FL

Knott's Berry Farm has truly been a great influence on the American theme park industry. Hundreds of parks, both independent and corporate owned, started to develop following the birth of Knott's. Creator Walter Knott may have figured out why amusement parks became so popular so quickly. He has been quoted as saying, "The more complex the world becomes, the more people turn to the past and the simple things in life. We [as in the amusement park operators] try to give them some of those things."[1] Even with the ever-increasing competition, Knott's continues to attract guests with its authentic historical artifacts, relaxed atmosphere, emphasis on learning, famous food, varied entertainment, innovative rides, and specialty shopping.[2]

Size and scope of the theme park industry

Visiting **theme parks** has always been a favorite tourist activity. Theme parks create an atmosphere of another place and time, and usually concentrate on one dominant theme. Theme parks and **attractions** vary according to theme, which might be historical, cultural, geographical, and so on. Some parks and attractions focus on a single theme, like the marine zoological Sea World parks. Other parks and attractions focus on multiple themes, like Kings Island in Ohio, a family entertainment center divided into seven theme areas: International Street, October Fest, River-Town, Planet Snoopy, Coney Mall, Boomerang Bay and Action Zone. Another example is California's Great America, a 100-acre family entertainment center that evokes North America's past in five themes: Home Town Square, Yankee Harbor, County Fair, Planet Snoopy and Orleans Plaza.

There are an abundance of theme parks located throughout the United States. These parks have a variety of attractions, from animals and sea life, to thrill rides and motion simulators. There are parks with educational themes and parks where people go to simply have a good time.

A rollercoaster corkscrews at Sea World theme park in Queensland, Australia.

Many of the country's most well-known parks are located in Florida. Walt Disney World, SeaWorld, Watermania, Wet 'n Wild, and Universal Studios are just a few of the many parks located in Orlando. Busch Gardens and Adventure Island are both in Tampa.

Key players in the theme park industry

Discover Some Unique Theme Parks in the World of Attractions Book

Walt Disney World is composed of four major theme parks: Magic Kingdom, Epcot, Disney's Animal Kingdom, and Disney–MGM Studios, with more than 100 attractions; 22 resort hotels themed to faraway lands; spectacular nighttime entertainment; and vast shopping, dining, and recreation facilities that cover thousands of acres in this tropical paradise.[3]

Walt Disney World includes 25 lighted tennis courts, 99 holes of championship golf, marinas, swimming pools, jogging and bike trails, water skiing, and motor boating. The resort also offers a unique zoological park and bird sanctuary that is alive with birds, monkeys, and alligators; lots of restaurants, lounges, and food courts; a nightclub metropolis to please nearly any musical palate; a starry-eyed tribute to 1930s Hollywood; and even bass fishing. Walt Disney World is always full of new surprises: It now features the world's most unusual water adventure park, a "snow-covered" mountain with a ski-resort theme called Blizzard Beach.[4]

Three new Disney hotels are architecturally exciting and more affordable than ever. The fun-filled Disney's All-Star Sports Resort and Disney's colorful All-Star Music Resort are categorized as value-class hotels. Disney's Wilderness Lodge is one of the park's jewels, with its impressive tall-timber atrium-lobby and rooms built around a Rocky Mountain geyser pool.

For nighttime fun, there are numerous restaurants and nightclubs near Pleasure Island. In all, the park has a cast of thousands of hosts, hostesses, and entertainers famous for their warm smiles and commitment to making every night an especially good one for Disney guests.

Magic Kingdom

The heart of Walt Disney World is its first famous theme park, the Magic Kingdom, which is the "happiest land on earth," where "age relives fond memories" and "youth may savor the challenge and promise of the future." It is a giant theatrical stage, where guests become part of exciting Disney adventures. It is also the home of Mickey Mouse, Snow White, Peter Pan, Tom Sawyer, Davy Crockett, and the Swiss Family Robinson.

More than 40 major shows and ride-through attractions, not to mention shops and unique dining facilities, fill its seven lands of imagination. Each land carries out its theme in fascinating detail—architecture, transportation, music, costumes, dining, shopping, and entertainment are designed to create a total atmosphere where guests can leave the ordinary world behind. The seven lands include the following:[5]

> "Theme parks offer a place for the whole family to go—for a day or an entire vacation."
>
> Kristen Biggs, *Walt Disney World*, Orlando, FL

Main Street, U.S.A.—Turn-of-the-century charm with horse-drawn streetcars, horseless carriages, a penny arcade, and a grand-circle tour on Walt Disney World's Steam Railroad

Adventureland—Explore with Pirates of the Caribbean, a wild animal Jungle Cruise, the Swiss Family Treehouse, a Tropical Serenade by birds, flowers, and tikis

Frontierland—Thrills on Splash Mountain and Big Thunder Mountain Railroad, musical fun in Country Bear Jamboree, Shooting Gallery, Tom Sawyer Island caves and raft rides

Liberty Square—Steamboating on the Rivers of America, mystery in the Haunted Mansion, whooping it up in Diamond Horseshoe Saloon, viewing the impressive Hall of Presidents with the addition of President Bill Clinton in a speaking role

Fantasyland—Cinderella Castle is the gateway to the new Legend of the Lion King plus Peter Pan's Flight, Snow White's Adventure, Mr. Toad's Wild Ride, Dumbo the Flying Elephant, Alice's Mad Tea Party, musical cruise with doll-like dancers in It's a Small World, Cinderella's Golden Carousel, and Skyway cable car to Tomorrowland

Mickey's Toontown Fair—Mickey's House, Grandma Duck's Farm, Mickey's Treehouse playground, and private photo session in Mickey's Dressing Room

New Tomorrowland—Sci-Fi city of the future, new frightening Alien Encounter, Transportarium time machine travels in Circle-Vision 360, new whirling Astro-Orbiter, speedy Space Mountain, new production of Carousel of Progress, Grand Prix Raceway, elevated Transit tour, new Disney Character show on Tomorrowland Stage.[6]

Epcot

Epcot is a unique, permanent, and ever-changing world's fair with two major themes: Future World and World Showcase. Highlights include IllumiNations, a nightly spectacle of fireworks, fountains, lasers, and classical music.

Future World shows an amazing exposition of technology for the near future for home, work, and play in INNOVENTIONS. The newest consumer products are continually added. Major pavilions exploring the past, present, and future are shown in the Spaceship Earth story of communications. The Universe of Energy giant dinosaurs help explain the origin and future of energy. There are also the Wonders of Life with spectacular Body Wars, Cranium Command and other medical health subjects, the World of Motion soon-to-be test track, Journey into Imagination, the Land, with spectacular agricultural research and environmental growing areas, and The Living Seas, the world's largest indoor ocean with thousands of tropical sea creatures.

Around the World Showcase Lagoon are pavilions where guests can see world-famous landmarks, and sample the native foods, entertainment, and culture of 11 nations:[7]

- Mexico—Mexico's fiesta plaza and boat trip on El Rio Del Tiempo, plus San Angel Inn for authentic Mexican cuisine
- Norway—Thrilling Viking boat journey and Akershus Royal Banquet Hall
- China—Wonders of China Circle-Vision 360 film tour from the Great Wall to the Yangtze River, plus Nine Dragons Restaurant
- Germany—Authentic Biergarten restaurant
- Italy—St. Mark's Square street players and L'Originale Alfredo di Roma Ristorante
- United States—The American Adventure's stirring historical drama
- Japan—Re-creating an imperial palace, plus Teppanyaki Dining Rooms
- Morocco—Morocco's palatial Restaurant Marrakesh
- France—Impressions de France film tour of the French countryside, Chefs de France
- United Kingdom—Shakespearean street players, plus Rose & Crown Pub
- Canada—Halifax to Vancouver Circle-Vision 360 tour

Each showcase has additional snack facilities and a variety of shops featuring arts, crafts, and merchandise from each nation.

Disney–MGM Studios[8]

With 50 major shows, shops, restaurants, ride-through adventures, and backstage tours, the Disney–MGM Studios combines real working motion picture, animation, and television studios with exciting movie attractions. The newest adventure in the Sunset Boulevard theater district is the Twilight Zone™ Tower of Terror, with a stunning 13-story elevator fall. The famous Mann's Chinese Theater on Hollywood Boulevard houses the Great Movie Ride.

Other major attractions include a Backstage visits to Epcot, the Magic Kingdom, Disney's Hollywood studios, Disney's Animal Kingdom, the Walt Disney World Nursery and Tree Farm and Central Studios. All this and much more are what help make Walt Disney World the most popular destination resort in the world. What causes the most comment from guests is the cleanliness, the friendliness of its cast, and the unbelievable attention to detail—a blend of showmanship and imagination that provides an endless variety of adventure and enjoyment.

Animal Kingdom focuses on nature and the animal world around us. Guests can go on time-traveling rides and come face to face with animals from the prehistoric past to the present. Shows are put on featuring Disney's most popular animal-based films, such as Toy Story 3. Los Angeles's Animal Kingdom also offers safari tours that bring guests up close and personal with live giraffes, elephants, and hippopotamuses.

Walt Disney World's two water parks are Blizzard Beach and Typhoon Lagoon. Blizzard Beach has a unique ski resort theme, while Typhoon Lagoon is based on the legend that a powerful storm swept through, leaving pools and rapids in its wake. Both parks offer a variety of slides, tube rides, pools, and moving rivers that drift throughout the parks.

Universal Studios[9]

Universal Studios has been giving guided tours on its famous movie sets for over 30 years, and tens of thousands of people visit Universal every day. Since its founding, Universal Studios has become the most formidable competitor facing the Disney Company.

Opening in Orlando, Florida, Universal Studios has enjoyed huge success, despite encroaching into the "kingdom" of Disney. In addition to its Hollywood and Orlando parks, Universal has since expanded into Spain, China, and Japan. One reason for Universal's success is its adaptation of movies into thrill rides. Another is its commitment to guest participation. Guests

Universal Studios theme park, Orlando, Florida.

Universal Studios PortAventura in Spain offers five worlds of fun and entertainment, from China to Polynesia, Mexico, the Far West, and the Mediterranean, all with an array of thrilling rides and experiences for movie buffs of all ages.

Universal Studios Experience in Beijing, China, gives the visitor a tantalizing taste of Hollywood, and is known to be a fun and educational experience for the whole family. For the younger audience, the park also offers nightlife and entertainment, "American Style"!

Universal Studios Japan features 18 rides and shows, some brand new and others old favorites, plus great dining and shopping.

help make sound effects and can participate in "stunts," making Universal Studios more than just a "look behind the scenes."

Universal Studios is also a good example of what is predicted to occur in the future with regards to amusement and theme parks. It is offering more realistic thrill rides by combining new technologies and state-of-the-art equipment. Also, the company has realized that visitors tend to go to theme parks just because they happen to be in the area. By greatly expanding the experience, NBC Universal is hoping that its improvements will make travelers want to visit Universal Studios as a one-stop destination.

Let's take a closer look at the Universal theme parks:[10]

Universal Studios Hollywood was the first Universal park, and is now the world's largest movie studio and theme park. As part of its new studio tour, you will be taken into the Tomb of the Mummy, feel the hot breath of King Kong, experience a major earthquake, and find yourself in the middle of a Hollywood movie shoot. Afterwards, you can "chill" at the Universal CityWalk, a street that claims to offer the best in food, nightlife, shopping, and entertainment.

Universal Orlando is a destination in itself, with two theme parks, several themed resorts, and a bustling City Walk. In Universal Studios, like in the Hollywood park, you can explore the exciting world of movie making. *Islands of Adventure*, gives you the best in roller coasters and thrill rides, whereas *Wet 'n Wild* gives you the opportunity to enjoy a range of cool waterslides, among other things. If you're not already exhausted by the mere thought of it, you could check out CityWalk for some food, shopping, and a taste of the hottest nightlife in town. Myriads of venues, popular with tourists and locals alike, offer an amazing variety of cool bars, hot clubs, and live music.

SeaWorld Parks and Entertainment

HTi Explore a Variety of National Attractions with Splashtown's Marketing Director

SeaWorld Parks and Entertainment includes Busch Gardens and is a division of Blackstone Group. The animal parks not only offer guests from around the world the opportunity to see and experience the wonders of many marine and land animals, but they also have highly developed educational programs. These programs reach millions of people a year, in the parks, on TV, and over the Internet, informing them on topics such as endangered animals, the environment, and the wonders of the ocean. In addition, the SeaWorld Parks and Entertainment Corporation is active within conservation, research, and wildlife assistance worldwide.

The company is dedicated to preserving marine life. It uses innovative programs to research various wildlife dilemmas. It also participates in breeding, animal rescue, rehabilitation, and conservation efforts throughout the year. What the company does for the preservation of animals is important to the existence of their theme parks. This is because the parks' research and rescue programs are subsidized through guest revenue. Also, each park offers unique shows and attractions combining entertainment and education with a strong commitment to research and conservation.

Currently, the SeaWorld Parks and Entertainment Company runs the following parks in the United States:[11]

Sea World—The three Sea World parks are located in California, Florida, and Texas. Each park has various themes, marine and animal attractions, shows, rides, and educational exhibits. Sea World is based on the creatures of the sea. Guests can pet dolphins and other fish, watch shows featuring Shamu, the famous killer whale, and learn

Guests at a theme park petting dolphins.

all about the mysteries of the sea. Several rides are also available at Sea World, and countless exhibits feature everything from stingrays to penguins.

Busch Gardens—These theme parks feature both exciting thrill rides and attractions in addition to large zoos and safari parks. Busch Gardens, located in both Tampa, Florida, and Williamsburg, Virginia, is perhaps the most well known of the animal-themed parks. Busch Gardens is like a zoo with a twist. It features equal amounts of thrill rides and animal attractions. Guests can take a train ride through the Serengeti Plains, where zebras and antelope run wild, hop aboard a giant tube ride through the Congo River rapids, or ride on one of the parks' many world-record-holding roller coasters. The theme for the Williamsburg Park is that of the seventeenth century charm of the Old World European atmosphere.

Adventure Island is also located in Tampa and It is also the only water theme park on Florida's West Coast, featuring several unique water play areas and thrilling splash rides. The water park comprises more than 25 acres of fun-filled water rides, cafés, and shops.

Water Country USA—theme park is located in Williamsburg, Virginia. It is "the mid-Atlantic's largest water park, featuring more than 30 water rides and attractions, live entertainment, shopping, and restaurants." Like Adventure Island, Water Country has an educational atmosphere to help guests, especially children, learn water safety techniques. Everything in the park is set to the theme of the 1950s surfing era.

Sesame Place—This 14-acre park is located in Langhorne, Pennsylvania, and is dedicated totally to a Sesame Street theme. It is designed to stimulate children's natural curiosity to learn and explore, while helping them build self-confidence as they interact with other children.

Discovery Cove—Adjacent to Sea World in Orlando, Florida, Discovery Cove is an exclusive, reservations-only tropical paradise, offering up-close encounters with dolphins and other exotic sea life., Guests can swim with dolphins, snorkel through a coral reef, a tropical river, waterfalls, and an amazing freshwater lagoon.

Hershey's[12]

What does the name Hershey bring to mind? In 1894, Milton Hershey, a small-time candy manufacturer, decided he wanted to make chocolate to coat his caramels. He opened his new establishment in Lancaster, Pennsylvania, and named it Hershey Chocolate Company. In the 1900s, the company started to produce mass quantities of milk chocolate, which brought immediate success. Soon after, Hershey decided that there was a need to increase his production facilities. He built a new factory in the farmlands of south-central Pennsylvania in Derry Township. Many product lines were expanded in the following decades. In 1968, the company was renamed Hershey Foods Corporation. Today, the company is the leading manufacturer of chocolate, nonchocolate confectionery, and grocery products in North America. It exports to over 90 countries, has approximately 13,700 employees, and has net sales in excess of $4 billion.[13]

In 1907, Milton Hershey opened Hershey Park, a leisure park for employees of Hershey's Company. He wanted to create a place for his employees to relax and have some fun when they were not on the job. The park was small and simple, offering employees a place to picnic, canoe, and walk around the beautifully landscaped grounds. In 1908, the park started its soon-to-be huge expansion with the addition of a merry-go-round.

In the years to come, the park added more rides and attractions. As the park continued to expand, the company decided to open the park's doors to the public. It became a small regional park with a pay-as-you-ride policy.

In 1971, the park was redeveloped and became a large theme park. A one-time admission fee replaced the pay-as-you-ride policy, and the name "Hershey Park" was changed to Hersheypark. Today, the park sits on over 110 acres and offers visitors over 60 rides and attractions.[14]

Check Your Knowledge

1. What is Knott's Berry Farm?
2. Why did Walt Disney really create Disneyland?
3. Discuss your favorite theme park with your class. Explain why it is your favorite.

.inc | Corporate Profile

SIX FLAGS

Six Flags is a world-renowned theme park. The company owns and operates 21 different parks spread out over North America, Latin America, and Europe. Locations include Mexico City, Belgium, France, Spain, Germany, and most major metropolitan areas in the United States. In fact, having a park in 40 of the 50 major metropolitan areas in the United States has earned Six Flags the title of world's largest regional theme park company. Annually, millions entertain themselves at Six Flags theme parks worldwide. Six Flags prides itself in claiming that 98 percent of the U.S. population is within an eight-hour drive to any one of its many theme parks.

Who is behind this huge success? The founder of the first theme park was Angus Wynne, a Texas oil baron with a vision: to create a family entertainment park that was fun as well as affordable and, most importantly, within reachable distance to where people lived. Wynne transformed a simple amusement park into a theme park by adding innovative rides with theme presentations. He opened his first park in Texas in 1961 to huge crowds.

The park was named after the six different flags that flew over Texas at one time, representing the six different countries that marked Texas's past history. The theme park was divided into six different regions, each modeled after the country it represented. Visitors could marvel at Spanish haciendas or French bistros, all the while in the company of Southern belles and pirates.

Today, Six Flags has a licensing agreement with DC Comics and Warner Bros. This means that characters such as Batman, Superman, and Bugs Bunny and the gang can be found wandering around the parks and having their pictures taken with park visitors. With fantastic rides and show-stopping entertainment, the parks have become one of the first-choice amusement parks for entertainment-seeking families and individuals.

Funding for the expansion of the company was drawn primarily from the profits made from the first successful Six Flag parks, including the first one in Texas. In 1996, Six Flags went public, meaning that it allowed the public to purchase its stock as opposed to hand-picked private investors. The shares were sold at $18 each, and their purchase totaled nearly $70 million. Just one year later, the company had raised $200 million with its public offering. With these kinds of funds, Six Flags continued to buy land or old amusement parks to turn them into Six Flags theme parks, rapidly expanding its reach.

Six Flags now offers "print and go tickets" from home, making it easier for guests to enjoy the park experience by avoiding one lineup. Each location has different rides with names like Goliath, Boomerang, The Rattler, Superman, Gullywasher and Road Runner.

If you are looking for a job in the theme park business, you might be interested in knowing that Six Flags employs thousands of seasonal workers and about 3,500 full-time employees all over the world. Employees commit to providing a fun and challenging experience for visitors. Six Flags offer competitive wages as well as varied benefits suitable for different ages. Six Flags also offers exciting internships for college students. You can apply for seasonal jobs online at http://www.sixflagsjobs.com/.

> "The more complex the world becomes, the more people turn to the past and the simple things in life. We [as in the amusement park operators] try to give them some of those things."

Introducing Walt Disney

A Man Turns a Vision and a Dream into Reality

To All who come to this happy place: Welcome! Disneyland is your land; here, age relives fond memories of the past, and here youth may savor the challenge and promise of the future.

Disneyland is dedicated to the hard facts that have created America, with the hope that it will be a source of joy and inspiration to all the world.

—Disneyland Dedication Plaque, July 17, 1955

In 1923, at age 21, Walt Disney arrived in Los Angeles from Kansas City to start a new business with his brother Roy. The first venture was a series of "shorts" (short movies) called *Alice Comedies*, which featured a child actress playing with animated characters. Realizing that they needed something new to capture the audience, Walt Disney conjured up the concept of a mouse. Mickey and Minnie Mouse first appeared in *Steamboat Willie*, which also incorporated music and sound. Audiences were ecstatic about the Disney Brothers, who became an overnight success.

During the next few years, Walt and Roy made many Mickey Mouse films. This earned them enough money to develop other projects, including full-length motion pictures in Technicolor. Their first film was *Snow White and the Seven Dwarfs*. Several other movies followed, and then they launched the television program, *The Mickey Mouse Club* (which is still on today!).

Walt Disney said that Disneyland really began when his two daughters were very young. Saturday was always "Daddy's Day," and he would take them to the merry-go-round and sit on a bench eating peanuts while they rode. Sitting there, he felt that there should be some kind of a family park where parents and children could have fun together.

Walt's original dream was not easy to bring to reality. Walt had to deal with about 300 banks just to get Disneyland open; even on opening day there were challenges—larger than expected crowds, long lines at the popular rides, and a cash flow that was so tight that the cashiers had to rush the admission money to the bank in order to make payroll. Fortunately, since those early days, Disneyland and the Disney characters have become a part of not only Walt Disney, but also of the American dream.

By the early 1960s, Walt had turned most of his attention from film to real estate. Because he was upset when cheap motels and souvenir shops popped up around Disneyland, for his next venture, Walt Disney World, he bought 27,000 acres around the park. The center of Walt Disney World was to be the Experimental Prototype Community of Tomorrow (Epcot). Regrettably, Epcot and Walt Disney world were his dying dreams, as Walt Disney succumbed to cancer in 1966. The ensuing years have given Disney phenomenal success with Epcot, movies, a TV station, the Disney Channel, Disney stores, and Disney–MGM Studios theme park, Euro Disney, Tokyo Disneyland, and Disneyland Hong Kong.

Hopefully you will dream big and have success in turning your dream into reality.

Source: 1. Randy Bright, *Disneyland: Inside Story.* (New York: Abrams, 1987), p. 33.

REGIONAL THEME PARKS

Uncover the Importance of Regional Theme Parks

Dollywood[15]

In 1961, a small attraction with a Civil War theme called Rebel Railroad opened its doors to the public. The name Rebel Road was later changed to Goldrush Junction, and the theme was changed to resemble the Wild West. Today, this attraction is known across the world as Dollywood; in 1986, Dolly Parton became a co-owner of the park and changed the

❝ Dollywood brings in over 2.5 million visitors every year. ❞

name once again. The park sits on 125 acres in the foothills of the Great Smoky Mountains in Pigeon Forge, Tennessee. In addition to having all the rides of an amusement park, Dollywood is enriched with the culture of the Smoky Mountains. The park includes crafts such as blacksmithing, glass blowing, and wood carving. It also continues to host several festivals, concerts, and musical events. Today, Dollywood brings in over 2.5 million visitors every year and continues to be Tennessee's number one tourist attraction.

LEGOLAND[16]

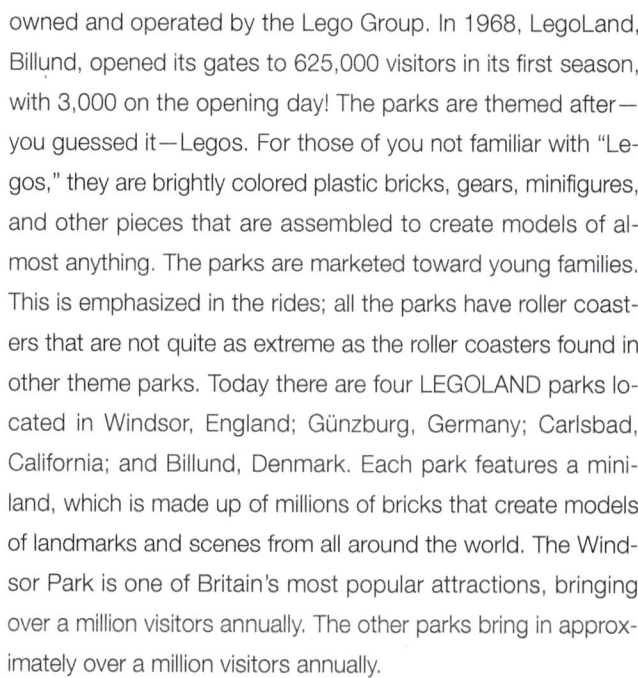

LEGOLAND is a theme park owned and operated by the Lego Group. In 1968, LegoLand, Billund, opened its gates to 625,000 visitors in its first season, with 3,000 on the opening day! The parks are themed after—you guessed it—Legos. For those of you not familiar with "Legos," they are brightly colored plastic bricks, gears, minifigures, and other pieces that are assembled to create models of almost anything. The parks are marketed toward young families. This is emphasized in the rides; all the parks have roller coasters that are not quite as extreme as the roller coasters found in other theme parks. Today there are four LEGOLAND parks located in Windsor, England; Günzburg, Germany; Carlsbad, California; and Billund, Denmark. Each park features a miniland, which is made up of millions of bricks that create models of landmarks and scenes from all around the world. The Windsor Park is one of Britain's most popular attractions, bringing over a million visitors annually. The other parks bring in approximately over a million visitors annually.

Gatorland[17]

Gatorland is a 110-acre theme park and wildlife preserve located in Orange County, Florida. Back after World War II, Owen Godwin decided that he wanted to build an attraction on his land that would provide a close-up view of Florida's animals in their native habitat. He bought a 16-acre plot located off of Florida's second most traveled highway, and opened the attraction's doors to the public under the name of the Florida Wildlife Institute in 1949. In 1954, Godwin once again changed the name of the attraction to what it is known as today—Gatorland.

The 1960s brought growth to the tourism industry in Florida. As the industry grew, Gatorland continued to expand by adding a number of exhibits and attractions. Today, Gatorland features alligators, crocodiles, a breeding marsh, reptilian shows, a petting zoo, a swamp walk, educational programs, and train rides. In addition, it offers various shows: Gators on the Go, a mobile show that allows younger kids a chance to interact with the parks cuddlier critters, Gator Jumparoo, which features alligators jumping four to five feet out of the water to retrieve food; Gator Wrestlin', in which wranglers catch an alligator by hand; and Upclose Encounters, where visitors meet wildlife from around the globe. One of the oldest attractions in the area, Gatorland is still privately owned by Godwin's family today.

Wet 'n Wild[18]

Wet 'n Wild was founded by George Millay in Orlando, Florida, in 1977. George Millay is also known as the creator of Sea World. Wet 'n Wild is considered the United States' first major water park. Millay received the first Lifetime Achievement Award from the World Waterpark Association for having created Wet 'n Wild: he was named the official "Father of the Waterpark."

Today, Wet 'n Wild is a chain of water parks with locations in Florida and North Carolina. The Wet 'n Wild North Carolina, located in Greensboro, features over 36 rides and attractions, which are classified "from mild to wild." Wet 'n Wild Orlando also offers something for everyone. Its rides fall into four categories: "Thrill Rides," "Multi-Person Rides," " Kids Rides," and "other activities." In 1998, Millay sold the Orlando Park to Universal Studios Recreation Group. The park was featured on Travel Channel's Extreem Waterparks and the park was also used for a music video by the Pet Shop boys.

THEME PARK MANAGEMENT

Managing theme parks is similar to managing other hospitality operations. The managerial process begins with the key elements of management: the first being *planning*, followed by *organizing*, *decision making*, *communicating*, *motivating*, and *controlling*. *Planning* for theme parks includes preopening. During the preopening stage, someone plans what type of park to

Sustainable Theme Parks

Because of their size, theme parks present both a challenge and an opportunity in terms of sustainability. One interesting new park is the Springs Preserve, which is a 180-acre green cultural park designed to commemorate Las Vegas's dynamic history and to provide a vision for a sustainable future. The Preserve features museums, galleries, outdoor concerts, and events such as green weddings, Easter Bunny Hops, and green meetings with environmentally responsible venues and practices. It also includes colorful botanical gardens and an interpretive trail system that meanders through scenic wetland habitat. The Springs Preserve is the largest commercial straw bale construction in the U.S. and is aiming for "platinum" LEED status (the highest possible) for seven of its buildings. It is even installing carpets made of recycled pop bottles.[19]

Matt Hickman writes in his blog:[20] One of the oldest amusement parks in the world, founded in 1843, is also one of the greenest: Tivoli Gardens in Copenhagen, Denmark. Although the Disneyland-inspiring park itself is not focused on sustainability—it's a rather old-fashioned amusement park with thrill rides, an aquarium, concert hall, and cultural attractions—Tivoli has long been keen on minding Mother Nature while entertaining and enchanting guests. Some of the green practices at Tivoli include a tram that runs on biofuel; an innovative, deposit-based recycling program that saves 1.2 million plastic cups from being landfilled annually; the use of ecofriendly cleaning products and the minimal use of chemical-based landscaping products; the widespread installation of LED light bulbs; in-park eateries that focus on the use of local, seasonal, and vegetarian ingredients; and special Climate and Energy Days. Most recently, in an ongoing attempt to go carbon neutral, Tivoli announced that it hopes to completely power the park via an offshore wind turbine that will be installed this year.[21]

Stateside, major theme parks are starting to give their inherently unsustainable operations a fresh, green sheen. Last year (along with bankruptcy), Six Flags announced a major greening campaign that includes partnering with Coca-Cola to add 3,000 more recycling bins to parks; partnering with Perf Green to replace plastic trash bags with biodegradable ones; doing away with diesel and reusing vegetable oil generated in park kitchens to power vehicles and trains; beefing up paper recycling efforts; and installing water-saving fixtures throughout the parks. The company is also considering installing "solar farms" that would provide clean power to adjacent parks.

Mickey Mouse and Co. are becoming more and more earth-friendly as Disney Parks continue to address ways to handle the not-so-magical environmental repercussions that come along with operating massive theme parks/resorts. Key focus areas include water and energy conservation, greenhouse gas emission reduction, waste minimization, ecosystem conservation, and eco-inspirational branding. Disney is also taking Tivoli's lead and looking at the possibility of wind power.[22]

---

open, where to open it, what kinds of rides and attractions to have, and predicts the number of people expected to come to the park. One of the challenges for park operators is in adding new rides and attractions to keep guests interested, because a high percentage of park guests are repeat guests.

Once the park is open, planning focuses on the operation of the park, including forecasting the number of daily visitors, and logistics such as traffic flow and wait times for rides. Once the park has calculated the attendance numbers, it can determine the sales figures. With the dollar sales amount forecasted, the sales departments can work on their budgets for expenses.

An important part of planning is staffing the park. With an idea of how many guests are likely to attend the park, managers can schedule the correct number of staff to serve guests. Parks have a number of full-time employees who are supplemented by part-timers and seasonal workers.

Organizing includes creating a structure so that the park's divisions have the right support teams in place to allow them to serve the guests. Departments include reservations, parking, guest services, rides, special events, stores, animals, foodservice, security, maintenance, uniforms, cleaning, and gardening. Depending on the size of the park, departments employ anywhere from several to hundreds of individuals.

Another example of organizing is the "fast pass." This idea came about because parks lose money when people are standing in line for a ride instead of spending money at stores

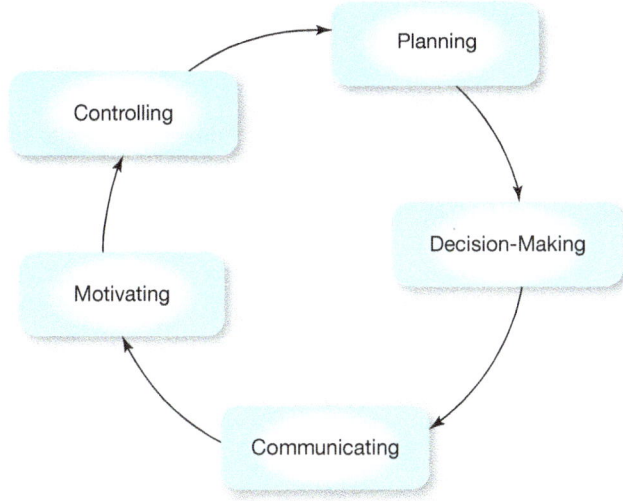

FIGURE 12–1 Elements of Management.

and restaurants. When guests swipe a fast pass at each ride, they are given a time to return, and they are allowed to then go to the front of the line. From the park's point of view, the less time guests spend in line, the more money they will spend.

Decision making includes the long-range decisions made by top and middle management and the short-range decisions made by frontline managers and supervisors. Managers and supervisors make lots of operational decisions every day; these decisions keep parks running smoothly and help enhance the guest experience.

Communicating in theme parks is done by computer, e-mails, and telephone (this includes "Bluetooth"-type headsets for hands-free communications). Employees get updates in pre-shift huddles.

Motivating employees is important to guest satisfaction. You have probably experienced a workplace where people were not motivated or happy, so you can appreciate an atmosphere where everyone is genuine in their desire to please you. The happiness of guests depends on the happiness of employees. Everyone is motivated in their own way, yet there is some commonality: to be motivated, people seek recognition, responsibility, achievement, advancement, and the creation of an excellent work climate.

Control provides information to management for decision-making purposes. For example, control gives management the number of guests visiting the park each day and the sales figures in all the areas: entrance, rides, food, beverage, shops, and other outlets. Control provides information on actual labor costs so that a comparison can be made with sales and the budget and any variance investigated. Control brings everything full circle by leading back to planning. Figure 12–1 shows the elements of management.

Check Your Knowledge

1. How did Dollywood begin?
2. Why did Milton Hershey open the leisure park?
3. What are the elements of theme park management?

> **The "fast pass" came about because parks lose money when people are standing in line for a ride instead of spending money at stores and restaurants.**

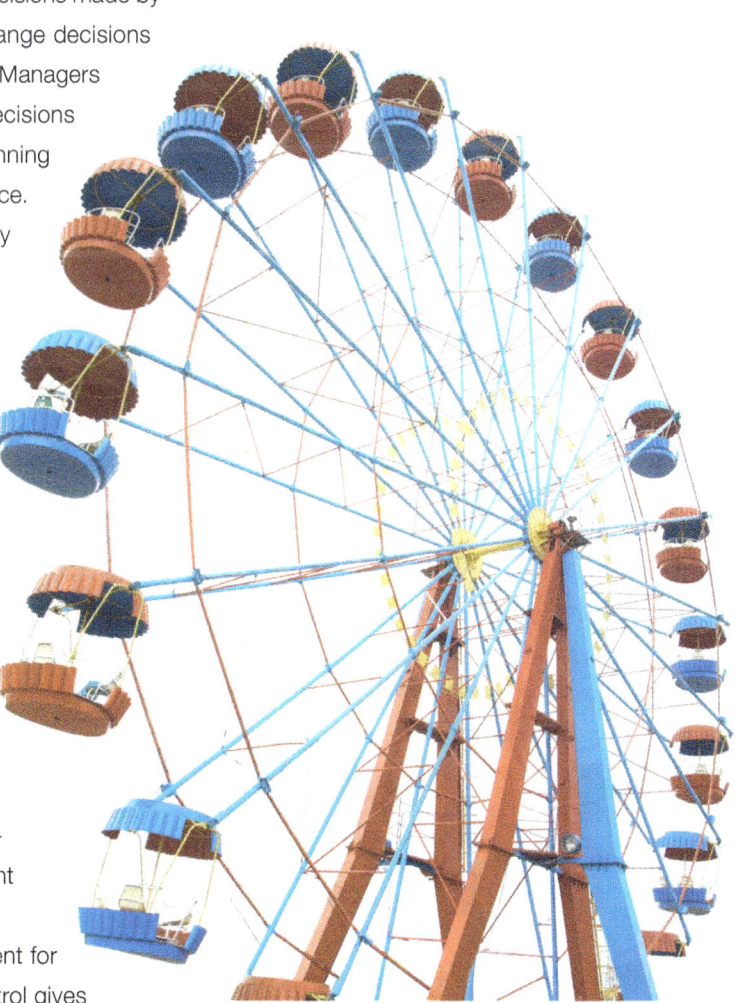

Fairs, festivals, and events

Oktoberfest celebration in Munich, Germany.

Believe it or not, but Woodstock, Gay Pride, the Olympic Games, and your local farmers' fair have something in common. They can all be described under the umbrella of **event tourism**. This is a relatively new term, and is defined as the systematic planning, development, and marketing of **festivals** and special events as tourist attractions, development catalysts, and image builders for attractions and destination areas. However, it is important to note that events often fall under more than one category (event/sports tourism, event/heritage tourism, and so on).

In each case, travel, accommodations, and restaurant meals become a part of the travel and tourism experience. Indeed, over the past few years, event tourism has been a rapidly growing segment of the tourism industry. **Fairs**, festivals, and events are public celebrations that are staged the world over, although it is often difficult to tell the difference among the three categories. In general, however, fairs are usually larger and extend over a longer period of time. Event tourism may range from local street festivals and fairs, to county, state, or provincial fairs, to the World Fairs. Each event enriches our lives and provides interesting career opportunities in such fields as event management.

Festivals or special events have a high degree of uniqueness, which distinguishes them from permanent attractions. Some festivals and events appear to be staged purely in order to attract tourists. Many cities in the United States are well known for their festivals, which bring in droves of vacationers year after year. In this section, we will examine some of the more notable festivals and events.

Oktoberfest

With its rivers of beer and rowdy people, Oktoberfest has taken on a life of its own. The first Oktoberfest was held on October 17, 1810, in Munich, in honor of the marriage of Crown Prince Ludwig of Bavaria to Princess Therese Von Sare-Hildburghausen. These days, the festival has become, above all, a celebration of German beer. The Lord Mayor of Munich opens the first barrel, and the 16-day festival begins. Both citizens and tourists flock to this event; it is marked by folk costume parades in which brewery horses pull floats and decorated beer wagons through the streets. Oktoberfest celebrations are modeled in North American cities. The Munich Oktoberfest—known by the locals as the "Wiesn"—is the biggest public festival in the world. Each year, about 6 million visitors attend Oktoberfest.[23]

The Carnival in Rio de Janeiro, Brazil

The world's most famous carnival is Rio's main event, and it happens at the peak of the Brazilian summer. This four-day celebration attracts thousands of people from all corners of the world, starting on a Saturday and ending on Fat Tuesday (Mardi Gras). The concept originated as a pagan celebration in ancient Rome or Greece, and was imported from Italy in the late nineteenth century. During Rio's Golden Age in the thirties, the famous Samba Parade was added—and is now the main attraction of the Carnival. The whole city participates in this free event.

Reggae on the River

Music festivals are held in virtually every state and province in the United States and Canada, each one attracting thousands of people. Whether some festivals are larger than others and travel from place to place—making it easier for leisure travelers to come to the event, like the Horde Festival—or whether they are smaller, like Benbow, California's Reggae on the River, all festivals are considerably important in the area of leisure travel.

Carnival in Rio de Janeiro, Brazil.

Reggae on the River's success is reflective of what is happening in the leisure travel industry. Leisure travel is beginning to encompass a larger market because more events, festivals, and other activities have sprung up to meet a variety of personal interests. For instance, when the Reggae festival first began in 1984, it attracted only 1,200 visitors. Today, however, the festival is known as the best reggae and world music festival in the United States. The festival's 10,000 tickets are always sold out in advance. It takes more than six months to plan, and requires the help of 1,000 volunteers.[24]

Mardi Gras

Mardi Gras began over 100 years ago as a carnival and has evolved into a world-renowned party. This festival in New Orleans is arguably the most flamboyant of all festivals, and takes place in January, February, and March. Festivities begin on January 6, with a series of private balls. The days leading up to Fat Tuesday are filled with wild parades, costume contests, concerts, and overall partying. The famous Bourbon Street is home to most of the party-going crowd and it is often too crowded to even walk down. Beads are big at Mardi Gras, and thousands are given out each year. The culture of New Orleans adds greatly to the festiveness of Mardi Gras, as traditional jazz and blues can always be heard on most street corners. The tempo picks up in the last two weeks of the carnival season, when streets are filled with some 30 separate parades. The parades consist of marching jazz bands and lavishly decorated two-story floats carrying people dressed in costume throwing beads out to the crowd. Each of the 20 or so floats in the parades is decorated to express a particular theme. The largest and most elaborate parades, the Krewe of Endymion and Bacchus parades, take place on the weekend before Mardi Gras, designated the "Day of Un-Rule."[25]

Grand Ole Opry

Another famous site of interest is the Grand Ole Opry in Nashville, Tennessee. The Grand Ole Opry is a live radio show in which country music guests are featured. Started over 75 years ago, the Grand Ole Opry is what made Nashville "Music City." Since the Opry's start, Nashville has created a theme park, Opryland, and a hotel, the Opryland Resort. Famous musicians come from all over the world to showcase their talents, and tourists flock from everywhere to hear the sounds of the Opry and see the sites that Nashville has to offer.[26]

Employment

Grasp the Economic Impact of Theme Parks on the Economy

There are over 350,000 workers in the theme park industry. These employees come to work every day because they like to be surrounded by people who are enjoying a fun and exciting experience. There are many different kinds of employees of theme parks including designers and artists, inspectors and repairers, scientists, and "other professionals."

Designers and artists come up with new ride concepts, develop technical plans for the ride, and paint and decorate the finished product. They also may create costumes for shows and backdrops for stage setups. They are usually creative individuals who enjoy working with a team to get a project done correctly.

It is helpful for designers in the industry to have some knowledge of computer programs, such as computer aided drafting (CAD), Adobe Illustrator, or Photoshop. Those who design new rides need a background in structural, mechanical, or electrical engineering.

There are many job opportunities for inspectors and repairers in the theme park industry. These employees are very important because they are the people who ensure the safety of everyone at the park. Safety inspectors and specialists are responsible for checking rides for comfort, safety, and durability.

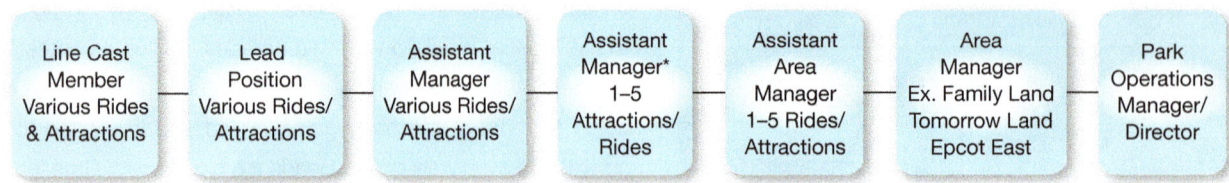

* Depending on the size of the operation.

FIGURE 12–2 A Career Path in the Theme Park Industry.

Safety inspectors must be certified through the **National Association of Amusement Ride Safety Officials.** After proper experience and education in the inspection area, one can advance to a senior or lead inspector. These people have a very strong background in any type of engineering and use special equipment and test dummies to evaluate rides. They conduct experiments that calculate the effect of physical forces on a passenger and do other calculations or experiments to discover whether a rider will get a headache or neck strain from the ride and the restraints.

Ride mechanics and maintenance managers are also integral to the operation of rides. They are responsible for identifying specific problems and fixing them. These jobs also require a background in structural or mechanical engineering.

Scientists of different types are also important to theme park operation. Horticulturists and landscape architects are needed to landscape the park. They maintain the grounds and often oversee large groups of people to be sure that all plants are healthy and cared for. They typically have associate's or bachelor's degrees in their field.

Biologists and zoologists play a huge role in many theme park operations. Many parks have wildlife attractions, and some even consider animals to be the main draw for crowds. These employees take care of the animals, oversee their habitats, and sometimes even participate in shows with the animals. The educational requirements for this field range from an associate's degree to a doctorate.

Most parks employ human resources and public relations specialists who communicate with other employees and the public. A strong background in communications or human resources is recommended for these positions.

> **There are over 350,000 workers in the theme park industry.**

Sales and marketing specialists also work at theme parks. They are responsible for promoting the amusement park and bringing in guests. They promote the park on a large scale, offering vacation packages to travel agents and large groups. They also analyze park data to determine the best marketing strategies. A background in sales and marketing is necessary for these jobs.

Theme park managers work in all areas and at all levels of the amusement park industry. General managers or upper-level managers oversee many different departments. They usually need a bachelor's or master's degree in business or management, as well as years of experience.

Beneath park managers are department managers, such as food and beverage service managers or ride operation managers. More managers may work within these departments. (For example, a manager for a particular restaurant works under the food and beverage service department manager.)

Salaries for theme park frontline managers range from $20,000 to $50,000 per year. Middle managers earn up to $75,000 and general managers make up to $100,000 annually. One big perk of being an employee of a theme park is that regardless of position, all employees usually receive free admission to the park and discounts on food, beverages, and merchandise. Figure 12–2 shows a possible career path in the theme park industry.

Check Your Knowledge

1. Define event tourism.
2. What is the difference between fairs and festivals?
3. Describe some career possibilities in theme parks.

TRENDS *in* THE THEME PARK INDUSTRY

- New parks focus on themes that are tied to the country or local region in which they are located.
- Theme parks are becoming more of a symbol for regional pride, culture, and technological advancement.
- New rides are being developed so that the riders can control the experience and intensity of the ride themselves.
- There is future expansion in the use of simulation virtual reality rides.
- There is a greater use of water-related activities with rides, landscaping, and attractions.
- Artificial environments continue to be developed so that parks can operate in all weather conditions.
- The expansion of theme parks will result in greater job opportunities.

CASE STUDY

Reducing Wait Time for Attractions and Rides

Guests of a major theme park are complaining about the long wait times for rides and attractions. You are a new member of management and are asked for your input in solving this problem.

DISCUSSION QUESTION

1. What suggestions can you come up with, and how much will they cost? What resources and expenditures will your solution entail?

CAREER INFORMATION

The operation of a theme park includes countless occupations. Anheuser-Busch, Disney, and others have excellent programs for employment during college. These programs provide information on career development. Upon graduation, careers may follow a number of paths. Graduates may start in any number of levels: operations management, marketing and sales, human resources, food service, planning and development, or information systems, to name but a few.

An internship is one of the best ways to get involved in the theme park industry. An internship provides valuable work experience and is a great way to learn more about various areas of the industry.

Interns are very appealing to potential employers. If you are a college student who is interested in spending a summer working for one of America's premier companies, visit the Disney College Program Web site at www.wdwcollegeprogram.com.

George Gonzalez, a theme park manager offers this advice:

"Theme parks and attractions offer excellent career opportunities for hospitality graduates. Parks and attractions are generally organized by divisions and departments: rides, shows, animal attractions, upclose tours, special events, dining, gift shop, group events, education and classes, and animal attractions.

If you are interested in theme parks, it is a good idea to work at one during the school year and in the summer months. By gaining experience in any department, you gain an overall impression of the park and hopefully learn if a career in the theme park industry would be a good fit you. Good luck whichever career path you take."

Related Web Sites
www.knotts.com
www.disney.go.com
www.universalstudios.com

SUMMARY

1. The theme park industry began in the 1920s in Buena Park, California, with a small berry farm and tea room.
2. After a gradual expansion, more than 80 years after its humble beginnings, Knott's Berry Farm has become the largest independent theme park in the United States.
3. Theme parks and attractions vary according to theme, which might be historical, cultural, or geographical. Some parks and attractions focus on a single theme, other parks and attractions focus on multiple themes.
4. Key players in the theme park industry include Disney, Universal Studios, Anheuser-Busch Companies, Six Flags, and Hershey.
5. Some of the better-known regional theme parks include Dollywood, LegoLand, Gatorland, and Wet 'n Wild.
6. Managing a theme park is similar to managing another hospitality operation.
7. The managerial process begins with the elements of management: the first being planning, followed by organizing, communicating, decision making, motivating, and controlling.
8. Fairs, festivals, and events all fall under the umbrella of event tourism.
9. Oktoberfest, The Carnival in Rio de Janeiro, Brazil, Reggae on the River, Mardi Gras, and the Grand Ole Opry are some of the larger fairs, festivals, and events.
10. There are over 350,000 workers in the theme park industry.
11. Designer and artists, inspectors and repairers, scientists, and other professionals are just some of the people who work in the theme park industry.

KEY WORDS AND CONCEPTS

Attractions
Event tourism
Fairs
Festivals
National Association of Amusement Ride Safety Officials
Theme parks

REVIEW QUESTIONS

1. Where are several of the most well-known parks located?
2. Who are the key players in the theme park industry?
3. Who is the most formidable competitor facing the Disney Corp.?
4. What association must safety inspectors have certification through?
5. What is the purpose of organizing in the managerial process?

INTERNET EXERCISES

1. Check the Web sites of at least two of the theme park corporations mentioned in the book. What news is coming up? Can you identify any current trends?
2. Go to the Web sites of one of the corporations mentioned above. Identify different career paths within the company.

APPLY YOUR KNOWLEDGE

1. Plan visits to two different theme parks and select rides in order of priority.
2. Research the history of Mardi Gras on the Internet. Write a description of the event and its cultural roots.

SUGGESTED ACTIVITY

1. In groups, create a new theme park, zoo, museum, or attraction for an existing theme park.

ENDNOTES

1. Personal correspondence with Knott's Berry Farms, April 2006.
2. Knott's Berry Farms Web site, http://www.knotts.com/real/real.htm, retrieved April 17, 2006.
3. www.waltdisneyworld.com, retrieved October 7, 2006.
4. Ibid.
5. http://disneyworld.disney.go.com/wdw/parks_parklisting?Id=MKAttractionListingPage.
6. Ibid.
7. www.waltdisneyworld.com.
8. www.disneyworld.disney.go.com/wdw_parks/parklanding?id=MGMLandingPage.
9. www.nbcuni.com/About_NBC_Universal_Company_Overview/.
10. Ibid.
11. www.blackstone.com, retrieved March 29, 2010.
12. www.thehersheycompany.com/.
13. 10_0018_Walker_CH12_typecode.dochttp://www.hershey.com/discover/visit.asp, retrieved March 29, 2010.
14. http://www.hershey.com/discover/history/company.asp, retrieved March 29, 2010.
15. www.dollywood.com/rides-attractions/.
16. www.legoland.com/.
17. www.gatorland.com/history/history.html.
18. www.wetnwild.com.
19. http://www.ecosherpa.com/uncategorized/sin-city-gambles-on-green-theme-park/.
20. http://www.good.is/post/do-green-amusement-or-theme-parks-exist.
21. http://www.good.is/post/do-green-amusement-or-theme-parks-exist.
22. http://www.good.is/post/do-green-amusement-or-theme-parks-exist#ixzz0iuqcLCzG.
23. www.muenchen.de/Tourismus/Oktoberfest/history_7552/index.html.
24. www.reggaeontheriver.com.
25. www.mardigras.com.
26. www.opry.com.

GAMING ENTERTAINMENT

13

LEARNING OUTCOMES

After reading and studying this chapter, you should be able to:

Outline the history of the gaming entertainment industry.

Describe the various activities related to gaming entertainment.

Explain how gaming entertainment converges with the hospitality industry.

Discuss the different positions within the gaming industry.

Describe the economic impact of tourism.

One of the most significant developments in the hospitality industry during the past two decades has been the astounding growth of the casino industry and its convergence with the lodging and hospitality industries. What has emerged from this development is an entirely new arena of hospitality known as the gaming entertainment industry. With its rapid expansion in North America and throughout the world, new opportunities have been created for hospitality careers. This chapter explores the gaming entertainment industry and details exciting developments yet to come in this dynamic and controversial segment of the hospitality business.

GAMING ENTERTAINMENT

For the purposes of this chapter, the term **gaming entertainment** refers to one subset of the gaming industry, that is, the casino industry. What used to be known as the casino business is now known as gaming entertainment. The dramatic growth of this part of the hospitality business has brought with it significant changes in how businesses in this industry operate and what they offer their guests. The changes have been so great that a new name had to be created to accurately describe all the amenities this industry provides.

The gaming industry includes 445 casinos in 11 states,[1] offering both land-based and riverboat casinos, card rooms, charitable games, lottery-operated games, and greyhound and horse races. The gaming industry as a whole is larger than most people can believe. Approximately $70 billion is *wagered,* or *bet,* on games or races every year, which is more than seven times what is spent on movie tickets. The total amount bet is called the **handle**. When a customer places a bet in any type of gaming activity, sometimes that customer wins and sometimes he or she loses. The total amount of all bets is the handle, and the net amount of spending by the customer is called the **win** by the gaming industry.

What is the difference between gambling and gaming? **Gambling** is playing a game of risk for the thrill of the "action" and the chance of making money. True gamblers spend a great

A themed gaming and slot machine area in a casino.

deal of time learning and understanding a favorite game of risk and enjoying its subtle attributes, and they find an enjoyable challenge in trying to "beat the house," or win more than they lose from a casino.

A gambler has little interest in anything other than the casino floor and the games it offers. It is true that the 40 million-plus visitors who go to Las Vegas, the more than 30 million who go to Atlantic City, and the hundreds of thousands who frequent other casino operations love the green felt tables, the whirling roulette wheels, the feel of the chips, and the thrill of the game. The rows of colorful slot machines sounding out musical tones and flashing lights, the distant sounds of someone hitting a jackpot, and the ringing bells and shouting guests create an environment of excitement and anticipation that can only be found on the casino floor. The gaming industry has exploded from just two jurisdictions in 1976 to some form of legal gambling in 48 states.

> **People go to casinos and gamble for a variety of reasons, whether it's for fun, excitement, the possibility of hitting a jackpot, or just to feel challenged.**

Read about Popular Casino Games in the *Casino Games Manual*

With the latest craze of the card game "Texas Hold'em," more and more people are watching such television shows as *Celebrity Poker* and the *World Series of Poker*.

Not long ago, the presence of a slot machine or blackjack table was all that was needed to lure visitors. However, with the rapid spread of **casinos** throughout North America, this is no longer true. The competitive nature of the casino business has created a bigger, better product to meet the needs of its guests. As Steve Wynn, owner of the Wynn Hotel and Resort puts it, the casino floor is "a thing which people pass on their way to visit the things that really matter to them." This product, "gaming entertainment," has evolved over the past decade.

Games of risk are only part of the total package of entertainment and leisure time activities found in gaming entertainment. Gaming entertainment serves a customer base of "social gamblers," customers who play a game of risk as a form of entertainment and a social activity, combining gambling with many other activities during their visit. Social gamblers, by this definition, are interested in many gaming entertainment amenities and take part in many diverse activities during a stay.

Gaming entertainment refers to the casino gaming business and all its aspects, including hotel operations, entertainment offerings, retail shopping, recreational activities, and other types of operations in addition to wagering on the gaming floor. The heart of gaming entertainment is what Glen Schaeffer, president of Circus Circus, has dubbed the "entertainment megastore" with thousands of rooms; dynamic, interesting, exterior architecture; and nongaming attractions—that is, it's a building on which someone can base a vacation, with 100,000 square feet or more of casino at its core. Schaeffer has said that this product "is to tourism what the Pentium chip is to technology," a dynamic new tourism product that serves as a destination attraction. Gaming entertainment is the business of hospitality and entertainment with a core strength in casino gaming.

According to this definition, a gaming entertainment business always has a casino floor area that offers various games of risk and that serves as the focal point for marketing to and attracting guests. Next in importance to the guests are high-quality food and beverage operations.

Gaming entertainment is one of the last hospitality concepts to support the full-service, table-side gourmet restaurant, in addition to the lavish buffet offerings that many casino locations offer. The number of foodservice concepts is wide and diverse—from signature restaurants featuring famous chefs, to ethnic offerings, to quick-service, franchised outlets. The gaming entertainment industry offers unlimited career opportunities in restaurant management and the culinary arts that were unheard of just a decade ago.

Explore Positions in the Gaming Entertainment Industry: Visit the Sea Wolfe Casino

Gaming entertainment also goes hand in hand with the lodging industry, because hotel rooms are part of the package. Full-service hotels are part and parcel of gaming entertainment. Rooms, food and beverage, convention services, banquet facilities, health spas, recreation, and other typical hotel amenities support gaming entertainment. Most of the largest and most complex hotels in the world are found in gaming entertainment venues, a number of which are described in detail later in this chapter.

Gaming entertainment offers a place where guests can gamble (the casino floor), eat and drink, sleep and relax, and maybe do some business. But there is much more: the entertainment ranges from live performances by the most famous entertainers to production shows that use the latest high-tech wizardry. Gaming entertainment includes theme parks and thrill

The fabulous Wynn hotel and resort, Las Vegas.

businesses in 48 states and seven Canadian provinces. These casinos take the form of commercially operated businesses, both privately and publicly held. Some are land based, meaning the casinos are housed in regular buildings. Others are on riverboats that cruise up and down a river, or on barges moored in water and do not cruise, called dockside casinos.

Casinos are also operated by Native American tribes on their reservations and tribal lands. These are land-based casinos and are often as complex as any operation in Las Vegas. Gaming entertainment is also popular on cruise ships, either as part of the cruise vacation product or on what are called "cruises to nowhere," where gaming and entertainment on board the ship are the main attraction.

Study the History of Casino Gaming and the Role of Native Americans

There is strong support for gaming in the marketplace as an entertainment activity. More than one-fourth or 54.1 million U.S. households gamble in casinos. U.S. households make 319 million visits annually to casinos. According to market research, more than 80 percent of U.S. adults say casino entertainment is acceptable for themselves or others.[2]

The demographic makeup of the typical gaming entertainment guest has remained consistent during the past several years. In comparison to the average American, casino players tend to have higher levels of income and education and are more likely to hold white-collar jobs. The customer profile of Las Vegas has gotten younger, and people who spend money want a total entertainment experience. According to the latest Las Vegas Visitor Profile Study, the average visitor to Las Vegas stays 3.4 nights, budgets $544 for gambling, and spends $86 per night on lodging, $248 on food and drink, $64 on local transportation, $124 on shopping, $47 on shows, and another $8 on sightseeing.[3]

rides, museums, and cultural centers. The most popular gaming entertainment destinations are designed around a central theme that includes the hotel and the casino operations.

Unlike its predecessor, the casino business, the gaming entertainment business has numerous revenue-generating activities. Revenue is produced from casino win, or the money guests spend on the casino floor. The odds of any casino game favor the house, some more than others. Casino win is the cost of gambling to guests, who often win over the house in the short run, and are therefore willing to place bets and try their luck.

Nongaming revenue comes from sources that are not related to wagering on the casino floor. As the gaming entertainment concept continues to emphasize activities other than gambling, nongaming revenue is increasing in importance. This is what gaming entertainment is truly about—hospitality and entertainment based on the attraction of a casino.

What forms does gaming entertainment take? The megaresorts of Las Vegas and Atlantic City garner the most publicity as the meccas of the gaming entertainment industry. However, there are smaller properties throughout Nevada and other casino-based

> Two decades ago, gambling in the United States was permitted in only two states. Today, only two states, Hawaii and Utah, do *not* permit some form of gambling!

HISTORICAL REVIEW OF GAMING ENTERTAINMENT

The precise origin of gambling is still unknown today. However, according to Chinese records, the first official account of the practice dates back to as far as 2300 B.C.! The Romans were also gamblers. They placed bets on chariot races, cockfights, and on dice throwing. This eventually led to problems: gambling, or "games of chance," were banned except for during the winter festival of Saturnalia.[4]

In the seventeenth century, casino-style gaming clubs existed in England and Central Europe. A public gambling house was legalized for the first time in 1626 in Venice, Italy, and one in Baden Baden, Germany, opened in 1748 and is still open today.[5] Soon, the upper class met in so-called "casinis" to socialize and gamble. In the first half of the nineteenth century, organized gaming casinos started to develop.

Las Vegas—the name alone summons images of neon lights, extravagant shows, outrageous performers, and bustling casinos, where millions are won and lost every night. Las Vegas is all of that, but much more. This city represents the American dream. A dusty watering hole less than 70 years ago, it has been transformed into one of the most elaborate cities in the world and one of the hottest vacation spots for the entire family. Las Vegas is second only to Walt Disney World as the favorite vacation destination in the United States.

The gaming entertainment business has its roots in Las Vegas. From the early 1940s until 1976, Las Vegas had a monopoly on the casino business, not the gaming entertainment business. Casinos had no hotel rooms, entertainment, or other amenities. The hotels that existed were just a place to sleep when a guest was not on the casino floor.

Las Vegas is rich with tales of Benjamin Hymen Siegelbaum, better known as Bugsy Siegel. Siegel was born February 28, 1906, in Brooklyn, N.Y. to a poor Austrian Jewish family. It is said that he began his career at a very young age by extorting money from pushcart peddlers. Eventually he turned to a life of bootlegging, gambling rackets, and murder-for-hire operations. In 1931, Bugsy was one of four men who executed Joe "the Boss" Masseria. Several years later, he was sent out West to develop rackets. In California, Siegel successfully developed gambling dens and ships. He also took part in narcotics smuggling, blackmail, and other questionable operations. After developing a nationwide bookmakers' wire service, Siegel moved on to build the well-known Flamingo Hotel and Casino in Las Vegas. The casino ended up costing $6 million, which forced Siegel to skim profits. This angered the Eastern bosses: Siegel subsequently died at his Beverly Hills home in June of 1947, hit by a barrage of bullets fired through his living-room window. At the same time, three henchmen walked into the Flamingo Hotel in Las Vegas and announced that they were the new owners.[6]

During the 1970s, Atlantic City was in an impoverished state, with high rates of crime and poverty. In an effort to revitalize the city, New Jersey voters in 1976 approved casino gambling in Atlantic City.[7] Later, casino gambling was legalized in the state of New Jersey by the Casino Control Act. The state looked to the casino hotel industry to invest capital, create jobs, pay taxes, and attract tourists, thus revitalizing the economy and creating a financial environment in which urban redevelopment could occur.

The act initiated a number of fees and taxes specific to the casino hotel business that would provide revenues to support regulatory costs, fund social services for the disabled and the elderly throughout the state, and provide investment funds for the redevelopment of Atlantic City. The Casino Control Act created the Casino Control Commission, whose purpose was not only to ensure the success and integrity of the Atlantic City casino industry, but also to carry out the objective of reversing the city's economic fortunes.[8]

Sensing that the objectives of the Casino Control Act were being fulfilled in New Jersey and wanting similar benefits for its state, but not wanting land-based casino gambling, Iowa legalized riverboat casinos 13 years later. Illinois, Mississippi, Louisiana, Missouri, and Indiana followed suit in rapid succession. As the casino industry spread throughout the United States and Canada, its competitive nature created a need for what is now known as gaming entertainment, and added noncasino attractions. Gaming entertainment is, therefore, a natural evolution of the casino industry.

Explore the Past and Discover the Future of Gaming in *The History and Future of Gambling Manual*

Native American Gaming

In *California v. Cabazon Band of Mission Indians et al.* (1987), the Supreme Court decided 6 to 3 that once a state has legalized any form of gambling, the Native Americans in that state have the right to offer and self-regulate the same games, without government restrictions. This ruling came about after the state of California and the county of Riverside sought to impose local and state regulations on card and bingo clubs operated by the Cabazon and Morongo bands of Mission Indians. The court clearly recognized the rights of tribes with regard to certain gaming activities.[9]

Congress, which some observers say was alarmed by the prospect of losing control over tribal gaming, responded to these court decisions by passing the **Indian Gaming Regulatory Act of 1988 (IGRA)**. The IGRA provides a framework by which games are conducted to protect both the tribes and the general public. For example, the IGRA outlines criteria for approval of casino management contracts entered into by tribes and establishes civil penalties for violation of its provisions. The act is clearly a compromise in that it balances the rights of sovereign tribal nations to conduct gaming activities with the rights of the federal and state governments to regulate activities within their borders.[10]

Gamblers at Caesars Palace, Las Vegas.

The three objectives of the IGRA are to (1) provide a statutory basis for the operation of gaming by Native American tribes as a means of promoting tribal economic development, self-sufficiency, and strong tribal governments; (2) provide a statutory basis for the regulation of gaming by a Native American tribe adequate to shield it from organized crime and other corrupting influences; and (3) establish an independent regulatory authority, the National Indian Gaming Commission (NIGC), for governing gaming activity on Native American lands.[11]

IGRA defines three different kinds, or classes, of Native American gaming activities: (1) class I gaming, consisting of social games played solely for prizes of minimum value or traditional forms of Native American gaming; (2) class II gaming, consisting of bingo, games similar to bingo, and card games explicitly authorized by the laws of the state; and (3) class III gaming, consisting of all forms of gaming that are neither class I nor class II gaming, and therefore including most of what are considered casino games.[12]

The significance of the definition of class III gaming activity is that it identifies the games that (1) must be located in a state that permits such gaming for any purpose by any person, organization, or entity and (2) are conducted in conformance with a compact that states are required to negotiate "in good faith" with the tribes.

While the federal gaming law precludes state taxation, the tribes in several states have made voluntary payments and also negotiated payments to state governments under certain circumstances. Often tribes give local governments voluntary payments in recognition of services the tribe receives, and some pay revenues in exchange for permission to maintain a casino gambling monopoly in a state. In Michigan, Connecticut, and Louisiana, tribes have agreed to make payments to the state as part of their comprehensive compacts for casino gambling. In almost all the states, the tribes make payments to the state for costs incurred by the states in regulating the casinos as provided for in the negotiated agreements.

There are 354 gaming facilities on reservation lands in 28 states, and Native American gaming has been the fastest-growing sector of casino gaming in the United States. Additional Native American gaming is conducted by the First Nations Bands of Canada.[13]

Check Your Knowledge

1. **Define the following:**
   a. Bet
   b. Handle
   c. Win
2. **Briefly describe the history of the gaming industry.**
3. **Where and when does the first official account of gaming practice date back to?**
4. **What does the Indian Gaming Regulatory Act of 1988 consist of?**

Size and scope of gaming entertainment

Why is the gaming/entertainment industry growing so quickly? Basically, because people like to wager and, historically, there has been more demand than supply for wagering opportunities. As public acceptance of legalized gaming has grown, and state and local governments have permitted gaming entertainment establishments to open, supply is beginning to meet demand.

The gaming entertainment industry pays billions of dollars per year in gambling privilege taxes to state governments.

Casino development has been credited with revitalizing economies through new capital investment, job creation, new tax revenue, and increased tourism.

Casino gaming has created thousands of direct and indirect jobs with billions paid in wages. When unemployment is high and an area is in economic despair, casinos create jobs. Casino gaming companies pay an average of 12 percent of total revenues in taxes. Casino gaming companies contribute to federal, state, and local governments through gaming-related and other taxes. Direct taxes include property, federal/state income, and construction sales and use taxes, which all industries pay, and gaming taxes, which are levied only on the gaming industry at rates ranging from 6.25 to 20 percent of gaming revenues.[14]

Key players in the industry

Learn about the Relationship between Gaming Entertainment and the Hospitality Industry

Today, there are only three industry giants: MGM Mirage, Harrah's, and Boyd Gaming. These companies all have diverse property portfolios, solid business practices, and are well respected by Wall Street.

Harrah's Entertainment and Caesars Entertainment have paired up to dominate the gaming industry and together are now the world's biggest casino operator. Harrah's Entertainment operates 40 casinos in three countries, under the Harrah's, Caesars, and Horseshoe brand names. Harrah's Entertainment, Inc., is the premier name in casino entertainment, and owns the following casinos: Harrah's, Caesars, Paris, Rio, Flamingo, Imperial Palace, and Horseshoe in Las Vegas. Harrah's history is a rich combination of casino expertise and quality, which was launched in northern Nevada in the late 1930s and has expanded across

.inc | Corporate Profile

MGM MIRAGE

MGM Mirage, one of the world's leading and most respected hotel and gaming companies, owns several casino resorts in Nevada, Mississippi, Michigan, and Australia. With the acquisition of Mandalay Resorts and the opening of CityCenter Las Vegas, the company now controls half of the Las Vegas strip. MGM Mirage has an impressive portfolio of properties which include ARIA, Vdara, Luxor, The Bellagio, MGM Grand Las Vegas, The Mirage, Treasure Island, and New York–New York, and several others.[15]

MGM Mirage prides itself on operating the world's largest hotel/casino. The MGM Grand Hotel, located on 113 acres along the Las Vegas strip, has more than 5,034 rooms and a 171,500-square-foot casino with some 3,700 slot machines, about 160 table games, some 50 shops, a theme park, and a special-events center featuring superstar acts. Across the strip is the MGM Mirage's 2,000-room New York–New York Hotel and Casino. The New York–New York Hotel and Casino includes an 84,000-square-foot casino, containing over 80 gaming tables and more than 2,000 slot machines. The Bellagio's lobby ceiling contains a breathtaking display of 2,000 hand-blown glass flowers created by world-renowned artist Dale Chihuly. A water ballet in front of the resort offers viewers a musical and visual spectacle performed by Bellagio's acclaimed water foundations. MGM Grand also runs a hotel/casino in northern Australia that caters to Asian gamblers. The company has agreed to develop casinos in Atlantic City, New Jersey, and South Africa.[16]

MGM Resorts International owns 50 percent of City Center Las Vegas. City Center includes: Aria Resort and Casino, Vdara, The Harmon Hotel, Mandarin Oriental, Veer Towers, and The Crystals. It is located in the heart of the Las Vegas Strip between the Bellagio and the Monte Carlo. In addition to the hotels and casino, the center includes 650 condominium-hotel units and 550,000 square feet of retail, dining, and entertainment space.[17]

Introducing Stephen A. Wynn

Chairman of the Board and CEO, Wynn Resorts

Casino developer Stephen A. Wynn is widely credited with transforming Las Vegas from a gambling venue for adults into a world-renowned resort and convention destination. As chairman of the board, president, and chief executive officer of Mirage Resorts, Inc., Wynn envisioned and built the Mirage, Treasure Island, and Bellagio—boldly conceived resorts that set progressively higher standards for quality, luxury, and entertainment. Now, as chairman of the board and chief executive officer of Wynn Resorts, Limited, Wynn developed Wynn Las Vegas, among the world's preeminent luxury hotel resorts. Wynn also developed the Wynn Macau, a flagship Asian casino resort in Macau, China, where his company has been awarded a 20-year concession by the Macau government.

Wynn began his career in 1967 as part owner, slot manager, and assistant credit manager of the Frontier Hotel. Between 1968 and 1972 he also owned and operated a wine and liquor importing company. But it was an entrepreneurial real estate deal with Howard Hughes in 1971 that produced sufficient profits for a major investment in the landmark Golden Nugget Casino. Once known only as a "gambling joint," he transformed it into a Four Diamond resort known for elegance and personal service. By 1973, at age 31, Wynn controlled the property and began developing the Golden Nugget as a complete resort hotel. In 1978, Wynn used the profits from the Golden Nugget in Las Vegas to build the Golden Nugget Hotel and Casino on the Boardwalk in Atlantic City. The resort became known for its elegant facilities, television ads featuring Frank Sinatra, and its impressive lineup of superstar entertainment. From its opening in 1979 until its sale in 1986, the Atlantic City property dominated the market in revenues and profits in spite of its smaller size. In 1987, Wynn sold the Atlantic City Golden Nugget, which had cost $160 million, to Bally for $450 million and turned his creativity to developing the elegant Mirage Resort, which opened in 1989. With its imaginative erupting volcano and South Seas theme, The Mirage ignited a $12 billion building boom that catapulted Las Vegas to America's number one tourist destination and fastest-growing city. In 1991, Golden Nugget Incorporated was renamed Mirage Resorts, Incorporated.

Following his staggering success at The Mirage, in 1993 Wynn opened Treasure Island, a Four Diamond property with a romantic tropical theme indoors and a full-size pirate ship used in the daily outdoor reenactment of the Battle of Buccaneer Bay. He raised the bar again in 1998, when he opened the opulent $1.6 billion Bellagio, one of the world's most spectacular hotels. Visitors line the street in front of the hotel to watch the Dancing Waters, shooting fountains choreographed to music that "dance" on the hotel's 8.5-acre man-made lake. He then brought Mirage Resorts' standard of style to historic Biloxi, Mississippi with the 1,835-room Beau Rivage, blending Mediterranean beauty and Southern hospitality.

In June 2000, Wynn sold Mirage Resorts, Incorporated to MGM for $6.6 billion and purchased Las Vegas's legendary Desert Inn Resort and Casino.

The Desert Inn was closed in August 2000, and on that site Wynn began developing Wynn Las Vegas, a 2,700-room luxury destination resort that has inspired yet another wave of development on the Strip.

For every property he develops, Wynn is known for assembling a dream team of highly motivated employees who keep guestrooms and public spaces impeccable, according to industry analysts. His properties are always exceptional, drawing a commanding share of a demanding market with an exceptionally high occupancy. He is confident that both his projects and Las Vegas will continue to thrive.

Today, Wynn is active in the Las Vegas community and has received honorary doctorate degrees from the University of Nevada, Las Vegas, and Sierra Nevada College in Northern Nevada. He is chairman of Utah's Moran Eye Institute; a trustee of his alma mater, the University of Pennsylvania; and a member of the board of the George Bush Presidential Library.

Courtesy of Stephen A. Wynn.

---

the continent. In the United States, Harrah's casinos are located in 13 states. One of the most geographically diverse casino companies, it also operates riverboat and dockside casinos in Illinois, Louisiana, Missouri, and Mississippi and Native American reservation casinos in Arizona and Washington.[18]

Boyd Gaming operates 15 gaming and hotel facilities in six states. Properties located in or close to Las Vegas include Main Street Station, Casino, Brewery and Hotel Hotel, Casino, & Brewery, the Orleans Hotel and Casino, Suncoast Hotel and Casino, Sam's Town Hotel and Gambling Hall, Fairmont Hotel and Casino, the California Hotel and Casino, Gold Coast Hotel and Casino, and the Fremont Hotel and Casino. Outside Nevada, Boyd operates Sam's Town Hotel and Gambling Hall, a dockside gaming and entertainment complex in Tunica

County, Mississippi; Blue Chip Casino Hotel in northwest Indiana; Sam's Town Hotel and Casino Shreveport, Delta Downs and the Treasure Chest Casino all located in Louisiana; and the Borgata Hotel, Casino, & The Water Club in New Jersey.[19]

Sustainable Casinos

Casinos can and do incorporate the same sustainable elements found in hotels and resorts. Sustainable guidelines for casinos include[20]

Greener Air

Customized room climate controls

Air filters

Smoke controls

Access to more fresh air

Co_2 Sensors for fresh air

"Smart" controls for ventilation

Greener Water

Water efficient and/or dual flush bathroom fixtures

50 percent recycled water and 100 percent rain water harvesting for irrigation

Optional linen and towel change

Greener Light

Energy efficient indoor and outdoor lights

Mood lighting with dimmers

Energy shut-off switch when room is not occupied

Bigger windows to allow more natural light

Greener Material

Nontoxic paints, carpeting and other materials

100 percent recycled stationary and other paper producer

100 percent biodegradable cleaning materials

Naturally grown bamboo, cotton, wool and silk fabrics

Reclaimed materials

Greener Energy

Low-energy heating and cooling systems

Reduced energy usage

Utilizing regional and domestic products

Greener Luxury

No plastics

Organic cotton bath towels

Passive solar design

Recycling by staff and customers

Composting kitchen food waste

These are only a few of many solutions to help minimize the demands placed on an already hard-pressed environment by a constantly expanding society. Conservation of natural resources needs to be an integral part of the development planning, execution, and operation of every building project.

Check Your Knowledge

1. Why is the gaming/entertainment industry growing so quickly?
2. Who are the top key players in the gaming industry?

Positions in Gaming Entertainment

Explore the Unlimited Career Opportunities in Gaming Entertainment

Careers in the gaming entertainment industry are unlimited. Students of the industry who understand the multidisciplinary needs of the business find five initial career tracks in hotel operations, food and beverage operations, casino operations, retail operations, and entertainment operations.

Hotel Operations

The career opportunities in gaming entertainment hotel operations are much like the career opportunities in the full-service hotel industry, with the exception that food and beverage can be a division of its own and not part of hotel operations. The rooms and guest services departments offer the most opportunities for students of hospitality management. Because gaming entertainment properties have hotels that are much larger than nongaming hotels, department heads have a larger number of supervisors reporting to them and more responsibilities. Reservations, front desk, housekeeping, valet parking, and guest services can all be very large departments with many employees.

Food and Beverage Operations

Gaming entertainment has a foundation of high-quality food and beverage service in a wide variety of styles and concepts. Some of the best foodservice operations in the hospitality industry are found in gaming entertainment operations. There are many career opportunities in restaurant management and the culinary arts. As with hotel operations, gaming entertainment properties are typically very large and contain numerous food and beverage outlets, including a number of restaurants, hotel room service, banquets and conventions, and retail outlets. Many establishments support gourmet, high-end signature restaurants. It is not unusual to find many more executive-level management positions in both front- and back-of-the-house food and beverage operations in gaming entertainment operations than in nongaming properties.

Casino Operations

Casino operations jobs fall into five functional areas. Gaming operations staff include slot machine technicians (approximately one technician for 40 machines), table-game dealers (approximately four dealers for each table game), and table-game supervisors. Casino service staff includes security, purchasing, and maintenance and facilities engineers. Marketing staff includes public relations, market research, and advertising professionals. Human resources staff includes employee relations, compensation, staffing, and training specialists. Finance and Administration staff includes lawyers, accounts payable, audit, payroll, and income control specialists.[21]

While there was little organized dealer training as recently as a decade ago, the explosive growth of the gaming industry has increased the need for trained dealers skilled at working a variety of table games including **blackjack**, **craps**, **roulette**, **poker**, and **baccarat**. Now, through the use of textbooks and videotapes combined with hands-on training at a mock casino, future dealers learn the techniques and fine points of dealing at classes offered by both colleges and private schools.

Retail Operations

Discover the Importance of Game Protection in the Industry

The increased emphasis on nongaming sources of revenues in gaming entertainment business demands an expertise in all phases of retail operations, from store design and layout to product selection, merchandising, and sales control. Negotiating with concession subcontractors may also be a part of the overall retail activities. Retail operations often support the overall theme of the property and can often be a major source of revenue; however, retail management careers are often an overlooked career path in the gaming entertainment industry.

Entertainment Operations

Because of the increased competition, gaming entertainment companies are creating bigger and better production shows to turn their properties into destination attractions. Some production shows have climbed into the $30 to $90 million range and require professional entertainment staffs to produce and manage them. Gaming entertainment properties often present live entertainment of all sorts, with headline acts drawing huge audiences. For example, at the MGM Grand, there are three entertainment showcases. These include the 15,000-seat Grand

---

TRENDS *in* THE GAMING ENTERTAINMENT INDUSTRY

Explore Trends in Gaming Entertainment

- Gaming entertainment is depending less on casino revenue and more on room, food and beverage, retail, and entertainment revenue for its profitability and growth.
- The gaming entertainment industry and lodging industry are converging, as hotel room inventory is rapidly expanding in gaming entertainment properties.
- Gaming entertainment, along with the gaming industry as a whole, will continue to be scrutinized by government and public policy makers as to the net economic and social impact of its activities.
- As the gaming entertainment industry becomes more competitive, exceptional service quality will become an increasingly important competitive advantage for success.
- The gaming entertainment industry will continue to provide management opportunities for careers in the hospitality business.

Arena, used for professional boxing matches and for superstars like Tina Turner; the smaller 1,700-seat theater that houses an elaborate production show called EFX; and a 700-seat theater that plays host to other stars.

As a result of this emphasis on entertainment, career opportunities exist for those interested in stage and theater production, lighting and box office management, and talent management and booking.

CASE STUDY

VIP

A frequent guest of the casino makes a last-minute decision to travel to your property for a weekend stay. The guest enjoys gaming as a leisure activity and is one of the casino's better customers. When he arrives at the casino, he is usually met by a casino host and treated as a very important person due to his level of wagering at the blackjack tables. This guest is worth approximately $50,000 in casino win per year to the hotel. Due to his last-minute arrangements, however, the guest cannot notify a casino host that he is on his way to the hotel. Upon arriving, he finds a very busy registration desk. He must wait in line for 20 minutes, and when he tries to check in, he is told that the hotel is full. The front-desk clerk acts impatient when the guest says that he is a frequent customer. In a fit of frustration, the would-be guest leaves the hotel and makes a mental note that all casinos have similar odds at the blackjack table and maybe another property will give him the respect he deserves.

DISCUSSION QUESTION

1. What systems or procedures could you institute to make sure this type of oversight does not happen in your property?

CASE STUDY

Negotiating with Convention Groups

Your convention sales department receives a call from a trip director for a large convention group. The group will use many function rooms for meetings during the day and will generate a substantial amount of convention services revenue. Likewise, the group's food and beverage needs are quite elaborate, so this will be good for the food and beverage department budget. However, the group is very sensitive concerning room price and is willing to negotiate the time of week for its three-night stay.

DISCUSSION QUESTION

1. What are the considerations that a gaming entertainment property must take into account when determining room rates for convention groups?

CAREER INFORMATION

In the past 25 years, the gaming industry in the United States has seen huge growth. Gambling, once considered illegal in almost every state, is now accessible throughout the country. Eleven states have commercial casino gaming and 29 states authorize Native American casino-style gaming. Gaming is now also available worldwide, even further expanding the opportunities for employment in the industry.

The gaming industry employs over 700,000 people. The vast expansion of the gaming industry has resulted in a variety of new job openings. People choose to work in the industry because it is known to place people first, whether they are employees or customers. The industry also has many opportunities for employees to learn new skills, which lead to growth and advancement in their careers.

Employees in the gaming industry may receive many tangible benefits. Most careers include impressive benefits packages and offer many career advancement opportunities. Casinos are known to hire from within, which gives current employees a greater chance to move into better positions over time. Because the gaming industry's positions are so varied, many educational and experiential backgrounds can be adapted to a specific casino's policies.

A variety of careers are specific to the gaming industry (see Figure 13–1), including dealer, slot attendant, marketing director, and casino surveillance. More opportunities are becoming available every day as new technology creates more openings. For example, systems such as MindPlay's Table Management System, IGT's EZpay technology, and the introduction of advance guest service technology will surely create new and exciting technical employment opportunities within the industry.

Although it may appear as if many gaming jobs have very specific qualifications, it is important not to focus too narrowly on one sector. Knowledge of all areas of the industry is integral for advancement. For example, today's casinos now rely on entertainment as well as gaming to bring in patrons. Therefore, an employee at such a casino also needs to have knowledge of

Croupier → Gain Experience at All Tables → Section Supervisor → Assistant Section Manager → Game Manager → Floor Manager → Casino Manager

FIGURE 13–1 A Career Path in the Gaming Industry.

the entertainment industry and how casinos operate such events.

Key to getting a job in the gaming industry, one must have very thorough knowledge of the legal, regulatory, and compliance issues related to daily operations in the casino. Broken laws can result in lawsuits and cost the company large sums of money. This can be avoided if all employees have the proper background knowledge.

Find Out More about the Importance of Customer Service

Even though observing daily activity in a casino provides invaluable work experience, it is also crucial to obtain a college or graduate degree. It is true that much of the necessary education can take place on the job; however, applicants who have received an outside education, as well as attended gaming certification programs, have a much better chance of standing out from their competition.

A general manager in the gaming industry earns a starting average annual salary of about $82,800. A casino operator begins at about $38,000, and marketing and sales employees start out at $55,000. Positions typically include full health benefits and yearly bonuses and other compensation, depending on the casino.

The multibillion dollar gaming entertainment industry is growing throughout the world. America will continue to see significant growth in the industry, but the extraordinary growth will occur internationally. Career opportunities will abound due to the gaming industry's growth, continuous operation, and labor-intensive nature.

Gaming entertainment offers careers in casino gambling, entertainment, foodservice, and lodging. Each area is an essential part of the gaming entertainment experience but it is important to remember that casinos still make the majority of their revenue from gambling! The other areas are designed to attract the customer and then keep them in the casino.

Management careers can be very different depending on your focus. If your interest is gaming management, it is important that you take courses in finance, law, human resources, management, and gambling. You also need to work in the gaming industry while in college, so that you can open doors for yourself through networking. Casinos still believe in promoting from within and so you will have to work your way up the corporate ladder. You also need to understand that because of the continuous operation of a casino, your work schedule will vary. It is not uncommon to work several 12-hour days straight, but the rewards for dedication and hard work can be very worthwhile. Casinos are exhilarating places where the rich and famous come to play and be entertained.

Dan Watson, vice president of gaming offers the following advice: "Casinos have many similar positions to hotels and resorts, plus gaming positions. Take a gaming promotions manager, for example. This position requires at least three years' experience in gaming industry promotions; a bachelor's degree in marketing; and the ability to lead a team in developing and planning promotional programs, setting departmental goals, and developing strategies to meet or exceed them. In addition, the position requires excellent written and verbal communication skills plus a detailed knowledge of and experience in gaming promotions planning and execution. A promotions manager must also have outstanding organizational skills and strong strategic and analytical skills. Gain experience while you are going to school and do an internship in one of the gaming areas—or both—to see if it is for you. Seek out a good mentor and plan the steps toward your career goal position. Remember that someone has to run Citycenter in Las Vegas—why not you?"

Related Web Sites

extranet.casinocareers.com/jobs/index.cfm—career bulletin board
www.casinoemployment.com/—employment bulletin board
www.harrahs.com/—gaming company information and employment
www.cltycenter.com—MGM Resorts International Las Vegas.
www.mgmresorts.com—MGM Resorts International

SUMMARY

1. The casino industry has developed into a new business called gaming entertainment, with the introduction of full-service hotels, retail, and entertainment offerings.
2. To operate gaming entertainment businesses, it is necessary to understand the relationship between the casino and other departments in the operation.
3. Gaming entertainment is strictly regulated by state governments, and the integrity developed over time by these regulations is necessary for the survival of the industry.
4. Nongaming revenue is increasing as a percentage of total revenue of gaming entertainment businesses.
5. Native American gaming entertainment businesses are a means for economic self-development by tribal people.

KEY WORDS AND CONCEPTS

Baccarat
Blackjack
Casino
Craps
Gambling
Gaming entertainment
Handle
Indian Gaming Regulatory Act (IGRA)
Poker
Roulette
Win

REVIEW QUESTIONS

1. Briefly describe the history of legalized gaming in the United States.
2. What defines a gaming entertainment business?
3. Explain the attraction of gaming entertainment to the destination of a tourist.
4. Why is it necessary for strict regulations to be in force on the casino floor?
5. How are hotel operations in a gaming entertainment business different from hotel operations in a nongaming environment?

INTERNET EXERCISES

1. Organization: Wynn Las Vegas
   Web site: www.wynnlasvegas.com
   Summary: Located on the Las Vegas Strip, the Wynn Las Vegas has a lot to offer. From gaming and concerts, to hosting some of the biggest conventions, the Wynn Las Vegas will certainly keep you busy.

   a. What are some of the gaming features that attract customers to the Wynn Las Vegas?
   b. What are the benefits to the different packages available under special offers?

2. Pick a casino in Las Vegas and look it up on the Internet. What does it offer that sets it apart from other casinos in Las Vegas and from other casinos in the United States? In what areas is it similar to other casinos?

APPLY YOUR KNOWLEDGE

1. Name the major gaming entertainment hotels in Las Vegas.
2. Give examples of nongaming revenue.

SUGGESTED ACTIVITY

1. Research careers in the gaming entertainment industry. Are there more opportunities than you realized? What careers in the industry interest you the most?

ENDNOTES

1. www.americangaming.org
2. Ibid.
3. www.Lvcva.com/getfile/vps-2005.
4. www.gypsyware.com/gamblinghistory.html.
5. www.14g.com/casino/knowledge/history_of_casinos_in_europe.
6. http://en.wikipedia.org/wiki/Bugsy_Siegel.
7. http://en.wikipedia.org/wiki/Atlantic_City,_New_Jersey.
8. Ibid.
9. Julia Glick, "Cabazon Indian Leader Who Pursued Gaming Rights Dies," *The Press-Enterprise*, January 4, 2007.
10. www.nicg.gov/LawsRegulations/IndianGamingRegulatoryAct/tabid/605/Default.aspx.
11. Ibid.
12. Op cit.
13. www.indiangaming.org/library/indian-gaming-facts/index.shtml.
14. www.americangaming.org/publications/AGA_studies.cfm.
15. www.mgmmirage.com, retrieved March 25, 2010.
16. Ibid.
17. Op. cit.
18. www.harrah's.com, retrieved March 25, 2010.
19. www.boydgaming.com/about, retrieved March 25, 2010.
20. http://www.casinoenterprise-management.com/articles/march-2010/green-architecture-creating-sustainable-world.
21. www.harrahs.com/about_us/community_relations/IPImpacts.pdf.

MEETINGS, CONVENTIONS, AND EXPOSITIONS

14

LEARNING OUTCOMES

After reading and studying this chapter, you should be able to:

Know about the major players in the convention industry.

Describe destination management companies.

Describe the different aspects of being a meeting planner.

Describe the different types of contractors.

Explain the different types of meetings, conventions, and expositions.

Know the various venues for meetings, conventions, and expositions.

HTi Describe the economic impact of tourism.

Development of the meetings, conventions, and expositions industry

People have gathered to attend **meetings, conventions**, and **expositions** since ancient times, mainly for social, sporting, political, or religious purposes. As cities became regional centers, the size and frequency of such activities increased, and various groups and associations set up regular expositions.

Associations go back many centuries: Guilds in Europe were created during the Middle Ages to secure proper wages and maintain work standards. Associations began in the United States at the beginning of the eighteenth century, when Rhode Island candlemakers organized themselves.

Size and scope of the industry

Today, according to the American Society of Association Executives (ASAE)—which has 23,000 members in the United States—about 6,000 associations operate at the national level, and a hundred thousand more function at the regional, state, and local levels. The association business is big business. Associations spend billions holding thousands of meetings and conventions that attract millions of attendees.

The hospitality and tourism industry itself consists of a number of associations, including the following:

- The American Hotel and Lodging Association
- The National Restaurant Association
- The American Culinary Federation
- The International Association of Convention and Visitors Bureaus
- Hotel Sales and Marketing Association International
- Meeting Planners Association
- Club Managers Association of America
- Professional Convention Management Association

> *Meetings, conventions, and expositions provide attendees and personnel in specialized areas an opportunity to discuss important issues and new developments with their peers.*
> — Laurel Ebert, *The Boylston Convention Center, Boylston, MA*

Associations are the main independent political force for industries like hospitality, offering the following benefits:

- Governmental/political voice
- Marketing avenues
- Education
- Member services
- Networking

Thousands of associations hold annual conventions at various locations across North America and the rest of the world. Some associations alternate the location of their conventions; others meet at fixed locations, such as the National Restaurant Association (NRA) show in Chicago or the American Hotel and Lodging Association (AH&LA) convention and show in New York.

Key players in the industry

Learn about Working with the CVB as a Meeting Manager

The need to hold face-to-face meetings and attend conventions has grown into a multibillion dollar industry. Many major and some smaller cities have convention centers with nearby hotels and restaurants.

> *Meetings provide managers the opportunity to give positive feedback to their employees, address employee concerns, and emphasize projects and/or goals.*
> — Lianne Wilhoitte, *Wilhoitte & Associates, Baltimore, MA*

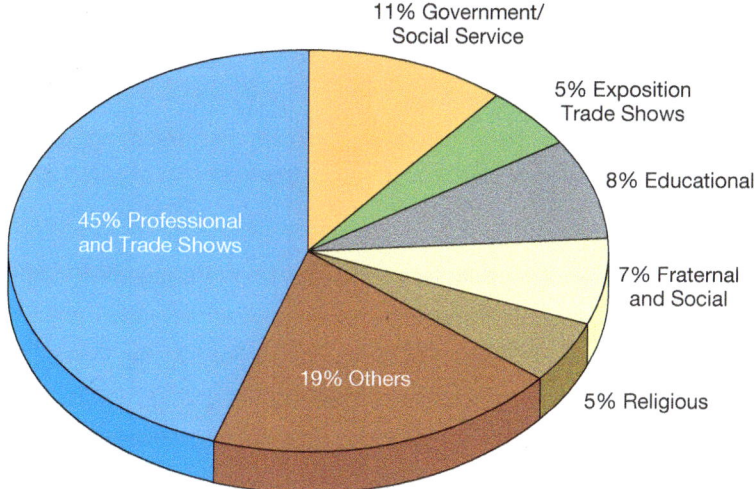

FIGURE 14–1 Major Players in the Convention Industry.

The major players in the convention industry are **convention and visitors bureaus (CVBs)**, meeting planners and their clients, convention centers, specialized services, and exhibitions. The wheel diagram in Figure 14–1 shows the number of different people and organizations involved with meetings, conventions, and expositions.

Convention and visitors bureaus are major participants in the meetings, conventions, and expositions market. The International Association of Conventions and Visitors Bureaus (IACVB) describes a CVB as a not-for-profit umbrella organization that represents an urban area that tries to solicit business- or pleasure-seeking visitors. The convention and visitors bureau comprises a number of visitor industry organizations representing the various industry sectors:

- Transportation
- Hotels and motels
- Restaurants
- Attractions
- Suppliers

The bureau represents these local businesses by acting as the sales team for the city. A bureau has five primary responsibilities:

1. To enhance the image of tourism in the local/city area.
2. To market the area and encourage people to visit and stay longer.
3. To target and encourage selected associations and others to hold meetings, conventions, and expositions in the city.
4. To assist associations and others with convention preparations and to give support during the convention.
5. To encourage tourists to partake of the historic, cultural, and recreational opportunities that the city or area has to offer.

The outcome of these five responsibilities is an increase in the cities' tourist industry revenues. Bureaus compete for business at trade shows, where interested visitor industry groups gather to do business. For example, a tour wholesaler who is promoting a tour will need to link up with hotels, restaurants, and attractions to package a vacation. Similarly, meeting planners are able to consider several locations and hotels by visiting a trade show. Bureaus generate leads (prospective clients) from a variety of sources. One source, associations, have national/international offices in Washington, D.C. (so that they can lobby the government) and Chicago.

A number of bureaus have offices or representatives in these cities or a sales team who will make follow-up visits to the leads generated at trade shows. Alternatively, they will make cold calls on potential prospects, such as major associations, corporations, and incentive houses. The sales manager will invite the meeting, convention, or exposition organizer to make a **familiarization (FAM) trip** to do a site inspection. The bureau assesses the needs of the client and organizes transportation, hotel accommodations, restaurants, and attractions accordingly. The bureau then lets the individual properties and other organizations make their own proposals to the client. Figure 14–2 shows the average expenditure per delegate per stay by the convention type.

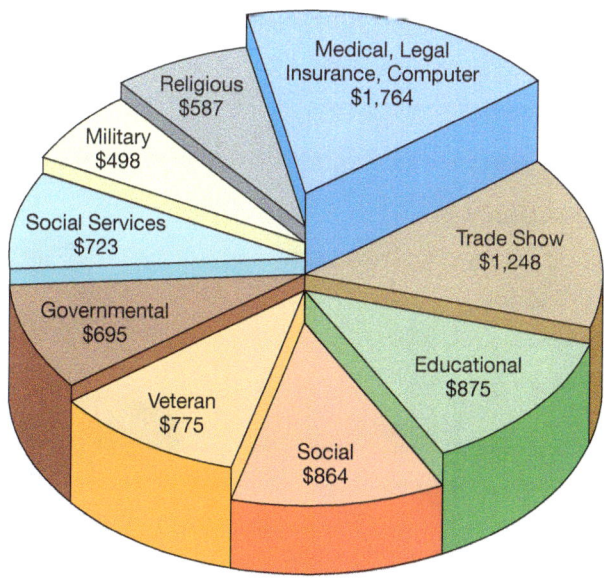

Average length of stay is 3.50 days

FIGURE 14–2 Average Expenditure per Delegate per Stay by the Convention Type.

Check Your Knowledge

1. According to the American Society of Association Executives (ASAE), how many associations operate at the national level in the United States?
2. What are the five primary responsibilities of a bureau?
3. What is the purpose of a familiarization (FAM) trip?

Destination Management Companies

Read *The Meeting Manager's Guide to Meetings*: Gain Insight into the Many Companies Involved in Meetings

A destination management company (DMC) is a service organization within the visitor industry that offers a host of programs and services to meet clients' needs. Initially, a destination management sales manager concentrates on selling the destination to meeting planners and performance improvement companies (incentive houses).

The needs of such groups may be as simple as an airport pickup or as involved as an international sales convention with theme parties. DMCs work closely with hotels; sometimes DMCs book rooms, and other times hotels request the DMC's know-how on organizing theme parties. Patricia Roscoe, chairperson of Patti Roscoe and Associates (PRA), says that meeting planners often have a choice of several destinations and might ask, "Why should I pick your destination?" The answer is that a DMC does everything, including airport greetings, transportation to the hotel, VIP check-in, theme parties, sponsoring programs, organizing competitive sports events, and more, depending on budget. Sales managers associated with DMCs obtain leads, which are potential clients, from the following sources:

- Hotels
- Trade shows
- Convention and visitors bureaus
- Cold calls
- Incentive houses
- Meeting planners

Each sales manager has a staff or team that would include the following:

- Special events manager, who will have expertise in sound, lighting, staging, and so on
- Accounts manager, who is an assistant to the sales manager
- A theme-events creative director
- Audiovisual specialist
- Operations manager, who coordinates everything, especially on-site arrangements, to ensure that what is sold actually happens.

For example, Patti Roscoe's destination management company organized meetings, accommodations, meals, beverages, and theme parties for 2,000 Ford Motor Company dealers in nine groups over three days for each group.

Roscoe also works closely with incentive houses, such as Carlson Marketing or Maritz Travel. These incentive houses approach a company and offer to set up incentive plans for companies' employees, including whatever it takes to motivate them. Once approved, Carlson contacts a destination management company and asks for a program.

In conclusion, thousands of companies and associations hold meetings and conventions all over the country. Many of these organizations use the services of professional meeting planners, who in turn seek out suitable destinations for the meetings and conventions. Meetings and conventions are now more international; several popular cities around the world draw large numbers of attendees.

Meeting Planners

Experience a Day in the Life of a Meeting Planner: Visit Nunally Meeting Room

Meeting planners may be independent contractors who contract out their services to both associations and corporations as the need arises, or they may be full-time employees of corporations or associations. In either case, meeting planners have interesting careers. According to the International Convention Management Association (ICMA), about 212,000 full- and part-time meeting planners work in the United States.

The professional meeting planner not only makes hotel and meeting bookings, but also plans the meeting down to the last minute, always remembering to check to ensure that the services contracted for have been delivered. In recent years, the technical aspects of audiovisual and simultaneous translation equipment have added to the complexity of meeting planning. The meeting planner's role varies from meeting to meeting, but may include some or all of the following activities:

Pre-Meeting Activities

- Estimate attendance
- Plan meeting agenda
- Establish meeting objectives
- Set meeting budget
- Select city location and hotel/convention site
- Negotiate contracts
- Plan exhibition
- Prepare exhibitor correspondence and packet
- Create marketing plan
- Plan travel to and from site
- Arrange ground transportation
- Organize shipping
- Organize audiovisual needs

On-Site Activities

- Conduct pre-event briefings
- Prepare VIP plan
- Facilitate people movement
- Approve expenditures

Postmeeting Activities

- Debrief
- Evaluate
- Give recognition and appreciation
- Plan for next year

As you can see, this is quite a long list of activities that meeting planners handle for clients.

Service Contractors

Read *The Event Planner's Guide* for Details on These Activities

Service contractors, exposition service contractors, general contractors, and decorators are terms that have at one time or another referred to the individual responsible for providing all of the services needed to run the facilities for a trade show. Just as a meeting planner is able to multitask and satisfy all the demands of meeting planning, a general exposition contractor must be multitalented and equipped to serve all exhibit requirements and creative ideas.

The service contractor is hired by the exposition show manager or association meeting planner. The service contractor is a part of the facilities management team and, in order to use the facility, the sponsor must use its service contractor. In other situations, the facility may have an exclusive contract with an outside contractor, and it may require all expositions to deal with this contractor. Today, there are Internet service companies that can take reservations, prepare lists, and provide all kinds of services online for meeting planners.

Check Your Knowledge

1. What is a destination management company?
2. What are the primary responsibilities of a professional meeting planner?

.inc Corporate Profile

HAWAI'I CONVENTION CENTER

The Hawai'i Convention Center (HCC) on the island of Oahu, Hawaii, is consistently recognized by meeting planners and conventioneers as the world's most desirable convention and meetings destination and has built its reputation around being a facility where business and *aloha* meet.

Hawaiian hospitality values are recognized as the most sophisticated and genuine in the world, and HCC offers each employee training in the Hawaii Institute of Hospitality, a program of the Native Hawaiian Hospitality Association (NaHHA). The seminar, headed by the Hawaii Institute of Hospitality, is just one element of a series of *Na Mea Ho'okipa* (Hawaiian hospitality) training for the staff at the center. More than teaching hospitality, *ho'okipa* advocates a personal behavior system based on Hawaiian values and a heightened "sense of place." "*Ho'okipa* is about understanding who we are and

.inc | Corporate Profile (Continued)

how we fit into this place, and the Hawai'i Convention Center has always had a fundamental sense of how it, as a viable economic powerhouse and ultimate host, fits successfully within Hawaii's cultural environment," says Peter Apo, director of NaHHA.

Ho'okipa training also includes a novel approach to orienting staff to the concept of place, the most integral element of the visitor experience. A walking tour through historic Waikiki reiterates that it is not merely high rises and hotels, but one of the most sacred, culturally important places in Hawaii. The "Hawai'i Advantage" is a strategy to position the Convention Center and Hawaii as the world's most desirable convention and meeting destination. This advantage is channeled through various facets, each one an instrumental consideration for meeting planners. The premise is that Hawaii as a destination expounds on aspects including, but not exclusive to, location, productivity, competitive shipping, value of facility, destination appeal, industry support, and customer service in a way that no other destination can. And of course, no other destination offers "business with aloha."

"The Hawai'i Advantage is a powerful concept that works on several levels; it distinguishes the Hawai'i Convention Center from other venues and is an initiative rooted in testimonials of past convention attendees," says Joe Davis, SMG general manager of the Hawai'i Convention Center. "The Convention Center and Hawaii offers conventioneers an unmatched experience. Once we get them here for the first time, we know they will rebook," says Davis.

Hawai'i Convention Center highlights include:

- One million square feet of meeting facilities, including an exhibit hall, theaters, and expansive conference rooms.
- Convention Television (CTV)—an exclusive service with the capability to broadcast convention information in 28,000 hotel rooms in Waikiki, as well as on screens within the Center. CTV is an expedient way for organizations to reach out to conventioneers with its message, as well as showcase sponsors, VIPs, and trade show participants.
- Designed with a "Hawaiian Sense of Place"—the Center captures the essence of the Hawaiian environment with a soaring, glass-front entry; a 70-foot misting waterfall; and mature palm trees.
- The facility also houses a $2 million Hawaiian art collection of unique pieces commissioned for specific locations within the building and features a rooftop outdoor function space complete with a tropical garden of native flora.
- The Center's state-of-the-art technical features include fiber-optic cabling, multilingual translation stations, satellite and microwave broadcast capability, and videoconferencing.
- The Center is marketed and managed by SMG, a company that manages 98 percent of the publicly owned exhibition space operated by private companies in North America.

The Hawai'i Convention Center's recent list of awards includes:

- Prime Site Award from *Facilities & Destinations* magazine
- Planners' Choice Award—Recognition for Excellence in the Hospitality Industry—*Meeting News* magazine
- Ranked as North America's most attractive convention center in the METROPOLL X study, Gerard Murphy & Associates
- Best Use of Nature in Design—*Tradeshow Week Magazine*

The Hawai'i Convention Center's Web site (http://www.hawaiiconvention.com/) offers the following information:

- Meeting planner testimonials
- Floor plans and facility services
- News and media kit
- 12-month event calendar

Types of Meetings, Conventions, and Expositions

Meet the Houseman: Discover More about Various Meeting Types

Meetings

Meetings are conferences, workshops, seminars, or other events designed to bring people together for the purpose of exchanging information. Meetings can take any one of the following forms:

- *Clinic:* A workshop-type educational experience in which attendees learn by doing. A clinic usually involves small groups interacting with each other on an individual basis.
- *Forum:* An assembly for the discussion of common concerns. Usually experts in a given field take opposite sides of an issue in a panel discussion, with liberal opportunity for audience participation.
- *Seminar:* A lecture and a dialogue that allow participants to share experiences in a particular field. A seminar is guided by an expert discussion leader, and usually 30 or fewer persons participate.
- *Symposium:* An event at which a particular subject is discussed by experts and opinions are gathered.
- *Workshop:* A small group led by a facilitator or trainer. It generally includes exercises to enhance skills or develop knowledge in a specific topic.

The reason for having a meeting can range from the presentation of a new sales plan to a total quality management workshop. The purpose of meetings is to affect behavior. For example, as a result of attending a meeting, a person should know or be able to do certain things. Some outcomes are very specific; others may be less so. For instance, if a meeting were called to brainstorm new ideas, the outcome might be less concrete than for other types of meetings. The number of people attending a meeting can vary. Successful meetings require a great deal of careful planning and organization. In a major convention city, convention delegates spend approximately $423 per day, almost twice that of vacation travelers. Figure 14–3 shows convention delegates' spending in a convention city.

Meetings are set up according to the wishes of the client. The three main types of meeting setups are theater style, classroom style, and boardroom style.

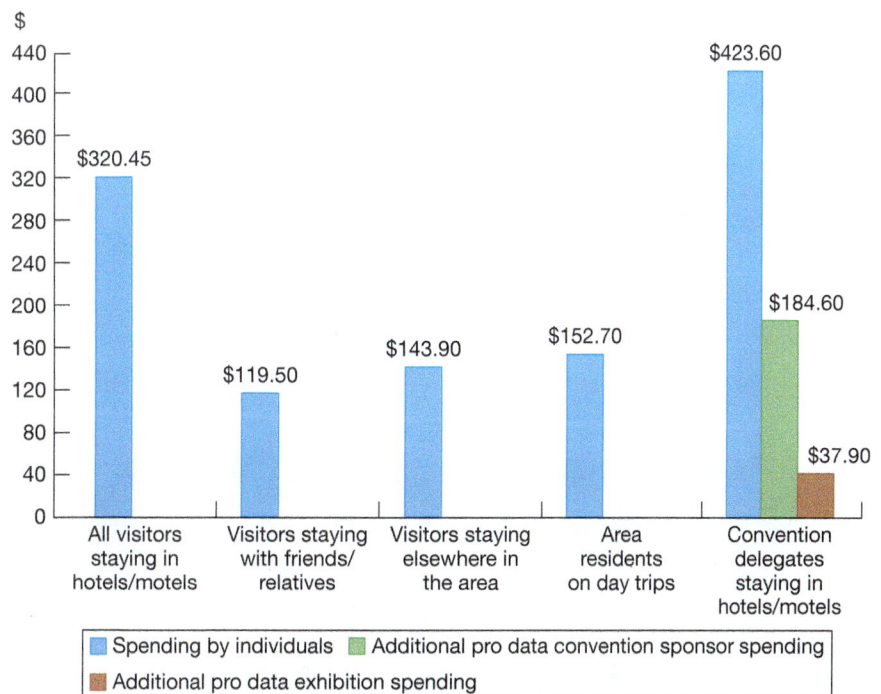

FIGURE 14–3 Convention Delegates' Spending in Convention City San Francisco.

- Theater style generally is intended for a large audience that does not need to make a lot of notes or refer to documents. This style usually consists of a raised platform and a lectern from which a presenter addresses the audience.
- Classroom setups are used when the meeting format is more instructional and participants need to take detailed notes or refer to documents. A workshop-type meeting often uses this format.
- Boardroom setups are made for small numbers of people. The meeting takes place around one block rectangular table.
- Boardroom setups are made for small numbers of people. The meeting takes place around one block rectangular table.

Association Meetings

Discover the Importance of Association Business in *The Meeting Manager's Guide to Meetings*

Every year, there are thousands of association meetings that spend millions of dollars sponsoring many types of meetings, including regional, special interest, education, and board meetings. When choosing a location, the association meeting planner considers the destination's availability of hotel and facilities, ease of transportation, distance from attendees, transportation costs, and food and beverage. Members attend association meetings voluntarily, so the hotel should work with meeting planners to make the destination seem as appealing as possible.

Conventions and Expositions

Conventions are generally larger meetings that include some form of exposition or trade show. A number of associations have one or more conventions per year. These conventions raise a large part of the association's budget. A typical convention follows a format like this:

- Welcome/registration
- Introduction of president
- President's welcome speech, opening the convention
- First keynote address by a featured speaker
- Exposition booths open (equipment manufacturers and trade suppliers)
- Several workshops or presentations on specific topics
- Luncheon
- More workshops and presentations
- Demonstrations of special topics (e.g., culinary arts for a hospitality convention)
- Vendors' private receptions
- Dinner
- Convention center closes

The Las Vegas Convention Center.

```
16:15:28                        San Diego                              Page: 1
                        Convention Center Corporation                  9506059
                              EVENT PROFILE

                             EVENT STATISTICS

       Event Name:    San Diego Apartment Association Trade Show    ID:              9506059
      Sales Person:   Joy Peacock                              Initial Contact:      8/3/2005
     Event Manager:   Trish A. Stiles                          Move In Date:         6/22/2009
     ConVis Contact:                                           Move In Day:          Wednesday
      Food Person:                                             Move In Time:         6:01 am
       Event Tech.:                                            First Event Date:     6/23/2009
     Event Attend.:                                            First Event Day:      Thursday
    Nature of Event:  LT Local Trade Show                      Start Show Time:      6:01 am
   Event Parameter:   60 San Diego Convention Center           End Show Time:        11:59 pm
    Business Type 1:  41 Association                           # of Event Days:      1
    Business Type 2:  91 LOCAL                                 Move Out Date:        6/23/2009
     Booking Status:  D Definite                               Move Out Day:         Thursday
     Rate Schedule:   III Public Show, Meetings and Location   Out Time:             11:59 pm
    Open to Public:   No                                       Date Confirmed:       8/3/2005
   Number Sessions:   1                                        Attend per Sesn:      3000
     Event Sold By:   F Facility (SDCCC)                       Tot Room Nights:      15
     Abbrev. Name:    /6/Apartment Assn                        Public Release:       Yes
   Est Bill Amount:   Rent – 6,060.00   Equip –                      0.00 Food –     0.00
    Last Changed On:  8/20/05 in: Comment Maintenance          By – Joy Peacock
  This Event has been in the facility before
```

CLIENT INFORMATION

Company: San Diego Apartment Assn, a non-profit Corporation
    Contact Name: Ms. Leslie Cloud, Sales and Marketing Coord.
        1011 Camino Del Rio South, Suite 200, San Diego, CA 92108   ID: SDAA
        Telephone Number: (619) 297-1000
        Fax Number: (619) 294-4510
        Alternate Number: (619) 294-4510

Company: San Diego Apartment Assn, a non-profit Corporation
    Alt Contact Name: Ms. Pamela A. Trimble, Finance & Operations Director
        1011 Camino Del Rio South, Suite 200, San Diego, 92108
        Telephone Number: (619) 297-1000
        Fax Number: (619) 297-4510

EVENT LOCATIONS

ROOM	MOVE IN	IN USE	ED	MOVE OUT	BS	SEAT	RATE	EST. RENT	ATTEND
A	6/22/09 6:01 am	6/23/09	1	6/23/09 11:59 pm	D	E	III	6,060.00	5000
AS	6/22/09 6:01 am	6/23/09	1	6/23/09 11:59 pm	D	E	III	0.00	10
R01	6/22/09 6:01 am	6/23/09	1	6/23/09 11:59 pm	D	T	III	0.00	450
R02	6/22/09 6:01 am	6/23/09	1	6/23/09 11:59 pm	D	T	III	0.00	350
R03	6/22/09 6:01 am	6/23/09	1	6/23/09 11:59 pm	D	T	III	0.00	280
R04	6/22/09 6:01 am	6/23/09	1	6/23/09 11:59 pm	D	T	III	0.00	280
R05	6/22/09 6:01 am	6/23/09	1	6/23/09 11:59 pm	D	T	III	0.00	460

FOOD SERVICES

ROOM	DATE	TIME	BS ATTEND	EST. COST FOOD SERVICE

There are No Food Services booked for this event

FIGURE 14–4 Convention Event Profile for a Trade Show.

Figure 14–4 shows a convention event profile for a trade show. Conventions are not always held in convention centers; in fact, the majority are held in large hotels over a three- to five-day period. The headquarters hotel is usually the one in which most of the activity takes place. Function space is allocated for registration, the convention, expositions, meals, and so on.

Associations used to be viewed as groups that held annual meetings and conventions with speeches, entertainment, an

16:15:28   San Diego   Page: 2
Convention Center Corporation   9506059

EVENT PROFILE

EVENT EQUIPMENT/SERVICES

ROOM	MOVE IN	IN USE	ED MOVE OUT	QUANTITY EQUIPMENT

There is No Equipment booked for this event

FOLLOW-UP/CHECKLIST ITEMS

FOLLOW-UP	DATE	ITEM	COMPLETED DATE	ASSIGN TO
	9/26/05	C DUE/date contracted		Vincent R. Magana
	8/22/05	c from sales	8/23/05	Sonia Michel
	8/22/05	c to licensee	8/23/05	Sonia Michel
	8/22/05	date c 1st printed	8/22/05	Sonia Michel

EVENT COMMENTS

8/3/05–JMP–This is a very strong hold for this group. CAD is pursuing a release of Hall A from Group Health and then this will be confirmed on a first option. Also holding an alternate date in April until this is released. All other rooms are clear.

200 BOOTHS – have used Carden in the past.
This is a trade show for the Apartment industry — products and services needed to keep a rental property in shape. Use Rooms 1–5 as seminar rooms. Trish has been the Event Coordinator for 2000–01.

8/18/05—JMP-CAD has been able to clear Hall A on a first option for move-in on 22nd from Group Health. Made definite and requested Sonia produce a contract. NOTE TO SONIA: Contract should be signed and mailed to alternate contact Pam Trimble. Meeting logistics only will go through Leslie. Note to housekeeping: we did the cleaning for the 2003 show.

LICENSE AGREEMENT REQUEST

EVENT COMMENTS

Requested:	Saturday, 08/20/07, 2:56 pm
License #:	9506059
Sales Person:	JMP
Nature of Event:	Local Trade
Full Legal Name of Licensee:	Yes
Insurance Y/N:	Yes
Deposit Schedule:	50-50
Special Arrangements or Directions:	Contract should be signed and sent to alternate contact Pam Trimble. Leslie is responsible for meeting logistics only.
Gross Revenues F/B Revenue:	$1000 concessions
In House A/V Revenue:	$600
Security Revenue:	$200
Telecom. Revenue:	$220

(Below, identify MI/MO or event days and attendance for each event).
Other business in Center: GROUP HEALTH, definite, Hall B-1 (m/o 22nd), 3000ppl; ALCOHOLICS ANON, definite, Hall B, move-in; SECURITY EXPO, tentative, Hall C (m/i 22nd, show 23rd), 6600ppl; ENTRP. EXPO, contracted, Ballroom (m/i 23rd), 2000ppl.

FIGURE 14–4 (*Continued*).

educational program, and social events. They have changed in activity and perception.

Expositions are events that bring together sellers of products and services at a location (usually a convention center) where they can show their products and services to a group of attendees at a convention or trade show. Exhibitors are an essential component of the industry because they pay to exhibit their products to the attendees. Exhibitors interact with

Introducing Jill Moran, CSEP

Principal and Owner, JS Moran, Special Event Planning & Management

In my life, there is no typical day. As the owner of a special event company, I provide a variety of services to corporate, nonprofit, and social clients. I must be able to communicate successfully with a client at one moment, a vendor at the next, and a prospect at another. My job also involves managing the growth of my company, hiring the right staff and vendors for projects, and getting each job done from start to finish in a professional and timely manner.

As a business owner, I am required to keep my eye on many facets of the company almost daily. Some areas are a must to attend to, such as billing, scheduling, and marketing. The squeakiest wheel that gets the most grease, though, is the actual ongoing projects. Once a project is secured, the contracting, planning, and execution stages quickly follow after the initial handshake. These components of meeting and event planning can be time and energy consuming as the details are planned out and put into motion. Event details may involve researching, attending meetings, generating event documents, developing creative concepts and themes, securing vendors to satisfy event details, or executing an event. In the planning of any given event or conference, I may be required to attend off-site visits with vendors, venues, or clients as well as use the computer or telephone to facilitate the planning process. Visits to art supply, furniture, fabric stores, or storerooms of linen or décor vendors are also key elements as theme and design elements are worked on. Review of entertainment or speakers, planning of room layouts or trade show and exhibition space, or discussion with graphic artists also fit into the necessary details covered during the planning phase of an event.

A typical day may involve early computer time to work on production schedules, timelines, e-mails to vendors or clients, follow-up on contracts, or focused time spent on a new proposal. I find early morning (before 9 A.M.) or evening (after 8 P.M.) to be the best time for these activities. This is when I get the fewest telephone interruptions, and it is before or after scheduled appointments that would require my time out of the office. During the typical business day, phone calls, planning activities and appointments occupy most of the day. If I am working on an international project, there is more flexibility with this due to the time differences.

While the execution phase of projects and events keeps me busy moment by moment, the strategic planning and business management of my company also demands attention as well. The challenge for me as a small business owner is to carve out time to prospect for new business while I am in the execution phase of events, so that when one project comes to an end, another is waiting in the wings. I do this by developing fresh marketing materials using photos or components of recent meetings and events; creating video or DVD-style materials to post on my Web site or to send to clients; making calls to colleagues, prospects, or venues to say "hello" or touch base; and attending luncheons or visits with past clients to keep in touch. I also try to spend time getting a pulse on new markets to explore or niche areas to develop. I subscribe to a wide variety of industry and professional magazines and try to end my day flipping through and tearing out articles that may be useful.

One thing I feel strongly about is keeping an eye on the future. I have owned a home-based business since 1988 and have seen the special events industry grow and change in many ways over the years. Passionate about the industry, I made a commitment to share my experience with those starting out, serving as a mentor, speaker, author, and industry leader. I continually examine the direction events and meetings are taking, gaps in the industry that need professional attention, and ways to improve the processes or offer new and better services to those who honor the value of events as vehicles for communication, education, or celebration. Whenever possible, I try to attend meetings and conferences, either in my local area or throughout the United States and internationally to get a feel for any new directions and changes in the industry. These meetings also give me ideas and feed my creative juices to approach new projects with an energized eye. I have met colleagues who are similar to me and share my challenges or are not at all like me and help me to consider different approaches to events. Many times, these gatherings offer terrific networking opportunities and ways to meet potential vendors or new clients.

Sometimes I feel that I eat, sleep, and live special events, and in many ways I do. But work doesn't take up every moment of my life. As a mother and wife, I still try to create a fun, loving home for my family by cooking dinner almost every night and by walking daily with my husband and two dogs. These breaks during the day give me downtime and a chance to regroup. I am also active in the music ministry at my local church as a youth choir director, which offers me spiritual and community involvement. I also belong to a book group (which I often attend without having completed the story!). There are only so many hours in the day, and I seem to use them up very quickly. But at the end of each day, I am always looking forward to the next!

Courtesy of Jill Moran

attendees with the intention of making sales or establishing contacts and leads for follow-up. Expositions can take up several hundred thousand square feet of space; this space is divided into booths for individual manufacturers or their representatives. In the hospitality industry, the two largest expositions are the American Hotel & Lodging Association's conference held in conjunction with the International Hotel/Motel & Restaurant Show (IHMRS) (held annually in November at the Jacob K. Javits Convention Center in New York) and the National Restaurant Association's annual exposition (held every May in Chicago). Both events are well worth attending.

Historical Associations

Today's associations find their roots in historical times. Ancient Roman and Oriental craftsmen formed associations for the betterment of their trade. In Medieval times, associations took the form of guilds, which were created to ensure proper wages and to maintain work standards.

Meetings, Incentive Travel, Conventions, and Exhibitions (MICE)

Meetings, incentive travel, conventions, and exhibitions (MICE) represent a segment of the tourism industry that has grown in recent years. The MICE segment of the tourism industry is very profitable. Industry statistics point to the fact that the average MICE tourist spends about twice the amount of money that other tourists spend.

Types of Associations

An association is an organized body that exhibits some variety of volunteer leadership structure, which engages in activities that the association members agree upon. The association is generally organized to promote and enhance that common interest, activity, or purpose. The association industry is significant in many respects—total employees, payroll, and membership—but is the undisputed leader when it comes to conventions and meetings.

The types of associations that participate in meetings, conventions, and expositions include the following:

Trade Association A trade association is an industry trade group that is generally a public relations organization founded and funded by corporations that operate in a specific industry. Its purpose is generally to promote that industry through PR activities such as advertising, education, political donation, political pressure, publishing, and astroturfing.[1]

> " About 6,000 associations operate at the national level, and a hundred thousand more function at the regional, state, and local levels. "

Professional Association A professional association is a professional body or organization, usually nonprofit, that exists to further a particular profession, to protect both the public interest and the interests of professionals.[2]

Medical and Scientific Associations These associations are professional organizations for medical and scientific professionals. They are often based on their specific specialties and are usually national, often with subnational or regional affiliates. These associations usually offer conferences and continuing education. They often serve in capacities similar to trade unions, and often take public policy stances on these issues.

Religious Organizations Religious organizations include those groups of individuals that are part of churches, mosques, synagogues, and other spiritual or religious congregations. Religion has taken many forms in various cultures and individuals. These groups may come together in meeting places to further develop their faith, to become more aware of others who have the same faith, to organize and plan activities, to recognize their leaders, fund-raising, and a number of other reasons.

Government Organizations There are thousands of government organizations in the United States made up of numerous public bodies and agencies. These types of organizations can range from federal, state, and local organizations. There are five basic types of local governments. Three of these are general-purpose governments; the remaining two include special-purpose local governments that fall into the category of school district governments and special district governments.

Types of Meetings

There are different types of meetings and purposes for having a meeting. There are annual meetings, meetings held by private or public companies or board and committees, there

Rediscover the Variety of Meetings and Meeting Groups

are fund-raisers, and there are professional and technical meetings. Popular types of meetings include:

Annual Meetings Annual meetings are meetings that are generally held every year by corporations or associations to inform their members of previous and future activities. In organizations run by volunteers or a paid committee, the annual meeting is generally the forum for the election of officers or representative for the organization.

Board, Committee Meetings, Seminars and Workshops, Professional and Technical Meetings Board meetings for corporations must be held annually and most corporations hold meetings monthly or four times a year. Of course, not all are held in hotels, but some are, and that brings in additional revenue. Committee meetings are generally held at the place of business and only occasionally are held in hotels. Seminars are frequently held in hotels as are workshops and technical meetings. To meet these needs, hotels and convention centers have convention and meeting managers who go over the requirements and prepare proposals and event orders and budgets.

Social, military, educational, religious, and fraternal groups (SMERF). Often these groups are price conscious, due to the fact that the majority of the functions sponsored by these organizations are paid for by the individual, and sometimes the fees are not tax deductible. However, SMERF groups are flexible to ensure that their spending falls within the limits of their budgets; they are a good filler business during off-peak times—meaning they frequently bring hotels business during otherwise quiet times.

Incentive Meetings The **incentive market** of MICE continues to experience rapid growth as meeting planners and travel agents organize corporate incentive travel programs to reward employees for reaching specific targets. Incentive trips generally vary from three to six days in length and can range from a moderate trip to an extremely lavish vacation for the employee and his or her partner. The most popular destination for incentive trips is Europe, followed closely by the Caribbean, Hawaii, Florida, and California. Because incentive travel serves as the reward for a unique subset of corporate group business, participants must perceive the

A computer software show.

destination and the hotel as something special. Climate, recreational facilities, and sightseeing opportunities are high on an incentive meeting planner's list of attributes to look for.

Check Your Knowledge

1. What are three different types of meetings described in this chapter and what is their purpose?
2. What is SMERF?

Meeting Planning

Read *The Event Planner's Guide to Meetings* for Pre-Meeting Planning

Meeting planning includes not only the planning, but also the successful holding of the meeting and the postmeeting evaluations. As we shall see, there are a number of topics and lots of details to consider.

Needs Analysis

Before a meeting planner can start planning a meeting, a *needs analysis* is done to determine the purpose and desired outcome of a meeting. Once this has been established, the meeting planner can work with the party to maximize the productivity of the meeting. The key to a productive meeting is a meeting agenda. The meeting agenda may not always fall under the responsibility of the meeting planner, but the meeting planner must be closely involved with the written agenda and with the core purpose of the agenda (which may be different from what is stated). For example, a nonprofit organization may hold a function to promote awareness of its objectives through a fun activity; however, its hidden agenda is to raise funds for the organization.

The meeting agenda provides the framework for creating *meeting objectives.* The meeting planner must know what the organization is trying to accomplish in order to successfully manage the meeting or conference. It is helpful for the meeting planner, regardless of what role he or she plays to plan the meeting with the meeting objectives in mind. The meeting's objectives provide the framework from which the meeting planner will set the budget, select the site and facility, and plan the overall meeting or convention.

Budget

Understanding your clients and knowing their needs are both extremely important, but the understanding the client's budget carries the most weight. Setting the *budget* for the meeting is more successful if the meeting planner is involved in the budget planning throughout and before any decisions are made about spending. Setting the budget for the meeting is not a simple task; however, knowing how much money is available and understanding the event's parameters will help the meeting planner guide clients. The amount of the budget needed varies for different sites and activities. Therefore, a working budget must be created to help with decisions about necessary changes. It is wise to inform the meeting planner of any changes in the budget so that the activity planning falls within budgetary constraints. Revenue and expenditure estimates must be accurate and as thorough as possible so that all possible expenditures are included in the budget prior to the event.

Income for a meeting, convention, or exposition comes from grants or contributions, event sponsor contributions, registration fees, exhibitor fees, sponsoring companies or organizations, advertising, and the sale of educational materials.

Expenses for a meeting, convention, or exposition may include (but are not limited to) rental fees, meeting planner fees, marketing expenses, printing and copying expenses, support supplies (such as office supplies and mailing), on-site and support staff, audiovisual equipment, speakers, signage, entertainment and recreational expenses, mementos for guests and attendees, tours, ground transportation, spousal programs, food and beverage, and on-site personnel.

Request for Proposal (RFQ) and Site Inspection and Selection

No matter how large or small a meeting, it is essential that clear meeting specifications are developed in the form of a written *Request for Proposal/Quote (RFQ)*, rather than contacting hotels by telephone to get a quote. Many larger hotels and convention centers now have online submission forms available.

The meeting planner evaluate several factors when he or she is selecting a meeting site, including location and level of service, accessibility, hotel room availability, conference room availability, price, city, restaurant service and quality, personal safety, and local attractions. Convention centers and hotels provide meeting space and accommodations as well as food and beverage facilities and service. The convention center and a hotel team from each hotel capable of handling the meeting will attempt to impress the meeting planner. The hotel sales executive will send particulars of the hotel's meeting space and a selection of banquet menus and invite the meeting planner for a site inspection. During the site inspection, the meeting planner is shown all facets of the hotel, including the meeting rooms, guest sleeping rooms, the food and beverage outlets, and any special facility that may interest the planner or the client.

Negotiation with the Convention Center or Hotel

The meeting planner has several critical interactions with hotels, including negotiating the room blocks and rates. Escorting clients on site inspections gives the hotel an opportunity to show its level of facilities and service. The most important interaction is normally with the catering/banquet/conference department associates, especially the services manager, maître d', and captains; these frontline associates can make or break a meeting. For example, meeting planners often send boxes of meeting materials to hotels expecting the hotel to automatically know which meeting they are for. On more than one occasion, they have ended up in the hotel's main storeroom, much to the consternation of the meeting planner. Fortunately, most meetings do not vary much from year to year. So, once meeting planners have taken care of one meeting, they know the drill.

Contracts

Once the meeting planner and the hotel or conference facility have agreed on all the requirements and costs, a contract is prepared and signed by the planner, the organization, and the hotel or convention center. The *contract* is a legal document that binds two or more parties. In the case of meetings, conventions, and expositions, a contract binds an association or organization and the hotel or convention center. The components that make up an enforceable contract include the following:[3]

1. *An offer:* The offer simply states, in as precise a manner as possible, exactly what the offering party is willing to do, and what he or she expects in return. The offer may include specific instructions for how, where, when, and to whom the offer is made.

2. *Consideration:* This is the payment exchanged for the promise(s) contained in a contract. For a contract to be valid, consideration must flow both ways. For example, the consideration is for a convention center to provide services and use of its facilities in exchange for a consideration of a stated amount to be paid by the organization or host.

3. *Acceptance:* The unconditional agreement to the precise terms and conditions of an offer. The acceptance must mirror exactly the terms of the offer in order for the acceptance to make the contract valid. The best way to indicate acceptance of an offer is by agreeing to the offer in writing.

Most importantly, to be considered legally enforceable, a contract must be made by parties who are legally able to contract, and the activities specified in the contract must not be in violation of the law. Contracts should include clauses on "attrition and performance," meaning that the contract has a clause to protect the hotel or convention facility in the event that the organizer's numbers drop below an acceptable level. Because the space reserved is supposed to produce a certain amount of money, if the numbers drop, so does the money, unless there is a clause that says something like, "there will be a guaranteed revenue of $$$ for the use of the room/space." The performance part of the clause means that a certain amount of food and beverage revenue will be charged regardless of whether it is consumed or not.

Organizing and Pre-Conference Meetings

The average lead time required to organize a small meeting is about three to six months; larger meetings and conferences take much longer and are booked years in advance. Some meetings and conventions choose the same location each year; others move from city to city, usually from the East Coast to the Midwest or West Coast.

A pre-conference meeting.

Conference Event Order

A conference event order includes all the information that department employees need about the details of the setup (times and layout) and the conference itself (arrival, meal times and what food and beverages are to be served) and the cost of items for billing purposes. An example of a conference event order is given in Figure 14–5.

Recognize Key Elements of the Event Order

Postevent Meeting

A postevent meeting is held to evaluate the event—what went well and what should be improved for next time. Larger conferences invite have staff from the hotel or convention center where the event will be held the following year so they can better prepare for the event when it is held at their facility.

EVENT DOCUMENT
REVISED COPY

/6/SAN DIEGO INTERNATIONAL BOAT SHOW
Tuesday, January 4, 2011–Tuesday, January 11, 2011

SPACE: Combined Exhibit Halls AB, Hall A – How Manager's Office, Box Office by Hall A, Hall B – Show Manager's Office, Mezzanine Room 12, Mezzanine Room 13, Mezzanine Rooms 14 A&B, and Mezzanine Rooms 15 A&B

CONTACT: Mr. Jeff Hancock
National Marine Manufacturers Association, Inc.
4901 Morena Blvd.
Suite 901
San Diego, CA 92117
Telephone Number: (619) 274-9924
Fax Number: (619) 274-6760
Decorator Co.: Greyhound Exposition Services
Sales Person: Denise Simenstad
Event Manager: Jane Krause
Event Tech.: Sylvia A. Harrison

SCHEDULE OF EVENTS:

Monday, January 3, 2011 5:00 am–6:00 pm   Combined Exhibit Halls AB
Service contractor move in GES,
Andy Quintena

Tuesday, January 4, 2011 8:00 am–6:00 pm   Combined Exhibit Halls AB
Service contractor move in GES,
Andy Quintena
12:00 pm–6:00 pm
Combined Exhibit Halls AB
Exhibitor move in

Wednesday, January 5, 2011 8:00 am–6:00 pm   Combined Exhibit Halls AB
Exhibitor move in
Est. attendance: 300

Thursday, January 6, 2011 8:00 am–12:00 pm   Combined Exhibit Halls AB
Exhibitor final move in
11:30 am–8:30 pm Box Office by Hall A
OPEN: Ticket prices, Adults $6, Children 12 & under $3

FIGURE 14–5 Conference Event Document.
(*Source:* Courtesy of the San Diego Convention Center Corporation.)

VENUES FOR MEETINGS, CONVENTIONS, AND EXPOSITIONS

Most of the time, meetings and functions are held in hotels, convention centers, city centers, conference centers, universities, corporate offices, or resorts; however, today more meetings are being held in unique venues, such as cruise ships and historical sites.

City Centers

Discover the Importance of Room Setup When Choosing a Venue

A city center is a good venue for some conferences, as it is convenient to reach by air and ground transportation. There is plenty of action in a major city center: attractions range from cultural to scenic beauty. Most cities have a convention center and several hotels to accommodate guests.

Convention Centers

Convention centers throughout the world compete to host the largest exhibitions, which may contribute several million dollars in revenue to the local economy. Convention centers are huge operations that include parking, information services, business centers, and food and beverage facilities.

Convention centers are usually corporations owned by county, city, or state governments and operated by a board of appointed representatives from the various groups that have a vested interest in the successful operation of the center. The board appoints a president or general manager to run the center according to a predetermined mission, and goals and objectives.

Convention centers have a variety of expositions and meeting rooms to accommodate both large and small events. The centers generate revenue from the rental of space, which frequently is divided into booths (one booth is about 100 square feet). Large exhibits may take up several booths. Additional revenue is generated by the sale of food and beverages, concession stand rentals, and vending machines. Many centers also have their own subcontractors to handle staging, construction, lighting, audiovisual, electrical, and communications.

In addition to the megaconvention centers, a number of prominent centers also contribute to the local, state, and national economies. One good example is the Rhode Island Convention Center. The $82 million center, representing the second-largest public works project in the state's history, is located in the heart of downtown Providence, adjacent to the 14,500-seat Providence Civic Center. The 365,000-square-foot center offers a 100,000-square-foot main exhibit hall, a 20,000-square-foot ballroom, 18 meeting rooms, and a full-service kitchen that can produce 5,000 meals per day.

Conference Centers

A conference center is a specially designed learning environment dedicated to hosting and supporting small- to medium-sized meetings, typically between 20 to 50 people.[4] The nature of a conference meeting is to promote a distraction-free learning environment. Conference centers are designed to encourage sharing of information in an inviting, comfortable atmosphere, and to focus sharply on meetings and what makes them effective. Although the groups that hold meetings in conference centers are typically small in terms of attendees, there are thousands of small meetings held every month. Increasingly, hotels are now going after executive meetings, where expense is not a major issue.

Hotels and Resorts

Hotels and resorts offer a variety of locations from city center to destination resorts. Many hotels have ballrooms and other meeting rooms designed to accommodate groups of various sizes. Today, they all have Web sites and offer meeting planners to help with the planning and organizing of conferences and meetings. Once the word gets out that a meeting planner is seeking a venue for a conference, there is plenty of competition amongst the hotels to get the business.

Cruise Ships

A nontraditional facility can provide a unique and memorable experience for the meeting attendee. However, many of the challenges faced in traditional venues such as hotels and convention centers are also applicable to these facilities. In some cases, planning must begin much earlier with alternative meeting environments than with traditional facilities. A thorough understanding of goals and objectives, budget, and attendee profile of the meeting is essential to negotiate the best package possible. A cruise ship meeting is uniquely different from the meeting setting and offers a number of advantages to the attendees, such as discounts, complementary meals, fewer outside distractions while at sea, entertainment, and the opportunity to visit more than one destination while unpacking only once!.[5]

Colleges and Universities

Alternative venues for meeting places also include colleges and universities and their campuses. The paramount consideration in contemplating the use of campus-based facilities is to know the nature of the target audience.[6] A certain knowledge and evaluation of the participants is inevitable and invaluable because the relative cost of campus-based meetings is usually less expensive than a medium-priced hotel.

TRENDS in MEETINGS, CONVENTIONS, AND EXPOSITIONS

- **Globalization/international participation:** More people are traveling abroad to attend meetings.
- **The cloning of shows:** Some international shows do not travel very well (i.e., agricultural machinery). Thus, organizations such as Bleinheim or Reed Exposition Group airlift components to create shows in other countries.
- **Competition:** Competitiveness has increased among all destinations. Convention centers will expand and new centers will come online.
- **Technology:** The industry needs to be more sophisticated. The need for fiber-optics is present everywhere.

- Shows are growing at a rate of 5 to 10 percent per year.
- Compared to a few years ago, large conventions are not as well attended, and regional conventions have more attendees.

CASE STUDY

Double-Booked

The convention bureau in a large and popular convention destination has jurisdiction over the convention center. A seasoned convention sales manager, who has worked for the bureau for seven years and produces more sales than any other sales manager, has rebooked a 2,000-person group for a three-day exposition in the convention center. The exposition is to take place two years from the booking date.

The client has a 15-year history of holding conventions, meetings, and expositions in this convention center and has always used the bureau to contract all space and services for them. In fact, the sales manager handling the account has worked with the client for 7 of the 15 years. The bureau considers this client a "preferred customer."

The convention group meeting planner has recently appeared in a magazine ad giving a testimony of praise for the convention bureau, this particular sales manager, and the city as a destination for conventions.

Shortly after the meeting planner rebooks this convention with the bureau, the bureau changes sales administration personnel, not once, but three times. This creates a challenge for the sales manager in terms of producing contracts, client files, and event profiles, and in the recording and distribution of information. The preferred customer who rebooked has a contract, purchase orders for vendor services, a move in and setup agenda, and an event profile, all supplied by the sales manager. The sales manager has copies of these documents as well. The two hotels where the group will be staying also have contracts for the VIP group.

Other sales managers at the bureau have been booking and contracting space for the same time period as the group that rebooked. In fact, the exhibit hall has been double-booked, as have the break-out rooms for seminars, workshops, and food and beverage service. The groups that were contracted later are all first-time users of the facility.

This situation remains undetected until 10 days prior to the groups' arrival. It is brought to the attention of the bureau and convention center only when the sales manager distributes a memo to schedule a pre-convention meeting with the meeting planner and all convention center staff.

Due to the administrative personnel changes, necessary information was not disseminated to key departments and key personnel. The convention center was never notified that space has been contracted for the preferred customer. The preferred customer has been told about this potentially catastrophic situation. Now there is a major problem to rectify.

DISCUSSION QUESTIONS

1. Ultimately, who is responsible for decision making in this situation?
2. What steps should be taken to remedy this situation?
3. Are there fair and ethical procedures to follow to provide space for the preferred customer? If so, what are they?
4. What measures, if any, should be taken in handling the seasoned sales manager?
5. What leverage does the meeting planner have to secure this and future business with the bureau?
6. What might the preferred customer do if they are denied space and usage of the convention center?
7. How can this situation be avoided in the future?

CAREER INFORMATION

Meetings, incentive travel, conventions, and expositions (the MICE segment) offer a broad range of career paths. Successful meeting planners are detail-oriented, organized people who not only plan and arrange meetings, but also negotiate hotel rooms and meeting space in hotels and convention centers.

Incentive travel includes aspects of organizing high-end travel, hotels, restaurants, attractions, and entertainment. With big budgets, this can be an exciting career for those interested in a combination of travel and hotels in exotic locations.

Conventions and convention centers offer several career paths, from assistants to sales managers to sales managers for a special type of account (e.g., associations) or territory. Senior sales managers are expected to book large conventions and expositions—yes, everyone has their quota. Event managers plan and organize the function/event with the client once the contract has been signed. Salaries range from $35,000 to $70,000 for both assistants on up to sales or event managers. Careers are also possible in the companies that service the MICE segment.

Someone has to equip the convention center, get it ready for an exposition, and supply all the food and beverage items. Off-premise catering and special events also offers careers for creative people who like to come up with concepts and themes around which an event or function may be planned.

For all career paths, it is critical to gain experience in the areas of your interest. Ask people you respect to be your mentor. Ask questions! When you show enthusiasm, people will respond with more help and advice. Figure 14–6 illustrates a career path to becoming a meeting planner; Figure 14–7 shows an event manager's job description at a convention center.

John Moors, former administrator of the Tampa Convention Center, offers the following advice: "The convention and meeting industry needs qualified candidates. Many come into the convention side of the industry with transferable skills from hotels and resorts with basic business principles. We hire personalities, not résumés. It does not take long to learn how to set up a meeting room. It does, however, take experience to learn how to lead people—this leadership aspect is very important. Get your degree! But remember, it's not only what you learn in the classroom, but also your-demonstrated ability to stick to something and achieve it. So get into the industry and find a mentor. Good luck!"

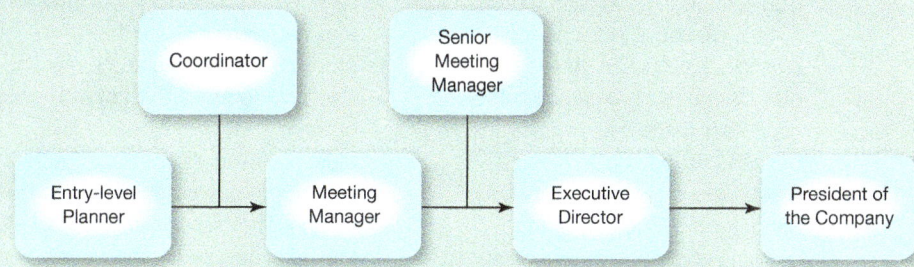

FIGURE 14–6 A Career Path to Becoming a Top-Level Event Manager.

EVENT MANAGER

DEFINITION

Under moderate direction from the services manager, plans, directs, and supervises assigned events and represents services manager on assigned shifts.

KEY RESPONSIBILITIES

- Plans, coordinates, and supervises all phases of the events to include set-ups, move ins and outs, and the activities themselves
- Prepares and disseminates set-up information to the proper departments well in advance of the activity, and ensures complete readiness of the facilities
- Responsible for arranging for all services needed by the tenant
- Coordinates facility staffing needs with appropriate departments
- Acts as a consultant to tenants and the liaison between in-house contractors and tenants
- Preserves facility's physical plant and ensures a safe environment by reviewing tenants' plans; requests and makes certain they comply with facility, state, county, and city rules and regulations
- Prepares accounting paperwork of tenant charges, approves final billings, and assists with collection of same
- Resolves complaints, including operational problems and difficulties
- Assists in conducting surveys, gathering statistical information, and working on special projects as assigned by services manager
- Conducts tours of the facilities

MINIMUM REQUIREMENTS

- Bachelor's degree in hospitality management, business, or recreational management from a fully accredited university or college, plus two (2) years of experience in coordinating major conventions and trade shows
- Combination of related education/training and additional experience may substitute for bachelor's degree
- An excellent ability to manage both fiscal and human resources
- Knowledge in public relations; oral and written communications
- Experienced with audiovisual equipment

225 Broadway, Suite 710 • San Diego, CA 92102 • (619) 239-1989
FAX (619) 239-2030
Operated by the San Diego Convention Center Corporation

FIGURE 14–7 An Event Manager's Job Description.

SUMMARY

1. Conventions, meetings, and expositions serve social, political, sporting, or religious purposes. Associations offer benefits such as a political voice, education, marketing avenues, member services, and networking.
2. Meetings are events designed to bring people together for the purpose of exchanging information. Typical forms of meetings are conference, workshops, seminars, forums, and symposiums.
3. Expositions bring together purveyors of products, equipment, and services in an environment in which they can demonstrate their products. Conventions are meetings that include some form of exposition or trade show.
4. Meeting planners contract out their services to associations and corporations. Their responsibilities include pre-meeting, on-site, and postmeeting activities.
5. The convention and visitors bureaus are nonprofit organizations that assess the needs of the client and organize transportation, hotel accommodations, restaurants, and attractions.
6. Convention centers are huge facilities, usually owned by the government, where meetings and expositions are held. Events at convention centers require a lot of planning ahead and careful event management. A contract that is based on the event profile and an event document is part of effective management.

KEY WORDS AND CONCEPTS

Associations
Convention
Convention and visitors bureaus (CVBs)
Convention center
Exposition
Familiarization (FAM) trip
Incentive market
Meeting
Meeting planner
Meetings, incentive travel, conventions, and exhibitions (MICE)
Social, military, educational, religious, and fraternal groups (SMERF)

REVIEW QUESTIONS

1. What are associations and what is their purpose?
2. List the number of different people and organizations involved with meetings, conventions, and expositions.
3. List the primary sources of revenue and expenses involved in holding a meeting, a convention, and an exposition.
4. Describe the main types of meeting setups.
5. Explain the difference between an exposition and a convention.
6. List the duties of CVBs.
7. Describe the topics a meeting planner needs to deal with before, during, and after a meeting.

INTERNET EXERCISES

1. Organization: Best of Boston
   Web site: www.bestboston.com
   Summary: Best of Boston is an event planning company that specializes in putting together packages for different events, such as conventions, corporate events, private parties, and weddings.
   a. Click on the company's Web site for events and list the different kinds of events they can organize.
   b. By simply browsing through the Web site, discuss the importance of networking in the meetings, conventions, and expositions industry.
2. Organization: M & C Online
   Web site: www.meetings-conventions.com
   Summary: This excellent Web site offers in-depth information on meetings and conventions from different perspectives, ranging from legal issues to unique themes and concepts.
   Click on Latest News (on the left, halfway down the page).
   a. What is the latest news?
   b. Click on "the current issue" to see what these stories include, then share your findings with your class.

APPLY YOUR KNOWLEDGE

1. Make a master plan that includes the necessary steps to hold a meeting or seminar on careers in hospitality management.

SUGGESTED ACTIVITY

1. Contact meeting planners in your area and, with permission of your professor, invite them to speak to the class about their work and how they do it. Prepare questions in advance so that they may be given to the speakers ahead of time.

ENDNOTES

1. http://en.wikipedia.org/wiki/Trade_association.
2. http://en.wikipedia.org/wiki/Professional_association.
3. Stephen Barth, *Hospitality Law: Managing Issues in the Hospitality Industry* (Hoboken, NJ: John Wiley & Sons, Inc., 2006), pp. 26–29.
4. *Professional Meeting Management*, (4th ed. The Professional Convention Management Association), 2004, pp. 557–561.
5. Ibid., pp. 564–565.
6. *Professional Meeting Management*, (4th ed. The Professional Convention Management Association, 2004), p. 552.

15 SPECIAL EVENTS

LEARNING OUTCOMES

After reading and studying this chapter, you should be able to:

Define a special event.

Describe what event planners do.

Classify special events.

Outline the skills and abilities required for event management.

Identify the main professional organizations and associations involved with the special event industry.

HTi

Describe the economic impact of tourism.

The **special events industry** is a dynamic, diverse field that has seen considerable growth and change over the past 40 years. Today, the industry employs professionals who work together to provide a broad range of services to create what is termed a special event. But, what is a special event? Dr. Joe J. Goldblatt, a leading academic and author in the special event field, distinguishes between a daily event and a special event in the following manner:

Daily Events	Special Events	Examples
Occur spontaneously	Are always planned	Convention
Do not arouse expectations	Always arouse expectations	Meeting
Usually occur without a reason	Are usually motivated by a reason for celebration	Festival Wedding

He uses these contributing factors to shape a definition of a special event: *"A special event recognizes a unique moment in time with ceremony and ritual to satisfy specific needs."*[1] The scope of this definition is very broad and encompasses many "moments." Special events include countless functions, such as **corporate seminars** and **workshops, conventions** and **trade shows, charity balls** and **fund-raisers, fairs and festivals**, and **social functions** such as **weddings and holiday parties**. It is for that reason, that the industry has seen such growth and presents so much potential for future careers and management opportunities.

Food, clothing, and shelter are the accepted basic physical needs that humans require. Following those needs is an emotional need to celebrate, which has a direct impact on the human spirit. All societies celebrate—whether it is publicly or privately, as individuals or in groups. The need to celebrate has been recognized by corporations, public and government officials, associations, and individuals. This has contributed to the rapid growth of the special event industry with a wide range of possible employment opportunities. When you consider all of the planners, caterers, producers, event sites, and others that become part of the "special event," you can only imagine the potential for future careers and employment possibilities.

Event management is a newcomer compared to the hotel and restaurant industries. Yet as you will soon learn, special events is a field that doesn't have rigid boundaries. Closely related fields that may overlap include marketing, sales, catering, and entertainment. Future growth trends in special event management provide plenty of career opportunities in all hospitality sectors.

This chapter presents an overview of the special events industry. You will learn about the various classifications of special events and where to look for future career opportunities. You will find information on the skills and abilities required to be successful in the field. Information on special event organizations, strategic event planning, and the future outlook of the industry will allow you to take a glimpse into this exiting, rewarding, and evolving field. As Frank Supovitz, vice president of special events for the National Hockey League says, "The stakes have never been higher. Sponsors are savvier. Audiences are more demanding. And, event producers and managers are held accountable by their clients to meet their financial and marketing goals more than ever before. . . . So, before the lights go down and the curtain rises, reach out for the experience and expertise and explore the opportunities in special event management."[2]

WHAT EVENT PLANNERS DO

Event planning is a general term that refers to a career path in the growing field of special events. Its forecast includes a growing demand for current and future employment opportunities. Like several other professions, event planning came about to fill a gap— someone needed to be in charge of all

> **“** Associations can be a valuable resource for students interested in a career in event management. Many offer scholarships and provide a great networking opportunity. **”**
>
> — Karen Harris

the gatherings, meetings, and conferences that were increasing in size, number, and spectacle among business and leisure sectors. Corporate managers had to step away from their assignments to take on the additional challenges of planning conventions and conferences. Government officials

Explore the Excitement of Event Planning: Read *The Event Planner's Guide to Meetings*

and employees were displaced from their assignments to arrange recruitment fairs and military events. Consequently, the planner became a person whose job description did not include "planning" whenever a special event was planned.

The title of **"event planner"** was first introduced at hotels and convention centers. Event planners are responsible for planning the event, from start to finish. This includes setting the date and location, advertising the event, providing refreshments or arranging catering services, speakers, or entertainment. Please keep in mind that this is a general list and will vary depending on the type, location, and nature of the event.

A VGM Career Book, *Opportunities in Event Planning Careers*, has the following to say about a good candidate: "In addition to good organizational skills, someone with a creative spirit, a flair for the dramatic, a sense of adventure, and a love of spectacle could expect to flourish in this field." Highlighted skills and characteristics of the professional event planner include:[3]

Someone has to manage this incredible event, the World Series.

- Computer skills
- Willingness to work a flexible schedule
- Willingness to work long hours
- Verbal and written communication skills
- Project management skills
- Ability to work with high-level executives
- Ability to initiate and close sales
- Ability to handle multiple tasks simultaneously
- Ability to interact with other departments
- Willingness to travel
- Experience in delegating
- Negotiating skills
- Enthusiasm
- Follow-through skills
- Budgeting skills
- Lots of patience
- Being a self-starter

EVENT MANAGEMENT

Event management can be as small as an office outing, or something larger, such as a music festival, Super Bowl or even the Olympics. Events can be on and off, annual or perennial (happening each year), or every four years (as with the Olympics). Events just do not happen by themselves; it takes a great deal of preparation to stage a successful event. To hold a successful event, the organizer should have a vision and leader–manager skills in key result areas: marketing, financial, operational, and legal. Getting good sponsorship is a big help. Sponsors provide money or in-kind contributions and receive recognition as a sponsor of the event, including use or display of their logo in the event's promotion. Sponsors expect to get something tangible in return for their sponsorship. Each year, thousands of people attend festivals and events of all kinds; most, if not close to all, events receive some sponsorship, because it is too costly to stage an event without sponsorship.

> **The art of networking will allow you to build a contact base that will help you succeed in the event industry.**
>
> Karen Harris

Event management requires special skills in marketing and sales (attracting the business in the first place); planning (ensuring that all details are covered and that everything will be ready on time); organization (making sure that key staff know what to do, why, when, where, and how); financial (creating and keeping to a budget); human resources and motivation (selecting, recruiting, training, and motivating the best people); lots of patience; and attention to detail. To gain business, an event manager prepares a proposal for the client's approval and contract signature. There are some important how-to's in preparing an event proposal: Find out as much information as possible about the event (if it has been previously held) or what the client has in mind. Ask organizers, attendees, providers, and others what went right, went wrong, or could be improved on. Write the proposal in business English, skipping the verbal foliage. Get creative—do something different and better and give them something to talk about; finally, do the numbers—nobody wants a surprise—create a pro-forma invoice so the client will know the costs, and surprise them by being on time and on budget.

An event can be expensive to put on; in addition to advertising there is a location charge, security costs, labor costs, and production costs (this may be food, beverage, and service, but also the staging and decor). Usually, the event manager has a good estimate of the number of ticket sales expected. She or he then budgets all costs, including entertainment, leaving a reasonable profit.

Event management also takes place at convention centers and hotels, where event managers handle all the arrangements after the sales manager has completed the contract. The larger convention center events are planned years in advance. As stated earlier, the convention and visitors bureau is usually responsible for the booking of conventions more than 18 months ahead. Obviously, both the convention and visitors bureau and the convention center marketing and sales teams work closely with each other. Once the booking becomes definite, the senior event manager assigns an event manager to work with the client throughout the sequence of pre-event, event, and postevent.

The booking manager is critical to the success of the event: he or she books the correct space, and works with the organizers to help them save money (by allocating only needed space and allowing the client to set up on time). A contract is written based on the event profile. The event profile stipulates in writing the client's requirements and gives the relevant information, such as which company will act as decorator/subcontractor to install carpets and set up the booths.

The contract requires careful preparation because it is a legal document and as such guarantees certain provisions. For example, the contract may specify that the booths may only be cleaned by center personnel or that food may be prepared for samples only, not for retail. After the contract has been signed and returned by the client, the event manager will make occasional follow-up calls until about six months before the event, when arrangements such as security, business services, and catering will be finalized. The event manager is the key contact between the center and the client. She or he will help the client by introducing approved subcontractors who are able to provide essential services.

Two weeks prior to the event, an event document is distributed to department heads. The event document contains all the detailed information that each department needs to know in order for the event to run smoothly. About 10 days before the event, a WAG meeting (week at a glance) is held. The WAG meeting is one of the most important meetings at the convention center because it provides an opportunity to avoid problems—like two event groups arriving at the same time or additional security for concerts or politicians. About this same time, a pre-convention or pre-expo meeting is held with expo managers and their contractors—shuttle bus managers, registration operators, exhibit floor managers, and so on. Once the setup begins, service contractors marshal the 18-wheeler trucks to unload the exhibits by using radio phones to call the trucks from a nearby depot. When the exhibits are in place, the exposition opens and the public is admitted.

The following information provides the stages in the event planning process.

Research

The first stage of event planning is to answer these simple questions:

1. Why should a special event be held?
2. Who should hold it?
3. Where should it be held?
4. What should the focus of the event be?
5. What outcomes are expected?

Once answers to these questions are available we can move to the second stage.

Design

The second stage in the event planning process can be the most exciting and challenging—at the same time. It is the area that allows freedom in creativity and the implementation of new ideas that support the objectives of the special event. The design process is a time when an event manager or team can brainstorm new innovative ideas or develop adaptations to previous

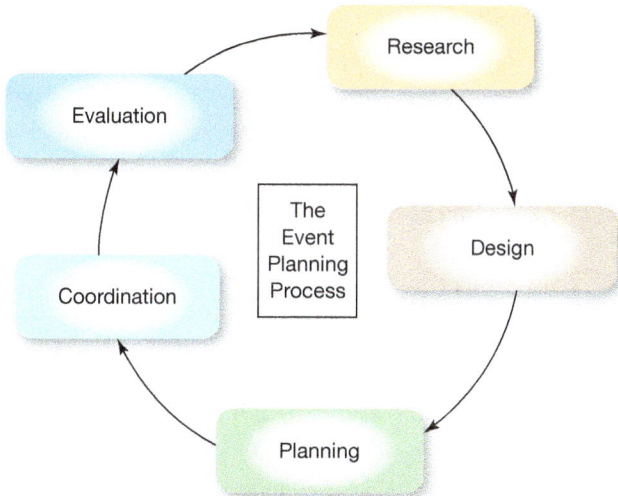

FIGURE 15–1 Event Planning Process Diagram.

events to make them better, grander, and more exciting for the attendees. The design process seeks to obtain original and fresh ideas that will create an event worth investing in. The event may be a corporate meeting or it may be a beachside wedding, yet the design of the event will have a lasting impression on those who attend it.

Planning

Planning, the third stage in the event planning process, is often led by the determined budget for the event. The planning process includes contracting out services and arranging all other activities that will become part of the event. The planning process may include:

- Determining the event budget
- Selecting the event site
- Selecting the hotel accommodations
- Arranging transportation
- Negotiating contracts
- Arranging catering
- Arranging speakers, entertainment, music
- Organizing audiovisual needs
- Creating a marketing plan for the event
- Preparing invitations or event packets

The type and size of the event will ultimately determine the steps required for the planning process. The information you learn about planning from your other courses and studies will help you if you choose to pursue a career in event management.

Coordination

The process of **coordination** can be compared to a director leading a band. The band may have rehearsed a piece of music countless times, and yet during a concert the director still has the ability to "direct" or control the number being performed. Similarly, the event manager coordinates the event as it unfolds. This may be a stressful, due to unforeseen problems that occur, or it may be a truly rewarding time, with a flawless execution. Regardless, coordination of the event may require the planner's decision-making skills and abilities as the event progresses.

Coordination of the special event also includes an aspect of human resources. Event managers are leaders, who motivate others through example. As an event manager, you will coordinate staff and/or volunteers to carry out the event's planned objectives and goals. As mentioned earlier, empowering your staff will create a positive environment and make your job of coordinating their efforts that much easier.

Evaluation

Evaluation should take place during each stage of the event planning process; as a final step, it measures the success of the event in meeting goals and objectives. The event planning process is continuous, as you can see in Figure 15–1. Outcomes are compared to expectations, and variances are investigated and corrected.

CHALLENGES FOR EVENT PLANNERS AND MANAGERS

If you're considering a professional career in event management, there are event-planning tools to help you as you pursue a career in this field. Professional event managers face four primary challenges: time, finance, technology, and human resources.

Time management plays an important role in event planning; remember to budget your time in the same way that you would your finances. Delegating tasks to the appropriate people, keeping accurate records and lists, preparing agendas

Guests mingle at a charity event in Coral Gables, Florida.

Learn More about Special Events at the Nunally Meeting Room

before meetings, and focusing on what items deserve top priority are examples of how to use time management effectively.

As an event planner, you will dabble in financial management: evaluating financial data, management fees, vendor fees, etc. You do not have to be a financial wizard; however, knowledge in this area will greatly enhance your opportunity to make profitable and sound decisions. You can take advantage of resources such as advice from a financial professional, or technology to help in event accounting.

Technology can assist event managers in the areas of time management and finances. Word processing programs, and financial and database management software can help in daily tasks and event planning. Other technology tools used by event professionals include laptop computers, cell phones, hand-held devices, event management software, and the Internet.

One more tool relates to the effective management of human resources. Empowering your employees is the key to success. As a manager and leader, you must train your employees and/or volunteers and give them the necessary information to perform their jobs. It is critical to select the right people, "empower" them, and develop their skills. This will ultimately help you succeed in accomplishing your goals. Empowering event staff can help them make important decisions—successful events involve many decisions, and you as a manager will not have the time to make all of them. Empowering your team is the best way to become an effective leader and improve the performance of your staff.

Classifications of Special Events

The development of the special events industry has been divided up into the following classifications:

- Corporate events (seminars, workshops, meetings, conferences)
- Association events (conventions, trade shows, meetings)
- Charity balls and fund-raising events
- Social functions (weddings, engagement parties, holiday functions)
- Fairs and festivals
- Concert and sporting events

Explore the World of Special Events and Event Planning

In a poll taken from a wide variety of event professionals in the industry, *Event Solutions Black Book* listed the following as the most popular types of event sites used:[4]

Site	Percentage
Hotel/Resort	62.0%
Convention Center	32.5%
Tent/Structure	32.6%
Banquet Hall	29.0%
Outdoors	21.8%
Corporate Facility	28.4%
Museum/Zoo/Gardens	12.4%
Arena/Stadium/Theatre	18.0%
Restaurant	16.1%
Private Residence	22.8%
Club	16.7%

With those figures in mind, we will now take a closer look at the various classifications that make up this exciting industry. Each category has its own unique characteristics, rewards, and challenges. As a human resource specialist would say, "It's important to put the right person in the right position." That statement also holds true here. Any career selection, and especially for a person seeking a management level, should look for the correct "fit." With such a vast array of options, you may find one that ignites your passion, find several that are the wrong size before you find the right one, or decide that this is not the right match for your personality and goals.

Check Your Knowledge

1. Give some differences between a daily event and a special event.
2. What are event planners responsible for?
3. Name the stages in the event planning process.

Corporate Events

Corporate events continue to lead the industry in terms of event business. About 80 percent of the event market is corporate events.

Corporate event managers are employed by the company to plan and execute the details of meetings for the corporation's employees, management, and owners. The growing use of special events in the corporate arena created the need for positions dedicated to the planning and management of them. Corporate event planners are involved in the planning and organizing of the event, and they also play a key leadership role. Planners must be skilled in communications, have the ability to coordinate various activities, and pay careful attention to detail.

Corporate events include annual meetings, sales meetings, new product launches, training meetings and workshops, management meetings, press meetings, incentive meetings, and awards ceremonies.

Corporate events benefit several sectors of the hospitality industry. For example, a client may hold an event at a major attraction like SeaWorld or at a resort like The Breakers. Each corporate client can spend tens of thousands of dollars on the hotel, restaurants, airlines, and other businesses in the destination's economy. When using a hotel, corporate event planners consider the factors that are most important to the attendees, such as corporate account rates for lodging, amenities like fitness centers and business centers, airport transportation, and quick check-in and check-out at the hotel. Therefore, corporate event planners should have strong negotiating skills to book lodging and convention services as needed.

Association Events

There are over 6,500 associations in the United States alone (the American Medical Association and the American Dental Association are two of the most recognized examples). The majority of the large association conventions are planned two to five years ahead of time, and the destination is a determining factor in the planning process. In the hospitality industry, the National Restaurant Association (NRA), American Hotel and Lodging Association (AH&LA), and at a global level the International Association of Convention and Visitors Bureaus are few of the many associations relating to special events. Associations account for about $60 billion annually in revenue generated from the 32.6 million people that attend an estimated 315,000 meetings and conventions in the U.S. For example, the American Marketing Association holds over 20 conferences each year, generating approximately $2 million. One hotel alone receives half of the revenues generated by the conference.[5]

Read about Association Events in *The Meeting Planner's Guide to Meetings*

Association events may range from a monthly luncheon at a private club or hotel to a yearly convention consisting of educational seminars where association members can network

Microsoft Chairman Bill Gates introduces Jay Leno at a corporate function.

with each other. Associations generally hire full-time paid planners to manage the yearly national membership meeting that is required as part of most associations' bylaws. Larger associations with greater financial resources often hire full-time meeting and convention management professionals who are involved in the large association events as well as other association events, including board meetings, educational seminars, membership meetings, professional meetings, and regional meetings.

Other opportunities for employment are widespread. They may include a position as a convention manager, special event manager in a hotel, conference manager, or a special event manager at a private club for events held by local associations.

In the event planning industry, professional associations have a great impact in contributing to the development of their members in the training, certification, networking, and assistance with business plans and other consulting services that they provide.

Associations can be a valuable resource for students. Many offer scholarships and provide a great networking opportunity. I received a scholarship from the American Association of University Women, and was therefore prompted to join as a student affiliate. Students interested in a career in event management can gain valuable experience by attending the meetings, and more importantly, by becoming involved. Volunteering is rarely turned down!

—Karen Harris

Charity Balls and Fund-Raising Events

Charity balls and fund-raising events provide a unique opportunity for an event manager to work with a particular group or charity. A theme is typically chosen for the event. The event manager is responsible for selecting the location and coordinating all of the details that will determine the success of the event, including catering, entertainment, decor, lighting, floral arrangements, invitations, rentals, public relations, transportation, security, and technical support.

One key skill that a person entering this category must possess is the ability to plan the event on a set and often limited budget. Why is this so critical? The purpose of these kinds of events is to raise funds for a group or charity; every dollar spent on the event means one less that could go toward the cause. Nevertheless, these events are expected to be extravagant—so a little creativity can go a long way in planning and implementing a theme. The event manager should also have strong negotiating skills to bargain with vendors for reduced rates or in some cases donated services or products. A smart planner knows how to market the positive public relations that the event could provide its vendors.

> " About 80 percent of the event market is corporate events. "

The demand for fund-raising event planners/managers holds solid ground. To prove this point, *Opportunities in Event Planning Careers* quoted an in-house event planner as stating: "One of the major advantages of working for a nonprofit as an in-house planner for almost six years was that I never had to look for work. There were always new events to take on."[6]

Volunteering is one of the best ways to gain experience in the event industry: charity/fund-raising events provide a great opportunity for this. I recently volunteered as a banquet server for the "Star Night Gala." More importantly, however, I had the chance to meet various people involved in the planning, and to ask questions! Check your local paper for "upcoming events"; you also look for a local charity register that provides a calendar of events for the upcoming year.

"Volunteers are not paid. Not because they are worthless, but because they are priceless . . ."—University of South Florida, Circle K International motto

The ability to learn as a volunteer truly is priceless!

—Karen Harris

Social Events

Social function planners or managers work on a broad variety of events, including the traditional wedding (which most of us are familiar with). Other events in this category include engagement parties, birthday parties, anniversary parties, holiday parties, graduation parties, military occasions, and social gatherings. A social event planner/manager is usually responsible for selecting the venue, determining any themes and or design schemes, ordering or planning decorations, arranging for catering and entertainment, and having invitations printed and sent out.

SMERF, which stands for social, military, educational, religious, and fraternal organizations, is a category of organizations that also fall into the social event category. Individuals of these organizations often pay for the events, meaning they are price sensitive. Needless to say, budgeting skills are important for anyone working with these groups.

A wedding is the most widely recognized social event, and a wedding planners is a key player in the social event category. The title seems glamorous, yet planning a wedding involves strict attention to detail. Don't forget that the planner is responsible for creating what is considered to be the most important day of a couple's life. "Realize that this is a business," says Gerard J. Monaghan, president of the Association of Bridal Consultants. "A fun business to be sure, but a business, nonetheless." An effective wedding planner makes contacts or a variety of services, including venues (like hotels), wedding locations, decorating, catering, bridal shops, musicians, photographers, and florists.

Weddings are more expensive than ever, and they often last longer. They have become true "special events" due to the willingness of family and friends to travel greater distances to celebrate with the bride and groom. Many weddings today have become "mini vacations" for the guests.

Check Your Knowledge

1. What event business continues to lead the industry?
2. When are the majority of large association conventions planned?
3. What key skills must a person entering the charity ball category possess?
4. What is SMERF?

Fairs and Festivals

Refresh Your Knowledge of Fairs and Other Planned Play Environments

The word "fair" is likely to evoke memories of cotton candy, funnel cakes, Ferris wheels, and other games. These memories are very important to why a fair is considered a special event, but the purpose of most fairs in the United States is usually related to the agriculture industry. These fairs are usually produced by a professional staff chosen by an elected local committee. Fairs are generally held at the local, county, or state level.

Festivals are planned events with a theme that often relates to the celebration's purpose. Cultures, anniversaries, holy days, and special occasions are commonly celebrated as a festival. Mardi Gras, for example, celebrates the beginning of Lent. Food and entertainment are greatly emphasized when planning a festival. Festivals.com is a Web site that allows you to search for festivals held around the world. The variety of festivals is astounding—art, music, sporting, literary, performing arts, air shows, science, and even children's festivals. Festivals.com describes cultural festivals as, "Magical parades. Fabulous feasts. Dizzying dancing. The spirit of celebration crosses languages, oceans, continents and cultures, as people revel in their heritages and communities."[7]

The following is a small sampling of festivals—some are commonly known; others are surprising.

Oktoberfest	Mardi Gras	Biketoberfest
Hispanic Heritage Festival	Street Music Festival	American Dance Festival
Polar Bear Jumpoff Festival	Gilroy Garlic Festival	Bagelfest

One of the key strategies in planning special events for fairs and festivals is to determine the purpose of the event early on. It is important to analyze the "available manpower" in the form of both professionals and volunteers who will assist in staging the event. The **International Festival & Events Association (IFEA)** provides an opportunity for event managers from around the world to network and exchange ideas on how other festivals excel in sponsorship, marketing, fund-raising, operations, volunteer coordination, and management. (The IFEA will be highlighted later in the chapter.)

Concerts and Sporting Events

Learn about Event Production at the Sea Wolfe Arena

Concert promoters are an alternate career choice relating to special events. (We will focus on smaller concert and music events here.) Woodstock, in 1969, was a large music festival that has been labeled as a transformational event—it altered the lives of the participants, and society as a whole. Many concerts are planned as fund-raisers, such as Live Aid, which was a rock concert held in 1985 that raised millions of dollars to benefit starving people of Africa. On a smaller scale, universities may provide a concert as a special event.

The sporting events' opening ceremonies, halftime, and postgame shows provide another "arena" for an event manager to select as a career path. These shows are highly visible due to the large number of sporting events that are televised. This provides a unique challenge for the event manager—to satisfy the millions of television viewers as well as those watching in the stadium (or whatever the venue may be).

Sporting events have historically been more popular than other forms of entertainment. This is probably due to our competitive nature and a desire to watch those who compete—a kind of flashback to the gladiator days of old. It is important to remember when planning special events in the sports environment that the primary attention should remain on the athletes and the competition. Therefore, the special event should be

CASE STUDY

Where Do Event Planners Work?

- Hotels/Resorts
- Private Corporations
- Associations
- Caterers
- The Government
- Private Clubs
- Convention Centers
- Bridal Businesses
- Event Production Companies
- Nonprofit Organizations
- Advertising Agencies
- Self-Employed

Discover the Excitement of Booking Sporting Events at the Sea Wolfe Arena

staged to "add to" and not "subtract from" the sport itself. Special events may even attract additional viewers and fans to the sport. The role of special events in the sports category has plenty of room for growth and expansion, as professional sports become more and more competitive.

Sports entertainment will likely see considerable growth in the future. After all, someone has to plan, organize, and run the halftime shows, as well as the events before and after the game. A large audience awaits your Super Bowl–sized imagination, which can ensure that every sporting event is a winning experience for the most important player of all—the fan.

Mega Events

Mega sporting events are some of the biggest moneymakers in the industry. Both large and small communities embrace mega sporting events because of their positive economic impact. Sports is a thriving industry. According to the Sports Tourism International Council, "$13.4 is spent on sport and recreational equipment, $14 billion is spent on sports supplies, and $6.2 billion is spent on theme parks and attraction attendance yearly."

Read about the Challenges of Booking and Scheduling Events

The *Olympic Games* is the hallmark of all sporting events, attracting over 6 million people to its host city. That is a lot of people traveling, staying in hotels, eating in restaurants, and possibly looking at the host city's attractions. The Olympics is an international sporting event that takes place every four years and it consists of both summer and winter games. The Olympics attract more people than any other sporting event, making it is easy to see why the Olympics play an important role in the industry.

The *World Cup* is an international competition that takes place every four years and features the best soccer teams in the world. Qualifying rounds take place during the three years before the final rounds, in which the championship is awarded. Close to one million people actually attend the World Cup, and millions more tune in via television or the Internet.

The *Super Bowl* is an annual competition between the two best American football teams. The game is traditionally held on "Super Bowl Sunday," which, over the years, has become a holiday for many Americans. The Super Bowl is one of the most-watched U.S. broadcasts of the year, but people don't just tune in for the game. They want to see the millions of dollars spent on the commercials! Viewers are also interested in the halftime show, which features some of the most popular musical artists. Another interesting fact is that this day is the second-largest food consumption day in the United States (the largest day is of course Thanksgiving). It is estimated that about 44 million people attend 7.5 million Super Bowl parties each year!

The *World Series* decides who has the best baseball team. This Major League Baseball (MLB) championship series occurs every year, starting in October, after the regular season is over. The series is a match between the American League and National League champions. The Series winner is determined through a best-of-seven playoff. The winning team is awarded the World Series Trophy, and each player receives a World Series ring.

There are four men's golf championships that are collectively known as *the Majors*. The *Masters Tournament* is an annual gathering of the world's best golf players on the Augusta National Golf Course. Champions of the Masters are automatically invited to play in the other three majors for the following five years, and earn a lifetime invitation to the Masters. The *U.S. Open Championship* is a men's open championship held in June of each year and is part of the official schedule of the PGA Tour and the European Tour. The U.S. Open takes place on a variety of golf courses. The *British Open* is the oldest of the four major championships in men's golf. It is played annually on a links course (which are located in coastal areas causing

Introducing Suzanne Bailey

Suzanne Bailey graduated from Southern Utah University with a BA in business administration, marketing in 1996. Eager to get her career started, she accepted an entry-level position at Bowl Games of America, a student travel/special event production company that produces several NCAA bowl game halftime shows, including the Orange Bowl (Miami, FL), Sugar Bowl (New Orleans, LA), Liberty Bowl (Memphis, TN), Alamo Bowl (San Antonio, TX), and Gator Bowl (Jacksonville, FL). BGA recruits high school marching bands and dance groups to perform in the field shows along with guest stars. The students earn an opportunity to perform with BGA by excelling in competition and working fund-raisers to pay for their three- to five-day trip. Within a year, Bailey found a role as an executive assistant within the division of the company that interested her most—the tiny but growing dance division of Bowl Games of America, BGA Performance.

Learn More about Careers in Sports Management

Bailey worked with the director of BGA Performance to create an entirely new marketing strategy, which eventually led to great success within the dance division. Rather than working with small high school dance groups exclusively, they set up a commission system with large private dance competition companies, which would market the bowl game performance opportunities to their competition winners. That marketing strategy led to 300 percent growth in the first year.

Bailey worked her way up the ladder to associate director and eventually director of BGA Performance. The work changes dramatically with the seasons. During dance competition season, the marketing effort is immense—it's time to make the big sales push. As director of BGA Performance, Bailey created and sent hundreds of invitation packets to private dance competition companies and made as many sales phone calls as possible. She also reviewed audition tapes and selected dancers for the bowl game halftime shows.

Once the dancers had signed up for the bowl game in which they would perform, Bailey's work shifted to roles in customer service and show production. She managed the numerous phone calls from dancers (and their directors and parents) with questions about their trip. She also worked with a BGA Performance operations director who books hotel rooms and arranges for transportation and meals for the dancers. Meanwhile, she hired a choreographer for each show and worked with the show's producer to create a show concept that included guest stars, props, lighting, music, and costumes.

Bailey traveled to each city a few months prior to the event with the dance directors and/or chaperones to give them a preview. These trips were always a lot of fun—"schmoozing" them with elegant dinners and fun activities. These included day cruises, and of course, a tour of the football stadium. The last few weeks of December were always the most hectic of the year for Bailey. Making sure everything was in place for the bowl games involved confirming choreography, rehearsal sites, costume orders, prop production, and final itinerary packets for the performers.

And finally, the events would take place. Bailey became an event director during the actual events. She would travel to the destination city a few days before the dancers arrived to confirm the schedule and details with hotel group sales managers, caterers, rehearsal site workers, and bowl game executives. She would meet and direct her on-site staff (choreography team and event staff). The workdays of these events can be long and exhausting, filled with excitement and anticipation. Much of the time is devoted to rehearsals, with some fun activities also included (for example, catered lunches, beach parties, and evening dinner/dance parties for the group at famous spots like Mardi Gras World in New Orleans). The dancers enjoy every minute of their week, including the long, hard rehearsals in the sun (rain, or snow, depending on the location). Game day (or show day) is always the most exciting. After much hard work and preparation, the dancers go out on the field for their five minutes of fame. They perform, along with famous guest stars and the BGA recruited marching bands, to a live stadium audience in the tens of thousands, and often a national television audience. This is when the position of director of BGA Performance really pays off. The excitement of the show outweighs all the frustrations and the logistics of putting it all together. It is extremely rewarding to watch these children have the time of their lives! For Bailey, the day after the performance was usually spent traveling to the next bowl game city and the process would starts all over again. . . .

Bailey had worked on bowl game halftime shows for about six years when the 2002 Olympics came to Salt Lake City, her hometown. As she had worked with the dance choreographer and other directors of the Olympic opening and closing ceremonies team for bowl game shows, she accepted a position with the ceremonies production team as senior production coordinator, volunteer cast. The Olympic opening ceremony is truly the pinnacle of any live production anytime, anywhere. Bailey helped manage a team of 15 cast coordinators, who

(Continued)

> worked with over 4,000 volunteer cast members and 200 production staff volunteers. She facilitated communication between choreographers, stage managers, the producers, and the cast. She managed all aspects of casting for the ceremonies, from recruitment to auditions to performer selection to the actual live performance. This was truly an opportunity of a lifetime for Bailey, and she enjoyed every minute of it.
>
> After the Olympics, Bailey started a family. She now accepts work as a subcontractor for specific events and shows. She enjoys tackling one project at a time according to her own schedule. The special events world is an exciting, exhausting, and fun place to work.

frequent wind, on sandy soil, often amid dunes, with few water hazards and few if any trees). The *U.S. PGA Championship* is the final championship of the year held in August. PGA champions are also automatically invited to play in the other three majors for the next five years, and are exempt for life from qualifying for the PGA Championship.

A number of boat races are held on an annual basis. *America's Cup*, held every four years, is perhaps the most famous of yachting races, and is also a test of boat design, sail design, fund-raising, and people. The races are held in a series that currently involves a best-of-nine of match racing (a duel between two boats).

Cruise lines also offer specialized sports cruises that invite spectators and participants to enhance their skills, meet professional athletes, attend major events, and simply immerse themselves in their favorite sports.

Required skills and abilities for event management

Special events management, like any other form of management, requires certain skills and abilities. The act of carrying out a successful event takes more than just an idea—it takes leadership, communication, project management, effective negotiating and delegating skills, the ability to work within a budget, the ability to multitask, enthusiasm, social skills, and even the ability to make contacts. The following information will provide an overview of skills critical to effective event management.

Leadership Skills

Leadership ability is the number one skill for successful event managers. The goal of an event manager is to become a leader who can direct a team of employees and/or volunteers who will respect, admire, and follow his or her direction to accomplish the established goals. As a leader, the event manager wears many hats. The first is to inspire the staff and volunteers by providing valid reasons as to why they should want to help achieve the established goals for the event. In this role, the event manager will also act as a salesperson. The second hat represents the event manager's responsibility to provide tools for the staff and volunteers to achieve the goals. This includes training and coordination. The third hat is that of coach. As a leader, the event manager will act as a mentor and provide a support system to build a team. Staff and volunteer motivation is an important factor for effective event management.

Effective event leadership can transform the people on your team. Empowering the members of your event team to find their own solutions will benefit both the people and the event. This will allow the team members to create new opportunities for themselves and stimulate personal growth. During the event, empowerment enables goals and objectives to be quickly achieved. Dr. Joe Jeff Goldblatt, CSEP, offers these event leadership tips:

- Event leadership enables your team members to find the motivation to continue achieving the event goals and objectives.
- You cannot motivate others; they must motivate themselves by identifying clear personal goals and objectives.
- Volunteers are the lifeblood of most events. Recruiting, training, coordinating, and rewarding are critical to the success of this activity.
- The three styles of event leadership are democratic, autocratic, and laissez-faire. Each style may be used during the course of the event.
- Policies, procedures, and practices serve as the blueprint for event decision-making.[8]

Ability to Communicate with Other Departments

The success of an event manager greatly depends on the ability of involved individuals to communicate effectively with one another. Communication can be oral, written, and electronic. It is very important for event managers to become effective communicators in order to maintain clear communications with all staff, volunteers, stakeholders, and other departments.

Written communications are an essential tool for record keeping and providing information to be mass distributed. Meetings are another tool that can be used to communicate with other departments.

Meeting planners coordinating events during a meeting.

Project Management Skills

Event planning and management can be time consuming. Therefore, a good planner should have effective project management skills and be equipped to balance all of the elements of one event (or more, if there are other events going on at the same time). Project management is the act of completing the project(s) on time and within budget. Project management is a perfect fit for the special event industry, where the entire event or components of an event can be managed as projects. These management tools, suggested by George G. Fenich, author of Meetings, Expositions, Events and Conventions, may be used to assist in event project management:

- Flow charts and graphs used for scheduling programs that will happen at the event. Look at any program of a meeting, and you will see the start and end times of seminars, when coffee breaks occur, when and where lunch is held, and when meetings resume. This charting of activities helps guide your attendees and guests.
- Clearly defined work setup and breakdown schedules for the event. This provides the event manager with an opportunity to determine tasks that may have been overlooked in the initial planning process for the event.
- Policy statements guide in the decision-making process and the fulfilling of commitments, including to human resources, sponsorships, security, ticketing, volunteers, and even to paid personnel for the event.[9]

Negotiating Skills

Negotiation is the process by which a meeting planner and supplier (hotel representative, for example) reach an agreement on the terms and conditions that will govern their relationship before, during, and after a meeting, convention, exposition, or event. An effective negotiator will enter the negotiation with a good idea of what he or she wants.

A negotiator gives the following tips:

- Do your homework. Develop a "game plan" of the outcomes sought, and prioritize your needs and wants. Learn as much about the other side's position as you can.
- Keep your eyes on the prize. Do not forget the outcome sought.
- Leave something on the table. It may provide an opportunity to come back later and renew the negotiations.
- Do not be the first one to make an offer. Letting the other person make the first move sets the outside parameters for the negotiation.
- Bluff, but do not lie.
- When there is a roadblock, find a more creative path. Thinking "outside the box" often leads to a solution.
- Timing is everything. Remember that time always works against the person who does not have it, and that 90 percent of negotiation usually occurs in the last 10 percent of the time allocated.
- Listen, listen, . . . listen and do not get emotional. Letting emotions rule a negotiation will cause one to lose sight of what result is important.[10]

The planning and execution of a special event may involve the negotiation of several contracts. The most important is generally the one with the facility or event site. Contracts with other services may include destination management, entertainment, catering, temporary employees, security, and audiovisual equipment, to name a few. An event manager should keep the following two words in mind to strengthen his or her negotiating skills and position: information and flexibility.

Coordinating and Delegating Skills

The management of staff and volunteers involves coordinating their duties and job performance to enable you to accomplish the goals of the event. As the manager, you are responsible for assigning supervisors or group leaders to oversee the performance of the employees and/or volunteers. It is important to provide coaching and mentoring when working with staff and volunteers to arrive at the event's goals and objectives. When employees can see the purpose and value of their work, as well as the outcomes, they usually become more excited about achieving the goals and objectives.

Budgeting Skills

Budgeting is an activity that allows managers to plan the use of their financial resources. In the event industry, the event planner may be working with a fixed budget determined by an association, SMERF group, or an individual (a wedding or engagement). In other cases, the budget may be more flexible—a large corporation, for example, that has greater financial resources. Budgeting is a required skill in all hospitality fields, including the special event industry.

The financial history of previous identical or similar events, the general economy and your forecast of the future, and the income expenses you reasonably believe you can expect with the resources available are all factors to be considered in creating an event budget. Even though most event managers will view the budgeting aspect as the least interesting in their job, it is an area that should be carefully managed and that is critical for success. The better you become with budgeting skills, the more you will be able to use resources for other "more creative" activities.

Ability to Multitask

Due to the nature of the business, an effective event manager should have the ability to multitask. During the planning and staging of the event, your ability to administrate, coordinate, market, and "manage" will be put to the test. Your job is ultimately to conduct and take control of whatever needs to be done to carry out your goals and objectives. You may encounter several problems arising at the same time, and an effective solution would be to delegate tasks accordingly.

Enthusiasm

As you've probably heard time and time again, in any hospitality field, the risk of burnout is high and the work is demanding. At the same time, however, the rewards are great—as is the satisfaction when the event is a complete success. As perfectly stated by Norman Brinker, chairman of the board of Brinker International, "Find out what you love to do and you'll never work a day in your life. . . . Make work like play, and play like hell!" Enthusiasm and passion. Drive and determination. These are all qualities that will contribute to the success of an event manager/planner. As shown in the profile of Suzanne Bailey, the special event industry is an "exciting, exhausting, and fun place to work." For those with the right enthusiasm and passion, it can be a truly rewarding career path.

Effective Social Skills

Social skills are an important trait for any management position, including one in the special event industry. Social skills are critical in making those you do business with feel comfortable, handling situations appropriately, and eliminating barriers that get in the way of accomplishing your goals. Communication is a critical social skill as is the other skill—listening. Social etiquette is another skill that can make or break a career, and it is a practiced skill that can be acquired. Social etiquette is defined as exhibiting good manners established as acceptable to society and showing consideration for others. Professionals in the hospitality industry, including the special event field, must be proficient in proper social etiquette. Service is one of the largest products offered; therefore, social skills and etiquette are required to

> " American Marketing Association holds over 20 conferences annually, which generates approximately $1,000,000 alone for one hotel that receives half of the business generated by the conference. "

be successful. Proper social etiquette is required in planning special events, and correct social manners are key to business success.[11] Effective social skills are also critical to leading a motivated group of staff and/or volunteers. How well you communicate, coach, instruct, lead, and listen are reflections of how well you will succeed as a manager.

Ability to Form Contacts

Many of us have heard the phrase: "It's not what you know, but who you know." Does this statement hold any value in the special event industry? It certainly does. An event may require various services, vendors, suppliers, or products. Here's how it works: An event planner prepares a specification of what is required and requests potential suppliers to submit their prices. The event planner then goes over this information with the client and they make a decision as to who will provide the services. Over time, event planners quickly find out who is the best provider and therefore the one they prefer to work with.

> ### Check Your Knowledge
> 1. **What does the International Festival & Events Association (IFEA) provide?**
> 2. **What is project management?**
> 3. **Define the process of negotiation.**

Wedding Planning

Weddings tend to be stressful and emotional. Remember the movie *The Wedding Planner*? Jennifer Lopez plays the role of a wedding planner and must handle many "situations." Because couples are either too busy or do not have the resources or know-how to plan and successfully organize a wedding, they hire a professional wedding planner. The wedding planner helps the couple, and their families, through the planning of the event to its organization and management.

Wedding planners need to:[12]

1. Be very clear to your client about what you will *not* do. By having an agreement in writing, there is less confusion and misunderstandings.
2. Be competitive in your pricing. Be honest with yourself and your ability to manage multiple tasks.

A good wedding consultant is able to skillfully and tactfully inject good taste into the basest of events. As a planner, your experience can give couples great ideas and fantastic scenarios that they may have otherwise over looked. Additionally you will have to act as mediator at some point in time during the planning stages. Knowing how to be subtle yet confident in your statements will go a long way in fostering better interpersonal relationships for your client and other families.[13]

Professional wedding planners need the following skills and knowledge:[14]

- Basic business management
- Basic accounting/bookkeeping
- Marketing and demographics
- Business English
- Business math
- Word processing/database management
- Art history
- Culinary techniques
- Color and design techniques
- Basic photography
- World religion
- Basic psychology and sociology
- Fashion history

The wedding planner's role is to make the planning and organization of the wedding go perfectly, and for there to be many happy memories for the bride and groom and their families. Wedding planners have a range of services that they can offer and have special relationships with vendors that can lead to discounts on pricing. Wedding planners need to have back-up plans and to "think on a dime." One tip is never to allow grandma to make the cake—the author once set up a three-tiered wedding cake only to find that the icing was so soft the cake actually fell over. At another wedding, an obviously short-sighted elderly server put salt in the sugar bowls; when the guests at the head table began to eat their fruit, their faces turned sour, one by one. Remember to have someone to act as the "master of ceremonies," or you may end up being one!

> We've all heard the term "networking." It is a practice worth the time and effort. Networking is one of the benefits of joining an association (explained in the next section). The art of networking will allow you to build a contact base that will help you succeed in the event industry. What would happen if your caterer backed out of a contract at the last minute? First of all, make sure you have a contract. Beyond that, having a strong contact base will allow you to plan for those "unexpected" occurrences that are bound to happen at some point in your career.
>
> —Karen Harris

Special Event Organizations

Like other hospitality industries, professional associations are a key contributor to the professional development of the special event field. Professional associations provide training and prestigious certification to their members, and membership provides an opportunity to network with other professionals in the field. Furthermore, associations can help members connect with vendors that provide products and services relating to special events.

International Festivals & Events Association

The International Festivals & Events Association (IFEA) has provided fund-raising and modern developmental ideas to the special events industry for 45 years. The IFEA began the program to enhance the level of festival management training and performance with a certified festival & event executive (CFEE) in 1983. Those seeking to achieve this distinguished title are committed to excellence in festival and event management, are using it as a tool for career advancement, and are in the search to further their knowledge. The organization currently has more than 2,700 professional members who are informed through IFEA publications, seminars, an annual convention and trade show, and ongoing networking.[17]

In accordance with an IFEA statement, "The CFEE program is a four-part process based on festival and event management experience, achievements and knowledge. Enrolling in the program and fulfilling the requirements listed above is the first step. Completing the application is next. Successfully completing an oral interview with member(s) of the CFEE Commission is the third. After achieving the CFEE designation, the fourth step is to maintain the designation through continuing education and participation in the profession."

The benefits of joining this association and meeting the CFEE requirements include being able to negotiate a better income or financial package, recognition by other industry professionals, and the "inside" knowledge that it provides for the

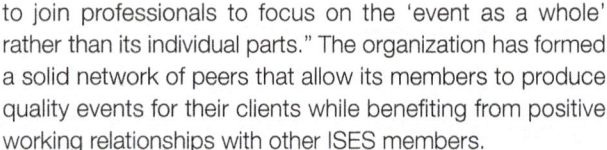

Corporate Profile

INTERNATIONAL SPECIAL EVENTS SOCIETY

The **International Special Events Society (ISES)** was founded in 1987, and now has grown to involve nearly 4,000 members who are active in 38 chapters around the world. The organization has professionals representing special event producers (from festivals to trade shows), caterers, decorators, florists, destination management companies, rental companies, special effects experts, audiovisual technicians, party and convention coordinators, hotel sales managers, specialty entertainers, and many others.

The ISES was founded with a goal to "foster enlightened performance through education while promoting ethical conduct. ISES works to join professionals to focus on the 'event as a whole' rather than its individual parts." The organization has formed a solid network of peers that allow its members to produce quality events for their clients while benefiting from positive working relationships with other ISES members.

The ISES awards a designation of certified special events professional (CSEP), which is considered to be the benchmark of professional achievement in the special events industry. "It is earned through education, performance, experience, service to the industry, portfolio presentation and examination, and reflects a commitment to professional conduct and ethics," as stated by the ISES. The program includes a self or group study program, point assessment of experience and service, application form, and exam.[15] Visit the ISES Web site at www.ises.com for further information.

Professional associations also help their members create a business plan and provide other forms of consultation. Job banks and referral services are even provided by some associations. The following information provides a brief overview of the key associations relating to the special event industry.

ISES Mission Statement

The mission of ISES is to educate, advance, and promote the special events industry and its network of professionals along with related industries.
To that end, we strive to . . .

- Uphold the integrity of the special events profession to the general public through our "Principles of Professional Conduct and Ethics"
- Acquire and disseminate useful business information
- Foster a spirit of cooperation among its members and other special events professionals, and . . .
- Cultivate high standards of business practices.[16]

festival industry. Visit the IFEA Web site at www.ifea.com for further information.

Meeting Planners International

Meeting Planners International (MPI) is a Dallas-based association with nearly 19,000 members. As stated on the MPI Web site, "As the global authority and resource for the $102.3 billion meeting and event industry, MPI empowers meeting professionals to increase their strategic value through education, clearly defined career pathways, and business growth opportunities." MPI offers professional development in two certification programs:

- Certified meeting professional (CMP)
- Certification in meeting management (CMM)

The CMP program is based on professional experience and academic examination, which then allows the professional to use the CMP designation after his or her name on business cards, letterheads, and other printed items. Additionally, studies show that CMPs earn up to $10,000 more annually than non-CMPs.[18]

Certification in meeting management is directed toward senior-level meeting professionals and provides an opportunity for continuing education, global certification and recognition, potential career advancement, and a networking base.[19] Visit the MPI Web site at www.mpiweb.org for more information.

Local Convention and Visitors Bureaus

A convention and visitor bureau (CVB) is a not-for-profit organization that is located in almost every city in the United States and Canada. Many other cities throughout the world also have a CVB or convention and visitors association (CVA). Simply stated, the CVB is an organization with the purpose of promoting tourism, meetings, and related business for their city. The CVB has three primary functions:

Discover the Importance of Marketing and the Sales Process at Little Wolfe Island CVB

- Encourage groups to hold meetings, conventions, and trade shows in the city or area it represents
- Assist those groups with meeting preparations and during the event
- Encourage tourists to visit the historic, cultural, and recreational opportunities the destination offers

The CVB does not engage in the actual planning or organizing of meetings, conventions, and other events. However, the CVB assists meeting planners and managers in several ways. First of all, it will provide information about the destination, area attractions, services, and facilities. Second, it provides an unbiased source of information to the planner. Finally, most of the services offered by the CVB are at no charge because they are funded through other sources including hotel occupancy taxes and membership dues. Therefore it can provide an array of services to event planners and managers. A sample of general services provided by a CVB include:

- CVBs act as a liaison between the planner and the community
- CVBs can help meeting attendees maximize their free time through the creation of pre- and postconference activities, spouse tours, and special evening events
- CVBs can provide hotel room counts and meeting space statistics
- CVBs can help with meeting facility availability
- CVBs are a network for transportation—shuttle service, ground transportation, and airline information
- CVBs can assist with site inspections and familiarization tours
- CVBs can provide speakers and local educational opportunities
- CVBs can provide help in securing auxiliary services, production companies, catering, security, and so forth

Sustainable Special Events

Sustainable events combine many of the elements that each of the preceding chapters offer. Some of the more noticeable efforts of sustainable events include:[20]

- Holding the event at a sustainable location—a certified green building.
- Utilizing the services of a certified green restaurant or caterer.
- Adopting Seven-Star turn-key green event services for environmentally Responsible and socially Respectful (eR/sR) festivals, trade and consumer expositions, conferences, and concerts.
- Joining and participating in the Green Meeting Industry Council.
- Develop and implement an operational and product usage plan.

Sustainability is gaining momentum in the hospitality industries and this trend will likely continue. As awareness of sustainability increases, special event clients will expect greener events and seek out those who offer them. Organizations like Seven-Star offer services like event production, budgeting, requests for proposal (RFPs) site inspections, venue and vendor contracts, floor plan design, policies, regulations and compliance, carbon footprint tracking and more—all in a shade of green.

The special event job market

Becoming a special event consultant or an off-premise catering/event specialist requires a delicate balance of many skills. Experience gained from several avenues will propel you to the heights of success. As with any career, an "experience ladder" must be climbed.

First, allow yourself to gain all the experience you can in the food and beverage aspect of the hospitality industry. If time and resources permit, it is highly recommended that you gain knowledge from a culinary arts program. Second, experience gained as a banquet food server in a high-volume convention or resort hotel property is invaluable. Also, paying your dues as a guest service agent at a hotel front desk or as a concierge provides you with the opportunity to hone your customer service skills. Promote yourself to a banquet manager or a CSM (convention service coordinator), which provides the opportunity to learn and perfect organizational skills—the ability to multitask and deal with hundreds of details simultaneously. After all, the business of special events is the business of managing details.

The next step is obtaining a sales position. An excellent appointment to aspire to is an executive meeting manager, sometimes called a small meeting manager, in a convention or conference hotel. Here, you are responsible for booking small room blocks (usually 20 rooms or fewer), making meeting room arrangements, meal plans, and audiovisual requirements. On a small scale, hundreds of details are coordinated for several groups at any one time. From this position, you may laterally move to a catering sales position within a hotel.

The catering sales position in a hotel will expose you to many different kinds of events: weddings, reunions, corporate events, holiday events, and social galas and balls. In this position, one either coordinates or has the opportunity to work with various vendors. This is where the florists, prop companies, lighting experts, entertainment agencies, rental companies, and audiovisual wizards come into play. Two to three years in this capacity grooms you for the next rung on the ladder.

Now, you can pursue several different angles: a promotion to a convention service manager within a hotel, moving into off-premise catering as a sales consultant, joining a production company, or perhaps affiliating yourself with a destination management company (DMC). Typically, without sales experience within a DMC, your first experience with them will be as an operations manager. Once proficient in this capacity, you then join the sales team.

After another two years creating and selling your heart out, you will be ready for the big leagues. The palette is now yours to paint your future. How about aspiring to be the next Super Bowl halftime creator and producer? Or perhaps creating the theme and schematics for the Olympics is in your future. Many avenues are available for exploring. Call on your marketing ideas, your business sense, your accounting skills, your aptitude for design, or your discriminating palette to create unique entertaining and dining concepts. Continually educating yourself and discovering fresh ideas through adventurous experiences is essential to designing and selling special events. Don't forget to embark on as many internships as you can in the name of gaining knowledge and experience. Show your enthusiasm for what is different and unconventional. Know that creativity has no boundaries. Visualize the big picture and go for it! Figure 15–2 shows a career path for an event manager.

Event Experience as a Cook and Server — Event Food Preparation Chef — Supervisor of Event Foodservice — Manager of Event Foodservice — Event Staffing Manager — Event Manager — Event Server Manager

FIGURE 15–2 A Career Path to an Event Manager.

TRENDS *in* THE SPECIAL EVENT INDUSTRY

- The special event industry is forecast to grow, as clients want ever-more spectacular events.
- Events are increasingly more complex, involving multimedia presentations, elaborate staging, and frequently upscale food and beverage service.
- Technology presents both an opportunity and a challenge: an opportunity in that it can facilitate event planning and management, and a challenge in that new software programs must be mastered.

Not Enough Space

Jessica is the event planner for a large convention center. A client has requested an exhibition that would not only bring excellent revenue but is an annual event that several other convention centers would like to host.

Exhibitions typically take one or two days to set up, three or four days of exhibition, and one day to break down. Professional organizations handle each part of the setup and breakdown.

When Jessica checks the space available on the days requested for the exhibition, she notices that another exhibition is blocking part of the space needed by her client.

DISCUSSION QUESTION

1. What can Jessica do to get this exhibition to use the convention center without inconveniencing either exhibition too much?

CASE STUDY

CAREER INFORMATION

The special event industry is growing, dynamic, and fast-paced. There are several career paths to consider: Starting as an intern, you could learn which aspect of the business you like most at this time and later apply for that kind of position. Remember, many internships lead to full-time positions upon graduation. It is always best to gain as much experience while going to school as possible. It is also important to start at the bottom and work your way up. So, volunteer next time an opportunity comes your way. Begin by working as an "extra" for some events, then look to get involved with the organization as an assistant to someone, and after a while become a coordinator, then meeting manager or event manager. Event management companies, destination management companies, meeting management companies, and hotels and convention centers are all good places to seek opportunities.

Judi Gallagher, Chef, Caterer, author, and TV personality offers this advice: "For success in special events, you need to be very organized. The best special events managers and caterers are the most organized, and they make every event very personal. For employment, I look for character, passion, and the ability to accept direction, multitask, work as a team, and be a leader. Keep a strong ethical position. The old saying, 'Don't eat the lasagna where you make it,' can be interpreted in many ways, but the message is to keep it professional."

SUMMARY

1. Special events differ from daily events. They occur spontaneously, invite expectations, are planned, and recognize a unique moment in time with ceremony and ritual to satisfy specific needs.
2. The special event industry is a growing field that will provide many professional career opportunities in event management and planning.
3. Special event planners and managers have filled a "need" that was first introduced at hotels and convention centers. They are responsible for planning the event, from start to finish.
4. The special event industry can be grouped into several smaller classifications including corporate events, association events, charity balls and fund-raising events, social functions, fairs and festivals, and concert and sporting events.
5. The event planning process includes the following steps: research, design, planning, coordination, and evaluation.
6. Special event planners can work in a variety of settings. They range from hotels/resorts, convention centers, and private clubs to self-employment.
7. Critical skills and abilities that are required for a career in special event management include leadership skills, effective communication, project management skills, negotiating skills, coordinating and delegating skills, budgeting skills, multitasking abilities, enthusiasm, effective social skills, and the ability to form contacts.
8. The special event industry has its own selection of professional associations that offer certification, continuing education, and networking to their members. The International Special Events Society (ISES), International Festivals & Events Association (IFEA), and Meeting Planners International (MPI) are three of the largest and most recognized professional associations in the field. Local convention and visitors bureaus (CVBs) are organizations that can be a valuable resource to the special event industry. A CVB has the purpose of promoting tourism, meetings, and related business for their city.
9. The management of time and finances, along with the utilization of technology and human resources, are event planning tools that can be used to your advantage as you pursue a career in this field.
10. The special events industry does not have rigid boundaries. Closely related fields that may overlap include catering, marketing, sales, and entertainment.

KEY WORDS AND CONCEPTS

Charity balls
Conventions
Coordination
Corporate events
Corporate seminars
Event planner
Event planning
Fairs and festivals
Fund-raisers
International Festival & Events Association (IFEA)
International Special Events Society (ISES)
Meeting Planners International (MPI)
Social functions
Special events industry
Trade shows
Weddings and holiday parties
Workshops

REVIEW QUESTIONS

1. What do event planners do?
2. What are the challenges for event planners and managers?
3. Describe three of the classifications of special events.
4. Explain the skills and abilities required for event management.

INTERNET EXERCISES

1. Go to www.ises.com and click on "Education." Look for Event World to see what an ISES Event World can do for professional development, and who should attend.
2. Go to www.mpiweb.org/home and click on career development—see what Career Connections has to offer job seekers?

APPLY YOUR KNOWLEDGE

1. Make a plan for a local event in your area. List all the headings and formulate a budget.

SUGGESTED ACTIVITY

1. Attend a special event. Write a brief report on the event and its planning and organization.

ENDNOTES

1. Joe J. Goldblatt, *Special Events: Best Practices in Modern Event Management,* 2d ed. (New York: John Wiley and Sons, 1997), p. 2 and *Special Events: The Art and Science of Celebration* (New York: Van Nostrand Reinhold, 1990), pp. 1–2.
2. Frank Supovitz, Forward in Joe J. Goldblatt, *Special Events: Best Practices in Modern Event Management,* 2d ed. (New York: John Wiley and Sons, 1997), p. iv.
3. Blythe Cameson, op. cit., pp. 4–7.
4. *Event Solutions–2004 Black Book* (Tempe, AZ: Event Publishing, 2004), p. 22; www.event-solutions.com.
5. John R. Walker, *Introduction to Hospitality Management* (Upper Saddle River, NJ: Pearson Education, 2007), p. 470.
6. Blythe Cameson, op. cit., p. 115.
7. www.festivals.com.
8. Joe J. Goldblatt, *Special Events: Best Practices in Modern Event Management,* 2d ed. (New York: John Wiley & Sons, Inc., 1997), pp. 129–139.
9. George G. Fenich, *Meetings, Expositions, Events, and Conventions: An Introduction to the Industry* (Upper Saddle River, NJ: Pearson Education, Inc., 2005), pp. 181–182.
10. Ibid., p. 366.
11. Judy Allen, *Event Planning Ethics and Etiquette: A Principled Approach to the Business of Special Event Management* (Etobicoke, Ontario: John Wiley and Sons, 2003), p. 79.
12. http://careerplanning.about.com/gi/o.htm?zi=1/XJ&zTi=1&sdn=careerplanning&cdn=careers&tm=37&gps=98_189_987_561&f=11&su=p284.9.336.ip_p554.12.336.ip_&tt=2&bt=1&bts=1&zu=http%3A//www.melanet.com/awg/wedpros/want_to_be1.html.
13. Ibid.
14. Rachel Pritchett, *McClatchy-Tribune,* Business News, Washington, March 29, 2010, 1-52010 http://proquest.umi.comezproxy.lib.usf.edu/pqdweb?did=1933289841&sid=1&Fmt=3&clientId=20178&RQT=309&VName=P, retrieved January 5, 2010.
15. www.ises.com.
16. Ibid.
17. www.ifea.com.
18. Blythe Cameson, op. cit., pp. 36–41.
19. www.mpiweb.org.
20. http://sevenstarevents.com/, retrieved March 29, 2010.

The Final Chapter of the Hospitality Story and Your Career Plan

At the beginning of this text, we stated our primary goal: help prepare students to advance their hospitality careers by giving a foundation of service and product knowledge with an extensive array of features. So far, you have enjoyed a taste of tourism, lodging, cruising, food and beverage, club management, attractions, recreation, assemblies, and event management. These are the major areas of the industry that most students and the public relate to. However, there are numerous other complementary positions that are vital to the industry, which we will now introduce. These career roles may be of interest to you, the inquisitive student, who is considering a more business–related career. This final chapter will explore some of these areas.

There are inherent risks in every business, large or small. The hospitality industry thrives on innovative and creative, independent or corporate entrepreneurs, who use critical thinking skills to increase incremental revenues, decrease unnecessary costs, and maximize profits. These individuals lead their successful businesses by focusing on certain basic business principles and positions: strategic business plans; marketing research and sales campaigns; financial analysis; attractive, functional, affordable design/architect; engineering and construction critical paths; management information systems; quality control; and human resource culture. Additionally, many companies opt to rely on supporting specialists for certain critical operational or sales consulting functions: strategic planners, trend/concept analysts, website designers, theme specialists, mystery shoppers, energy conservationists, asset managers, and internal/external auditors. Could you see yourself in any of these positions, as they relate to successful hospitality entities?

While not unique to the hospitality industry, each successful business needs a written vision (where are we going) and mission (what is our purpose and how will achieve the vision). The business plan is the vehicle to help accomplish the vision and mission, and experience dictates that certain steps are critical for a business to succeed. The business plan is accomplished before any new venture is initiated and is updated at least annually for existing hospitality companies. Many companies will update this living document semi-annually or even quarterly. The person(s) who accomplish this vital document may be the proprietor, partners, corporate C-level executives (CEO, COO, CFO, CMO, etc.) or a dedicated strategic planner for mega-companies. These person(s) will share the plan format, provide macro and micro level social/technological/economic/ political/ environmental information, monitor the collection of the market and competitive information, and schedule sessions to brainstorm the potential future of the entity. Then he/she will develop a game plan with financial projections for the upcoming 1–5 year period.

A typical hospitality business plan includes:

Executive Summary—a recap of the entire plan, including many details as outlined below

Business description—a description of the venture, who will be involved, the market segment served, and the timing of all aspects

Environmental analysis—a market analysis, competitive analysis, entry and exit barriers, supplier analysis, availability of technology, and overall economic factors of the area, and relevant government regulations.

Functional plans—a marketing plan, an operations plan, a management plan, research and development plan, personnel training plan, management information strategy, financial/capital plan for funding and major equipment/renovations

Financial projections—proforma for revenues, expenses and profits; balance sheet estimates; projection of cash flows; and the overall return on investment expectations

Implementation schedule—time frame for accomplishing various activities

Exit-strategy—a plan to let investors know when they can expect to exit the venture

Risk Analysis—evaluates potential "risk versus reward"

Business plans are used extensively by developers. The term **developer** refers to someone who makes improvements of some kind to real property, thereby increasing its value. The developer may be an individual, but is more often a partnership, limited liability company, or corporation. There are two major categories of real estate development activity: land development and building development (also known as project development). Building developers acquire raw land, improved land, and/or redevelopable property in order to construct building projects. The buildings are then sold entirely or in part to others, or retained as assets to produce cash flow via rentals and other means. Some building developers have their own internal departments for designing and constructing buildings (more common among larger developers), while others subcontract these parts of the work to third parties (typical of small developers).

Many experienced developers will create their own business plans. However, if a developer has a need for a business plan for a new-build, as opposed to a renovation or restoration, then the risk tends to be greater. In such cases, many developers will obtain the services of an asset manager and feasibility or viability consultant/team. The asset manager can perform property reviews, on-site inspection services, asset condition analysis, franchise compliance, recommendations regarding yield management, capital improvements, etc. Feasibility/viability teams are experts in strategic business planning, design, architecture, and/or land-use. Additionally, these consultants may be well-trained to investigate the existing competitive set and market in order to determine whether the project can be financially successful. These experts are referred to as feasibility (or viability) consultants. By utilizing the expertise of external asset managers and consultants/teams, the developer/s gain four advantages:

1. The consultant is more objective regarding the existing competitors;
2. They may have information regarding new competitors on the horizon;
3. YThey are knowledgeable about the market and of similar markets; and they are experts in their field; and
4. While these experts may charge $10,000–$100,000 per study, they can ultimately save the potential developer/owner millions by steering her/him away from a "sour" deal.

If the decision is made to move forward with the project, then the developer will contract the services of a conceptual team to consider one or more alternative best-use scenarios for the project: hotel, timeshare, condo-hotel, restaurant, rental car, theme park, golf course, retail/office space, etc. He/she may hire the conceptual consultant to collaborate with the developer, while considering the proper market segments to attack, the type of theming or experience to provide for the particular market segment, the ideal number of units (rooms, seats, vehicle spaces) and the appropriate features and benefits to incorporate into the project. It is particularly important to understand the present and future possibilities of technological developments, so that the construction and engineering teams will make proper physical modifications for these electronics.

The everyday use of computers has dramatically changed the way in which hospitality management world operates and has increased the career opportunities for "techies." The integration of computer information technology has allowed the hospitality industry to efficiently manage large amounts of data, which in turn allows organizations to run more efficiently. The challenge of integrating computer systems into hospitality operations is to not lose focus on the personal service element that guests have come to expect. When the guest is reduced to being just a number in an automated service setting, the essence of hospitality is lost. In the 1980s, when hospitality organizations began moving towards computerization, many people feared that guest services would suffer as computers took over the jobs that people had done in the past. Most of these fears proved unfounded and the successful companies understood the essence of hospitality and could integrate computers into an existing system and allow workers to continue their interaction with guests. In addition, computers enhanced a worker's ability to do their job quicker. Computers have actually improved service over the years by allowing workers to get away from the routine tasks (e.g., sorting hotel registration cards, balancing guest accounts) and be able to spend more time with guests and provide them with the personalized service that they expect.

Many people mistakenly believe that Management Information Systems (MIS) are synonymous with computer systems. In fact, MIS predates the development and implementation of computers. MIS is generally defined as the "systematic formal assemblage of components that perform data processing operations"

(Burch and Strater). A more commonly accepted definition of MIS in hospitality management is that "A well-designed (management) information system gets the right information, to the right person in the right format at the right time, so that it adds value to that person's decision. The right person typically is the guest, the employee or both" (Ford & Heaton). An example of this might be the hotel information television channel guests can view in their hotel room. Most hotels operate a separate television channel allowing the guest to view information on time, weather, hotel amenities and events that are scheduled in the hotels conference space. Hotels have even advanced this MIS technology to the point that a guest can view their account balance, provide guest constructive feedback, and even check-out, all from the comfort of their hotel room. Prior to this advance in technology, guests would have had to either call or visit the front desk to perform these simple tasks. The use of MIS helps the guests and employees work more efficiently, which in turn leads to better guest services.

Ironically, utilizing MIS properly does not reduce the guest's experience to a cold production line approach, but rather the opposite. MIS can enable employees to personalize the guest's experience and improve the perception of hospitality. For example, many hotel phone switchboards are integrated with the front desk computer system allowing the phone operator (with the help of caller ID) to see the name and room number of the caller. With this information, the operator will typically address the guest by their name (i.e. Mr. Smith or Mrs. Jones) instead of the generic "sir" or "ma'am." Guest opinion studies have consistently shown that guests enjoy being identified by their name and state that being recognized by the staff is one of the factors that leads them to return to a hotel.

In the world of theme parks, ride designers are utilizing MIS to enhance rides and provide their guests with a unique experience. The ET ride at Universal Studios Florida was one of the first theme park attractions to utilize computer technology to personalize the experience. Upon entering the building, guests are provided with a card, similar to a hotel room key card, that has their first name encoded on it. This card is inserted into the ride vehicle at the loading zone and allows ET to say goodbye to each of the riders by name. New computer technology in the future will allow attraction rides to become interactive, compared to the passive experiences of the past. Both the Men in Black-Alien Attack attraction at Universal Studios Florida and the Buzz Lightyear's Space Ranger Spin at the Magic Kingdom at Walt Disney World have guests shoot targets along the ride to score points that are totaled at the end. The result is that the riders often return to the same ride multiple times in an attempt to beat their high score. This new technology adds a challenging aspect to the traditional rides and has been proven to be a crowd pleaser at the theme parks.

The decrease in the cost of technology and the ease of accessing the Internet suggest the Internet will forever change the way in which people book their travel arrangements. The development of the Internet as a user-friendly application allowed non-technical consumers to use the computer to perform many different tasks that previously required person to person contact. Recent studies confirmed that continued consumer acceptance of electronic commerce has lead to an increase in usage of the Internet for booking travel arrangements (Weber &

Roehl). It is anticipated that in 2007 more travelers will utilize the Internet to book their arrangements than all other methods combined. This is largely attributed to the different range of distribution channels through which hotels, airlines, and rental cars can be booked and the influence of effective marketing and advertising.

The creation of Internet travel web sites and online travel agencies has created a distribution channel referred to as Internet Enabled Distribution Channels (IDECs) (Choi & Kimes, 2002). IDECs produce the same results as traditional distribution channels, only through electronic means. IDECs require both the supplier and the consumer to utilize the computer in order to complete the transaction. The travel supplier offers the general public the ability to check rates and availability electronically. The consumer, in turn, has the ability to secure a reservation from the supplier electronically and receive confirmation of the booking. Electronic distribution channels allow hospitality enterprises the ability to provide better exposure to potential customers and sell more rooms and/or seats during slower times.

Computer technology and the Internet are positioned to continue to change the way in which people book and enjoy their hospitality, travel and tourism arrangements. These arrangements include restaurant reservations, rental car GPS, golf tee times, airline seat selection, theme park attraction crowd control, safety and security devices, etc. The future hospitality manager must not only be aware of these changes, but also be able to capitalize on this technology in order to ensure the success of their enterprise.

Internal hospitality technology positions are initiated daily and outsourced enterprises are spawning everyday, and include website designers, audio and event technologist, web content analyst, casino IT Director, business systems analyst, hotel operations technical expert, data base administrator, cruise line senior programmer analyst, internal/external technology auditors, etc.

Now that we have reviewed the business approach to hospitality concepts, design, construction and technology, we need to consider how to maintain the facility at peak product, operations and service levels. Total quality management is an issue for the franchisor, the franchisee or the independent entrepreneur. The business is only as good as any one weak link or poor guest experience. Therefore, a sharp hospitality business leader will establish certain checks and balances to ensure maximum levels of quality control.

Consider the needs of an entrepreneur who owns an independent/non-franchise operation. Because they do not rely on corporate policies, procedures, and handbooks, the independent operator can be successful by utilizing a proprietor's approach: set a clear vision, share the vision, model the vision, and monitor the vision by building the operation one "moment of truth" at a time. It is critical to demonstrate hands-on skills and knowledge and incorporate MBWA (management by wandering around). However, it is easy to lose objectivity. Therefore, the independent operator may consider hiring the services of a mystery shopper to "shop" their operation and the competitive set. Mystery shopping is a tool used by market research companies to measure quality of retail service. Companies send mystery shoppers to act as shoppers of the hospitality products and services. They are hired by a company to pose as a customer, evaluate the services or purchase pre-selected merchandise, and provide feedback.

Instructions to mystery shoppers can include a script of behavior, questions to ask, complaints to give, purchases to make, and measures to record, such as the time it takes to receive attention from a housekeeping employee or to be served in the restaurant, for example. The purpose of mystery shoppers is to help businesses increase sales and improve employee customer service awareness by providing a more realistic picture of how their customers perceive their company. The shopping service may simply "tel-shop" by posing as a potential guest attempting to make a telephone reservation, or they pose as a business group, who are seeking a block of hotel rooms. The shopper will follow a prescribed script by asking structured questions and evaluating accordingly. Or the shop may be a one or two day resort visit, which might include evaluation of the overnight accommodations, food and beverage (e.g. bartender honesty), and amenities (spa, golf, retail). At the end of the shop, the outside mystery shopper will present evidence to support all of their encounters with the staff, the product, and the environment in general. This evidence includes written comments, video tape, microphone replay, photographs, etc. Mystery shopping can be a valuable service with an attached cost, but it can lead to increased revenues in the long term.

The large hospitality franchisors and corporations also are concerned with product and service consistency and they can devote a department solely to this. When a franchisor signs an agreement with the franchisee, the franchisor entrusts that the franchisee will operate to the standards provided in the franchise agreement. To ensure that the franchisee is in compliance with the franchise agreement, the franchisor establishes two positions to maintain the quality control in the field where the franchisee operates their restaurant or hotel or car rental: the franchise service director and the quality control inspector. The franchise service director (FSD) is a single point of contact for the franchisee and is responsible for guiding them through the opening process, providing revenue-generating assistance, as well as operations support for their property. The FSD will help them fully utilize all training, services, resources, and programs, and assist in the development of action plans for operational and marketing enhancements. They also provide onsite training at the franchisee's request and monitor adherence to quality assurance standards for the franchisor's brand, training, and day-in day-out operations.

Additionally, most franchisors establish and maintain a Quality Control Department, and they are charged with inspecting the products and services of all franchisees' properties on a scheduled basis (annually, quarterly, or monthly) with the intention to review all aspects of quality control. They have a list of items that are used to rate the facility to determine if the property passes the franchisor's standards. Examples might include ingredients in a restaurant menu, service script at an airline ticket counter, the number of threads per square inch in a pillow cover, or the number of times an air conditioning unit has been cleaned in a quarterly period. The quality control inspectors will provide their findings and rating to the franchisee. If necessary, the franchisee is expected to improve the score at the following inspection, most of which are unannounced.

This overview has explored several positions that you, the hospitality student, may want to pursue. There remain dozens of other critical hospitality positions that are valuable to the industry: international franchise brokers, hospitality specific attorneys, landscape architects, environmentalists, telecommunications, costume/uniform creators, suppliers, vendors, hospitality financial specialists for real estate, mortgages, and pension plans, and on and on. Clearly, there are a multitude of career opportunities in the world of hospitality. Take advantage of the largest and fastest growing industry and enjoy the adventure!

Burch and Strater. *Information Systems: Theory and Practice*. Hamilton Publishing Co., Santa Barbara, CA, 1974, p.71.

Choi, S. & Kimes, S. (2002). Electronic distribution channel's effect on hotel revenue management. *Cornell Hotel and Restaurant Administration Quarterly*, 43 (3), 23–32.

Ford, R. & Heaton, C (2000). *Managing the Guest Experience in Hospitality*, Delmar Publishers., Albany, NY. p. 250–251.

Weber, K & Roehl W. (1999). Profiling People Searching for and Purchasing Travel Products on the World Wide Web. *Journal of Travel Research*, 37 (3), p.291–299.

Glossary

A

Adventure cruise Cruises that explore a number of adventurous areas, including Alaska, the Amazon River, the Orinoco River, Antarctica, Greenland, the Galapagos Islands, the South Pacific, and the Northwest Passage.

Air-cruise packages Packages that include air and cruise travel in one price.

American service Food is prepared and appealingly placed onto plates in the kitchen, carried into the dining room, and served to guests. American service is a less formal—yet professional—approach that is preferred by today's restaurant guests.

Associations Groups of individuals and corporations who come together for purposes of representing their industry segment to legislators and for the benefit of members in education and other operational benefits.

Attractions Places that provide entertainment offered to the public.

Average daily rate (ADR) One of the key operating ratios that indicates the level of a hotel's performance. The ADR is calculated by dividing the dollar sales by the number of rooms rented.

Average guest check The average amount each group spends; used primarily in a restaurant setting.

B

Baccarat A traditional table game in which the winning hand totals closest to nine.

Back-of-the-house operations The support areas behind the scenes in a hotel or motel, including housekeeping, laundry, engineering, and foodservice. Also refers to individuals who operate behind the scenes to make a guest's stay pleasant and safe.

Batch cooking The cooking of food in quantities for consumption throughout a meal period. Used in noncommercial foodservice to avoid putting out all the food at 11:30 and having it spoil. Batches are cooked for readiness at 11:30, 12:00, 12:30, and so on.

Beer A brewed and fermented beverage made from water, barley malt, yeast, and other starchy cereals and flavored with hops.

Beverage cost percentage Similar to food cost percentage, except that it relates to beverages.

Blackjack A table game in which the winning hand is determined by whether the dealer or the player gets cards that add up to a number closest to or equal to 21 without going over.

Brandy Brandy is distilled from wine and is served as an after-dinner beverage or mixed in cocktails.

Business travel Travel for business purposes.

C

Captain The highest ranking position on a cruise ship, receiving most of the perks. The captain also makes virtually every executive decision dealing with the ship.

Casino An area in which gaming activities involving table games and slot machines take place.

Casual dining Relaxed dining; includes restaurants from several classifications.

Chain restaurant Restaurant that is one of a chain of restaurants.

Champagne Sparkling wine made in the Champagne district of France.

Charity ball Events are used to raise funds toward a set group or charity, and every dollar that is spent on the event is thereby one less dollar that could go toward the cause.

Chief purser Part of the hotel operations department on a cruise ship responsible for supervising all other departments on board, with the exception of deck and engine.

Chief steward The individual in a hotel, club, or foodservice operation who is responsible for the cleanliness of the back of the house and dishwashing areas, and for storage and control of china, glassware, and silverware.

City ledger A client whose company has established credit with a certain hotel. Charges are posted to the city ledger and accounts are sent once or twice monthly.

Clarify Wine is clarified by adding either eggwhite or bentonite.

Club management The management of clubs.

Club Manager's Association The professional organization to which many of the club managers of the 6,000 private country clubs belong. The association's goal is to advance the profession of club management by fulfilling the educational and related needs of the club managers.

Coastal cruises Offered in Northern Europe, the United States, and Mexico. Significantly smaller than the average floating resort, they sail closer to land, seeking out areas not accessible to larger ships.

Cognac The finest brandy only made in the Cognac region of France.

Commercial foodservice Operations that compete for customers in the open market.

Committees A person or group of persons elected or appointed to perform some service or function, as to investigate, report on, or act upon a particular matter.

Contractor A company that operates a foodservice for the client on a contractual basis.

Convention A generic term referring to any size of business or professional meeting held in one specific location, which usually includes some form of trade show or exposition. Also refers to a group of delegates or members who assemble to accomplish a specific goal.

Convention and visitors bureau 1. An organization responsible for promoting tourism at the regional and local level. 2. A not-for-profit umbrella organization that represents a city or urban area in soliciting and servicing all types of travelers to that city or area, whether for business, pleasure, or both.

Convention center A large meeting place.

Cooking line "The line" is a term used to describe the final cooking and plating area of the kitchen.

Coordination of activities The process of achieving unity of action among interdependent activities.

Core competencies A defined level of expertise that is essential or fundamental to a particular job.

Corporate events Annual meetings, sales meetings, new product launches, training meetings and workshops, management meetings, press meetings, incentive meetings, and awards ceremonies.

Corporate seminars A corporate meeting for an exchange of ideas, a conference.

Country clubs Clubs that offer golf and sometimes tennis and/or swimming for members' recreation along with restaurants and social activities.

Craps A game in which two dice are thrown and in which a first throw of 7 or 11 wins, a first throw of 2, 3, or 12 loses, and a first throw of 4, 5, 6, 8, 9, or 10 can be won only by throwing the same number again before throwing a 7.

Crossings Implies sailing across the Northern Atlantic Ocean either to or from the Americas, although it can take place across any major ocean.

cruise director In charge of all on-board entertainment and activities, creates, coordinates, and implements all daily activities, and acts as master of ceremonies at all social activities and evening shows.

Cruise Lines International Association (CLIA) A marketing and training organization composed of 19 of the major cruise lines serving North America.

Cultural tourism Tourism motivated by interest in cultural events like festivals, activities like theatre, history, arts, sciences, museums, architecture, and religion.

D

Daily rate The amount of money required to pay for each person's foodservice a day.

Daily report A report prepared each day to provide essential performance information for a particular property to its management.

Dinner house restaurant A restaurant with a casual, eclectic décor that may promote a particular theme.

Dram shop legislation Laws and procedures that govern the legal operation of establishments that sell measured alcoholic beverages.

E

Ecotourism Responsible travel to natural areas that conserves the environment and sustains the well-being of the local people.

Empowerment The act of giving employees the authority, tools, and information they need to do their jobs with greater autonomy.

Ethics The study of standards of conduct and moral judgment; also, the standards of correct conduct.

Ethnic restaurant A restaurant featuring a particular cuisine such as Chinese, Mexican, or Italian.

Event planner Event planners are responsible for planning the event, from start to finish. This includes: setting the date and location, advertising the event, providing refreshments or arranging catering services, and speakers or entertainment.

Event planning A general term that refers to a career path in the growing field of special events. Its forecast includes a growing demand for current and future employment opportunities.

Event tourism Defined as the systematic planning, development, and marketing of festivals and special events as tourist attractions, development catalysts, and image builders for attractions and destination areas.

Executive committee A committee of hotel executives from each of the major departments within the hotel generally made up of the general manager, director of rooms division, food and beverage director, marketing and sales director, human resources director, accounting and/or finance director, and engineering director.

Expeditions and natural cruises Cruises that visit exotic and exciting places. Passengers play an active part in every aspect of the trip, which tends to be oriented toward visiting interesting destinations, exploring, and studying nature. These cruise lines hire special lecturers, naturalists, and historians.

Exposition An event held mainly to promote informational exchanges among trade people. A large exhibition in which the presentation is the main attraction, as well as being a source of revenue for an exhibitor.

F

Fairs and festivals Planned events that are often themed to the celebration's purpose.

Familiarization (FAM) trip A free or reduced-price trip given to travel agents, travel writers, or other intermediaries to promote destinations.

Fine dining restaurant Upscale dining, usually with white tablecloths, à la carte menus, and table service.

Fining The process by which wine that has matured is filtered to help stabilize it and remove any solid particles still in the wine.

First-in, first-out (FIFO) The supplies that are ordered first are used first.

Focus groups A group of people questioned together about their opinions of a service or product.

Food and beverage manager Person in charge of all the areas that serve food and beverages onboard the ship. They also are in charge of food costs and the overall quality of the food and beverages on board the ship.

Food cost percentage A ratio comparing the cost of food sold to food sales, which is calculated by dividing the cost of food sold during a given period by food sales during the same period.

Fortified wine Wine to which brandy or other spirits have been added to stop further fermentation or to raise its alcoholic content.

Franchising A concept that allows a company to expand quickly by allowing qualified people to use the systems, marketing, and purchasing power of the franchiser.

Front-of-the-house operations Comprises all areas with which guests come in contact, including the lobby, corridors, elevators, guest rooms, restaurants and bars, meeting rooms, and restrooms. Also refers to employees who staff these areas.

Fund-raisers Events that are used to raise funds toward a set group or charity, and every dollar that is spent on the event is thereby one less dollar that could go toward the cause.

Fusion Combining usually widely differing ethnic or regional ingredients, styles, or techniques.

G

Gambling To bet money on the outcome of a game of chance.

Gaming entertainment industry Businesses that offer games of risk as part of a total package of entertainment and leisure time activities, including resort hotel, various foodservice concepts, retail shopping, theme parks, live entertainment, and recreational pursuits.

Guest counts (covers) The number of guests dining in a restaurant.

Guest satisfaction The desired outcome of hospitality services.

H

Handle The dollars wagered, or bet; often confused with "win." Whenever a customer places a bet, the handle increases by the amount of the bet. The handle is not affected by the outcome of the bet.

Heritage tourism Tourism motivated by historic preservation—a combination of the natural, cultural, and architectural environment.

Hops The dried, conical fruit of a special vine that imparts bitterness to beer.

Hotel manager Person in charge of all hotel operations on board the ship which consist of Administration, Cruise Staff, Entertainment, Food & Beverage, Dining Room, and Housekeeping. The hotel manager is also in charge of training the hotel staff and financial operations.

Hub-and-spoke system A system by which airline passengers can travel from one small city to another via a hub at a major city.

I

Incentive market A market for incentive travel.

Independent restaurant A nonfranchise restaurant, privately owned.

Indian Gaming Regulatory Act (IGRA) A federal act that created a statutory basis for the operation of gaming by Indian tribes in order to promote tribal economic development, self-sufficiency, and strong tribal governments.

Infrastructure The basic, constructed services like water, gas, electric, sewage, drainage, roads, airports, cruise, bus and rail terminals.

Initiation fee The initial charge to belong to an association or organization.

Inseparability The linkage of hospitality products and services.

Intangible Hospitality service is intangible; it cannot be sampled prior to purchase.

Interdependency of tourism and hospitality Tourism and hospitality are interdependent.

International Festival & Events Association (IFEA) An organization that provides an opportunity for event managers from around the world to network and exchange ideas on how other festivals excel in sponsorship, marketing, fund-raising, operations, volunteer coordination, and management. They also provide fund-raising and modern developmental ideas to the special events industry.

International Special Events Society (ISES) An organization that works to join professionals to focus on the "event as a whole" rather than its individual parts. The organization has formed a solid network of peers that allow its members to produce quality events for their clients while benefiting from positive working relationships with other ISES members.

Inventory control A method for keeping track of all resources required to produce a product.

L

Liaison personnel Workers who are responsible for translating corporate philosophy for the contractor and for overseeing the contractor to be sure that he or she abides by the terms of the contract.

Luxury market Consists of people with incomes higher than $80,000.

M

Malt Germinated barley.

Managed services Services that can be leased to professional management companies.

Management contract A written agreement between an owner and an operator of a hotel or motor inn by which the owner employs the operator as an agent (employee) to assume full responsibility for operating and managing the property.

Mashing In the making of beer, the process of grinding the malt and screening out bits of dirt.

Mass market Consists of people with incomes in the $30,000 to $60,000 range.

Meeting A gathering of people for a common purpose.

Meeting planner An individual who coordinates every detail of meetings and conventions.

Meetings Planners International (MPI) A Dallas-based association with nearly 19,000 members. MPI offers professional development in two certification programs, Certified Meeting Professional (CMP), and Certification in Meeting Management (CMM).

MICE Meetings, incentive travel, conventions, and exhibitions (MICE) represent a segment of the tourism industry that has grown in recent years. The MICE segment of the tourism industry is very profitable. Industry statistics point to the fact that the average MICE tourist spends about twice the amount of money that other tourists spend.

Middle market Consists of people with incomes in the $60,000 to $80,000 range.

Monthly dues Fees charged on a monthly basis.

Multiplier effect A concept that refers to new money that is brought into a community to pay for hotel rooms, restaurant meals, and other aspects of leisure. To some extent, that income then passes into the community when the hotel or restaurant orders supplies and services, pays employees, and so on.

N

National Association of Amusement Ride Safety Officials An association that certifies ride safety inspectors.

National Restaurant Association (NRA) The association representing restaurant owners and the restaurant industry.

National School Lunch Program (NSLP) The program that provides free lunches to students from a certain income level.

Nature tourism Tourism motivated by nature, such as a visit to a National Park.

Night auditor The individual who verifies and balances guests' accounts.

Nonalcoholic beverage A beverage without alcohol.

Nutrition education programs Programs ensuring that food served in school cafeterias follows the nutrition standards set by government programs.

O

Order specification Established standards for each product to be ordered.

P

Pacific Area Travel Association (PATA) An association for the promotion of excellence in travel within, and to and from, the Pacific region.

Par stock The level of stock that must be kept on hand at all times. If the stock on hand falls below this point, a computerized reorder system automatically reorders a predetermined quantity of the stock.

Perishability The limited lifetime of hospitality products; for example, last night's vacant hotel room cannot be sold today.

Pleasure travel Travel for pleasure, including leisure, recreation, vacations, and visiting friends and family.

Poker A card game in which participants play against each other instead of the casino.

Private clubs Where members (only) gather for social, recreational, professional, or fraternal reasons.

Product specification The establishment of standards for each product, determined by the purchaser. For example, when ordering meat, the product specification includes the cut, weight, size, percentage of fat content, and so forth.

Production control sheet A checklist/sheet itemizing the production.

Prohibition The period from 1919 to 1933 when alcohol was banned in the United States.

Proof A figure representing liquor's alcohol content.

Property management system (PMS) A computerized system that integrates all systems used by a lodging property, such as reservations, front desk, housekeeping, food and beverage control, and accounting.

Purchase order An order to purchase.

Q

Quality control Error detection and prevention, based on TQM or Continuous Quality Improvement, an important part of delivering exceptional service to guests.

Quick-service restaurant A restaurant that offers quick service.

R

Rack rate The price a hotel charges for a room before any discount has been taken into account. The published rate for a room, sometimes set artificially high and used to calculate a variety of discounts.

Real Estate Investment Trust (REIT) A method that enables small investors to combine their funds and protects them from the double taxation levied against an ordinary corporation or trust; designed to facilitate investment in real estate in much the same way a mutual fund facilitates investment in securities.

Receiving The back-of-the-house area devoted to receiving goods.

Regional cruises The most popular of cruises. They sail in the Caribbean, the Mediterranean, and to a lesser extent, the Baltic Sea and other small seas. The majority of cruise lines offer regional cruises, and many specialize in one area such as the Caribbean, or switch between the Mediterranean during summer and the Caribbean during winter.

Restaurant forecasting The process of estimating future events in the restaurant.

Rev par See Revenue per available room.

Revenue per available room (Rev par) Total Rooms Revenue for Period divided by Total Rooms Available During a Period.

Room occupancy percentage (ROP) The number of rooms occupied divided by rooms available; a key operating ratio for hotels.

Rooms division The rooms division is made up of the following departments: front office, communications, reservations, guest services, concierge, and housekeeping.

Roulette A traditional table game in which a dealer spins a wheel and players wager on which number a small ball will fall.

S

Sail-cruises Cruises that rely on their sails at least part of the time.

Self-operator A company that manages its own foodservice operations.

Service industry The hospitality industry is a service industry; we take pride in caring about others as well as ourselves. Ensuring that guests receive outstanding service is a goal of the service industry.

SMERF Social, military, education, religious, and fraternal.

Social functions Events that include weddings, engagement parties, holiday functions.

Sparkling wine Wine containing carbon dioxide, which provides effervescence when the wine is poured.

Special events industry An industry that employs professionals who work together to provide a broad range of services to create what is termed a special event.

Specialty and theme cruises Often culture-rich, off-the-beaten-path itineraries built around passengers' special interests and hobbies, and high on enrichment and adventure. The target customers are the experienced cruisers who are looking for something more than the conventional cruise experience.

Spirits Distilled drinks.

Standardized recipe A recipe that specifically describes the exact, measurable amount of ingredients and the method of preparation needed to consistently produce a product.

Steam boating A concept unique to the USA, and takes you along the Mississippi River, as well as other major rivers, of-fering passengers a unique chance to see America's Heartland.

Suggestive selling Servers in a restaurant increase sales by suggesting appropriate additional items to customers. For example, a server may suggest a Mondavi fumée blanc to complement a fish dish.

Sustainable tourism Tourism that has minimal impact on the environment and culture of the host community.

T

Theme park A recreational park based on a particular setting or artistic interpretation; may operate with hundreds or thousands of acres of parkland and hundreds or thousands of employees.

Theme restaurant A restaurant distinguished by its combination of decor, atmosphere, and menu.

Total quality management (TQM) A managerial approach that integrates all of the functions and related processes of a business such that they are all aimed at maximizing guest satisfaction through ongoing improvement.

Tourism Travel for recreation or the promotion and arrangement of such travel.

Tray line The lineup of trays on which all the food for hospital patients is placed.

U

United Nations Educational, Scientific, and Cultural Organizations (UNESCO) Encourages international peace and universal respect by promoting collaboration among nations. Conducts studies, facilitates knowledge sharing, and develops standards.

V

Vacation ownership Offers consumers the opportunity to purchase fully furnished vacation accommodations in a variety of forms, such as weekly intervals or points in point-based systems, for a percentage of the cost of full ownership.

Vintage The year in which a wine's grapes were harvested.

W

Weddings and holiday parties Social gatherings. Weddings are the most widely recognized social event.

White spirits Gin, rum, vodka, and tequila.

Win Dollars won by the gaming operation from its customers. The net spending of customers on gaming is called the win, also known as *gross gaming revenue (GGR)*.

Workshops An educational seminar or series of meetings emphasizing interaction and exchange of information among a usually small number of participants.

World Tourism Organization A specialized agency of the United Nations made up of 146 countries that aim to play a decisive role in tourism promotion, sustainability, and socioeconomic development.

Wort In the making of beer, the liquid obtained after the mashing process.

Y

Yeast Yeast converts sugar to ethyl alcohol.

Index

A

AAA Diamond-Rating Guidelines, 81
Adams, John, 224
Adams, Ryan, 108
Adventure cruises, 134
Air-cruise packages, 129
Air travel, 33–35
Airlines/airports foodservice, 188–190
Airport hotels, 84
Albrecht, Karl, *At America's Service*, 10
Albrecht, Karl and Ron Zemke, *Service America!*, 12
Alcohol-related highway deaths, 230
All-suite extended-stay hotels, 87
American Automobile Association, 37–38, 80, 96
American Dental Association, 311
American Express, 46
American Express and National Trust for Historic Preservation, *Getting Started: How to Succeed in Heritage Tourism*, 65
American Golf, 240
American Hotel and Lodging Association, 22, 80, 83, 119, 311
American Marketing Association, 311, 318
American Medical Association, 311
American service in dining, 165–166
American Society of Association Executives, 284
American Society of Travel Agents, 45
Americans with Disabilities Act, 122
America's Cup, 316
Amtrak, 36, 37
Andrews, Sudhir, *Hotel Housekeeping*, 112
Annual meetings, 295
Aramark, 200
Arison, Ted, 137
Aromatic wines, 213
Art and tourism, 64–65
Association events, 311–312
At America's Service (Albrecht), 10
Athletic clubs, 237–238
Atlantic City, 273
Attractions. *See* Theme parks and attractions
Aust, Suzie, 56
Automobile associations, 37–38
Average daily rate, 106, 107
Average guest check, 165
Avery, John, 32
Avis Budget Group, Inc., 79

B

Babb, Jason, 12
Baccarat, 278
Back of the house, 11, 167–176
Back-to-basics cooking, 157
Bailey, Suzanne, 315–316
Barges, 134
Bars, 227–229
    operations of, 116
Basham, Robert, 151
Batch cooking, 188
Beck, Robert A., 24
Bed and breakfast inns, 8, 87–88
Beer, 218–221, 224
Beverage industry, 210–233
    alcohol-related highway deaths, 230
    bars, 227–229
    beer, 218–221, 224
    bottled water, 227
    carbonated soft drinks, 226
    career information, 231–232
    cocktails, 222–223
    coffee, 224–226
    cost percentage, 177
    juices, 226
    liquor liability and the law, 229–230
    nonalcoholic beer, 224
    nonalcoholic beverages, 224–227
    power (energy) drinks, 226–227
    spirits, 222–223
    tea, 226
    trends in, 230
    wines, 212–218. *See also* Wines
Bier, Godfrey, 100
Biggs, Kristen, 253
Blackjack, 278
Board meetings, 295
Boo, Elizabeth, *Ecotourism: The Potential and Pitfalls*, 58
Booth, Brian, 84
Bottled water, 227
Bourbon, 222
Bowl Games of America, 315
Boyd Gaming, 276–277
Branding, 157
Brandy, 223
Brewing beer, 217–221
Bryant, Chris, 96

Budget in meeting planning, 296
Budgeting skills, 318
Bus travel, 38–39
Business/industry foodservice, 202–203
Business travel, 56, 141
Business Week, 16

C

Caballos-Lascuráin, Héctor, 58
Calhoun, John, 237
California Association of Wine Grape Growers, "Code of Sustainable Winegrowing Practices," 214
California v. Cabazon Band of Mission Indians, 273
Canadian Automobile Association, 38
Capacity requirements of tourists, 62
Capsule Hotel, 91
Captain, 137
Car travel, 37–38
Carbon footprint reductions, 94
Carbonated soft drinks, 226
Career goals, 20–21
Career information
    airline industry, 71
    assistant restaurant manager job description, 171
    beverage industry, 231–232
    car rental business, 72
    club industry, 242, 243, 247–248
    convention center managers, 72
    cruise industry, 71, 142–143
    gaming entertainment, 277–278, 279–280
    hotel development and classification, 96
    hotel operations, 123–124
    managed services, 207
    meetings/conventions/expositions industry, 301
    Opportunities in Event Planning Careers, 312
    restaurant industry, 158–160
    restaurant manager job analysis, 180–182
    restaurant operations, 171, 183
    special events industry, 312, 314, 322–323
    theme parks and attractions, 263–264, 265
    tourism industry, 26, 50

Career path, 20
  advice for students, 23
  beverage industry, 232
  career ladders, 8–9, 72
  club management, 248
  cruise industry, 143
  event manager, 301
  event managers, 323
  gaming industry, 280
  hospitality industry, 4
  lifetime salaries by education level, 8
  in lodging management, 124
  managed services, 207
  professionalism and etiquette, 21–22
  restaurant industry, 159, 182
  self-assessment and personal philosophy, 21
  theme park industry, 164
Carême, Marie-Antoine, 149
Carlson Companies, 16
Carlson Credo, 175
Carlson, Curtis L., 16
Carnival Cruise Lines, 129–130, 137–138
Carnival in Rio de Janeiro, 262
Carvalho, Holly, 63
Case studies
  becoming a captain, 142
  building a convention center, 71
  chaos in the kitchen, 206
  club management, 247–248
  double-booked, 300
  ecotourism, 63
  franchising, 95
  in gaming entertainment, 279
  gas leak, 206
  hotel overbooking, 123
  the infidels' drink, 224
  Java Coffee House, 231
  national park overpopulation, 49
  not enough space, 323
  promotion from within, 26
  short staffed in the kitchen, 158
  shortage in stock, 183
  wait time for attractions and rides, 265
Casino Control Act, 273
Casino hotels, 85
Casinos, 271, 278
Catering department, 117–118
Catering event orders, 117, 118
Causal dining, 152–153
Celebrity restaurants, 151
Centralized reservation system, 79
Cerminia, Cherry, 196
Certified travel counselor, 47
Chain restaurants, 148
Champagne, 212
Channel Tunnel, 36
Charity balls and fund-raisers, 306, 312
Chief purser, 138
Chief steward, 138
Chihuly, Dale, 275

Choice Hotels, 77
Circus Circus, 271
City center hotels, 84
City centers, 299
City clubs, 237
City ledger, 104
Clarion Hotel Bayview daily report, 107
Classical cuisine, 149
Clefs d'Or (Golden Keys), 112
Clement VIII, Pope, 224
Climate change impacts, 93–94
Club industry, 234–249
  career information, 242, 243, 247–248
  club manager's job description, 242
  code of ethics, 243
  committees, 241–242
  country club organization chart, 244
  food and beverage management, 242, 244
  golf course superintendent, 244–246
  golf professional, 246
  golf shop, 246
  historical overview, 236
  key players in, 238–240
  management in, 238–247
  management structure, 240–242
  sustainable golf course management, 246
  trends in, 247
  types of clubs, 237–238
Club Managers Association of America, 230, 248
  Code of Ethics, 243
Club Med, 60–61
ClubCorp, 239, 248
Coastal cruises, 134
Coca-Cola, 8, 226, 260
Cocktails, 222–223
Code of Ethics, Club Managers Association of America, 243
Coffee, 224–226
Coffee shops, 229
Cognac, 223
College/universities foodservice, 193–196
Colleges and universities, 299
Collins, Jim, 4
Colpitts, Gary, 159
Commercial foodservices and managed services, 188
Commissions for travel agents, 46
Committee meetings, 295
Committees, 241–242
Communications CBX or PBX, 111
Communication abilities, 317
Compass Group, 202, 204
Concerts and sporting events, 313–314
Concierge, 112
Condé Nast Traveler, 112
Condotels, 87
Conference centers, 299
Conference event document, 298

Conference event order, 297
Contract management, 194, 319
Contracts, 297
Convention and visitors bureaus, 44, 285, 321
Convention centers, 299
Convention delegates spending in San Francisco, 289
Convention hotels and resorts, 85, 299
Conventions. *See* Meetings/conventions/expositions industry
Coordinating and delegating skills, 318
Coordination, 309
Core competencies, 240, 241
Corporate events, 311
Corporate seminars and workshops, 306
Corporate travel managers, 47
Cost control, restaurant operations, 176–179
Costello, John, 248
Council of the World Economic Forum, 16
Country club organization chart, 244
Country clubs, 237
Craps, 278
Crossings, 135
Cruise director, 138
Cruise industry, 126–145
  air-cruise packages, 129
  career information, 142–143
  cruise market, 130–133
  destinations, 139–142
  development of, 128–129
  first cruise ships, 128
  key players, 129–130
  ship organization, 137–139
  shore excursions, 139
  sustainable cruising, 140
  terminology, 135
  trends in, 142
  types of cruises, 133–136
Cruise Lines International Association, 130
Cruise ships, 299
Cultural impact of, 57
Cultural tourism, 63–65, 141
Cunningham, Ann Pamela, 66

D

Daily rate, 193
Daily report, 106, 107
Davidson, Dave, 200
Davis, Joe, 288
Day, Cecil B., 77
Deluxe cruising, 135–136
Demographics, 157
Destination management companies, 48, 286
Destinations Magazine, 39
Di Bona, Joanne, 57

Dining clubs, 238
Dinner house restaurants, 152
Director of housekeeping, 138
Disney approach to service, 15–19, 65
Disney-MGM Studios, 254
Disney Theme Parks and Resorts College Program, 19
Disney, Walt, 18, 258
Disney World, 253–254
    Disney-MGM Studios, 254
    Epcot, 254
    Magic Kingdom, 253
    sustainable theme parks, 260
Diversity, 122
Drake Hotel, 84
Dram shop legislation, 229–230

E

Early inns, 100
Ebert, Laurel, 284
Ebony magazine, 83
Economic impact of tourism, 44–45
Economy/budget hotels, 86
Ecotourism, 58–62, 141. *See also* Sustainable lodging
Ecotourism: The Potential and Pitfalls (Boo), 58
Education level, lifetime salaries by, 8
Education tourism, 141
Elementary/secondary schools foodservices, 191–192
Empowerment, 15
Energy Star, 120
English Common Law, 24
Entertainment operations, 277
Enthusiasm, 318
Environmental impact of tourism, 61–62
Epcot, 254
Escoffier, Auguste, 149
Ethics in hospitality industry, 22–24
Ethics in Hospitality Management (Hall), 24
Ethnic restaurants, 152–153
Etiquette, 21–22, 236
Eurail, 36
European Union, 92
Event planning, 306–310
Event tourism, 262
Executive committee, in lodging operations, 100, 101
Expeditions and natural cruises, 134
Expositions. *See* Meetings/conventions/expositions industry
Extended-stay hotels, 86–87

F

Fairmont Hotels, sustainable lodging, 93–94
Fairs and festivals, 262, 306, 313
Familiarization trips, 285
Family restaurants, 152
Ferguson, Valerie, 83–84
Festivals, 262
Fine dining, 149
Fining in wine, 214
First in-first out (FIFO) system, 173
Fisher, William, 23
Fishman, Bill, 200
Five Steps of Leadership, 18
Focus groups, 156
Food, matching with wines, 214–216
Food and beverages
    career ladder, 9
    management, 115, 138, 242, 244, 277
Food cost control process, 172
Food cost percentage, 176
Food delivery services, 155
Food pyramid, 192
Ford, Henry, 37
Forecasting restaurant sales, 165
Fortified wines, 213
Fortune magazine, 16
Franchises, 76–79, 149
Fraternal clubs, 238
Frazier, Raquel, 205
Freeway hotels and motels, 84–85
French service in dining, 165
Front of the house, 11, 164–167
Front-office manager, 103
Front-office organizational chart, 102–105
Full-service hotels, 85–86
Fusion cuisine, 150, 157

G

Gallagher, Judi, 323
Gambling. *See* Gaming entertainment
Gaming entertainment, 268–281
    background of, 270–272
    career information, 277–278, 279–280
    casino operations, 277
    casinos, 271
    entertainment operations, 277
    food and beverage operations, 278
    historical overview, 272–274
    hotel operations, 277
    key players, 275–277
    Las Vegas, 273
    Native American gaming, 272, 273–274
    positions in, 277–278
    retail operations, 278
    size/scope, 274–275
    trends, 278
Gannon, Tim, 151
G.A.P Adventures, 41–42
Gates, Bill, 311
Gatorland, 259
GDP (gross domestic product), 31, 32
General manager role, in lodging operations, 100–101
Getting Started: How to Succeed in Heritage Tourism, American Express and National Trust for Historic Preservation, 65
Gin, 222
Global Code of Ethics for Tourism, 30
Globalization, 157
Godwin, Owen, 259
Gold Bond Stamp Company, 16
Goldblatt, Joe Jeff, 316
Golf course superintendent, 244–246
Golf professional, 246
Golf shop, 246
Gonzalez, Carmen, 11
Gonzalez, George, 265
Government organizations, 294
Grand Ole Opry, 263
Green lodging, 92
Green Restaurant Association, 155, 156
Green Restaurant Certification 4.0 Standards, 156–157
Green Seal, 120
Greening the guestroom, 121–122
Gross domestic product (GDP), 31, 32
Group booking curve, 110
Guest bikes, 121
Guest counts or covers, 165
Guest cycle, 103
Guest satisfaction, 7
Guest service associate, 103
Guest services, 111

H

Hall, Stephen S.J., *Ethics in Hospitality Management*, 24
Handle in gambling industry, 270
Harrah's, 275–276
Harris, Karen, 306, 312, 319
Hawaii, 140–142
Hawai'i Convention Center, 287–288
Hawaii Tourism Authority, 141
Health and wines, 217
Health care facilities foodservices, 198–202
Health tourism, 141
Heritage tourism, 65–70
    benefits of, 66
    challenges in, 66–67
    fit between community and, 67
    steps in, 67–70
Hershey, Milton, 256
Hershey's, 256
Hickman, Matt, 260
Highest altitude hotel, 91
Hilton Hotels, 13
Historical associations, 294
Hobbs, Ray, 120
Holiday Corporation, 76
Holiday Inns, 76

Holiday parties, 306
Hops in brewing beer, 218
Hospitality industry
  career path in, 4
  characteristics of, 7–9
  ethical dilemmas in, 24
  and ethics, 22–25
  professional organizations and associations, 22
  salaries, 9
  service. *See* Service
  shift work in, 7
  and tourism interdependency, 5–6, 33
  trends in, 25
Hospitality spirit, 4
Hosteur (Webzine), 22
Hotel del Corondo, 108
Hotel Housekeeping (Andrews), 112
Hotel manager, 137
Hotel operations, 277
Hotels. *See* Lodging
HOTELS magazine, 13
Housekeeping, 112–114
Hub-and-spoke system, 34–35
Hyatt Hotels Corporation, 13, 83, 105–106

I

Ice Hotel, 91
Identification procedures, 114
Incentive market, 295
Indian Gaming Regulation Act (1988), 273–274
Indies, 148
Infrastructure, 58
Initiation fees, 237
Inseparability of services, 7
Intangible services, 7
Intercontinental Hotel Corporation, 76, 77
International Association of Convention and Visitors Bureaus, 311
International Council on Hospitality Education, 22
International development organizations, 41
International Ecotourism Society, 59
International Festivals & Events Association, 313, 320
International Hotel Association, 122
International perspective in lodging, 92
International Special Events Society, 22, 320
International Tourism Partnership Sustainable Hotel Manual, 94
Ishikawa Medal, 13

J

Jefferson, Thomas, 149
Jones, Donald, 11
Jordan, Charlotte, 4
Juices, 226

K

Kitchen/food production, 167–170
Kitchen in lodging operations, 115
Knott's Berry Farm, 252
Kroc, Ray, 164, 181

L

La Guide Culinaire, 149
Las Vegas, 273
Le livre des Menus, 129
Leadership, 13–14
  Five Steps of, 18
Leadership in Energy and Environmental Design (LEED) standards, 94
Leadership skills, 316
LEGOLAND, 259
Leisure and recreation foodservice, 203–204
Leno, Jay, 311
Leopold Center for Sustainable Agriculture, 155
Lettuce Entertain You Enterprises, Inc., 156
Lifetime salaries by education level, 8
Light beverage wines, 212
Liquor liability and the law, 229–230
Lobbyist, origin of term, 101
Lodging, 74–97
  AAA Diamond-Rating Guidelines, 81
  best hotel chains, 91
  centralized reservation system, 79
  food and beverage career ladder, 9
  franchising, 76–79
  hotel development and ownership, 76, 96
  hotels by price segments, 76, 77, 82, 84
  international perspective, 92
  largest chains in franchised and managed contract hotels, 78
  management career ladder, 8
  management contracts, 77–79
  rating and classification of hotels, 80–82, 96
  real estate investment trusts, 80
  rooms division career ladder, 9
  trends in hotel development, 95
  types and locations of, 84–90
  unusual hotels, 91
  vacation ownership (time-share), 89–90
  see also Lodging operations; Sustainable lodging
Lodging Magazine, 22
Lodging operations, 98–125
  bars, 116
  catering department, 117–118
  communications CBX or PBX, 111
  concierge, 112
  departments, 102–109
  early inns, 100
  executive committee, 100, 101
  food and beverage management, 115
  front office organizational chart, 102–105
  functions and departments, 100
  general manager role, 100–101
  guest cycle, 103
  guest services, 111
  housekeeping, 112–114
  kitchen, 115
  management structure, 101–102
  night auditor, 105–109
  property management systems, 109
  reservations, 111
  restaurants, 116
  revenue management, 109–110
  room service/in-room dining, 119
  rooms division organizational chart, 102
  security/loss prevention, 114
  stewarding department, 116
  trends in, 122
  types of rates, 104
  see also Lodging; Sustainable lodging
Lopez, Jennifer, 319
Lorenz, James, 169
Lotts, Heather, 10
Lu, Amy, 168
Luxury cruise market, 133

M

Ma Cuisine, 149
Magic Kingdom, 253
Maglevs, 37
Majors (golf championships), 314–315
Malcolm Baldrige National Quality Award, 14, 91
Malt in brewing beer, 218
Managed services, 186–209
  airlines/airports, 188–190
  business/industry, 202–203
  career information, 207
  college/universities, 193–196
  and commercial foodservices, 188
  contract management, 194
  elementary/secondary schools, 191–192
  health care facilities, 198–202
  leisure and recreation, 203–204
  military, 190
  operating statement, 198–199
  responsibilities in, 196–198
  seniors, 204
  stadium points of service, 203–204
  student unions, 194
  sustainable, 204–205
  technology, 206
  trends in, 205

Management
  career ladder in, 8
  contracts in lodging, 77–79
  involvement/follow-up in restaurant operations, 170
  skills for, 316–319
  structure in lodging operations, 101–102
  theme parks and attractions, 258–260
Marco Polo, 100
Mardi Gras, 263
Marriott, Bill, 14
  The Spirit to Serve: Marriott's Way, 4
Marriott Corporation, 78
Mashing in brewing beer, 220
Mass cruise market, 133
Mayers, John, 159
McManemon, Jim, 96
McWilliams, Louise, 103
Medical and scientific associations, 24
Meeting planners, 286–287
Meeting Planners International, 321
Meeting planning, 295–298
  budget, 296
  conference event order, 297
  contracts, 297
  needs analysis, 295–296
  negotiation with convention center, 296–297
  organizing and pre-conference meetings, 297
  postevent meeting, 297
  request for proposal (RFQ), 296
  site inspection and selection, 296
  see also Meetings/conventions/expositions industry
Meetings/conventions/expositions industry, 282–303
  associations, 284, 290, 294
  career information, 301
  conference event document, 298
  convention delegates spending in San Francisco, 289
  conventions and expositions, 290–292, 294
  destination management companies, 286
  development/size/scope, 284
  key players, 284–287
  meeting planners, 286–287
  meetings, 289–290, 294–295
  MICE, 294
  service contractors, 287
  trade show profile, 291–292
  trends, 300
  venues, 298–299
  see also Meeting planning; Special events industry
Meetings, incentive travel, conventions, and exhibitions (MICE), 294
Mega events, 314–316

Melman, Richard, 156
Méthode champenoise, 212
Meyer, Danny, 10, 150, 166
MGM Mirage, 275
Microbreweries, 228
Middle cruise market, 133
Military clubs, 238
Military foodservice, 190
Mini vacations, 55
Mixed-use hotel development, 87
Money Magazine, "The Six Rudest Restaurants in America," 10
Monthly dues, 237
Moran, Jill, 293
Motels, 6, 77
Motorcoach associations, 39
Multi-Unit Foodservice Operators Conference, 151
Multiplier effect in tourism, 44–45
Multitasking, 318

N

National Association of Amusement Ride Safety Officials, 264
National Association of College Auxiliary Services, 193
National Association of Homebuilders, 239
National Historic Preservation Act (1966), 66
National Offices of Tourism, 48
National Restaurant Association (NRA), 5, 22, 311
  annual restaurant show, 7–8
  Educational Foundation, 13
  restaurant manager job analysis, 180–182
  statistics, 148, 155–156
National School Lunch Program, 191
National Society of Minorities in Hospitality, 22
National Trust for Historic Preservation, 65
National Women's Business Council, 16
Native American gaming, 272, 273–274
Natural cruises, 134
Nature tourism, 70
Needs analysis, 295–296
Negotiating skills, 317
Negotiation with convention center, 296–297
Nelson, Marilyn Carlson, 16
Night auditor, 105–109
Nightclubs, 227–228
Nonalcoholic beer, 224
Nonalcoholic beverages, 224–227
North America Hotel Guest Satisfaction Index Study, 120
North American Free Trade Agreement, 92
Norwegian Cruise Line, 129, 130
Nutrition education programs, 192

O

Oktoberfest, 262
Olympic Games, 314
One-pot cooking, 157
Operating statement, 198–199
Opportunities in Event Planning Careers, 312
Order specification in restaurant operations, 172
Organization chart in restaurant operations, 164
Organization for Economic and Development, 41–42
Orzoff, Jerry A., 145
Osika, Adena, 207
Outback Steakhouse, 151

P

Pacific Area Travel Association, 42
Pannel Kew Foster, 96
Par stock, 172
Paris, 39–40
Pepsi, 226
Perishability of product, 7
Philosophy, personal, 21
Pineapple tradition, 5
Pleasure travel, 54–56
Poker, 278
Portman, John, 106
Power (energy) drinks, 226–227
Price, Margaret, 76
Pritzker, Nicholas, 105
Private clubs, 236
Product specification, 170, 172
Production control sheets, 169
Professional and technical meetings, 295
Professional clubs, 237
Professional Convention Management Association, 22
Professional organizations and associations, 22, 294
  in meetings/conventions/expositions industry, 284, 290, 294
  special events industry, 320–322
  in tourism, 40–44
Professionalism and etiquette, 21–22
Project management skills, 317
Proof in spirits, 222
Property management systems, 109
Proprietary clubs, 238
Puck, Wolfgang, 150, 151
Purchase order, 172
Purchasing, 170–172

Q

Quality control, 15
Queen Elizabeth II, 129
Quick-service/fast-food restaurants, 153–155

R

Rack rate, 109
Radisson Hotels, 10
Rail Passenger Service Act (1970), 36
Rail travel, 35–37
Rating and classification of hotels, 80–82, 96
Real estate investment trusts, 80
Receiving, 172–173
Recycling, 121
Reggae on the River, 262–263
Regional cruises, 133
Regional theme parks, 258–259
Religious organizations, 294
Rental cars, 38
Request for proposal, 296
Reservations, in lodging operations, 111
Resort Condominiums International, 89, 90
Resort hotels, 88–89
Restaurant and hotel bars, 227
Restaurant industry, 146–161
   background and statistics, 148
   career information, 158–160
   classical cuisine, 149
   classification of, 148–157
   delivery services, 155
   franchises, 149
   Green Restaurant Certification 4.0 Standards, 156–157
   sustainable restaurants, 155–157
   top market shares by restaurant type, 153
   trends in, 157
   see also Restaurant operations
Restaurant management career ladder, 9
Restaurant manager job analysis, 180–182
Restaurant operations, 162–185
   assistant restaurant manager job description, 171
   back of the house, 167–176
   career information, 171, 183
   cost control, 176–179
   first in-first out (FIFO) system, 173
   food cost control process, 172
   forecasting restaurant sales, 165
   front of the house, 164–167
   kitchen/food production, 167–170
   management involvement/follow-up, 170
   order specification, 172
   organization chart, 164
   par stock, 172
   product specification, 170, 172
   production control sheets, 169
   purchase order, 172
   purchasing, 170–172
   receiving, 172–173
   restaurant manager job analysis, 180–182
   service, 165–166
   standardized recipe, 172
   storing/issuing, 173
   suggestive selling, 164, 166–167
   sustainable, 1780179
   trends in, 182
   see also Restaurant industry
Retail operations, 278
Rev par (revenue per available room), 110
Revenue management, 109–110
Revere, Paul, 224
Rigan, Bill, 205
Ritz-Carlton Hotel Company, 4, 13, 14, 76, 83, 91
River cruises, 134
Robinson, Chris, 175–176
Room occupancy percentage, 106, 107
Room service/in-room dining, 119
Rooms division career ladder, 9
Rooms division organizationsl chart, 102
Roscoe, Patricia L., 43, 48, 286
Roulette, 278
Rousseau, Jean-Jacques, 224
Royal Caribbean Cruises, 129, 130
Rum, 223
Russian service in dining, 165

S

Sail-cruises, 134–135
Salaries, 8, 9
Sandwich restaurants, 155
Saputo, John, 231
Scandinavian Airline System, 12
Schaeffer, Glen, 271
Schrock, Jay R., 216
Schulze, Horst, 13
Scotch whiskey, 222
Sea World Parks and Entertainment, 255–256
Security/loss prevention, 114
Security officers, 114
Self-assessment and personal philosophy, 21
Seminars and workshops, 295, 306
Seniors foodservice, 204
Seraton Grande Torrey Pines catering event order, 118
Service
   Disney approach to, 15–19
   focus on, 10–19
   inseparability of, 7
   intangibility of, 7
   perfecting, 13
   "Seven Deadly Sins of Service," 10
   success in, 11–12
   and total quality management, 14–15
Service America! (Albrecht and Zemke), 12
Service contractors, 287
Service in restaurant operations, 165–166
Service-oriented people, 21
"Seven Deadly Sins of Service," 10
Shaughnessy, Edward J., 245
Shift work, 7
Ship organization, 137–139
Shore excursions, 139
Siegal, Bugsy, 273
Siegal, Jonathan W., 170
Silverman, Henry, 89
Six Flags, 257
"Six Rudest Restaurants in America, The," *Money Magazine*, 10
Smart rooms, 85–86
Smith, Debbie, 236
Smith, Ralph, 130
Social and cultural impact, 57
Social clubs, 237
Social events, 312–313
Social functions, 306
Social, military, educational, religious, and fraternal groups, 295
Social skills, 318
Sodexho, 189, 196
Southern Living Magazine, 138
Souza, Ana, 196
Spacey, Richard, 131–132
Sparkling wines, 212–213
Special events industry, 304–325
   association events, 311–312
   background, 306
   career information, 312, 314, 323
   charity balls and fund-raising, 312
   concerts and sporting events, 313–314
   corporate events, 311
   event planning, 306–310
   fairs and festivals, 313
   job market, 233–323
   mega events, 314–316
   professional organizations, 320–322
   skills required for management, 316–319
   social events, 312–313
   sustainable aspects, 322
   wedding planning, 319
   see also Meetings/conventions/expositions industry
Specialty Coffee Association of America, 224
Specialty and theme cruises, 135
Spirit to Serve, The: Marriott's Way (Marriott), 4
Spirits, 222–223
Sporting events, 313–314
Sports Bars, 228–229
Sports tourism, 141
Stadium points of service, 203–204
Standardized recipe, 172
Starbucks Coffee Company, 225
Steakhouses, 151–152
Steam boating, 134
Stewarding department, 116
Stillman, Alan, 173

Storing/issuing, 173
Student unions foodservice, 194
Suggestive selling, 164, 166–167
Sullivan, Chris, 151
Super Bowl, 314
Superstructure, 58
Sustainable aspects
   in brewing beer, 220–221
   of coffee, 225, 226
   Gold Medal for Corporate Achievement in Sustainable Development, 225
   in golf course management, 246
   in managed services, 204–205
   of restaurant operations, 155–157, 178–179
   special events industry, 323
   theme parks, 260–261, 261
   theme parks and attractions, 260–261
   in tourism, 32, 58
   wines, 214
Sustainable lodging, 92–94
   carbon footprint reductions, 94
   climate change impacts, 93–94
   Fairmont Hotels, 92–93
   green lodging, 92
Sustainable lodging operations, 120–121
   Energy Star, 120
   Green Seal, 119
   greening the guestroom, 121–122
   guest bikes, 121
   model for, 119
   recycling, 120
   water conservation, 120

T

Tea, 226
Technology, 122, 206
Tequila, 223
T.G.I. Friday's, 173–175
Thackeray, William Makepeace, 128
Theme cruises, 135
Theme parks and attractions, 250–267
   career information, 263–264, 265
   development of, 252
   fairs/festivals/events, 262–263
   key players, 253-258. *See also* Disney World
   management, 260–261
   regional theme parks, 259–260
   size/scope, 252
   sustainable, 260
   trends, 265
Theme restaurants, 150
Time-share (vacation ownership), 89–90
Tip, Bruce Poon, 41
Titanic, 128
Tivoli, 260
Top market shares by restaurant type, 153

Total quality management, 14–15
Tour operators, 45
Tourism, 28–51
   air travel, 33–35
   and art, 64–65
   benefits of, 32
   bus travel, 38–39
   car travel, 37–38
   categorization and classification of, 31
   convention centers and visitors bureaus (CVBs), 44
   economic impact of, 44–45
   environmental impact of, 61–62
   Global Code of Ethics for Tourism, 30
   gross domestic product (GDP), 31, 32
   historic highlights of, 30
   and hospitality industry interdependency, 5–6, 33
   multiplier effect, 44–45
   organizations, 40–44
   promoters of, 45–48
   social and cultural impact of, 57, 65
   sustainable, 31–32
   Tourism 2020 Vision, 32–33
   train travel, 35–37
   trends in, 49
   United Nations World Tourism Organization, 30–31
   World Travel and Tourism Council, 31
   see also Why people travel
Tourism 2020 Vision, 32–33
Trade associations, 294
Trade show profile, 291–292
Trade shows, 306
Tradeshow Week Magazine, 288
Train travel, 35–37
Travel. *See* Cruise industry; Lodging; Tourism; Why people travel
Travel agencies, 45–46
Travel Agent magazine, 16
Travel and tour wholesalers, 47
Travel corporations, 46–47
Travel Industry Association of America, 16
Travel Weekly Magazine, 45
Tray line, 199
Treetops Hotel, 91
Trends
   beverage industry, 230
   club industry, 247
   cruise industry, 142
   gaming entertainment, 278–279
   hospitality industry, 25
   hotel development, 95
   lodging operations, 122
   managed services, 205
   meetings/conventions/expositions industry, 300
   restaurant industry, 157
   restaurant operations, 182

   theme parks and attractions, 265
   tourism, 49, 71
Trotter, Charlie, 150
Turner, Jessica, 197

U

Underwater hotel, 91
Union Professionelle des Portiers des Grand Hotels, 112
Union Square Hospitality Group, 10
United Nations Development Program, 41
United Nations Educational, Scientific, and Cultural Organizations, 63
United Nations World Tourism Organization, 30–31
United States Green Building Council, 94
Universal Studios, 254–255
University clubs, 238
Unusual hotels, 91

V

Vacation ownership (time-share), 89–90
Venetian Hotel, 90
Venues, meetings/conventions/expositions industry, 298–299
Vintage wines, 214
Vodka, 223
Voltaire, 224

W

Wachtveilt, Kurt, 5
Wall Street Journal, 106, 228
Water conservation, 119
Waters, Alice, 150
Watson, Dan, 280
WCI Communities, 239
Weaver, David, 59
Wedding planning, 319
Weddings, 306
Weil, Bob, 123
West Paces Hotel Group, 13
Westfall, Rob, 219
Wet 'n Wild, 259
Whiskies, 222
White spirits, 222
Why people travel, 52–73
   business travel, 56
   cultural tourism, 63–65
   ecotourism, 58–62. *See also* Sustainable lodging
   heritage tourism, 65-70. *See also* Heritage tourism
   list of reasons, 54, 55
   mini vacations, 55
   motivational forces for, 72
   nature tourism, 70
   pleasure travel, 54–56
   sustainable tourism, 58
   trends in travel, 71
   see also Tourism

Wilhoitte, Lianne, 284
Wilkie, Susan, 15
Willard Intercontinental Hotel, 101
Willis, Martha, 205
Wilson, Kemmons, 76
Win in gambling industry, 270
Wine tasting, 216
Wines, 212–218
   aromatic, 213
   fortified, 213
   and health, 217
   history of, 213
   light beverage, 212
   major wine-producing countries, 217–218
   making of, 214
   matching with food, 214–216
   sparkling, 212–213
   sustainable production, 214
   wine tasting, 216
Working Mother magazine, 16
World Bank, 41
World cruises, 135
World Cup, 314
World Series, 314
World Tourism Organization, 40, 90
World Travel and Tourism Council, 31–32, 44
Wort in brewing beer, 220
Wright, James, 111
Wyndham Worldwide, 77
Wynn, Stephen, 276
Wynne, Angus, 257

Y

Yamaguchi, Roy, 141–142
Yeast in brewing beer, 218

Z

Zagat's America's Top Restaurants, 155

Photo Credits

Chapter 1

pp. 2–3: Michael Moran © Dorling Kindersley
p. 5 (top): Geoff Dann © Dorling Kindersley
p. 5 (bottom): Demetrio Carrasco © Dorling Kindersley
p. 7: Francesca Yorke © Dorling Kindersley, Courtesy of the Coyote Cafe, Santa Fe
p. 10: Robert Fried/robertfriedphotography.com
p. 11: Courtesy of Carmen Gonzalez
p. 12: hans.slegers/Shutterstock
p. 13: Courtesy of Horst Schulze
p. 14: © Jodi Hilton/Corbis
p. 16: Courtesy of Marilyn Carlson Nelson
p. 19: Dan Bannister/Rough Guides Dorling Kindersley
p. 20: J. Helgason/Shutterstock
p. 25: Coprid/Shutterstock

Chapter 2

pp. 28–29: Mark Green
p. 30: r.nagy/Shutterstock
p. 31: Mark Green
p. 33: © Dorling Kindersley
p. 34: © JNTO
p. 35: Rob Wilson/Shutterstock
p. 36: Mike Dunning © Dorling Kindersley
p. 37: Demetrio Carrasco © Dorling Kindersley
p. 39: © Dorling Kindersley
p. 40: Max Alexander © Dorling Kindersley
p. 41: G.A.P Adventures
p. 42: Mark Green
p. 43: Courtesy of Patti Roscoe
p. 44: James Steidl/Shutterstock
p. 46: Prentice Hall School Division
p. 48: Ilin Sergey/Shutterstock

Chapter 3

pp. 52–53: Rick Pawlenty
p. 55 (top): © JNTO
p. 55 (bottom): Rick Pawlenty
p. 57 (top): Courtesy of the San Diego Convention and Visitor's Bureau
p. 57 (bottom): Linda Whitwam © Dorling Kindersley
p. 60: Robert Armstrong/Photolibrary.com
p. 61: Rick Pawlenty
p. 62: John Walker
p. 63 (top): Kurhan/Shutterstock
p. 63 (bottom): Courtesy of Holly Carvalho
p. 65: Mark Green
p. 66: Rick Pawlenty
p. 67: John Coletti © Dorling Kindersley
p. 70: Mark Green

Chapter 4

pp. 74–75: Gunter Marx © Dorling Kindersley
p. 77: Jakub Pavlinec/Shutterstock
p. 78: Nigel Hicks © Dorling Kindersley
p. 79: Courtesy of Cendant
p. 80 (top): Nigel Hicks © Dorling Kindersley
p. 80 (bottom): Jim Warych © Dorling Kindersley
p. 83: Courtesy of Valerie Ferguson
p. 85 (top): Peter Wilson © Dorling Kindersley
p. 85 (bottom): Wynn Las Vegas
p. 86: Tony Souter © Dorling Kindersley
p. 87: Rob Reichenfeld © Dorling Kindersley
p. 88: Linda Whitwam © Dorling Kindersley
p. 89: Uranov/Shutterstock
p. 91: Peter Hanneberg © Dorling Kindersley
p. 92: James Steidl/Shutterstock
p. 94: Zdorov Kirill Vladimirovich/Shutterstock

Chapter 5

pp. 98–99: Chen Chao © Dorling Kindersley
p. 101: Angus Osborn © Rough Guides
p. 104: Pearson Education/PH College
p. 105: Chen Chao © Dorling Kindersley
p. 108: Courtesy of Ryan Adams
p. 109: Clara/Shutterstock
p. 112: Terry Carter © Dorling Kindersley
p. 113: James Steidl/Shutterstock
p. 114: Jakub Pavlinec/Shutterstock
p. 116: © Dorling Kindersley
p. 117: Cindy Charles/PhotoEdit Inc.
p. 119: Jackson Gee/Shutterstock

Chapter 6

pp. 126–127: Mark Green
p. 129: James Steidl/Shutterstock
p. 130: Bel Kambach
p. 131: Courtesy of Richard Spacey
p. 133: Mark Green
p. 134: Gabor Barka © Dorling Kindersley
p. 137: AP Wide World Photos
p. 139 (top): photomak/Shutterstock
p. 139 (bottom): Bel Kambach
p. 140: Rob Reichenfeld © Dorling Kindersley
p. 141: Lisa F. Young/Shutterstock

Chapter 7

pp. 146–147: Joanne DiBona, San Diego CVB
p. 148: Sedin/Shutterstock
p. 150 (top): Charlie Trotter
p. 150 (bottom): Chris Stowers © Dorling Kindersley, courtesy of Corvette Diner
p. 151: John Walker
p. 152: Dorling Kindersley
p. 153: Chris Stowers © Dorling Kindersley
p. 154: Britta Jaschinski © Dorling Kindersley, Courtesy of Hasir restaurant, Adalbertstrasse, Berlin
p. 155: Studiotouch/Shutterstock
p. 156: Courtesy of Richard Melman

Chapter 8

pp. 162–163: Ian O'Leary © Dorling Kindersley
p. 164: Vladyslav Danilin/Shutterstock
p. 165: Magnus Rew © Dorling Kindersley, Courtesy of Sushi Hatsu, Orlando
p. 166: Pearson Education/PH College
p. 167: Joanne DiBona, San Diego CVB
p. 168: Burke/Triolo Productions/Jupiter Images-PictureArts Corporation
p. 169: Courtesy of James Lorenz
p. 170: Pearson Education/PH College
p. 173 (top): Pearson Education/PH College
p. 173 (bottom): TGI Friday's
p. 175: Pearson Education/PH College
p. 179: Johann Helgason/Shutterstock
p. 181: Givaga/Shutterstock

Chapter 9

pp. 186–187: Tony Weller/Getty Images-Digital Vision
p. 188: Chris Stowers © Dorling Kindersley
p. 189: Sodexho
p. 191: Michael Gaffney/Silver Burdett Ginn
p. 193: Patrick White/Merrill Education
p. 194: L Barnwell/Shutterstock
p. 196 (top): Courtesy of Cherry Cerminia
p. 196 (bottom): Lisa F. Young/Shutterstock
p. 200: Aramark
p. 201: Pearson Education/PH College
p. 202 (top): The Compass Group
p. 202 (bottom): Sodexho
p. 203: Aramark
p. 207: Rob Byron/Shutterstock

Chapter 10

pp. 210–211: Ian O'Leary © Dorling Kindersley
p. 212: Ian O'Leary © Dorling Kindersley
p. 213: Linda Whitwam © Dorling Kindersley
p. 214: Philippe Giraud © Dorling Kindersley
p. 215: Ian O'Leary © Dorling Kindersley
p. 216 (right): Arkady Ten/Shutterstock
p. 216 (left): Jay R. Schrock
p. 218: Petr Vaclavek/Shutterstock
p. 219: Courtesy of Rob Westfall
p. 220: © Dorling Kindersley
p. 221: Bjorn Heller/Shutterstock
p. 222: Perkus/Shutterstock
p. 223 (top): Steve Gorton © Dorling Kindersley
p. 223 (bottom): Perkus/Shutterstock
p. 224 (top): Dave King © Dorling Kindersley/Courtesy of Big Cup, New York
p. 224 (bottom): Vasca/Shutterstock
p. 225: Starbucks
p. 226: Aptyp_koK/Shutterstock
p. 227: Evgeny Karandaev/Shutterstock
p. 228: Paul Chesley/Stone/Getty Images
p. 230: Dmitrijs Mihejevs/Shutterstock

Chapter 11

pp. 234–235: Gerard Brown © Dorling Kindersley
p. 236: Linda Whitwam © Dorling Kindersley
p. 237: Gerard Brown © Dorling Kindersley
p. 238: Kletr/Shutterstock
p. 239: Nigel Hicks © Dorling Kindersley
p. 241: Steve Cukrov/Shutterstock
p. 245: Courtesy of Edward J. Shaughnessy
p. 246: Bartlomies Zaranek © Dorling Kindersley

Chapter 12

pp. 250–251: Dave King © Dorling Kindersley
p. 252: Rob Reichenfeld © Dorling Kindersley
p. 255: Stephen Whitehorn © Dorling Kindersley
p. 256: Stephen Whitehorn © Dorling Kindersley
p. 257 (top): Bill Aron/PhotoEdit Inc.
p, 257 (bottom): Margo Harrison/Shutterstock
p. 258: © Disney Enterprises, Inc.
p. 259: tavi/Shutterstock
p. 261: Vakhrushev Pavel/Shutterstock
p. 262: Katarzyna and Sergiusz Michalscy © Dorling Kindersley
p. 263: Alex Robinson © Dorling Kindersley
p. 264: Margo Harrison/Shutterstock

Chapter 13

pp. 268–269: © Dorling Kindersley, Courtesy of The Venetian, Las Vegas
p. 270: New York, New York Hotel and Casino
p. 271: Chistoprudov Dmitriy Gennadievich/Shutterstock
p. 272: Wynn Las Vegas
pp. 272–273: Stephen Coburn/Shutterstock
p. 274: Alan Keohane © Dorling Kindersley
p. 275: © Dorling Kindersley, Courtesy of the Hotel Bellagio, Las Vegas
p. 276: Wynn Las Vegas
p. 277: dekede/Shutterstock
p. 278: Michael C. Gray/Shutterstoc

Chapter 14

pp. 282–283: Nigel Hicks © Dorling Kindersley
p. 286: StockLite/Shutterstock
p. 287: Tatiana Popova/Shutterstock
p. 288: Peter French/PacificStock.com
p. 290: Alan Keohane © Dorling Kindersley
p. 293: Courtesy of Jill Moran
p. 294: Cristovao/Shutterstock
p. 295: Nigel Blythe/Robert Harding World Imagery
p. 296: grekoff/Shutterstock
p. 297: Photolibrary.com
p. 300: Shutterstock

Chapter 15

pp. 304–305: Nigel Hicks © Dorling Kindersley, Courtesy of the International Olympic Committee
p. 306: James Steidl/Shutterstock
p. 307: AP Wide World Photos
pp. 308–309: John Denver/Shutterstock
p. 310: Jeff Greenberg/PhotoEdit, Inc.
p. 311: Gary Stewart/AP Wide World Photos
p. 312: Picsfive/Shutterstock
p. 314: MishAl/Shutterstock
p. 315: Courtesy of Suzanne Bailey
p. 317: Triangle Images/Getty Images-Digital Vision
p. 318: GalaxyPhoto/Shutterstock
p. 320: Stephen Whitehorn © Dorling Kindersley